D1797452

Development Economics and Policy: Readings

Development Economics and Policy: Readings

Edited by
IAN LIVINGSTONE
Professor of Development Economics, University of East Anglia

London
GEORGE ALLEN & UNWIN
Boston Sydney

First published in 1981

GEORGE ALLEN & UNWIN LTD
40 Museum Street, London WC1A 1LU

British Library Cataloguing in Publication Data

Development economics and policy readings.
1. Underdeveloped areas—Economic conditions
—Addresses, essays, lectures
I. Livingstone, Ian
330.9′172′4 HC59.7 80–40944

ISBN 0–04–382025–5
ISBN 0–04–382026–3 Pbk

Set in 9 on 10 point Times by Typesetters (Birmingham) Limited, Birmingham, and printed in Great Britain by Lowe & Brydone Printers Limited, Thetford, Norfolk

Contents

Acknowledgements

Permission to reproduce the Readings in this volume is acknowledged from the following sources:

Reading 1 Institut für Weltwirtschaft an der Universität Kiel and Professor P. T. Bauer.
Reading 2 Macmillan, London and Basingstoke, and P. Streeten
Reading 3 Istanbul University, Faculty of Economics, and J. H. Habakkuk
Reading 4 Oxford University Press and S. P. Schatz
Reading 5 Basil Blackwell, Publishers, and T. Balogh and P. Streeten
Reading 6 North-Holland Publishing Co. and M. S. Ahluwalia
Reading 7 Frank Cass & Co. Ltd and W. C. Robinson
Reading 8 McGraw-Hill Book Company and Eicher & Witt
Reading 9 The Johns Hopkins University Press and D. W. Jorgensen
Reading 10 Cambridge University Press and K. Hart
Reading 11 Pergamon Press Ltd and E. O. Edwards
Reading 12 American Economic Association, and J. R. Harris and M. P. Todaro
Reading 13 Cambridge University Press and H. Myint
Reading 14 Cambridge University Press and M. J. Flanders
Reading 15 Institute of Development Studies and D. Evans
Reading 16 Inter American Affairs Press
Reading 17 University of Chicago Press and C. Glezakos
Reading 18 American Economic Association and Professor T. Dos Santos
Reading 19 Oxford University Press and S. Lall
Reading 20 Pakistan Institute of Development Economics
Reading 21 Pakistan Institute of Development Economics
Reading 22 Institut de Science Economique Appliquée and F. Perroux
Reading 23 Oxford University Press and N. Rosenberg
Reading 24 Macmillan, London and Basingstoke, and F. Stewart
Reading 25 *The Journal of Economic History* and B. F. Hoselitz
Reading 26 *Quarterly Journal of Economics* and A. K. Sen
Reading 27 *Finance and Development*
Reading 28 Basil Blackwell, Publishers
Reading 29 Longman Group Ltd and A. P. Thirlwall
Reading 30 University of Chicago Press and B. Balassa and D. M. Schydlowsky
Reading 31 Frank Cass & Co. Ltd and M. Lipton
Reading 32 The Agricultural Economics Society
Reading 33 University of the West Indies
Reading 34 *Journal of Asian Studies*
Reading 35 Council on Foreign Relations Inc.
Reading 36 Food Research Institute
Reading 37 The Agricultural Economics Society
Reading 38 Manchester University Press
Reading 39 International Monetary Fund and A. H. Chandavarkar

Introduction

This volume is a successor to my earlier collection of Readings, *Economic Policy for Development* (Penguin, 1971), which, like a large part of the Penguin series unfortunately, has gone out of print. Some of the articles which users seem to have found it particularly convenient to have made available via the Penguin have been retained but, naturally, as time moves on, this is substantially a new collection.

The primary purpose of the collection is to make available in the handy form of a single relatively low-priced volume some of the articles which are most likely to be relevant to undergraduate and postgraduate courses in development economics at the present time. To this pedagogic end recommended reading lists for a large number of such courses being conducted in British universities were scrutinised and some of the most heavily used articles picked out. This pedagogic objective is carried further by including a number of useful surveys of a field, such as those on disguised unemployment by Kao, Anschel and Eicher and by Jorgensen (Readings 8 and 9), those on import-substituting industrialisation by Bruton (Reading 20) and on transnational enterprises by Lall (Reading 19), and that on inflation by Kirkpatrick and Nixson (Reading 38). Some of the particularly seminal articles which have stimulated a great deal of subsequent discussion are those by A. K. Sen on the choice of technique (Reading 26), by Harris and Todaro on rural–urban migration (Reading 12), by Hart on the concept of the informal sector (Reading 10) and by Perroux on growth poles (Reading 22). Then, as in the case of the Penguin but rather less so, perhaps, some preference has been given to good articles which were for various reasons less accessible than others, such as the article by Perroux, translated for the first time from the French, and that by Habakkuk (Reading 3).

The primary criterion, however, has been that these are what I considered to be good and valuable articles which I felt should be essential reading. Secondly, I have tried to include the whole of the article wherever possible, except where sheer length did not permit this, on grounds that readers generally prefer to see articles as they were written, rather than a series of excerpts. This is therefore not an attempt to produce a textbook by means of scissors and paste but could be considered as complementary to Meier's excellent *Leading Issues*.

The title, *Development Economics and Policy*, like that of the Penguin, reflects the fact that if the study of development has not succeeded so far, in the editor's opinion, in producing convincing broad theories and basic models of development, development economists have raised a series of crucial policy issues for development. Do we emphasise agriculture or industry? Capital goods or consumer goods industries? Import-substitution industries or export industries? Plantations or peasant production? How can fiscal policy be best designed for development? How can monetary policy and interest rate policy be used? What investment criteria should be applied? What education and manpower policy should be followed? This volume is, therefore, like development economics itself, policy-oriented and issue-oriented.

IAN LIVINGSTONE
University of East Anglia
September 1979

Part One

Causal Factors and Theories of Development

As stated in the Introduction, development economics as a subject has not produced very convincing theories or models of development. However, generations of thinkers have asked themselves whether there is a particular ingredient essential to development or 'missing factor' resulting in under-development, such as lack of capital or lack of entrepreneurship. Habakkuk (Reading 3) discusses the last of these, while Schatz (Reading 4) raises some searching questions regarding the role of capital. Balogh and Streeten (Reading 5) similarly demonstrate that increases in physical inputs of capital and labour cannot themselves fully explain increasing output but identify a substantial 'coefficient of ignorance' in the equation. Streeten (Reading 2) questions whether we should be looking for a single factor at all, rather than a constellation of forces, and thus levels a fundamental criticism at 'single barrier' theories in general. If not much progress has been made on a general theory, however, the concept of a 'vicious circle' constraining development is well established in the literature: the damage done to the concept by Bauer (Reading 1) underlines the need for more careful testing of theories and hypotheses in development economics. Ahluwalia (Reading 6) examines the evidence regarding the relation between development and inequality.

Reading 1

The Vicious Circle of Poverty

P. T. Bauer

Weltwirtschaftliches Archiv, vol. 95, no. 2, 1965, pp. 4–20.

1

I intend to discuss the validity of the widely held notion that underdeveloped (or poor) countries are caught in a vicious circle of poverty and stagnation, or as it has been put rather pithily by Professor Nurkse, that a country is poor because it is poor. The upsurge of interest in the last twenty years or so in the economics of countries and of their development has so far not yielded many illuminating generalizations. The thesis usually known as the vicious circle of poverty is perhaps the principal generalization of this literature. It is not as dominant now as it was a few years ago. But it is still prominent in the academic, official and popular literature in this general area. It also acts as the background or as the basis for important policy proposals and more notably for the suggestion that appreciable economic progress of poor countries requires drastic sacrifices at home, supplemented by aid from abroad.

The thesis states that poverty itself sets up well nigh unsurmountable obstacles to its own conquest. It is presented in several distinctly different variants, which, however, are not exclusive but cumulative. The most frequent is that the low level of income renders saving impossible, thus preventing the capital accumulation necessary for an increase in income. Others include the suggestion that the narrow markets of these countries obstruct the emergence and extension of the specialists necessary for higher incomes; that demand is too small to permit progressive and productive investment; that government revenues are insufficient for the establishment of effective public services; that malnutrition and ill-health keep productivity low, which prevents a rise in income; and there are others as well. International private investment cannot alleviate the situation, since one aspect of the vicious circle is a lack of productive private investment opportunities.

I quote at some length from influential sources to show the importance of the thesis in the literature, to illustrate the reasoning behind it and to forestall criticism that I am quoting out of context.

One source is a study submitted to a United States Senate Committee by the Center for International Studies of the Massachusetts Institute of Technology (1957, p. 37), a well-known and very influential organization in this field. '. . . the general scarcity relative to population of nearly all resources creates a self-perpetuating vicious circle of poverty. Additional capital is necessary to increase output, but poverty itself makes it impossible to carry out the required saving and investment by a voluntary reduction in consumption'.

Another formulation which has often been quoted is by the late Professor Nurkse (1953) whose book is one of the best known and most influential writings in this field. He writes under the heading 'The vicious circle of poverty'.

> In discussions of the problem of economic development, a phrase that crops up frequently is 'the vicious circle of poverty'. A situation of this sort, a vicious circle of poverty, relating to a country as a whole can be summed up in the trite proposition: 'a country is poor because it is poor'.
>
> Perhaps the most important circular relationships of this kind are those that afflict the accumulation of capital in economically backward countries. The supply of capital is governed by the ability and willingness to save; the demand for capital is governed by the incentives to invest. A circular relationship exists on both sides of the problem of capital formation in the poverty-ridden areas of the world.
>
> On the supply side, there is the small capacity to save, resulting from the low level of real income. The low real income is a reflection of low productivity, which in its turn is due largely to the lack of capital. The lack of capital is a result of the small capacity to save and so the circle is complete.
>
> On the demand side, the inducement to invest may be low because of the small buying power of the people, which is due to their small income, which again is due to low productivity. The low level of productivity, however, is a result of the small amount of capital used in production, which in its turn may be caused at least partly by the small inducement to invest.
>
> The low level of real income, reflecting low productivity, is a point that is common to both circles.

Such quotations could be multiplied easily from the writings of well-known authors such as Professor Gunnar Myrdal, Dr H. W. Singer, and many others.

It will be readily realized that this thesis can be expressed in the form of a model, that is, an analytical device setting out the crucial variables in the explanation of particular phenomena. The model of the vicious circle of poverty and underdevelopment is a particular model designed to explain the continuation through time of a zero or negligible rate of economic growth. The crucial variables and relationships in most growth models are these: the growth of income is a function of the rate of capital accumulation, that is, of investment; investment depends on saving; and saving is a function of income. Hence the growth of income depends on the growth of capital and the growth of capital depends on the growth of income. Thus the model behind the thesis of the vicious circle of poverty pivots on the suggestion that the low level of income itself prevents the capital formation required to raise income.

This thesis is demonstrably and indeed obviously invalid. If it were valid, innumerable individuals, groups and communities could not have risen from great poverty to riches as they have done throughout the world in both rich and poor countries. This in itself should be sufficient to disprove the thesis as a general proposition. The thesis is refuted also by the very existence of developed countries all of which started poor, with low incomes per head and low levels of accumulated capital, i.e. with the economic features which define underdeveloped countries today. Yet they have advanced, usually without appreciable outside capital and invariably without external grants. This would have been impossible on the arguments of the vicious circle of poverty and stagnation. As the world is a closed system and clearly began in a state of underdevelopment the thesis is indeed inconsistent with the phenomenon of development.

It is also refuted by the rapid economic advance of many underdeveloped countries in recent decades which for obvious reasons is particularly relevant in this context. I shall give some instances of this progress in broader terms and others in more detailed and specific terms.

2

According to the statistics of the Economic Commission for Latin America over the period 1935 through 1953 the gross national product in Latin American countries increased at an annual rate of 4·2 per cent, and output per head by 2 per cent (UN, Department of Economic and Social Affairs, 1955a, p. 10). Over the period 1945 through 1955 the rate of growth was even faster, as total output increased by about 4·9 per cent annually and output per head by 2·4 per cent, an appreciably higher rate than in the United States (UN, Department of Economic and Social Affairs, 1955b, p. 3). Latin America is largely pervaded by the money economy so that statistics of the gross national product are somewhat more meaningful than for most underdeveloped countries.

South-east Asia, and in particular Malaya, and West Africa, are other underdeveloped regions where there has been rapid and readily demonstrable progress since the latter part of the nineteenth century. In these areas there are no series of national income figures going back before the Second World War and the present figures are somewhat hazardous. The national income of Malaya (gross domestic product per head per year) was about £100 in 1961, the latest year for which official figures are available, and in Ghana it was about £75 in 1962, again the latest available figure. These are low figures by Western standards but they nevertheless reflect substantial advance since the beginning of the century, when these were essentially subsistence economies.

Regardless of the availability or limitations of national income statistics, there is no lack of information on the rapid progress of these economies in these years. The rubber industry of south-east Asia began only around 1900. In 1963 it produced about two million tons of rubber annually (in spite of the disorganization in Indonesia, the country with the largest area under rubber), worth about £400 million. More than two-thirds of the output is on Asian-owned properties. In 1900 total domestic exports from Malaya were worth about £8 million annually; in 1963 they were about £300 million. In 1900 there were no exports of plantation rubber from Malaya; in 1963 they exceeded 800,000 tons, rather more than half from Asian-owned properties. There has also been a very rapid increase in the entrepôt trade of the country, which reflects largely the spread of exchange economy in south-east Asia. Thus while total Malayan (including Singapore) exports and imports together (including re-imports) in 1900 were around £50 million, in 1963 they were about £1000 million.

In West Africa the progress of Ghana (the Gold Coast until 1957) and Nigeria since the end of the nineteenth century has been striking, rapid and well documented. There is ample evidence of this progress from sporadic national income figures and, more relevant and revealing, from statistics of population growth, foreign trade, government revenues, literacy, health, infant mortality, and so on. The rapid progress of Ghana is reflected in statistics which are somewhat more reliable and meaningful than elsewhere in Africa or Asia. As already noted, by the early 1960s the national income per head was about £75; in real terms it had doubled since 1910 and quadrupled since 1890. The total population approximately quadrupled between 1890 and 1960 from about 1·6 million to about 6·5 million.

Statistics of foreign trade are of particular interest for West Africa because well over 99·5 per cent of the population is African: all agricultural exports (the bulk of all exports) are produced by them and practically all imports are destined for their use. To take Gold Coast–Ghana first. In 1890 there were no exports (or production) of cocoa; by the mid-1930s these were about 300,000 tons annually, and by the early 1960s they were over 400,000 tons, all from farms established, owned and operated by Africans; there are no foreign-owned cocoa farms. In 1890 combined imports and exports were less than £1 million annually; by the 1930s both imports and exports were in tens of millions; since the mid-1950s imports and exports have each been around £100 million annually. Over this period there was a spectacular increase in imports of both consumer and capital goods. In 1890 there were no imports, or negligible imports of flour, sugar, cement, petroleum products or iron and steel. In recent decades most of these have been on a massive scale. In the early 1890s there were about 3000 children at school; by the mid-1950s there were over half a million. In the 1890s there were neither railways nor roads, but only a few jungle paths, and transport of goods was entirely by human porterage and by canoe. By the 1930s there was a substantial railway mileage and a good road system; by then journeys by road required fewer hours than they had required days in 1890.

Substantially the same applies to Nigeria. Around 1900 exports and imports were each around £2 million annually; by the 1930s they were in tens of millions and since the mid-1950s they have been around £150–200 million annually. Here again practically all exports are produced by Africans and practically all imports are destined for their use. In 1900 there were no exports (or production) of cocoa from Nigeria and exports of oil-palm products were one tenth of their present volume. And here again there has been a phenomenal increase in imports of mass consumer goods and capital goods over this period; in recent years there has also been a substantial increase in the local production of commodities previously imported.

The economic development of West Africa is only the most striking instance of a more general experience in Africa since the end of the nineteenth century. There has been substantial material advance in many parts of the continent, those parts with which the developed world has established contact. And the advance has taken place from extremely backward and indeed savage conditions. By Western standards, sub-Saharan Africa was materially almost unimaginably backward in the third quarter of the nineteenth century. For instance, there were no schools and no man-made communications in the interior (with the irrelevant exception of a few primitive paths chiefly cut by slave-traders or raiders). Apart from slave-trading and raiding there was then little contact between the different parts of the interior of Africa because of the absence of communication facilities which have since been developed in many parts of the continent.

Statistical information of the kind just presented can be multiplied easily. But by itself it cannot convey the profound and pervasive changes which have taken place in many parts of the underdeveloped world in recent decades, and which have changed the conditions of existence. In many areas this progress has meant the suppression of slavery and tribal warfare and the disappearance of famine and of the worst epidemic and endemic diseases. It has meant the development of communications, the replacement of local self-sufficiency by the possibilities of exchange and the emergence and growth of cities. For instance Malaya, which in the 1890s was a sparsely populated country of Malay hamlets and fishing villages, has been completely transformed by the rise of the rubber industry, and has developed into a country with populous cities, thriving commerce and an excellent system of roads. In West Africa slave raiding and slavery were still widespread at the end of the nineteenth century; in 1900 the towns of northern Nigeria, which are now centres of the groundnut trade, were important slave markets.

One further specific example. Hong Kong was an empty, barren rock in the first half of the nineteenth century. By the end of the century it was a port and a minor entrepôt centre. In recent years it has become a major manufacturing centre, exporting manufactures on a large scale throughout the Western world. Severe barriers have come to be erected against imports from Hong Kong to protect the domestic industry of the United States, Great Britain, Germany and France from the unsubsidized competition of the industries of Hong Kong, an underdeveloped country, 8000 or more miles away. This rapid progress has occurred in spite of the presence in Hong Kong of three features often said to reinforce the vicious circle of poverty, namely lack of natural resources, extremely severe population pressure, and a very restricted domestic market.

The level of income in underdeveloped countries is by definition low, but this is compatible with advance, indeed even rapid advance, if that advance has begun only comparatively recently, and has started from a very low level. This is the position in many underdeveloped countries.

The thesis of the vicious circle of poverty postulates either that low average levels entail zero rates of change, which is readily refuted by observation; or, alternatively, the thesis identifies a low level with a zero rate of change, which is a simple error in logic. It is remarkable that such a crude notion should have been so widely accepted.

3

I now turn to two points which may be of some interst in their own right but which are also designed to forestall possible objections.

First, the foregoing discussion is not intended to

suggest that there has been material progress throughout the underdeveloped world. There are substantial groups and large areas in the underdeveloped world which have progressed little in recent times. They include the aborigines in many parts of the world, the desert peoples of the Sahara and elsewhere, and the tribal populations of central and east Africa. And over large areas of south and east Asia (including large parts of rural India, Pakistan and China), progress has been comparatively slow, and much of it has been absorbed in the form of increased populations. These are areas largely of subsistence agriculture. There is nothing abnormal or unexpected even in extreme material poverty in these circumstances. In particular, it has nothing to do with a generally operative vicious circle of poverty. There is no general rule or prescriptive right ensuring that all countries or regions should reach the same level of economic attainment or the same rate of progress at any given time or over any given period. Economic progress and achievement depend very largely on human qualities and attitudes, on social and political institutions which derive from these, on historical experience and also on natural resources and on various other factors. There is nothing surprising, abnormal or reprehensible in differences in economic attainment.

Second, recognition of the material progress in so many parts of the underdeveloped world is not a plea for *laissez faire* or for any other policy. The advance has often created formidable problems calling for government action. The progress which has occurred has often been rapid and generally also uneven, both in the sense that it has affected certain areas and sectors earlier and more pervasively than others, and also in that its impact has been much greater on some activities, attitudes and institutions than on others. This latter aspect in particular has often set up considerable strains. The resulting problems are often acute but they are totally different from those of stagnation. Problems of changes in land-tenure arrangements and in property rights and inheritance, personal and social problems arising from detribalization and from the transformation of a subsistence into a money economy, and problems of congestion and delay in ports and on the railroads, are pressing issues in a number of underdeveloped countries, which would not arise in a stagnant economy caught in a vicious circle of poverty. Indeed, the insistence on the vicious circle of poverty has served to obscure these other problems, and to divert attention and energy from attempts to deal with them.

4

The standard current ideology or orthodoxy of underdeveloped countries, of which the thesis of the vicious circle is an integral and indeed principal part, refers to the underdeveloped world almost wholly in terms of stagnation, starvation, retrogression and so forth. However, there also exists a substantial and authoritative body of writings, chiefly by anthropologists, historians, administrators and even some economists, which discusses the rapid changes in these countries since the end of the nineteenth century, and the problems associated with them. This literature discusses prominently the difficulties of adapting institutions and attitudes to fast-changing conditions: the transition from communal to individual tenure of land; the results of detribalization and disintegration of communal life and values; and the difficulties of rapid urbanization; and other related problems. Here are a few examples.

The following is a typical passage from the writings of Mary H. Kingsley, a traveller and humanitarian of the turn of the century who studied the impact of the culture of nineteenth-century Europe on the African whose outlook was that of much earlier cultures: 'If you will try Science [i.e. anthropology], all the evils of the clash between the two culture periods could be avoided and you could assist these West Africans in their thirteenth century state to rise into their nineteenth century state without their having the hard fight for it that you yourself had' (Kingsley, 1901, quoted in Hancock, 1942, p. 333).

In 1926, well before African development became a major international issue, Dr A. McPhee published a book with the revealing title: *The Economic Revolution in British West Africa*. The following passage epitomizes his conclusion:

> In fact, the process since the 'nineties of last century has been the superimposition of the twentieth century after Christ on the twentieth century before Christ, and a large part of the problem of native policy is concerned with the clash of such widely different cultures and with the protection of the natives during the difficulties of transition. . . . The transition has been from the growth of subsistence crops and the collection of sylvan produce to the cultivation of exchange crops, with the necessary implication of a transition from a 'natural' economy to a 'monetary' economy, and the innumerable important reactions from the latter phase (1926).

Much the same conclusions were reached by Sir Keith Hancock, judicious and critical historian of African development. This is what he says:

> In some periods of European history – in our own day, for example, or in the day of the first steam-engines and power mills – the European world has seemed to be transformed; Europe nevertheless has remained the same world, spinning very much faster. But in Africa change means more than acceleration. Europe's commerce and its money-measurements really have brought the African into a new world. . . . He retains something of his old social and religious and mental life and habit – these things are very slow

in dying – but they are distinct from his new economic life and habit (1942, p. 283).

The problems of policy were particularly baffling in the area of land tenure (though by no means confined to it), notably whether individual rights in the cultivation and ownership of land should be permitted to replace communal or tribal tenure wholly or in part, again a problem which would not arise in a static or stagnant society. According to Professor S. Herbert Frankel, well-intentioned but mistaken decisions in this field, taken before the First World War, have had far-reaching consequences in East and South Africa, retarding the more secure advance of the Africans in East Africa and leading South African policy into its present impasse. He writes in a recently published and closely argued paper:

> Looking back from the vantage point of our own times, it is clear that the root cause of the economic backwardness of various African territories as well as of the Native areas in the Union lies in the failure to modify customary control of land occupation and tenure, which has prevented the emergence of land use and ownership compatible with modern forms of commercialized production in a money economy. The failure to make of the land a viable economic factor of production has condemned the peoples on it to eke out a precarious subsistence. . . . As long as communal systems of land tenure and the ban on Native purchase of land in European areas continued, those able and willing to embark upon new methods of production were unable to obtain land holdings of suitable size, adequately protected against tribal rights and authority, and ensuring to the owner the undisturbed fruits of his labour for himself and his heirs. The enterprising, the unemployed, or the redundant were, therefore, condemned to wander to the towns or to other European areas to sell their labour (1960, p. 7).

Nor is this literature confined to Africa. The problems and strains of rapid advance are a major theme of J. S. Furnivall who deals extensively with the experience of Burma:

> The dissolution of the political structure is only the first stage in social dissolution, and it is completed by the second, or economic, stage, breaking up the village into individuals. In this process two factors are operative: economic forces are released; and the checks controlling their action are relaxed. . . . In such circumstances there remains no embodiment of social will or representative of public welfare to control the economic forces which the impact of the West releases (1956, pp. 297 et seq.).

These writers were not simple sentimentalists deploring the passing of the good old days; they noted the very rapid changes and the problems created by them.

5

The discussion of the preceding sections bears on the suggestion that the international inequality of income is constantly and necessarily widening because the underdeveloped world is caught in a vicious circle of poverty while the developed countries are progressing steadily and often rapidly. And this ever widening inequality is said to be both morally reprehensible and politically explosive. If the thesis of the vicious circle were valid, the conclusion would be simple, irresistible and meaningful. But once it is recognized that the thesis is invalid no such simple conclusion is possible.

The following considerations are among those germane to this issue. Whether the international inequality of income between developed and underdeveloped countries is widening or not depends among other factors on where the line between them is drawn, which is arbitrary. For instance, a number of countries which used to be classified as underdeveloped are no longer so regarded; familiar examples include Japan and Hong Kong. This is, of course, quite apart from the fact that all developed countries began as underdeveloped. Again, for a large part of the underdeveloped world there were until recently no statistics whatever of national income or production, and the present statistics are often of very limited meaning.

In particular, these statistics often greatly exaggerate differences in incomes and standards of living between developed and underdeveloped (rich and poor) countries. This arises chiefly because the rates of exchange normally used in comparing national outputs greatly understate the domestic purchasing power of the currencies of the underdeveloped countries (relatively to those in developed countries), because they are based on the purchasing power of money over internationally traded goods, in which the comparative advantage of developed countries is much greater than over non-traded goods and especially services. Moreover, many of the goods and services conventionally included in the national income are more properly regarded as cost, rather than as output or income, and these are relatively much more important in developed than in underdeveloped countries. Further, intra-family services are usually excluded from national income estimates. In underdeveloped countries the concept of the family is much wider than in developed countries, and a much larger proportion of economic activity takes place within the family so that this omitted category is much more important in the underdeveloped than in developed countries. Yet again, a large part of subsistence output and of services connected with subsistence or near-subsistence production are either wholly ignored or undervalued and these are much more important in underdeveloped than in developed countries. And there are also other reasons for the relative underestimate of income in poor countries. These considerations obviously bear on comparisons both of income levels and of rates of progress.[1]

The profound changes in the conditions of life which have occurred in many parts of the underdeveloped world over the last century also much affect the meaningfulness of discussions whether the differences in real income per head between rich and poor countries have widened or narrowed over this period. Indeed it is doubtful whether the concept of income conventionally measured is helpful in indicating or expressing such profound changes.

The inadequacy of national income estimates for comparative purposes is reinforced by the great increase in population which has occurred throughout the underdeveloped world over the last fifty to eighty years, over which period the population of most of these countries has increased by a factor of between two and five. This has come about largely as a result of suppression or reduction of famine, disease, infant mortality, slave raiding and tribal warfare. As a result, very large numbers of people have survived who otherwise would not be there, which obviously bears on the relevance and meaningfulness of discussions on differences in average or median incomes between developed and underdeveloped countries.

Economic progress is usually measured by the growth of real income per head. This procedure implies various judgments which are generally covert and unrecognized. The increase in population in underdeveloped countries has been brought about by the fall in the death rate (especially, but not only, among children) and this implies a longer expectation of life. The position of those who have failed to die has certainly improved as has the situation of those whose children continue to live. Thus there is here an obvious and real psychic income. Its reality is clear from people's readiness to pay for the satisfaction of the postponement of death. Thus the usual way of drawing conclusions from income per head obscures important conceptual problems of the defined and measured income. It also implies a judgement that a high birth rate is a sign of an inability rather than of an unwillingness to control birth.

Over considerable periods in recent times, notably since 1930, the rates of population growth in many underdeveloped countries have been higher than in most developed countries. A differential rate of population increase in rich and poor countries brings about a change in relative numbers; as a result, the mean incomes could fall for the whole world, or for the underdeveloped world, even if incomes have everywhere increased. Indeed, the difference between the mean incomes in rich and poor countries could widen even if incomes in the latter rise faster than in the former, if the difference in the rates of population growth is greater than that in the rise in incomes. These statistical results of a change in the relative importance of component elements of an aggregate are familiar or should be familiar.[2]

Of course, even if international inequality in some specified sense or other were widening for such reasons, as for instance the relatively greater ability of the populations of the developed countries to take advantage of technical progress, or other differences in economic qualities and attitudes, this would not mean that the higher incomes have been extracted from the underdeveloped countries or otherwise secured at their expense, as is commonly suggested in contemporary discussion. The higher incomes and living standards in developed countries have been created there and not extracted from the rest of the world. In the material sense at any rate, contact[3] with the developed world has benefited the poorer countries. Throughout the underdeveloped world the most advanced and rapidly advancing areas are those with which the developed countries have established contact. Conversely, the poorest and most backward are those with least contact with the developed world.

6

In recent years a variant of the general thesis of the vicious circle of poverty has gained considerable influence. This is the suggestion that the presence of the developed countries sets up an international demonstration effect which serves to obstruct further any capital formation in underdeveloped countries which might otherwise take place. This is regarded as a further obstacle to capital formation and to economic development, in effect substituting another vicious circle of poverty and underdevelopment should the first vicious circle be broken through in some way or other. This was first advanced by Professor Nurkse who argued that contact with advanced economies is damaging to underdeveloped countries by raising the propensity to consume, thus discouraging saving and preventing investment. To quote:

> Knowledge of or contact with new consumption patterns opens one's eyes to previously unrecognized possibilities. . . . In the poorer countries such goods are often imported goods, not produced at home; but that is not the only trouble. The basic trouble is that the presence or the mere knowledge of new goods and new methods of consumption tends to raise the general propensity to consume. . . . The vicious circle that keeps down the domestic supply of capital in low-income areas is bad enough by itself. My point is that it tends to be made even worse by the stresses that arise from relative as distinct from absolute poverty (Nurkse, 1953, pp. 61 et seq., 70).

In fact, however, the effects of contact with more advanced countries are usually very different from those assumed by the international demonstration effect. It almost invariably accelerates economic growth in less developed countries by encouraging production for the market, by suggesting new wants, new crops, and improved methods generally. This indeed is a commonplace of economic history. And at present throughout the underdeveloped world the more advanced sectors and areas are those which are in contact with the more developed countries.

The usual formulation of the international demonstration effect omits to note that the new types of consumer goods can be bought only if incomes are first earned to purchase them. Indeed, until quite recently the absence of new wants, and the inelasticity of consumption and of standards of living, were regarded as major obstacles to economic development; and the role of new categories of consumer goods, often termed incentive or inducement goods, was emphasized as an instrument of economic progress. The demonstration effect resulting from contact with more developed economies usually induces a higher economic performance, more effort, more productive work, more enterprise, and often also additional and more productive saving and investment, especially direct investment in agriculture for production for the market. This influence is reinforced because the contact usually not only suggests new wants but also acquaints the population with new crops and methods of production, the adoption of which makes possible the satisfaction of the new wants. Moreover, by generating cash incomes this process also promotes investment in other parts of the economy; public investment made possible by increased revenues is only one obvious example.

The usual exposition of the international demonstration effect seems to assume that the exchange economy has already permeated the entire economy, or at any rate that the supply of effort to the exchange sector and its rate of expansion are not affected by the attractiveness of the rewards obtainable in that sector. These assumptions are inapplicable to most underdeveloped countries.

Notes: Reading 1

1 The relative underestimate in the conventional statistics of incomes and living standards in underdeveloped countries has been known for some time. An up-to-date and systematic discussion, both of the extent of exaggeration in the conventional comparisons and of the reasons for it, are to be found in an article by Dan Usher (1963). He writes: 'For example, the conventional comparison shows that the *per capita* national income of the United Kingdom is about fourteen times that of Thailand. Recomputations made by the author to allow for various biases in the comparison suggest that the effective ratio of living standards is about three to one. Even if the recomputed ratio is doubled, the change in order of magnitude is large enough to affect our way of thinking about the underdeveloped countries' (p. 140).

2 The discussion in the text bears on some quite specific ideas in the most influential current literature on underdeveloped countries. For instance, Professor Gunnar Myrdal (1956, p. 2) writes: 'As Mr H. W. Singer has rightly pointed out, world real income *per capita*, and with it the standard of living of the *average* human being, is probably lower now than twenty-five years ago, and perhaps lower than in 1900, because the nations that have rapidly raised their economic standards have been a shrinking proportion of the total world population.' (My italics.) The relevant passage in Mr Singer's article quoted verbatim reads: 'If we define the "average" world income as that of the median world citizen, the spectacular improvement which has occurred at one extreme and which has fascinated economists and other observers becomes irrelevant.' Apart from the absence or the severe limitations of statistics of income, these passages rest on a misleading and unwarranted use of the concepts of average.

3 The reference here, as elsewhere in this paper, is of course to peaceful contact, not to military conquest.

References: Reading 1

Center for International Studies of the Massachusetts Institute of Technology (1957), study submitted to the state committee investigating the operation of foreign aid.

Frankel, S. H. (1960), 'The tyranny of economic paternalism in Africa: a study of frontier mentality, 1860–1960', *Optima* supplement, December.

Furnivall, J. S. (1956), *Colonial Policy and Practice: A Comparative Study of Burma and Netherlands India* (Cambridge University Press).

Hancock, W. K. (1942), *Survey of British Commonwealth Affairs*, Vol. 2, *Problems of Economic Policy, 1918–1939*, pt 2 (Oxford University Press).

Kingsley, M. H. (1901), *West African Studies* (Macmillan).

McPhee, A. (1926), 'The economic revolution in British West Africa', *Studies in Economic and Political Science*, no. 89 (London School of Economics and Political Science).

Myrdal, G. (1956), *An International Economy: Problems and Aspects* (Routledge & Kegan Paul).

Nurkse, R. (1953), *Problems of Capital Formation in Underdeveloped Countries* (Blackwell).

UN, Department of Economic and Social Affairs (1955a), *Analyses and Projections of Economic Development* (UN).

UN, Department of Economic and Social Affairs (1955b), *Economic Survey of Latin America* (UN).

Usher, D. (1963), 'The transport bias in comparisons of national income', *Economica*, new series, Vol. 30, pp. 130 *et seq.*

Reading 2

Single Barrier Theories of Development

P. Streeten

The Frontiers of Development Studies, by P. Streeten (Macmillan, 1972), pp. 13–20.

There is no scarcity of economic theories which attempt to explain the absence of development or its difficulties. Many of them share certain presuppositions. The reasoning commonly takes the following form. It is assumed that all men prefer higher incomes and therefore higher production to lower incomes. Since the knowledge of advanced methods of production is available and need only be transferred from the industrialised countries of the West, there is a presumption that these methods would be adopted everywhere. Since in fact we observe many countries which have not adopted these methods and therefore do not enjoy high incomes, there must be obstacles to development. Many of these theories then single out one obstacle.

Marxian versions see in colonialism and imperialistic exploitation the chief barrier. It is the vested interests of powerful monopolies which prevent the transfer of modern technology and the rise in incomes. But it is not difficult to point to countries and periods where development did not occur, although they were not dominated by colonial powers.

Non-Marxian theories have stressed a number of economic barriers. According to one group of writers, lack of savings keeps down investment, which in turn confines production to primitive techniques, which result in low productivity, low incomes and inability to save. The vicious circle of poverty can be broken only by somehow raising the savings ratio to the point of 'take-off'. Yet, in many of these societies distribution is very unequal and there should be no difficulty, if we ignore political factors, in extracting savings from the richest groups. There is also evidence that even the poorest set aside a part of their income for non-essential purposes, spending it on gold, jewellery, festivities, etc. Very poor countries are known to have been able to save quite considerable proportions for defence or war, for building cathedrals, temples, pagodas or pyramids. All this suggests that in few societies are levels of income so low that all income must be devoted to current expenditure on essentials.

A refinement of this argument says that it was easier for the Egyptians to build pyramids and for medieval princes and kings to build cathedrals because they did not have to keep up with any rich Joneses whose consumption levels made their mouths water and weakened the sinews of saving. It is the so-called international Demonstration Effect – the evidence of high living in rich countries – which presents a barrier to higher savings in poor countries. In particular, the élites in the less developed countries, it is argued, take their bearings from the high consumption societies of the West, emulating them on the beaches in the South of France or in Miami, on yachts, or in cadillacs in Paris or Rome. But this theory leaves unexplained why the élites seek to imitate luxury living but not habits of scientific research, experiment, hard work, rational management and entrepreneurial initiative. Savings, as well as consumption, are higher in advanced countries and the demonstration effect could apply to either.

Another theory sees the main obstacle to development in the lack of incentives to invest in productive plant and equipment. According to this theory, savings are, or would be, available, but they are wasted on non-productive investment, such as the acquisition of land, the maintenance of a large number of useless retainers, on palaces and luxury housing, or they are tucked away safely abroad. The incentive to invest, according to this theory, is weak because productive equipment must be put up with a minimum capacity to be efficient, but markets are too small to justify this minimum capacity. Once again, there is a vicious circle: low incomes cause small markets and small markets prevent the installation of capacity which would raise productivity and incomes and which would widen the market.

But first, it is possible to find many countries in which domestic markets could quite easily be created by cutting off imports. Second, there are numerous manufacturing activities which can be carried out economically in quite small-scale enterprises. Third, many of these countries pride themselves on having development plans. They could co-ordinate the investment decisions and ensure that markets are provided for large-scale investment projects, by their being undertaken jointly.

Another theory attributes the blockage to the

difficulty of constructing overhead capital. Roads, railways, harbours, power stations, require large lumps of capital. Poor countries cannot afford these. But without them, development cannot proceed. Although such projects can be very useful in promoting development, they can often be constructed with labour-intensive methods and, initially, on a relatively small scale and piecemeal. Where large-scale projects have been carried out with foreign aid, they have often turned out to be badly managed and underutilised.

A more recent group of writers, impressed by the inadequacy of explanations that concentrate on physical capital as the main condition for accelerating development, has stressed 'inadequate investment in human resources', or, more simply, lack of education and skills. Yet, it is evident that many underdeveloped countries spend too much on the wrong kind of education and, failing to take other necessary measures, have produced a class of educated unemployed who provide a fertile ground for reactionary rather than economic activity.

Others again have attributed considerable responsibility to deteriorating terms of trade and trading opportunities generally. Yet, countries which enjoy large oil revenues or have a plentiful supply of foreign exchange for other reasons have not been more successful in accelerating development.

The argument so far has been that, although many of these theories point to important obstacles, and although some may be true for certain regions at certain times, they certainly do not show that the removal of these barriers is a sufficient condition for development. In addition, it is possible to point to successful development which occurred in spite of the presence of many of these barriers. Development has taken place even though trading opportunities were unfavourable, even though no foreign loans were available, where the population had not been educated, etc. Even although rising savings and investment ratios have normally accompanied development, it is as plausible to argue that they were the *result* of development as it is to say that they were its *cause*.

Such considerations suggest scepticism towards any single-barrier explanation. Obstacles are numerous and interrelated, though clearly some are more important at certain times and in certain places than others.

It is helpful to look at the situation in underdeveloped countries as a social system. In this system a large number of 'conditions' are causally interrelated, in the sense that a change in any one condition will cause changes in some or all the others. It is possible to group these conditions into the following six broad categories:

1 Output and incomes.
2 Conditions of production.
3 Levels of living (including nutrition and housing and facilities for health, education and training).
4 Attitudes to work and life.
5 Institutions.
6 Policies.

The first three categories comprise what are usually called 'economic' conditions, while categories 4 and 5 would normally be called 'non-economic', psychological, social, and cultural conditions. Category 6 is a mixture and is regarded as 'economic' if policies aim at changing categories 1, 2 and 3, but not if they aim at changes in human attitudes and social institutions. Sometimes only categories 1 and 2 are considered proper topics of 'economic' analysis.

This particular ordering is arbitrary. Since conditions are interdependent, there can be no 'primary' and 'secondary' conditions, no categories that are more fundamental than others. For certain purposes entirely different categories may be appropriate.

When we speak of an 'underdeveloped society', we imply that the conditions 1 to 6 are undesirable, judged from the point of view of the ideal of development.

This is not the place to discuss the manner of interaction of these conditions. A change in any one condition can change others either in the same or in the opposite direction and a very great variety of different outcomes are possible. Some of these give rise to a stable equilibrium, others to an unstable equilibrium (a cumulative process upwards or downwards). The types of questions which one would wish to discuss include the following:

i Is this particular classification the most convenient? Does it cover the ground or does it omit any important category? In particular, is it convenient to include facilities for health, education, and training in 'levels of living'?
ii Is it possible to use quantitative indexes for these categories and will it be possible to assign coefficients of interdependence to the relationships?
iii Can these relationships be studied independently of the direction of change, the previous history of the system and the simultaneous conditions in other social systems which have reached higher stages of development?
iv Is the distinction between 'economic' and 'non-economic' conditions tenable? If not, does this distinction contain a systematic bias which is liable to be reflected in biased policy recommendations?

One important advantage of presenting the conditions of development in this way is to reduce the emphasis laid a decade ago on the accumulation of physical capital. But, from another point of view, it is possible to widen the concept 'capital' so as to include anything that yields a stream of production and income over time. A generalised approach to capital accumulation may help to correct both biases. It may help to approach different investment complexes (the components of which are complementary) as substitutes in a strategy for development. The returns of such complexes or packages could, in principle, be compared. But it would amount to the evaluation of different large strategic decisions, not of marginal or infinitesimal moves.

The Role of Agriculture

The system may be illustrated by asking what are the prerequisites for [a] breakthrough in agriculture.

1 Agricultural output and incomes both determine and depend upon:
2 Conditions of production:
assuming an adequate infrastructure of roads, irrigation, etc., it is necessary to increase inputs such as chemical fertilisers, insecticides and farm tools; and to improve the skills of farmers by training.
3 Levels of living:
it is necessary for the farmer to have a minimum level and the right kind of education, health and nutrition.
4 Attitudes to work and life:
it is necessary to increase availability of incentive goods, i.e. things which the farmer and his family would work harder to get; the resistance to work in the country on the part of urban youth and technicians must be broken down.
5 Institutions:
there must be a system of land tenure which permits the farmer to reap the benefits of his efforts; credit must be available at low rates of interest to make him change the composition of his crops and raise productivity; the marketing organisation should prevent middle-men from creaming off so much as to leave the farmer inadequate incentive to switch from export crops to domestic food production; diversification often depends on more efficient marketing.
6 Policies:
the farmer must be assured of a steady and remunerative price; technical assistance relevant to his soil, weather conditions and change in technology must be made available *on the spot*.

It can be seen that these conditions interact. Better education, of the right kind, makes farmers more receptive to technical assistance and ready to use irrigation, better seeds, fertilisers and tools. The result of their improved efforts must be marketable at a stable and remunerative price, which reinforces confidence in further improvements and strengthens inducements to undergo the right kind of training.

It has become part of the current orthodoxy to say that agricultural reform must be given the highest priority. It is, however, not always made clear why precisely this breakthrough in agriculture is considered to be crucial, nor how advance on this front is related to advances on other fronts. In addition, much talk of agricultural reform seems to be a rationalisation of an urban, industrial bias, which insists that surpluses of workers, food and savings be squeezed out of the rural sector to advance the industrial sector.

A widespread view, therefore, is that agricultural progress is necessary in order to supply, firstly, *a surplus of labour* for industry, secondly, *a marketable surplus* of food for industrial workers and, thirdly, an *investible surplus* of savings for urban industry.

The doctrine of the need for a *labour surplus* is no longer tenable. The problem in the foreseeable future is not labour shortage but shortage of jobs. The need to provide employment opportunities in agriculture and in rural industry calls for technological research, because the available technology is adapted to a shrinking, not an expanding, rural labour force. It also calls for land reform, extension services, irrigation and drainage, improved seeds, fertilisers and pesticides, improved storage, transport, credit and marketing facilities and more reliable prices for the produce sold. It would be quite illusory to believe that urban industry can wholly absorb the growing labour force. If we assume that the rate of population growth is the same in agriculture as in industry, say 3 per cent, that the labour force grows at the same rate as population and that 80 per cent of the labour force are in the rural sector and 20 per cent in urban industry, urban industry's demand for labour would have to grow at 15 per cent in order to absorb the whole growth of the labour force. The high growth of the labour force will continue for the next thirty years, however effective birth control were to become now. The need for the creation of employment opportunities in the rural sector is aggravated by the facts: (*a*) that population grows more rapidly in the rural sector than in the urban sector, (*b*) that there is already substantial rural underutilisation of labour, and (*c*) that the technology used in the urban sector saves labour in relation to capital. It follows that the emphasis on agricultural and rural employment opportunities, far from presenting a case against industrialisation, shows the importance of agricultural advance as a necessary condition for industrialisation. Rural underutilisation of labour damages in a number of ways the prospect of successful industrialisation.

The doctrine of the need for a *marketable surplus*, to feed and supply with raw materials the rapidly, and indeed increasingly rapidly, growing proportion of the labour force in industry, unlike the doctrine of the labour surplus, has not been seriously questioned.

There can be no doubt that it is essential to improve the diet and to raise levels of living, both because these are objectives worth pursuing for their own sake and because this would improve the quality of the labour force by reducing apathy and increasing health, strength and vigour. In particular, there is a crying need to improve the diet and level of living of the *rural* population in underdeveloped countries who, while ministering to the basic needs of life, suffer from the most depressed levels of consumption. It is they – the landless labourers, the small tenant farmers, the share-croppers and the peasants with tiny plots of land – who form the proletariat of the world today. Compared with them, the employed industrial workers in the under-developed countries are an aristocracy. Rural reform would therefore, in addition to breaking the main development bottleneck, contribute to a reduction of the most glaring social inequality.

But the application of the doctrine of the marketable surplus may make the fate of the small subsistence farmer, the share-cropper and the landless labourer worse rather than better. The stimulation of urban market opportunities, though clearly desirable, if pursued ruthlessly, benefits the big farmer rather than the small man, may increase rural inequalities and may worsen rural malnutrition. Many of the recent agricultural success stories do not survive the test of rural welfare, reduced inequality and advance on a wide front.

Finally, the doctrine of the need to squeeze an *investible surplus* out of agriculture, in order to finance urban industrial investment, ignores the potentially higher returns to some forms of investment in agriculture. Typically, 20 per cent of investment is allocated to the rural sector, comprising 70 per cent of the population. While it is now generally accepted that higher investment is not a sufficient condition for agricultural growth and while some glaringly bad agricultural investment projects stare one in the eye, it is equally clear that the absorptive capacity for capital in agriculture can be substantially raised. The division into agriculture and industry is probably too aggregative and crude to provide sound investment criteria. One agro-industrial investment complex may show high returns, while other projects, both in agriculture and industry, may yield low returns. Calculations of sectoral capital–output ratios are no substitute for careful project selection. But none of this can be used as an argument to squeeze savings out of agriculture into urban industry. The need to secure agricultural savings is clear. But the place to reinvest these may well be within the agricultural sector. Big farmers must be taxed, not in order to finance industry, but in order to secure a wider spread of agricultural progress.

The endowment per worker of capital, calories and protein is lower in the villages than in the towns. Increases in any of these will yield more extra output. Equality, growth and development in this area do not conflict; they reinforce one another. Not only justice, but also economic progress require that savings and food surpluses should be kept in the rural areas.

Agricultural reform can be used in some cases to reduce balance-of-payments strains. This can be done by raising the supply of exports, either directly by producing domestic food and raw materials for those engaged in exporting manufactured goods, or by substituting domestic food and raw materials for imports.

The ability of the rural sector to supply food and raw materials to industry, through the maximisation of this surplus, implies that the rural sector provides a market for industrial products. The higher the productivity of the rural sector, the higher will be its demand for industrial products. If industry adopts methods of mass production and exploits economies of scale, a prosperous rural sector, by providing an ever-widening market, is a condition for progress in industry. But the need for greater emphasis on agriculture and rural development has been used to reinforce policies which discriminate against the rural poor and the rural tillers of the land.

Reading 3

The Entrepreneur and Economic Development

J. Habakkuk

Lectures on Economic Development, by J. Habakkuk (University of Istanbul, 1958).

There is no simple formula for economic development. Rapid and sustained economic advance has become a common state of affairs only in relatively recent times. A great part of the human race has existed for thousands of years without achieving any perceptible degree of economic progress. Even today, assured progress is confined to a few areas. And the course of development within these areas has been very far from uniform. One cannot generalize even about the most important economic variables. Some of the developing countries were, at the start, sparsely populated, e.g. the USA and Canada; some were very densely populated, e.g. Holland and Belgium. In some countries economic development has been accompanied by a high rate of population growth, e.g. the United Kingdom and Japan; in others like Sweden the growth of population has been slow. In most countries economic development was accompanied by a high rate of capital accumulation: in Japan, e.g. between 1913 and 1939, real capital is estimated to have increased between five- and six-fold. But in France over a similar period there was probably no increase in aggregate capital and capital per head of the working population (see Clark, 1957, p. 506).

The undeveloped countries are even more diverse. They include areas like India and China with long traditions of civilization, as well as the African tribal societies. They number countries rich in mineral resources and land, like many parts of Latin America, and countries badly endowed by nature: countries which will certainly become rich and countries which will probably remain poor. They include not only the densely populated countries of Asia, but sparsely populated countries like Brazil; not only areas which are desperately short of capital, but countries like Venezuela and Iraq in which funds are plentiful. And when we ask why one country has enjoyed rapid economic progress whereas another has remained backward, the answer is not always obvious. Why should the USA have become a great industrial power, but not Brazil, why Japan but not China?

Moreover there are countries which appeared to enter upon a period of economic development, which was then arrested. Mexico for example between 1900 and 1910 made quite rapid progress, but it was halted by revolution and has not since been resumed at anything like the same rate. Argentina is, perhaps, a similar case. These countries had their ‘take-off’, to use Professor Rostow’s phrase. They became air-borne. But they ‘bumped down’ again.

All these facts suggest that economic development is an immensely complicated process. It is not just a matter of natural resources, capital and labour. It is part of the whole social development of a society; it depends not merely on economic circumstances but on social structure and the attitudes of people to life as a whole.

Of all the many influences on economic development, I have chosen to consider the entrepreneur, the business leader, not necessarily because he is the most important influence, but because he has been the immediate agent of economic development in the USA and in western Europe, and because he is the point at which the wider social influences are most directly brought to bear upon the economic process. I confine my attention to the entrepreneur in industry.

I shall consider first the circumstances which favoured the rise of a class of vigorous entrepreneurs among the western industrial nations. I shall then consider what relevance this experience may have for the under-developed countries of the modern world.

1

In western industrial civilization, in its formative stages, the entrepreneurs were people who took the key decisions. One naturally thinks of the famous names. In England, men like Arkwright, who revolutionized the cotton textile industry, Boulton who made the steam engine a commercial proposition, Bessemer, who saw the possibilities of cheap steel; in Germany men like

Strousberg, the great builder of railways, creators of German heavy industry like Thyssen and Krupps, founders of her electrical industry like Siemens; in America the railway kings like Gould and Harriman, steel magnates like Andrew Carnegie, and Ford who revolutionized the motor-car industry. But besides these clearly exceptional personalities, there was a large number of men who made minor but still important innovations, and many more were imitators and followers, but those imitations involved a considerable degree of initiative and vigour. It is not the appearance of a handful of remarkable 'captains of industry' which has to be explained, but the emergence of a large social group.

The entrepreneurs of western industrial society have not been all of a single type. A German like Rathenau was moulded in a different intellectual tradition from an Englishman like Lord Leverhulme. The railway kings were a race apart, much more interested in quick speculative gains than were the leaders in most other fields. The great iron masters—and they were more typical of the industrial entrepreneur—identified themselves with long-term projects. But, despite these differences, most entrepreneurs had certain common characteristics: a flair for identifying and seizing opportunities for profit, an eye for the possibilities of new products, unexploited raw material supplies, untapped markets; willingness to take considerable risks; vision, drive and initiative; the ability to devote their whole energies completely to attain their ends. In the early phases of industrialization, they owned as well as managed their concerns; most of them had a very strong urge to accumulate; the most characteristic of them eschewed the full possibilities of increased personal consumption which success brought, and ploughed back their profits. Their distinguishing characteristic was that they thought in terms of reinvesting income in factories and machines, ships and rails, and it was their habits which were in the first instance responsible for the high rates of capital accumulation achieved by western industrial society. Many of them were ruthless; few of them were pleasant to live with; but they accomplished great economic changes, and up to 1914 they were the men whose decisions primarily determined the rate of economic advance.

The great age of such men was the century before 1914. At the present time, to an increasing extent, industrial leadership in America and Europe comes from the great corporations and companies, from managers rather than owners; the new lines of advance are explored systematically by the research laboratory and not left to the flair of individual entrepreneurs. But even now, the old style entrepreneur still plays some part; he has been important, for example, in the aircraft industry and in television. One of the key figures in the American shipbuilding industry, Mr Henry Kaiser, was an entrepreneur of the old type. And the executives of the great corporations often display the same concentration of energy as the nineteenth-century entrepreneur, the same subordination of life to a single end. They are managers rather than owners, and their interests are therefore somewhat different from those of the classic entrepreneur; but there are resemblances in character and personality. And it is this type of character, and the conditions which encourage its development that we have to explain.

It calls for explanation, for it has been rare in human history; the willingness to 'scorn delights and live laborious days', the ability to concentrate one's whole life on building up a great industrial concern and ceaselessly expanding its boundaries—these are qualities that are not come easily to human beings. Most of us, when we have got a reasonable amount of money, prefer to enjoy ourselves.

These entrepreneurs are, of course, not to be considered only as the causes of economic development, they are also a product, a consequence, of economic development. Shall we say that economic progress was rapid in a particular country because the entrepreneurs of that country were unusually adventurous, or that the entrepreneurs were successful because the country was developing rapidly for quite independent reasons? The entrepreneurs of the United States have, as a class, been highly successful; but is this because by nature they are unusually enterprising, or because America is rich in natural resources and has a large homogeneous market? In the later nineteenth century German entrepreneurs were, in general, more vigorous than the French. But was this because their original attitudes were different, or simply because, for straightforward economic reasons, the rewards of enterprise were greater in Germany? It is always difficult to know how much importance we should attribute to the entrepreneur and how much to the economy in which he works, to the nature of the market he supplies, to the character of his labour supplies and the extent of the natural resources. The entrepreneur is not a *deus ex machina*: he is part of a complicated social process. In isolating him I do not wish to suggest he has been the only, or the most important, factor in economic development.

How are we to explain men of the entrepreneurial type? What conditions favoured their appearance in large numbers in western Europe and the United States in the nineteenth century? There are really two questions we have to answer. Why were there so many of them, i.e. what factors have influenced the supply of entrepreneurs? And what determines their pattern of behaviour once they have become entrepreneurs?

The supply of entrepreneurs may be limited by economic circumstances, by social structure, and by social attitudes towards entrepreneurs, and we shall consider each of these influences in turn. In Europe and the United States the strictly economic limitations were not of major importance. These areas had all had considerable industries, organized on the 'domestic system', long before the period of the classic industrial revolution. Such industries were training grounds for entrepreneurs. Moreover, since economic progress consisted of the gradual development of new techniques, not the taking over in a body of techniques from outside, the entrepreneurs of these countries accumulated a body of experience which enabled them to assess the risks of industrial investment, and to identify the most fruitful lines of advance.

So far as social structure was concerned, the position was exceptionally favourable in the United States. In that country, there was no long-established class system to impede social mobility. The possibility of rising to the top was believed to be much greater than anywhere else in the world, and, indeed, this belief corresponded to the facts. This belief in an open avenue to wealth is one of the main reasons for the amount of ability that has been devoted—and is being devoted—to entrepreneurship in the United States. Even now, in America, the ambition to own one's own business is widespread among manual workers (see Sutton, 1954, p. 13). Moreover, in the United States, there were—and are—few competitors to business success as a source of social prestige. There was no large and powerful bureaucracy, no hereditary aristocracy. There was no professional military class and soldiers were not held in high esteem. Horatio Alger, the hero of the American success story, wanted to be a businessman not a general or a civil servant or a great landowner. The men of ambition and ability turned naturally to business, not only because of the gains which might be made there—though they were sometimes certainly enormous—but because businessmen, a Rockefeller, or a Pierrepont Morgan, were the leading men of the country.

In western Europe conditions were more complicated. There were strongly entrenched social systems which limited social mobility, social systems inherited from the pre-industrial times when landowners were the ruling groups. Moreover, there were sources of power and prestige besides business. Landownership, bureaucracy, the army and the professions were all powerful competitors of business for the services of the able men. Thus, in France it has been argued that, because of the power and prestige of the bureaucracy, too many able men became civil servants. In Germany the prestige of the military class may have had the same effect. In England—and to some extent in Germany—there was a haemorrhage of capital and ability from industry and trade into landownership and politics. Robert Peel and Gladstone both came of entrepreneurial families, but their abilities were devoted to politics, not to industry and trade.

In all three countries the high social standing of the professions has drawn off a large number of the ablest men. One of the most successful British entrepreneurs of the twentieth century, Lord Nuffield, entered a business career only because his father was unable, for economic reasons, to fulfil his original intention to make him a surgeon. Undoubtedly in England in the first forty years or so of this century, the professions attracted too many able people and business too few. After 1902, there was a vast increase in educational opportunities in England, but the majority of those who profited from such opportunities up to 1939 became teachers or lawyers, doctors or architects rather than businessmen. Why were the professions more attractive? Certainly not because they yielded higher incomes; it was partly because, for a person with no personal contacts in business, the professions were more accessible, and partly because business in general lacked the social prestige of the professions. Moreover, in the present century a business career, the acquisition of profit, became actively disapproved of among the many people who were influenced by socialist ideas about capitalism and the profit motive.

In western Europe therefore business has had to face greater competition for the able men than it has had to face in the USA. But in this respect, Europe is becoming more like America. Two wars have reduced the prestige of the army in Germany, and to some extent in France. Post-war Germany has been rebuilt by her businessmen. Inflation has depressed the professions and elevated the entrepreneur. Even the socialist measures in Great Britain, by reducing the importance of hereditary wealth, have made current income and achievement more important. And, all things taken together, the upward path in western European countries in the last hundred years has been less obstructed than in most other parts of the world. Historically great entrepreneurs have been recruited from almost every social group—from landed aristocrats to wage-earners. The wider, therefore, the circle from which a country draws its businessmen, the more likely it is to produce great entrepreneurs. In western Europe, the feudal system and the obstacles it presented to the rise of 'new men' had disappeared before the main phase of industrialization; in the United States these obstacles had never existed. The conditions were eminently suitable for the growth of a large class of entrepreneurs.

I have now come to the second and more difficult question. Let us suppose that there are few obstacles in the path of men who attempt to become businessmen. What determines their behaviour when they have become businessmen? This depends partly on the motives of the entrepreneur, on his own psychology. It depends partly on the value which other people in his society place upon his activities.

Consider the motives of the entrepreneur first. Max Weber (1930) attributed the peculiar character of the western-type entrepreneur to religious changes—to Calvinism. For the Calvinist, success in his 'callings', in his occupation, was the measure of his real worth. He worked not merely for worldly ends, but because business success was a sign of spiritual grace. This belief, Weber argued, provided the psychological foundation for the creation of a large class of entrepreneurs. It gave them the necessary self-discipline to devote themselves heart and soul to their occupation. Weber has been much criticized. But his thesis does point to an important condition for the rise of a class of effective entrepreneurs. It is difficult to overcome the natural inclination of men to spend their money and enjoy their leisure, difficult to induce them to devote all their life to their work and to reinvest their gains on the interests of the future which they will not live to enjoy. To do so involves a fundamental change in a man's whole attitude to life, and so great a change is most easily brought about by a change in religious belief. It is significant that the periods of most vigorous entrepreneurial activity have been accompanied by ideological changes. An almost religious faith in democracy and free enterprise reinforced the drive and thrust of American entrepreneurs. The devotion to Marxism may have played a somewhat similar role in Soviet Russia. Nationalism has often provided the extra energy required for great entrepreneurial effort, as the achievement of national unity did in nineteenth-century Germany. A simple desire to make profits will not by itself produce the intense concentration of effort required for sustained entrepreneurial achievement. It needs to be reinforced by a belief that the business leader is serving a wider purpose. Calvinism certainly created such a belief, and some ideology with its roots outside the economic sphere is probably necessary for the purpose.

But the entrepreneur's behaviour does not depend upon his own motives alone. It depends also on the way other people in his society regard his activities, on the general climate of opinion in which he works, on the amount of social approval given to the entrepreneur. What determines a man's social standing? Sometimes birth, memberhip of a certain type of family or racial group. Sometimes the type of education a man has had. Sometimes the way he behaves, his manners and his accent. Sometimes the whole range of a man's achievements and abilities, his physical strength or weakness, the way in which he orders his life, his capacity to paint, or to play instruments, his whole character and personality. Sometimes a man's success in his occupation. In most societies each of these influences play some part in determining a man's standing in society. But they are not always of equal importance; birth, for example, is more important in India than it is in Europe; the type of education and accent are more important in Britain than they are in America. Some societies have valued supremely the 'all-round man'; the ideal of Renaissance Europe, for example, was the ideal of the aristocratic gentleman, the man of well-developed competence in many fields, who could do many things well. In other societies the main emphasis is placed on success in one's job, as measured primarily by income.

In the United States, from almost the beginning, birth and hereditary status were of small influence, and the highly efficient performance of a specific and limited function was the mark of a man's social standing. There the man who concentrates his energies on a single goal and achieves success in his occupation is the man who commands respect; the accepted ideal is that he should rise as far in terms of wealth as his abilities can carry him. A man's success in his occupation is not invariably judged by the amount of money he makes. Some occupations are very highly regarded which do not yield very high rewards, e.g. a Justice of the Supreme Court, but income is certainly an important criterion of occupational success. Most of the signs of social standing, e.g. the current model of an expensive car, can be acquired with money.

The industrial countries of western Europe are not in quite the same position. There are still strong pre-industrial elements in their social attitudes. In Europe, with its more complicated social traditions, birth and family are more important than in the USA. The ideal of the 'all-round man' still lingers. There are still many marks of social standing, like accent, which a man may possess even though he has little money, and which a man may not be able to acquire even though he has a great deal of money. Considerable social standing attaches to certain of the professions, even though the money rewards are small. But even in many parts of western Europe over the last hundred years, birth, family education, general attainments, have tended to yield before occupational success as the rod by which people are judged. And it is evident that industrialization itself has weakened the power of these 'competitors to occupational performance', these alternative ways of judging a man's social standing. Industrialization has been accompanied by the growth of towns, and by considerable geographical movements of population; and both have weakened the traditional criteria of social position. A family may have an inherited social importance in a small village with a static population; it will find it difficult to retain it in a large town with a mobile population. Industrialization has brought—has necessitated—wider educational opportunities. When clever boys can go to the University, no matter what their family, their family origin matters less. With heavy death duties, inherited wealth becomes less important, and the income a man earns for himself becomes more important. In the way a man is judged, in the importance placed on efficiency in a job, western Europe has, in varying degrees, for the last fifty years been developing along American lines.

Where social standing depends on birth or accent, i.e. on qualities which cannot be bought by current income, the incentive to devote the whole personality to the acquisition of wealth is weak. But where social standing depends on success in one's occupation, a man has a very strong incentive to devote all his energies to his occupation, particularly if success is measured by income.

The activity of entrepreneurs in western industrial society has thus not been determined solely by economic facts. It is the result of the fact that social mobility was relatively easy, that the insuperable barriers to social mobility had been removed before industrialization began. It was the result also of social attitudes which took long to establish themselves, attitudes among the entrepreneurs as well as in the society in which they operated; the result especially of the high degree of social approval accorded to success in business.

2

The question now arises how far these are essential conditions for the appearance of vigorous private entrepreneurs. In many underdeveloped countries at the present time society is stratified; there are a great variety of social obstacles to a man who attempts to rise. And in these countries the prevailing attitudes to business success are different. There is often hostility to private businessmen—by the government and by the intelligentsia. Of modern India, for example, it has been said that 'leadership in the civil services, the professions, the Universities, the All-India Congress, and the trade union movement has come largely from an intelligentsia who have played little part in Indian business. Often they disparage business, regarding its purposes as somehow alien to what they believe are authentic Indian values' (Lamb, 1955). Will entrepreneurship in such societies be frustrated by their social systems? Or will it appear, but in different forms and from other sources than in the West? Or will entrepreneurs of the Western type emerge and by their activity revolutionize the social structure and attitudes of such societies?

It is clearly possible for a country to produce first rate entrepreneurs, even though its social mobility is small and business achievement as such is not accorded high social prestige. There were plenty of aristocratic entrepreneurs in pre-industrial Europe. In the modern world the classic case is Japan where the industrial entrepreneurs were drawn from the landowners. 'This swift transformation of an old-type aristocracy into a new-type capitalist class was profoundly important in increasing the supply of entrepreneurship in Japan in the crucial last quarter of the nineteenth century' (Lewis, 1955, p. 237).

It may be argued further that, in an undeveloped country, a closed class system, i.e. an authoritarian system in which people are prepared to accept subordination, is very well adapted to produce the type of entrepreneurial activity which such a country needs. While the need in a developed industrial economy is to devise and adopt entirely new ways of doing things, producing existing products by better methods or producing goods hitherto unknown, the need in an undeveloped economy is to choose from among the methods already existing in the advanced economies those which best suit its particular circumstances. Provided *somebody* in the undeveloped country is prepared to take this initiative, the authoritarian, cohesive character of the society may positively facilitate the subsequent process of imitation and diffusion of techniques. Thus the Japanese habits of class subordination may have assisted the adoption of Western techniques.

But is not Japan an exceptional case? The experience of India may be more relevant. There have been, for a long time, a number of great entrepreneurial families in India, e.g. the Birlas and Tatas, but they have had very few followers. They have been generals without an army. It seems a characteristic of successful businessmen in such countries that they do not stay in a single industry; they start in one industry and then go on to some entirely unrelated industry. In this way the same group may initiate and develop a number of industries, but they do not inspire imitators. In India, the three great business communities—Parsis, Gujaratis and Marwaris—are still preponderant in Indian industry and banking, and within them a small number of industrial families still retain their hold.

It is clear that in underdeveloped countries the supply of entrepreneurs is limited in the first place by economic circumstances. In such countries, even where the long-term prospects for industrialization are favourable, the risks of investment in industry are substantial; an industrialist has to commit his resources for a long period to uses that cannot easily be changed, and the risks of such a long-term commitment is great, for there is no body of experience to enable the entrepreneur to assess the risks correctly and no institutions designed to reduce them. In such countries, therefore, the men with capital and ability tend to put their money into trade or land; into trade, where the turnover of capital is rapid, into land which is both more secure and more liquid than factories. The very unequal distribution of wealth, found in many undeveloped countries, reinforces the emphasis on commerce; the best and most assured markets are provided by the small number of wealthy people who buy imported goods, i.e. goods supplied by the trader not the local industrialist. Thus, for a variety of reasons, potential entrepreneurs are diverted away from industry. Most of the great industrial entrepreneurs of the Western world have had technical knowledge, and many of them have risen from among the skilled artisans. Where entrepreneurs have appeared among the indigenous populations of underdeveloped areas they have generally been recruited from among the commercial element.

It is clear, secondly, that in many undeveloped countries, the social structure imposes barriers to the emergence of a class of business entrepreneurs. In the case, for example, of the tribal societies of East Africa, the embryo entrepreneur is hampered by his obligations to his kindred. A caste system, like that of India, which constricts a man to the caste into which he was born, obviously makes it extremely difficult to draw upon the supplies of entrepreneurial ability. Still more the values of such stratified and hierarchical societies limit the supply of entrepreneurs. In many of these societies birth is still of major importance in determining social standing. A man is born into a class, with customary rights and duties, and traditional stages of personal development, and he is judged by the efficiency with which he performs his traditional role.

Where, for these economic and social reasons, the indigenous supply of entrepreneurs is deficient, one possible method of meeting the situation is the import of foreign entrepreneurs. This has historically been an important source of enterprise. German entrepreneurs developed certain branches of English mining in the sixteenth century. British entrepreneurs established textile factories and iron foundries in nineteenth-century Europe. Immigrants also have sometimes provided entrepreneurs in conditions where the local supply of business enterprise was small; thus in 1938 more than 60 per cent of the industry of Argentina was controlled by first-generation immigrants, presumably because, among other reasons, they were less influenced by traditional value-systems.

This method of supplying a local scarcity of enterprise has had a long and successful history in economies where the other prerequisites of economic development were present. The foreign entrepreneurs, where successful, have often called forth supplies of local entrepreneurial ability; they have stimulated competition and imitation; they have provided opportunities for the local inhabitants to acquire industrial techniques and administrative skills. This happened in Germany around the middle of the nineteenth century. It is likely to happen wherever the gap between the technical and educational levels of the foreigner and the native is not too large. There may, of course, be difficulties about this method. Where the foreigner is greatly superior, he may become entrenched and the local inhabitants will find it difficult to enter the field; he may moreover concentrate on types of enterprise which do not necessarily have the greatest contribution to make to a long-term development (see Belshaw, 1955). But there are many parts of the world where this method has still a major part to play.

The second main possibility is that the state shall perform entrepreneurial functions. The industrializations of the USA and western Europe were spontaneous; in most countries, the state played a positive role by creating conditions in which private entrepreneurs could work, but in general it did not itself take the initiative in starting industries. This is true even of Germany. In the less developed areas of the present day, the scope and the need for state action are likely to be wider. What is not clear is the precise scope and purpose of state action. It may well be that some undeveloped countries will only have a 'take-off' if the government takes vigorous action to start new industries and to impose on the country—by inflation and taxation—a high rate of capital accumulation. This 'shock treatment' may be the quickest way of achieving a fundamental change in social structure and attitudes. But it can be an extremely painful way, as the experience of the USSR shows; it may inflict intense hardship upon the peasantry, at whose expense a rapid outburst of capital investment is apt to take place. And the cost of this method in social and political disturbance is extremely difficult to estimate beforehand. We have too little experience of rapid enforced industrialization in backward countries to enable us to judge the margins of tolerance where social strains are concerned. One cannot avoid social strains by doing nothing; rapid population growth in a stagnant economy may well ultimately produce strains and stresses as great as those which may be brought about by enforced development. What pace of economic development will prove compatible with social stability is obviously a question to which there can be no answer of general application; the problem is one which has to be solved by trial and error in the light of the conditions of each country. It is a problem for which, in many under-developed countries, the state has assumed responsibility.

This question of *speed* of development is, however, logically distinct from the question of *method*, from the question of the extent of state action. One can imagine a government promoting, by subsidies and creation of liberal credit conditions, a rapid rate of capital accumulation while leaving industry entirely in private hands. It is also possible to conceive of an economy owned by the state but characterized by a low rate of capital accumulation. On the question of *method*, I believe that the private entrepreneur has a greater part to play in the economic development of the undeveloped areas than some prevalent fashions on this matter suggest. He is not likely, of course, to build the great public utilities; they fall to the lot of the state, as indeed they usually did even in the nineteenth century. But over a considerable field of industry the acquisitive instinct of the businessmen can still be an immensely powerful agent of economic advance. I believe that in many areas a large part of government policy could profitably be devoted to the creation of conditions favourable to the emergence of a large class of entrepreneurs devoted to industrial investment. This is more difficult now than it was in the nineteenth century for it involves a generous attitude towards profit, and, as Professor W. A. Lewis has observed, 'the less developed countries have awakened into a century where everybody wishes to ride two horses simultaneously, the horse of economic equality and the horse of economic development'. It may also involve a deliberate effort by the state to divert entrepreneurial talent into industry. It involves finally an attempt to promote among the people at large attitudes favourable to entrepreneurial achievement.

References: Reading 3

Belshaw, C. S. (1955), 'The cultural milieu of the entrepreneur', *Explorations in Entrepreneurial History*, Vol. 7, No. 3 (Princeton University Press).

Clark, C. (1957), *The Conditions of Economic Progress*, 2nd edn (Macmillan).

Lamb, H. B. (1955), 'The role of business communities in the evolution of an Indian industrialist class', *Pacific Affairs*, June.

Lewis, W. A. (1955), *The Theory of Economic Growth* (Allen & Unwin).

Sutton, F. X. (1954), 'Achievement norms and the motivations of entrepreneurs', in Cole (ed.), *Entrepreneurship and Economic Growth* (Harvard Research Center in Entrepreneurial History, mimeo.).

Weber, M. (1930), *The Protestant Ethic and the Spirit of Capitalism* (Scribner).

Reading 4

The Capital Shortage Illusion: Government Lending in Nigeria

S. P. Schatz

Oxford Economic Papers (Oxford University Press, 1965), pp. 309–16.

A shortage of capital is usually considered one of the most immediate and pressing as well as most fundamental obstacles to domestic private investment and thus to economic growth in the less-developed economies. In Nigeria, the country which provides empirical support for the thesis presented here, this opinion is widely held and it is certainly the belief of the indigenous businessmen themselves. A survey of Nigerian businesses indicates that 'most Nigerian businessmen believe that inadequate capital is their main or sole business handicap'.[1]

The thesis of this article is that frequently the belief that a capital shortage is the effective or operating impediment to indigenous private investment is mistaken, that it is an illusion created by a large false demand for capital, and that what really exists is not an immediate shortage of capital at all, but a shortage of viable projects, i.e. projects that, all things considered, promise to be sufficiently profitable to attract indigenous private investment. Let me point out that I use the term 'viability' in a broad sense here. When a project is considered unlikely to be commercially successful for any reason—whether the project itself is badly conceived, or because the applicant has insufficient entrepreneurial ability, or because conditions external to the enterprise are unfavourable—then the project is 'not viable'.[2]

The chief source of evidence used in this article is the loans experience of Nigeria's Federal Loans Board (FLB) from its establishment in 1956 to December 1962. The FLB is a development bank, operated by the Federal Government of Nigeria, which makes loans to indigenous entrepreneurs for undertakings in fields other than agriculture or trade. The commercial viability of projects submitted to the FLB is rather carefully investigated by the Industries Division of the Federal Ministry of Commerce and Industry. This Division then presents its recommendations to the FLB, which generally accepts them. Approved loans are subject to the further requirement before they are finally sanctioned that the potential borrower must have adequate collateral to secure the loan. Security is investigated only after the project has passed the viability test.

Since some of the lending activities of the Regional Governments' Loans Boards in the Federation of Nigeria have been greatly influenced by political considerations, it is worth making the point at the outset that this has not been true of the Federal Loans Board. This is analytically important because it allows us to carry on an analysis of the *economics* of the Board's lending activities free from the complicating effects of political factors. The relative insulation of the FLB from political considerations is best shown by the fact that, for the period covered by my observations, the Board accepted the recommendations of the Industries Division officials in 96 per cent of the applications that came before it. All evidence indicates that the recommendations of these Industrial Officers, most of whom were non-Nigerian, were based on economic rather than political considerations. This is universally agreed upon by those who are familiar with the situation, Nigerians as well as Europeans.

1 False Shortage of Capital

We examine the thesis of this article by scrutinizing all applications first considered by the FLB by August 1961. This cut-off date allows time to follow up on the eventual disposal of the applications. Two hundred and ninety applications were judged by the criterion of commercial viability.[3] Of these, 229 (79 per cent) were rejected ('Viability rejectees') and 61 (21 per cent) were approved ('viability approvees'). Of the sixty-one viability approvees, 54 (89 per cent) had acceptable security while seven (11 per cent) were refused loans because of inadequate security.

We see a false demand for capital consisting of two parts. The apparent demand for FLB loans funds, or what may simply be called the apparent demand for capital, is represented by the 290 applications judged on the basis of viability.[4] The first and major segment of the false demand for capital comprises the 229 viability rejectees. They do not constitute part of the genuine demand for capital because, obviously, loans are not made simply on the basis of the aspiring borrowers' estimates of the prospects of their projects. Those with projects which the potential lenders have adjudged unworthy have a *desire* for capital but not an effective demand for capital. The seven security rejectees constitute the second and much smaller segment of the false demand for capital.[5] These are eliminated from the genuine demand for capital because would-be borrowers who cannot produce security acceptable to the lender will not be given loans. The security rejectees also have a desire but not an effective demand for capital.

Table 1 **Federal Loans Board Action on Loans Applications**

Total number of applications judged on the basis of viability	290
Rejected	229 (79%)
Approved	61 (21%)
Of those whose viability was approved	
Security also approved	54 (89%)
Security rejected	7 (11%)

Thus, taking the viability and the security rejectees together, 236 of the 290 applicants have a false demand for capital, while only 54 have a genuine demand. Assuming applications of equal size, 18 per cent of the demand for capital is genuine and 82 per cent is false. If we use the actual average sizes of applications, however, the false demand for capital is larger. The average loan requested by the viability rejectees was £16,648; the average loan requested by the viability approvees was £9,620. Using these figures, we find that 89 per cent of the capital demand was false while 11 per cent was genuine, i.e. the false demand for capital was eight times as large as the genuine.

These figures understate the relative magnitude of the false demand for capital in Nigeria in several ways. Many FLB applications fall by the wayside before they reach the Board because it is made clear in preliminary discussions that the applicant has no chance of success. Moreover, we will see that the FLB, under pressure to make loans, has sometimes gone to considerable lengths to find projects loanworthy. It is also willing to finance projects which are not quite promising enough to be accepted by commercial lenders. We will also see that the prospective viability of some marginal applications is enhanced and the appraisal made more sanguine than it would be if potential investments were considered purely on their own merits because various kinds of government assistance will be rendered to the applying firm. These factors tend to reduce the number of viability rejectees and/or increase the number of viability approvees that emerge from the FLB loan appraisal process.

The number of inadequate security cases is also understated. When a promising project is held up because of inadequate security, the FLB, reluctant to retard economic development, often waters down its security requirements substantially. Where there appeared to be no alternative other than rejection of a promising project, the FLB has sometimes simply approved loans with no security at all.

2 Real Shortage of Viable Projects

We have said that Nigeria manifests a large false demand for and therefore a large false shortage of capital. In this section we discuss reasons for believing that what really exists in Nigeria is a shortage of viable projects.

In terms of loans disbursed, FLB activity was quite limited. The FLB made only forty-four loans to the firms whose applications it first considered during its first five-and-a-quarter years.[6] The aggregate amount of money lent was slightly more than £400,000.

The amount loaned was as small as this despite the fact that the FLB searched assiduously for viable projects. Responding to deep-seated popular desires for rapid development, the FLB frequently judged projects leniently in an effort to find some that could be considered loanworthy. The Board has sometimes gone to great lengths to carve a promising part out of a generally unacceptable application. A firm that engaged in sawmilling and hand production of furniture, for example, applied for a loan of more than £20,000 for log-handling equipment, furniture-making machinery, and the construction of a building. Investigation by an Industrial Officer indicated that the firm had incurred a net loss the previous year, that it had a substantial number of debts, that the proprietor had little or no knowledge of machine-produced furniture (which line of production was, in any case, overcrowded), and that the firm's hand-furniture business was not viable. The sawmilling project was much more promising, but the applicant was adamant about applying for the furniture business as well. The FLB nevertheless refrained from rejecting the application; it deferred its decision and informed the applicant that the Board would probably be favourably inclined to an application for the sawmilling project only. When the applicant acted upon this advice, he was approved for a loan of close to £9,000. The FLB will also sometimes disregard unfavourable factors for a particularly promising entrepreneur. For example, an application was submitted for a loan to enable completion of a partly built hotel by an experienced and capable hotel manager, who also ran a successful enterprise of his own. The report on the application, however, stated that the hotel business was already well served in the area of the prospective enterprise, and any ordinary applicant would probably have been rejected. It was felt, however, that this man would be successful despite the competition, and the FLB approved the loan. The FLB will also pay less than full heed to its own policy rules of thumb for a promising entrepreneur. Thus, because the sawmilling industry was already well developed and competition in the industry was keen, the Board had expressed a reluctance to make loans for this purpose. Nevertheless, when a (different) sawmill proprietor who was already running his existing business successfully and whose prospects for successful expansion were good applied for a loan, his application was approved. The FLB's leniency with respect to security and its practice of taking into account the salutary effects of prospective government assistance to borrowers also increased the proportion of applicants who received loans.

The shortage of viable projects is shown most clearly, perhaps, by the record of the loan recipients. I have examined the FLB progress reports and various other materials on the forty-four FLB borrowers in order to assess the success of their loan financed projects. The results are shown in Table 2.

For sixteen of the firms, mainly those which received their loans most recently, no assessment of business success can yet be made. Of the remaining twenty-eight firms, ten (36 per cent) are proceeding successfully so far. Eleven (39 per cent) have proved unsuccessful. These are cases in which the loan approved project can be judged with confidence to have been unsuccessful. Many of these firms have been taken to court as loan defaulters. Seven (25 per cent) of the projects are shaky, i.e. they are having serious difficulties but may pull out of them.

Table 2 **Success of Projects**

	Forty-four FLB loan recipients			
Year loan was issued	*Successful*	*Unsuccessful*	*Shaky*	*No assessment*
1956/7	1	1	0	0
1957/8	6	4	2	1
1958/9	3	5	0	0
1959/60	0	0	3	1
1960/1	0	1	2	3
1961/2	0	0	0	8
1962/3	0	0	0	3
Total	10	11	7	16

There is a supplementary group of borrowers under FLB jurisdiction whose business performance we can also assess. This group consists of four FLB loan recipients approved at early meetings for which no records were available and seven other loan recipients which were transferred to the FLB jurisdiction after having received loans from the FLB's predecessor, the Colony Development Board.

The records of the supplementary group of loan recipients as well as the overall record of the two groups combined (omitting the no assessment cases) are shown in Table 3.

Table 3 **Success of Projects**

	Enlarged group of FLB loan recipients		
	Successful	*Unsuccessful*	*Shaky*
Basic group . . .	10	11	7
Supplementary group . .	5	5	1
Overall record	15 (38%)	16 (41%)	8 (21%)

This record is a poor one.

It may be countered that such a judgement is unduly harsh, for many small businesses fail in the highly developed economies also. But the loan recipients are not new businesses, which provide the bulk of the business failures in developed economies, for the FLB does not make loans to new firms. These were businesses that survived the high mortality rates of the first years. Moreover, this was not a random sample of Nigerian businesses. The loan recipients constituted a select group. They had gone through a selective process which eliminated 82 per cent of the applicants. Fragmentary evidence indicates that similar select groups have fared much better in other countries.[7] Third, the loan recipients have had their loans for only a short time. The median loan, in terms of date disbursed, was made in the 1958–9 fiscal year, about 4½ years before the data of this study were collected, and many of the firms experienced considerable delays in receiving equipment, etc., so that they were unable to start on their projects until many months after they received their loans. It must therefore be expected that not only many of the shaky firms, but also some of those operating successfully so far will fail. Fourth, considerable government assistance has been provided to the loan recipients. The borrower is helped to spend his money wisely. For example, a furniture producer who planned to spend £2,500 for his machinery was steered to equipment that was not only more suitable, but which also cost about half as much. Technical advice and assistance have been given on such matters as the availability of servicing facilities, installation of equipment, and production techniques. Marketing assistance has also occasionally been provided. Loan recipients have sometimes been shielded from competition. While a continual shortage of staff has caused the flow of assistance to be much smaller than the FLB would have liked it to be, it was nevertheless far from negligible.

Thus, a highly selected group of indigenous firms—firms which had already been well established, which had projects that had been carefully reviewed and approved, which had, moreover, received special government assistance—have produced a most disappointing scorecard of success and failure, a record which, furthermore, is bound to deteriorate since many of the loan recipients have not yet had time to come to grief.

The facts that (1) so few of those who completed applications (after many of the weaker firms had been headed off during the preliminary stages) had acceptable projects, and (2) that such a large proportion of the acceptable projects failed despite efforts to help them combine to indicate that the significant shortage in the indigenous sector of the Nigerian economy is one of profitable projects. The large false demand for capital creates the illusion that there is a shortage of capital. But the record indicates that, *rather than a large number of viable projects vainly seeking capital, capital has been vainly seeking viable private projects.*

I suggest that this is true not only of Nigeria, but of many other of the more economically underdeveloped countries as well.

Notes: Reading 4

1 Sayre P. Schatz and S. I. Edokpayi, 'Economic attitudes of Nigerian businessmen', *Nigerian Journal of Economic and Social Studies*, vol. IV, no. 3, December 1962, p. 266.

2 I have argued elsewhere that the chief impediment to private investment in West Africa is not lack of entrepreneurial ability, but a wide range of factors that may be summed up as the economic environment. 'Economic environment and private enterprise in West Africa', *Economic Bulletin* (Ghana), vol. VII, no. 4, December 1963.

3 There were 336 applications altogether. I have judged that forty-six of the rejected applications were not appraised on the basis of probable commercial viability, but were rejected on other grounds, for example, because they were for projects that were beyond the FLB jurisdiction.

4 It could well be argued that the forty-six applications rejected on grounds other than viability, and perhaps other groups as well, should also be included in the apparent demand for capital. In order to avoid some rather esoteric discussions, I am omitting these; their inclusion, however, would strengthen my thesis.

5 The relatively small number of security rejectees results partially from the FLB's application procedure. The FLB judges applications on a viability basis first, and then goes on to appraise the security offered by the viability approvees only.

6 Ten of the fifty-four loans that were approved for both viability and security remain unissued for various reasons.

7 See Nathaniel H. Engle, *Industrial Development Banking in Action: A Study of Organisation, Operations, Procedure of Private Development Banks in India, Iran, Pakistan, Turkey*, mimeographed, Pakistan Industrial and Credit Corporation (?), 1962, pp. 275–8, 51, 16, and Shirley Boskey, *Problems and Practises of Development Banks*, published for the International Bank for Reconstruction and Development by the Johns Hopkins Press, Baltimore, 1959, p. 101.

Reading 5

The Coefficient of Ignorance

T. Balogh and P. P. Streeten

Bulletin of the Oxford Institute of Economics and Statistics, 1963, pp. 307–42.

Carefully directed social expenditure can have a much higher total yield (including all secondary effects) than types of expenditure which may result in some imposing visible structure, but whose effects on output in other sectors of the economy are zero or negative. Expenditures on the health, education and feeding of workers, on the provision of information, the creation of skills, etc., can raise output considerably, if properly directed and linked with improved equipment and appropriate institutional reforms. But these expenditures have for long been recalcitrant to theoretical treatment because

(*a*) they are permissive, creating opportunities for output growth without being its sufficient condition;
(*b*) their direct output is often not easily measurable;
(*c*) their effects are widely diffused;
(*d*) their effects are spread over a long time;
(*e*) there exists no determinate functional relationship between inputs and outputs, partly because success is contingent on complementary measures;
(*f*) independent value, as well as instrumental value, is attached to both the initial expenditure and the resultant flow of satisfactions;
(*g*) considerations of 'deserved social rewards' enter into the determination of costs (e.g. teachers' salaries);
(*h*) they cut across the traditional distinction between investment and consumption (on which many growth theories are built), according to which a sacrifice in current consumption can make future consumption greater than it would otherwise have been;
(*i*) they are frequently correlated with other causes of higher productivity from which they are not easily separated.

Although many of these considerations apply, perhaps to a lesser extent, also to expenditure on physical capital, they are more glaring when social expenditure is considered and therefore social expenditures have been, until recently, unpopular with model builders. But the bias which emphasizes allegedly measurable, separable and determinate, and neglects other types of relationship is unwarranted. Actions about whose results it is possible to make only the vaguest guesses may be much more important than actions whose trivial effects are supposed to be precisely foreseeable. The challenge of estimating the returns on certain types of social expenditure has been accepted, but in the process of analysing them the same mistakes have been made which have vitiated the use of more traditional concepts and relations, both in analysis and in their application to development planning.

In the last few years models have been constructed which attempt to isolate the contribution to growth made by expenditure on research, education, health, provision of information, etc. The starting point has usually been the addition of one term to the Cobb Douglas production function. $Y = aK^{\alpha}L^{\beta}H^{\gamma}$ where Y is national income, K capital, L labour and H a ragbag term for 'human factor' including 'improved knowledge', improved health and skills, better organisation and management, economies of scale, external economies, changes in the composition of output, etc. a, α, β and γ are constants, and $\alpha + \beta = 1$. Thus whatever is not caught in variations of K and L is attributed to H. 'Improvement in knowledge' is a name for what has rightly been called 'coefficient of our ignorance'.[1]

Whatever the value of these models for advanced Western countries, and however welcome the attempt to get away from preoccupation with physical investment, their application to the problems of underdeveloped countries has bred confusion.[2]

The reasoning behind these new models can be briefly summarised in this way: the increased use of one factor of production, while others are kept constant and 'knowledge' and 'skills' are given, will yield diminishing marginal returns. If the growth of national product over several decades is such that the expansion of land, labour and capital does not account for the whole increase, the remainder must be due to 'investment in human beings'.

Another approach has attempted to estimate the returns in the form of higher earnings to the educated in relation to expenditure on their education in the USA. Both these approaches and others have seemed to show that the returns to this type of 'investment' are substantially above the returns to physical investment.

The conclusion is then drawn that expenditure on education and on other ways of improving knowledge and skills should be carried out by planners in other countries, and particularly in underdeveloped countries.[3]

The pitfalls and fallacies in this admittedly over-simplified chain of reasoning are too numerous to be discussed here in detail. In the models of an aggregate production function a relationship, based on static economic models, is *assumed* between capital, labour and output; the historically *observed* relationship in *advanced* countries is seen to diverge widely from the *assumed* relationship, and the difference is *postulated* to be due solely to 'improvements in knowledge'. This conclusion is then bodily *transferred* to a totally different technical, historical, cultural, religious, institutional and political setting. Even if improved knowledge were a necessary condition for production growth, it might yield output only if incorporated in machines, exploited in specific ways, or combined with other policies, but not if occurring in isolation. Nor is education a homogeneous input. The teaching of Sanscrit has different results from the teaching of land cultivation. The teaching of book-keeping may increase the efficiency of manual labour, while the teaching of certain religions may reduce it. Isolation of 'education' from other measures ignores the importance of co-ordinating policies, and aggregating all types of 'education' obscures the type of education required for development. The concept therefore suffers both from illegitimate isolation and from misplaced aggregation.

Similar objections must be raised to the models attempting to calculate the returns to education by discounting the excess earnings of the educated over those of the uneducated. The American data, which are mostly used, do not provide evidence as to whether expenditure on education is *cause* or *effect* of superior incomes; they do not show, even if we could assume it to be a condition of higher earnings, whether it is a *sufficient* or a *necessary* condition of growth, and they do not separate *monopolistic* and *other forces* influencing differential earnings which are correlated with, but not caused by, differential education.

The calculations based on these data ignore both the indirect (financial and non-financial) returns accruing to others than the educated individual, and the direct non-financial returns to the individual. On the other hand, they pay a good deal of attention to 'income forgone during study' which constitutes a large proportion of the costs of 'investment'. But neither the income forgone by other groups in society (housewives, voluntary workers, people such as some university teachers—accepting a lower income than they could get in other occupations), nor the non-financial benefits enjoyed during education are estimated. Since the time-flow over a lifetime of the earnings of the educated is quite different from that of the uneducated, lifetime earnings now must be calculated as returns on education in the nineteen-twenties. To conclude from those returns anything about today's returns is like identifying a crystal radio set with Telstar.

Assuming that the ratio of returns to costs reflected something significant, it would be rash to attribute it to education. Expenditure on education is highly correlated to income and wealth of parents, to ability and motivation, to educational opportunities such as urban residence and proximity to educational centres, to access to well-paid jobs through family and other connections, any one of which could, either by itself or in conjunction with any of the others, account for the superior earnings.

But monopolistic elements enter not only in the differential advantages enjoyed by the children of wealthy parents, but also in reaping the rewards of an education. How much of the differential earnings of lawyers and doctors is due to 'investment in men' and how much to restrictive practices concealed as requirements of qualifications? Much of the higher earnings is not a return on education but a monopoly rent on (1) the scarcity of parents who can afford to educate their children well and (2) the restrictions on members permitted into a profession in which existing members have a financial interest in maintaining scarcity.

If anybody attempted to use these models for calculating the returns to education in many underdeveloped countries he would discover even higher rates of return. All this would show, however, is that pay scales in the civil service, in universities and in the professions are still governed by the traditional standards of a feudal or colonial aristocracy and by natural or artificial restrictions. It would provide no clue as to how public money ought to be distributed between 'investment' in 'physical capital' and in 'people'.

This approach, though logically weak, not only appeals to the snobbery and flatters the self-esteem of the educated, appearing to provide an economic justification of existing income differentials, but also buttresses vested interests. The specific measures that would be required to make expenditure on technical and agricultural education effective are painful, they violate vested interests and run into numerous inhibitions of the planners and obstacles put up by the planned. What a relief then to be served by econometricians with an elegant model, and how convenient to elevate a statistical residual to the engine of development, thus converting ignorance into 'knowledge'. Instead of having to specify *which type of education combined with what other measures* (such as investment in improved methods of cultivation, provision of the right equipment), creating skills and ability and willingness to work efficiently, and *complemented by what other* policies reforming attitudes and institutions (land reform, reform of the credit system, the civil service, price guarantees, transport), one item is singled out, either as the necessary and sufficient condition, or as a principal strategic variable of development. But the wrong kind of education, unaccompanied by the required complementary actions, can check or reverse the process of development. An unemployed or unemployable intelligentsia can be a source of revolutionary rather than economic activity, and young people brought up to despise manual work can reinforce the resistances to development.[4] Growth rates derived from the experience of the United States cannot be used to calculate the returns on education in the entirely different setting of underdeveloped countries. The same 'input' could result in refusal to work on farms, an increase in urban unemployment, subversion and collapse. The wrong type of education can also produce a ruling elite which gives the wrong kind of advice, as well as setting up ideals that stand in the way of development. It can encourage ignorance of and contempt for the professional and technical qualifications which are a condition of economic development.

Aggregation of all 'investment in human capital' and its separation from 'investment in physical capital' not only obscures the complementary nature of most subgroups of the two, but also serves as an intellectual and moral escape mechanism from unpleasant social and political difficulties.

New types of models are beginning to appear in which the returns yielded by expenditure on research and development, on training in management and administration, perhaps even on psychological treatment to transform tradition-bound into 'achievement-motivated' personalities are calculated. But as long as crucial distinctions are blurred by aggregation, crucial connections severed by isolation, and historical and geographical differences neglected, the results will be useless or misleading.

One group of critics have attacked the sordidly mercenary approach to activities of high intrinsic value, saying that it is a perversion of values to calculate rates of return on what is, or should be, the ultimate end of all production. But these criticisms miss the point. The chief conclusion of most of the recent researches is that not enough is spent on education. The high independent value of education itself and of the consequent flow of independently (i.e. not instrumentally) valued satisfactions may be used as an argument against not spending enough, but it cannot be used as an argument against spending at least as much as would yield a return equal to that on physical capital. It could, of course, be said that once mercenary calculations are admitted, the relative values of different kinds of education will be assessed by the wrong standards, and that the sense of the *value* of education will be lost, the more accurately its *price* is known. Already some authors argue that the returns on education in certain countries are lower than those on physical capital.

But the fact that we attach both independent and instrumental value to certain activities and that we attempt to estimate, if and when this is possible, the instrumental value, need not detract from the independent value. If the two reinforce each other, there can be no cause for complaint, and if they don't, it is surely rational to know the costs of policies promoting independent values.

The objection to the models is therefore not that they degrade education and equate human beings to machines. Better knowledge of the productive potential of human beings would raise, not lower, human dignity, human choice and human freedom. The objection is that the models approach the problem in the wrong way.

The faulty isolation of one tributary to the stream of production and the aggregation of different channels, some of which flow in opposite directions, some of which are stagnant and some of which do not contain any liquid, does not imply a disparagement of the need for detailed quantitative planning, including the planning of education, which has particularly long gestation periods. Whether a particular theoretical model is worth constructing depends upon whether we can give sufficient precision to the definition of the parameters and the variables and whether we can estimate the numerical relations between them. The rigour which is claimed for mathematical models is an illusion if the terms which they contain have no clear reference to the relevant items.

In the process of criticizing misplaced aggregation, such as that which lumps all education into a single category, we are led to the formulation of less general concepts: education is subdivided according to where it takes place, in what subjects, at what level and to whom. The purpose of such decomposition, disaggregation and subdivision is not to restrict analysis to less general concepts. We are, indeed, first trying to get rid of ragbag terms which do not correspond to anything observable and to replace them by 'boxes' that can be 'filled'. But as the boxes are being filled and as we gain fuller empirical knowledge, we may look forward to the formulation of new aggregates and to the recomposition of the decomposed material in a different form. The new 'packages' or 'boxes' will differ from the old. Some of the new distinctions will cut across the old ones. Thus when we examine the forcees determining labour utilisation in underdeveloped countries ('unemployment' and 'under-employment' are as misleading as 'education'), we shall discover that certain forms of education improve the quality of work and its efficiency, as well as, by improving hygiene and sanitation, the duration of work. Capital equipment may extend the duration (co-operation enforcing discipline) and efficiency. Instead of separating 'equipment' from 'labour' and aggregating each, we may arrive at a new abstraction in which skill and knowledge are infused through the introduction of machines.[5]

The formulation of long-term plans of economic development for underdeveloped countries which must incorporate the planning of education, must meet, in addition to these conceptual, certain other requirements.

(i) A long-term plan must embrace a study of how and

how far traditional educational patterns have contributed to the failure of social and economic progress in the past. The study must discover whether the attitudes which are hostile to economic progress have been the result of a specific structure of education, and what modifications of that structure are needed to accelerate development. In both the formerly British and the formerly French territories a disdain of technical education has grown up which has been strengthened by the low status of technical schools and the restricted openings for their pupils. So long as the Civil Service and the appointments controlled or influenced by it are the preserve of the non-technically educated, the best ability will be diverted into non-technical education. This will both justify and strengthen the initial disdain and tender progress more difficult. On the basis of this study of obstacles a new educational structure can be planned which will raise the status of those who meet the requirements of accelerated growth. Thus both diversion of the best talent and an increase in the supply of the required skills will be achieved.

(ii) The second requirement is a concrete idea of the size and composition of long-term development, based upon knowledge of the concrete endowments of the economy and a clear formulation of specific objectives and ideals. From these the future pattern of manpower distribution can be derived and thus an indication of the measures and the timing needed for educational development. The long gestation period of much education and training requires that starts are made now in order to reap results after 15, 20 and 25 years. Neither general formulae of ill-defined and irrelevant aggregates and their unverifiable relationships, nor even the occupational composition experienced at comparable stages of development in advanced industrial countries are of much use. Past experience of non-Soviet countries relates to spontaneous growth (or its failure). It cannot be assumed that deliberate efforts to accelerate growth by a series of policies would show the same requirements. The problem is to overcome *specific* difficulties, which differ from country to country and from time to time, while historical experience from now advanced countries points to broadly *similar* categories. From the long-term plan the quantities and types of educated personnel in detailed categories can be derived. Since changes in technology, demand, international policies, etc., will continually change these requirements, the long-term plan should be a 'rolling' plan, reviewed continually and at least annually, and adapted to new information. It should provide the framework for the 5-year (or seven-year) plans and for the annual budgets, so that policies which will not bear fruit until after more than five or seven years do not get neglected. To avoid superimposing new rigidities upon often already rigid economies, all three plans, the annual budget, the 'plan' and the perspective plan should be reviewed continually, and carried forward, so that they apply always to the next year, five years, fifteen years.

(iii) A number of measures will have to be taken which lie outside the scope of conventional economic considerations. Thus if training takes place abroad, the return of the trained men will have to be insured; if they have acquired the required skills, it will be necessary that they use them in isolated rural areas and reluctance to live there has to be overcome; the type of training provided must fit the available technology and not be appropriate to a more advanced form, etc.

(iv) Because of the narrow margins of tolerance and the closeness of many underdeveloped countries to misery and starvation, it is crucially important that minimum needs are estimated and that the required combination of measures are planned and executed. Failure to execute complementary measures can spell disaster. The isolation of 'educational' expenditure distracts attention from the urgent need, not only to select the right type of education, but also to combine it with the provisions of better seeds, drainage and fertilisers, with land reform and price stabilisation, with improvements in transport and birth control, with a reform of recruitment to the Civil Service and business management. The waste involved in not planning for the required complementarities, and pushing education too far, can be catastrophic.

(v) The detailed planning of education and training will have to make explicit political judgments about the distribution of the benefits between classes and over time. One of the costs of raising output later above what it would otherwise have been is the use of resources now to support the educational system required at a later stage. Since the social rate of time discount will tend to be high in countries where many are on the verge of starvation, extreme care is required in the expenditure on education. Financially conservative advice will be politically difficult and unpopular and may in many areas give rise to accusations of racial discrimination. Efforts are therefore needed to remove prejudices against quick-yielding and applied types of education. Education has to be used to get the right kind of education accepted. The larger the area for which collective planning can be initiated, the greater will be the scope for, and the less will be the danger of, indivisible highly specialised institutions which are expensive, not directly related to current progress, but imposing and prestige-yielding. The division of labour, in this field too, is limited by the extent of the market, and the larger and richer the area the more scope is there for specialised units conducting 'basic' research. Although it is true that the practical use of 'pure' research is unpredictable and that conscious direction of education and research to 'applied' field does not always yield higher returns earlier than some initially 'pure' research, it cannot be denied that it takes time between a discovery, its application by engineers and its exploitation by entrepreneurs and their followers. Only a large and rich economy with a low rate of time discount can afford to devote much energy to basic or pure scholarship. It must not be forgotten, moreover, that the adaptation of *known* techniques by poor developing countries could raise substantially their real income. Training rather than research would yield maximum returns.

The choice of the distribution over time is related to the choice between types of education with a high ratio of instrumental to independent value and those with a low ratio. The pursuit of knowledge for its own sake, wherever it may lead, is highly valued in many cultures, but it is not costless. This decision will in turn depend upon the political judgments made about the rate of growth of real income compared with that of leisure and the form in which leisure is to be enjoyed. These political value judgments will not be given once for all, but will themselves change as the plan is executed. But without a specification of concrete valuations and concrete manpower requirements, the calculation of 'returns to education' suppresses these value judgments in a pseudo-scientific formulation, buries the factual judgments in misplaced aggregation and severs crucial connexions by illegitimate isolation.

Notes: Reading 5

1 Mr E. F. Denison, in his book *The Sources of Economic Growth*, Committee for Economic Development, 1962, simultaneously assumes a linear homogeneous production function and perfect competition in order to use average return per unit of factor as a measure of its marginal value product, and attributes a substantial proportion of 'residual' growth to economies of scale.

2 For a brief discussion of and reference to these attempts, see John Vaizey, *The Economics of Education*, London, 1962, ch. III. For criticism of the application of these models to underdeveloped countries, see T. Balogh, 'Balance in educational planning: some fallacies in current thought', *Times Educational Supplement*, 8 June 1962, and 'Misconceived educational programmes in Africa', *Universities Quarterly*, 1962.

3 Thus Mr Adiseshia, Unesco's Acting Director-General, at a United Nations Association in Cambridge said: 'So my thesis is that accelerated economic growth is, to a large degree, a function of adequate and commensurate development of human resources . . . the expenditure in formal education, in training, in mass media and in research and development leads to increased returns both to the individual and to the community . . . The return from education over a twelve-year period to the individual, expressed in terms of the relation between the amount invested by him and/or his parents and his higher earnings in the future, can be averaged at 16 per cent gross or, if allowance is made for income forgone while at school or college, the net average would be 11 per cent. Similarly, a two-year training course increases future earnings by around 6 per cent gross or 3 per cent net.' *War on Want*, Pergamon Press, 1962.

4 'Wilfrid Malenbaum, for instance, found that unemployment in India varies directly with the degree of higher education. See "Urban Unemployment in India", *Pacific Affairs*, vol. XXX, no. 2, June 1957, p. 146.' Quoted in Gustav Ranis, 'Economic development: a suggested approach', *Kyklos*, vol. XII, no. 3, 1959, p. 445.

5 An interesting attempt to construct a model in which all productivity change is embodied in new investment was made by Professor Robert M. Solow.

Reading 6

Inequality, Poverty and Development

M. S. Ahluwalia

Journal of Development Economics, no. 3, 1976, pp. 307–42 (North-Holland Publishing Co.).

1 Introduction

The relationship between the distribution of income and the process of development is one of the oldest subjects of economic enquiry. Classical economic theory accorded it a central position in analysing the dynamics of economic systems, and while this pre-eminence was somewhat obscured in the heyday of neoclassical theory, in recent years it has again come to occupy the center stage of development economics. The purpose of this paper is to explore the nature of this relationship on the basis of cross country data on income inequality. The use of cross country data for the analysis of what are essentially dynamic processes raises a number of familiar problems. Ideally, such processes should be examined in an explicitly historical context for particular countries. Unfortunately, time series data on the distribution of income, over any substantial period, are simply not available for most developing countries. For the present, therefore, empirical investigation in this field must perforce draw heavily on cross country experience.

The results presented in this paper are based on a sample of 60 countries including 40 developing countries, 14 developed countries and 6 socialist countries.[1] In the established tradition of cross country analysis, the approach adopted is essentially exploratory. We have used multivariate regression analysis to estimate cross country relationships between the income shares of different percentile groups and selected variables reflecting aspects of the development process which are likely to influence income inequality.[2] The estimated equations are then used as a basis for broad generalisations about the relationship between income distribution and development. The difficulties inherent in this methodology are well known, although all too often ignored. It is self-evident that the relationships thus identified are primarily associational. They do not necessarily establish the nature of the underlying causal mechanism at work for the simple reason that quite different causal mechanisms might generate the same observed relationship between selected variables. Such alternative mechanisms (or hypotheses) are observationally equivalent in the sense that our estimated equations do not always permit us to choose between them.

The cross country relationships presented in this paper must be viewed in this perspective. We should treat them as 'stylised facts' which can be observed, but which still need to be explained, by an appropriate theory. The documentation of such 'stylised facts' is obviously not the same thing as the development of a tried and tested theory, but it may contribute to the development of such a theory in two ways. Firstly, the observed relationships may suggest hypotheses about the nature of the underlying causal mechanisms at work, which then need to be further tested and fashioned into a broader theory. Secondly, they provide yardsticks for verifying theories of distribution and development by defining the observed 'behaviour' that such theories must explain.

What, then, do we know of the 'stylised facts' about income distribution and development? A logical point of departure for our investigation is the hypothesis, originally advanced by Kuznets (1955, 1963), that the secular behaviour of inequality follows an inverted 'U-shaped' pattern with inequality first increasing and then decreasing with development. Following Kuznets, the proposition that the distribution of income worsens with development, at least in the early stages, has received considerable attention.[3] More recently it has been advanced in a much stronger formulation, which states that the process of development may lead not just to increasing relative inequality, but also to the absolute impoverishment of the lower income groups.[4]

These issues, together with several others, are examined in this paper. Section 2 presents the cross section evidence on the relationship between inequality and the level of development, showing a distinct U-shaped pattern as hypothesised by Kuznets. Section 3 extends our search for stylised facts by including a number of other correlates of inequality in an expanded regression equation. Section 4 reviews the implications of the expanded regression equations for the U-shaped curve and the hypothesis of absolute impoverishment. Section 5 examines the relationship between inequality and the rate of growth as a short-term relationship and attempts to draw some implications for policy.

2 Kuznets' hypothesis: The 'U-shaped curve'

We begin by documenting the evidence for Kuznets' hypothesis that inequality tends to widen in the early stages of development, with a reversal of this tendency in the later stages. Following convention, we have tested this hypothesis by taking the per capita GNP of each country (in US$ at 1965–1971 prices) as a summary measure of its level of development and including it as an explanatory variable in regression equations in which the income share of different percentile groups is taken as the dependent variable.

The cross country regressions provide a substantial measure of support for the hypothesis that there is a U-shaped pattern in the secular behaviour of inequality. Table 1 reports the estimated equations describing the relationship between income shares of five different percentile groups (the top 20 per cent, the next or 'middle' 40 per cent, the lowest 60 per cent, the lowest 40 per cent and the lowest 20 per cent) and the logarithm of per capita GNP.[5] Two equations are reported for each income share, one estimated from the full sample of 60 countries and the other estimated from the restricted sample of 40 developing countries only. For the full sample, we have included a dummy variable for the socialist countries in order to take account of the much higher degree of equality observed in these countries.[6] The results obtained can be summarised as follows:

(i) Taking the results from the full sample to begin with, there is clear evidence of a nonmonotonic relationship between inequality and the level of development. The estimated equations test for a quadratic relationship with the logarithm of per capita GNP. We find that in all cases, both terms of the quadratic are significant[7] and the coefficients have the appropriate opposite signs to generate the U-shaped pattern hypothesised by Kuznets. Income shares of all percentile groups except the top 20 per cent first decline and then increase as per capita GNP rises. Income shares of the top 20 per cent display a corresponding opposite pattern.

(ii) The turning point for income shares implied by the estimated equations are also reported in Table 1. It is interesting to note that this turning point occurs at different levels of per capita GNP for different income groups. In the case of the full sample, the turning point for the income share of the top 20 per cent occurs at per capita GNP levels of US$ 364 (for the economy as a whole) after which the income share of this group begins to decline. However, the income shares of the middle 40 per cent appear to improve after a per capita GNP level of US$ 291 is reached. As shown in Table 1, the turning point of income shares shifts systematically further out as we go down the percentile groups, with the lowest 20 per cent having to wait until per capita GNP levels of about $600 are reached. Taking these estimates at face value (i.e. ignoring the question whether these estimated differences are significant), the cross section evidence suggests that the reversal of the 'deteriorating phase' of relative inequality begins fairly early, first for the middle income group and much later for the lower income groups. It appears that if there is a 'trickle down' process, then it takes substantially longer to reach the bottom!

(iii) The basic pattern described in (i) and (ii) above can also be discerned in the equations estimated from the restricted sample of 40 developing countries, with slight differences. Except for the equation explaining income shares of the middle 40 per cent, the coefficients on both terms in the quadratic are again significant and have the same sign patterns as in the full sample, indicating a U-shaped pattern in the income shares of the lower income groups offset by an opposite pattern in the income shares of the top 20 per cent. The absolute magnitudes of the estimated coefficients in these equations are, however, somewhat different, implying that there are differences in the shape of the Kuznets' curve obtained in the two cases. The exclusion of the developed countries and socialist countries from the sample has the effect of (a) shifting the turning point of the Kuznets' curve slightly inwards and (b) increasing the steepness of the observed U-shape in both phases. The extent of the shift can be seen in Fig. 1, which compares the curve of estimated income shares for the lowest 40 per cent at different levels of per capita GNP from eq. (A.4), with the curve of estimated shares from eq. (B.4), which includes developing countries only. We note that the improvement in relative income shares in the later phases of development appears markedly more modest if we look at the full sample than at the reduced sample of developing countries only. This is because the quadratic formulation forces a symmetry of shape with respect to the logarithm of per capita GNP and this allows the equations for the restricted sample to fit a steeper U curve in conformity with the steepness observed over the $75–500 range, which is where most of the developing countries are concentrated (see Appendix, Table 8). By contrast, the equation for the full sample is forced to fit a somewhat less steep curve to reflect the relatively modest improvement in equality observed between the middle income countries at the bottom of the U and the developed countries of today.

(iv) A major problem in interpreting the U shape revealed in cross country data is the possibility that it may be generated solely by the fact that the middle income range is dominated by countries with particular characteristics which generate high inequality. If so, the U shape has little relevance to

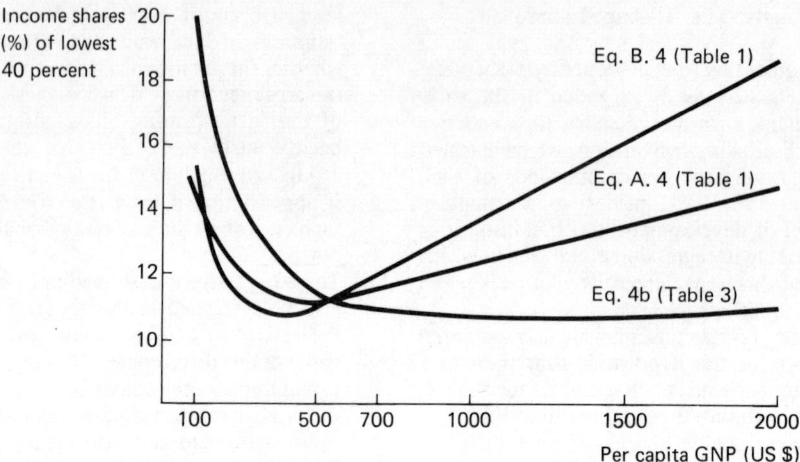

Fig. 1

the long-term prospect facing the low income countries of today, unless these countries share the same characteristics. Thus it is sometimes argued that the U shape simply reflects the concentration in the middle income range of Latin American countries, which display greater inequality because of particular historical and structural characteristics not applicable to others. We have tested for this

Table 1 **The Kuznets curve**

Dependent variable	*Estimated coefficients on explanatory variables*[a]							
Income shares of:	*Constant*	*Log per capita GNP*	*[Log per capita GNP]*^{2}	*Socialist Dummy*	R^2	*F*	*D.W.*[b]	*Turning point per capita GNP US$ (1965–71)*
(A) Full sample								
(1) Top 20 per cent	−57.58 (2.11)	89.95 (4.48)	−17.56 (4.88)	−20.15 (6.83)	0.58	27.9	2.05	364
(2) Middle 40 per cent	87.03 (4.81)	−45.59 (3.43)	9.25 (3.88)	8.21 (4.20)	0.47	18.6	2.08	291
(3) Lowest 60 per cent	119.4 (5.85)	−73.52 (4.90)	14.06 (5.23)	17.52 (7.95)	0.61	31.4	1.97	412
(4) Lowest 40 per cent	70.57 (5.38)	−44.38 (4.61)	8.31 (4.82)	11.95 (8.45)	0.59	29.8	2.04	468
(5) Lowest 20 per cent	27.31 (4.93)	−16.97 (3.71)	3.06 (3.74)	5.54 (8.28)	0.54	24.3	1.93	593
(B) Developing countries only								
(1) Top 20 per cent	−99.74 (1.56)	123.80 (2.35)	−24.18 (2.26)		0.12	3.6	2.24	363
(2) Middle 40 per cent	92.93 (2.12)	−49.13 (1.36)	9.65 (1.32)		0.01	1.4	2.19	351
(3) Lowest 60 per cent	171.50 (3.79)	−116.40 (3.12)	22.72 (2.99)		0.22	6.5	2.20	364
(4) Lowest 40 per cent	106.80 (3.83)	−74.69 (3.25)	14.53 (3.10)		0.24	7.2	2.20	371
(5) Lowest 20 per cent	44.15 (3.43)	−31.33 (2.96)	6.07 (2.81)		0.22	6.3	1.98	381

[a] *t*-statistics in parentheses.

[b] In estimating these equations the observations were entered in ascending order of per capita GNP. The Durbin–Watson statistic therefore gives some idea of the pattern of residuals with this ordering. The lack of serial correlation of residuals in the above equations provides some reassurance that the quadratic formulation captures the underlying nonlinearity reasonably well.

'Latin America effect' by including a dummy variable for the Latin American countries in each of the equations (A.1)–(A.4). We find that the coefficient on this dummy variable is insignificant in all cases and its inclusion leaves both the sign pattern and the significance of the coefficients on the income quadratic largely unaffected. Similarly, Papanek (1976) has argued that the observed U shape disappears when the 'strongly dualistic' countries are excluded from the sample. We note that our sample excludes South Africa, Rhodesia, Libya, Niger and Trinidad, four of the seven dualistic cases identified by Papanek, but this does not affect the significance of the U shape.

These results are broadly in line with the findings of Adelman and Morris (1973) and Chenery and Syrquin (1975). They point to a marked decline in the relative income shares of the lower income groups in the early stages of development and they also suggest that the decline is most prolonged for the poorest groups. We will examine the welfare implications of this pattern in section 4. For the moment, we continue our examination of the U-shaped curve in order to determine how far it tells the whole story. Judging this by goodness of fit, there is little doubt that the equations in Table 1 leave much to be desired. In the sample of developing countries, the estimated equations explain just over a quarter of the observed variation in income shares of the lower income groups and much less than this for the top 20 per cent. The R^2's for the equations estimated from the full sample are much higher, but this is to some extent due to the fact that the inclusion of socialist countries in this sample adds substantially to the inter-country variance in income shares and the dummy variable for these countries also 'explains' most of this added variance.

The relatively limited explanatory power of these estimated equations is hardly surprising. The true relationship between inequality and development must be fairly complex, reflecting the impact of a number of processes of structural change occurring with development. Such a complex relationship obviously cannot be 'reduced' into a relationship with a single explanatory variable. Per capita GNP is a useful summary measure of the level of development[8] in the sense that it is correlated with most of the processes occurring with development, and as such, it may capture the net effect of these processes as observed in cross country experience. The resulting estimated relationship is undoubtedly of some interest as a possible indicator of the secular behaviour of inequality, but it tells us nothing about the specific mechanisms through which development affects the degree of inequality. Since it is precisely these mechanisms that are of interest, from the analytical as well as the policy point of view, we need to extend our search for stylised facts to take account of them to the extent possible. The next section is devoted to an exploration of the cross country data along these lines.

3 Income distribution and economic structure

Our search for the specific mechanisms through which development affects the degree of inequality is necessarily limited by the availability of cross country data on explanatory variables. The explanatory variables we were able to use are reported in Table 2, where they are grouped according to various aspects of the development process which are measured (albeit somewhat crudely) by these variables. The relationship between income inequality and these different aspects of development was explored by experimenting with alternative combinations of these explanatory variables in explaining cross country variation in the income shares of the different percentile groups.

In general, we find that three aspects of the development process appear to be systematically related to the degree of inequality. These are:

(1) Intersectoral shifts involving a relative decline of the traditional agricultural sector and a parallel shift of population to the urban sector.
(2) Expansion in the educational and skill characteristics of the population.
(3) The 'demographic transition' involving a reduction in the rate of growth of population.

Inclusion of explanatory variables reflecting these processes in our regression equations substantially improves the goodness of fit obtained and the estimated relationships also conform to *a priori* expectations about the impact of these processes upon income inequality.

Table 3 provides an overview of the results obtained by the expanded regression equations which include additional explanatory variables reflecting the impact of these aspects of development. Equation (a) is a general form applied to all income shares and includes variables with coefficients that are not always significant. Equation (b) for each income share contains only those variables that are found to be significant in equation (a). Clearly, the expanded equations have greater explanatory power than the equations reported in Table 1, in which development was measured solely in terms of per capita GNP. They explain between two-thirds and three-fourths of the observed variation in income shares compared to just over half in the case of the simpler formulation.[9]

A general problem in exploring these relationships is that the explanatory variables used to reflect different aspects of development are all highly correlated with per capita GNP (see Table 2) and this makes it difficult to attribute observed associations in a particular equation to the impact of one or the other variable. This is an

Table 2 **Explanatory variables used in cross country regressions**

Variables	*Correlation coefficient with log of per capita GNP*
(1) *Level and pace of development*	
Logarithm of per capita GNP (constant 1971 US$)	1.00
Dummy variable for all developed countries	0.73
Rate of growth of GNP over the past 5–10 years (percentage)	0.03
(2) *Education and human resources*	
Literacy rate (percentage)	0.81
Primary school enrollment rate (percentage)	0.62
Secondary school enrollment rate (percentage)	0.85
(3) *Structure of production*	
Share of agriculture in GDP (percentage)	−0.88
Share of urban population (percentage)	0.83
(4) *Demographic characteristics*	
Total Population	−0.03
Rate of growth of population (percentage)	−0.55
(5) *Government activity*	
Share of government revenue in GDP (percentage)[a]	−0.24
(6) *Other common variables reflecting structural commonality*	
Dummy variable for Latin American countries	0.01
Dummy variable for Socialist countries	0.12
Gini coefficient for land distribution[a]	−0.02

[a]This variable is not available for all countries in the full sample. The correlation coefficient relates to the subsample for which observations are available.

example of the problem of 'observational equivalence' of hypotheses mentioned in the introduction (section 1) and there is no satisfactory solution to this problem. The approach we have adopted is to examine the relationship with each variable under alternative specifications of the regression equation in order to determine which relationships appear more stable in the face of inclusion and exclusion of other explanatory variables.[10]

3.1. *Intersectoral shifts*

Intersectoral shifts occurring with development have long been recognised as a possible mechanism through which the process of development affects inequality. This was first pointed out by Kuznets (1963), who argued that development typically involves accelerated growth in the high income nonagricultural sectors, which slowly absorb population from the low income, relatively stagnant, agricultural sector. Kuznets showed that such a process would lead to an increase in relative inequality in the early stages of development and, under certain conditions, would generate precisely the U-shaped behaviour discussed above.

This effect of intersectoral shifts on overall inequality can be easily illustrated by a simplified two-sector example.[11] Taking the variance of the logarithms of income as a measure of inequality, the variance V for the population as a whole can be decomposed into component terms as follows,

$$V=s_u V_u+(1-s_u)V_r+s_u(\bar{Y}_u-\bar{Y})^2+(1-s_u)(\bar{Y}_r-\bar{Y})^2, \quad (1)$$

where s_u is the population share of the urban (or non-agricultural) sector, V_u and V_r are the variances of logarithms of income within the urban and rural sectors respectively, and $\bar{Y}_u$, $\bar{Y}_r$, $\bar{Y}$ are mean logarithms of income for the two sectors and the whole economy respectively. Using $\bar{Y}=\bar{Y}_u s_u+\bar{Y}_r(1-s_u)$, eq. (1) can be rewritten,

$$V=V_r+s_u[V_u V_r)+(\bar{Y}_u-\bar{Y}_r)^2]-s_u^2[\bar{Y}_u-\bar{Y}_r]^2. \quad (2)$$

It is easily shown that on certain restrictive assumptions, the intersectoral shifts described above generate a U-shaped pattern in inequality. Suppose, for example, that inequality within sectors remains constant and incomes in the two sectors grow at the same rate so that $(\bar{Y}_u-\bar{Y}_r)$ remains constant. In this case, if there are no population shifts, our inequality measure V remains constant. However, if development involves a progressive shift of population into the high income sector then eq. (2) becomes a quadratic in s_u (the terms in square brackets being constants). This function reaches a maximum for V at an urban population share given by

$$s_u = \frac{1}{2} + \frac{V_u - V_r}{2[\bar{Y}_u - \bar{Y}_r]^2} \qquad (3)$$

Clearly, development generates the familiar U shape in inequality provided the maximum occurs within the relevant range $0<s_u<1$. A sufficient condition for this is that $|V_u - V_r| < [\bar{Y}_u - \bar{Y}_r]^2$, i.e. the squared difference between sectoral means is greater than the differences between the within sector variances.[12]

The assumptions of constant inequality within sectors and equal growth rates in sectoral incomes are obviously unrealistic. In fact we would expect both the degree of inequality within sectors and mean income differences between sectors to change systematically with development. Interestingly, there are plausible reasons for supposing that these changes might reinforce the U-shaped pattern in overall inequality. For one thing, inequality in the urban sector may itself follow a U-shaped pattern. It may increase initially, as accelerated economic growth creates a strong demand for skilled labour, in the face of acute scarcities, with the result that skill differentials expand. In the later stages, we can expect urban income to become more equal as labour skills improve and become more widely dispersed in the population leading to both an increase in wage share, as well as greater equality in the distribution of wage income (see subsection 3.2 below).

The ratio of mean incomes between sectors may also follow a U-shaped pattern with intersectoral differences widening in the early stages, as scarce capital and other resources are pre-empted by the modern (and typically privileged) urban sector, to the detriment of productivity and income levels in the traditional sector. These differentials can be expected to narrow in the later stages of development for two reasons. Firstly, as capital becomes less scarce, more resources are likely to be made available to improve productivity in the low income sectors. Secondly, as the size of the modern

Table 3 **Inequality and development**

Dependent variable	*Estimated coefficients on explanatory variables*[a]												
Income shares of:	*Constant*	*Log per capita GNP*	*[Log per capita GNP]*^{2}	*Share of Agri-culture in GDP*	*Share of Urban popula-tion in total*	*Literacy rate*	*Secondary school enroll-ment*	*Popula-tion growth rate*	*Socialist dummy*	R^2	*F*	*D.W.*[b]	*Turn-ing point US$*
(1) Top 20 per cent													
(a)	−8.711	49.620	−7.975	−0.258	−0.090	−0.094	0.146	3.611	9.443	0.75	23.4	1.90	1291
	(0.26)	(2.24)	(2.10)	(2.15)	(1.58)	(2.29)	(2.63)	(4.28)	(3.27)				
(b)	−1.592	43.580	−7.157	−0.225		−0.107	−0.160	3.48	−9.287	0.75	25.7	1.95	1108
	(0.05)	(1.97)	(1.87)	(1.87)		(2.60)	(2.86)	(4.09)	(3.17)				
(2) Middle 40 per cent													
(a)	34.27	−5.819	0.977	0.226	0.035	0.045	0.115	−2.448	0.751	0.70	18.0	1.82	
	(1.57)	(0.40)	(0.39)	(2.86)	(0.93)	(1.68)	(3.14)	(4.43)	(0.40)				
(b)	30.46			0.172			0.154	−2.51		0.70	45.8	1.88	
	(14.63)			(4.08)			(6.49)	(5.48)					
(3) Lowest 60 per cent													
(a)	105.3	−57.70	9.212	0.115	0.078	0.080	0.084	−2.50	10.43	0.74	22.47	1.96	1355
	(4.02)	(3.30)	(3.08)	(1.22)	(1.72)	(2.45)	(1.91)	(3.77)	(4.59)				
(b)	126.3	−68.470	10.68		0.068	0.076	0.089	−2.425	11.05	0.74	25.2	1.92	1605
	(6.38)	(4.53)	(3.88)		(1.53)	(2.35)	(2.03)	(3.65)	(4.96)				
(4) Lowest 40 per cent													
(a)	74.500	−43.850	7.009	0.032	0.055	0.049	0.031	−1.161	8.702	0.68	16.48	2.06	1343
	(4.01)	(3.54)	(3.30)	(0.48)	(1.73)	(2.13)	(1.0)	(2.47)	(5.40)				
(b)	85.660	−51.440	8.41		0.057	0.056		−1.155	9.184	0.68	22.0	2.04	1144
	(6.59)	(5.29)	(4.96)		(1.85)	(2.61)		(2.48)	(5.98)				
(5) Lowest 20 per cent													
(a)	35.110	−21.24	3.337	−0.004	0.027	0.021	0.001	−0.333	4.697	0.58	11.37	1.83	1522
	(3.73)	(3.38)	(3.10)	(0.12)	(1.67)	(1.82)	(0.08)	(1.40)	(5.75)				
(b)	34.520	−21.00	3.315		0.027	0.022		−0.336	4.685	0.60	15.7	1.83	1454
	(5.31)	(4.32)	(3.91)		(1.77)	(2.01)		(1.44)	(6.10)				

[a]*t*-statistics in parentheses.

[b]In estimating these equations the observations were entered in ascending order of per capita GNP. The Durbin–Watson statistic therefore gives some idea of the pattern of residuals with this ordering. The lack of serial correlation of residuals in the above equations provides some reassurance that the quadratic formulation captures the underlying nonlinearity reasonably well.

sector increases in the later stages of development, its continued expansion has a proportionately larger impact on reducing the pressure of population in the low income sector. Both factors lead to an accelerated increase in productivity in the traditional sector in the later stages of development and can be expected to reduce income differentials between sectors.

A systematic exploration of the impact of intersectoral shifts on inequality obviously calls for data on inequality within each sector, sectoral mean incomes and sectoral population shares. In the absence of such data we have used two explanatory variables which capture some aspects of the process. These are the *share of agriculture in GDP*, which declines with development as the nonagricultural sector grows at an accelerated rate, and the *share of the urban population*, which can be expected to rise as population shifts away from the traditional agricultural sector. These two variables are obviously closely related but they do reflect somewhat different aspects of the same process. The share of agriculture in GDP reflects the extent to which the income generating capacity of the economy has shifted into nonagricultural activity while the share of the urban population reflects the extent to which this shift has been accompanied by increased absorption of population into the nonagricultural sectors.

Our first step was to consider if either of the structural shift variables are associated with the U shape in inequality. Table 4 summarises the results on this count. We note that either of the intersectoral shift variables generate a U-shaped behaviour in inequality when entered in quadratic form in the regression equations. It is obviously difficult to determine if the estimated relationships reflect the effect of these variables or the effect of per capita GNP with which both variables are highly correlated (see Table 2). However it is worth noting that these results are slightly worse than those reported in Table 1, in which the quadratic is defined in

Table 4 **Intersectoral shifts and inequality**

Dependent variable		*Estimated coefficients on explanatory variables*[a]									
Income shares of:		*Constant*	*Log per capita GNP*	*[Log per capita GNP]*^{2}	*Share of agriculture in GDP*	*[Share of agriculture in GDP]*^{3}	*Share of urban population*	*[Share of urban population]*^{2}	*Socialist dummy*	R^2	*F*
(1) Top 20 per cent	(a)	39.54			1.155	−0.018			−20.110	0.49	19.8
		(13.73)			(5.01)	(4.63)			(6.33)		
	(b)	52.08					0.28	−0.005	−18.140	0.43	15.8
		(15.25)					(1.62)	(2.53)	(5.39)		
	(c)	36.06	80.42	−15.64	−0.279	0.002	0.068	−0.005	−19.66	0.59	13.3
		(0.73)	(2.29)	(2.64)	(1.17)	(0.66)	(0.20)	(0.92)	(6.59)		
(2) Middle 40 per cent	(a)	41.89			−0.671	0.010			8.453	0.34	10.9
		(21.55)			(4.31)	(3.77)			(3.94)		
	(b)	31.860					−0.050	0.002	7.066	0.28	8.5
		(14.00)					(0.43)	(1.36)	(3.15)		
	(c)	70.140	−41.88	8.870	0.093	0.002	0.249	−0.002		0.50	9.4
		(2.16)	(1.81)	(2.27)	(0.40)	(0.55)	(1.59)	(1.25)			
(3) Lowest 60 per cent	(a)	36.58			−0.867	0.014			17.24	0.55	24.5
		(17.38)			(5.15)	(4.91)			(7.42)		
	(b)	29.49					−0.310	0.004	15.99	0.50	20.4
		(11.99)					(2.46)	(3.28)	(6.54)		
	(c)	109.0	−65.67	12.12	−0.171	0.004	0.123	−0.000	17.50	0.62	14.8
		(2.95)	(2.49)	(2.73)	(0.65)	(1.08)	(0.69)		(7.84)		
(4) Lowest 40 per cent	(a)	18.56			−0.484	0.008			11.660	0.56	26.3
		(14.25)			(4.64)	(4.61)			(8.11)		
	(b)	16.060					−0.232	0.003	11.070	0.54	24.1
		(10.71)					(3.04)	(3.69)	(7.50)		
	(c)	66.010	−38.60	6.780	−0.162	0.003	0.031	0.000	12.090	0.61	14.4
		(2.80)	(2.30)	(2.39)	(1.0)	(1.17)	(0.27)		(8.49)		
(5) Lowest 20 per cent	(a)	6.02			−0.159	0.003			5.370	0.54	24.2
		(10.11)			(3.35)	(3.68)			(8.18)		
	(b)	6.10					0.107	0.001	5.221	0.53	23.0
		(9.00)					(3.12)	(3.39)	(7.82)		
	(c)	27.570	−15.02	2.39	−0.112	0.002	0.011	0.000	5.712	0.57	12.1
		(2.48)	(1.90)	(1.79)	(1.41)	(1.40)	(0.21)		(8.51)		

[a] *t*-statistics in parentheses.

terms of the logarithm of per capita GNP. We also find that the U shape defined in terms of per capita GNP is more stable. When the quadratic formulation in either of the intersectoral shift variables is included, together with the quadratic in the logarithm of per capita GNP, the coefficients on the structural shift variables are no longer significant while the quadratic formulation in the per capita GNP remains significant. Table 4 reports one equation in which the quadratic formulations in all three variables are included in the same regression equation. Again we find that the quadratic in per capita GNP remains significant.

These results suggest that the U-shaped relationship is better explained by per capita GNP than the structural shift variables. We have, therefore, retained the quadratic formulation in per capita GNP and entered the two structural shift variables as additional explanatory variables, but not in quadratic form. When this is done we find that these variables are significantly related to income inequality. The estimated relationships obtained are broadly comparable to those reported in our expanded 'best' equations in Table 3 (which include some additional explanatory variables). Our general results on the impact of structural shifts on inequality can, therefore, be summarised with reference to the results reported in Table 3.

(i) We find that the share of agriculture in GDP and the urban share of total population are both significantly related to the pattern of income inequality, but their effects on income shares of different groups are not identical. The share of agriculture in GDP is not significantly related to the income shares of the lowest groups, but it is positively related to the income shares of the middle groups and negatively related to the income share of the top 20 per cent (equations (2b) and (1b) in Table 3). By contrast, the share of the urban population in the total has no significant effect on the income share of the middle group, but is significantly positively associated with the income shares of the lowest groups and negatively associated with the income shares of the top 20 per cent (equations (3b), (4b), (5b) and (1b) in Table 3).

(ii) These results point to an interesting asymmetry in the distributional impact of the intersectoral shifts that occur with development. As the share of agriculture in GDP declines with development, there appears to be a relative shift of income away from the middle group and towards the upper groups. Alongside this 'disequalising' process, however, development also generates a shift of population to the modern or urban sectors. According to the cross section results, this latter process appears to favour the lowest income groups at the expense of the rich.

The proposition that increasing urbanisation may raise the income shares of the lowest income groups is consistent with *a priori* expectation. Given the dualistic nature of the development process, a higher rate of urbanisation, other things being the same, reflects a wider access to productive employment opportunities in the expanding nontraditional sector and a correspondingly lower pressure of population in the rural areas. Both forces can be expected to operate in favour of the lower income groups.[13]

The observed 'disequalising' impact of the decline in the share of agriculture in GDP in terms of a shift from the middle income groups to the top is less easily explained. One possibility is that as the relative size of agricultural activity diminishes, compared to nonagricultural activity, there is a shift towards greater concentration of income and wealth because the nonagricultural sector typically promotes larger size production units for both institutional and technological reasons. A shift from small to large scale production can be expected to generate an increased concentration of income in the upper income groups at the expense of the middle. We can also speculate that the observed adverse effect on the middle groups is due to the fact that the decline in the relative importance of agriculture probably has its strongest impact on small and middle sized land holding cultivators who dominate the middle income groups. The slower growth rate in agriculture implies a slower growth in income for these groups, which is in turn reflected in a declining income share of the middle income group in the economy. The difficulty with this argument is that it implies that the poorest rural groups (e.g. landless labourers, artisans, etc.) may also be adversely affected by the slower growth of agriculture and this should be reflected in a positive relationship between the share of agriculture in GDP and income shares of the lowest 40 per cent or lowest 20 per cent. Our results provide no evidence of such a relationship. The equations in Table 3 suggest that the income share of the poorest groups are affected by the level of development as measured by per capita GNP, but not by the relative importance of agriculture at a given level of development. One possible explanation is that the poorer, landless groups are relatively more mobile than landowning cultivators and are more willing to shift from agriculture into unskilled employment in urban areas so that their income share is not affected by the relative size of agricultural production. Note that since our equations indicate that income shares of the lower groups fall as per capita GNP rises in the early stages of development, the above result suggests only that the extent of the fall is independent of the relative size of the agricultural sector.

3.2. *Education and labour skills*

Improvements in the educational characteristics and skill endowments of the labour force provide another mechanism through which development affects inequality. The usual argument is that this mechanism operates to promote income equality in the long run. The reasons underlying this optimism are worth reviewing before considering our empirical results.

The central assumption underlying this view is that there is substantial scope for substituting skilled for unskilled labour in the production process (particularly in a dynamic context) without a decline in the marginal productivity in the former. This view of production and technological change, combined with the conventional marginal productivity theory of factor rewards, implies that a more skilled labour force will produce a shift from low paid, unskilled employment to high paid, skilled employment. This shift, it is argued, produces higher labour incomes, a reduction in skill differentials, and an increase in the share of wages in total output.[14] This mechanism, combined with economic policies that do not discriminate against labour-using and skill-intensive production sectors, is often described as the key to the success of countries such as Taiwan and Korea in achieving a rapid rate of development together with high growth rates of employment and relatively equal income distribution.

In addition to the technological assumptions about factor productivity, there is also the argument that skill intensive development patterns are less prone to income concentration than capital intensive patterns. This is because of the peculiar characteristic of human capital —unlike physical capital—that expansion in the stock of human capital in the economy necessarily involves dispersion across a wider population. There is a limit beyond which human capital cannot be accumulated in a single person, and at any rate it cannot be bequeathed across generations in the same manner as physical capital. Both factors, it is argued, combine to generate strong pressures towards equality in income distribution as the human resource endowment expands with development.

The available data permit us to examine the education-inequality relationship in terms of three explanatory variables which provide crude approximations to the level of human resource development—the *literacy rate*, the *primary school enrollment ratio* and the *secondary school enrollment ratio*. Because of the high correlation among these variables, it is necessary to be somewhat selective in our choice of explanatory variables. We have chosen the literacy rate as a measure of the basic education level of the stock of the population and the secondary school enrollment rate as a measure of the degree of educational achievement beyond this basic level.[15] Two points about the exclusion of the primary school enrollment rate are worth noting. First, the literacy rate provides us with a better measure of the basic educational level, being a measure of the stock and not future additions to the stock. Secondly, we observe in our sample that there is relatively little variation in the primary school enrollment rate across countries beyond the middle level of development by when fairly high enrollment ratios are achieved in most countries. The lack of variation obviously makes it less attractive as an explanatory variable.

The results obtained can be summarised as follows:

(i) There is clear evidence that education is significantly positively correlated with equality. When the two education variables chosen—the literacy rate and the secondary school enrollment rate—are entered in the regression equations without per capita GNP (equations (1a), (2a), (3a), (4a) and (5a) in Table 5), we find that the secondary schooling variable is associated with shifts in income from the top 20 per cent to all other groups except the lowest 20 per cent. The literacy rate is not significant in any of the equations. When these variables are included together with the quadratic in per capita GNP the pattern changes in important respects. As shown in Table 5, the secondary schooling variable retains its positive impact on the middle groups but the literacy rate variable now has a positive impact on the income shares of the three lowest groups. It is tempting to conclude that the relationship thus revealed reflects the true impact of literacy on inequality, which was previously swamped by the bias introduced by the exclusion of per capita GNP.[16] This basic pattern remains unchanged when the equations are expanded to include other explanatory variables (see Table 3).

(ii) The positive impact of education on relative equality appears to be quantitatively fairly substantial. For example, an increase in the literacy rate from 10 per cent to 60 per cent is associated with a 2.8 percentage point increase in the share of the lowest 40 per cent. This should be compared to an average share for this group of about 16 per cent at low levels of development. Similarly, an increase in secondary school enrollment from 10 per cent to 40 per cent is associated with an increase of 4.6 percentage points in the income share of the middle 40 per cent compared to an average share of 34 per cent for this group at low levels of development.

(iii) The fact that the secondary schooling variable benefits the middle groups while the literacy rate benefits the lower group calls for some explanation. The most plausible explanation is in terms of the likely beneficiaries of expansion in secondary schooling and expansion in literacy in our sample. In general, the observed variation in secondary school enrollment (between 5 and 40 per cent for most developing countries) is not such that the benefits of expansion in secondary school enrollment are likely to have reached the poorer groups. Since access to secondary schooling almost certainly expands from the top downwards, the observed range of variation for most of the countries in our sample suggests that the lower income groups are excluded from secondary schooling. By contrast, the variation in literacy

Table 5 **Education and inequality**

Dependent variable		*Estimated coefficients on explanatory variables*[a]							
Income shares of:		*Constant*	*Log per capita GNP*	*[Log per capita GNP]²*	*Literacy rate*	*Secondary school enrollment rate*	*Socialist dummy*	R^2	*F*
(1) Top 20 per cent	(a)	58.76			0.022	−0.219	−14.85	0.56	25.9
		(28.60)			(0.49)	(4.32)	(4.92		
	(b)	−57.340	85.150	−14.420	−0.085	−0.172	−16.46	0.67	24.4
		(2.11)	(4.16)	(3.84)	(1.81)	(2.70)	(5.92)		
(2) Middle 40 per cent	(a)	29.54			−0.014	0.152	5.16	0.52	22.3
		(23.27)			(0.51)	(4.86)	(2.77)		
	(b)	81.080	−37.860	6.430	−0.033	0.130	5.900	0.57	16.7
		(4.45)	(2.76)	(2.55)	(1.05)	(3.04)	(3.16)		
(3) Lowest 60 per cent	(a)	23.09			−0.015	0.143	13.50	0.54	24.5
		(14.25)			(0.40)	(3.58)	(5.67)		
	(b)	124.40	−74.330	12.60	0.078	0.102	14.91	0.68	26.1
		(6.54)	(5.25)	(4.44)	(2.20)	(2.10)	(7.09)		
(4) Lowest 40 per cent	(a)	11.70			−0.008	0.066	9.69	0.51	21.0
		(10.99)			(0.11)	(2.53)	(6.05)		
	(b)	76.32	−47.35	8.00	0.052	0.042	10.57	0.65	22.5
		(5.58)	(4.60)	(4.24)	(2.21)	(1.29)	(7.55)		
(5) Lowest 20 per cent	(a)	4.259			0.002	0.012	6.49	0.44	17.2
		(8.47)			(0.18)	(0.97)	(6.46)		
	(b)	31.32	−19.67	3.27	0.024	0.005	5.10	0.57	16.8
		(4.67)	(3.90)	(3.53)	(2.12)	(0.33)	(7.44)		

[a] *t*-statistics in parentheses.

rates observed in our sample (between 10 to 80 per cent for most developing countries) is such that the observed expansion in literacy across different countries clearly does reach the lowest groups.

(iv) It is interesting to note that in the case of each of the education variables, the income share of the relevant beneficiary group expands at the expense of the income share of the top 20 per cent. This can be said to be an unambiguous improvement from the welfare point of view.

These results are broadly in line with earlier cross section studies—notably Adelman and Morris (1973) and Chenery and Syrquin (1975)—in that they testify to the close relationship between the process of educational and skill improvement, which occurs with development, and the increase in relative equality. As we have seen, there are persuasive reasons for arguing that the correlation reflects an important causal process, although even so the argument does depend upon some fairly crucial assumptions (see note 14) which may not hold in a number of circumstances. Sceptics will also want to point out that the observed correlation may even reflect the reverse direction of causation, i.e. educational levels may be determined by the degree of inequality. We can only record that the cross section data are also consistent with this hypothesis.[17]

3.3. *Population growth and inequality*

The reasons for expecting a particular relationship between income inequality and the rate of growth of population are much less clear than the reasons for expecting the relationships discussed above. For one thing, our understanding of the role of population growth in the development process is fairly limited. In any case, most of the debate in this area has been focused on the relationship between population growth and the pace of development, while its impact on the degree of inequality has received relatively less attention.[18]

In these circumstances, it is appropriate to begin with observed cross country experience—the stylised facts —and then consider how far we have a theory to explain them. Our estimated results unambiguously show high growth rates of population to be systematically associated with greater income inequality. As shown in Table 3, the rate of growth of population has a significant positive impact on the income share of the top 20 per cent, and a significantly negative impact on the income shares of all other groups (except the lowest 20 per cent for which group the negative coefficient on the population variable is not significant). This general pattern remains valid when the regressions are run with different combinations of other explanatory variables and also with the reduced sample of developing countries only.

In interpreting this result, it is important to note that the relationship identified above holds after controlling for other explanatory variables such as per capita GNP. In other words, we need to ask ourselves why an economy with faster population growth would show greater inequality *when it reaches a given level of per capita GNP* than another with a slower growth of population observed *at the same level of development*. The literature suggests two possibilities, neither of which has been fully explored:

(i) Perhaps the most important link between population growth and income inequality is provided by the fact that different income groups grow at different rates, with the lower income groups typically experiencing a faster natural rate of increase in population. Although we have not allowed explicitly for intergroup differences in population growth (data on this subject are simply not available) it is arguable that high growth rates in total population reflect greater differentials in population growth across groups, which in turn generate greater inequality. The argument can be summarised as follows. It is well known that the process of development produces a 'demographic transition'. Suppose that this transition takes the form of a reduction in the natural rate of population growth of each group as per capita income in the group rises, and there is a flattening out of this response at high income levels. In that case, declines in the rate of growth of total population will occur with development as the various groups slide down this curve, and the flattening of the curve implies that this process will produce a narrowing of intergroup differentials in population growth. The argument can be carried even further if we allow for the fact that high population growth rates in some low income countries reflect an initial acceleration in population growth as a result of lower mortality, after which they can be expected to go through a 'demographic transition' as birth rates decline. It is reasonable to assume that this type of acceleration in population growth occurs mainly in the low income groups where the mortality rate is highest. These factors suggest that countries with high growth rates of population probably suffer from larger intergroup differentials in population growth compared to countries with low growth rates of population. It follows that in countries with high growth rates of population, per capita income of the poorer groups will grow more slowly compared to per capita income of the rich, leading to higher inequality at given levels of per capita GNP.

(ii) A second link between population growth and inequality is suggested by the fact that higher growth rates of population imply greater pressure of labour supply on other productive factors with a consequent deterioration in the share of labour in total output. This is especially so in the presence of fixed factors such as land, which are likely to be particularly important in developing countries. A higher population density generated by faster population growth is likely to produce a higher rental share, which in turn generates greater inequality given the typically concentrated pattern of land ownership. A similar argument can be advanced in the case of capital as a productive factor. It has been argued that high growth rates of population lead to higher dependency burdens which reduce the flow of private savings and also places a larger claim on scarce public resources for 'nonproductive' public investment.[19] Both factors tend to lower the ratio of productive capital to labour. If we accept the conjecture that economies with a faster rate of growth of population have lower 'equilibrium' capital–labour ratios at any level of development, it is very likely that they will also have lower labour shares.[20]

3.4. *Socialist countries*

A consistent finding in all the equations estimated is that the six socialist countries in the sample display substantially greater equality than is predicted by the cross country regression line. The coefficient on the dummy variable for these countries is significantly negative in all the equations explaining income shares of the top 20 per cent and it is significantly positive for all other groups. This is precisely what one would expect, given the absence of the disequalising effect of income from property (i.e. land and capital), which is typically highly concentrated.

It is also of interest to consider how the absolute size of the coefficient on the dummy variable changes as we allow explicitly for the impact of particular aspects of development. Taking the various equations explaining the income share of the lowest 40 per cent, for example, we find that the coefficient on the dummy variable for socialist countries is about 12.0 in the case of the basic equation reported in Table 1. It drops to 9.7 when the educational variables are included in Table 5 and is further reduced to 8.7 by the inclusion of all the other explanatory variables in the expanded equations reported in Table 3. Thus a part of the much greater equality of the socialist countries observed in the sample may be due to the fact that in these countries, the progress made in expanding education levels and reducing the rate of growth of population is much greater than for other countries at their income levels. However, it is clear that even after allowing for these specific factors, the socialist countries display markedly greater equality.

In concluding this section, it is appropriate to remind the reader of some caveats. The results discussed above serve to identify some of the correlates of inequality which provide a basis for speculating about causal mechanisms. But it is important to note that our equations do not take account of some of the crucial factors determining cross country differences in income inequality. Two of these deserve special mention.

The most important omission from this point of view is our inability to examine the role of differences in the concentration in ownership of productive assets, including land. This aspect of economic structure is rightly regarded as a crucial determinant of income inequality, and indeed the greater equality observed in socialist countries testifies to this fact. Countries differ widely in the degree of concentration in productive assets both in terms of the initial conditions in this respect and the institutional and policy framework which determines the evolution of concentration patterns over time. Unfortunately, for most countries, lack of data on patterns of concentration of wealth makes it impossible to quantify this relationship directly.[21] We note that we have experimented with the Gini coefficient of the distribution of agricultural land (which is available for about thirty countries) as an explanatory variable, but no significant relationship was identified between this variable and income inequality. This is not really surprising, given that the direct impact on overall inequality will depend upon the size of the rural sector (in terms of both population share and income share), which varies substantially across countries.

A second limitation of our exercise is the lack of explicit recognition of the role of the institutional framework in which development takes place. The distribution of income generated by an economic system is ultimately the result of a complex interaction between economic and socio-political forces. Indeed, it can be argued that the very distinction between these forces results from arbitrary classifications, which are adopted for 'analytical convenience,' at some risk of oversimplification. For example, the distributional impact of an initial concentration of land depends not merely upon the resulting concentration of 'equilibrium' factor incomes, but also on its impact on the equilibrium itself, through the dominant position accorded to landowners in a whole range of transactions. Similarly, improvement in labour incomes and labour shares in total income, occurring with development, depends not only on the upgrading of skills and technological 'factor productivities' as discussed above, but also on the growth of labour power through social and political institutions. These socio-political factors are not easily quantified on an ordinal scale, let alone the cardinal scale needed for regression analysis.[22] Apart from the introduction of a dummy variable for socialist countries, we have made no allowances for subtler differences in socio-political structure. We note in passing that we have attempted to test for the effect of the scale of government activity, as measured by the ratio of tax revenues to GNP, but no significant relationship was discernible.

4 Relative Inequality, Absolute Poverty and Development

In the previous section, we showed that income inequality across countries is related not merely to per capita GNP, but also to other variables measuring particular aspects of development. An important feature of these results is that the inclusion of these additional explanatory variables does not swamp the observed relationship between inequality and per capita GNP. The expanded equations reported in Table 3 show a clear U-shaped pattern with respect to per capita GNP, with the coefficients on the two terms of the quadratic being significant and of opposite signs in the case of the top 20 per cent, as well as the three lower income groups—the lowest 60 per cent, the lowest 40 per cent, and the lowest 20 per cent. In this section, we turn to the implications of these results for the long-term path of inequality and the welfare implications of this path.

4.1. The U-shaped curve revisited

The first point to note about the expanded equations reported in Table 3 is that although they confirm the U-shaped pattern, the absolute magnitudes of the coefficients on the quadratic terms are substantially altered, implying a change in the curvature of the estimated U shape.

The nature of this change can be seen in Fig. 1, which compares the estimated U shape in the income share of the lowest 40 per cent as derived from the equations in Table 1 with the U shape as derived from the expanded equation in Table 3.[23] The U-shaped curve in the expanded equation is substantially flattened out in the later phase when inequality declines. By comparison, the earlier phase of sharply increasing inequality remains relatively unchanged. This basic pattern of a flattening in the inequality reductions in the later phases of development is repeated in the case of the income shares of the lowest 60 per cent and the lowest 20 per cent, and there is a corresponding flattening of the inverted U shape for the top 20 per cent also. In all cases, the turning point is shifted substantially further out (compare results in Table 3 and Table 1).

The change in the estimated U shape suggests an interesting hypothesis for further study. It can be argued that the two phases of inequality conventionally characterised by the U-shaped curve arise from the operation of quite distinct forces. The reduction in inequality observed in the later phases of development appears to be associated with a number of particular processes occurring with development, such as the increasing absorption of labour in the relatively high income modern sector, the expansion in education and the improvement in human resources, and the reduction in population growth rates. Once we allow explicitly for the operation of these processes (as we have done in the expanded equations) the ascending phase of the U-shaped curve is almost completely damped. By contrast, we have not been able to isolate particular processes occurring with development which underlie the initial phase in which relative inequality deteriorates.

Can we explain this observed deterioration? Of the various relationships discussed in section 3, only the process of a declining share of agriculture in GDP is associated with a deterioration in inequality, and that too involves a shift from the middle group to the top, leaving the lower income groups unaffected. If we focus on the income shares of the lowest 40 per cent and the lowest 20 per cent, none of the additional explanatory variables with which we have experimented help to explain this particular 'stylised fact' of cross country experience. We must clearly look to country-specific studies for the answer.

4.2. The absolute impoverishment hypothesis

The prolonged decline in income shares of lower income groups in the early stages of development has important welfare implications. There is clearly a very strong presumption that the poor benefit from development much less than the rich. More seriously, it has been argued by Adelman and Morris (1973) that developing countries face the prospect not just of increasing relative inequality, but also of prolonged absolute impoverishment for the lower income groups. This view needs to be examined in some detail.

The proposition that development may lead to absolute impoverishment of the poorer groups obviously cannot be ruled out *a priori*. Such an outcome may result from the erosion of traditional economic structures as a consequence of the expansion of the modern sector. An aggressively expanding technologically advanced, modern sector, competing against the traditional sector for markets and resources (and benefiting in this competition from an entrenched position in the institutional and political context) may well generate both a relative and absolute decline in incomes of the poor. Needless to say, history provides numerous instances of the operation of such processes.

Against this bleak view of the development process, there is another explanation of the observed increase in relative inequality which is somewhat less pessimistic. On this view, increasing relative inequality is not due to absolute impoverishment but to unequal benefits from growth.

The differences between these two views of what lies behind the observed increase in relative inequality are crucial. In the one case we assume that the disruption of low income traditional economic activities is in some sense a necessary consequence (on some views it is even an essential pre-condition!) for the growth of the modern sector. In the other case, the problem is seen not as arising from a necessary contradiction.

Choosing between these views or, as is more likely, between an appropriate mix of these views is ultimately an empirical issue to be resolved for each particular country experience. Cross section analysis should not be used to derive general pronouncements to be applied to all cases, but in keeping with our objective, it can help to document the 'stylised facts' of cross country experience. The data permit two different tests of the absolute impoverishment hypothesis. The first consists of using the estimated income shares of the lower income groups from the regression equations described above to calculate the per capita absolute income of these groups at different levels of per capita GNP. The second test consists of calculating the average absolute income of the poorer groups for each country from the actual income shares, and then estimating a cross country relationship between this measure of average absolute income of the poor and the level of development.

We find that both tests reject the hypothesis that the process of development produces impoverishment in absolute terms:

(i) Table 6 presents estimates of average incomes of the lowest 60 per cent, the lowest 40 per cent and the lowest 20 per cent at different levels of development based on income shares for these groups predicted by eqs. (3b), (4b) and (5b), for the full sample of countries (Table 3) and from the same equations, estimated for the reduced sample of developing countries only. It should be noted that the predicted income shares for this exercise are obtained by holding all other explanatory variables constant at the mean value for the sample. In all cases, the estimated average absolute income of these groups increases with per capita GNP.

(ii) These results are further supported by the attempt to estimate regression equations using the logarithm of average absolute incomes of the three lower income groups as the dependent variable. Table 7 reports the results of this exercise for the full sample of 60 countries as well as for the reduced sample of developing countries only. The explanatory variables are the same as those used to explain income shares in the expanded equation in Table 3 and include a quadratic in the logarithm of per capita GNP in order to test for the existence of a phase of absolute impoverishment. We find that although the coefficient on the first term in the quadratic is negative in the equations for the lowest 40 per cent, and the lowest 20 per cent, it is not significant in either case. In any case, the coefficients imply no decline in absolute income over the relevant range.

Table 6 **Estimated average absolute income levels of low income groups**[a]

Per capita GNP in US$	Lowest 60 per cent: Full sample	Lowest 60 per cent: Developing countries	Lowest 40 per cent: Full sample	Lowest 40 per cent: Developing countries	Lowest 20 per cent: Full sample	Lowest 20 per cent: Developing countries
75	51.6	45.5	42.0	37.8	32.6	27.7
100	63.2	55.4	50.2	42.0	38.3	31.7
200	103.8	89.0	77.3	63.7	56.3	44.9
300	140.3	118.2	101.2	84.6	70.8	57.5
400	175.2	145.5	124.0	106.4	84.1	71.1
500	209.4	171.8	146.7	129.6	96.8	86.3
600	243.4	197.6	169.6	154.4	109.4	103.1
700	277.4	223.1	193.0	180.7	122.1	121.6
800	311.6	248.5	217.0	209.1	135.0	141.6
900	346.0	273.9	241.6	238.9	148.2	163.3
1000	380.7	299.4	266.9	270.2	161.8	186.5
1500	560.0		403.6		235.7	
3000	1158.9		909.1		519.1	

[a]The figures in the first column for each income group are based on income shares predicted by eqs. (3b), (4b) and (4c) from Table 3, and the figures in the second column are based on income shares predicted by the same equation estimated from the reduced sample of developing countries only. In the latter case, absolute incomes for per capita GNP levels above US$ 1000 are not shown because the predicting equation for income shares was estimated from a sample which did not extend beyond this level.

The behaviour of absolute income of the poor over the relevant range is perhaps best seen in terms of its elasticity with respect to per capita GNP. This can be directly obtained from the estimated equations in Table 7. Differentiating partially with respect to the logarithms of per capita GNP gives $\alpha + 2\beta$ [log per capita GNP] as the elasticity at that level of per capita GNP (where α and β are the coefficients on the two terms of the quadratic). As shown below, the elasticity for all three groups obtained from eqs. (1a), (2a) and (3a) from Table 7 is positive, albeit less than unity (reflecting the increase in relative inequality). Furthermore, it rises as per capita GNP rises.

	Elasticity of absolute income with respect to per capita GNP at:		
	Per capita GNP US$ 100 (1965–71)	Per capita GNP US$ 500 (1965–71)	Per capita GNP US$ 750 (1965–71)
Lowest 60 per cent	0.64	0.73	0.89
Lowest 40 per cent	0.45	0.77	0.85
Lowest 20 per cent	0.18	0.65	0.77

It is worth noting, however, that the elasticity for the lowest 20 per cent, although positive, is much lower than for the other groups and takes much longer to rise to unity.

We conclude that while the cross country evidence points to unequal benefits from growth, it does not support the hypothesis of a prolonged decline in absolute incomes for the poor as development proceeds.

5. Growth and Inequality: The Short-term Relationship

Thus far, our analysis has focused on what are essentially long-term relationships between inequality and development. The worsening in relative inequality observed in our cross-country data occurs over the phase of development presented by the transition from per capita GNP levels of US$ 75 to per capita GNP levels of around US$ 750. For an economy experiencing growth in per capita GNP at the rate of about 2.5 per cent per year, this transition would take about a hundred years. While long-term relationships are of considerable interest, it is important to note that some of the debate in this area has focussed on much more short-term impacts.

The importance of making a distinction between the secular relationship between inequality and levels of development on the one hand and the short-term relationship between inequality and growth on the other, is not always clearly recognised. For example, it has been suggested that high growth rates in some of the developing countries observed over comparatively short periods—e.g. Brazil between 1960 and 1970—have led to a marked increase in income inequality. To some extent, the long-term relationship discussed above would produce precisely such an outcome – a higher rate of growth observed over a given period raises the level of development above what it would otherwise be, and this in turn affects inequality. However, the debate on this issue has a somewhat different flavour. There is a definite suspicion that there are short-run mechanisms which are quite distinct from any structural or long-term factors, and which generate greater inequality as a direct consequence of faster growth. This raises the question of whether the degree of inequality may be affected not

Table 7 **Cross country regressions using absolute average income**

Dependent variable — *Logarithms of average absolute income of:*	*Estimated coefficients on explanatory variables*[a] — *Constant*	*Log per capita GNP*	*(Log per capita GNP)*^{2}	*Share of agriculture in GDP*	*Share of urban pop. in total*	*Literacy rate*	*Secondary school enrollment*	*Population growth rate*	*Socialist dummy*	R^2	*F*	*D.W.*[b]
(1) Lowest 60 per cent												
(a) Full sample	0.959	0.070	0.143	0.002	0.001	0.001	0.001	−0.052	0.106	0.98	444.8	2.03
	(2.10)	(0.23)	(2.75)	(1.05)	(1.55)	(2.60)	(1.81)	(4.47)	(2.68)			
(b) Developing countries	0.720	0.252	0.111	0.002	0.001	0.002	0.001	−0.061		0.94	87.8	2.02
	(0.79)	(0.35)	(0.79)	(1.16)	(0.86)	(2.32)	(1.21)	(3.80)				
(2) Lowest 40 per cent												
(a) Full sample	1.620	−0.475	0.231	0.001	0.001	0.002	0.001	−0.047	0.189	0.97	214.7	2.02
	(2.47)	(1.09)	(3.08)	(0.28)	(1.32)	(2.36)	(1.01)	(2.80)	(3.31)			
(b) Developing countries	1.828	−0.697	0.289	0.001	0.001	0.002	0.001	−0.055		0.88	41.2	2.04
	(1.41)	(0.69)	(1.44)	(0.50)	(0.56)	(2.16)	(0.49)	(2.42)				
(3) Lowest 20 per cent												
(a) Full sample	2.479	−1.183	0.340	−0.001	0.002	0.002	0.001	−0.269	0.32	0.91	75.8	1.72
	(2.31)	(1.65)	(2.77)	(0.27)	(1.11)	(1.83)	(0.39)	(1.00)	(3.46)			
(b) Developing countries	3.216	−1.967	0.534	0.001	0.001	0.003	0.000	−0.036		0.72	15.3	1.83
	(1.55)	(1.21)	(1.66)	(0.20)	(0.32)	(1.85)		(0.99)				

[a]*t*-statistics in parentheses.
[b]In estimating these equations the observations were entered in ascending order of per capita GNP.

only by the level of development but also by the speed at which this level is achieved.

A plausible reason for the existence of such a relationship may be found in a number of short-term pressures associated with high growth rates. For example, the existence of lags in factor mobility across regions or sectors will ensure that as opportunities for accelerated growth arise in particular regions or sectors, economic expansion creates factor market disequilibria which may generate significant income differentials. Such disequilibria are likely to be more severe in a high growth situation than in a more stable low growth situation.

The cross country data permit only a crude test for the existence of a short-term relationship of this type. We can include the rate of growth of GDP for each country over the ten years preceding the point at which the distribution is measured as an additional explanatory variable in our regression equations and consider if (other things being the same) faster growing countries display greater inequality. The results obtained from this exercise reject the hypothesis that a faster rate of growth leads to greater inequality.

One interpretation is that while there may be a secular time path for inequality which developing countries must traverse, and which contains a phase of increasing inequality, there is at least no evidence that countries which traverse this path at a fast pace are worse off *at the same level of development* than countries which traverse it at a slower pace. Such a proposition, if accepted, has dramatic policy implications. It suggests that policymakers are perhaps best advised to think of the rate of growth as determining essentially the speed of transition through the different phases of development and inequality: higher growth rates accelerate this transition without necessarily generating greater inequality than can be expected given the structural characteristics of the economy at each level of development.

It would be naïve to pretend that so important a conclusion can be firmly established on the flimsy basis of the lack of an observable relationship between inequality and the rate of growth. A major limitation of our methodology is that it does not permit us to go beyond the simple measurement of rates of growth to examine differences in the type of growth achieved in different situations. But if we cannot deny that certain types of high growth processes lead to greater inequality than can be structurally expected, we can at least assert that the cross section evidence does not suggest that *all fast growers* systematically display this pattern. The experience of Brazil, where the high growth was accompanied by worsening relative inequality, can be contrasted with the experience of Taiwan, where substantial growth has taken place with an actual reduction in income inequality.

Recognising this diversity of country experience is perhaps the most important lesson to be learned from the data. At the very least, it shifts attention from an unquestioning suspicion of high growth rates as such towards an examination of the particular nature of growth in different countries and the implications of different types of growth for inequality. A systematic investigation along these lines can only be conducted in the context of in-depth analysis of the historical experience of particular countries.

6. Conclusions

It was stated at the outset that the objective of this paper is primarily exploratory. It could not be otherwise, given the limitations of cross country analysis. The results presented above therefore should not be viewed as definitive either in defining the prospects facing particular developing countries or in providing unambiguous policy guidelines. They are best viewed as a useful documentation of empiricial regularities—the so-called 'stylised facts' of cross country experience. More ambitiously, they can also be viewed as providing some clues to the mechanisms through which the development process affects the degree of inequality. They can be no more than clues precisely because the essential complexity of a dynamic process, and its great variety across countries, cannot be adequately captured in a single equation.

Subject to these limitations, our cross country results can be summarised as follows:

(i) There is strong support for the proposition that relative inequality increases substantially in the early stages of development, with a reversal of this tendency in the later stages. This proposition holds whether we restrict the sample to developing countries or expand it to include developed and socialist countries. Furthermore, it appears that the process is most prolonged for the poorest group.

(ii) There are a number of processes occurring *pari passu* with development which are correlated with income inequality and which can plausibly be interpreted as causal. These are intersectoral shifts in the structure of production, expansion in educational attainment and skill level of the labour force, and reduction in the rate of growth of population. The operation of these processes appears to explain some of the improvement in income distribution observed in the later stages of development, but they do not serve to explain the marked deterioration observed in the earlier stages.

(iii) The cross section results do not support the stronger hypothesis that the deterioration in relative inequality reflects a prolonged absolute impoverishment of large sections of the population in the course of development. The cross country pattern shows average absolute incomes of the lower percentile groups rising as per capita GNP rises, although slower than for upper income groups.

(iv) Finally, the cross section results do not support the view that a faster rate of growth is systematically associated with higher inequality than can be expected given the stage of development achieved.

Appendix: Data sources and problems

The income distribution data used in this paper are summarised in Table 8. The sample of 60 countries was selected from a recent compilation of available cross country data undertaken in the World Bank's Development Research Center and reported in Jain (1975). The source for each observation is given by the number in parentheses which corresponds to the source number reported in Jain (1975).

The quintile shares given in Table 8 differ slightly from those implied by the decile shares reported in Jain (1975). This is because the latter are obtained from a Lorenz curve fitted to the original data. Our figures are read off a Lorenz curve plotted through individual points recorded in the original source. The main reason for preferring this method is that the fitted curve does not necessarily pass through the observed points and since these points correspond to deciles or quintiles in many cases, it is arguably more appropriate to use the exact figures. All equations reported in the paper have also been estimated using the data reported in Jain (1975) and the results are substantially unaffected.

The choice of 60 countries from a potential total of 71 countries was dictated by particular judgments about the reliability of data in some cases. Although multiple observations were available for some countries, we have restricted our data set to one observation per country on the grounds that adding more than one observation for some countries would give too much weight to particular country experience. Wherever available, household distributions have been used, but in many cases we have had to use the distribution of individuals.

It is important to emphasise that our selection process does not necessarily ensure that the sixty observations selected come up to some objective standard of quality. Income distribution data are notoriously deficient and the many sources of error affecting them are well known. The sources of error may be broadly grouped into three categories:

(i) There are a number of conceptual and definitional problems in measuring income inequality and available surveys do not display any uniform practice in handling these problems. For one thing, the concept of income that is relevant for the study of inequality is not easy to define uniquely. It should obviously include subsistence income (valued appropriately) and the case can even be made that it should refer in some sense to 'permanent' income, smoothing out both life cycle variations as well as purely stochastic variations around the life cycle profile. There are also obvious problems associated with inequality measures using money incomes for groups facing very different price levels.

(ii) There are well-known sampling problems which limit the reliability of measures of income inequality based on survey data. These problems are aggravated by the fact that many of the available surveys on which inequality measures are based were not originally designed to provide reliable measures of income inequality.

(iii) Finally, quite apart from sampling errors, there are non-sampling errors that are particularly serious in measuring income distribution. It is well known that response bias may lead to intentional understatement of incomes at the upper end of the income range and there may also be some overstatement at the lower end. More generally, it is widely recognised that surveys which include only a few questions on income are likely to elicit highly inaccurate statements about actual incomes from most people.

The data we have used are undoubtedly subject to all these limitations and the result is that our estimates of income distribution are subject to substantial measurement error. In defense of the use of such data for cross section analysis we have only the familiar excuse: the presence of random error in the data serves only to hide cross country patterns rather than to generate spurious patterns. Such patterns as can be discerned despite these errors therefore deserve serious, if critical, consideration.

Table 8 **Income distribution at different levels of development**

		Income shares of quintiles				
Country	*Per capita GNP in US$ (1970 prices)*	*Bottom 20%*	*Second quintile*	*Third quintile*	*Fourth quintile*	*Top 20%*
Developing countries						
1. Chad 58 (1)	79.5	7.5	10.5	17.0	22.0	43.0
2. Malawi 69 (1)	80.0	5.8	9.1	13.3	18.6	53.2
3. Dahomey 59 (1)	91.3	5.0	10.5	14.5	20.0	50.0
4. Pakistan 63–64[a]	93.7	6.5	11.0	15.5	21.5	45.5
5. Tanzania 67 (1)	103.8	5.0	9.0	12.0	17.0	57.0
6. Sri Lanka 69–70 (3)	108.6	6.0	11.0	16.5	20.5	46.0
7. India 63–64 (4)	110.3	5.0	11.0	13.0	19.0	52.0
8. Malagasy 60 (1)	138.7	5.5	8.0	9.5	16.0	61.0
9. Thailand 62 (1)	142.8	5.7	7.2	11.9	17.5	57.7
10. Uganda 70 (1)	144.3	6.2	10.9	13.9	21.9	47.1
11. Kenya 69 (1)	153.2	3.8	6.2	8.5	13.5	68.0
12. Botswana 71–72 (1)	216.6	1.0	5.9	14.5	19.7	58.9
13. Philippines 65 (1)	224.4	3.9	7.9	12.5	20.3	55.4
14. Egypt 64–65 (1)	232.8	4.2	9.8	15.5	23.5	47.0
15. Iraq 56 (1)	235.5	2.0	4.8	9.2	16.0	68.0
16. El Salvador 61 (1)	267.4	5.5	6.5	8.8	17.8	61.4
17. Korea 70 (5)	269.2	7.0	11.0	15.0	22.0	45.0
18. Senegal 60 (1)	281.8	3.0	7.0	10.0	16.0	64.0
19. Honduras 67–68 (1)	301.0	2.0	4.4	9.1	19.5	65.0
20. Tunisia 70 (2)	306.1	4.1	7.3	12.0	21.6	55.0
21. Zambia 59 (1)	308.2	5.6	9.0	11.9	16.5	57.0
22. Ecuador 70 (1)	313.6	2.5	3.9	5.6	14.5	73.5
23. Turkey 68 (1)	322.2	3.0	6.5	11.1	18.8	60.6
24. Ivory Coast 70 (2)	328.7	3.9	6.2	11.8	20.9	57.2
25. Guyana 55–56 (1)	350.8	4.0	10.0	16.8	23.5	45.7
26. Taiwan 68[b]	366.1	7.8	12.2	16.3	22.3	41.4
27. Colombia 70 (7)	388.2	3.5	5.9	12.1	19.1	59.4
28. Malaysia 70 (3)	401.4	3.4	8.0	12.6	20.1	55.9
29. Brazil 70 (4)	456.5	3.1	6.9	10.8	17.0	62.2
30. Jamaica 58 (1)	515.6	2.2	6.0	10.8	19.5	61.5
31. Peru 70 (4)	546.1	1.5	5.0	12.0	21.5	60.0
32. Lebanon 55–60 (1)	588.3	5.0	8.0	10.0	16.0	61.0
33. Gabon 68 (2)	608.1	3.3	5.5	7.9	15.8	67.5
34. Costa Rica 71 (2)	617.1	5.4	9.3	13.7	21.0	50.6
35. Mexico 69 (5)	696.9	4.0	6.5	9.5	16.0	64.0
36. Uruguay 67 (1)	720.8	4.3	10.0	15.1	23.2	47.4
37. Panama 69 (2)	773.4	2.9	6.5	12.5	18.8	59.3
38. Spain 64–65 (1)	852.1	6.0	11.0	15.7	22.1	45.2
39. Chile 68 (1)	903.5	4.5	8.5	12.7	17.5	56.8

Table 8 (*continued*)

Country	Per capita GNP in US$ (1970 prices)	Income shares of quintiles: Bottom 20%	Second quintile	Third quintile	Fourth quintile	Top 20%
40. Argentina 61 (1)	1004.6	7.0	10.3	13.1	17.6	52.0
41. Puerto Rico 63 (1)	1217.4	4.5	9.2	14.2	21.5	50.6
42. Japan 68 (2)	1712.8	4.6	11.3	16.8	23.4	43.8
43. Finland 62 (1)	1839.8	2.4	8.7	15.4	24.2	49.3
44. Netherlands 67 (2)	2297.0	3.1	10.5	16.4	21.5	48.5
45. France 62 (1)	2303.1	1.9	7.6	14.0	22.8	53.7
46. Norway 63 (1)	2361.9	4.5	12.1	18.5	24.4	40.5
47. United Kingdom 68 (2)	2414.3	6.0	12.8	18.2	23.8	39.2
48. New Zealand 70–71 (3)	2501.5	4.4	12.5	18.6	23.5	41.0
49. Denmark 63 (1)	2563.9	5.0	10.8	16.8	24.2	43.2
50. Australia 67–68 (1)	2632.4	6.6	13.5	17.8	23.4	38.7
51. Germany, W. 70 (2)	3208.6	5.9	10.4	15.6	22.5	45.6
52. Canada 65 (1)	3509.6	6.4	13.6	16.5	23.3	40.2
53. Sweden 70 (2)	4452.2	5.4	9.9	17.6	24.6	42.5
54. United States 70 (3)	5244.1	6.7	13.0	17.4	24.1	38.8
Socialist countries						
55. Bulgaria (1)	406.9	9.8	15.2	18.0	22.0	35.0
56. Yugoslavia 68 (2)	602.3	6.5	12.0	17.0	23.0	41.5
57. Poland 64 (1)	660.8	9.8	13.6	18.1	22.5	36.0
58. Hungary 67 (1)	872.7	8.5	15.5	19.0	23.5	33.5
59. Czechoslovakia 64 (1)	887.7	12.0	15.6	19.0	22.4	31.0
60. Germany, E. 70 (1)	2046.3	10.4	15.8	19.8	23.3	30.7

[a]The income distribution for Pakistan is for East and West Pakistan taken together as reported in source 1 for Pakistan from Jain (1975).

[b]The income distribution for Taiwan is from W. Kuo, 'Income distribution by size in Taiwan area – Changes and causes,' in: Income Distribution, Employment and Economic Development in South East and East Asia, papers and proceedings of the seminar sponsored by the Japan Economic Research Center and the Council for Asian Manpower Studies, vol. 1.

Notes: Reading 6

1 See Appendix for data sources and a brief discussion of data problems.

2 We have used income shares as the dependent variables instead of summary indices of inequality such as the Gini coefficient because this permits us to focus on the impact of the development process over different ranges of the income distribution. The Gini coefficient is also a relatively insensitive measure and its limited variation across countries makes it difficult to identify statistically significant relationships. See, for example, Papanek (1976).

3 See, for example, Kravis (1960), Oshima (1962), Adelman and Morris (1973) and Chenery and Syrquin (1975). For a recent review of this literature see Paukert (1973) and Cline (1975).

4 This is argued in Adelman and Morris (1973, pp. 179–83).

5 The logarithmic transformation gives equal weight to equal proportional differences in GNP in measuring 'levels of development'. This has an intuitive appeal since growth occurs at a compound rate over time.

6 Our results on this score are discussed in detail in section 3.

7 Throughout this Reading the term significant will be used to indicate that the estimated coefficients are significantly different from zero with the sign indicated at least at the 10 per cent level for a two-tailed test. The critical value of t for this level of significance is 1.68 for our sample size.

8 There are, however, major problems of comparability across countries in using per capita GNP as a measure of the level of development. The use of official exchange rates to convert GNP measured in domestic currency to GNP measured in US$ introduces obvious errors since exchange rates typically do not reflect purchasing power parity. Kravis *et al.* (1975), investigating this problem, found that the use of official exchange rates understates GNP in developing countries compared to developed countries. Furthermore, within the developing countries studied, the degree of understatement varies across countries sufficiently to create a switch in per capita GNP rankings. These results indicate that there must be substantial measurement error in our explanatory variables.

9 The increase in the variation explained is statistically significant at the 5 per cent level in all cases.

10 It should be emphasised that this approach does not provide a rigorous basis for choosing between alternative hypotheses. It is essentially a heuristic exploration of alternative patterns.

11 For a fuller discussion see Robinson (1976).

12 As pointed out by Robinson (1976), it is not essential for urban inequality to be greater than rural inequality for the

U shape to exist, provided the intersectoral mean differences are large enough. As equation (3) makes clear, $v_u > v_r$ only ensures that the turning point occurs when more than half the population is in urban areas.

13 Note that this is not to deny that in many circumstances the extent of migration may be excessive compared to available employment possibilities. The urban population share variable measures the total absorption of population in the urban areas which largely reflects expansion in employment opportunities. These data provide no basis for measuring the degree of excess migration.

14 Note that the assumption that a greater supply of skilled labour will not produce a sharp decline in its marginal product is obviously crucial. Otherwise, skill upgrading will not have much effect upon total output, and while it may reduce relative wage differentials it may also reduce the share of labour in total income, thus contributing to an increase in overall inequality. Indeed in these circumstances it is even likely that skill differentials will not narrow because of the resistance of organised labour, and the result will be either open unemployment of skilled labour or displacement of unskilled labour by skilled labour in the unorganised sector of the market. The existence of 'over-educated' manpower in many developing countries may reflect just such a phenomenon. Proponents of the importance of education are usually undismayed by this phenomenon and explain it away as an expansion in the 'wrong kind of education'.

15 Measuring the educational and skill levels of the labour force is no simple task. Ideally we would need to develop appropriate definitions of skill levels and to measure the skill structure of the labour force in each country. Data of this sort relating to the stock of labour are not available for most of the countries in our sample. The use of the school enrolment rate has obvious limitations since it is a flow variable and not a stock variable.

16 Recalling that the decline in income shares with respect to per capita GNP was most prolonged in the case of the lowest income groups (see section 2), it is reasonable to assume that the literacy rate, which is correlated with the per capita GNP variable, is picking up the negative impact due to per capita GNP through most of the early stages of development.

17 A regression of the literacy rate and the secondary school enrolment rate on per capita GNP and the income shares of the middle and lower groups yields significant positive coefficients on the latter.

18 The conventional wisdom in this area (which has been extensively aired in recent years) states that there is a mutually reinforcing relationship between the pace of economic development and reductions in the rate of growth of population. For an unconventional – and on the whole implausible – view that population growth may actually provide the impetus to economic expansion in otherwise stagnant societies, see Boserup (1965).

19 See, for example, Leff (1969).

20 This relationship between labour shares and capital–labour ratios follows from standard neo-classical assumptions, providing the elasticity of substitution is less than unity.

21 For a review of the importance of this aspect of economic structure in determining income inequality in the economy and its overwhelming importance in the agricultural sector, see Chenery *et al.* (1974).

22 For an attempt at examining these relationships using analysis of variance techniques suitable for ordinally measurable variables, see Adelman and Morris (1973). Measurement of this type inevitably involves a high degree of subjective evaluation.

23 In each case, the curve corresponds to the estimated share predicted by the regression equation for different levels of per capita GNP, holding all other explanatory variables at their mean value for the sample and holding the dummy variable for socialist countries at zero.

References: Reading 6

Adelman, I., and Morris, C. T. (1973), *Economic Growth and Social Equity in Developing Countries* (Stanford University Press).

Adelman, I., and Robinson, S. (1976), *Income Distribution Policy in Developing Countries: The Case of Korea* (Stanford University Press).

Ahluwalia, M. S. (1974), 'Income inequality: some dimensions of the problem', in Chenery *et al.* (1974).

Boserup, E. (1965), *The Conditions of Agricultural Growth: The Economics of Agrarian Change with Population Pressure* (Chicago).

Chenery, H. B., and Syrquin, M. (1975), *Patterns of Development – 1950–70* (Oxford University Press).

Chenery, H. B., Ahluwalia, M. S., Bell, C. L. G., Duloy, J. H., and Jolly, R. (1974), *Redistribution with Growth: An Approach to Policy* (Oxford University Press).

Cline, W. R. (1975), 'Distribution and development', *Journal of Development Economics*, Vol. 1, no. 4, pp. 359–402.

Jain, S. (1975), *The Size Distribution of Income: A Compilation of Data* (Johns Hopkins University Press).

Kravis, B. (1960), 'International differences in the distribution of income', *Review of Economics and Statistics*, November.

Kravis, B., Kennessey, Z., Heston, A., and Summers, R. (1975), *A System of International Comparisons of Gross Product and Purchasing Power* (Johns Hopkins University Press).

Kuznets, S. (1955), 'Economic growth and income inequality', *American Economic Review*, March.

Kuznets, S. (1963), 'Quantitative aspects of the economic growth of nations: VIII distribution of income by size', *Economic Development and Cultural Change*, January.

Leff, N. H. (1969), 'Dependency rates and savings rates', *American Economic Review*, December.

Oshima, H. (1962), 'The international comparison of size distribution of family incomes with special reference to Asia', *Review of Economics and Statistics*, November.

Papanek, G. F. (1976), 'Economic growth, income distribution, and the political process in less developed countries', paper presented at a symposium on Income Distribution and Economic Inequality, Bad Homburg, West Germany, June.

Paukert, F. (1973), 'Income distribution at different levels of development', *International Labour Review*, August–September.

Robinson, S. (1976), 'A note on the U hypothesis relating income inequality and economic development', *American Economic Review*, June.

Part Two

Population, Labour and Employment

In relation to population Robinson (Reading 7) suggests that conventional approaches to assessing the benefits of population control, such as Enke's cost-benefit analysis, neglect the problem of response to population programmes, and suggests that responsiveness will differ substantially between different country categories. Continuing the discussion of Part One, some theorists such as Arthur Lewis have suggested that unemployment and underemployed labour of developing countries afford an important potential for development: Readings 8 and 9 together survey a substantial amount of empirical work regarding the extent of such underemployment and confirm that the potential may be more circumscribed than previously thought. Hart (Reading 10) argues that between the formally employed and the unemployed there is in fact a substantial and quite heterogeneous category of 'informal' sector employment which merits much more attention. Following a succinct contribution by Edwards (Reading 11) on education and development, the section ends with the widely discussed article by Harris and Todaro (Reading 12) on the determinants of the migration of population from the rural to urban sector, which has been recognised as an increasingly serious problem in developing countries.

Reading 7

Population Control and Development Strategy

W. C. Robinson

Journal of Development Studies, 1972, pp. 104–17.

Introduction

Population continues to be one of the most widely discussed and poorly understood aspects of economic and social development.

Socio-economic Factors and the Vital Rates

There is a general recognition that the vital demographic processes—fertility, mortality, and others—are determined in some basic socio-psychological fashion by the structure of the physical and social environment in which people live. As this environment changes so do the vital processes. High mortality and high fertility go with a particular set of social and economic institutions; they are characteristics of what may be called pre-modern, pre-industrial societies. As a society changes its basic structure and becomes more urban and more industrial, as income and education levels rise and as man increasingly begins to shape his environment instead of the other way around, there is every reason to think that mortality and also fertility will begin to decline.

Roughly speaking, this is what happened in the West and this has been generalized into the so-called 'Theory of the Demographic Transition'. Ansley Coale has summed up this experience as follows:

> In barest outline the sequence of events, according to the theory of the demographic transition, can be summarized as follows: The agrarian low-income economy is characterized by high birth and death rates—the birth rates relatively stable, and the death rates fluctuating in response to varying fortunes. Then as the economy changes its form to a more interdependent and specialized market-dominated economy, the average death rate declines. It continues to decline under the impact of better organization and improving medical knowledge and care. Somewhat later the birth rate begins to fall. The two rates pursue a more or less parallel downward course with the decline of the birth rate lagging behind. Finally as further reduction of the death rate becomes harder to attain, the birth rate again approaches equality with death rate and a more gradual rate of growth is re-established, with, however, low risks of mortality and small families as the typical pattern. Mortality rates are now relatively stable from year to year and birth-rates—now responsive to voluntary decisions rather than to deeply imbedded customs—may fluctuate from year to year. This short description fits the experience of most countries whose economies have undergone the kind of reorganization we have been calling economic development.[1]

The cause of the 'turning points' in mortality and fertility in Western history is of great interest. On mortality there is general agreement that the beginning of the decline in mortality in the West far antedated really effective public health or preventive medicine. Record and McKeown, concluding their classic study of the mortality changes in Great Britain during the eighteenth and nineteenth centuries, note:

> . . . the death rate fell between 1770 and 1900 and the chief reason for the fall was improvement in the environmental conditions of living and health.[2]

The United Nations *Determinants and Consequences* volume reaches a similar conclusion:

> It is clear, however, that the general improvement in the mortality experience of the Western nations during the eighteenth and first part of the nineteenth centuries was due more to a rising level of living, better working conditions and broad social reforms than to the development of scientific methods for control of diseases.[3]

The other important change, the decline in fertility,

also appears to have been due largely to 'natural means'. For a time in the 1930s Carr-Saunders, Fairchild and others talked about the nineteenth century 'technological breakthrough', the availability of cheap, thin but strong sheet rubber, as the important factor which made possible the widespread adoption of family planning. However, Stix, Notestein and others argued in contrast to 'appliance methods' that 'folk methods'—*coitus interruptus* and advancing age at marriage—were more important in explaining the beginning of the fertility decline. The Royal Commission Report of 1948 which showed that 80 per cent of those who had been practising contraception in Great Britain prior to 1910 had been using the folk methods effectively ended the debate.

Thus one can generalize and say that the important changes in birth rate and death rate in the Western demographic transition took place *before* modern medical science and its multitude of applications had begun to exert much influence on the vital processes. This is not to say that medical science has not been responsible for the fall in the death rate in recent decades and for the fact that it will continue to fall; nor is it to deny that modern science has made 'folk methods' of contraception obsolete and largely unused today. But, if we limit ourselves to the turning-points of the transition we do conclude that 'natural' rather than 'technological' forces seem to have dominated.

Experience in Developing Areas

The transferability of the Western experience to the developing areas of the world has been debated at some length. Judith Blake sees two main approaches which she calls: (*a*) the 'economic development' approach, and (*b*) the 'family planning' approach. These she describes as follows:

> The first [economic development] sees decreases in family size as the long-range resultant of a complete socio-economic overhauling which, in turn, leads to a desire for fewer children. The second [family planning] overlooks the institutionalization of reproduction entirely and assumes that education and communication regarding birth control will eventually reduce births to a level in keeping with low mortality.[4]

But, regardless of one's point of view, it seems clear, as Kirk has pointed out,[5] that a new 'tradition' has in fact begun to occur. That is, at one pole there are many countries (most underdeveloped areas) which have high fertility and at the other pole another group (a majority of the developed nations) which have low fertility. In the last decade a middle group of 'transitional' populations with fertility rates between the extremes have begun to appear. Some of these are countries with notably successful population control programmes.

It will not be necessary for us to attempt a review of each of these programmes or countries. This has already been done[6] and there is growing agreement about the socio-economic pattern which emerges. In general, one can say that the 'successes' have been in countries in which substantial socio-economic progress had already been made. After reviewing 'transitions' in several underdeveloped areas, Irene Taeuber concludes:

> . . . economic and social development and demographic modernization are an inter-related if not an integrated process. Culture is a conditioning factor, but, if there is participating in a modernizing economy and society, there is declining fertility. The extent of that decline is more explainable in terms of economic and social status and dynamics than in relation to region, culture, religion or political form.[7]

And Freedman writes:

> Let me say in summary that I expect fertility to decline first and most rapidly under the following conditions: (1) where significant social development has already occurred; (2) where mortality has been relatively low for some time; (3) where there is evidence that many people, wanting moderate-sized families, are beginning to try to limit family size; (4) where there are effective social networks transcending local communities through which family planning ideas and services and other modernizing influences can be disseminated; (5) where there are large-scale, effective *organized* efforts to disseminate family-planning ideas and information; (6) where such new contraceptives as the intra-uterine devices or contraceptive pills are effectively available. . . . Obviously, the first four conditions are relevant both to the past and to current situations. The last two . . . introduce new elements for which history provides no specific guide-lines.[8]

Generalizing, one can suggest that the 'successes' achieved to date suggest the following conclusions:

> First, nearly all the 'successes' of family planning . . . have been in areas where considerable progress towards modernity had already occurred. Typically, death rates in these areas are low (10 or under), female literacy high (50 per cent or over) and education, occupational change, urbanization and such other factors rather far advanced. The studies also indicate that not infrequently the populations concerned were already beginning to practise family planning and that their initial pre-programme fertility was already declining or at least below unrestricted fertility levels. The introduction of family planning as a policy seems then to have reinforced and accelerated trends already in existence.
>
> Second, there is evidence that in the case of large-scale national family planning programmes, conven-

> tional contraceptives have not proved the answer. In Taiwan, the 'cafeteria approach' (as Freedman calls it) quickly led to the realization that the I.U.D.s were the most favoured method. . . . Even where the socio-economic factors are favourable there appears to be a danger in expecting too high a degree of motivations and persistence on the part of still semi-literate population; and where initial motivation is strong, the I.U.D. or other clinical methods are likely to be preferred from the outset.
>
> Third, in rural areas lacking any vestige of modernity, the degree of success has been limited. Expression of interest and willingness to accept supplies can not be taken as the same thing as a firm determination to practise birth control.[9]

This brief review also suggests that we would be quite wrong to think that the 'successes' so far amount to a totally new technological breakthrough. All that we can definitely say is that in some areas the population has proved receptive to improved contraceptive techniques. This has been especially true of areas in which health conditions were good, education and income rising, and transport and medical facilities available. But, fertility rates in these areas were probably already declining and we cannot be sure to what extent the use of the newer techniques simply represent a change in method. This is not altogether bad since the newer methods (the I.U.D. or the orals) are likely to be more effective than the ones which they are replacing and the fertility decline is thus accelerated. But, this does not constitute the kind of success for which we hope from a new technology. In fact, so far, the evidence rather bears out the argument that fertility declines and social and economic change occur simultaneously or in some kind of related chain-reaction sequence.[10]

Benefits and Costs of Population Control Programmes

Coale and Hoover, in their now classic book on India's prospects, first performed the relatively simple exercise of showing the impact on *per capita* income of some assumed reduction in fertility. That is, making projections of income to some target date in the future and then indicating the *per capita* income implied if population growth continued unchecked or if it declined by some stated amount. (For periods of up to twenty years it can be assumed that decreases in population do not affect output since the births not occurring would have been contributing to output in this period in any case. If one assumes a zero marginal product for additional members of the labour force then the same logic can be applied to the longer-run periods of over twenty years also.) Coale and Hoover also ignored the question of the cost of the population control scheme, assuming that it was part of the regular investment programme of the public sector. In the case of such a costless reduction in fertility, the impact on *per capita* income in the short-run is unambiguously favourable and in the long-run also favourable if one assumes the marginal product of workers in the future is less than average product today.

A more realistic approach must take into account the fact that a population control programme will involve costs of an incremental sort. Demeny[11] takes such an approach and begins by making two sets of population projections, one with constant fertility, the other with declining fertility. He next derives the income to the future point based on various assumptions concerning the principal economic parameters (savings ratio, capital-output ratio, etc.) and finds in consequence the *per capita* incomes associated with the higher and the lower population estimates. If *per capita* income is even slightly higher, then the population is better off and will prefer this situation, he reasons; and since the lower growth population will have a higher *per capita* income, Demeny reasons that the society should be willing to spend that part of total income represented by the difference in *per capita* income between the two figures times the difference in population. That is, it would be willing to spend its gains to cover the costs of obtaining those gains so long as anything is left over. The figure resulting then is at least an upper limit to the amount which could be spent to prevent population growth.

Meier, Enke, Bower, Zaidan[12] and others have employed the more familiar cost-benefit apparatus to calculate the actual return per dollar spent so that this figure can then be compared to other investment possibilities open to the society. This approach again focuses on the relatively short-run period (less than twenty years) in which case additional population creates only costs and no increment to output. (It is also true that in the longer run if one argues for a zero (or even very low) marginal product of labour, the same answer results.) In any case, the 'benefits' of the fertility reduction are the costs which society does not have to incur because births do not occur. These include: (i) social overhead costs involved in providing for maternal and prenatal care and facilities for the incremental pregnancies and births; (ii) subsistence costs of the added population (food, clothing, shelter, etc.); (iii) social overhead costs of eduction plus perhaps also the extra strain placed upon general overhead items such as transportation, power, and so on.

These costs would have been incurred over time from now (the time the family planning programme is launched) until the end of their period under consideration. Thus, viewed as a stream of benefits (costs not incurred) they are still future benefits and must be discounted back to the present to make a benefit-cost calculation in the present. The selection of the relevant discount rate is difficult but not impossible, and the problem is manageable analytically.

The costs of the programme are less easily handled. Several sorts of costs are relevant and these include the direct money costs of the programmes including the costs of the appliances involved, the cost of the supporting personnel, the publicity and overhead costs, and also the costs of the incentive bonus payments, if any, paid to the public to participate in the programme. Enke, in some of his writings[13] draws a distinction between 'resources costs' (costs of contraceptives and personnel) and 'transfer costs' (costs of bonus payments). He makes the explicit assumption that the 'transfer' costs can be disregarded since domestic taxes can be increased to cover them and these tax proceeds would have not been used for some other development-related project. This is a highly unrealistic assumption which, as Demeny has pointed out,[14] avoids the real issue of choice between population control schemes versus other programmes by assuming them to be non-competing financially speaking. In fact, for any kind of expenditure on family planning, there are very important opportunity cost elements which should be taken into account. These are the decreases (or increases which do not occur) in other programmes which will be deferred or cut back to finance family planning. Such programmes will almost certainly be in the health and welfare area. In other words, it is not likely that the defence budget will be cut back to allow family planning to begin, but it is very likely that malaria control or rural public health will be cut back. Family planning is thought of as 'health and welfare' and is directly competitive with other programmes in this area. Now, such welfare programmes when successful probably affect an improvement in the efficiency of labour. Malaria control, for example, has been shown to work dramatic increases in labour productivity and the same may be said for campaigns against many other debilitating diseases. To the extent that such potential increases in output per worker are not realized because of other programmes these lost 'benefits' must fairly be seen as costs of the family planning itself.[15]

Even if it be objected that family planning costs are minimal because of foreign exchange help, or local currency grants from foreign countries (even including grants in kind of the necessary appliances) the point remains valid in a qualitative way. For the key shortage may not be funds but administrators. The family planning scheme will almost certainly draw some if not all of its key people from other programmes and, even if budgets are not effected, the other programmes must still be affected. Thus, even without financial limitations one could argue that the family planning scheme will have sharply negative 'spill overs' for other programmes.

Few actual efforts have been made to calculate costs for programmes. Demeny does not make such an attempt, satisfying himself instead with establishing the upper limits to how much economies with certain stated parameters should be willing to pay. Enke's efforts are largely hypothetical and consistently ignore or underestimate important cost elements. Thus, Enke's estimate that it costs 20 cents to prevent a pregnancy using 'withdrawal' compared to 50 cents using 'rhythm' is, to say the least, startling.[16] His estimate that I.U.D.s cost $1.11 to prevent one birth is similarly completely conjectural. The only detailed cost estimate of any ongoing programme (that in Taichung, Taiwan, in 1963) suggested costs ranging up to $6.48 U.S. per I.U.D. inserted.[17] Experience on Taiwan suggests a ratio of 5 I.U.D. inserted per birth prevented thus giving a figure of $25.00 to $30.00, and this range would represent costs under the conditions where, as has been discussed above, setting factors and social infrastructure were highly positive.

In fact, we actually know very little about the costs of family planning programmes per unit of final payoff. The number of national or even large-scale demonstration programmes yet launched are few and data for these are typically not available in such a form as to permit true costs-benefit or performance analysis.

Another aspect of the cost-benefit approach which Enke and other authors do not mention is that the payoff the births prevented must be viewed in probabilistic terms. The programme may or may not be a complete success. If the budget is viewed as fixed then a 50 per cent successful programme will mean a 100 per cent increase in the unit-cost of the payoff. Figure 1, which is an adaptation of the familiar returns curve of economic analysis, illustrates this. Each curve represents a given set of setting factors. The most unfavourable situation (a) brings (A births prevented for OX expenditure for a per unit cost of OX/OA; situation (b) shows OX/OB costs per unit; while the most favourable; (c), shows costs per unit of OX/OC. Hypothetical benefit-cost analyses will yield quite different results depending upon which of the return curves one assumes to be the actual one.

Figure 1 illustrates another important but little-discussed aspect of the cost-benefit question. Costs per unit of payoff are not likely to be constant. Along all the returns curves shown in Figure 1 costs per unit change with the volume or scale, eventually rising sharply as marginal returns begin to asymptotically approach zero. The shape and slope of the curves of Figure 1 are, however, also purely hypothetical and it is possible to imagine other type functions. Figure 2 illustrates some of these in terms of average costs per unit. Curve A in Figure 2 would be consistent with the cost functions shown in Figure 1; curve B of Figure 2 would simply be a constant cost per unit up to some point at which, because perhaps of a bottleneck shortage of some critical input, costs would rise sharply. Curve C indicates that costs per unit fall continuously even after high volumes of operations have been reached. One cannot say with any assurance on *a priori* grounds which function is most likely to be the actual one experienced. The usual explanation in economic terms for the falling average costs with volume is the necessity for some overhead (fixed capital) regardless of the volume of operation. As volume rises, the fixed cost is spread more thinly over larger number of units, bringing down average costs. This is likely to be true for family planning programmes also and thus a moderately declining average cost per unit should be expected. If all other inputs are assumed to be available at present prices in virtually unlimited quantities, then costs per unit would fall gradually, levelling off as the impact of spreading the fixed cost became more and more diffused over a very large volume. If costs of some inputs are allowed to rise, however, because of a shortage, then

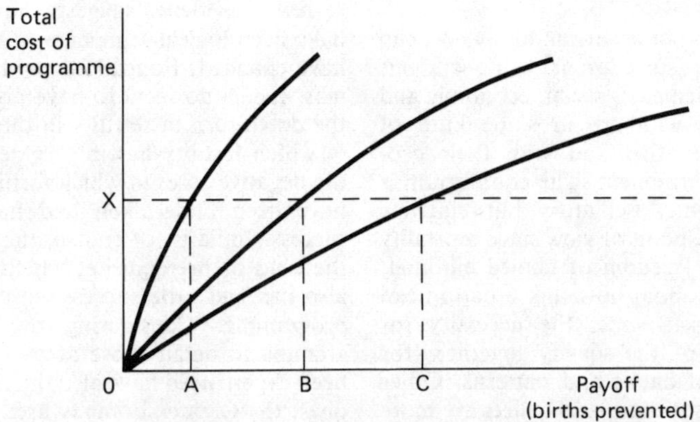

Figure 1

costs per unit would begin to rise also. Perhaps, on all these counts, curve D in Figure 2 represents the most plausible expected average cost per unit (birth prevented) curve.

The foregoing considerations are intended as qualifications or extensions to the usual cost-benefit analysis as applied in the area of population control programmes. Allowing more fully for all costs and allowing for the

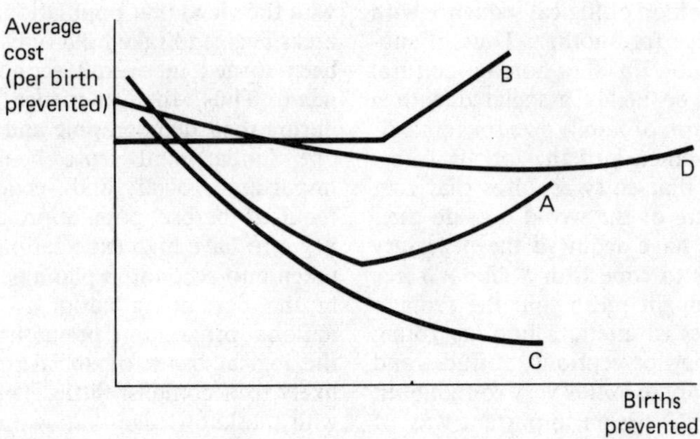

Figure 2

probabilistic outcome of the programmes might or might not change the answer which cost-benefit analysis would give in particular cases. Given the high upper limit which Demeny's model suggests for costs, one suspects that most programmes would still show positive benefits. However, the benefits might very well be much lower than is usually assumed. In any case, taking all these difficulties and unknowns into account, one must be dubious of flat unqualified statements to the effect that a dollar invested in family planning brings social returns several hundred times greater than the same dollar invested in any other way.

The Question of Prerequisites and Linkages

The process of development is a complex, many-sided series of changes in basic social and economic institutions and behaviour patterns in society. We lack a well-articulated theory of how and also why such changes take place. Indeed, such a theory covering all types of societies may not be possible except at such a level of generalization as to be trivial.

In any case, change does not occur randomly. We can think of the 'traditional' societies as being systems containing a complex of elements, social, economic and political, which to begin with are in some kind of equilibrium one with the other and with their geographical and climatic environment. The equilibrium is stable perhaps, even if slightly oscillatory, but relatively undesirable from a welfare point of view since mortality is high, income low, and freedom of choice minimal. Economic development is about how this situation can be changed. Some theorists stress the necessity for changing large segments of the society together, for changing whole clusters of habits and patterns. Other writers argue that some institutions and beliefs are more easily changed than others and that this should be encouraged. Whatever approach is followed, it is clear that the disruption of the original equilibrium is dangerous and tends to release forces destructive to true growth and development as well as those beneficial to it.

It is clear that 'balance' in growth is vital, but it is also clear that if all the fundamental social and economic institutions of the country change at once, or change very rapidly, social disorganization and political chaos may well be the result. Permanent changes in institutions usually occur in some kind of logical sequence with one change setting the stage for another. Thus, if substantial female participation in the non-agricultural labour force is found to be highly associated with a reduction in the desired norm of family size for females, then the goal is to get women into the labour force. However, it may also be that entry requires that first females have become aware of the world outside their own home or village and have acquired the necessary self-confidence and ability to cope with a labour force situation. This, in turn, might mean that the females must have left their homes to attend school as young girls and had thus gained new perceptions, attitudes and abilities. Thus, one might argue in this very roundabout way that education of females is an important way of affecting the population growth rate in such societies. The linkages and relationships are complex. If all the assumptions made in the above example are, in fact, correct, then educating girls and denying them access to the labour market would still have no effect. Or, attempting to recruit females into the labour force when they had not gone through the earlier experience of having schooling outside home would be equally useless.

Of course, none of this is absolute. Indeed, one can argue that development planning is explicitly aimed at making it possible to skip steps in such a long and drawn-out chain of preconditions. Perhaps women in the home, literate and employed or not, can be reached by determined family planning propaganda. If so, then a large number of intervening steps may be skipped. But, surely, there is also a limit to the number of steps which can be skipped.

Turning to the question of family planning, the above review of evidence suggests that at least thus far, there have been logical sequences to the way in which events have changed. Education, public health, and access to mass media do seem to have preceded the beginning of the down-turn in fertility in those developing countries in which fertility has in fact declined. There also exist the negative cases in which fertility control programmes have been undertaken and have shown little or no success. India is, of course, the prime case. India lacks the kind of prerequisites which Taiwan had and India also has had little success with her population control programme. Considering the regional Indian programme in detail those areas where some success has been experienced have also the relatively more advanced ones: the Greater Bombay area, Hoogly District in the Calcutta area, Madras and one or two others. These areas have typically shown above average literacy, per cent of the labour force in industry and low mortality rates. The experience of the developing areas reviewed by Taeuber, Freedman, Glass. and the others quoted above makes clear that there is some concensus on this point.

There are two interesting conclusions to be drawn from these arguments that social economic change will occur in some kind of sequential ordering. First, the evidence supports the view (or at least is not inconsistent with the view) that population control in the developing areas begins to take hold only after a certain corner has been turned in overall economic and social development. Thus, the experience of the Western nations during their demographic and economic transition is in one fundamental sense being repeated. Second, if important social and economic infrastructure is required before population control programmes can begin to have high expectations of payoff, this must be taken into account in planning any official programmes in the developing nations. To launch an ambitious national programme prematurely, ahead of its place in the logical order of social and economic changes, is likely to accomplish little. The planner must be armed with the knowledge that A must precede B and that B must come before C.[18] Much as he might like to proceed directly to C, over the longer run this will simply not be good planning.

Conclusions: A Suggested Strategy for Population Control

Let us now see what can be said, in the light of the foregoing, about an optimum strategy for population control. The countries of the high-fertility lesser-developed world fall into three groups: first, those countries which have already made substantial strides towards development and in which the various indices of modernity—literacy, especially female literacy, income, exposure to outside media or information, non-agriculture economic pursuits, and so on—are relatively favourable. In such countries one would suspect that a close study of fertility will show that fertility has already started to decline for some groups, and for some areas. Contraception (with methods however inefficient) is being practised. Such countries are then 'ready' and a well-planned campaign would presumably accelerate and strengthen the existing trend towards lower fertility. Several Latin American countries are undoubtedly at this stage now, including Mexico and Chile, where in the latter case the classic folk method of preventing births—abortion—has been growing in importance.

A second group of countries would be those in which some modernization has occurred but in which the bulk of the population still have not been effectively reached by the forces of change. Here the necessary conditions for widespread acceptance of fertility limitation—natural or technological—simply are not to be found. For the present, then, emphasis should be placed on mounting an effective health programme to reduce the mortality rate so that one important (and quite rational) reason for larger families is removed, and on education to make the population more susceptible to new ideas.

In this group of countries also, undoubtedly some family planning already exists, too, although in smaller degree, and probably concentrated in certain geographic areas (cities) or socio-economic strata (industrial workers, civil servants). Such pockets should be encouraged with clinics and by subsidized distribution of the newer techniques. But, ambitious programmes in the rural areas will probably not be good investments.

A third group of countries are those which are still at the very beginning stage of development and here the main emphasis must be on such fundamental infrastructure as transport and communications as well as health and education. Family planning will be largely a waste of time, except for some very small part of the urban population (it may be taken for granted that a modest clinic programme in the larger urban areas will always be a good idea regardless of the overall setting).

Two sorts of objections to the strategy outlined above can be put forward. First, why not do everything at once anyway just in case we have misread the signs about the logical ordering of change. To this we must answer that you cannot do everything at once because resources are limited. The opportunity cost of a family planning programme is the other programmes you forgo in order to launch it. And if the programmes forgone are ones needed to help create a favourable environment for family planning then we are in another of the vicious circles for which such countries are famous.

A second argument against this line of reasoning is that time is so short. In ten years, a country growing at 2.5 per cent annually will have added a third to her population. Something simply must be done now. This may seem an unanswerable argument but it is essentially irrelevant. What we have suggested is that for certain areas and under certain conditions we must accept the likelihood that population growth will continue and even increase in the foreseeable future. This fact should not discourage us excessively nor should it distract us from continuing the work of helping such countries to reshape as quickly as possible their basic economic and social structures. With skill and luck the problem of population along with many of the other problems will in time become manageable.

Notes: Reading 7

1 Ansley J. Coale and E. M. Hoover, *Population Growth and Economic Development in Low-Income Countries*, Princeton University Press, 1958, pp. 12–13.

2 T. McKeown and R. E. Record, 'Reasons for the decline in mortality in England and Wales during the 19th century', *Population Studies*, vol. 16, no. 2, November 1962, p. 70.

3 United Nations, Department of Economics and Social Affairs, Population Studies No. 17, *Determinants and Consequences of Population Trends*, p. 80.

4 Judith Black, 'Demographic science and the redirection of population policy', in M. Sheps and J. C. Ridley (eds), *Public Health and Population Change*, Pittsburgh University Press, 1966, p. 67.

5 Dudley Kirk, 'The growing "transition" in world population', paper delivered at 1966 Population Association of America meetings.

6 See Bernard Berelson (ed.), *Family Planning and Population Programs*, Chicago University Press, 1966.

7 Irene B. Taeuber, 'Demographic modernization: continuities and transitions', *Demography*, vol. 3, no. 1, 1966, p. 108.

8 Ronald Freeman, 'The transition from high to low fertility: challenge to demographers', in M. Sheps and J. C. Ridley (eds), *Public Health and Population Change,* Pittsburgh University Press, 1966, p. 418.

9 Warren C. Robinson, 'Family planning in Pakistan's third five year plan', *Pakistan Development Review*, vol. VI, no. 2, Summer 1966, pp. 274–5.

10 Interestingly enough, there is also some evidence that the impact of modern medical 'miracles' in causing the decline in death rates in developing areas may also have been overrated. See Harald Frederiksen, 'Dynamic equilibrium of economic and demographic transition', *Economic Development and Cultural Change*, vol. 14, no. 3, April 1966; also Harald Frederiksen, 'Determinants and consequences of mortality and fertility trends', *Public Health Reports*, vol. 81, no. 8, August 1966.

11 Paul Demeny, 'Investment allocation and population growth', *Demography*, vol. 2, 1965.

12 R. L. Meier, *Modern Science and the Human Fertility Problem*, Wiley, 1959, ch. 4; George Zaidan, 'The foregone benefits and costs of a prevented birth', IBRD Economics Dept Working Paper No. 11, 23 January 1968; S. Enke, 'The economics of slowing population growth', *Economic Journal*, vol. 76, no. 301, February 1965; L. G. Bower,

'The return from investment in population control in less developed countries', unpublished paper presented at 1967 meeting of Population Association of America, Cincinnati, Ohio. For a critical summary of this literature, see Warren C. Robinson and David E. Horlocher, 'Evaluating the economic benefits of fertility reduction', *Studies in Family Planning*, forthcoming.

13 S. Enke, 'The economics of government payments to limit population', *Economic Development and Cultural Change*, vol. VIII, no. 2, July 1960.

14 P. Demeny, 'The economics of government payments to limit population: a comment', *Economic Development and Cultural Change*, vol. IX, no. 2, July 1961.

15 For an excellent review and discussion of the recent literature on the economic effects of health programmes, see Mark Perlman, 'On health and economic development: some problems, methods, and conclusions reviewed in a perusal of the literature', *Comparative Studies in Society and History*, vol. 8, July 1966.

16 S. Enke, 'The economics of slowing population growth', *Economic Journal*, vol. 76, no. 301, March 1966, p. 49.

17 Population Council, *Studies in Family Planning*, no. 10, February 1966, p. 7.

18 David Glass writes:

> As for the action programs themselves . . . the fact that surveys have shown the existence of an apparent interest in controlling family size does not mean that the mere distribution of contraceptives will be sufficient . . . In such circumstances, to rush into the establishment of a large-scale program of family planning centers or similar units might well be a waste of resources.

D. V. Glass, 'Population growth and population policy', in M. Sheps and J. C. Ridley (eds), *Public Health and Population Change*, University of Pittsburgh Press, 1966, p. 22.

Reading 8

Disguised Unemployment in Agriculture: A Survey

C. H. C. Kao, K. R. Anschel and C. K. Eicher

Agriculture in Economic Development (McGraw-Hill, 1964), pp. 129–44.

Introduction

This paper is divided into three sections. In the first, disguised unemployment is discussed in historical perspective. The second examines the theoretical foundation of disguised unemployment with special references to contributions by Nurkse,[33] Lewis,[24] Eckaus,[7] Leibenstein,[21, 22] and Mellor.[29] Since the presence or absence of disguised unemployment is an empirical issue, the final section examines recent empirical studies to appraise methodological advances in measuring disguised unemployment in less developed countries.

Disguised Unemployment in Historical Perspective

Joan Robinson coined the words 'disguised unemployment' in 1936 to describe workers in developed countries who accepted inferior occupations as a result of being laid off from industries suffering from a lack of effective demand.[43, 44] She was referring to workers having a low rather than a zero marginal product of labor.

Studies by Buck,[2] Warriner,[55] and Rosenstein-Rodan[45] in the 1930s and 1940s in less developed countries presented statistical data for China and Southeastern Europe to suggest that a large percentage of agricultural labor was idle for substantial periods of the year. In fact, Buck collected data on over 15,000 farms in China during the years 1929–1933 which revealed that only 35 per cent of the men between fifteen and sixty years of age had full-time jobs. Buck's labor utilization approach,[2] of course, did not reveal anything about the marginal product of labor. Doreen Warriner followed in 1939 with a widely quoted study[55] which revealed that before World War II in 'Eastern Europe as a whole, one-quarter to one-third of the farm population is surplus . . .' (p. 68). Next, in 1943, Rosenstein-Rodan[45] wrote that twenty to twenty-five million of the 100 to 110 million people in Eastern and Southeastern Europe were either wholly or partially unemployed (p. 202). In 1945, Mandelbaum[26] estimated that from 20 to 27 per cent of the active rural workers in Greece, Yugoslavia, Poland, Hungary, Rumania, and Bulgaria were redundant; he presented a 'mechanical' model of planned industrialization to absorb the surplus labor within one generation. The studies cited so far all measured labor utilization in agriculture in many countries in the 1930s and 1940s and are widely cited as support for the existence of disguised unemployment in agriculture. In fact, the widely quoted 1951 United Nations report[53] by a group of experts including W. Arthur Lewis, T. W. Schultz, and D. R. Gadgil cited these studies and added that it seems 'safe to assume that for many regions of India and Pakistan, and for certain parts of the Philippines and Indonesia, the surplus [rural population] cannot be less than the pre-war average for the East European Region' (p. 9). The experts advanced this definition of disguised unemployment: zero marginal product of agricultural labor and the condition of *ceteris paribus*, which has been adopted by Leibenstein,[21, 22] Viner,[54] Rosenstein-Rodan,[46] and many others.

The presence or absence of disguised unemployment is partly an issue of definition. While the writers mentioned above accept a zero marginal product of labor and the condition of *ceteris paribus*, Navarrete and Navarrete in a 1951 article[32] relaxed the *ceteris paribus* assumption and included the introduction of some capital into the production function in their definition of underemployment. Obviously the greater the reorganization of agriculture and the greater the introduction of capital, the larger the volume of workers who can be transferred out of agriculture without affecting agricultural output.

In 1953, Nurkse[33] introduced a theory of economic development on the assumption that disguised unemployment was present over a wide portion of Asia. Nurkse stated that development could be initiated and accelerated in these countries, by forming capital through the employment of redundant rural labor. Farm output does not fall, in the Nurkse schema, when workers are shifted to nonfarm tasks, because he relaxes the static assumptions slightly to permit better organization through 'consolidation of scattered strips and plots of land' (p. 33). The Egyptian economist Koestner was among the first to criticize the disguised unemployment doctrine when, in an article written in 1953,[20] he strongly criticized Nurkse's position.

Lewis presented another version of disguised unemployment in 1954, when he introduced a model of capital formation and development in which the capitalist sector grew by drawing on cheap rural labor without any significant reduction in agricultural output.[24, 25] This is discussed in more detail in the next section of this paper. Next, Eckaus explained the existence of disguised unemployment by limited technical substitutability of factors of production in agriculture.[7]

Concentrated opposition to disguised unemployment came from Warriner in 1955[57] and Schultz in 1955 and 1956.[47, 48] Warriner reversed her earlier position in *Land and Poverty in the Middle East*[56] in which she showed that 50 per cent of the Egyptian rural population was surplus by noting that she had omitted the labor requirement for capital maintenance in agriculture (p. 26). Schultz[47] wrote that 'all too much attention is being directed to taking up the existing slack in countries that now have a poor collection of resources on the assumption that there are many underemployed resources readily available for economic growth' (p. 373). While Schultz cited examples in Latin American countries where the removal of agricultural labor resulted in a decline in agricultural output,[47] he argued on a broader scale and wrote, 'I know of no evidence for any poor country anywhere that would even suggest that a transfer of some small fraction, say 5 per cent, of the existing labor force out of agriculture, with other things equal, could be made without reducing its [agricultural] production' (p. 375). Viner was the next strong opponent of disguised unemployment.[54] Writing in 1957, he criticized writers such as Eckaus[7] who contended that disguised unemployment could exist in agriculture because of limited technical substitutability of factors of production, by noting:[54]

> I find it impossible to conceive a farm of any kind on which, other factors of production being held constant in quantity, and even in form as well, it would not be possible, by known methods, to obtain some addition to the crop by using additional labor in more careful selection and planting of the seed, more intensive weeding, cultivation, thinning, and mulching, more painstaking harvesting, gleaning and cleaning of the crop (p. 347).

In an unpublished dissertation in 1957, Kenadjian reviewed a wide range of studies of disguised unemployment and concluded:[18]

> . . . that almost invariably the estimates of surplus labor have been inflated and the opinions about the extent of redundance in a particular country have contained elements of gross exaggeration in all the countries about which quantitative information can be found to any significant extent. In particular, assertions that disguised unemployment exists in proportions as high as 25 to 30 per cent of the labor force in any sector of the economy of even the most overpopulated countries of the world appear to be entirely without foundation (p. 259).

Haberler joined the attack in 1957[12] and 1959[13] and criticized disguised unemployment, basing his reasoning on the propositions earlier advanced by Schultz and Viner.

Our discussion so far has summarized the important literature in the disguised unemployment debate, with the exception of theoretical developments by Eckaus, Leibenstein, Lewis, Nurkse, Georgescu-Roegen and Mellor, which are inspected more fully in the next section. Five empirical studies will be discussed in detail in the final section.

The Theoretical Foundation of Disguised Unemployment

This section will examine the assumptions and theoretical foundation underlying the concept of disguised unemployment. Almost all economists define disguised unemployment as the existence of a portion of the labor force which can be removed without reducing output. Most also assume that no other changes occur (*ceteris paribus*). The theoreticians must suggest answers to the following questions if they are to explain why disguised unemployment exists contrary to the expectations of orthodox theory. First, if labor is unemployed or otherwise wasted, why are techniques not introduced which use less land and capital relative to labor? Second, with given technology (fixed capital-land-labor ratios), why is labor used to the point where no returns are forthcoming? Employers of hired labor lose money when they pay a wage to labor whose product is zero or negligible. The self-employed who produce nothing would do better to hire out their surplus labor for a wage. Third, why are wages higher than the marginal product? If large numbers of people produce nothing or very little, wages normally would be bid down to the marginal product of labor.

We will attempt to outline how several economists deal with one or more of the above questions. Eckaus[7] discusses only the first; Lewis,[24] Georgescu-Roegen,[11] Leibenstein,[21, 22] and Nurkse[33] propose solutions to the second and third. Mellor,[29] on the other hand, pursues a different path by arguing that unemployment may be related to a deficiency of demand.

Eckaus, writing in 1955,[7] is the only one who systematically analyzes the technological restraints which might lead to disguised unemployment. He says that disguised unemployment exists when 'with agricultural techniques remaining unchanged, withdrawal of farm labor would not reduce output' (p. 545). He then asks why, if labor is in surplus, more labor-intensive techniques are not in use. He believes that even the most labor-intensive agricultural process requires some minimum amount of capital per unit of labor; there is some minimum ratio of capital to labor, but many underdeveloped nations have less capital than is required to utilize their whole labor force. Hence, a portion of the available labor supply is unused. Eckaus left it to others to explain why labor is used until its marginal product is zero, but continues to be paid a positive wage.

Lewis, in his well-known article[24] 'Economic Development with Unlimited Supplies of Labor,' analyzes the relationship between the subsistence and capitalist sectors of an underdeveloped country. In his model, surplus labor is available in both rural and urban areas. The rural labor surplus is disguised in the sense that everyone is working, but if some portion is withdrawn output will not fall; the remaining workers will just work harder. The urban surplus labor is openly unemployed: porters waiting for the next ship to come in, retail traders waiting for a customer, messengers sitting in the courtyard. Workers, rural and urban, do not receive their marginal product, but a higher traditional wage. Lewis suggests that the average product per worker in agriculture determines the traditional wage. Labor employed in the capitalist sector will also be paid the traditional wage as long as there is a surplus of labor in the subsistence sector. The low and constant wages permit large profits for potential reinvestment in the capitalist sector. The economy grows at a faster rate, because profits grow relative to the size of the capitalist sector and an increasing proportion of national income is reinvested.

In this article, Lewis's chief contribution to the concept of disguised unemployment is his explanation of the existence of a greater than zero wage when the marginal product of labor is zero. He explains by tradition and lack of alternatives the existence of self-employed labor which receives a positive wage, but whose marginal product is negligible. In peasant agriculture, each family member receives the family's average product regardless of contribution. Since there are no opportunities for receiving a wage higher than the average product on the family's farm, there is no motivation to leave the farm and the average product will be greater than the marginal product.

Georgescu-Roegen provides an alternative explanation of zero marginal product of agricultural labor.[11] Georgescu-Roegen contends that neither capitalism not socialism is an efficient form of organizing agriculture in an overpopulated country. Under capitalism, labor will not be employed beyond the point where its marginal product equals the wage rate and, as a result, a portion of the labor force will remain idle and the total agricultural output will not be maximized. Feudalism, as Georgescu points out, provided such an institutional framework because the family maximized employment beyond the point where its marginal product equaled wages. Today feudalism has been replaced by individual peasant holdings and the total agricultural output is still maximized because the employment of the peasant family is governed by maximizing total family output rather than by the principle of marginal productivity. Hence, marginal product is zero when the total output of the family farm is maximized.

Leibenstein provides another explanation of a greater than zero wage rate. When labor is unemployed and the labor market is competitive, wages would be bid down to very low levels. He explains the phenomenon of greater than zero wages through an interaction between labor productivity and wage rates. Since output per man increases due to improved nutrition when wage rates increase, landlords find it profitable to hire all available labor to prevent wage rates being bid down, poor nutrition, and the resulting small output per man. Although net revenue would be higher if only a portion of the labor force were utilized, wages would fall, causing productivity to decline.

Nurkse defines disguised unemployment as zero marginal product of labor when some organizational changes are introduced. If minor changes such as consolidation of landholdings are permitted, then a substantial amount of agricultural labor can be used in other pursuits, such as building dams and rural roads, without reducing agricultural output. Nurkse explains that labor is used until no more output is forthcoming, because family labor is not paid. He assumes a free-holding peasant agriculture in which food is shared among all family members. Nurkse does not believe that significant savings of labor can be made through the reduction of leisure time or through the exertion of greater effort by the remaining workers, but must be obtained through better use of labor time. Owing to poor organization, much time is spent on essentially inefficient tasks, such as walking from place to place, transporting materials and products, and organizing and supervising other workers. He suggests that through reorganization enough labor time can be saved to make feasible the utilization of labor in other capacities.

Nurkse's early optimism for releasing surplus labor through changes in agricultural organization was qualified somewhat in 1958[35] when he wrote that such changes in agricultural organization 'are a major undertaking and cannot be lightly taken for granted' (p. 262).

The last approach to disguised unemployment to be discussed assumes a deficiency of demand. Mellor[29] is the chief proponent of this position. He argues that the peasant in the underdeveloped country works hard to achieve some traditionally determined minimum standard of living, but has no motivation for increasing his income above that level because of tradition-bound consumption patterns.

Mellor's deficient demand approach is similar to the concept of unemployment advanced by Joan Robinson in her demand deficiency theory. There are few empirical data to support Mellor's position. For a survey of literature rejecting the notion of tradition-bound peasant consumption patterns in Africa, for example, see the recent article by Jones.[17]

Empirical Studies of Disguised Unemployment

Five empirical studies of disguised unemployment in Thailand, India, Italy, and Greece are examined in this section (References 30, 31, 40, 46, and 49). Three are on the micro level. Two are on the macro level. Discussion will center on two aspects: the methodology adopted in these studies and their empirical results.

Generally speaking, two methods are available to measure disguised unemployment. The first is the direct method, which is based upon a sample survey. This method uses the labor utilization and the labor productivity approaches. The labor utilization approach presents an inventory of what labor is used in the field or in other farm tasks as a percentage of the available supply. The labor productivity approach goes a step further and examines the relationship between the quantity of labor used and/or available and the level of production.[29]

The indirect method, which relies on secondary data, is the second method of measuring disguised unemployment. The three variants of this method measure (1) the difference between the number of labor hours required to produce a given output and the number of labor hours available from the active agrarian population, (2) the difference between the density of population deemed adequate for a given type of cultivation and the actual density of population, and (3) the difference between the number of acres or hectares required under a given type of cultivation to provide one person with a 'standard income', in contrast to the number of available acres or hectares and available agrarian population. (See Reference 46, p. 2.)

Mellor and Stevens's study in Thailand

Mellor and Stevens undertook a study of the average and marginal product of farm labor in Thailand, which was based on labor income records obtained by personal interviews in 104 rice farms at Bang Chan, Thailand, and published in 1956.[30] All farms were assumed to have a similar rice production function. The total output of rice was estimated with a high degree of accuracy because most of the rice was taken to the local miller for polishing. Labor inputs were measured in terms of man equivalents on the basis of interviews concerning the number of persons available for farm work on each farm. In their analysis, Mellor and Stevens[30] said: '. . . labor that is available for farm work but is doing no work is counted as part of labor input. Labor that is actually on the field but contributing no increment in output through its efforts is not treated differently from labor that is not working but is available for such work' (p. 785). To estimate the productivity of labor they used a least-square linear regression equation. The equation is $Y = 30.4 + 13.5X$ (Y = total product, X = man equivalent). The b (slope) value in the equation of 13.5 tang (which is equal to approximately 24 pounds or 0.54 bushel) is not significantly different from zero at the 5 per cent level of significance. They write.[30] 'This is consistent with the hypothesis that in this type of area, the marginal product of labor will be zero or close to zero' (p. 987). Thus, disguised unemployment existed in this area. More recently, Mellor[29] commented on this village study and stated that the data were inadequate for more than a rough approximation of disguised unemployment (p. 3). Given the assumptions of labor homogeneity and a uniform production function, this study represents a valid method of measuring marginal labor productivity.

Harry T.Oshima, commenting recently on the Mellor and Stevens's study, stated:[37]

> There is one empirical study, . . . of 104 farms in one Thai village. In this pioneer study, the conclusion is reached that there is substantial zero MPP farm workers. I feel it is hazardous to regard this study as conclusive for either theoretical or policy use. The spread of the data in the scatter diagram relating rice yields to labor input for each of the 104 farms suggests to me, not a linear regression line as it does to the authors, but inadequate data and/or dubious assumptions. For example, they assume that rice production functions for each of the 104 farms were the same. In estimating labor input, the authors exclude working children under 15 years old and include all persons 15 years and above, whether working or not (p. 450).

Mujumdar's study in India

In a recent book, Mujumdar studies two facets of underemployment in agriculture, namely, disguised and seasonal unemployment.[31] Attention here is given to the empirical results of disguised unemployment.

Field investigation covering three months in 1954–1955 was conducted in nine selected villages of the Bombay Karnatak region to measure the degree of disguised unemployment. The author interviewed village officers and studied village records to determine the population, occupations, land use, number of livestock, labor movements, work schedule, and standard cultivated holdings in each village. Also, twenty-five families in each village were intensively interviewed to determine family size, occupation, sources of income, size of holdings, and annual work schedule.

The author uses the standard cultivated holding as his most important tool in estimating underemployment. He defines it as 'the area of land which is sufficient to absorb, in given conditions of techniques and type of farming, the labour of an average farm family working with a pair of bullocks' (pp. 83–84). Unfortunately, Mujumdar does not tell us how he determined the standard holding. He simply states: 'When once the standard holding is defined for a village or area, the intensity of employment can be measured against the standard so determined. The ideal case being that of full employment when the cultivated holding is of the size of the standard unit or above. All other cases come under disguised unemployment . . .' (p. 202).

Mujumdar finds in his nine-village study of small farmers that 'roughly about 71 per cent of the farmers are affected by disguised unemployment' (p. 208). Thus, this figure, 'in spite of all the limitation, present[s] in concrete terms the alarming proportions which the phenomenon of disguised unemployment has assumed' (p. 208).

There are at least three shortcomings of Mujumdar's methodology. First, the standard holding is essentially an arbitrary unit. It assumes that bullocks are used in producing all crops and allows no alternative production techniques. Nor does it recognize the possibility that bullocks may be labor-replacing, and hence uneconomical, on farms with large amounts of available family labor relative to land. In addition, Mujumdar makes no adjustments for differences in capital, land fertility, and irrigation on each farm. Second, Mujumdar makes no special attempt to quantify the labor input and include it in his analysis. He assumes that all farms are using the most labor-intensive techniques available. Yet, this, he admits, is not true of India. Third, Mujumdar, like many other economists, fails to relate his empirical definition to his theoretical definition of disguised unemployment which is defined as 'taking the size of labour force as given, disguised unemployment may be described as a situation in which the withdrawal of a certain quantity of the factor labour to other uses, will not diminish the total output of the sector from which it is withdrawn, *given* a measure of reorganization in the sector' (p. 39).

Mujumdar's empirical definition classifies any worker on a farm of less than the standard holding as underemployed; he sees no need to estimate his productivity or the productivity of the group. Using the standard holding rather than the marginal productivity technique, Mujumdar arrives at the dubious conclusion that more than 70 per cent of the agricultural population could be removed from the region without lowering production.

Rosenstein-Rodan's study in southern Italy

In 1957, Rosenstein-Rodan[46] wrote that it was his firm belief that disguised unemployment of more than 5 per cent exists in many—though not all—underdeveloped countries; he supported this belief by measuring disguised unemployment in southern Italy (p. 1). He used the static concept of disguised unemployment.

The following major assumptions and criteria were used: (1) Only agricultural small holdings of peasant owners and tenants were included. (2) The active population was assumed to be between fourteen and sixty-five years of age. Coefficients of labor efficiency of men, women, and children were used for each type of cultivation. (3) Surplus workers were assumed to be involuntarily unemployed. (4) Labor hours required for each type of cultivation over the whole year, month by month, were counted and compared with available labor hours. An average of 270 available workdays per year was assumed. (5) A distinction was made between (*a*) removable disguised underemployment or disguised unemployment, (*b*) disguised fractional underemployment, that is, labor hours not used throughout the whole year which do not add up to an entire labor unit (persons in this category cannot be moved out of agriculture), and (*c*) seasonal underemployment due to climatic factors. These distinctions were taken into account in calculating the number of laborers, affected by disguised unemployment. (6) A slight deviation from the static concept was allowed in the analysis. The author used the direct method of questionnaires to distinguish different types of cultivation, different sizes and forms of property, the composition of the labor force, and the number of labor hours required and supplied.

Rosenstein-Rodan[46] found that 'more than 10 per cent of the active labor force in southern Italian agriculture is surplus . . .' (p. 4). Later, however, Kenadjian[18] discussed this matter with Rosenstein-Rodan and reported: 'When Rosenstein-Rodan observes that in southern Italy around 10 to 12 per cent of the actual population in agriculture are removable, he is including among the removable surplus the individuals who are needed for 50 days or less. If the more rigid definition, which is also the more sensible one, is adopted, the removable surplus is reduced to 5 per cent' (p. 250).

This clearly illustrates that a careful appraisal of the definition is necessary before one so blindly accepts an author's statement that 10, 20, or 70 per cent of the labor is redundant in agriculture.

Schultz's study in India

As was pointed out earlier, T. W. Schultz supported the validity of the disguised unemployment concept in the United Nations report[53] in 1951 (p. 9) and later rejected the existence of disguised unemployment in publications in 1956.[47, 48] In his recently published book, he reinforced this position by turning to the influenza epidemic of 1918–1919 in India to test the hypothesis that the marginal product of a part of the labor force in agriculture was zero.[49] This incident was used because the epidemic struck suddenly; the death rate reached a peak within weeks and then diminished rapidly. Those who survived were not debilitated for very long. Schultz estimated the existence of disguised unemployment by comparing the reduction in acreage sown with the reduction in the labor force. Such a comparison assumes that if any disguised unemployment exists, the acreage sown will not be reduced as a result of a sudden reduction in the labor force. The rationale for such a comparison is[49] 'where there are many people relative to land and much land is cultivated intensively, the expectation would be that acreage sown would be less sensitive to a decrease in the labor force than total yield' (p. 11). Therefore, the acreage sown 'would be a more decisive test than . . . a reduction of the same percentage in agricultural production' (p. 11). Schultz found that the agricultural labor force in India was reduced by about 9 per cent, while:[49]

> The area sown in 1919–20 was, however, 10 million acres below, or 3.8 per cent less than that of the base year 1916–17. In general, the provinces of India that had the highest death rates attributed to the epidemic also had the largest percentage decline in acreage sown to crops. It would be hard to find any support in these data for the doctrine that a part of the labor force in agriculture in India at the time of the epidemic had a marginal product of zero (p. 67).

The influenza epidemic test was a unique laboratory technique to use in measuring disguised unemployment. An advantage of this approach was that the influenza epidemic did not directly affect animals, and therefore the only change in the factors of production was in the number of workers. Since India's population grew 44 per cent from 1921 to 1961 as compared with 5 per cent from 1894 to 1921,[59] the population pressures in India today are much different from those of the period studied by Schultz. Therefore, one wonders whether Schultz needs more observations from India in the post-1920 period and from other countries in the 1960s before he can conclude 'a part of the labor working in agriculture in poor countries [today] has a marginal productivity of zero . . . is a false doctrine' (p. 13).

Pepelasis and Yotopoulos' study in Greece

Pepelasis and Yotopoulos[40] recently published a macro level study which was designed to measure the volume of removable surplus labor as well as that seasonal surplus labor in Greek agriculture for the period from 1953 to 1960. Removable (chronic) surplus labor was defined as the amount of labor which could be removed for at least one year without any change in the quantities of other factors of production and without leading to any reduction in output (p. 86). The authors measured surplus labor by comparing the labor available with the labor required for a given volume of output within the agriculture sector. The indirect method, using secondary data, was employed to derive estimates of labor availability and labor requirements.

The labor available was calculated from the total size of the agricultural population from fifteen to sixty-nine years old, as measured by the Census. This estimate was converted into a labor potential and into homogeneous Man Productive Units on the basis of conversion coefficients measuring the workday of an adult male farm worker. Finally the Man Productive Units were converted into Man Productive Days available during the period from 1953 to 1960 (Chapter Four).

Separate estimates of the annual agricultural labor requirements for farming, husbandry, forestry, fishing, and agricultural transport were computed. Given each year's agricultural activities, Pepelasis and Yotopoulos derived annual labor requirements by product by applying a 'labor-intensity coefficient', that is, a labor/land and/or a capital output ratio. The labor coefficients were 'expressed in terms of man and supplementary . . . nine-hour workdays estimated to be used per *stremma* of animal or unit of output to produce the given volume of agricultural output of the year' (p.108). The authors found that 'chronic surplus labor in Greek agriculture is virtually nonexistent. From the eight years of our series, it existed only in 1953 and 1954 to a degree of 3.5 and 2.3 respectively. The other years of the period are marked by a seasonal shortage of labor' (p. 136). The authors commented on the feasibility of removing the chronically unemployed by noting 'if in one village of 100 working agricultural population the surplus labor is 2 per cent, this does not imply that we can remove for a whole year two workers without decreasing the total output of the village' (p. 138). This is so because that labor is not divisible, for both physical and institutional reasons. The 2 per cent, for example, may consist of fractions of labor in surplus spread among a number of families; therefore, 'we cannot exactly determine how much chronic surplus labor it is feasible to remove. . . . Its size can only be determined through a *disaggregative microeconomic investigation based on the direct method of studying a sample of farm households*' (p. 138). The important point of this study is the nonexistence of disguised unemployment in Greek agriculture since 1954.

Summary

We have pointed out that the existence of disguised unemployment is largely a matter of definition and the assumptions about the institutional forces involved. Nevertheless, some writers agreed upon the zero product of labor definition in the early 1950s, and it is an understatement to say that the development literature in this period was optimistic about development through the transfer of redundant agricultural labor to other occupations. We have shown that the empirical studies supporting this optimism were often poorly conceived.

In addition, we have noted that by considering temporary rather than permanent labor transfers and by allowing some reorganization of production, various writers have arrived at a high percentage of disguised unemployment. To date, there is little reliable empirical evidence to support the existence of more than token—5 per cent—disguised unemployment in underdeveloped countries as defined by a zero marginal product of labor and the condition of *ceteris paribus*.

References: Reading 8

1 Barber, William J., 'Disguised unemployment in underdeveloped economies', *Oxford Economic Papers*, vol. 13, pp. 103–15.

2 Buck, John Lossings, *Chinese Farm Economy* (University of Chicago Press, 1930).

3 Buck, John Lossings, *Land Utilization in China* (University of Chicago Press, 1937).

4 Cho, Yong Sam, *Disguised Unemployment in South Korean Agriculture* (University of California Press, 1963).

5 Dandekar, V. N., 'Economic theory and agrarian reform', *Oxford Economic Papers*, vol. 14, February 1962, pp. 69–80.

6 Enke, S., 'Economic development with unlimited and limited supplies of labor', *Oxford Economic Papers*, vol. 14, June 1962, pp. 158–72.

7 Eckaus, R. S., 'Factor proportions in underdeveloped countries', *American Economic Review*, vol. 45, September 1955, pp. 539–65.

8 Ezekiel, Hannan, 'An application of Leibenstein's theory of underemployment', *Journal of Political Economy*, vol. 68, October 1960, pp. 511–17.

9 Fei, J. C. H., and Ranis, Gustav, 'Capital accumulation and economic development', *American Economic Review*, vol. 53, June 1963, pp. 283–313.

10 Frankel, S. Herbert, *The Economic Impact on Underdeveloped Societies* (Blackwell & Mott, 1953).

11 Georgescu-Roegen, N., 'Economic theory and agrarian economics', *Oxford Economic Papers*, vol. 12, February 1963, pp. 1–40.

12 Haberler, Gottfried, 'Critical observations on some current notions in the theory of economic development', *L'Industria*, no. 2, 1957, pp. 3–13.

13 Haberler, Gottfried, 'International trade and economic development', Fiftieth Anniversary Commemoration Lectures, Lecture III, National Bank of Egypt, Cairo, 1959.

14 Hsieh, Chiang, 'Underemployment in Asia: nature and extent', *International Labor Review*, vol. 55, January–June 1952, pp. 703–25.

15 Hsieh, Chiang, 'Underemployment in Asia: its relation to investment policy', *International Labor Review*, vol. 56, July–December 1952, pp. 30–9.

16 International Labor Office, *Measurement of Underemployment* (Geneva, 1957).

17 Jones, William O., 'Economic man in Africa', *Food Research Institute Studies*, vol. 1, May 1960, pp. 107–34.

18 Kenadjian, Berdj, 'Disguised unemployment in underdeveloped countries', unpublished doctoral dissertation, Harvard University, 1957.

19 Khan, Nasir Ahmad, *Problems of Growth of an Underdeveloped Economy – India* (Asia Publishing House, 1961), ch. VII.

20 Koestner, N., 'Comments on Professor Nurkse's capital accumulation in underdeveloped countries', *L'Egypte Contemporaine*, vol. 44, April 1953 (Cairo), pp. 1–8.

21 Leibenstein, Harvey, 'The theory of underemployment in backward economies', *Journal of Political Economy*, vol. 65, April 1957, pp. 91–103.

22 Leibenstein, Harvey, *Economic Backwardness and Economic Growth* (Wiley, 1957).

23 Leibenstein, Harvey, 'Underemployment in backward economies: some additional notes', *Journal of Political Economy*, vol. 66, June 1958, pp. 256–8.

24 Lewis, W. Arthur, 'Economic development with unlimited supplies of labour', *Manchester School of Economic and Social Studies Bulletin*, May 1954, pp. 139–92.

25 Lewis, W. Arthur, *The Theory of Economic Growth* (Allen & Unwin, 1955).

26 Mandelbaum, K., *The Industrialization of Backward Areas* (Blackwell & Mott, 1945).

27 Mazumdar, Dipak, 'The marginal productivity theory of wages and disguised unemployment', *Review of Economic Studies*,vol. 26, June 1959, pp. 190–7.

28 Mazumdar, Dipak, 'Underemployment in agriculture and the industrial wage rate', *Economica*, vol. 26, November 1959, pp. 328–40.

29 Mellor, John W., 'The use and productivity of farm family labor in early stages of agricultural development', *Journal of Farm Economics*, vol. 45, August 1963, pp. 517–34.

30 Mellor, John W., and Stevens, Robert D., 'The average and marginal product of farm labor in underdeveloped economies', *Journal of Farm Economics*, vol. 38, August 1956, pp. 780–91.

31 Mujumdar, N. A., *Some Problems of Underemployment* (Popular Book Depot, Bombay, 1961).

32 Navarrete, Alfredo, Jr, and Navarrete, Ifigenia M., 'Underemployment in underdeveloped economies', *International Economic Papers*, no. 3, London 1953, pp. 235–9, translated from *El Trimestre Economico*, vol. 17, no. 4, October–December 1951.

33 Nurkse, Ragnar, *Problems of Capital Formation in Underdeveloped Countries* (Oxford University Press, 1953).

34 Nurkse, Ragnar, 'Excess population and capital construction', *Malayan Economic Review*, vol. 2, October 1957, pp. 1–11.

35 Nurkse, Ragnar, 'Epilogue: the quest for a stabilization policy in primary producing countries', *Kyklos*, vol. 11, no. 2, 1958, pp. 261–2.

36 Oshima, Harry T., 'Underemployment in backward economies: an empirical comment', *Journal of Political Economy*, vol. 66, June 1958, pp. 259–64.

37 Oshima, Harry T., 'The Ranis-Fei model of economic development: comment', *American Economic Review*, vol. 53, June 1963, pp. 448–52.

38 Parthasaratry, Gogula, 'Underemployment and Indian agriculture', unpublished doctoral dissertation, University of Wisconsin, 1957.

39 Patel, K. R., 'The nature and extent of under-employment of the self-employed cultivators', unpublished doctoral dissertation, University of Bombay, 1962.

40 Pepelasis, Adam A., and Yotopoulos, Pan A., *Surplus*

Labor in Greek Agriculture, 1953–1960, Center of Economic Research, Research Monograph Series 2, Athens, 1962.

41 Ranis, Gustav, and Fei, John C. H., 'A theory of economic development', *American Economic Review*, vol. 51, September 1961, pp. 553–8.

42 Ranis, Gustav, and Fei, John C. H., 'The Ranis-Fei model of economic development: reply', *American Economic Review*, vol. 53, June 1963, pp. 452–4.

43 Robinson, Joan, 'Disguised unemployment', *Economic Journal*, vol. 46, June 1936, pp. 225–37.

44 Robinson, Joan, *Essays in the Theory of Employment* (Oxford University Press, 1947).

45 Rosenstein-Rodan, P. N., 'Problems of industrialization of eastern and south-eastern Europe', *Economic Journal*,vol. 53, June–September 1943, pp. 202–11.

46 Rosenstein-Rodan, P. N., 'Disguised unemployment and underemployment in agriculture', *Monthly Bulletin of Agricultural Economics and Statistics*, vol. 6, July–August 1957 (FAO, Rome), pp. 1–7.

47 Schultz, Theodore W., 'The role of government in promoting economic growth', in Leonard D. White (ed.), *The State of the Social Sciences* (University of Chicago Press, 1956), pp. 372–83.

48 Schultz, Theodore W., 'The economic test of Latin America', *New York State School of Industrial and Labor Relations Bulletin 35* (Cornell University, Ithaca, August 1956), pp. 14–15.

49 Schultz, Theodore W., 'The doctrine of agricultural labor of zero value', *Transforming Traditional Agriculture* (Yale University Press, 1964).

50 Sen, A. K., *Choice of Techniques* (Blackwell & Mott, 1960).

51 Singh, Tarlok, *Poverty and Social Change* (Longmans, Green, 1945).

52 Sovani, N. V., 'Underemployment, micro and macro, and development planning', *Indian Economic Journal*, vol. 2, no. 4, April 1955, pp. 301–10.

53 United Nations, *Measures for the Economic Development ofUnderdeveloped Countries* (Department of Economic and Social Affairs, New York, 1951).

54 Viner, Jacob, 'Some reflections on the concept of disguised unemployment', *Contribucoes a Analise do Desenvolvimento Economico* (Livraria Ager Editora, Rio de Janeiro, 1957); reprinted under the same title in *Indian Journal of Economics*, vol. 38, July 1957, pp. 17–23.

55 Warriner, Doreen, *Economics of Peasant Farming* (Oxford University Press, 1939).

56 Warriner, Doreen, *Land and Poverty in the Middle East* (Royal Institute of International Affairs, London, 1948).

57 Warriner, Doreen, 'Land reform and economic development', Fiftieth Anniversary Commemoration Lectures, National Bank of Egypt, Cairo, 1955.

58 Wonnacott, Paul, 'Disguised and overt unemployment in underdeveloped economies', *Quarterly Journal of Economics*, vol. 76, May 1962, pp. 279–97.

59 See A. Coale and E. Hoover, *Population Growth and Economic Development in Low-Income Countries: A Case Study of India's Prospects* (Princeton University Press, 1958).

Reading 9

Testing Alternative Theories of the Development of a Dual Economy

D. W. Jorgensen

J. Adelman and E. Thorbecke (eds), *The Theory and Design of Economic Development* (Johns Hopkins University Press, 1967).

Introduction

As a branch of general economic theory, that of development of a dual economy is of relatively recent origin. It is widely recognized that under contemporary conditions most backward economic systems have important relations with advanced economies, either through international trade or through the establishment of a modern 'enclave' in an otherwise backward social and economic setting. Either relationship gives rise to economic and social 'dualism' in which a given economic or social system consists of two component parts – an advanced or modern sector and a backward or traditional sector. Neither theories of economic growth for an advanced economy nor theories of development for a backward economy are directly applicable to the development of a dual economy.

In a previous paper we have described two alternative approaches to the theory of development of a dual economy (Jorgensen, 1965). In order to facilitate comparison of the two approaches, we attempted to develop both within the same framework. The basic differences between the two are in assumptions made about the technology of the agricultural sector and about conditions governing the supply of labor. In the 'classical' approach it is assumed that there is some level of the agricultural labor force beyond which further increments to this force are redundant. In the 'neo-classical' approach the marginal productivity of labor in agriculture is assumed to be always positive so that labor is never redundant. In the 'classical' approach the real wage rate, measured in agricultural goods, is assumed to be fixed 'institutionally' so long as there is disguised unemployment in the agricultural sector. In the 'neo-classical' approach the real wage rate is assumed to be variable rather than fixed; it is further assumed that at very low levels of income the rate of population growth depends on the level of income. These are the basic differences between the 'neo-classical' and 'classical' approaches to the theory of development of a dual economy.

The neo-classical and classical theories differ in characterization of the backward or traditional sector of the economy. These differences have implications for the behavior of the backward sector. Among the implications we may note that according to the classical approach, the agricultural labor force must decline absolutely before the end of the phase of disguised unemployment; in the neo-classical approach the agricultural labor force may rise, fall, or remain constant. The differences between the two approaches also have implications for the behavior of the advanced sector; unfortunately, these implications depend on the actual behavior of the terms of trade between the backward and advanced sectors. In the neo-classical approach the terms of trade may rise or fall; in the classical approach, they cannot be determined endogenously. Alternative assumptions about the course of the terms of trade may be made. Corresponding to each assumption, there is an alternative theory for the behavior of the advanced sector. Since any assumption about the course of the terms of trade is consistent with the classical approach, the behavior of these terms cannot provide a test of this approach. The classical approach may be tested only by deriving the implications of this approach for the advanced sector, given the observed behavior of the terms of trade, and confronting these implications with empirical evidence.

We have developed the classical theory in detail only on the assumption that the terms of trade between the backward and advanced sectors remain constant. Proceeding on this assumption, we have derived the following implications of the classical approach:

1 Output and employment in the advanced sector grow at the same rate so long as there is disguised unemployment in the backward sector, that is, labor productivity in the advanced sector remains constant.
2 Capital grows at a slower rate than output and labor so that the capital – output ratio falls.
3 The rates of growth of manufacturing output, employment and capital increase during the phase of disguised unemployment.

For the neo-classical approach, the corresponding results are:

1 Output and capital in the advanced sector grow at the same rate, asymptotically, so that the capital – output ratio remains constant.
2 Manufacturing employment grows more slowly than either output or capital so that labor productivity in the advanced sector rises.
3 The rates of growth of manufacturing output and employment decrease throughout the development process.

Since the classical approach reduces to the neo-classical approach after the phase of disguised unemployment is completed, the two approaches have different implications only for situations where it is alleged that disguised unemployment exists.

In view of the similarities between classical and neo-classical approaches to the development of a dual economy, it is not surprising that many implications of one model are also implications of the other. For example, both models imply that, if the proportion of manufacturing output to agricultural output increases, the share of saving in total income also increases. Thus, either model suffices to explain an increase in the fraction of income saved in the course of economic development. The fact that the implications of the two approaches for the share of saving are identical is of considerable significance. According to Lewis (1954, p. 155): 'The central problem in the theory of economic development is to understand the process by which a community which was previously saving and investing [4 or 5 per cent] of its national income or less, converts itself into an economy where voluntary saving is running at about [12 to 15 per cent] of national income or more. This is the central problem because the central fact of economic development is rapid capital accumulation (including knowledge and skills with capital).' Both classical and neo-classical theories of the development of a dual economy provide an explanation of an increase in the share of saving. In each case the explanation is based on the relationship between saving and industrial profits. Disguised unemployment is neither necessary nor sufficient to generate a sustained rise in the share of saving. Ultimately, a sustained increase in the saving share depends on a positive and growing agricultural surplus and not on the presence or absence of disguised unemployment.

We conclude that tests of the classical versus the neo-classical approach to the development of a dual economy can be carried out only for situations in which it is alleged that disguised unemployment exists. For all other situations the implications of the two approaches are identical. Even where disguised unemployment is alleged to exist, some implications of the two approaches are identical. The implications that are different may be classified into two groups: direct implications of the basic assumptions about agricultural technology and the conditions governing the supply of labor; and indirect implications about the behavior of both backward and advanced sectors of the economy. In reviewing the evidence pertaining to the development of a dual economy, we will first discuss the evidence for and against the existence of disguised unemployment and historical evidence for and against the constancy of the real wage rate in certain historical circumstances where disguised unemployment allegedly exists. Secondly, we will discuss the evidence for and against the indirect implications of the two alternative approaches. Since the indirect implications refer mainly to historical trends in economic development, we will concentrate on the historical development of the Japanese economy, which is cited in support of the classical approach by Fei and Ranis (1964, pp. 263–4) and by Johnston (1962).

Evidence: Direct Implications

In Lewis's original presentation of the classical approach the scope of validity of the assumption of disguised unemployment is delimited as follows: 'It is obviously not true of the United Kingdom, or of north-west Europe. It is not true either of some of the countries usually now lumped together as under-developed; for example, there is an acute shortage of male labour in some parts of Africa and of Latin America. On the other hand it is obviously the relevant assumption for the economies of Egypt, of India, or of Jamaica' (1954, p. 140). In *The Theory of Economic Growth*, Lewis (1955, p. 327) characterizes the phenomenon of disguised unemployment as follows: 'This phenomenon is rare in Africa and in Latin America, but it repeats itself in China, in Indonesia, in Egypt, and in many countries of Eastern Europe.' In a later presentation he states: 'More than half of the world's population (mainly in Asia and in Eastern Europe) lives in conditions which correspond to the classical and not to the neo-classical assumptions' (1958, p. 1). Fei and Ranis are not so specific in delimiting the scope of application of their version of the Lewis model. However, they state: 'The empirical support of both our theory and policy conclusions draw heavily on the experience of nineteenth-century Japan and contemporary India' (1964, p. 6).

Lewis's allegations that disguised unemployment exists in Asia and Eastern Europe are based on a substantial literature on the problem dating from the 1930s and early 1940s. This literature has been surveyed by Kao, Anschel and Eicher (1964). Estimates of disguised unemployment in the early literature are based on what Kao, Anschel and Eicher call the 'indirect method' of measurement. Labor requirements for production of the current level of agricultural output and labor available from the agrarian population are estimated; the difference between labor available and labor required is called 'disguised unemployment'. One fallacy underlying this method is that agricultural work in all countries is highly seasonal. Substantial parts of the agricultural labor force may be unemployed in agriculture during a part of the year without being redundant. The critical test is whether the agricultural labor force is fully employed during peak periods of demand for labor such as planting and harvesting. Only if labor is redundant during periods of peak demand could the agricultural labor force be reduced without reducing agricultural output. A second fallacy underlying the indirect method is that all members of the agricultural population older than some minimum age, usually fifteen, are treated as members of the labor force and that younger members of the population are not treated as members of the labor force. All of the studies of the 1930s and early 1940s are based on the indirect method of measurement. Examples are provided by the work of Buck (1930) on China and of Warriner (1939), Rosenstein-Rodan (1943) and Mandelbaum (1945) on south-eastern Europe. More recent examples may be found in the work of Warriner (1948) on Egypt, Mellor and Stevens (1956) on Thailand, and Rosenstein-Rodan (1957) on southern Italy.

Warriner (1955) has subsequently withdrawn from her position on disguised unemployment in Egypt, noting that her earlier estimate was based on a fallacious set of assumptions. Kenadjian (1961) has corrected Rosenstein-Rodan's estimate of disguised unemployment for southern Italy to take into account seasonal demands for labor. By this single adjustment the estimate of disguised unemployment is reduced from between 10 and 12 per cent of the agricultural labor force to less than 5 per cent. Pepelasis and Yotopoulos (1962) have attempted to measure disguised unemployment in Greece from 1953 to 1960, taking into account the seasonal pattern of demand for labor. Their conclusion is the following: 'From the eight years of our series, [disguised unemployment] existed only in 1953 and 1954 to a degree of 3.4 and 2.3 [per cent] respectively. The other years of the period are marked by a seasonal shortage of labor' (quoted in Kao, Anschel and Eicher, 1964, p. 140). A corrected version of Buck's estimate of disguised unemployment has been presented by Hsieh: 'The conclusion that in the majority of the localities . . . there was at the seasonal peak a shortage of male labour, which had to be reinforced by a large number of female workers, probably applies not only to many other areas of China but also to other Asian countries. Field investigations of several other localities in China and the rural districts of Bengal in India reveal a similar situation. Considering the extremely intensive input of labour in their farm operations, this is not unexpected.' (See Oshima, 1958; Oshima cites Hsieh, 1952, the passage quoted being from pp. 716–17.) We conclude that estimates of disguised unemployment based on the so-called indirect method of measurement always over-estimate the amount of disguised unemployment. When these estimates are corrected to take into account the seasonality of demands for agricultural labor, the situation in south-eastern Europe, Egypt, China and south-east Asia appears to be one of labor shortage rather than labor surplus.

Almost all of the evidence for the existence of disguised unemployment is based on the indirect method of measurement. However, attempts have been made to test for the existence of disguised unemployment by examining historical instances in which substantial parts of the agricultural labor force have been withdrawn in a short period of time. This type of test is always subject to the criticism that one cannot generalize from isolated historical examples. Nonetheless, the evidence is worth reviewing. One class of examples consists of studies of agricultural production after labor is withdrawn for a public works project. Two such examples are summarized by Schultz: 'In Peru a modest road was recently built down the east slopes of the Andes to Tingo Maria, using some labor from farms along the way mostly within walking distances; agricultural production in the area dropped promptly because of the withdrawal of this labor from agriculture. In Belo Horizonte, Brazil, an upsurge in construction in the city drew workers to it from the nearby countryside, and this curtailed agricultural production' (1956, p. 375; see also Schultz, 1964, p. 62).

Another class of examples consists of studies of the effects of famines and epidemics. Schultz has studied in detail the effects of the influenza epidemic of 1918–19 in India on agricultural production. He summarizes the results:

> The agricultural labor force in India may have been reduced by about 8 per cent as a consequence of the 1918–19 epidemic. The area sown to crops was reduced sharply the year of the influenza, falling from 265 million in 1916–17 to 228 million in 1918–19. This drop, however, is confounded by some adverse weather and by the many millions of people who became ill and who were therefore incapacitated for a part of the crop year. For reasons already presented, 1919–20 is the appropriate year to use in this analysis. The area sown in 1919–20 was, however, 10 million acres below, or 3.8 per cent less than that of the base year 1916–17. In general, the provinces of India with the highest death rates attributed to the epidemic also had the largest percentage declines in acreage sown to crops. It would be hard to find any support in these data for the doctrine that a part of the labor force in agriculture in India at the time of the epidemic has a marginal productivity of zero (1964, pp. 66–7).[1]

A third type of evidence used to test for the existence of disguised unemployment consists of anthropological studies of peasant agriculture. Eighteen studies by anthropologists and economists are cited by Oshima in support of the following position:

> Despite the limitations of the empirical material, there is no denying the general picture that emerges for Asia. The labor requirement during busy seasons exceeds the male, adult population so that female and juvenile labor must be recruited into the labor force. And, from the description found in the books cited, no part of this larger labor requirement seems redundant, given the existing technology and organization. A withdrawal of portions of the labor force may be expected to reduce total output (in the sense that insufficient plowing, inadequate planting, and untimely harvesting will diminish the size of the final crop) (1958, p. 261).

The studies reviewed by Oshima refer to India, China, and south-east Asia. Schultz gives a detailed summary of two exceptionally complete anthropological studies, that of Panajachel, Guatemala, by Sol Tax and that of Senapur, India, by W. David Hopper. Schultz (1964, p. 52) concludes 'that no part of the labor force working in agriculture in these communities has a marginal productivity of zero'.

Evidence from anthropological studies is subject to the same criticism as the examination of historical instances of rapid withdrawal of agricultural labor, namely, that one cannot generalize from particular examples. However, the consistency of the evidence from indirect estimates of disguised unemployment for the entire agricultural labor force of countries such as Greece, southern Italy, Egypt and China, with the evidence from both historical and anthropological studies, leads to the conclusion that disguised unemployment simply does not exist for a wide range of historical and geographical situations where it has been alleged to exist. Lewis admits that disguised unemployment is not typical of Africa and Latin America. This is consistent with the historical and anthropological evidence for Brazil, Mexico and Peru cited by Schultz. Lewis claims that disguised unemployment exists in south-eastern Europe, Egypt and Asia. But this is inconsistent with the evidence from indirect measurement in the case of south-eastern Europe, Egypt and China and with both historical and anthropological evidence in the case of India, China, and south-east Asia. We may conclude, with Kao, Anschel and Eicher (1964, p. 141), that

> it is an understatement to say that the development literature [in the early 1950s] was optimistic about development through the transfer of redundant agricultural labor to other occupations. We have shown that the empirical studies supporting this optimism were often poorly conceived. In addition, we have noted that by considering temporary rather than permanent labor transfers, and by allowing some re-organization of production, various writers have arrived at a high percentage of disguised unemployment. To date, there is little reliable empirical evidence to support the existence of more than token – 5 per cent – disguised unemployment in underdeveloped countries. . . .

Evidence: Indirect Implications

We have reviewed the evidence for and against the existence of disguised unemployment. The indirect evidence suggests that the conditions governing the supply of labor in south-eastern Europe and Asia are no different from those in Latin America and Africa to which Lewis refers. This evidence does not demonstrate that disguised unemployment never exists in any historical or geographical circumstances, but only that the scope of applicability of the classical approach to the development of a dual economy is severely limited. More specifically, the classical assumptions do not apply to Latin America, Africa, south-eastern Europe, India, China or the remainder of south-east Asia. Thus far we have reviewed direct evidence for most of Asia except for Japan, for which it is possible to check out the indirect implications of the classical and neo-classical approaches for historical trends in economic development. Japan is the only Asian country for which long-term data exist for trends in agricultural and non-agricultural labor force, agricultural and non-agricultural output, and capital formation. Furthermore, Japanese historical development has been cited in support of the classical approach by Fei and Ranis (1964, pp. 134, 263–4) and by Johnston (1962). Fei and Ranis state that: 'Continuous capital shallowing in Japanese industry between 1888 and the end of World War I is evidence that Japan made maximum use of her abundant factor, surplus agricultural labor' (p. 132). They continue: 'The empirical evidence on Japan . . . indicates clearly that . . . a change of regime from capital shallowing to capital deepening occurred at about the end of World War I. Moreover, we have convincing evidence that Japan's unlimited supply of labor condition came to an end at just about that time. . . . The virtual constancy before and rapid rise of the real wage after approximately 1918 is rather startling. We thus have rather conclusive evidence in corroboration of our theoretical framework' (pp. 263–4). Since the Japanese data are the only empirical support Fei and Ranis offer for their assumption of an unlimited labor supply at a constant real wage, Japanese economic development up to 1918 provides an important test case for the classical approach to the theory of development of a dual economy.

We first consider the indirect implications of the classical approach for the agricultural sector. For this sector Fei and Ranis assume that there is an institutionally fixed real wage, equal to the initial average productivity of labor (p. 22). Ohkawa and Rosovsky (1964, p. 52) provide data from which real labor income *per capita* in agriculture for the period 1878–1917 may be estimated. The share of rents in agricultural income fluctuates during this period, beginning at an average level of 59 per cent in 1878–87 and ending at an average level of 58 per cent in 1908–17. Labor income may be estimated by deducting the share of rents from real income *per capita*. This results in the series for labor income presented in Table 1. Total real income *per*

Table 1 **Real Labor Income per capita in Japanese Agriculture, Five-Year Averages, 1878–1917**

1878–82	18.0
1883–87	18.1
1888–92	18.2
1893–97	21.1
1898–1902	27.0
1903–7	31.3
1908–12	39.4
1913–17	42.0

Source: Computed from Ohkawa and Rosovsky (1964, pp. 129–43).

capita is 100.0 in 1913–17 (Ohkawa and Rosovsky, 1964, p. 55). We conclude that for the period 1878–1917, the assumption of a constant real wage rate in the agricultural sector is inconsistent with the evidence. The hypothesis of a constant real wage rate in the agricultural sector where disguised unemployment exists is the most important assumption underlying the classical approach to the theory of development of a dual economy. The classical approach stands or falls on this hypothesis.

A second implication of the classical approach for the behavior of the agricultural sector is that the agricultural labor force must decline absolutely as redundant labor leaves the land and later as disguised unemployment is eliminated. This decline must include all of the redundant labor force, together with that part of the labor force with marginal productivity less than the real wage rate. The typical pattern of economic development in Europe is a constant or moderately rising agricultural labor force until just before or just after the relative importance of non-agricultural population surpasses that of agricultural population. Subsequently, the agricultural labor force begins to fall (see Dovring, 1959, pp. 1–11). In short, absolute reductions in the size of the agricultural labor force occur after industrialization is well under way rather than during its early states. This pattern also characterizes Japan. The agricultural labor force is essentially constant from 1878–82 to 1903–7, falling slightly from an average level of 15,573,000 to 15,184,000 over this period of twenty-five years. From 1903–7 to 1913–17 the agricultural labor force falls from an average level of 15,184 thousand to an average of 14,613 thousand. The total decline over the thirty-five years period is 7 per cent (Ohkawa and Rosovsky, 1964, p. 46). Since Fei and Ranis date the end of the surplus labor period at 1918, we may conclude that 7 per cent can serve as an upper bound for the percentage of the labor force that could be classified as redundant at any time during the period 1878–1917. A second useful comparison may be made between the number of farm households in 1884, a total of 5,437 thousand, and the number in 1920, 5,573 thousand, a slight increase (Ohkawa and Rosovsky, 1964, p. 49). The movement of labor from the rural areas to the advanced sector did not involve the transfer of a reserve army of the disguised unemployed. The process is described by Ohkawa and Rosovsky (1964, p. 48): 'During the early period of industrialization necessary increases in the labor force did indeed come from the rural areas. But laborers were usually young and left single. There was only very little movement in terms of family units, and no formation of an agricultural proletariat. Thus, a fairly typical Asian type of agriculture remained in existence and was utilized to promote impressive increases in productivity, while Western technology was making rapid progress in manufacturing.' The Japanese pattern may be regarded as similar to that of many European countries, including countries of north-western Europe, where the period preceding the predominance of the non-agricultural labor force in the total labor force is characterized by a stable agricultural labor force, rising or declining at very moderate rates throughout the period of initial industrialization. This pattern is inconsistent with the hypothesis of redundant labor or of disguised unemployment. However, the pattern is entirely consistent with the neo-classical theory of the development of a dual economy. We may conclude with Ohkawa and Minami (1964, p. 8) that 'in the light of Japanese experience with the initial phase of economic development, traditional agriculture based on household production grew at a considerable rate in terms of both output and productivity; technological progress had taken place and the level of living and wage rates increased to a certain extent. These responses occurred together with the increase in population. In view of this, it seems that the features of models of the Lewis type are too rigorous to be applied to such historical realities.'

We have discussed the empirical validity of the implications of the classical approach to the theory of development of a dual economy for the agricultural sector. These implications – the constancy of the real wage rate, measured in agricultural goods, and the absolute decline of the agricultural labor force during the phase of disguised unemployment – are directly contradicted by the evidence we have reviewed. In particular, the interpretation of Japanese economic development prior to 1917 by Fei and Ranis is inconsistent with the evidence on real labor income in agriculture. The pattern of development of the agricultural labor force up to 1917 is inconsistent with the existence of substantial surplus labor in the agricultural sector during the initial period of industrialization. The development of the agricultural labor force follows the pattern of most European countries and is fully consistent with the neo-classical approach to the development of a dual economy. At this point we turn to the development of the advanced or non-agricultural sector of the Japanese economy during the period preceding 1917. As we have already pointed out, the implications of the classical approach for the advanced sector depend on the historical development of the terms of trade between agriculture and industry. Data on the terms of trade are presented by Ohkawa and Rosovsky (1964, p. 48, Table 4). These data are consistent with the assumption that the terms of trade are essentially constant throughout the period before 1917. Accordingly, the implications of the classical approach on this assumption may be confronted with data on the development of the non-agricultural sector of the Japanese economy for this period.

The first implication of the classical approach for the advanced sector is that labor productivity remains constant during the phase of disguised unemployment. The corresponding implication of the neo-classical approach is that labor productivity is always rising. Real income per member of the labor force in secondary and tertiary industry for the period 1878–1917 are given by Ohkawa (1957, p. 34) (see Table 2). The data show an increase in labor productivity from 1878–82 to 1913–17 of 239 per cent in secondary industry and 213 per cent in tertiary industry. These increases in productivity are inconsistent with the implication of the classical theory

Table 2 **Real Income per capita in Japanese Industry, Five-Year Averages, 1878–1917**

	Secondary industry	*Tertiary industry*
1878–82	137	156
1883–7	173	199
1888–92	189	197
1893–7	217	227
1898–1902	268	261
1903–7	237	261
1908–12	266	313
1913–17	327	333

Source: K. Ohkawa (1957, p. 34).

that labor productivity remains constant throughout the phase of disguised unemployment. Increases in labor productivity are a direct implication of the neo-classical approach. We conclude that the data on labor productivity provide very powerful support for the neo-classical theory.

A second implication of the classical approach for the advanced sector is that the rates of growth of output and employment increase over time. The corresponding implication of the neo-classical approach is that rates of growth of both variables decline over time. Rates of growth of real income and occupied population in secondary and tertiary industry for the period 1878–1917 are presented in Table 3. The rate of growth of real income has a substantial downward trend for this period, which is inconsistent with the implications of the classical approach. The rate of growth of the non-agricultural labor force shows a high initial value but declines monotonically as development proceeds. This trend is also inconsistent with the implications of the classical approach. We conclude that data on the rates of growth of output and employment provide additional support for the neo-classical theory. It should be pointed out that for the period subsequent to 1918, the date at which disguised unemployment disappears, according to Fei and Ranis, there is an increase in the rates of growth in the secondary and tertiary sectors. This is evidence neither for nor against the classical as opposed to the neo-classical approach, since the implications of these approaches are identical for periods in which there is no disguised unemployment.

A third implication of the classical approach for the advanced sector is that the capital–output ratio falls throughout the phase of disguised unemployment and that the rate of growth of capital increases over time. The corresponding implications of the neo-classical approach are based on asymptotic results; the capital–output ratio eventually becomes constant since the rate

Table 3 **Rates of Growth of Output, Employment and Capital in Japanese Industry, Five-Year Averages, 1878–1917**

	Output	*Employment*	*Capital*
1878–82 to 1883–7	10.1	5.4	—
to 1888–92	4.4	4.4	4.7
to 1893–7	6.3	3.8	5.2
to 1898–1902	6.7	3.4	5.7
to 1903–7	1.9	3.0	4.6
to 1908–12	5.8	2.6	6.5
to 1913–17	5.2	2.4	5.8

Source: Rates of growth of output and employment computed from Ohkawa (1957, pp. 20, 34); rate of growth of capital computed from Ishiwata (n.d., p. 12).

of growth of output and the rate of growth of capital tend to the same limit. Data on net capital stock for the period 1883–1917 are given by Ishiwata (n.d., p. 12).

Rates of growth computed from these data are presented in Table 3. There is essentially no trend in the rate of growth of capital during this period. We conclude that data on the rate of growth of capital stock are inconsistent with the implications of the classical approach.

Table 4 **Capital–Output Ratio in Japanese Industry, Five-Year Averages, 1883–1917**

	Ohkawa real income	*Ishiwata real income*
1883–7	1.96	1.56
1888–92	1.99	1.51
1893–7	1.88	1.53
1898–1902	1.80	1.52
1803–7	2.03	1.72
1909–12	2.10	1.82
1913–17	2.24	1.79

Source: Computed from Ohkawa (1957, p. 34) and Ishiwata (n.d., p. 15).

The capital–output ratio for the advanced sector may be computed from the data on capital given by Ishiwata and the data on real income given by Ohkawa. The resulting capital–output ratios are presented in Table 4, along with the capital–output ratio for the advanced sector computed by Ishiwata (n.d., p. 15) from an alternative set of data on real income. For the period as a whole, both series of capital–output ratios show a substantial increasing trend. For Ishiwata's series of capital–output ratios the trend is especially strong. We conclude that the implication of the classical approach of 'capital-shallowing' throughout the period prior to 1917 is inconsistent with the evidence. The data on capital–output ratios provide additional support for the neo-classical theory.

Summary and Conclusion

We have considered implications of the classical and neo-classical approaches to the development of a dual economy for both agricultural and non-agricultural sectors. The assumption of a constant real wage rate in the agricultural sector made in the classical approach is inconsistent with the evidence presented by Ohkawa and Rosovsky. Real labor income *per capita* in agriculture more than doubles during the period 1878–1917. The implication of the classical approach that the agricultural labor force must decline absolutely as redundant labor leaves the land is also inconsistent with the evidence. Data on the occupied population in agriculture show a decline from 1878–1917 of only 7 per cent; data on the number of farm households show a 2.5 per cent increase. The Japanese pattern is similar to that of many European countries where the agricultural labor force is essentially stable throughout the period of initial industrialization.

Implications of the classical approach for the non-agricultural sector are also inconsistent with the evidence. Firstly, the implication that labor productivity remains constant is inconsistent with the data presented by Ohkawa; these data show an increase in labor productivity over the period 1878–1917 of 239 per cent in secondary industry and 213 per cent in tertiary industry. Secondly, the implication that rates of growth of output and employment increase over time is inconsistent with evidence on the growth of real income and employment in the non-agricultural sector presented by Ohkawa. Finally, the implications that the rate of growth of capital increases over time and that the capital–output ratio falls is inconsistent with the data of Ishiwata on capital stock for the period 1883–1917. The rate of growth of capital stock shows no trend over this period; the capital–output ratio actually rises substantially over the period 1883–1917.

The evidence on Japanese economic development from 1878–1917 supports the neo-classical rather than the classical approach to the theory of development of a dual economy. The basic assumptions of the classical approach are inconsistent with the evidence. The implications of the classical approach are also inconsistent with the evidence, while the implications of the neo-classical approach are strongly supported. Our knowledge of Japanese economic development corroborates the evidence we have reviewed for and against the existence of disguised unemployment in Latin America, Africa, south-eastern Europe, India, China and south-east Asia. We conclude that the neo-classical theory of the development of a dual economy is strongly supported by the empirical evidence and that the classical approach must be rejected.

Note: Reading 9

1 Amartya K. Sen has pointed out to me that the estimates of changes in working-age population used by Schultz are too high, since only deaths between 1917–18 and 1918–19 are recorded as changes in the labor force. The natural increase of the population from 1916–17 and 1919–20, the base dates for the measurement of acreage sown, are ignored. Taking 8.35 per cent per decade as the rate of natural increase, Schultz's estimates of changes in the agriculture labor force should be reduced by 2.4 per cent. Making these changes, Sen obtains an estimate of the labor coefficient of 0.412 ± 0.252. Sen's estimate is closer to the *a priori* value of 0.4 given by Schultz than Schultz's own estimate of 0.349 ± 0.152. Both results support the conclusion cited in the text.

References: Reading 9

Buck, J. L. (1930), *Chinese Farm Economy* (University of Chicago Press).

Chambers, J. D. (1953), 'Enclosure and labour supply in the industrial revolution', *Econ. Hist. Rev.*, vol. 5, no. 3.

Dovring, F. (1959), 'The share of agriculture in a growing population', *Monthly Bull. Agri. Econ. Stat.*, vol. 8, nos. 8–9.

Ellis, H. S. (1961), 'Las economias duales y el progreso', *Revista de Economia Latinoamericana*, vol. 1, no. 3.

Fei, J. C. H., and Ranis, G. (1964), *Development of the Labor Surplus Economy* (Irwin).

Hsieh, C. (1952), 'The nature and extent of underemployment in Asia', *Internat. Lab. Rev.*, vol. 65, no. 6.

Ishiwata, S. (n.d.), 'Estimation of capital stocks in pre-war Japan, 1868–1940', unpublished paper D27, Institute of Economic Research, Hitotsubashi University, Tokyo.

Johnston, B. F. (1962), 'Agricultural development and economic transformation: a comparative study of the Japanese experience', *Food Research Institute Studies*, vol. 3, no. 3.

Jorgensen, D. W. (1961), 'The development of a dual economy', *Econ. J.*, vol. 71, June.

Jorgensen, D. W. (1965), 'Subsistence agriculture and economic growth', paper presented to the Conference on Subsistence and Peasant Economies, Honolulu, Hawaii, 5 March.

Kao, C. H. C., Anschel, K. R., and Eicher, C. K. (1964), 'Disguised unemployment in agriculture: a survey', in C. K. Eicher and L. W. Witt (eds), *Agriculture in Economic Development*, (McGraw–Hill).

Kenadjian, B. (1961), 'Disguised unemployment in underdeveloped countries', *Zeitschrift für Nationalökonomie*, vol. 9.

Lewis, W. A. (1954), 'Economic development with unlimited supplies of labour', *Manchester Sch. Econ. Soc. Studies*, vol. 22, May.

Lewis, W. A. (1955), *The Theory of Economic Growth* (Allen & Unwin).

Lewis, W. A. (1958), 'Unlimited labour: further notes', *Manchester Sch. Econ. Soc. Studies*, vol. 26, no. 1.

Mandelbaum, K. (1945), *The Industrialization of Backward Areas* (Blackwell).

Mellor, J. S., and Stevens, R. D. (1956), 'The average and marginal product of farm labor in underdeveloped economies', *J. Farm Econ.*, vol. 38, no. 3.

Ohkawa, K. (1957), *The Growth Rate of the Japanese Economy since 1878* (Kinokuniya Bookstore Co., Tokyo).

Ohkawa, K., and Minami, R. (1964), 'The phase of unlimited supplies of labor', *Hitotsubashi Journal of Economics*, vol. 6, no. 1.

Ohkawa, K., and Rosovsky, H. (1964), 'The role of agriculture in modern Japanese economic development', in C. K. Eicher and L. W. Witt (eds), *Agriculture in Economic Development* (McGraw–Hill).

Oshima, H. (1958), 'Underemployment in backward economies: an empirical comment', *J. Polit. Econ.*, vol. 66, no. 3.

Pepelasis, A. A., and Yotopoulos, P. A. (1962), *Surplus Labor or Greek Agriculture, 1953–60*, Centre of Economic Research, Research Monograph Series 2, Athens.

Rosenstein–Rodan, P. N. (1943), 'Problems of industrialization of eastern and south-eastern Europe', *Econ. J.*, vol. 53, June–September.

Rosenstein–Rodan, P. N. (1957), 'Disguised unemployment and underemployment in agriculture', *Monthly Bull. Agri. Econ. Stat.*, vol. 6, nos 7–8.

Schultz, T. (1956), 'The role of the government in promoting economic growth', in L. D. White (ed.), *The State of the Social Sciences* (University of Chicago Press).

Schultz, T. (1964), *Transforming Traditional Agriculture* (Yale University Press).

Spaventa, L. (1959), 'Dualism in economic growth', *Banca Nazionale del Lavoro Quarterly Review*, no. 51.

Warriner, D. (1939), *Economics of Peasant Farming* (Barnes & Noble).

Warriner, D. (1948), *Land and Poverty in the Middle East* (Institute of International Affairs, London).

Warriner, D. (1955), 'Land reform and economic development', Fiftieth Anniversary Lectures, National Bank of Egypt, Cairo, p. 26.

Wharton, C. W. J., Jr (ed.) (1969), *Economic Development in Subsistence and Peasant Agriculture* (Aldine).

Reading 10

Informal Income Opportunities and Urban Employment in Ghana

Keith Hart

The Journal of Modern African Studies, vol. II, no. I, 1973, pp. 61–89.

This article originated[1] in the study of one Northern Ghanaian group, the Frafras, as migrants to the urban areas of Southern Ghana. It describes the economic activities of the low-income section of the labour force in Accra, the urban sub-proletariat into which the unskilled and illiterate majority of Frafra migrants are drawn.

Price inflation, inadequate wages, and an increasing surplus to the requirements of the urban labour market have led to a high degree of informality in the income-generating activities of the sub-proletariat. Consequently income and expenditure patterns are more complex than is normally allowed for in the economic analysis of poor countries. Government planning and the effective application of economic theory in this sphere has been impeded by the unthinking transfer of western categories to the economic and social structures of African cities. The question to be answered is this: Does the 'reserve army of urban unemployed and underemployed' really constitute a passive, exploited majority in cities like Accra, or do their informal economic activities possess some autonomous capacity for generating growth in the incomes of the urban (and rural) poor?

The Economic Situation of the Urban Sub-Proletariat in Accra

International and long-distance migrants comprised 29 per cent of Ghana's labour force in 1960, while intra-regional migrants accounted for a further 24 per cent. As far as Accra was concerned, many of these mobile workers were housed in the slum on the northern outskirts, of which the centre is Nima. Over a third of the Accra labour force came to live in such areas – which included New Town and Sabon Zongo – but the Nima district alone in 1960 constituted some 8 per cent (31,000) of the city's population of just under 400,000. Nima's workforce (those aged 15 years or more) was then enumerated as 20,800 (males 63 per cent, females 37 per cent); but, of these, only 16,000 (77 per cent) were listed as 'economically active'.

Table 1 shows that, while the public and private sectors have a roughly equal share of wage employment among the economically active population, over half the total is listed as self-employed, non-wage earning, and unemployed. In addition, a quarter of the working-age population is described as not economically active (mostly female home-makers, plus some students, disabled persons, and others). Leaving aside problems of definition and of accuracy of enumeration, it is clear that a very large part of the urban labour force is not touched by wage employment: 40 per cent of active males and 95 per cent of active females in Nima. The question is, How many are truly unemployed? Census statistics cannot help us here.

The great differences between males and females of various ages are well illustrated by Table 2. Taking the active labour force alone, unemployment seems to fall heaviest on teenage boys (38 per cent) and girls (31 per cent), young men (22 per cent), and men in their prime (15 per cent). But this tripartite classification into employed (including self-employed), unemployed, and non-active may well be unreliable. Let it suffice to indicate the sheer size of the population which does not earn wages in Accra.

The range of occupations filled by Nima inhabitants is restricted. In 1960, 80 per cent of employed women were sales workers, the remainder being scattered through various manual occupations, of which tailoring provided the only significant percentage; but 90 per cent were self-employed. Male workers were concentrated in manual occupations also, mostly as artisans (32 per cent) and labourers (31 per cent); white collar occupations accounted for less than·8 per cent.

The pattern of economic life

Evidence for Ghana in the 1960s shows declining real incomes for urban wage-earners. Thus, three separate indices of real earnings revealed decreases over the

Table 1 **Economic Situation of Working Age Population in Accra and Nima, 1960**[a]

						Percentage
	Males		Females		Total	
Economic situation	*Accra*	*Nima*	*Accra*	*Nima*	*Accra*	*Nima*
Public-sector employee	30.3	29.3	6.9	2.6	22.4	22.9
Private-sector employee	31.6	31.2	6.3	2.7	23.0	24.6
Employer/self-employed	21.5	18.2	67.5	81.6	37.1	32.9
Other non-wage earning	4.2	2.7	3.9	2.4	4.1	2.7
Unemployed	12.4	18.7	15.5	10.8	13.5	16.9
Total economically active	100.0	100.1	100.1	100.1	100.1	100.0
Not economically active (as % of working age population)	15.1	6.3	42.0	52.0	26.6	23.3

Table 2 **Nima: Sex, Age, and Economic Situation, 1960**[b]

	Total		Employed		Unemployed		Non-active	
Age group	*Number*	*%*	*Number*	*%*	*Number*	*%*	*Number*	*%*
Males	13,110		10,040		2,240		830	
15–19		11.1		46.6		28.6		24.8
20–24		20.4		73.6		20.4		6.0
25–44		57.9		83.0		14.9		2.1
45 +		10.6		79.1		10.8		10.1
Females	7,720		3,280		420		4,020	
15–19		18.1		32.3		14.3		53.4
20–24		26.2		37.7		3.1		59.2
25–44		46.8		47.2		3.6		49.2
45 +		8.9		52.0		4.7		43.3
Total	20,830		13,320		2,660		4,850	

[a]Source: *Census of Population, 1960.*
[b]Source: ibid.

5-year period 1960–1 to 1965–6 of 55 per cent, 46 per cent, and 36 per cent respectively.[2]

The chronic imbalance between income from wage employment and expenditure needs is only partly mitigated by the generosity of kinsmen and neighbours, and only temporarily deferred by manipulation of the credit system. A more lasting solution may be sought from supplementary income sources; and it is with the analysis of these opportunities, rather than consumption patterns and the structure of dependency relationships, that this article is mainly concerned.

One solution to the inadequacy of urban wages, however, lies in duplication of wage employment within the organised labour force. The practice of holding down more than one job at a time, doubling up of shifts worked, 'moonlighting', and similar examples of industry, were extremely common in Nima. The incidence of this phenomenon is of some significance for urban labour statistics; for widespread job duplication would raise the already substantial residue calculated by subtracting the number of enumerated jobs from the total economically active population. 'One man, one job' is a risky assumption, especially when low-paid, low hours employment is involved.

It is erroneous to assume that such behaviour is typical only of short-term 'target' migrants. Seasonal or yearly migration has become a much less common contributor to the urban labour supply in recent years. This is largely attributable to the difficulty of obtaining employment under present-day conditions in cities like Accra. While a few may retain relatively fixed, immediate goals, for most workers long-term residence (sometimes of an intermittent nature) in the urban areas of Southern Ghana is the norm. The system of rewarding lengthy service, particularly in the public sector, by gratuities and pensions is an important stabilising element. The desire of migrants to improve their living standards, and to accumulate against retirement in the country, is not easily satisfied; as a result, most stay for a number of years, perhaps for all their working lives, in pursuit of a goal which for many is simply unrealisable.[3]

The 'way out' of this persistent dilemma for urban workers is seen by many to lie in emulating the role of the small-scale entrepreneur, as exemplified by the success of some of their fellows who started off with similar life-chances. Rouch made this point in relation to the immigrants of 1953–4:

> A comparison between the wages paid unskilled workers and the earnings of traders shows that the same migrants can attain to more profitable situations . . . In a month or two a *kayakaya* (market porter) can hope to become a truck boy and make 10*s*. a day . . . Finally the migrant has all around him the encouraging example of the great success of his comrades (cattle, timber and transport operators). One can understand why the emigrants try as quickly as possible to amass a small nest-egg in wage-earning employment so that they can also enter into trading careers.[4]

Petty capitalism, often as a supplement to wage-employment, offers itself as a means of salvation. If only the right chance came, the urban workers could break out of the nexus of high living costs and low wages which is their lot. This hope is comparable with the promise of wealth which a large win on the football pools holds out for the British worker over-burdened by hire-purchase payments. As it is, the monthly equation of income and expenditure is usually negative, and few manage to escape from the spiral of ever-increasing debt. But the lives of the majority are sustained by hopes of this kind and, as a result, most are ready to involve themselves, both on a casual and regular basis, in petty enterprises of all types ranging in scale from the most trivial activities to major businesses.

Another way of putting this is to say that, denied success by the formal opportunity structure, these members of the urban sub-proletariat seek informal means of increasing their incomes. This is not unique: of many prominent examples, we may compare the dilemma of slum-dwellers in the United States,[5] and of those who live in the 'culture of poverty' in Central America[6] – and, perhaps above all, the high degree of informality in the economic lives of the nineteenth-century London poor.[7] It is this world of economic activities outside the organised labour force which is the subject of detailed examination here.

The Informal Sector

The distinction between formal and informal income opportunities is based essentially on that between wage-earning and self-employment. The key variable is the degree of rationalisation of work – that is to say, whether or not labour is recruited on a permanent and regular basis for fixed rewards. Most enterprises run with some measure of bureaucracy are amenable to enumeration by surveys, and – as such – constitute the 'modern sector' of the urban economy. The remainder – that is, those who escape enumeration – are variously classified as 'the *low-productivity* urban sector', 'the reserve army of *underemployed and unemployed*', 'the urban *traditional* sector', and so on. These terms beggar analysis by assuming what has to be demonstrated.

A typology of urban income opportunities

It has been shown for Accra that the number of those outside the organised labour force is very large. The significance of the activities of this residue is subject to some dispute, however. The semi-automatic classification of unorganised workers as 'underemployed shoe-shine boys and sellers of matches' contrasts with a view which stresses the important part played by these workers in supplying many of the essential services on which life in the city is dependent. I have discussed elsewhere the role of small operators in distribution, transport, and other tertiary activities in Ghana.[8] In practice, informal activities encompass a wide-ranging scale, from marginal operations to large enterprises; whether their productivity is relatively high or low remains a question for empirical verification.

Moreover, a consideration of income opportunities outside formal employment must include certain kinds of crime. The incidence of illegitimate activity in Nima was, to my knowledge, all-pervasive. It was difficult indeed to find anyone who had not at some time transgressed the law, usually with some profitable result, if undetected. The following typology, therefore, distinguishes between legitimate and illegitimate activities in the informal sector. It should be emphasised that the typology refers to activities or roles, *not* persons: actual individuals are often to be found on both sides of the analytical divide and in more than one capacity.

Formal income opportunities

(*a*) *Public sector wages.*
(*b*) *Private sector wages.*
(*c*) *Transfer payments* – pensions, unemployment benefits.

Informal income opportunities: legitimate

(*a*) *Primary and secondary activities* – farming, market gardening, building contractors and associated activities, self-employed artisans, shoemakers, tailors, manufacturers of beers and spirits.

(*b*) *Tertiary enterprises with relatively large capital inputs* – housing, transport, utilities, commodity speculation, rentier activities.
(*c*) *Small-scale distribution* – market operatives, petty traders, street hawkers, caterers in food and drink, bar attendants, carriers (*kayakaya*), commission agents, and dealers.
(*d*) *Other services* – musicians, launderers, shoeshiners, barbers, night-soil removers, photographers, vehicle repair and other maintenance workers; brokerage and middlemanship (the *maigida* system in markets, law courts, etc.); ritual services, magic, and medicine.
(*e* *Private transfer payments* – gifts and similar flows of money and goods between persons; borrowing; begging.

Informal income opportunities: illegitimate

(*a*) *Services* – hustlers and spivs in general; receivers of stolen goods; usury, and pawnbroking (at illegal interest rates); drug-pushing, prostitution, poncing ('pilot boy'), smuggling, bribery, political corruption Tammany Hall-style, protection rackets.
(*b*) *Transfers* – petty theft (e.g. pickpockets), larceny (e.g. burglary and armed robbery), peculation and embezzlement, confidence tricksters (e.g. money doublers), gambling.

This list is by no means exhaustive, but it serves to illustrate the range of income opportunities widely available to the urban sub-proletariat living in areas such as Nima. An important consideration is the degree of regularity (one might say of professionalism) with which the individual is engaged in informal activities. Only in the case of regular involvement can we talk of 'informal employment' as distinct from casual income flows of an occasional nature.

Primary and secondary activities

Many urban dwellers purchase, rent, or occupy plots of land to farm on as a sideline. One migrant even once remarked that 'the trouble with Accra is that there is not enough land to farm on'! Despite this, a good number manage to find a small place on the outskirts of the city to grow corn and vegetables. The high cost of food makes gardening, whether for one's own consumption or for sale, a profitable business. Cannabis is also grown openly in city gardens. Similarly many raise fowls and small livestock even in the heart of a slum like Nima. Access to these income sources is limited primarily by the availability of space.

Artisans need not only small capital sums in order to set up their own sewing machine, bench and tools, or other equipment, but also a considerable amount of learned expertise. For those who have such training, practice of their craft is not necessarily burdened with heavy overheads in rents and the like – the weather is predictable enough to permit work in the open under a shady tree, while others may establish themselves on a verandah, or even partition off working-space in their own living quarters. The same applies to female gin-distillers and beer brewers operating from their small compounds. These occupations are, by definition, not available to unskilled workers, but a young man or woman may acquire the necessary skills by informal apprenticeship (with scanty pay) to one of these operators over a lengthy period of time.

Tertiary enterprises

Entrepreneurial activities in the services sector – transport operators, landlords, cornmill owners, commodity speculators, and so on – represent the apex of informal economic opportunities to the sub-proletariat. Their essential characteristic is that they are frequently part-time roles, entered by individuals who have accumulated savings by some other means and, in the absence of an advanced capital market, re-invest income under their own management in taxis and lorries, accommodation, bulk purchases of maize, and the like. Successful performance is not, however, solely dependent on capital supplies or bureaucratic knowledge (many are illiterate); these constraints are overshadowed by the need for specialised 'know-how' and the ability, through diversification of investments and delegation of tasks, to accommodate the considerable risks attendant on these one-man enterprises. Though income from such activities may be very high, they are often combined with a formal job.

Small-scale distribution

Traders fall into a number of groups. There are [several] axes of differentiation [in trade], such as the nature of the trading medium (market stalls, roadside booths, hawking) and, more importantly, the commodity being traded. Frafras specialise in fowls, Northern artifacts of straw and leather, and also as bread-sellers. It is common to find a small niche in the distribution system dominated by one ethnic group in this way. Possibly by access to supply sources, and certainly through information control, trust and co-operation, these social segments in the city acquire competitive advantage over others in relation to specific commodities. A further differentiating factor is the trader's position in the chain of distribution of his chosen commodity: some are carriers, some are middlemen; some buy and sell in bulk, others buy on credit and retail in small quantities; bread-sellers retail on a commission basis for bakeries, while some cattle dealers act merely as brokers. All maintain a flexible attitude to their trading role and are apt to switch from one to another, or to combine several at once. Finally, they differ in the time-input and scale of their activities. Petty traders, brokers, wholesale merchants, commission agents, and occasional dealers – all these roles are played in varying degrees by large numbers of the urban sub-proletariat.

Occasional buying and selling of consumer goods is a common means of increasing one's income. Most urban workers are 'out for a quick buck' and, given the chance, an individual with some cash to spare will buy an object for which he thinks he can find a buyer at a higher price, preferably after he himself has had some use of it. The objects most commonly traded are consumer items ranging from wrist-watches to refrigerators, and running the gamut of clothing, furniture, and household effects. Some have refined this trade into a lucrative art, the main aim of which is to place oneself between the owner and a would-be purchaser. Naturally, in a place like Nima, these activities often shade into the receiving of stolen goods. The main assets for this occupation are a well-tried sense of value and a wide range of contacts: an individual with both may, by maintaining a fast flow of single items through his hands, achieve considerable profits without needing much capital or storage space.

Distribution has been discussed at length owing to its significance in urban economic life. One frequently reads that ease of entry into trade in cities like Accra is so total that, with the consequent proliferation of small operatives, returns to the individual are less than for an equivalent time spent in formal wage employment at the minimum rate. The low opportunity cost of labour thus justifies the classification of most traders as 'underemployed' and, incidentally, argues for the efficiency of the system through the effects of competition on prices. For example, in a study of peasant marketing in Java, the author remarks that profits are kept down, since, if people thought profits were high, they would go in for trading themselves.[9] This assumption discounts constraints on entry such as social networks, informal skill, and knowledge, as well as the availability of time, capital, or credit.

The pervasiveness of credit at all levels, and the difficulties of trading without literate aids, make this an activity which must be learnt just as any other skilled or, at least, semi-skilled occupation. Ethnic group concentrations of the kind already mentioned also act as informal rings inhibiting entry into certain commodity trades. The whole of meat distribution, from cattle trading to butchering, is dominated by the Islamic Hausa community, and non-Muslims have great difficulty breaking in, even at the lowest level. It must be acknowledged, however, that opportunities for trading on a regular or casual basis are extremely widespread in Accra, if not completely unrestricted in their modes of entry. Moreover, the trading role (part-time as well as full-time) offers potentially much higher returns than wage employment of the kind available to the urban proletariat.

Other services

Secondary occupations are a marked feature of rural society in Ghana. The Frafra homeland is no exception – the farming season there is so short and the fruits so meagre that most men derive some earnings from the practice of a learned skill. It is not surprising, therefore, that many migrants to the towns of Southern Ghana continue to derive supplementary income from these skills. An expert musician or praise-singer is rewarded handsomely at parties and drinking houses. There is also a good market for diviners and other ritual specialists: the urban employment potential for religious and related workers is at least as great as in rural areas. Islamic teachers (*mallams*) would also fall into this category of the full-time informally employed. Payment for such services is irregular, but frequently lucrative. For skilled, semi-skilled, and unskilled service occupations – fitters, barbers, and washerwomen, etc. – learned expertise and small capital/overhead requirements restrict entry to a varying degree. Unskilled service occupations, such as night-soil remover, are available freely within the limits of market demand and personal distaste.

Private transfer payments

The ability of an individual to draw on the resources of others, either consistently (as a client to a patron, or as a dependant to a highly paid worker) or in emergencies, involves the entire structure of rural–urban and urban community relationships. Last of all, of course, there is begging on the streets: there are no limits, save personal pride, to the availability of this expedient. But in Accra, begging is largely restricted to disabled persons and children.

Illegitimate activities

Nima is notorious for its *lack* of respectability, for the dominance of a criminal element, and for the provision of those goods and services usually associated with any major city's 'red-light district'. In this environment, the availability of certain illegitimate means (particularly of a casual, rather than a professional kind) is scarcely less than infinite; moreover these activities, while recognised as illegal, and therefore somewhat risky, meet with little of the opprobrium found elsewhere in the city. These illegitimate activities may be classified into 'services' and 'transfers' for the reason that, while the former constitute deviant forms of services which may be said to be purchased, the victims of the latter cannot be said to have voluntarily initiated the income flows concerned.

Some Choices Facing the Urban Poor

Recruitment to formal and informal employment is, of

course, determined on a far from random basis, even allowing for differences in the qualifications of would-be aspirants to the various jobs. The uneven distribution of economic opportunities between the regional/ethnic groups of Ghana is striking, thus while 21 per cent of Gas (the dominant tribe of Accra) had a white-collar job in 1960, only 1 per cent of the northern Mole-Dagbani group of tribes fell into this category. The extremes are well illustrated by comparing the 200 Frafra white-collar workers with the 5,000 from the smaller number of Akwapims in Southern Ghana; the latter rate is 75 times the former. These differences, which add an explosive regional/tribal element to Ghana's emergent class structure, are largely attributable to differing lengths of exposure to colonial rule and the spread of western education.

Job-seeking

Frafras and other groups like them, when seeking employment in the South, are very conservative; few will apply for a job where they have no particularistic relationship – such as a previously employed kinsman – and perhaps their view of the recruitment process is justified. Information about vacancies tends to travel along informal social networks rather than through employment exchanges, and nepotism is not unknown in Ghana. The result is that migrants from one village or area tend to be clustered occupationally – out of 22 Accra residents from one village section, 20 were employed as cooks; from another section, half were employed as construction workers, and so on. This is perhaps why virtually none of the 5,000 adult male Frafras in Accra-Tema were employed in factories during the mid-1960s. We have already seen the same phenomenon in specialised commodity trading. Thus, a significant constraint limiting access to urban employment of all kinds is the actor's perception of the competitive advantage or disadvantage to himself of ethnic or kin-group membership.

All types of work in the city are therefore viewed differently according to the standpoint of the job-seeker. Apart from ethnic affiliation, the status-ranking of occupations varies between other social categories; thus, while the Islamic community, for example, may accord high prestige to commercial success, others look down on all informal occupations. The education variable is, of course, extremely significant in this respect. The high rates of 'unemployment' recorded among the young in the 1960 Census – see Table 2 – undoubtedly reflect the influence of exposure to western education. If, to the illerate Frafra migrant, informal opportunities offer a ladder out of poverty, to the educated youth, with his eyes on a conventional bureaucratic career, such employment may seem both socially inferior and undesirable. However, an increasing number of middle-school leavers in the urban labour market find their qualifications inadequate for scarce white-collar jobs, so that they must compete with illiterates for manual work. Under these circumstances, informal occupational roles take on a more favourable aspect as a substitute for, or complementary to, forms of employment with a low wages ceiling. One may speculate on the result, when literacy comes to be widely added to existing aptitudes in the pursuit of informal means of advancement.

Combinations of income sources

If job duplication in the formal sector is common, multiple informal employment – both with and without simultaneous wage employment – is almost universal in the economic behaviour of Accra's sub-proletariat. Only rarely is an individual or family dependent on one source of income. This preference for diversity of income streams has its roots in the traditional risk-aversion of peasants under conditions of extreme uncertainty, and is justified by the insecurity of urban workers today. The most salient characteristic of wage employment in the eyes of the sub-proletariat is not the absolute amount of income receipts but its reliability. For informal employment, even of the legitimate variety, is risky and expected rewards highly variable. Thus, for subsistence purposes alone, regular wage employment, however badly paid, has some solid advantages; and hence men who derive substantial incomes from informal activities may still retain or desire formal employment. An acquaintance in Nima earned on an average over £100 a month from rents, receiving stolen goods, and a host of trading operations (though the dispersion of his earnings from month to month was very wide); yet he referred to himself as an 'unemployed cook/steward', the occupation which he had left some five years before. Time is an important constraint for successful operators and, in the absence of scope for delegation, the opportunity cost of time foregone for the sake of keeping on a job may be too high. A particular aspect to be noted is that informal employment may act as a buffer, for those who are 'out of work', against destitution or dependence on others.

How easy is it for someone who lacks alternative means of supporting himself to find work of this kind? The answer, of course, will vary according to the type of work. Nevertheless, despite the constraints on entry to informal occupations, the range of opportunities available outside the organised labour market is so wide that few of the 'unemployed' are totally without some form of income, however irregular. By any standards many of them are poor, but then so are large numbers of wage-earners.

The Structure of Urban Employment

It is generally understood that growing residual under-employment and unemployment in the cities of developing countries is 'a bad thing'. But why should this be so? In what way precisely does this phenomenon constitute a *problem*? Is it from the viewpoint of poverty (inadequate personal or family incomes), social disorganisation and public morality (the crime rate or prostitution), overcrowding (pressure on social infrastructure in towns), political unrest (the danger to politicians of a concentration of frustrated slum-dwellers), rural depopulation (reductions in agricultural capacity)? Or, expressed in terms of the productivity of labour, is it an economist's problem (inefficient utilisation of manpower or reduced contribution to growth in national income)?

Rethinking employment policy

Employment policy frequently confronts all of these questions and some objectives may be seen to be in conflict. But by focusing on 'unemployment', with its attendant western folk images of Tyneside or New York in the 1930s, of dole queues and Keynesian solutions, the goals of employment policy are confused, when they should be made explicit. What happens if the problem is restated in terms of formal and informal employment structures? The question becomes not 'How can we create work for the jobless?', but rather 'Do we want to shift the emphasis of income opportunities in the direction of formal employment for its own sake, or only to reduce participation in socially disapproved informal activities and in those informal occupations whose marginal productivity is too low?' Perhaps it will be argued that some movement should be encouraged away from tertiary activities (both formal and informal) towards primary and secondary production in town and countryside. These are matters of political economy and empirical verification which demand a more sophisticated approach to *all* forms of employment, both inside and out of the formal or wages sector.

Several examples from Ghana's recent history illustrate these points. In the early 1960s the Workers' Brigade was seen as a partial solution to the employment problem – a public-sector, para-military organisation which provided opportunities for work in primary and secondary production. Recruitment in urban areas heavily favoured women, as an explicit measure to diminish prostitution by providing alternative sources of income for city girls. The success of this may be judged by the observation, which was commonplace in Nima, that Workers' Brigade girls were 'easier game' than most, and more ready to extend credit to their lovers when they already had a steady income from their job.

Another failure was the Lonrho *pito* brewery, a capital-intensive concern set up in Tamale to compete with petty manufacturers of a beer made from northern millet. Other examples of a more general kind may be multiplied – food supermarkets, automatic car-washers, and so on – most of which diminish the dependence of the urban middle classes on goods and services supplied by the informal sector. In view of the factor endowments of cities like Accra, is the justification for such developments (that the 'productivity' of labour so employed is high) sufficient to offset the cost of reduced demand for informal goods and services?

In the midst of this haphazard modernisation, one strand of employment policy emerges as the cornerstone of government planning in many African states: that is, the goal of maximising employment opportunities through keeping down the wages of those who are already employed – job creation with wage restraint. As long as urban wage-earners could be described as an 'aristocracy of labour' – the lucky few who had won a passport from unemployment (or, at best, underemployment) to the automatic affluence of a job – any policy aimed at reducing the queue of those playing the 'urban lottery' would be demonstrably rational. The only problem is then to stem the tide of farmworkers rushing to town in pursuit of these lucrative jobs, an objective to which modern sector wage restraint is admirably suited. Unfortunately this view of the situation, in Ghana's case at least, has for long been so far removed from reality as to invite political catastrophe.

Who are the unemployed and underemployed?

This article has attempted to show that for many urban wage-earners poverty is ever present, and that the informal sector provides opportunities of improving real incomes for this category as well as for the 'jobless'. The difficulty of placing many individuals unequivocally in either the formal or informal sectors (owing to the widespread incidence of multiple income sources), when combined with the low ceiling to wage employment relative to informal maximum incomes, makes it empirically and theoretically absurd to maintain the notion of a significant status transition from unemployment or underemployment to full-time employment through the mere acquisition of a job in the organised labour force.

We must re-examine and refine our terms. Most urban workers lacking formal employment and therefore 'out of work' may be said to be, in the most basic sense, unemployed. For they would usually take a wage job, as long as it did not seriously limit the scope for continuing informal activities, on the grounds that the income provided is *secure*, i.e fixed, regular, and relatively permanent. But the urgency of their plight varies, and this may be measured by the amount of time which is spent, while out of work, actively canvassing for formal employment. The truly 'unemployed' are those who will not accept income opportunities open to them for which they are qualified, and this often means rejecting informal means of making a living. It may be that in Accra only educated youths contain a high proportion of persons who would fall into this category.

All the residue of the unorganised urban work-force is commonly subsumed in the term 'underemployed', which is grounded in an assumption about their level of productivity. But these are vague, value-laden concepts – what criteria are being used? Is it to be taken for granted that income returns to a given time input, at a certain level of skill, are usually lower in the informal than in the formal sector? Few are as 'underemployed' by this criterion as full-time workers employed at the government minimum wage. And, when a wage job alone cannot provide for a family's subsistence needs, the question of poverty and income levels in general becomes more relevant than the definition of underemployment.

Some questions about the informal sector

Informal activities are recognised as typical of economic life in the cities of developing and developed countries, but their overall significance could be dismissed as negligible – except, of course, for the unfortunate individuals forced to live in this way. The Jamaican urban unemployed are thus said to make a living from 'scuffling . . . a hand-to-mouth existence which includes begging, borrowing, stealing, finding, receiving as gifts, with a little casual work and selling thrown in'.[10] All of this counts as income from the individual viewpoint, but it is mostly transfers combined with productive activities of little aggregative consequence. The informal sector has therefore been assumed to depend on demand created by current levels of activity in the formal sector, as measured by movements in gross national product or total formal wage expenditure. Such a picture leaves many questions unresolved, although it allows economists to equate significant economic activity with what is measured.

Just what is the relationship between the formal and informal sectors of the urban economy? Do they move in parallel? – or does the level of some informal activities vary inversely with formal trends? In particular, what are the effects of transfers through urban crime? In looking at the determinants of growth in informal output we need to distinguish between demand and supply constraints. Is the demand curve perfectly elastic or downwards sloping? If the latter, by how much is average income decreased by the addition of labour seeking work in the informal sector? Is the urban economy relatively stable or dynamic in this respect? Might not the removal of some supply constraints push the demand curve outwards? What is the state of trade between formal and informal sectors? Does the informal economy resemble *in scale* the US or UK economies in its dependence on outside factors? How much income is generated by internal transactions, and how much by export activity? Finally, is there a net transfer of resources either way between the formal and informal sectors? What about relationships with the rural sector? Inasmuch as the informal sector is identifiable with a socio-economic category (the sub-proletariat living in Accra's slums and earning a maximum from wage employment of £15 to £20 per month), what are the income distribution effects of informal activities?

So many of the goods and services purchased in the city are informally produced that their exclusion from economic analysis is unwarrantable. This article cannot provide empirically determined answers, but it is possible to suggest ways of conceptualising these problems in a fairly rigorous way.

An input–output approach to income flows

One way to chart income flows within the urban economy would be to set up an input–output matrix of formal and informal activities (using a typology such as that drawn up on pp. 77–8) based on surveys of income and expenditure patterns. Additional rows and columns would account for trade and transfers with the rural sector and the 'rest of the world'. Ignoring measurement problems and the question of short- and long-term changes (which could be resolved only by time-series data), this mode of analysis arguably refines the questions and generates testable hypotheses.

Thus, all informal purchases paid for from wages earned in the formal sector would be classified as 'exports'; set against this would be the volume of 'imports', i.e. purchases in the formal sector financed by informal incomes. The 'balance of payments' between the sectors would be completed by net transfers, particularly those occasioned by theft. Assuming that the formal sector monopolises trade with the 'rest of the world', the only other relevant balance of payments for the informal sector would then be that with the rural sector. A current account surplus in favour of the informal sector *vis-à-vis* the formal might be offset by capital flows in the opposite direction, or by a deficit with the rural sector – there are several possibilities here.

Apart from import–export activities, a most significant question relates to the amount of income generated by transactions *within* the informal sector; the 'spread effects' of informal purchases or transfers could be quantified by an analysis of expenditure patterns. Demand creation thus depends on the internal income multiplier, as well as on sales to the formal sector. Informal occupations might therefore be classified according to their 'export coefficients'. Whatever its drawbacks, at least this approach has the merit of directing attention to all income flows in the urban economy.

The structure of the urban economy

The informal sector may be identified for heuristic purposes with the sub-proletariat of the slum – a reasonable assumption despite the participation of many in the wage economy, and of a few members of higher income groups in certain lucrative informal activities.

On inspection, the informal sector seems to support a high level of export activity: much primary and secondary production, as well as many service activities (distribution, transport, and so on), are for the general market and therefore paid for in large measure by those living outside the slum. The biggest export coefficients (combining services and transfers in this context) are to be found in such illegitimate occupations as prostitute, burglar, embezzler, and con-man, in contrast with the hustler, moneylender, drug-pusher, and gambler, whose customers are generally sub-proletarians also.

Most current expenditures are internal transactions – rents, profits from food and similar sales, personal services, and entertainments are paid for mainly within the informal economy. Public transfers are of negligible significance in Accra, and private transfers circulate within the sub-proletariat, with some leakage to the rural sector; but illegitimate transfers are borne predominantly by the urban middle classes. We may hypothesise, therefore, that the current-account balance of payments between the informal and formal economies favours the former, and that informal activities constitute a net addition to the income resources of the sub-proletariat.

Urban crime may then be seen as a redistribution of wealth with income effects throughout the informal economy. 'Loot' – or static wealth lying idle in the homes of the bourgeoisie – is a stock, independent of current income flows, which is mobilised through theft into direct and indirect income for sub-proletarians. In this sense, increases in crime may act as a buffer against falls in GNP, since national income accounting does not normally include transfers by theft. The tie-up between urban unemployment and crime rates in Africa is receiving much press publicity at present. It is interesting that Ghana's repatriation of many foreign nationals in 1969, which has been interpreted by at least one commentator as a response to growing unemployment, should have been conducted with references by the Government to the 'lawlessness' of the immigrant community. This area of analysis clearly deserves a more comprehensive approach than it has hitherto been accorded.

When we turn to the question of internal income distribution in the slum, the informal economy emerges as a source of differentiation within the sub-proletariat which far surpasses the homogeneous impression given by the range of wages in formal employment. These differences in life-style, wealth, and social status are, however, mitigated by the system of patronage and familial/ethnic obligation which ensures a more equitable distribution. It is the 'big men' of each ethnic division of the sub-proletariat who provide the newcomer and the newly out of work with a certain refuge, where food and a place to sleep may always be found in emergencies.

Finally, what can be said about the relationship between wage-employment levels and the informal sector? It is clear that an increasing surplus to the labour requirements of the formal sector (whether occasioned by rural–urban migration, or by redundancies in a period of deflation), must increase the supply of labour to the informal economy. Not only that – if wage incomes are inadequate, the needs of the 'employed' create added pressures on the supply side. The question is, Does the informal sector have any autonomous capacity for growth?

The dynamics of informal growth depend on a number of factors: changes in the pattern of final demand in favour of goods and services produced informally, changes in the rates of savings and capital formation in the informal sector, and on the volume of transfers via theft which is independent of demand. The possibility that the informal economy, with its emphasis on tertiary activities, may be developing at a rate faster than other sectors of the national economy, and thus taking up some of the slack created by inadequate rates of growth in the well-documented modern sector, cannot be dismissed on *a priori* grounds. When half of the urban labour force falls outside the organised labour market, how can we continue to be satisfied with indicators of economic performance which ignore their productive activities?

Understanding urban drift

The implied criticisms of the previous section apply to no field more strongly than to the analysis of urban drift in developing countries. One theory which incorporates wage-employment levels in comparing the expected real incomes of rural–urban migrants is M. P. Todaro's often-quoted East African model.[11] Stated in terms of the subjective probability of improving real incomes, this model may account for much of the variation in rural–urban movements, *provided that* the measurements chosen for the income and probability factors approximate to reality.

This article has argued that wage incomes are only part of the urban opportunity structure, and we need not think all of those who enter informal occupations do so as a result of failure to obtain a wage job. The magnetic force of the town may be derived from the multiplicity of income opportunities rather than merely from wage levels. A decision to come to the city would then have some objectively rational motive if, despite the paucity of formal employment opportunities and the low ceiling to wage remunerations, the migrant could look to the prospect of accumulation, with or without a job, in the informal economy of the urban slums.

Conclusions

This article lacks an overview of informal urban activities in relation to underdevelopment of the

Ghanaian type. Socialists may argue that foreign capitalist dominance of these economies determines the scope for informal (and formal) development, and condemns the majority of the urban population to deprivation and exploitation. More optimistic liberals may see in informal activities, as described here, the possibility of a dramatic 'bootstrap' operation, lifting the underdeveloped economies through their own indigenous enterprise. Before either view – or a middle course stressing both external constraint and autonomous effort – may be espoused, much more empirical research is required.

It may be that an important source of variance is the level of industrial activity as a proportion of total urban employment and consequent differences in the structure of wages. Old cities like Accra, lacking significant industrial development, may be contrasted with newer urban complexes such as the Zambian Copperbelt in the scope and relative attractiveness of informal opportunities – a contrast which is sustainable for western cities in the industrial revolution, for example between London and Manchester in the nineteenth century. One thing is certain: Accra is not unique, and a historical, cross-cultural comparison of urban economies in the development process must grant a place to the analysis of informal as well as formal structures. It is time that the language and approach of development economics took this into account.

Notes: Reading 10

1 The anthropological fieldwork was undertaken during 1965–8, and the ethnographic present, whenever used, refers to this period.

2 See Douglas Rimmer, 'Wage politics in west Africa', University of Birmingham, 1970. All three indices showed a slight upturn in real earnings for 1967–8, following an 8 per cent increase in the minimum wage.

3 The empirical basis for these statements concerning the length of stay in urban areas is contained in my unpublished PhD thesis: J. K. Hart, 'Entrepreneurs and migrants – a study of modernisation among the Frafras of Ghana', University of Cambridge, 1969.

4 See Jean Rouch, *Notes on Migrations into the Gold Coast*, Paris, 1954; English translation by P. E. O. and J. B. Heigham, Accra, 1956.

5 W. F. Whyte, *Street-Corner Society*, Chicago, 1943.

6 O. Lewis, *La Vida*, New York, 1966.

7 H. Mayhew, *London Labour and the London Poor*, vols. 1–4, London, 1851.

8 See J. K. Hart, 'Small-scale entrepreneurs in Ghana and development planning', *Journal of Development Studies*, July 1970, pp. 103–20.

9 See A. Dewey, *Peasant Marketing in Java*, Glencoe, Ill., 1962, p. 85.

10 See K. Norris, *Jamaica: The Search for Identity*, London, 1962, p. 40.

11 See M. P. Todaro, 'A model of labor migration and urban unemployment in less developed countries', *American Economic Review*, vol. 69, no. 1, March 1969 (Providence, R.I.).

Reading 11

Investment in Education in Developing Nations: Policy Responses when Private and Social Signals Conflict

E. O. Edwards

World Development, vol. 3, no. 1, January 1975, pp. 41–5.

It has been typical of educational systems in developing nations that they have responded to the most obvious private and social signals confronting them. The private signals can be encapsulated as the *aggregate private demand* for education which rests on private perceptions of educational benefits and costs – the benefits the beneficiaries of education expect to receive and the costs which they (or their families) expect to bear. The social signals can be summarized as the *net social benefit* from education which reflects judgments about the full social benefits and costs of education – judgments which may be based on crude estimates of social need, manpower studies or sophisticated cost–benefit analyses. These two sets of signals will seldom correspond exactly – some social benefits may escape private detection; private perceptions may exaggerate benefits; and the costs borne privately (including earnings foregone while attending school) are typically a small portion of full educational costs – but they may point in the same direction. The problem of appropriate political response arises when they point to different educational policies.

Consider the experience of the last three decades. So long as the private and social signals were mutually reinforcing and indicated educational expansion, the substantial allocations of development expenditures to education were politically secure, the risk of social and economic error not being an obvious signal. Nations achieving independence since World War II (most of the LDCs in Asia and Africa) immediately perceived social needs to expand education in preparation for indigenously managed growth – to replace expatriate civil servants and private-sector employees, to diminish dependence on foreign training and to meet the normal requirements of growth and replacement. These social needs were strongly reinforced by a pent-up private indigenous demand for education. In these circumstances, the rate of educational expansion, particularly at higher levels, was naturally and justifiably in excess of the rate which could be sustained by normal requirements of growth and replacement alone. Unfortunately, as the unusual needs for expatriate replacement and the substitution of domestic for foreign training subsided, many educational systems nevertheless continued their rapid growth, seriously overproducing in terms of the social and economic requirements of normal growth.

Today the obvious signals are mixed. The dominant social signal is that there are too few jobs for those emerging from most educational systems suggesting that a larger share of future development expenditures should go to job creation and that the rate of educational expansion at secondary and higher levels should diminish. The aggregate private demand for secondary and higher education, on the other hand, continues strong, reflecting for the most part (1) distortions in urban/rural and occupational income differentials which serve to exaggerate the benefits of education as privately perceived and (2) subsidies to education so that only a small proportion of educational costs is borne by the private beneficiaries of education.[1]

The benefits of education, as measured by the wage differentials related to education, will typically be discounted privately by the probability of employment.[2] But so long as those differentials persist at exaggerated and institutionally determined levels and higher education is heavily subsidized by governments, the aggregate private demand for education must exceed the social need for it. Thus the conflict between expanding education and creating employment opportunities becomes a real policy dilemma.

In these circumstances of conflict the obvious signals provide no clear-cut single guide to national educational policies. An 'imminent danger' philosophy of government would suggest a first accommodation of educational supply to the visible pressures of the aggregate private demand for education. Later (and it will involve a substantial lag), when growing unemployment itself poses an imminent threat to political stability, that challenge may be given priority. Evidence on educational expansion over the last two decades in many LDCs is consistent with this hypothesis of political behavior.[3] But that evidence also suggests that the greater threat is unemployment and it would be socially desirable to attend to it at an earlier stage.

The contradiction in that earlier stage between the social need and the private demand for education raises three questions which seem to have easy, though in some cases unsatisfactory, answers:

1. To which set of signals *should* the educational system (and the development budget) respond? (Answer: Net social benefit.)

2. Which set has greatest influence on political feasibility? (Answer: Aggregate private demand.)

3. Which force takes precedence? (Answer: Aggregate private demand.)

Even a summary examination of these questions will lead us to others which are more complex and less easily answered.

The aggregate private demand for education, particularly at higher levels, is usually clearly and forcibly expressed. The net social need at any time is more ambiguous, less precise in its dimensions, and often lacking in powerful sponsors. One outcome of the growing conflict between the two sets of signals has been the demand for more careful analyses of educational needs, benefits and costs. When the obvious signals were mutually reinforcing, such analyses could be treated casually – as a basis for refining, but not as a guide for establishing, basic policy. But if at that earlier stage the tools of sophisticated analysis were treated too cavalierly, perhaps today too much is expected of them.

The bag of tools to which policy-makers are turning is cost–benefit analysis. But the value of cost–benefit analysis as applied to educational planning lies not so much in its accuracy, or indeed in its utility for investment decisions as in the kinds of information it seeks to disclose and in the hints to be gleaned from this information about an extensive array of economic policies extending beyond the educational sector itself. Indeed, if these hints about price distortions and cost incidence are not heeded, the likelihood that cost–benefit-based investment decisions can be implemented is extremely small.

The three elements of cost–benefit analysis to which we call attention are (1) its effort to embrace all benefits and costs regardless of how widely they may be shared or to whom they may accrue, (2) its intent to value all benefits and costs in monetary terms and at social rather than private values, bearing in mind that most of the relevant values must be estimated for an array of future dates, and (3) its attempt to find objective means (discounting) of standardizing benefits and costs for the time differentials related to their occurrence as a means of facilitating comparison. Perhaps such a stark summary makes the principal limitations of cost–benefit analysis all too apparent – to identify all of the benefits and costs of education is a large task; to assign money values to many of them is a hazardous undertaking; to estimate social values when these are not thrown up by the market-place and when they lie in the future rather than the present is certainly ambitious; and to attempt to compare values across time is a tricky task. Accuracy is not a feasible objective of cost–benefit analysis.

What it does offer is a time perspective and an attempt at objectivity, both of which should improve investment decisions as compared to decisions based on either crude social imbalances or uneven private perceptions of the costs and benefits of education. Crude social imbalances such as unemployment or obvious mismatches between types of education and job requirements are probably not bad indicators of needed policy change and they can undoubtedly be improved upon through analysis of first differences, the rates at which such indicators are changing. But because of the long gestation period in education, decisions on *future* school output based on *present* imbalances may obviously turn out to be deficient when measured against future needs.

On the other hand, aggregate private demand is excessive not only because the incomes associated with higher levels of education often overvalue higher education (partly because differentials established when education was scarce tend to be perpetuated), but also because these benefits accrue to the relatively few who receive higher education, while the subsidies to education (as opposed to student fees and the opportunity costs of foregone employment) are shared widely through the tax system falling most heavily on those who do not benefit.[4] Thus the gains are fully counted by those who receive them, but as costs are shared with others, beneficiaries count only a portion of them in determining the aggregate private demand for education.

The foregoing argument also contains the elements to justify the easy answers to questions (2) and (3). As the benefits are clearly associated with education and become the private property of the beneficiaries, present and potential beneficiaries constitute a strong, influential and vocal group favoring educational expansion and the retention of subsidies. On the other hand, because the subsidies are widely diffused and not clearly earmarked for education, those who bear those costs are stillborn as a political lobby. The voices raised all favor educational expansion. It is not surprising if those who listen in the political market-place respond. Typically, they do; educational systems expand, particularly at higher levels; and costs are subsidized, much more at higher than at lower levels.

It is, however, one advantage of cost–benefit analysis that it surfaces educational costs – for decision-makers at any rate – and relates them to educational benefits. This information may stir the consciences of policy-makers and temper the rate of expansion of higher education despite growing pressures from aggregate private demand. But it is just at this stage that our scenario becomes interesting and instructive. Suppose that net social benefit considerations are fully persuasive to policy-makers, and they are moved, despite the educational lobby, to seek to reduce the rate of expansion of higher levels of education in favor of a more rapid expansion of productive employment opportunities. An apparent social triumph may yet slip away; the problems confronting both the investment decision and its implementation may be formidable.

In the first place, in deciding how to use the funds released from investment in education, policy-makers must confront another set of political pressures. Employment creation suggests on the available evidence a dispersion of those funds to rural infrastructure, to small farmers, to decentralized functions of government, and to small-scale industrial and service activities in both urban and rural areas, *not* an indiscriminate allocation of funds to make-work civil service employment at the center or to large, capital-intensive forms of industrial and agricultural enterprises. But the effective lobbies concerned with the reallocation of these investment funds are likely to be composed of those who will benefit from large-scale, urban development – and the policy-makers themselves may be members. The promotion of small-scale, capital-economizing activities may fall by the wayside, even though they are more productive, in the face of political pressures for continuing capital concentration which is beneficial to the influential. While the social value of reducing the rate of educational expansion in favor of promoting dispersed, small-scale, employment-creating activities may be reasonably clear, the social value of shifting funds from education to capital-intensive, large-scale undertakings may be a matter of considerable doubt. The easy answer to question (1) may not be conclusive after all.

In the second place, even if policy-makers make the right social decision on reallocating investment funds, the political pressures which inhibited that decision in the first place will continue unabated, and indeed may grow in force and magnitude. *There is nothing in the investment decision itself which will modify the price signals determining the private demand for education or the demand of the influential for capital-intensive projects.* These continuing pressures may frustrate implementation, turn policy-makers out of office or force a reversal of the decision. Indeed, some within both local and central governments who disapprove of the decision may assist in circumventing it, as in the early years of the Harambee school movement in Kenya. In any event, the decision will entail the rationing of educational opportunities and a consequent opportunity for discrimination.

In the third place, the decision controls directly only public investment and any attempt to implement it as a *national* policy, as opposed to only a public sector policy, implies means of enforcement which extend into the private sector. Secondary and higher education is not a public good in the sense that its benefits cannot be 'resold' by the beneficiaries; it follows that profits may be made by those who supply educational services. In these circumstances the tendency exists for the aggregate private demand for education to spill over into the private sector and for enterprising entrepreneurs to find means for supplying it, as in the Philippines. A decrease in public investment in education may simply lead to an increase in private investment and, so long as the price signals determining aggregate private demand are distorted, aggregate private and public investment in education will continue to be socially excessive.

The conclusion seems inescapable that for most developing nations the making of 'socially correct' investment decisions with regard to education, whether on the basis of crude social signals or more refined cost–benefit analyses, will not in and of itself alleviate, and indeed may aggravate, the political and economic counter-pressures stemming largely from a distorted private demand for education. Moreover, if unpopular decisions are in fact taken in the face of such pressures, the obstacles confronting effective implementation in both public and private sectors will seriously distort the desired outcome.

The alternative is to look beyond the educational investment decision itself to those policies which will tend to make conflicting private and social signals converge, thus modifying the aggregate private demand for education. To the extent that the social costs and benefits of education can be internalized, the private demand for education will reflect choices based on consumer preferences in confrontation with a more realistic set of both costs and benefits. The gap between private and social perceptions may not be fully closed, but the area of conflict should shrink and the likelihood that social need and private demand will point toward similar rather than different rates of expansion of education should be increased. Policies which may narrow the gap between private and social signals fall in three categories.

1. *Policies to adjust labor-market price signals and hiring practices so that market price differentials accord more closely with social realities (shadow-price differentials) and education is not privately overvalued.* The use of shadow prices for decision-making is usually implicitly premised on the existence of control mechanisms which transcend the market, as in allocation decisions internal to the firm. Equally effective control mechanisms are not readily available for enforcing unpopular educational investment decisions; the rationing of education opportunities, for example, is usually discriminatory and in any event may only squeeze unsatisfied private demand into the private and local government sectors. Adjusting relative market signals toward shadow-price counterparts will reduce the need for and pressure on such control mechanisms.

The policy adjustments referred to here are therefore desirable whether education is supplied in either the public or private sector or in both.

2. *Policies to recover from the beneficiaries of higher education a greater proportion of the costs of providing it in the public sector*. That part of education which is not a public good, its benefits becoming private property whose services can be marketed, should be financed by its beneficiaries out of future income differentials or through public service. Such policies should diminish discrimination by parents' incomes (because it is the beneficiary who pays), temper the private demand for education, and recover a portion of educational costs for other public sector purposes.

3. *As an alternative or supplement to (2), policies to encourage the supply of 'private good' higher education in the private sector*. Such policies will ensure that the costs of some higher education opportunities (those in the private sector) enter the private calculus. The major disadvantage is that, unless such policies are supplemented by a public-sector loan program, the distribution of the benefits of private-sector education will depend heavily on parents' incomes, rather than on the prospective incomes of the beneficiaries of higher education.

To bring us full circle, the question must be posed: 'What political forces will an attempt to introduce *these* policies encounter?' The first may encounter resistance from those who benefit from capital subsidies and high wages, the capital-intensive industries and the labor unions, the force depending of course on the form remedial efforts assume. The second will confront the higher education lobbies of which many civil servants and policy-makers are members. The third should encounter less resistance if proper quality control is exercised. But such changes can all be introduced gradually and may on that account be less painful and encounter less resistance than the rationing of school places. The point is, of course, that policies such as these should not only promote better decisions on educational investment but should also increase employment opportunities for those who emerge from educational systems at every level.

Policies such as these should not be interpreted as a 'complete guide' to educational decision-making. Two points are immediately apparent. First, nothing has been said about the cost, quality and content of education – the internal effectiveness of educational systems. Second, to the extent that educational benefits are a public good (promoting national unity, cohesiveness and communication, for example) and are not entertained in the private calculus, the conversion of all social costs into private costs raises a risk contrary to the one to which this paper is addressed, namely, that the aggregate private demand for education may turn out to be less than what is socially optimal.

Notes: Reading 11

1 For a more extensive and rigorous discussion of the conflict between the need for jobs and the demand for education and of the rationing dilemma this conflict raises, see E. O. Edwards and M. P. Todaro, 'Educational demand and supply in the context of growing unemployment in less developed countries', *World Development*, March–April 1973.

2 Michael P. Todaro, 'A model for labor migration and urban unemployment in less developed countries', *American Economic Review*, March 1969.

3 See, for example, the illuminating evidence of such behaviour in the ILO report, *Matching Employment Opportunities and Expectations: A Program of Action for Ceylon*, Geneva, 1971.

4 An excellent exposition of this and related issues can be found in Jagdish Bhagwati, 'Education, class structure and income equality', *World Development*, May 1973.

Reading 12

Migration, Unemployment and Development: A Two-Sector Analysis

J. R. Harris and M. P. Todaro

American Economic Review, 1970, pp. 126–40.

Throughout many less developed economies of the world, especially those of tropical Africa, a curious economic phenomenon is presently taking place. Despite the existence of positive marginal products in agriculture and significant levels of urban unemployment, rural-urban labor migration not only continues to exist, but indeed appears to be accelerating. Conventional economic models with their singular dependence on the achievement of a full employment equilibrium through appropriate wage and price adjustments are hard put to provide rational behavioral explanations for these sizable and growing levels of urban unemployment in the absence of absolute labor redundancy in the economy as a whole. Moreover, this lack of an adequate analytical model to account for the unemployment phenomenon often leads to rather amorphous explanations such as the 'bright lights' of the city acting as a magnet to lure peasants into urban areas.

In this paper we shall diverge from the usual full employment, flexible wage-price models of economic analysis by formulating a two-sector model of rural-urban migration which, among other things, recognizes the existence of a politically determined minimum urban wage at levels substantially higher than agricultural earnings.[1] We shall then consider the effect of this parametric urban wage on the rural individual's economic behavior when the assumption of no agricultural labor surplus is made, i.e. that the agricultural marginal product is always positive and inversely related to the size of the rural labor force. The distinguishing feature of this model is that migration proceeds in response to urban-rural differences in *expected earnings* (defined below) with the urban employment rate acting as an equilibrating force on such migration. We shall then use the overall model for the following purposes:

1 to demonstrate that given this politically determined high minimum wage, the continued existence of rural-urban migration in spite of substantial overt urban unemployment represents an economically rational choice on the part of the individual migrant;

2 to show that economists' standard policy prescription of generating urban employment opportunities through the use of 'shadow prices' implemented by means of wage subsidies or direct government hiring will *not* necessarily lead to a welfare improvement and may, in fact, exacerbate the problem of urban unemployment;

3 to evaluate the welfare implications of alternative policies associated with various back-to-the-land programs when it is recognized that the standard remedy suggested by economic theory—namely, full wage flexibility—is for all practical purposes politically infeasible. Special attention will be given here to the impact of migration cum unemployment on the welfare of the rural sector as a whole which gives rise to intersectoral compensation requirements; and, finally,

4 to argue that in the absence of wage flexibility, an optimal policy is, in fact, a 'policy package' including *both* partial wage subsidies (or direct government employment) and measures to restrict free migration.

1. The Basic Model

The basic model which we shall employ can be described as a two-sector internal trade model with unemployment. The two sectors are the permanent urban and the rural. For analytical purposes we shall distinguish between sectors from the point of view of production and income. The urban sector specializes in the production of a manufactured good, part of which is exported to the rural sector in exchange for agricultural goods. The rural sector has a choice of either using all available labor to produce a single agricultural good, some of which is exported to the urban sector, *or* using only part of its labor to produce this good while *exporting* the remaining labor to the urban sector in return for wages paid in the form of the manufactured good. We are thus assuming that the typical migrant retains his ties to the rural sector and, therefore, the income that he earns as an urban worker will be considered, from the standpoint of sectoral welfare, as accruing to the rural sector. However, this assumption is not at all necessary for our demonstration of the rationality of migration in the face of significant urban unemployment.

The crucial assumption to be made in our model is that rural-urban migration will continue so long as the *expected* urban real income at the margin exceeds real agricultural product—i.e. prospective rural migrants behave as maximizers of *expected* utility. For analytical purposes, we shall assume that the total urban labor force consists of a permanent urban proletariat without ties to the rural sector, plus the available supply of rural migrants. From this combined pool or urban labor, we assume that a periodic *random job selection process* exists whenever the number of available jobs is exceeded by the number of job seekers. Consequently, the expected urban wage will be defined as equal to the fixed minimum wage (expressed in terms of manufactured goods) times the proportion of the urban labor force actually employed (see equation (6)). Finally, we assume perfectly competitive behavior on the part of producers in both sectors with the further simplifying assumption that the price of the agricultural good (defined in terms of manufactured goods) is determined directly by the relative quantities of the two goods produced.

Consider now the following formulation of the model.

Agricultural Production Function:

(1) $$X_A = q(N_A, \bar{L}, \bar{K}_A),\ q' > 0,\ q'' < 0$$

where,

X_A is output of the agricultural good,
N_A is the rural labor used to produce this output,
$\bar{L}$ is the fixed availability of land,
$\bar{K}_A$ is the fixed capital stock,
q' is the derivative of q with respect of N_A, its only variable factor.

Manufacturing Production Function:

(2) $$X_M = f(N_M, \bar{K}_M),\ f' > 0,\ f'' < 0$$

where,

X_M is the output of the manufactured good,
N_M is the total labor (urban and rural migrant) required to produce this output.
$\bar{K}_M$ is fixed capital stock, and
f' is the derivative of f with respect to N_M, its only variable factor.

Price Determination:

(3) $$P = \rho\left(\frac{X_M}{X_A}\right),\qquad \rho' > 0$$

where,

P, the price of the agricultural good in terms of the manufactured good (i.e., the terms of trade), is a function of the relative outputs of agricultural and manufactured good when the latter serves as numeraire.

Agricultural Real Wage Determination:

(4) $$W_A = P \cdot q'$$

where,

W_A, the agricultural real wage, is equal to the value of labor's marginal product in agriculture expressed in terms of the manufactured good.

Manufacturing Real Wage:

(5) $$W_M = f' \geqq \bar{W}_M.$$

The real wage in manufacturing, expressed in terms of manufactured goods, is equated with the marginal product of labor in manufacturing because of profit maximization on the part of perfectly competitive producers. However, this wage is constrained to be greater than or equal to the fixed minimum urban wage. In our analysis, we shall be dealing only with cases in which $f' = W_M$ (i.e. there is never an excess demand for labor at the minimum wage).

Urban Expected Wage:

(6) $$W_u^e = \frac{\bar{W}_M N_M}{N_u},\qquad \frac{N_M}{N_u} \leq 1,$$

where the *expected* real wage in the urban sector, W_u^e, is equal to the real minimum wage W_M adjusted for the proportion of the total urban labor force (permanent urban plus migrants, denoted as N_u) actually employed, N_M/N_u. Only in the case of full employment in the urban sector ($N_M = N_u$) is the expected wage equal to the minimum wage (i.e. $W_u^e = \bar{W}_M$).

Labor Endowment:

(7) $$N_A + N_u = \bar{N}_R + \bar{N}_u = \bar{N}$$

There is a *labor constraint* which states that the sum of workers actually employed in the agricultural sector (N_A), plus the total urban labor force (N_u), must equal the sum of initial endowments of rural ($\bar{N}_R$) and permanent urban ($\bar{N}_u$) labor which in turn equals the total labor endowment ($\bar{N}$).

Equilibrium Condition:

(8) $$W_A = W_u^*$$

Equation (8), an equilibrium condition, is derived from the hypothesis that migration to the urban area is a positive function of the urban-rural *expected* wage differential. This can be written formally as

(9) $$\dot{N}_u = \psi\left(\frac{\overline{W}_M N_M}{N_u} - P \cdot q'\right),$$

$$\psi' > 0, \ \psi(0) = 0$$

where $\dot{N}_u$ is a time derivative. Clearly then, migration will cease only when the expected income differential is zero, the condition posited in (8).[2] It is important to note that this assumes that a migrant gives up only his marginal product.

We thus have 8 equations in 8 unknowns X_A, X_M, N_A, N_M, W_A, W_u^e, N_u and P. Given the production functions and fixed minimum wage $\overline{W}_M$, it is possible to solve for sectoral employment, the equilibrium unemployment rate and, consequently, the equilibrium expected wage, relative output levels and terms of trade. Let us analyze how such an unemployment equilibrium can come about.

The essence of our argument is that in many developing nations the existence of an institutionally determined urban minimum wage at levels substantially higher than that which the free market would allow can, and usually does, lead to an equilibrium with considerable urban unemployment. In our model migration is a disequilibrium phenomenon. In equilibrium $\overline{W}_M N_M / N_u = Pq'$ and migration ceases. Now we know from equation (5) that in the competitive urban manufacturing sector, $\overline{W}_M = f'$. We also know from equation (7) that $\overline{N} - N_A = N_u$ and from equation (3) that $P = \varrho(X_M/X_A)$. Therefore, we can rewrite our equilibrium condition (8) as

(8′) $$\Phi = \varrho\,(X_M/X_A)q' - \frac{f' N_M}{\overline{N} - N_A} = 0.$$

Since X_M and X_A are functions of N_M and N_A respectively, Φ is an implicit function in N_A and N_M which, for any stated minimum wage, can be solved for the equilibrium combination of agricultural and manufacturing employment. From this solution the levels of urban unemployment and commodity outputs can also be determined. There will be a unique equilibrium associated with each possible value of the minimum wage, and the locus of these equilibria is plotted in Figure 1 as the line $\Phi = 0$ in N_A, N_M space. The line $N_A + N_M = \overline{N}$ in Figure 1 is the locus of full-employment points.

Point Z is the only equilibrium full-employment point in Figure 1 at which N_M^* workers would be employed in manufacturing and N_A^* in agriculture. Points on the locus $\Phi = 0$ east of Z are infeasible and will not be considered further, while points to the west of Z are associated with minimum wages higher than the full-employment wage. There is a monotonic mapping such that higher minimum wages are associated with points on $\Phi = 0$ lying farther to the west. Thus we can demonstrate that the setting of a minimum wage above the market-clearing level causes an economy to settle at a point such as H in Figure 1. At H, N'_A workers are employed in agriculture, N'_M in manufacturing, and $N_u - N'_M$ workers are unemployed. It is evident that the minimum wage causes a loss of employment and hence output in both sectors.[3]

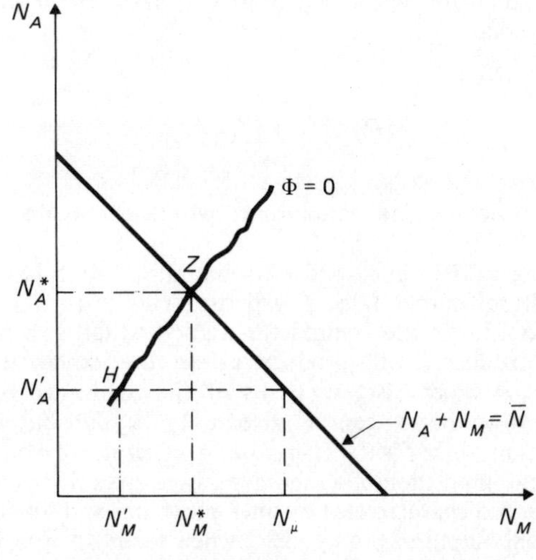

Figure 1

It is important to note that even though an equilibrium at point H represents a suboptimum situation for the economy as a whole, it does represent a rational, utility maximizing choice for individual rural migrants given the level of the minimum wage.

One final point might be raised at this juncture. So far we have assumed that the urban minimum wage is fixed in terms of the manufactured good. What if, instead, the minimum wage were fixed in terms of the agricultural good? We would then substitute for equation (5):

(5′) $$W_M = \frac{f'}{P} \geq W_M.$$

Substituting (4), (5′), and (6) into (8) we get the equilibrium relationship:

(11) $$\underline{Pq'} = \frac{\frac{f'}{P} \cdot N_M}{\underline{N}u}.$$

We can then imagine an economy starting initially at the point on the production possibilities frontier at which

X_M is that for which equation (5′) is satisfied and assume that

$$\underline{Pq}' < \frac{\left(\frac{f'}{p}\right).N_M}{N_u}$$

at that point. The equilibrium point will again be reached through a simultaneous raising of Pq' and lowering of W^e_u in response to migration. As relative agricultural output falls, P will rise. This in turn will cause output of the manufactured good to fall as well, since producers will produce up to the point that $f' = \overline{W}_M P$ which rises in terms of the manufactured good. Note that f' can be raised only through output restriction (since $f''<0$). Therefore, in general, we would find that imposition of a minimum wage gives rise to an equilibrium characterized by unemployment and loss of potential output of both goods. A new locus $\Phi' = 0$ will be defined in Figure 1 such that the point on Φ' corresponding to any given minimum wage will be west of the corresponding point on Φ.

Although our initial assumption is a bit easier to handle, the principal conclusion remains unaffected if we make the minimum wage fixed in terms of the agricultural good. Equilibrium is only achievable with unemployment. Actual minimum wage setting is usually done with reference to some general cost of living index, and food is the largest single item in the budget of most urban workers. (See Massell and Heyer, and the Nigeria report.) Hence, the second case may be somewhat more realistic. Note that in the first case the 'true' real wage was reduced somewhat by the rising agricultural price, while in the latter case it is increased by the falling relative price of the manufactured good.

2 Implications for Development Policy

A. *Planning in terms of shadow prices*

The standard solution to the problem of an institutionally determined wage that is higher than the equilibrium level is to employ labor in the public sector according to a shadow wage and/or to grant a payroll subsidy to private employers that equates private costs with this shadow wage. Two main problems arise with this prescription: first, how can one determine the appropriate shadow wage? And, secondly, what are the implications of executing such a scheme when the institutional wage will continue to be paid to the employed? Our model can shed light on both of these issues.

In a static framework the appropriate shadow wage is the opportunity cost of labor hired by the industrial sector. Hence, if labor is hired to the point that its marginal product in industry is equated with the shadow wage which in turn is equated with the marginal product in agriculture, marginal productivity of labor will be equal in both sectors, a necessary condition for an optimal allocation of resources. Naturally, this assumes a positive marginal product in agriculture and sufficient factor mobility to ensure full employment of labor. The existence of urban unemployment, however, suggests that there may be a pool of labor that can be tapped without sacrificing output. Consequently, it might be suggested that even though agricultural labor is fully employed at peak seasons, the appropriate shadow wage for urban labor is likely to be one that is lower than the marginal product in agriculture. This would be correct if the two labor forces, urban and rural, were separate noncompeting groups. In linear programming terms, there are two labor constraints and each may well have a different associated shadow wage.

Now, the essence of our model is that the two sectors *are* intimately connected through labor migration. If one additional job is created in the industrial sector at the minimum wage, the expected wage will rise and rural-urban migration will be induced. It can be shown that more than one agricultural worker will be likely to migrate in response to the creation of one additional industrial job. Hence, the opportunity cost of an industrial worker will exceed the marginal product of an agricultural worker. On the other hand, an increase in agricultural income will induce reverse migration with no diminution of industrial output. Thus, the opportunity cost of labor is lower to the agricultural than to the industrial sector!

The literature has been strangely silent for the most part about the full implications of using shadow-wage criteria. In a static context, Stolper has pointed out that financing subsidies or losses of public enterprises gives rise to fiscal problems, but unfortunately this issue has not yet been pursued in sufficient detail. If the problem is considered at all, the analyst usually assumes that a system of nondistorting lump-sum taxes is available. Little, Lefeber, and Little and Mirrlees have pointed out that in a dynamic setting, the extra consumption arising from payment of the institutional wage diverts resources from investment to consumption; thus some of the foregone future consumption should be considered in calculating the shadow wage. In our model, payment of the minimum wage to additional industrial workers will induce more rural-urban migration. Therefore, implementation of a shadow-wage employment criterion will have important effects on the level of agricultural output and on urban unemployment. The argument can be clarified with reference to Figure 2.

The initial equilibrium, given the minimum wage, is at point D with output of the manufactured good restricted to OX^*_M. If individuals did not migrate in response to expected wage differentials, the economy could produce at point E, but migration reduces agricultural output to the level OQ. The theory of shadow pricing suggests that with an appropriate wage subsidy (or public-sector-hiring rule) the economy could

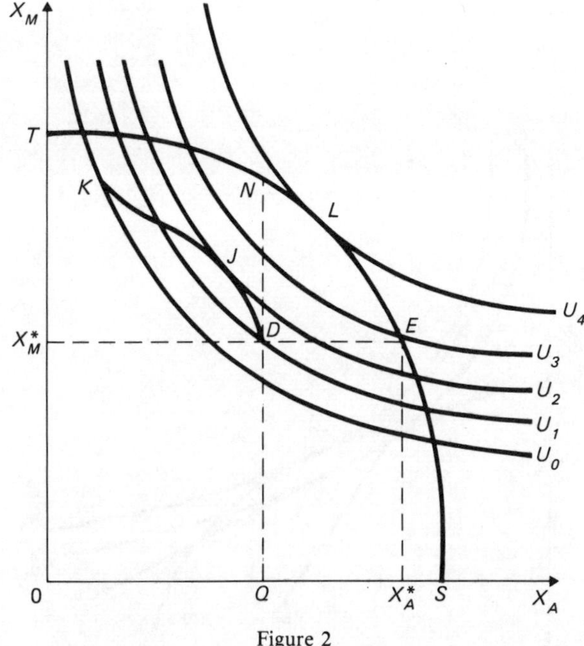

Figure 2

move to point L on the production possibilities frontier which, with the posited social indifference map, is the optimum position. Welfare would be increased from a level U_1 to a higher level U_4.

In the context of our model, such a point is unattainable. The effect of implementing a shadow wage will induce some additional migration from the rural sector and therefore agricultural output will fall. Hence, movement from D can only be in a northwest direction. The line DK in Figure 2 is the locus of all such attainable points, and it is evident that there is only one point, K, at which there can be full employment of the economy's labor resources. At that point the expected wage will be equal to the minimum wage since there is no urban unemployment. Therefore, the marginal product in agriculture will have to be equal to the minimum wage. But, with the subsidy, the marginal product of labor in manufacturing will be lower than in agriculture, hence K lies inside the production possibilities frontier. (In the extreme case in which marginal productivity in agriculture can never be as high as the minimum wage, K will coincide with T, the point of complete specialization in manufactures.) This situation will certainly not meet the conditions for a general optimum which can be met only at L. Thus, implementing a shadow wage criterion to the point that urban unemployment is eliminated will not generally be a desirable policy.

However, some level of wage subsidy will usually lead to an improvement. In Figure 2 it is clear that point J, with a welfare level U_2, will be preferable to D. The criterion for welfare maximization is the following:

$$f' = Pq' \left(\frac{dN_u}{dN_M}\right) \tag{12}$$

Note what this means. Creating one additional job in the industrial sector increases output by f' but, since increased employment will raise the expected urban wage, migration will be induced in an amount dN_u/dN_M. The right-hand side of equation (12) states the amount of agricultural output sacrificed because of migration. Thus the shadow wage will be equal to this opportunity cost of an urban job and the amount of subsidy will be $W_M—f'$. So long as $f' > Pq'(dN_u/dN_M)$, aggregate welfare can be increased by expanding industrial employment through subsidy or public sector hiring. Clearly the more responsive is migration to industrial employment, the higher is the social cost of industrialization and the smaller is the optimal amount of subsidy. In many African economies it is likely that dN_u/dN_M exceeds unity. If so, it will be optimal for the marginal product of labor in industry to be higher than in agriculture and urban unemployment will be a persistent phenomenon so long as minimum wages are set above a market-clearing level.

The discussion so far has ignored two other adverse effects of using a shadow wage. As mentioned earlier, several writers have noted that payment of a subsidized minimum wage to additional workers will increase total consumption, thereby reducing the level of resources available for investment. If foregone future consumption is positively valued, the opportunity cost of industrial labor will be higher than indicated in equation (12) and the shadow wage will be raised correspondingly. Furthermore, wage subsidies or public enterprise losses must be financed and if revenue cannot be raised through costless lump sum taxes, the opportunity cost of raising taxes must be considered. Both of these effects will reduce the desirable amount of subsidized job creation in the industrial sector.

It is interesting to note that this model implies different opportunity costs of labor to the two sectors. While the creation of an additional job in the urban area reduces agricultural output through induced migration, additional employment can be generated in the agricultural sector without reducing manufacturing output. If this phenomenon is not taken into account, standard application of investment criteria is likely to be biassed in favor of urban projects.

B. *Migration restriction*

An alternative approach to the problem of urban unemployment is to physically control migration from the rural areas. Such controls have recently been introduced in Tanzania and have been used for some time in

South Africa. Other countries, such as Kenya, are giving serious consideration to instituting such a policy. Although we personally have grave reservations about the ethical issues involved in such a restriction of individual choice, and the complexity and arbitrariness of administration, it seems desirable to investigate the economic implications of such a policy.

Looking at Figure 2 it is obvious that with the minimum wage such that industrial output is OX_M^*, prohibition of migration in excess of the labor required to produce that output will allow the economy to produce at point E. The movement from D to E arising from the restriction of migration leads to an unambiguous aggregate welfare improvement providing appropriate lump-sum redistribution is effected. Since such compensation is notoriously difficult to carry out in practice, it will be useful to examine the welfare implications of such a move on each of the two sectors in the absence of compensation.

Recall that the two sectors were defined to be a permanent urban group and a rural sector that produces both agricultural goods and exports labor to the urban area in exchange for wages in the form of manufactured goods.[4] In Figure 3 the line $T'S'$ represents production possibilities for the agricultural sector when labor export is allowed. If its entire labor endowment is devoted to agricultural production, it can produce a quantity OS'. However, by exporting its labor, the agricultural sector can 'produce' the manufactured good (wages are paid in the form of this good). Hence this production possibilities frontier depends on market forces (wage levels and unemployment) as well as on purely technological factors. The amount of agricultural output foregone if a unit of labor is to be 'exported' is its marginal product; the amount of manufactured goods obtained by the exported labor unit depends on the wage, the amount of employment obtained by the exported unit, and its effect on employment of previously exported units.

In addition to these production possibilities, the rural sector also has the opportunity to trade some of its agricultural output with the permanent urban sector in exchange for manufactured goods. Corresponding to each point on the production possibilities frontier $T'S'$, there is a determinate price of the agricultural good. The manner in which alternative constellations of production and trade affect the sector's welfare can be illustrated by Figure 3.

D' corresponds to the initial unemployment equilibium D (Figure 2). At that point the rural sector as a whole 'produces' $X_A{}^0$ and $X_M{}^0$ of the two goods. It also has the opportunity to trade at the price P^0. By trading some of its agricultural output to the permanent urban sector for additional manufactured goods, it consumes $\hat{X}_A{}^0$, $\hat{X}_M{}^0$ and achieves a welfare level of U_1^R. Restriction of migration results in the sector's producing $X_A{}'\ X_M{}'$. If it could still trade at price P^0, the agricultural sector would clearly be better off. But this is

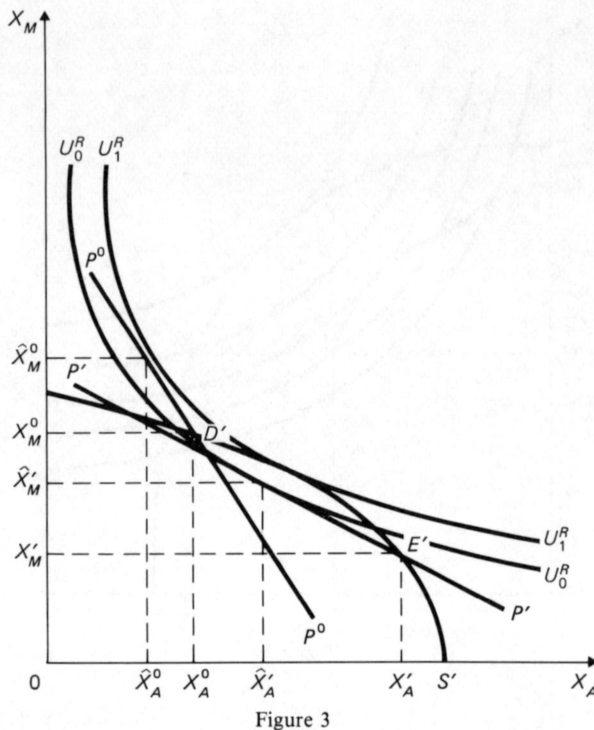

Figure 3

impossible. At E' (which corresponds to E in Figure 2), the price of agricultural good will fall to P' and with trade the best consumption bundle attainable by the sector is $\hat{X}_A$, $\hat{X}_M$ which corresponds to a lower level of welfare U_0^R. (Note that if P' did not cut $T'S'$ there could be no incentive to migrate at E'.)

It can be shown that $Pq'\ (1 - 1/\eta)$ (where η is the price elasticity of demand for the agricultural good) is the amount of the manufactured good sacrificed by the rural sector as a result of removing one worker from producing the agricultural good which could have been exchanged for the manufactured good at the market price $1/P$. This quantity is less than the value of labor's marginal product in agriculture (Pq'), since the reduction in output has a favorable terms-of-trade effect. If the demand for the agriculture good is inelastic (η<1) we reach the startling conclusion that the sacrifice becomes negative! This is, of course, the familiar proposition that aggregate farm income may be increased by reducing output. The *direct* gain in manufactured goods achieved by the rural sector through exporting an additional unit of labor is $\overline{W}_M N_M / N_u$, the expected urban wage. But additional migration, by increasing unemployment, reduces the earnings of *all* migrants already in the urban labor force by a factor $(1 - R)$, where R is the fraction of the total urban labor force supplied by the rural sector.

As long as $Pq'\ (1 - \eta) < \overline{W}_M N_M / N_u\ (1 - R)$ the welfare of the rural sector will be increased by allowing migration even though unemployment ensues and the economy as a whole sacrifices output. Since Pq' and $\overline{W}_M N_M/N_u$ are always positive and $R \leq 1$, additional migration will always benefit the rural sector when $\eta < 1$. In general, the lower is Pq', η, or R and the higher is $\overline{W}_M N_M/N_u$, the more will the rural sector benefit from the opportunity to migrate.

From the foregoing, one can conclude that although migration restriction will improve aggregate welfare of the economy, given plausible values of η and R, substantial compensation to the rural sector will be required if it is not to be made worse off by removing the opportunity for free migration. The permanent urban labor force clearly will be made better off by becoming fully employed at the high minimum wage while also being able to buy food at a lower price. Each unit of labor exported by the rural sector will similarly earn more, but this gain will be offset by reduced total labor exports and lower agricultural prices. Whether or not this will be true depends, of course, on the values of the specific parameters of the economy. If η is sufficiently high, the rural sector could be made better off by restricting migration in the absence of compensation, but this seems very unlikely.

C. *A combination of policies*

It has been shown that either a limited wage subsidy or a migration-restriction policy will lead to a welfare improvement. Which of the two policies will lead to the better position cannot be determined without knowing all the relevant parameters for a particular economy. It is clear, however, that neither policy alone is capable of moving the economy to the optimum that could be achieved with competitive wage determination (point L in Figure 2).

At first sight it may seem strange that with a single market failure, the wage level, a single policy instrument is unable to fully correct the situation. The reason is that the wage performs two functions in this model. It determines *both* the level of employment in the industrial sector *and* the allocation of labor between rural and urban areas. While a subsidy changes the effective wage for determination of industrial employment, so long as the wage actually received by workers exceeds agricultural earnings there will be migration and urban unemployment. Restriction of migration prevents the minimum wage having its effect on unemployment but does nothing to increase the level of industrial employment. Therefore, if the optimum position is to be achieved, a combination of both instruments will have to be used. In order to reach point L a wage subsidy must be instituted such that industrial employment will increase to the extent that with full employment the marginal product of labor will be equal in manufacturing and agriculture. The subsidy will be positive and equal to the difference between the minimum wage and marginal productivity. At that point $W_u^e = \overline{W}_M$ and $\overline{W}_M > Pq'$. Therefore, individuals would still find it in their interest to migrate and the point will not be attainable unless migration is restricted.

The agricultural sector has to be better off at L than at E since each additional unit of labor exported earns the full minimum wage, marginal productivity in agriculture is less than the minimum wage, and the price of the agricultural good rises. Whether the agricultural sector is better off at L than at D, however, depends again on the parametric values of the model. It can be stated with certainty that the amount of compensation needed to make the rural sector *no worse off* than at D will be less at L than at E, and furthermore it should be easier to finance since total income is greater.

Even so the fiscal requirements of subsidy (or public enterprise losses) and compensation cannot be taken lightly. A government may find it difficult to find non-distorting taxes capable of raising sufficient revenue. Perhaps a head-tax on all urban residents would be feasible, although this too raises the question of how minimum wages are set (unions in tropical Africa have, in some cases, successfully fought to maintain the real after-tax wage). A tax on rural land is ruled out if there must be *net* compensation to the rural sector which, in the absence of pure profits in manufacturing, leaves an urban land tax as the remaining potential ideal tax.

All of the above suggests that altering the minimum wage may avoid the problems of taxation, administration, and interference with individual mobility attendant to the policy package just discussed. Income and wages policies designed to narrow the rural-urban wage gap have been suggested by D. P. Ghai, and Tanzania has formally adopted such a policy along with migration restriction. In the final analysis, however, the basic issue at stake is really one of political feasibility, and it is not at all clear that an incomes policy is any more feasible than the alternatives.

Notes: Reading 12

1 For some empirical evidence on the magnitude of these real earnings differentials in less developed economies, see Reynolds, Berg, Henderson, and Ghai.

2 $\Psi(0) = 0$ is purely arbitrary. If, instead, we assume $\Psi(\alpha) = 0$ where α can take on any value, migration will cease when the urban-rural expected wage differential is equal to α. None of the subsequent analysis is affected qualitatively by specifying $\alpha = 0$. Equation (8) would merely be written as $W_A + \alpha = W_u^e$.

3 If $dN_A/dN_M < 0$, which we believe to be empirically unlikely, this statement would have to be modified. In such a case, increasing the minimum wage will decrease manufacturing employment but will increase agricultural employment and output. Unemployment will result from the imposition of a minimum wage, but we can no longer assert that the level of unemployment will increase concomitantly with the level of the minimum wage.

4 In considering the welfare of the rural sector as a whole we are making the tacit assumption that there is redistribution

of goods between individuals in this sector. This is a very strong assumption. Yet there is considerable evidence from tropical Africa that employed urban migrants repatriate substantial portions of their earnings to their kinsmen remaining in the rural areas, and conversely that income both in cash and kind is received by unemployed migrants from kinsmen remaining on the farm. To the extent that the extended family system does redistribute goods between members, this assumption may be tenable as a first approximation. As Gugler (1968, p. 480) has pointed out, it is appropriate to view the extended family as maximising its income by allocating its members between agriculture and urban wage employment. Although there is some evidence that growing numbers of urban workers are settling permanently and gradually eliminating rural ties, it will be many years before such ties are completely severed.

References: Reading 12

Bardham, P. K. (1964), 'Factor market disequilibrium and the theory of protection', *Oxford Econ. Pap.*, new series, no. 16, October, pp. 375–88.

Berg, E. J. (1969), 'Wage structure in less developed countries', in A. D. Smith (ed.), *Wage Policy Issues in Economic Development* (London).

Callaway, A. (1965), 'From traditional crafts to modern industries', *ODU, University of Ife Journal of African Studies*, no. 2, July.

Chakravarty, S. (1964), 'The use of shadow prices in programme evaluation', in Rosenstein–Rodan (ed.), *Capital Formation and Economic Development* (London).

Cho, Y. S. (1960), *Disguised Unemployment in Developing Areas, with Special Reference to South Korean Agriculture* (Berkeley, Calif.).

Eckaus, R. S. (1955), 'The factor-proportions problem in underdeveloped areas', *Amer. Econ. Rev.*, no. 45, September, pp. 539–65.

Erickson, J. (1969), 'Wage employment relationships in Latin American industry: a pilot study of Argentina, Brazil, and Mexico', International Labour Office, typescript.

Fei, J., and Ranis, G. (1964), *Development of the Labor Surplus Economy* (Illinois).

Ghai, D. P. (1968), 'Incomes policy in Kenya: need, criteria and machinery', *East Afr. Econ. Rev.*, no. 4, June, pp. 19–35.

Gugler, J. (1968), 'The impact of labour migration on society and economy in sub-Saharan Africa. Empirical findings and theoretical considerations', *African Social Research*, no. 6, December, pp. 463–86.

Hagen, E. E. (1958), 'An economic justification of protectionism', *Quart. J. Econ.*, no. 72, November, pp. 496–514.

Harris, J. R., and Todaro, M. P. (1968), 'Urban unemployment in east Africa: an economic analysis of policy alternatives', *East Afr. Econ. Rev.*, no. 4, December, pp. 17–36.

Harris, J. R., and Todaro, M. P. (1969), 'Wages, industrial employment, and labour productivity: the Kenyan experience', *East Afr. Econ. Rev.*, new series, no. 1, June, pp. 29–46.

Henderson, J. P. (1968), 'Wage policy in Africa', paper prepared for delivery at the African Conference on Economics, Temple University, April, mimeo.

Hutton, C. R. (1969), 'The causes of labour migration', in Gugler (ed.), *Urbanization in Sub-Saharan Africa* (Kampala).

Kao, C. H. C., Anschel, K. R., and Eicher, C. K. (1964), 'Disguised unemployment in agriculture: a survey', in C. K. Eicher and L. W. Witt (eds), *Agriculture in Economic Development* (New York), pp. 129–44 (Reading 8).

Katz, J. M. (1968), 'Verdoorn effects; returns to scale, and the elasticity of factor substitution', *Oxford Econ. Pap.*, no. 20, November, pp. 342–52.

Lefeber, L. (1968), 'Planning in a surplus labor economy', *Amer. Econ. Rev.*, no. 58, June, pp. 343–73.

Lewis, W. A. (1954), 'Economic development with unlimited supplies of labour', *Manchester Sch. Econ. Soc. Stud.*, no. 22, May, pp. 139–91.

Little, I. M. D. (1964), 'The real cost of labour, and the choice between consumption and investment', in P. N. Rosenstein–Rodan (ed.), *Pricing and Fiscal Policies: A Study in Method* (Cambridge), pp. 77–91.

Little, I. M. D., and Mirrlees, J. A. (1969), *Manual of Industrial Project Analysis, Vol. II, Social Cost Benefit Analysis* (Paris).

Massell, B. F., and Heyer, J. (1969), 'Household expenditure in Nairobi: a statistical analysis of consumer behaviour', *Econ. Develop. Cult. Change*, no. 17, January, pp. 212–34.

Nigeria, *Report of the Commission on the Review of Wages, Salary and Conditions of Service of the Junior Employees of the Governments of the Federation and in Private Establishments 1963–64*.

Reynolds, L. G. (1965), 'Wages and employment in a labor-surplus economy', *Amer. Econ. Rev.*, no. 55, March, pp. 19–39.

Stolper, W. F. (1966), *Planning Without Facts: Lessons in Resource Allocation from Nigeria's Development* (Cambridge).

Todaro, M. P. (1969), 'A model of labor migration and urban unemployment in less developed countries', *Amer. Econ. Rev.*, no. 59, March, pp. 138–48.

Part Three

Trade and Investment

Much of development economics is in fact concerned with strategies for development agriculture or industry, balanced or unbalanced growth, import substitution or export promotion – or 'tactics' for development, as one might describe policy choices regarding tax systems, interest rates and educational structures. However, choice of strategy and tactics as above depends first and foremost on views held regarding the existing international pattern of specialisation and division of labour, and the extent to which it is desirable to attempt structural transformation at the national level alongside fundamental change at the international level. Accordingly, theoretical and applied analysis of the effects of trade on the position and prospects of the less developed countries might be said now to provide the theoretical core of development economics itself: hence this substantial section focusing on international trade theory. The papers by Myint (Reading 13), Flanders (covering Prebisch's theory, Reading 14) and Evans (Reading 15) all review and criticise the theory of comparative advantage from either more or less radical viewpoints. Apart from the pattern of trade, developing countries have been concerned with the long-run terms of trade (Reading 16) and the short-term stability of trade prices (Reading 17). Particularly with the rise of the transnational company (Reading 19), however, it is no longer satisfactory to separate issues of international trade from those of international investment, dependency (Reading 18) being a product of both.

Trade and Investment

Reading 13

The 'Classical Theory' of International Trade and Underdeveloped Countries

H. Myint

Economic Journal, vol. 68, 1958.

There has recently been a considerable amount of controversy concerning the applicability of the 'classical theory' of international trade to the underdeveloped countries.[1] The twists in this controversy may be set out as follows. The critics start with the intention of showing that the 'nineteenth-century pattern' of international trade, whereby the underdeveloped countries export raw materials and import manufactured goods, has been unfavourable to the economic development of these countries. But instead of trying to show this directly, the concentrate their attacks on the 'classical theory' which they believe to be responsible for the unfavourable pattern of trade. The orthodox economists then come to the defence of the classical theory by reiterating the principle of comparative costs which they claim to be applicable both to the developed and the underdeveloped countries. After this, the controversy shifts from the primary question whether or not the nineteenth-century pattern of international trade, as a historical reality, has been unfavourable to the underdeveloped countries to the different question whether or not the theoretical model assumed in the comparative-costs analysis is applicable to these countries. Both sides then tend to conduct their argument as though the two questions were the same and to identify the 'classical theory' with the comparative-costs theory.

It will be argued in this paper that this has led to the neglect of those other elements in the classical theory of international trade which are much nearer to the realities and ideologies of the nineteenth-century expansion of international trade to the underdeveloped countries.

1

The neglected elements in the classical theory of international trade may be traced to Adam Smith (1776), particularly to the following key passage in the *Wealth of Nations.*

> Between whatever places foreign trade is carried on, they all of them derive two distinct benefits from it. It carries out that surplus part of the produce of their land and labour for which there is no demand among them, and brings back in return for it something else for which there is a demand. It gives a value to their superfluities, by exchanging them for something else, which may satisfy a part of their wants, and increase their enjoyments. By means of it, the narrowness of the home market does not hinder the division of labour in any particular branch of art or manufacture from being carried to the highest perfection. By opening a more extensive market for whatever part of the produce of their labour may exceed the home consumption, it encourages them to improve its productive powers, and to augment its annual produce to the utmost, and thereby to increase the real revenue and wealth of society (vol. I, p. 413).

There are two leading ideas here. Firstly, international trade overcomes the narrowness of the home market and provides an outlet for the surplus product above domestic requirements. This develops into what may be called the 'vent for surplus' theory of international trade. Later we hope to remove some of the prejudice aroused by this 'mercantilist' sounding phrase. Secondly, by widening the extent of the market, international trade also improves the division of labour and raises the general level of productivity within the country. This develops into what may be called the 'productivity' theory. We shall be mainly concerned with the 'vent for surplus' theory and the light it throws upon the growth of international trade in the underdeveloped countries in the nineteenth century. But first it is necessary to consider the 'productivity' theory briefly.

The 'productivity' doctrine differs from the comparative-costs doctrine in the interpretation of 'specialization' for international trade.

1 In the comparative-costs theory 'specialization' merely means a movement along a static 'production possibility curve' constructed on the given resources and the *given techniques* of the trading country. In contrast, the 'productivity' doctrine looks upon international trade as a dynamic force which, by widening the extent of the market and the scope of the division of labour, raises the skill and dexterity of the workmen, encourages technical innovations, overcomes technical indivisibilities and generally enables the trading country to enjoy increasing returns and economic development.[2] This distinction was clearly realized by J. S. Mill, who regarded the gains in terms of comparative-costs theory as direct gains and the gains in terms of Adam Smithian increases in productivity as 'indirect effects, which must be counted as benefits of a high order'. Mill even went on to extend this doctrine to countries at 'an early stage of industrial advancement', where international trade by introducing new wants 'sometimes works a sort of industrial revolution' (1848, p. 581).

2 In the comparative-costs theory 'specialization', conceived as a reallocation of resources, is a completely reversible process. The Adam Smithian process of specialization, however, involves adapting and reshaping the productive structure of a country to meet the export demand, and is therefore not easily reversible. This means that a country specializing for the export market is more vulnerable to changes in the terms of trade than is allowed for in the comparative-costs theory. We shall come back to this point later.

In the expansive mental climate of the late nineteenth century the 'productivity' aspect of international specialization completely dominated the 'vulnerability' aspect. At a semi-popular level, and particularly in its application to the underdeveloped countries, Smith's 'productivity' doctrine developed beyond a free-trade argument into an export-drive argument. It was contended that since international trade was so beneficial in raising productivity and stimulating economic development, the State should go beyond a neutral and negative policy of removing barriers to trade and embark on a positive policy of encouraging international trade and economic development. Under its influence, many colonial governments went far beyond the strict *laissez-faire* policy in their attempts to promote the export trade of the colonies. Further, although these governments were frequently obliged to use 'unclassical' methods, such as the granting of monopolistic privileges to the chartered companies or the taxing of the indigenous people to force them to take up wage labour or grow cash crops, they nevertheless sought to justify their policy by invoking the Adam Smithian doctrine of the benefits of international division of labour. This partly explains why some critics have associated the 'classical theory' with 'colonialism' and why they have frequently singled out Adam Smith for attack instead of Ricardo, the founder of the official classical free-trade theory.

It is fair to say that Smith's 'productivity' doctrine is instructive more in relation to the ideological than to the actual economic forces which characterized the nineteenth-century expansion of international trade to the underdeveloped countries. It is true, as we shall see later, that both the total value and the physical output of the exports of these countries expanded rapidly. In many cases the rate of increase in export production was well above any possible rate of increase in population, resulting in a considerable rise in output per head. But it is still true to say that this was achieved not quite in the way envisaged by Smith, namely, a better division of labour and specialization leading on to innovations and cumulative improvements in skills and productivity per man-hour. Rather, the increase in output per head seems to have been due to once-and-for-all increases in productivity accompanying the transfer of labour from the subsistence economy to the mines and plantations, and secondly, what is more important, as we shall see later, to an increase in working hours and in the proportion of gainfully employed labour relatively to the semi-idle labour of the subsistence economy.

The transfer of labour from the subsistence economy to the mines and plantations with their much higher capital–output ratio and skilled management undoubtedly resulted in a considerable increase in productivity. But this was mostly of a once-and-for-all character for a number of reasons. To begin with, the indigenous labour emerging from the subsistence economy was raw and technically backward. Moreover, it was subject to high rates of turnover, and therefore not amenable to attempts to raise productivity. Unfortunately, this initial experience gave rise to or hardened the convention of 'cheap labour', which regarded indigenous labour merely as an undifferentiated mass of low-grade man-power to be used with a minimum of capital outlay (see Frankel, 1938, pp. 142–6, and Macmillan, 1940, pp. 48–50). Thus when the local labour supply was exhausted the typical reaction was not to try to economize labour by installing more machinery and by reorganizing methods of production but to seek farther afield for additional supplies of cheap labour. This is why the nineteenth-century process of international trade in the underdeveloped countries was characterized by large-scale movements of cheap labour from India and China (see Knowles, 1924, pp. viii, 182–201). This tendency was reinforced by the way in which the world-market demand for raw materials expanded in a series of waves. During the booms, output had to be expanded as quickly as possible along existing lines, and there was no time to introduce new techniques or reorganize production; during the slumps it was difficult to raise capital for such purposes.

This failure to achieve Adam Smith's ideal of specialization leading on to continuous improvements in skills can also be observed in the peasant export sectors. Where the export crop happened to be a traditional crop, e.g. rice in south-east Asia, the expansion in export production was achieved simply by bringing more land under cultivation with the same methods of cultivation used in the subsistence economy. Even where new export crops were introduced, the essence of their success as peasant export crops was that they could be produced by fairly simple methods involving no radical departure from the traditional techniques of production employed in subsistence agriculture.[3]

Thus instead of a process of economic growth based on continuous improvements in skills, more productive recombinations of factors and increasing returns, the nineteenth-century expansion of international trade in the underdeveloped countries seems to approximate to a simpler process based on constant returns and fairly rigid combinations of factors. Such a process of expansion could continue smoothly only if it could feed on *additional* supplies of factors in the required proportions.

2

Let us now turn to Smith's 'vent for surplus' theory of international trade. It may be contrasted with the comparative-costs theory in two ways.

1 The comparative-costs theory assumes that the resources of a country are given and fully employed before it enters into international trade. The function of trade is then to reallocate its given resources more efficiently between domestic and export production in the light of the new set of relative supply functions. With given techniques and full employment, export production can be increased only at the cost of reducing the domestic production. In contrast, the demand function theory assumes that a previously isolated country about to enter into international trade possesses a surplus productive capacity of some sort or another. The function of trade here is not so much to reallocate the given resources as to provide the *new effective demand* for the output of the surplus resources which would have remained unused in the absence of trade. It follows that export production can be increased without necessarily reducing domestic production.

2 The concept of a surplus productive capacity above the requirements of domestic consumption implies an inelastic domestic demand for the exportable commodity and/or a considerable degree of internal immobility and specificness of resources. In contrast, the comparative-costs theory assumes either a perfect or, at least, a much greater degree of internal mobility of factors and/or a greater degree of flexibility or elasticity both on the side of production and of consumption. Thus the resources not required for export production will not remain as a surplus productive capacity, but will be reabsorbed into domestic production, although this might take some time and entail a loss to the country.

These two points bring out clearly a peculiarity of the 'vent-for-surplus' theory which may be used either as a free-trade argument or as an anti-trade argument, depending on the point of view adopted. From the point of view of a previously isolated country about to enter into trade, a surplus productive capacity suitable for the export market appears as a virtually 'costless' means of acquiring imports and expanding domestic economic activity. This was how Adam Smith used it as a free-trade argument. From the point of view of an established trading country faced with a fluctuating world market, a sizeable surplus productive capacity which cannot be easily switched from export to domestic production makes it 'vulnerable' to external economic disturbances. This is in fact how the present-day writers on the underdeveloped countries use the same situation depicted by Smith's theory as a criticism of the nineteenth-century pattern of international trade. This concept of vulnerability may be distinguished from that which we have come across in discussing the 'productivity' theory of trade. There, a country is considered 'vulnerable' because it has adapted and reshaped its productive structure to meet the requirements of the export market through a genuine process of 'specialization'. Here, the country is considered 'vulnerable' simply because it happens to possess a sizeable surplus productive capacity which (even without any improvements and extensions) it cannot use for domestic production. This distinction may be blurred in border-line cases, particularly in underdeveloped countries with a large mining sector. But we hope to show that, on the whole, while the 'vulnerability' of the advanced countries, such as those in western Europe which have succeeded in building up large export trades to maintain their large populations, is of the first kind, the 'vulnerability' of most of the underdeveloped countries is of the second kind.

Let us now consider the 'vent-for-surplus' approach purely as a theoretical tool. There is a considerable amount of prejudice among economists against the 'vent-for-surplus' theory, partly because of its technical crudeness and partly because of its mercantilist associations. This may be traced to J. S. Mill, who regarded Smith's 'vent-for-surplus' doctrine as 'a surviving relic of the Mercantile Theory' (1848, p. 579).

The crux of the matter here is the question: why should a country isolated from international trade have a surplus productive capacity? The answer which suggests itself is that, given its random combination of natural resources, techniques of production, tastes and population, such an isolated country is bound to suffer from a certain imbalance or disproportion between its productive and consumption capacities. Thus, take the case of a country which starts with a sparse population in relation to its natural resources. This was broadly true not only of Western countries during their mercantilist period but also of the underdeveloped countries of south-east Asia, Latin America and Africa when they were opened up to international trade in the nineteenth century. Given this situation, the conventional international-trade theory (in its Ohlin version) would say that this initial disproportion between land and labour would have been equilibrated away by appropriate price adjustments, i.e. rents would be low and, relatively, land-using commodities would have low prices, whereas wages would be high and relatively labour-using commodities would have high prices. In equilibrium there would be no surplus productive capacity (although there might be surplus land by itself) because the scarce factor, labour, would have been fully employed. Thus when this country enters into international trade it can produce the exports only by drawing labour away from domestic production. Now this result is obtained only by introducing a highly developed price mechanism and economic organization into a country which is supposed to have had no previous economic contacts with the outside world. This procedure may be instructive while dealing with the isolated economy as a theoretical model. But it is misleading when we are dealing with genuinely isolated economies in their proper historical setting; it is misleading, in particular, when we are dealing with the underdeveloped countries, many of which were subsistence economies when they were opened to international trade. In fact, it was the growth of international trade itself which introduced or extended the money economy in these countries. Given the genuine historical setting of an isolated economy, might not its initial disproportion between its resources, techniques, tastes and population show itself in the form of surplus productive capacity?

Adam Smith himself thought that the pre-existence of a surplus productive capacity in an isolated economy was such a matter of common observation that he assumed it implicitly without elaborating upon it. But he did give some hints suggesting how the 'narrowness of the home market', which causes the surplus capacity, is bound up with the underdeveloped economic organization of an isolated country, particularly the lack of a good internal transport system and of suitable investment opportunities.[4] Further, his concept of surplus productive capacity is not merely a matter of surplus land by itself but surplus land combined with surplus labour; and the surplus labour is then linked up with his concept of 'unproductive' labour. To avoid confusion this latter should not be identified with the modern concept of 'disguised unemployment' caused by an acute shortage of land in overpopulated countries. Although Smith described some cases of genuine 'disguised unemployment' in the modern sense, particularly with reference to China, 'unproductive' labour in his sense can arise even in thinly populated countries, provided their internal economic organization is sufficiently underdeveloped. In fact, it is especially in relation to those underdeveloped countries which started off with sparse populations in relation to their natural resources that we shall find Smith's 'vent-for-surplus' approach very illuminating.

3

Let us now try to relate the 'vent-for-surplus' theory to the nineteenth-century process of expansion of international trade to the underdeveloped countries. Even from the somewhat meagre historical information about these countries, two broad features stand out very clearly. Firstly, the underdeveloped countries of south-east Asia, Latin America and Africa, which were to develop into important export economies, started off with sparse populations relatively to their natural resources. If North America and Australia could then be described as 'empty', these countries were at least 'semi-empty'. Secondly, once the opening-up process had got into its stride, the export production of these countries expanded very rapidly, along a typical growth curve,[5] rising very sharply to begin with and tapering off afterwards. By the Great Depression of the 1930s, the expansion process seems to have come to a stop in many countries; in others, which had a later start, the expansion process may still be continuing after the Second World War.

There are three reasons why the 'vent-for-surplus' theory offers a more effective approach than the conventional theory to this type of expansion of international trade in the underdeveloped countries.

1 The characteristically high rates of expansion which can be observed in the export production of many underdeveloped countries cannot really be explained in terms of the comparative-costs theory based on the assumption of given resources and given techniques. Nor can we attribute any significant part of the expansion to revolutionary changes in techniques and increases in productivity. As we have seen in section 1, peasant export production expanded by extension of cultivation using traditional methods of production, while mining and plantation sectors expanded on the basis of increasing supplies of cheap labour with a minimum of capital outlay. Thus the contributions of Western enterprise to the expansion process are mainly to be found in two spheres: the improvements of transport and communications[6] and the discoveries of new mineral resources. Both are methods[7] of increasing the total volume of resources rather than methods of making the given volume of resources more productive. All these factors suggest an expansion process which kept itself going by drawing an increasing volume of hitherto unused or surplus resources into export production.

2 International trade between the tropical underdeveloped countries and the advanced countries of the temperate zone has grown out of sharp differences in

geography and climate resulting in absolute differences of costs. In this context, the older comparative-costs theory, which is usually formulated in terms of qualitative differences (see Viner, 1953, pp. 14–16) in the resources of the trading countries, tends to stress the obvious geographical differences to the neglect of the more interesting quantitative differences in the factor endowments of countries possessing approximately the same type of climate and geography. Thus while it is true enough to say that Burma is an exporter of rice because of her climate and geography, the more interesting question is why Burma should develop into a major rice exporter while the neighbouring south India, with approximately the same type of climate and geography, should develop into a net importer of rice. Here the 'vent-for-surplus' approach which directs our attention to population density as a major determinant of export capacity has an advantage over the conventional theory.

3 Granted the importance of quantitative differences in factor endowments, there still remains the question why Smith's cruder 'vent-for-surplus' approach should be preferable to the modern Ohlin variant of the comparative-costs theory. The main reason is that, according to the Ohlin theory, a country about to enter into international trade is supposed already to possess a highly developed and flexible economic system which can adjust its methods of production and factor combinations to cope with a wide range of possible variations in relative factor supplies (see section 2 above). but in fact the economic framework of the underdeveloped countries is a much cruder apparatus which can make only rough-and-ready adjustments. In particular, with their meagre technical and capital resources, the underdeveloped countries operate under conditions nearer to those of fixed technical coefficients than of variable technical coefficients. Nor can they make important adjustments through changes in the outputs of different commodities requiring different proportions of factors because of the inelastic demand both for their domestic production, mainly consisting of basic foodstuff, and for their exportable commodities, mainly consisting of industrial raw materials. Here again the cruder 'vent-for-surplus' approach turns out to be more suitable.

Our argument that, in general, the 'vent-for-surplus' theory provides a more effective approach than the comparative-costs theory to the international trade of the underdeveloped countries does not mean that the 'vent-for-surplus' theory will provide an exact fit to all the particular patterns of development in different types of export economies. No simple theoretical approach can be expected to do this. Thus if we interpret the concept of the surplus productive capacity strictly as pre-existing surplus productive capacity arising out of the original endowments of the factors, it needs to be qualified, especially in relation to the mining and plantation sectors of the underdeveloped countries. Here the surplus productive capacity which may have existed to some extent before the country was opened to international trade is usually greatly increased by the discovery of new mineral resources and by a considerable inflow of foreign capital and immigrant labour. While immigrant labour is the surplus population of other underdeveloped countries, notably India and China, the term 'surplus' in the strict sense cannot be applied to foreign capital. But, of course, the existence of suitable surplus natural resources in an underdeveloped country is a pre-condition of attracting foreign investment to it. Two points may be noted here. Firstly, the complication of foreign investment is not as damaging to the surplus-productive-capacity approach as it appears at first sight, because the inflow of foreign investment to the tropical and semi-tropical underdeveloped countries has been relatively small both in the nineteenth century and the inter-war period (see Nurkse, 1954, pp. 744–58, and the United Nations report on *International Capital Movements during the Inter-War Period*). Secondly, the nineteenth-century phenomenon of international mobility of capital and labour has been largely neglected by the comparative-costs theory, which is based on the assumption of perfect mobility of factors within a country and their imperfect mobility between different countries. The surplus-productive-capacity approach at least serves to remind us that the output of mining and plantation sectors can expand without necessarily contracting domestic subsistence output.

The use of the surplus-productive-capacity approach may prove in particular to be extremely treacherous in relation to certain parts of Africa, where mines, plantations and other European enterprises have taken away from the tribal economies the so-called 'surplus' land and labour, which, on a closer analysis, prove to be no surplus at all. Here the extraction of these so-called 'surplus' resources, by various forcible methods in which normal economic incentives play only a part, entails not merely a reduction in the subsistence output but also much heavier social costs in the form of the disruption of the tribal societies (see United Nations report on the *Enlargement of the Exchange Economy in Tropical Africa*, pp. 37, 49–51).

When we turn to the peasant export sectors, however, the application of the 'vent-for-surplus' theory is fairly straightforward. Here, unlike the mining and plantation sectors, there has not been a significant inflow of foreign investment and immigrant labour. The main function of the foreign export-import firms has been to act as middlemen between the world market and the peasants, and perhaps also to stimulate the peasants' wants for the new imported consumers' goods. As we have seen, peasant export production expanded by using methods of production more or less on the same technical level as those employed in the traditional subsistence culture. Thus the main effect of the innovations, such as improvements in transport and communications[7] and the introduction of the new crops, was to bring a greater area of surplus land under cultivation rather than to raise the physical productivity per unit of land and labour. Yet peasant export production usually managed to expand as rapidly as that of the other sectors while remaining self-sufficient with respect to basic food crops. Here, then, we have a fairly close approximation to the concept of a pre-existing surplus productive capacity which can be tapped by the world-market demand with a minimum addition of external resources.

Even here, of course, there is room for differences in interpretation. For instance, there is evidence to suggest that, in the early decades of expansion, the rates of increase in peasant export production in south-east Asian and west African countries were well above the possible rates of growth in their working population.[8] Given the conditions of constant techniques, no significant inflow of immigrant foreign labour and the continuing self-sufficiency with respect to the basic food crops, we are left with the question of how these peasant economies managed to obtain the extra labour required to expand their export production so rapidly. A part of this labour may have been released by the decline in cottage industries and by the introduction of modern labour-saving forms of transport in place of porterage, but the gap in the explanation cannot be satisfactorily filled until we postulate that even those peasant economies which started off with adequate land relatively for their population must have had initially a considerable amount of underemployed or surplus labour. This surplus labour existed, not because of a shortage of co-operating factors, but because in the subsistence economies, with poor transport and little specialisation in production, each self-sufficient economic unit could not find any market outlet to dispose of its potential surplus output, and had therefore no incentive to produce more than its own requirements. Here, then, we have the archetypal form of Smith's 'unproductive' labour locked up in a semi-idle state in the underdeveloped economy of a country isolated from outside economic contacts. In most peasant economies this surplus labour was mobilized, however, not by the spread of the money-wage system of employment, but by peasant economic units with their complement of 'family' labour moving *en bloc* into the money economy and export production.

The need to postulate a surplus productive capacity to explain the rapid expansion in peasant export production is further strengthened when we reflect on the implications of the fact that this expansion process is inextricably bound up with the introduction of the money economy into the subsistence sectors. To the peasant on the threshold of international trade, the question whether or not to take up export production was not merely a question of growing a different type of crop but a far-reaching decision to step into the new and unfamiliar ways of the money economy.

Thus let us consider a community of self-sufficient peasants who, with their existing techniques, have just sufficient land and labour to produce their minimum subsistence requirements, so that any export production can be achieved only by reducing the subsistence output below the minimum level. Now, according to the conventional economic theory, there is no reason why these peasants should not turn to export production if they have a differential advantage there, so that they could more than make up for their food deficit by purchases out of their cash income from the export crop. But, in practice, the peasants in this situation are unlikely to turn to export production so readily. Nor is this 'conservatism' entirely irrational, for by taking up export production on such a slender margin of reserves, the peasants would be facing the risk of a possible food shortage for the sake of some gain in the form of imported consumers' goods which are 'luxuries' to them. Moreover, this gain might be wiped off by unfavourable changes in the prices of both the export crop they would sell and the foodstuffs they would have to buy and by the market imperfections, which would be considerable at this early stage. Thus, where the margin of resources is very small above that required for the minimum subsistence output, we should expect the spread of export production to be inhibited or very slow, even if there were some genuine possibilities of gains on the comparative costs principle.

In contrast, the transition from subsistence agriculture to export production is made much easier when we assume that our peasants start with some surplus resources which enable them to produce the export crop *in addition* to their subsistence production. Here the surplus resources perform two functions: firstly, they enable the peasants to hedge their position completely and secure their subsistence minimum before entering into the risks of trading; and secondly, they enable them to look upon the imported goods they obtain from trade in the nature of a clear net gain obtainable merely for the effort of the extra labour in growing the export crop. Both of these considerations are important in giving the peasants just that extra push to facilitate their first plunge into the money economy.

Starting from this first group of peasants, we may picture the growth of export production and the money economy taking place in two ways. Firstly, the money economy may grow extensively, with improvements in transport and communications and law and order, bringing in more and more groups of peasants with their complements of family labour into export production on the same 'part-time' basis as the first group of peasants. Secondly, the money economy may grow intensively by turning the first group of peasants from 'part-time' into 'whole-time' producers of the export crop. In the first case, surplus resources are necessary as a lubricant to push more peasants into export production at each round of the widening circle of the money economy. Even in the second case, surplus resources are necessary if the whole-time export producers buy their food requirements locally from other peasants, who must then have surplus resources to produce the food crops above their own requirements. Logically, there is no reason why the first group of peasants who are now whole-time producers of the export crop should buy their food requirements locally instead of importing them. But, as it happens, few peasant export economies have specialized in export production to such an extent as to import their basic food requirements.

The average economist's reaction to our picture of discrete blocks of surplus productive capacity being drawn into a widening circle of money economy and international trade is to say that while this 'crude' analysis may be good enough for the transition phase, the conventional analysis in terms of differential advantages and continuous marginal productivity curves must come into its own once the transition phase is over. Here it is necessary to distinguish between the expansion phase and the transition phase. It is true in most peasant export economies the expansion process is tapering off or has come to a stop, as most of the surplus land suitable for the export crop has been brought under cultivation. This, of course, brings back the problem of allocating a fixed amount of resources, as we shall see in the next section when we consider issues of economic policy. But even so, the surplus-productive-capacity approach is not entirely superseded so long as the transition from a subsistence to a fully developed money economy remains incomplete. In most underdeveloped countries of Asia and Africa this transition seems not likely to be over until they cease to be underdeveloped.

The continuing relevance of the surplus-productive-capacity approach may be most clearly seen in the typical case of a peasant export economy which with its natural resources and methods of production has reached the limit of expansion in production while its population continues to grow rapidly. According to the surplus-productive-capacity approach, we should expect the export capacity of such a country to fall roughly in proportion as the domestic requirement of resources to feed a larger population increases. This common-sense result may, however, be contrasted with that obtainable from the conventional theory as formulated by Ohlin. Firstly, it appears that the Ohlin theory puts to the forefront of the picture the *type* of export, i.e. whether it is more labour-using or land-using as distinct from the total export capacity measured by the ratio of total exports to the total national output of the trading country. Secondly, in the Ohlin theory there is no reason why a thickly populated country should not also possess a high ratio of (labour-intensive) exports to its total output.

The ideal pattern of trade suggested by the Ohlin theory has a real counterpart in the thickly populated advanced countries of Europe, which for that very reason are obliged to build up a large export trade in manufactures or even in agriculture as in the case of Holland. But when we turn to the thickly populated underdeveloped countries, however, the ideal and the actual patterns of international trade diverge widely from each other. Indeed, we may say that these countries remain underdeveloped precisely because they have not succeeded in building up a labour-intensive export trade to cope with their growing population. The ratio of their export to total production could, of course, be maintained at the same level and the pressure of population met in some other way. But given the existing conditions, even this neutral pattern may not be possible in many underdeveloped countries. Thus, in Indonesia there is some evidence to suggest that the volume of agricultural exports from the thickly populated Java and Madura is declining absolutely and also relatively to those of the Outer Islands, which are still sparsely populated. Of course, there are other causes of this decline, but population pressure reducing the surplus productive capacity of Java seems to be a fundamental economic factor; and the decline spreads from peasant to plantation exports as more of the plantation lands, which were under sugar and rubber, are encroached upon by the peasants for subsistence production.[9] In general, given the social and economic conditions prevailing in many underdeveloped countries, it seems fair to conclude that the trend in their export trade is likely to be nearer to that suggested by the surplus-productive-capacity approach than to that suggested by the theory of comparative costs.

4

This paper is mainly concerned with interpretation and analysis, but we may round off our argument by touching briefly upon some of its policy implications.

We have seen that the effect of population pressure on many underdeveloped countries, given their existing social and economic organization, is likely to reduce their export capacity by diverting natural resources from export to subsistence production. If we assume that these natural resources have a genuine differential advantage in export production, then population pressure inflicts a double loss: firstly, through simple diminishing returns, and secondly, by diverting resources from more to less productive use. Thus, if Java has a genuine differential advantage in growing rubber and sugar, she would obtain a greater amount of rice by maintaining her plantation estates instead of allowing them to be encroached upon by peasants for subsistence rice cultivation. The orthodox liberal economists, confronted with this situation, would, of course, strongly urge the removal of artificial obstacles to a more systematic development of the money economy and the price system. Now there are still many underdeveloped countries which are suffering acutely from the economic rigidities arising out of their traditional social structure and/or from discriminatory policies based on differences in race, religion and class. Here the removal of barriers, for instance, to the horizontal and vertical mobility of labour, freedom to own land and to enter any occupation, etc., may well prove to be a great liberating force. But our analysis has suggested that it is much easier to promote the growth of the money economy in the early stage when a country is newly opened up to international trade and still has plenty of surplus land and labour rather than at a later stage, when there are no more surplus resources, particularly land, to feed the growth of the money economy.

We have seen that the rapid expansion in the export production of the underdeveloped countries in the nineteenth century cannot be satisfactorily explained without postulating that these countries started off with a considerable amount of surplus productive capacity consisting both of unused natural resources and underemployed labour. This gives us a common-sense argument for free trade which is especially relevant for the underdeveloped countries in the nineteenth century: the surplus productive capacity provided these countries with a virtually 'costless' means of acquiring imports which did not require a withdrawal of resources from domestic production but merely a fuller employment for their semi-idle labour. Of course, one may point to the real cost incurred by the indigenous peoples in the form of extra effort and sacrifice of the traditional leisurely life and also to the various social costs not normally considered in the comparative-costs theory, such as being sometimes subject to the pressure of taxation and even compulsory labour and frequently of having to accommodate a considerable inflow of immigrant labour creating difficult social and political problems later on. One may also point to a different type of cost which arises with the wasteful exploitation of natural resources. But for the most part it is still true to say that the indigenous peoples of the underdeveloped countries took to export production on a voluntary basis and enjoyed a clear gain by being able to satisfy their developing wants for the new imported commodities.

Notes: Reading 13

1 Of the very extensive literature on the subject, we may refer to two notable recent works, the first stating the orthodox position and the second the position of the critics: Viner (1953) and Myrdal (1956).

2 See Williams (1929, bk 1, chs 2 and 3). This aspect of Smith's theory has been made familiar by Professor Allyn Young (1928).

3 Thus A. McPhee (1926, pp. 39–40) wrote about the palm-oil and ground-nut exports of West Africa: 'They made little demand on the energy and thought of the natives and they effected no revolution in the society of West Africa. That was why they were so readily grafted on the old economy and grew as they did.' Some writers argue that there was a studied neglect of technical improvements in the peasant sector to facilitate the supply of cheap labour to other sectors. See, for example, Lewis (1954).

4 Smith (1776, Vol. I, pp. 21, 383).

5 For instance, the annual value of Burma's exports, taking years of high and low prices, increased at a constant proportional rate of 5 per cent per annum on the average between 1870 and 1900. Similar rates of expansion can be observed for Siam and Indonesia (see Furnivall, 1956, Appendix 1; Boeke, 1942, p. 184; and Ingram, 1955, Appendix C). African export economies started their expansion phase after 1900, and the official trade returns for the Gold Coast, Nigeria and Uganda show similar rates of increase after that date, although the expansion process was arrested by the depression of the 1930s.

6 This is what Professor Knowles (1924, pp. 138–52) described as the 'Unlocking of the Tropics'.

7 It may be noted that the expansion of some peasant export crops, notably rice in South-East Asia, depended to a much greater extent on pre-existing indigenous transport facilities, such as river boats and bullock carts, than is generally realized.

8 For instance, cocoa output of the Gold Coast expanded over forty times during the twenty-five year period 1905–30. Even higher rates of expansion in cocoa production can be observed in Nigeria, combined with a considerable expansion in the output of other export crops. Both have managed to remain self-sufficient with regard to basic food crops (see West African Institute of Economic Research, 1953, especially the chart between pp. 96 and 98; Perham, 1946, Vol. 1, pt 2). In lower Burma, for the thirty-year period 1870–1900, the area under rice cultivation increased by more than three times, while the population, including immigrants from upper Burma, doubled (see Furnivall, 1956, pp. 84–5).

9 The same tendency to transfer land from plantation to subsistence agriculture may be observed in Fiji with the growing population pressure created by the Indian immigrant labour originally introduced to work in the sugar plantations. The outline is blurred here by the decline in the sugar industry. The reason why this tendency does not seem to operate in the West Indies is complex. But it may be partly attributable to the tourist industry, which helps to pay for the food imports of some of the islands.

References: Reading 13

Bauer, P. T., and Yamey, B. S. (1951), 'Economic progress and occupational distribution', *Econ. J.*, vol. 61, December, p. 743.

Boeke, J. H. (1942), *The Structure of Netherlands Indian Economy* (Institute of Pacific Relations, New York).

Boeke, J. H. (1948), *Outwikkelingsgang en Toekomst van Bevolkings – en Ondernemingslandbouus in Nederlandsch-Indie* (Leiden).

Frankel, S. H. (1938), *Capital Investment in Africa* (Oxford University Press).

Furnivall, J. S. (1956), *Colonial Policy and Practice: A Comparative Study of Burma and Netherlands India* (Cambridge University Press).

Hazlewood, A. D. (1954), 'Economics of colonial monetary

arrangements', *Soc. Econ. Studies*, December (Jamaica).
Ingram, J. C. (1955), *Economic Change in Thailand since 1850* (Stanford University Press).
Knowles, L. C. A. (1924), *The Economic Development of the British Overseas Empire*, Vol. 1 (Routledge & Kegan Paul).
Lewis, W. A. (1954), 'Economic development with unlimited supplies of labour', *Manchester Sch. Econ. Soc. Studies*, vol. 22, May.
MacDougall, D. (1957), *The World Dollar Problem* (St Martin's Press).
Macmillan, W. M. (1940), *Europe and West Africa* (Oxford University Press).
McPhee, A. (1926), *The Economic Revolution in British West Africa*, Studies in Economic and Political Science, no. 89 (London School of Economics and Political Science).
Mill, J. S. (1848), *Principles* (Longman).
Myrdal, G. (1956), *An International Economy: Problems and Aspects* (Routledge & Kegan Paul).
Nurkse, R. (1954), 'International investment today in the light of nineteenth-century experience', *Econ. J.*, vol. 64, December.
Perham, M. (ed.) (1946), *The Native Economies of Nigeria* (Faber).
Robinson, J. (1956), *The Accumulation of Capital* (Macmillan).
Royal Commission (1953), *Report on East Africa* (HMSO).
Sidgwick, H. (1883), *Principles of Political Economy* (Macmillan), bk. 3, ch. 5.
Smith, A. (1776), *The Wealth of Nations*, 6th edn, ed. E. Cannan (Methuen, 1950).
UN (1949), *International Capital Movements during the Inter-War Period* (UN).
UN (1954), *Enlargement of the Exchange Economy in Tropical Africa* (UN).
Viner, J. (1953), *International Trade and Economic Development* (Clarendon Press).
West African Institute of Economic Research (1953), *Annual Conference* (Economic Section, Achimota).
Williams, J. H. (1929), 'The theory of international trade reconsidered', *Econ. J.*, vol. 39, June.
Williams, J. H. (1951), 'International trade theory and policy – some current issues', *Amer. Econ. Rev.*, papers and proceedings, vol. 41, no. 2.
Young, A. (1928), 'Increasing returns and economic progress', *Econ. J.*, vol. 38, December.

Prebisch on Protectionism: An Evaluation

M. J. Flanders

The Economic Journal, June 1964, pp. 305–26.

In the area of international trade and payments theories, one of the most important issues today, from the point of view of relevance to contemporary world problems and application to policy-making decision, is that of determining the optimum commercial policy of under-developed or, more euphemistically, 'developing' countries. Many professorial economists have addressed themselves to this problem, but none seems to have attracted as much attention among his colleagues nor have had so widespread an influence on thinking outside the profession as Professor Raul Prebisch, until recently the Executive Secretary of the United Nations Economic Commission for Latin America and presently Secretary-General of the United Nations Conference on Trade and Development. Because of the interest which his pronouncements have evoked, it is worth some time and effort to examine his arguments more thoroughly than has heretofore been done; for, interestingly enough, though his writings have been much discussed, most of this discussion revolves around only one part of his multi-faceted argument, and much of it stems from a misinterpretation of even that one part. In what follows we propose to discuss his work and to show that there is not one single 'Prebisch thesis' or model, but many, and that it is by no means obvious that they are consistent with one another.

It is usual to begin a critical evaluation of a writer's work by summarising it, but one of the implications of our contention that there are a number of 'Prebisch theses' is that his work, by its very nature, defies any attempt to present a single, simple, summary statement of it. There have, indeed, been many exegeses of his text, but in the main these have involved emphasis on one or two aspects of his argument, ignoring the others. It is necessary, therefore, to consider his arguments one by one. The discussion that follows will be based on the two well-known and oft-cited essays, which will be referred to as Prebisch I[1] and Prebisch II[2] respectively.

The most frequently heard view of Prebisch's thesis is that peripheral countries have experienced (and presumably will continue to experience) long-run deterioration in their terms of trade with the centre and that they should counteract this by imposing tariffs on industrial imports. Much of the discussion,[3] therefore, has dealt with the questions of whether in fact the terms of trade of the periphery did fall; and if they fell, what were the reasons for the decline (alleged differences in market structure between peripheral and central countries being the most oft-mentioned issue here). It should be noted, incidentally, that a careful reading of Prebisch shows him to be much less of an 'autarkist' than either his detractors or his supporters seem to think.

One of our purposes here is to discover what in the Prebisch model(s) would tend to cause a deterioration in the periphery's terms of trade. Another is to find the connection between the declining terms of trade and the protectionism he proposes. In other words, what precisely are the benefits which the periphery can be expected to reap from protectionism? In broad categories, there are three types of benefits which Prebisch seems to expect.

One is the 'rationing' effect. In Prebisch I this is closely tied in with the world-wide 'dollar shortage', so that tariffs are simply one method of rationing limited supplies of United States dollars (p. 3; Chapter III; Chapter IV). In 1950, of course, Prebisch was not the only economist who was misled into expecting the dollar shortage to continue for ever—or at least for a very long time. By Prebisch II the dollar shortage has dropped from the discussion, but he is still disturbed by the low import coefficient of the United States (p. 266) and the low capacity to import, because of inadequate foreign-exchange earnings, of the Latin American countries (p. 267). The high income elasticity of demand for imports into the periphery, combined with the low income elasticity of demand for imports into the centre, will force the periphery to achieve balance-of-payments equilibrium by either of the unattractive alternatives of growing more slowly than the centre, or of restraining its demand for imports, preferably by imposing tariffs.

Now, the latter alternative may well be the less unpleasant of the two, but a tariff system designed to ration scarce foreign exchange, not to decrease the total demand for imports, cannot be expected to cause an improvement in the terms of trade. At best it might slow down future deterioration in the terms of trade.[4]

This brings us to Prebisch's second type of benefit from protectionism, that of preventing further deterioration in the terms of trade (or reversing past losses?) by 'countervailance'. As we shall see, this raises a number of highly complicated issues regarding what Prebisch is really assuming as to market structure, income distribution and wage-rate determination in the periphery and the centre respectively. But there are also some 'macro' problems involved. The usual 'monopoly' argument for tariffs is presented in terms of a two-country model. Now, even if we assume, with Prebisch, that there is only one centre country and one peripheral country, and even if we assume that they are of roughly comparable economic size, we must recognise that in fact the centre's biggest customer is itself, not the periphery. That is, if we think of two 'countries', the centre and the periphery, 'domestic' demand will have a greater influence on the prices of export goods, relatively to foreign demand, in the centre than it will in the periphery. Hence, protection in the periphery cannot be expected to cause a significant reduction in the prices of its imports. Furthermore, Prebisch insists that protection should be highly 'selective' (Prebisch II, p. 257). But then the industrial product (or products) to be protected will be different in each peripheral country. Thus the 'countervailing' effects of the tariffs will be diffused among many industries in many countries of the centre, and will thus be even less likely to influence the prices of industrial imports.

There is one further difficulty with the 'countervailance' argument, in terms of consistency with other parts of the model. The past deterioration of the terms of trade of the periphery is attributed in large measure to the downward inflexibility of prices and wages in the centre as contrasted with the periphery.

If this is so, a downward shift in the periphery's demand function for centre exports will result in making the centre worse off, through unemployment, without making the periphery better off through improvement in the terms of trade. In fact, by lowering the income and employment levels in the centre this would actually hurt the periphery by reducing the demand for its exports; however small the income elasticity of demand for imports in the centre may be, there is no reason to expect it to be negative.

The third category of benefits from protection, according to Prebisch, is an 'allocative' one. This, like the first, is only indirectly associated with the simple terms of trade argument, and it will be discussed more fully when we examine the formal model(s) in detail.

There is one important expected benefit from protection which Prebisch does not discuss systematically; however, he mentions it at several points, though only incidentally. This is the whole class of benefits that may accrue to a country which is industrialised—the changes in economic 'structure', the flexibility, vitality, the changes in social structure and 'personality' of a country that many people are convinced comes with, and only with, an increase in the proportion of industrial production to total output of a country. There has been much written on this subject, and many of the arguments are highly plausible. Those who advocate protectionism for this type of reason may well be right. But it is important to note and remember that this is independent of, and very different from, any of the arguments Prebisch advances.[5]

As suggested above, only a part of Prebisch's argument in favour of some protection in the periphery devolves on the assertion that '. . . the great industrial centres not only keep for themselves the benefit of the use of new techniques in their own economy, but are in a favourable position to obtain a share of that deriving from the technical progress of the periphery' (Prebisch I, p. 14). We shall argue that the validity of this assertion is not necessary as a support of his policy recommendations. Nevertheless, this notion is worth examining carefully, for two reasons. First, because this is the part of his analysis that has attracted the most attention and the greatest amount of comment, both critical and favourable. It seems to many writers, and apparently to Prebisch himself, to be the main line of his argument, upon which the validity of everything else he says depends. And secondly, it is that part of his argument which elicits the most emotional response, again both from critics and supporters. The notion that, whether deliberately or not, the developed countries have 'exploited' the periphery and will, unless counteracting measures are taken, continue to do so, is not one to be passed over lightly.

Let us examine first the argument presented in Prebisch I (pp. 8–14). Table 2 (p. 11) is a hypothetical illustration of both the actual and the 'ideal' '. . . distribution of the benefits of technical progress between the centre and the periphery, . . . in which it is assumed that the indexes of productivity, per man, are greater [rise more] in industry than in primary production. For the sake of simplification, both are supposed to make an equal contribution to the finished product.' (This last assumption is difficult to interpret in the light of differential rates of productivity change in the two kinds of activity.) In the illustration productivity *per man* in primary production increases by 20% as a result of technical progress. In the centre technical progress in industrial production raises productivity by 60%. Since industry and primary production contribute equally to the value of the final product, productivity per man, in world output of finished products, rises by 40%. Now, he says, if all productivity changes are reflected in declining prices, and (money?) income does not rise at all, primary producers experience an increased purchasing power of 16.7% per unit of primary product. Since, with a given work force, they can now produce 20% more output, their total buying power of finished goods, that is, their total real income, has risen by 40%. In the centre, on the other hand, the purchasing power of a unit of output has fallen to 87.5% of its original value. But since a given number of workers can now produce 60% more than previously, the total real income of the centre has risen by 40%, and the centre and the periphery have shared equally the fruits of the technical progress. 'The benefits of technical progress would thus have been distributed alike throughout the world, *in accordance with the implicit premise of the schema of the international division of labour*, and Latin America would have had no economic advantage in industrializing. On the contrary, the region would have suffered a definite loss, until it had achieved the same productive efficiency as the industrial countries.'[6]

This argument seems to be based on the factor-price equalisation theorem, but it is a fallacious and naïve interpretation. Quite apart from the many well-known restrictions to any *practical* application of that theorem to the 'real world', Prebisch's hypothetical example involves a misapplication of the results of that theorem. As he does elsewhere, he seems to be identifying wages with personal income, that is, assuming that there is only one factor of production in the world, labour. If that is the case, however, the factor-price equalisation theorem is not relevant and the equalisation of income throughout the world is not an '. . . implicit premise of the schema of the international division of labour'. Alternatively, if there are two factors of production the theorem is valid only when both countries produce both commodities. This is a difficult assumption to make when one country is the periphery and the other is the centre; in any case, Prebisch, in the example we are discussing, specifically assumes that there is complete specialisation.

Prebisch seems to be arguing here: (1) that 'technical progress', defined by him as an increase in productivity per man, just 'happens' and is not the result of an increase in any other input; the benefit derived from such progress, then, is presumably analogous to 'unearned' land rent; and (2) that from the point of view of justice and equity in distribution, such 'unearned' benefits should be distributed equally throughout the world. Both of these propositions are highly questionable. The opportunity cost of technical progress is by no means negligible, even if we include only the direct outlay for research and development made by private business in the countries of the centre. Nor should one ignore the benefits of the centre's progress which accrue to the periphery by means other than the decline in the prices of final products which Prebisch argues should have taken place; the opportunity for peripheral countries to exploit such natural resources as rubber, for example, grew in the first place out of the development in the centre of industries requiring such primary products as inputs. In any case, however, neither of the propositions stated above follows naturally, as Prebisch argues, from the traditional theory of comparative advantage and international specialisation.

Having contrasted what he thinks 'should' have happened with what in fact, he asserts, did happen, namely the movement of the terms of trade against, rather than in favour of, the periphery, Prebisch goes on to explain the mechanism by which this took place.

> The existence of this phenomenon cannot be understood, except in relation to trade cycles and the way in which they occur in the centres and at the periphery, since the cycle is the characteristic form of growth of capitalist economy, and increased productivity is one of the main factors of that growth (p. 12).

At this point profits come into the picture, not, however, as a return to a factor of production, but rather as a windfall due to temporary emergence of excess demand.

> As prices rise, profits are transferred from the entrepreneurs at the centre to the primary producers of the periphery. The greater the competition and the longer the time required to increase primary production in relation to the time needed for the other stages of production, and the smaller the stocks, the greater the proportion of profits transferred to the periphery. Hence follows a typical characteristic of the cyclical upswing; prices of primary products tend to rise more sharply than those of finished goods, by reason of the high proportion of profits transferred to the periphery.
>
> If this be so, what is the explanation of the fact that, with the passage of time and throughout the cycles, income has increased more at the centre than at the periphery?
>
> There is no contradiction whatsoever between the two phenomena. The prices of primary products rise more rapidly than industrial prices in the upswing, but also they fall more in the downswing, so that in the course of the cycles the gap between prices of the two is progressively widened (p. 13).

What he must mean here, though not explicitly stated, is that the fall in prices in the downswing (in the periphery as compared with the centre) is greater than the relative rise in the upswing (in the centre as compared with the periphery). Otherwise there would not be the long-run ratchet effect that he speaks of. This is subsequently explained in terms of the wage mechanism at the centre. Some of the rising profits in the upswing are mopped up by higher wages;[7] in the downswing wages are rigid, however, so that prices of raw materials are forced down by more than the previous rise. But greater price-wage rigidity at the periphery would not alleviate the difficulty; it would, in fact, intensify it,

> . . . since, when profits in the periphery did not decrease sufficiently to offset the inequality between supply and demand in the cyclical centres, stocks would accumulate in the latter, industrial production contract, and with it the demand for primary products. Demand would then fall to the extent required to achieve the necessary reduction in income in the primary producing sector (pp. 13–14).

There is a peculiar asymmetry here. The rigidity of wages in the periphery, if it existed, would result in a decline in employment, presumably, as demand for primary products decreased. Thus income would be decreased in the periphery by means of unemployment rather than by means of lower prices and real wages. This reasoning is unobjectionable, but surely it should be applied also to the centre. It is not, however. In the centre, *per capita* income is identified, apparently, with wages and the terms of trade, that is, with real wages, and no allowance is made for the declining income *per capita* which is the obvious concomitant of mass unemployment (p. 13).

In Prebisch II (pp. 258–61) the '. . . process of transfer of real income through the deterioration in the terms of trade' (p. 258) is explained in terms of 'productivity ratios' and 'technological densities' rather than differences in market structure between the periphery and the centre. The basic concept involved here stems from Graham's[8] notion of a list of products, ranked in order of the degree of comparative advantage, the commodity at the top of the list being that in which the country has the greatest comparative advantage. Prebisch applies this by comparing the 'productivity ratio [which] expresses the relationship of physical productivity per man between the periphery and the center' with the wage ratio (p. 258). There is, of course, only one wage ratio and there are as many productivity ratios as there are commodities. A commodity will be exported by the periphery only if the productivity ratio is equal to or greater than the wage ratio. In order for it to export (or stop importing) a commodity for which the productivity ratio is less than the wage ratio wages must fall. However, Prebisch goes on to argue that the difference in productivity between the 'best' and the 'marginal' export good is transferred 'to the center through the free play of market forces' (pp. 258–9). But this assertion is valid only under highly restrictive assumptions. To determine the gains from trade by comparing wage ratios with ratios of physical productivity per man is possible only if labour is the sole factor of production and wage costs, therefore, the total cost of production. The parenthetical comment (p. 259) that land rental is excluded 'to avoid complications . . . since it cannot be transferred' is, to say the least, ingenuous. Economists make simplifying assumptions all the time, of course, but this one is analogous to 'simplifying' a study of oligopoly by assuming that there is only one firm! A comparison of wage ratios and productivity ratios might be admissible as a rough index of comparative advantage if: (*a*) both countries produced the goods that entered into trade, and (*b*) if they produced them with roughly the same combinations of labour with other inputs. (Even this is questionable in this instance, since Prebisch himself, as we have noted previously, argues that there is a significant 'profit' element included in wages in the centre but not in the periphery.) Thus, it is impossible to say that the productivity of labour (or of anything else) in coffee production is four times as high in Brazil as in Canada, because nobody knows what the productivity of labour in coffee production is in Canada. Furthermore, it would be wrong to say that if productivity per man in beef production in Argentina is three times as high as in the United Kingdom and wages in Argentina are half as high as in the United Kingdom, then beef must cost one-sixth as much in Argentina as in the United Kingdom. It would be wrong, because we know from this nothing about the relative amounts (and costs) of non-labour inputs—land, feed, shelter, etc., involved in beef production in the two countries. In fact, in such a case one could not even say with certainty that Argentina would export beef to the United Kingdom. Furthermore, if the world did indeed have only one factor of production, then the situation would be symmetrical, and the centre would also be transferring to the periphery its differential productivity for all exports for which the productivity ratio is higher than the wage ratio. In order, then, for the periphery to be at a disadvantage in this respect it would be necessary to show either that *only* at the periphery are there no factors of production other than labour or else that there is a systematic tendency for the periphery to have a greater 'productivity surplus' than the centre over and above the productivity in the last, infra-marginal export commodity. This is an empirical question, but apparently it is Prebisch's belief that there is in fact a tendency for the periphery to have a greater 'productivity surplus' than the centre. This is clearly what he means when he talks about 'disparities in technological densities' (p. 262).

This can best be explained by supposing that there are ten commodities, *A . . . J*, such that the ratio of country *P*'s productivity to country *C*'s productivity is highest for commodity *A* and lowest for commodity *J*. Then Graham's conclusions are: (1) that country *P* is better off in trade the smaller the number of commodities (in addition to *A*) that it actually exports, that is, the less far down the list it has to go in exporting in order to pay for its imports; but (2) *ceteris paribus*, *P* is better off the closer together the internal productivity ratios, *A*/*B*, *B*/*C*, *C*/*D*, etc. The closer together the productivities (in Prebisch's terminology, the more dense the technology), the less deterioration in its terms of trade a country will have to suffer in response to an increase in its demand for imports or a decrease in foreign demand for its current exports.

Suppose *P* is exporting *A* and *B* and importing commodities *C* through *J*. Now as productivity (in general?) in the periphery increases and growth occurs, there is surplus man-power in the periphery which must be employed by producing *C* domestically. Real wages must drop accordingly to maintain the equality of the wage ratio with the (marginal) productivity ratio. Since *P*'s technology is sparse (i.e. not 'dense'), the decline in the productivity as it moves to producing *C* is large. Since wages constitute the only cost of production, according to Prebisch, the price in terms of foreign currency of all exports must fall proportionately, and the 'differential productivity' of labour in the production of *A* and *B* is transferred abroad. But protection of *C*, the marginal industry, will not cure the transfer abroad of the productivity differential of *A* as compared to *B* which had been taking place all along. Furthermore, protection of this type is not only necessarily permanent, as Prebisch recognises it to be, it is also self-propagating. If *P* imposes a tariff on the import of *C*, Prebisch argues, then if productivity in the production of commodity *C* increases and protection is maintained, *P* can raise wages throughout. But if this is done, then *B* can no longer be exported without protection or subsidisation. So that protection, far from being temporary, must increase over time. Presumably Prebisch would argue that this would not be the case because productivity would also increase in *B*. But if that were the case, then wages could have been raised without the protection. This may be impossible, however, because of the surplus man-power (which, we shall argue, is the real villain of the piece); but then the increase of productivity in *C* will also generate surplus man-power, and it will be necessary to extend protection to D, and so on.

As noted, the real problem seems to lie with the surplus man-power; Prebisch seems to be thinking of an indefinitely large, and growing, population, with no relation whatever (even, apparently, at 'subsistence' wages) between the wage rate and the supply of labour. It is possible to make a strong case for protection in such a situation in order to stimulate, or at least permit, industrialisation, because of the beneficial social effects (and social external economies), including amelioration of the tendency towards population explosions. But this has nothing to do with the transfer-of-income argument.

Furthermore, it is not obvious why the surplus man-power should not be successfully utilised in the production of goods which are likely to be domestic goods regardless of the terms of trade (within any reasonably expected limits to the terms of trade) because of high transport costs: construction of all sorts, including that of social overhead capital, or various types of services. Nor is it obvious why there should not be an increase in agricultural production for domestic consumption, since poor nutrition and near-starvation are ubiquitous problems in peripheral countries. One is tempted to speculate that the objection to both of these alternatives would be in terms of the desirability of industrialisation as such. And again, it should be emphasised that the desire for industralisation is a respectable motive for protection, but is quite independent of the arguments Prebisch employs.

Thus far we have discussed essentially two versions of Prebisch's argument, both dealing with the notion that the periphery transfers abroad the fruits of its technological progress through deterioration in its terms of trade. In one instance this is due to the fact that prices and wages are flexible upward in the centre but not in the periphery; in the other case it is due to the 'technological density' of the centre as compared with the periphery. There is yet a third branch of the argument which is stated in Prebisch II (pp. 252–60). Assume that the centre and the periphery are growing at the same rate—presumably *per capita* income is increasing at the same annual rate in both. Then, at a given set of price levels and exchange rates, the periphery will tend to develop a balance-of-payments deficit because its marginal propensity to import is higher than that of the centre. It is therefore necessary to effect import substitution, which is '. . . defined here as an increase in the proportion of goods that is supplied from domestic sources and not necessarily as a reduction in the ratio of imports to total income' (p. 253). (It is difficult to comprehend this definition.) One fairly obvious way to achieve this is through devaluation, which Prebisch discusses at some length. The 'usual' type of objection to devaluation in such a system would be to argue that it would fail to increase foreign-exchange earnings if the demand for exports were inelastic with respect to price. Prebisch holds the view that price elasticity of demand for primary products is indeed low (p. 256), but this is not an important part of his argument. (The significance of price-inelastic demand for primary products has been given much more attention in the 'commentaries' than in Prebisch's own work.)

The objection to devaluation, in Prebisch's view, is that it will stimulate exports from the periphery beyond the point which is socially optimal from the point of view of any one peripheral country. Higher internal prices for exports (initially) would encourage an increase in the output of exports. Higher internal prices of imports would also encourage domestic production of import-substitutes. But exports would increase too much, because the perfectly competitive firms producing exports would equate marginal cost with price, whereas socially the appropriate calculation would be an equation of marginal cost with marginal revenue. Since the domestic prices of exports would fall (from the initial post-devaluation peak—whether they would fall to levels lower than before devaluation is not clear), social marginal revenue would be less than price. Since for some, at least, of the world's primary products, the demand function facing any individual exporting *country* is probably close to infinitely elastic, the assumption here must be that all the peripheral countries are pursuing the same policy and that either: (1) exports are produced under conditions of perfect competition in each country; or (2) the decision-making unit in each country is ignoring the policy being carried out in the other countries exporting the same commodity. One of these is essential to the mechanism, since supply of exports (which is the same thing, in Prebisch's model, as the output of exportables) is a function of price, not of marginal revenue.

For a 'demonstration' that devaluation would lead to an increase in exports beyond the socially optimum point, the reader is referred to the Appendix (Prebisch II, pp. 269–73). The analysis here, however, is extremely difficult to follow. First, he is referring here, not to the response to devaluation, but rather to

> . . . how the process of spontaneous industrialization might operate according to the classical mechanism, assuming that there is free mobility of labor and unrestricted competition. We are concerned here only with the alternative employment of the surplus man-power in export production and industrial activities: for the sake of simplicity, other aspects will be overlooked (p. 269).

Some of these 'other aspects', however, would seem to be fairly important. Thus for the sake of 'simplicity' it must be assumed that there is no domestic demand for the export good, nor for any (agricultural or primary) product which may be a very close substitute on the supply side for the export commodity. (Nor, *a fortiori*, can there be any new export good which is a close substitute in supply for existing exports.) All production not devoted to export must be industrial production. But even within this somewhat restrictive simplification it is not clear what the process is. 'Spontaneous industrialization' is not defined. All we know is that we start from a position in which there is some industrial production (which is able to compete with imports in the home market) and there is a given quantity of 'surplus man-power' which needs to be employed. Presumably productivity (in exports? industry? both?) has risen, so that with output constant there is redundant labour. The issue therefore is that of allocating this surplus labour between primary production for export and industrial production for home consumption.

Some additional production for export can take place without any decline in export prices. The extent to which this is possible depends upon the rate of growth at the centre and the centre's income elasticity of demand for imports of the primary product in question. Beyond a certain point, more exports can be sold only at lower prices. (There really should be no distinction made. The only significance of the point—point 0 in Prebisch's diagram—is that before that point is reached export prices are lower than they would otherwise have been; after the point is reached prices are actually falling.) It should be noted again that this does not depend on the demand for primary products being inelastic with respect to price. A larger output can be sold only at declining prices whenever the demand is less than infinitely elastic. Since marginal physical productivity is constant and profits *per unit* are constant (p. 271), wages are less than prices by a constant amount and the decline in export prices forces wages down in the export-producing sector. Since labour is mobile (and presumably, homogeneous) this forces wages down in the industrial sector as well, making additional, previously extra-marginal, industries competitive with imports. Equilibrium is attained when the average product in export production (which is declining because prices of exports are falling) equals the average product in industry (which is declining because as industrial production expands output is expanded and extended to activities where productivity is lower and lower). Wages, of course, are the same throughout, equal in each sector to average product less a constant. But marginal income per person in the export sector is less than wages and less than marginal (equal to average) income in industry. The reason for this is the declining price of exports, which means that marginal revenue is less than price. In industry, on the other hand, '. . . marginal income per person is the same as *per capita* income, from the point of view of the economy as a whole. . . . The fall of wages has brought also a decline of prices in existing industries; but this involves a purely internal transfer, whereas in export activities there is an external loss of income which reduces the increment of income due to the employment of the surplus man-power' (p. 272). The socially optimum allocation would be to stop increasing export production where marginal product in exports is equal to average product in industry. This can be achieved only by some interference with the free market. The problem, then, is not that the centre's demand is price- or income-inelastic—greater elasticity would postpone the day of reckoning, perhaps, but would not avert it. The problem stems from the fact that exports are produced under perfectly competitive conditions (which may be a valid assumption for parts of Latin America, but surely not for many other countries in the periphery); and that they are produced under conditions of constant marginal physical productivity of labour, which, for primary products, seems inconceivable.

When we apply this analysis to the effects of a devaluation the problem of explaining the origin of the 'spontaneous industrialization' is removed. The immediate effect of the devaluation is to raise the domestic prices of both exports and imports. Export production is therefore stimulated, as is the production of at least some of the import-competing goods. Since, as we have noted, there seems always in Prebisch's world to be a redundancy of labour, both of these sectors are able to increase simultaneously. The argument, then, is that the response of the free market to the devaluation would involve an increase in the output of exports that was larger than the optimum and, correspondingly, an increase in the output of industrial, import-competing goods, that was smaller than optimum. It is worth recalling what assumptions underlie this analysis.

1 The labour force is perfectly homogeneous and perfectly mobile.
2 The periphery as a whole is a monopolist in the market for its exports, or at any rate a sufficiently important seller so that it is faced with a downward-sloping demand curve.
3 The export commodity is produced under perfectly competitive conditions *or* the producers of the export commodity (whether private enterprise, government-owned or directed by governmental or para-governmental agencies, such as a marketing board) in each country ignore the fact that other peripheral countries producing the same commodity are also executing the same policies of devaluation and expansion of exports.
4 All increased output of the export commodity must be exported. Thus, not only is there no stock-piling of the commodity by marketing boards, but there is no domestic consumption of the export commodity, or else the domestic demand for the export commodity is totally inelastic with respect to both price and income.
5 Exports are produced under conditions of constant returns to scale.
6 Exports are produced under conditions of constant marginal physical productivity of labour, which in turn implies either: (*a*) that labour is the only factor of production; or (*b*) that the supply of the other factors of production is infinitely elastic at the prevailing price, which is the 'constant unit profit' mentioned above.

It is hardly necessary to point out that this is a rather formidable set of assumptions. The objections to assumptions 5 and 6, particularly in the case of agricultural and primary production, are obvious. Assumption 4 may be a reasonable approximation for some countries and some products in the form in which we have stated it here. But if it is interpreted more broadly it raises a host of new questions. For the assumption that exports are not consumed at home is the same as the statement that there are two sectors in the economy, an industrial, import-competing sector, and a primary-producing, export sector. This is not a 'dual economy' problem, since Prebisch raises neither the questions concerned with technological dualism, differences in factor substitutability and the like, nor those involving non-competing groups in the labour market. But the importance of assuming that there are two—and no more than two—sectors is that it limits the number of alternatives available. There is always redundancy in the labour market (though this does not affect the wage level) which can be employed only in the industrial sector, where it runs up against competition from imports which can be overcome only by protection or subsidisation, or else in the export sector, where it runs into decreasing real returns due to the transfer of income abroad which results from the decline in price of exports. As we have noted previously, there is no room in his discussion for an increase in the output of 'domestic goods', such as construction, with high transport costs; or of agricultural products for home consumption, which may be very close substitutes in production for the export commodity; or of 'social overhead capital'; or, for that matter, of new exports which may be close substitutes in production for existing export goods. On the other hand, there are a number of instances in which Prebisch does seem to be thinking of a third sector (Prebisch I, p. 18, *e.g.*) which consists of domestic services and the like, and in which productivity is very low, so that output in that sector should not be encouraged. In fact, in a number of cases it is this third sector which seems to be the source of the apparently indefinitely large supply of man-power.

An even more troublesome, though related problem, is the question of the wage-determination mechanism. In the discussion of the disadvantages resulting from not having 'technological density' and in the model presented in the Appendix which we have just examined, it seems clear that the real wage is equal to marginal (which equals the average) product in the export industry. Since this is constant, real wages in fact depend on the terms of trade. As the price of exports falls, wages fall, and this allows industrial activity, where productivity is lower, to expand. But elsewhere there is the notion that wages are determined by overall, or average, productivity, in the whole economy, as illustrated in footnote 1 on p. 318 and in the following:

> It was pointed out at the beginning of this section that there are two ways of increasing real income. One is through an increase in productivity and the other through a readjustment of income from primary production so as to lessen the disparity between it and income of the great industrial countries.
>
> The second result can be achieved only in so far as the first is accomplished. As productivity and the average real income from industry increase in the Latin-American countries, wages in agriculture and primary production in general will have to rise, as they have in other countries (Prebisch I, p. 47).

These quotations are from Prebisch I, and it is, of course, possible that Prebisch's views changed during the years intervening between publication of the two essays. But whatever the reason, it is clear that there is a difference between the two views of the wage-determination mechanism which needs to be explained. Furthermore, there seems to be a difference in Prebisch's estimation of the productivity in industry in the two cases. If overall productivity rises as a result of industrialisation, productivity in industry must be higher than in the production of exports, in which case it is not clear why there is a need for protection of industry. There are two possible explanations for this. One is that Prebisch is implicitly going from a static to a dynamic analysis (which, incidentally, he does frequently throughout both papers), and the rise in productivity which results from industrialisation is a long-run result of the working-out of the external economies of industrialisation and its overall socio-economic effects, that is, the infant industry, or 'infant economy' argument. A different explanation is that the higher productivity resulting from industrialisation results from the elimination, or at any rate the diminution, of the third sector, the low productivity domestic services. This is implied elsewhere in Prebisch I (p. 18). But this brings us back to the question of why this third sector cannot consist of 'domestic goods' with high transport costs, of agricultural production for home consumption and/or of high-productivity services. What is more serious, there is the problem of how to explain the existence of such a sector in an economy in which labour is mobile and the wage-rate uniform. If productivity in that sector is so low, why does labour not move out of it and into the production of exports until the wage level in exports is brought down (through falling exports prices) to that prevailing in domestic service?

Almost all of the preceding discussion has been directed at the formal, analytical structure of Prebisch's arguments. As we stated at the beginning, there is not one single model, but several. In this sense, we would argue, Prebisch has fallen short of making his case because he has over-stated it. The obvious question then is, can we ferret out from his argument a single, 'minimum' model which would be sufficient to justify the policies he proposes? The following is a simplified version which we believe to be logically consistent and sufficient. Its acceptability depends, of course, on its empirical relevance.

Consider two countries, *P* and *C*, which are alike with respect to rate of growth of population, rate of increase in *per capita* income (hence rate of increase in productivity per man and in the real wage rate) and technological density. At the existing exchange rate and wage rates in the two countries all of *P*'s exports are primary products and all of *C*'s exports are industrial goods. The only difference is that with growth in income the world demand function for *C*'s industrial exports is rising faster than the world demand function for *P*'s primary exports. As a result, an ever-increasing proportion of *P*'s incremental population *must* be allocated to industrial production, while in *C* an ever-increasing proportion of the incremental population *can*—and will—be allocated to industrial production. But *P*'s industrial output can compete (in *P*'s home market) with imports from *C* only if, through changes in the exchange rate or in the wage rate, *P* accepts a deterioration in its terms of trade. Thus part of the increase in productivity in *P* accrues to *C*. So far there has been no need to appeal to differences in market structure, the mechanism of wage determination or any other asymmetrical imperfections in the working of the market mechanism and perfect competition.

Analytically, the only question remaining is whether there is any tendency for the decline in the terms of trade to stop. Prebisch does not address himself explicitly to this problem, but one gets the impression that he considers the decline in the terms of trade to be a continuing process. There seem, however, to be two equilibrating forces at work. First, as the proportion of the labour force employed in industrial production in *P* increases, the demand for imports of industrial goods from *C* should increase at a decreasing rate. Secondly, the fact that the terms of trade for *P* are declining means that real income *per capita* is not growing as rapidly as in *C*, so that even with a high income elasticity of demand for imports the absolute increments in imports demanded by *P* should eventually equal the growth in demand for its exports. Prebisch himself is aware of the latter tendency (Prebisch II, pp. 253–4), but argues that as a result the periphery's growth rate will be less than it would be if the demand for its exports were more income-elastic (or more price-elastic) or the demand for imports less income-elastic. This, indeed, is the heart of the 'Prebisch thesis', and, we repeat, it stems from the assumption of different income elasticities of demand, not from alleged differences in market structure and the wage-price mechanism.

The problem thus far is essentially a balance-of-payments problem. Because of the disparities in income elasticities, income in *P* cannot grow as rapidly as income in *C* without generating a chronic deficit in the balance of payments. (The protectionism this suggests is of the 'exchange-rationing' type discussed on p. 108. Tariffs, multiple exchange rates, or various types of discriminatory controls are frequently proposed—as relatively simple alternatives to more difficult alterations in the internal tax structure—to prevent the high-income groups from 'frittering away' precious foreign-exchange reserves by exporting flight capital or importing luxury consumer goods. It would, indeed, be interesting to know the relationship between the apparently high income elasticity of demand for imports and the shape of the income distribution in *P*.) But the question still remains how fast real income *per capita* could grow in the absence of the balance-of-payments constraint. We are back to the traditional welfare propositions of international trade theory. Ignoring, as Prebisch does, a number of extremely important considerations, such as institutional patterns, the propensity to save and invest, the distribution of income, etc., the absolute growth at any one time is clearly a function of the level of real income. Furthermore, if our goal is to maximise income at some future date it is not obvious that maximising the rate of growth over the relevant time interval is the most appropriate means to that end. A slower rate of growth of a higher level of income may be better. If 'the free play of market forces' dictates an increase in exports, and if this maximises *P*'s income at any—and every—given point in time, this may be preferable to having a lower level of income which is growing at a more rapid rate.[9] Here the empirical questions of world (not domestic) market structure enter. The difficulty is that the periphery (as a group) is a monopolist but not a monopsonist: the world price of its imports is not a function of its demand for imports; and the demand for its exports is likewise independent of its demand for exports. But, though the demand *function* for *P*'s exports is independent of what *P* does, the *price* of *P*'s exports is directly dependent on the amount it offers for sale on the world market. In a static context this is the only possible interpretation of Prebisch's statement (Prebisch II, p. 255): 'It is not really a question of comparing the industrial costs with import prices but of comparing the increment of income obtained in the expansion of industry with that which could have been obtained in export activities had the same productive resources been employed there.' The two comparisons will yield the same solution (if the international market is in equilibrium) *unless* marginal value product is less than the average in exports and equal to the average (or less, but with a smaller differential) in domestic industrial production, and import prices are not affected. (In a dynamic framework the quoted sentence can be interpreted as a statement of the infant industry argument.)

We can therefore characterise the basic Prebisch thesis as consisting of two components: (1) A 'balance-of-payments' problem, with demand for imports in *P* tending to grow faster than import demand in *C*, so that equilibrium can be achieved only if *P* grows more slowly than *C*. This problem arises from *C*'s inelastic demand (for imports from *P*) with respect to *income*. (2) A 'real income' problem. This is frequently stated as *C*'s price-inelastic demand for imports from *P*, but more correctly should be attributed to *P*'s monopolistic position in the world market, which causes the demand for her exports to be less than infinitely elastic with respect to price. The result of this is that the 'free market', responding to existing relative prices, misallocates resources in *P* between export industries and import-competing industries, so that aggregate real income in *P* is not maximised.

Notes: Reading 14

1 Economic Commission for Latin America, *The Economic Development of Latin America and its Principal Problems*, United Nations, Department of Economic Affairs, New York, 1950.

2 'Commercial policy in the underdeveloped countries', *American Economic Review, Papers and Proceedings*, vol. XLIV, May 1959, pp. 251–73.

3 See, for example, Gottfried Haberler, 'Terms of trade and economic development', in *Economic Development for Latin America*, ed. Howard S. Ellis, Macmillan, 1961, pp. 275–97; Paul T. Ellsworth, 'The terms of trade between primary producing and industrial countries', *Inter-American Economic Affairs*, vol. X, Summer 1956; Werner Baer, 'The economics of Prebisch and ECLA', *Economic Development and Cultural Change*, vol. X, January 1962, pp. 169–82; and also a comment by M. June Flanders in a forthcoming issue of the same journal.

4 This would be the case if the imposition of tariffs, by preventing the demand for imports from rising as much as it otherwise would, discouraged the tendency for the periphery's exports to increase, causing a decline in the price of exports.

5 The name of Hans W. Singer is frequently joined with that of Prebisch in discussion of the issue. In his paper 'The distribution of gains between investing and borrowing countries', *American Economic Review, Papers and Proceedings*, vol. XL, May 1950, pp. 473–85, he does enunciate what is commonly referred to as 'the Prebisch thesis'. But he also stresses, and elaborates on, the importance in a dynamic context of industrialisation *per se*. He argues, for example, that '. . . the most important contribution of an industry is not its immediate product . . . and not even its effects on other industries and immediate social benefits . . . but perhaps even further its effect on the general level of education, skill, way of life, inventiveness, habits, store of technology, creations of new demand, etc. And this is perhaps precisely the reason why manufacturing industries are so universally desired by underdeveloped countries; namely, that they provide the growing points for increased technical knowledge, urban education, the dynamism and resilience that goes with urban civilization, as well as the direct Marshallian external economies. No doubt under different circumstances commerce, farming, and plantation agriculture have proved capable of being such "growing points", but manufacturing industry is unmatched in our present age' (pp. 476–7).

6 Prebisch I, p. 8. Italics added. The last sentence in the quotation is hard to understand in view of the benefits which would have accrued to the periphery from the technical progress of the centre.

7 'During the upswing, part of the profits are absorbed by an increase in wages, occasioned by competition between entrepreneurs and by the pressure of trade unions. When profits have to be reduced during the downswing, the part that had been absorbed by wage increases loses its fluidity, at the centre, by reason of the well-known resistance to a lowering of wages.' Is it generally accepted that this 'well-known resistance' existed throughout the period he refers to, from the 1870s to the 1930s? (Prebisch I, p. 13.)

8 Frank D. Graham, 'The theory of international values re-examined', *Quarterly Journal of Economics*, vol. XXVIII, November 1923, pp. 54–86.

9 This increase in exports may, of course, stop short of complete specialisation, since production of exports may begin to run into decreasing returns. Cf. Prebisch II, p. 263, discussing '. . . forces . . . of a Ricardian character'. This, incidentally, is one of the many examples of Prebisch's 'asides' belying the naivety of his assumptions and 'simplifications' in the formal analysis.

Reading 15

Unequal Exchange and Economic Policies: Some Implications of the Neo-Ricardian Critique of the Theory of Comparative Advantage

D. Evans

I. O. S. Bulletin, Volume 6, No. 4, March 1975. Reprinted in *Economic and Political Weekly, vol. XI*, nos. 5–7, February 1976.

1 Introduction

Over the last 150 years, there has been an endless stream of critical literature on the theory of comparative advantage. Why should one bother with yet another paper on the subject? It is the purpose of this paper to show that the recent upsurge of critiques of the standard theory of comparative advantage (as expressed in the classical Ricardian forms and in the highly refined neo-classical form) have far-reaching consequences, not only theoretically, but in the implications of the theories for policy and action in the concrete world. Since the full implications of these critiques are only just beginning to be worked out, only passing reference is made to some of the consequences.

In this paper, I deal only with what might be termed the neo-Ricardian critique of the theory of comparative advantage.[1] A more fully fledged development of the arguments presented here will appear in Evans (forthcoming).

Reasons for dissatisfaction with the prescription of specialisation in accordance with 'comparative advantage' in an ideal world of free trade and capital movements are not hard to find. Apart from revolutionary activity in the Third World, directed towards breaking many areas of the world from the world capitalist system, a most obvious source of discomfort to conventional wisdom is the rapid rise of inter- and intranational income inequality in the postwar era. This has occurred in spite of a massive increase in trade and capital flows, which, according to the neo-classical theory of comparative advantage, should have resulted in a more equal distribution of the fruits of the development of the forces of production. Over the last twenty-five years, free trade (or freer trade) policy prescriptions have been accepted by many capitalist governments; the Kennedy round tariff cut is perhaps the most shining example of the successful implementation of this type of policy. Such policies are usually implicitly or explicitly based on the neo-classical trade model. They have been implemented both with and without a supplementary package of policies designed to eliminate 'side effects' which are counter-productive, policies to offset other imperfections in the economy, and so on, as required to validate the free or freer trade policy. Whilst the neo-classical trade model generates the presumption of potential economic benefits from free trade, and the more equal distribution of such benefits, the fact that such predictions were not fulfilled need not necessarily be taken as evidence that the model was wrong. It is possible that in a second-best situation when special complicating real-world factors are included in the model (factors which in no way undermine the basic model), the observed outcomes are quite reconcilable with the model. Alternatively, the neo-classical model itself could be fundamentally flawed.

It will be argued in this paper that the problems with both the neo-classical and Ricardian models are more fundamental than has been generally admitted. It is not simply a matter of taking into account more realistic and complicating factors. It will be shown, for example, that under the most simple assumptions about the nature of the world economy, the general presumption in favour of free trade will be entirely removed from the theory of comparative advantage. This is a matter of enormous importance, for at this level of abstraction even Marx did not challenge Ricardo. Thus the neo-Ricardian critique is of crucial importance for all who work on the problem of international trade and value; an understanding of the neo-Ricardian critique of the theory of comparative advantage is a prerequisite for the development of a more satisfactory theory of international values.

2 Ricardian Theory and Neo-Classical Development

Ever since the publication of Ricardo's 'Principles of political economy and taxation', the law of comparative advantage has never been seriously challenged as the fundamental determinant of international trade and values, whether formulated in the Ricardian or in the neo-classical framework associated with the names of Heckscher, Ohlin and Samuelson, henceforth referred to as H-O-S. The challenges of a long list of protectionist theory and its associated free trade doctrine have been integrated into the main body of international trade theory.[2] By directing attention to correcting the malfunctioning of the market mechanisms which operate in one way or another to give incorrect 'signals' as to the direction of comparative advantage, the free trade argument has in general survived the onslaught. Protectionist arguments arising out of the work of Keynes, from which it can be shown that a single country can gain from protection in the presence of unemployment, do not constitute a challenge to the theory of comparative advantage. Such problems, it is argued, can be better dealt with by using fiscal policies to overcome the market malfunction which gives rise to unemployment.

Considerations arising from, the problem of decreasing costs and external economies have been dealt with by the identification of appropriate market interventions where the malfunctioning of competitive markets leads to specialisation against 'true' comparative advantage. More recently, there has been work stressing the dynamic nature of comparative advantage within the context of computable programming models designed to give planners the 'right' price signals for investment decisions.[3] Questions of domestic monopoly, factor price distortions, incorrectly valued exchange rates, have been treated as a market imperfection which can lessen the gains from trade arising from specialisation according to comparative advantage. In the production of new technology, monopoly is in fact often regarded as an essential market mechanism for attracting resources into 'R and D' (research and development) and for the realisation of a comparative advantage in R and D. Monopoly in foreign trade also leads to one of the few 'legitimate' arguments for export taxes or tariffs.

Ricardo's concern with international trade is related to but not integrated with his theory of capital accumulation in a closed economy. Behind his analysis of accumulation was a deep concern with the struggle for power in England between what he saw as a progressive and modernising industrial capitalist class and a reactionary landed gentry living mainly on the rents from their agricultural land. Ricardo's demonstration of the possibility of gains from free trade (especially from of the abolition of the Corn Laws) had the attractive feature of providing a favourable outcome for industrial capital with whose interests he closely identified. The removal of the Corn Laws would lower the cost of bread, thus removing an immediate cause for discontent amongst the working class. Free trade would provide the basis for the expansion of industrial capital without the shackles of the law of diminishing returns from land and the long-run redistribution of income to the landed classes.

Ricardo assumed that resources were mobile nationally but completely immobile internationally and that labour was the only factor of production considered explicitly, being employed in two branches of production exhibiting constant return to scale. Significantly, Ricardo claimed that free trade would lead to a gain for everybody in the society; in fact one can demonstrate that there will be some gains and losses with only a net potential gain for everybody. Given the supply of labour in each country, prices are proportional to relative labour inputs in internal trade. Once the possibility of international trade is introduced, then profitable trade can take place between the limits set by the internal price ratios, which are fundamentally determined by the technical conditions governing labour inputs in each economy. These technical conditions are, in turn, influenced by the availability of machines and natural resources which are only implicitly included in the formal model considered by Ricardo, the famous England–Portugal example. There is nothing in Ricardo's analysis to determine international values which are unhinged from the labour theory of value and are left indeterminate.

Before dealing with the classical mechanisms for the determination of international prices, several points should be noted. First, the opening of trade implies the possibility of complete specialisation in the production in each country. Whilst it is not hard to think of many reasons why complete specialisation will not take place, the assumption of costless labour mobility to an alternative branch of industry, even when complete specialisation does not take place, hides behind it a wealth of evidence of direct costs of trade to those thrown out of work by foreign competition – handicraft workers, small-scale producers, and so on – and indirect losses via the less dynamic external economies in such industries. The converse of this is that those engaged in the production of the exported good gain from the increased demand for their product. It is around this issue that much debate is generated, for the cost to those thrown out of work by trade may be, at best, unskilled wage work and, at worst, permanent underemployment. This consideration leads directly to the second point, that the argument so far only shows potential gain for all from trade and not, as Ricardo claimed, actual gain for all. For the latter to be achieved, it is necessary not for those workers who gain actually to compensate those who lose, but for the capitalists and landowners in the declining industry also to be bought off. Thirdly, it is assumed that the gains from trade will all be paid out in terms of higher wages to workers. However, there is no reason why some of this should not go to profits and into accumulation, as in the more dynamic analysis of distribution.

The classical solution to the determination of international values was found in Mills's law of reciprocal demand. The introduction of demand as the determinant of the equilibrium terms of trade in the Ricardian model emphasises the break from the labour theory of value as the determinant of international values. However, there are important considerations which modify this proposition, having profound implications for the analysis of the distribution of the gains from trade between countries within the framework of analysis as developed so far. If one retains a two-country split of the world, then there is a presumption that all of the gains from trade will go to the small country and that international values are 'determined' by the relative labour costs of the large country.

The happy proposition that the big, rich countries of the world do not gain as much from international trade as the poor, the small and the weak has been challenged within the context of the Ricardian theory. Once many commodities and many countries are introduced then there would no longer be a presumption that the international values will be determined by the cost conditions of the largest country.[4] Rather, prices would be determined by the ratio of labour costs of one of the many pairs of commodities produced in any one of many countries. Thus, it will no longer be so likely that all of the gains from trade will go to the smallest country, though the practical importance of this has been played down.

The differences between the Ricardian and neo-classical (H-O-S) theories of comparative advantage, at the level of comparative static analysis, lies mainly in the substitution of differing factor endowments as the primary determinant of comparative advantage as distinct from differences in techniques of production. In its most essential form, the neo-classical theory begins by demonstrating the possibility of gainful trade when the techniques of production are identical in all countries but the endowment of productive factors differs. Naturally, if techniques of production between two countries were in fact different, as in the Ricardian case, then there would be additional reason for differing pre-trade price ratios and the possibility of gain from trade. In addition, differences in demand patterns will also give rise to differences in pre-trade price ratios even if techniques and factor endowments are the same.

Whilst there is an elaboration of the types of factors which can lead to the possibility of profitable international trade, the types of conclusions reached with the aid of the static neo-classical model are very similar to those reached with a static Ricardian model. The extensions of the international division of labour leads to the potential gain of all members of society, with the given *technical* conditions of production and preferences of consumers. Further, it can readily be shown that if the standard neo-classical assumptions hold together with certain empirically plausible restrictions on the production conditions, the income of the owners of the factor used intensively in the exporting industry will increase both absolutely and relatively with the opening of trade, with the converse holding for the owners of the factor used relatively intensively in the import competing sector. The Ricardian propositions concerning the distribution of the gains from trade between a large rich and small poor country will tend to hold. This arises because it is more likely that the small poor country will end up with a very high degree of specialisation in production, since its factor endowments will be very different from those in the rich large country, leading to larger potential gain. Finally, there are two elaborations of the neo-classical model of special importance for later discussion.

First, factor immobility plays a crucial role in the Ricardian system, but this is not true for the neo-classical system. In fact, within the comparative static neo-classical world it has been shown that factor movements can substitute for commodity movements in achieving the potential gains from international interaction.[5] This proposition is of enormous importance when it is realised that there are serious barriers to trade and labour movements, and natural resources are not easily transportable. What better argument for the free flow for international capital? The importance of this proposition for those who identify with the interests of American and other rich country capital is quite similar to Ricardo's demonstration of the gains from free trade for manufacturing capital in nineteenth-century Britain.[6] In the 'ideal' neo-classical case, the international capital flow leaves the workers with the same income as with free trade, the domestic capitalists with the same returns, and the rest of the income is paid out to the foreign capitalists. Thus, the domestic factors in the country have the same relative (and absolute) income *either* with free trade *or* with no trade and an inflow of foreign capital. The same point applies to the international movements of labour, and lies behind much of the discussion of the 'brain drain' by neo-classical economists.

Secondly, there are some important neo-classical propositions which arise from the consideration of economic growth and technical change. Perhaps the most important proposition for consideration here is the concept of immiserising growth of factors of production, or growth which leaves a country with both a relative and an absolute lowering of income after growth.[7] This phenomenon can occur for a wide variety of reasons.

Consider first the effects of either technical progress

or balanced factor accumulation. At constant international terms of trade, relative factor prices are unchanged by growth, and consumption will increase by the same per cent as production. Now if the rate of balanced growth is higher than in the rest of the world (for the sake of argument, the rest of the world does not grow), then some of the benefit of growth must be lost via a deterioration in the terms of trade. If the rest of the world is not growing, then the only way in which the international markets will be cleared is for the price of exports of the growing country to fall and the price of imports to rise. The extent to which the terms of trade deteriorate will depend on (amongst other things) the elasticity of demand for the growing country's exports and the ease with which production is shifted from the export to the import competing industry. The more inelastic is the demand for exports and the more inelastic are the possibilities of substitution into import competing production, the greater will be the decline in the terms of trade. Further, if the growth is biased towards the export sector (say, from more rapid growth of the factor intensive in the export sector), then the greater will be the decline in the terms of trade. In essence this is the neo-classical analysis of the problem of the tendency over some periods of the terms of trade to move against poor primary producing countries, whose export industries tend to be labour intensive, and may experience relatively rapid technical change. Further, these countries often experience very rapid population growth and have inelastic demand for their products in export markets.

It is a short step from the above analysis to establish the conditions under which growth will lead to such a deterioration of the terms of trade that the country is *worse* off than before growth. For example, accumulation of the factor used intensively in export production (say, labour, the problem arising from a population explosion) will lead to an *absolute* decline in importable production at constant factor and commodity prices. This is because some of the factors used intensively in the importable sector must move into exportable production. Of course, the converse of this is that a lack of growth in such export industries will lead to a rapid improvement in the terms of trade, as has occurred over recent years in a number of countries exporting primary commodities.

A summary of the conditions for immiserising growth (where growth is defined in terms of the physical expansion of inputs rather than income derived from production) is as follows:

1 The rest of the world's offer curve must be inelastic.
2 Growth must be biased towards export production.

In addition, the following factors make immiserising growth more likely:

3 The ratio of total domestic production to imports is small.
4 The price elasticity of demand for imports is low.
5 The elasticity of supply of importables to a change in the price of importables is small.

The list of circumstances under which immiserising growth can occur has been considerably lengthened. Distortions in factor markets, tariffs and tariff-induced capital flows can all lead to immiserising growth. However, lest one despair that this destroys the basic argument of the neo-classicists, that free trade is best, it is important to note that in *all cases* immiserising growth can be overcome by some 'optimal' policy intervention. Further, the only case which requires 'deviation' from free trade is the case discussed in detail above, where the consequences of immiserising growth can be removed by an optimal tariff in conjunction with such measures as population control (if that is exacerbating the problem).[8]

A great deal of work has been done in recent years on fully dynamic extensions of the H-O-S model. There is little point in discussing these contributions, since the essential flavour of the neo-classical approach has been established well enough for our purposes and, as will now be shown, one of the crucial building blocks of the neo-classical approach is valid only on the most stringent assumptions about the nature of the capital.

3 Capital Theory Route to a Neo-Ricardian Critique

In all of the discussion of the neo-classical model so far, it has been implicitly assumed that, in principle, a unique measure can be found for aggregate capital endowments. Unfortunately for the H-O-S trade model, it is not possible to define capital as a part of 'factor endowment', unless it is assumed that capital goods are homogeneous (which obviously they are not). With heterogeneous capital goods, it is necessary to use some set of weights to construct an index to measure the sum of all types of capital endowments. An obvious set of weights is to use the labour required directly and indirectly to produce capital goods, but then one would no longer be dealing with capital as an independent 'factor' of production as is done under the neo-classical paradigm. An alternative which would enable one to aggregate different types of capital goods would be to use prices of capital goods. However, to be useful to the neo-classical trade model (which predicts the direction of trade on the basis of some measure of factor endowments), the index of capital must be invariant with respect to changes in factor prices. Otherwise, comparative advantage will be dependent on the distribution of income as well as factor endowments, the technical determinants of production techniques and preferences in consumption. An invariant measure of capital using price weights can only be made in the case in which the capital/labour ratios are the same in every industry, a restriction that attacks the very core of a theory which sets out to predict the patterns of trade in the simplest case where every industry produces throughout the world with identical techniques of production (but techniques of production differ between industries) and the only difference between countries is factor endowments.[9] It is ironical that the standard H-O-S version of neo-classical theory should fall apart on the very point which Marx was so heavily criticised for – the assumption of a constant organic composition of capital (constant capital/labour ratio) made in some parts of *Capital*.

A corollary of the demonstration that there is no measure of capital which is variant with respect to factor prices (or the distribution of income) is the de-bunking and demystifying of the marginal productivity theory of income distribution which lies behind the aggregate capital version of the H-O-S model. That is, it is no longer possible to identify a relationship between the incremental or marginal productivity of capital or labour and to call it either the rate of interest (or profit) and wages. Capitalists as recipients of a reward for their contribution to production and abstinence from consumption are decisively relegated to the realm of ideology without an independent 'scientific' validity. As a result of the capital theory point, the distribution of income becomes a central determinant of the possibility of gainful international trade and specialisation. Prices can no longer be taken as indicators of the relative scarcity of factors and an automatic drive towards full employment cannot be assumed. Thus the quest for squaring the observed reality of a worsening distribution of income in the postwar era with the neo-classical model by the elaboration and extension of the model to cover more complicated 'real world' factors is fundamentally mistaken. The capital theory point attacks at the very core of a factor-proportions theory of international trade, which includes aggregate capital, together with land, labour, and so on, as independent factors.

The theoretical literature on the neo-Ricardian theory of international trade developed out of the Cambridge, England, side of the capital theory debate has grown rapidly over the last eight years[10] (also referred to as the 'English' neo-Ricardians for convenience in later comparisons with 'unequal exchange' or 'French' neo-Ricardians). Theories of income distribution considered by the 'English' neo-Ricardians include a 'classical' theory of the determination of wages by subsistence or historically/socially/institutionally given norms, or a neo-Keynesian theory based on capitalist savings behaviour and the rate of growth.[11] Whilst some of the conclusions of the neo-classical theory carry over to the neo-Ricardian theory when capital is relegated to the role of a produced input, some of the most important propositions do not. For example, the neo-classical theory predicts that trade will raise the income of the factor intensively used in export productions. Whilst there are qualifications to the neo-classical theory which will make this result less likely, there remains a presumption that this will be the case. The neo-Ricardian theory entirely removes this presumption: a more realistic world of heterogeneous capital goods is more complex than the neo-classical homogeneous capital world. For example, it can be shown that opening trade between capitalist countries can lead to a loss of per capita consumption. This result is analysed in Metcalfe and Steedman (1974), Mainwaring (1974, 1976) and Samuelson (1975) and can be explained as follows.

In the neo-classical analysis, losses of economic welfare arise when there are imperfections in the competitive market mechanism, such as in the markets for capital and labour. Under these circumstances, it is quite possible for free trade to lead to specialisation away from 'true' comparative advantage, leaving economic welfare lower after trade than with no trade. This 'special case' in the H-O-S model is the general case in the neo-Ricardian model because of the differences in the specification of capital. In the H-O-S model, capital is a recipient of its 'marginal product' with no pure surplus or profit paid to capital over and above its 'reward'. On the other hand, in the neo-Ricardian model, capital only receives a pure surplus or profit, there being no relationship between 'marginal product' and the rate of profit. As a consequence of the different specification of capital, there exists in the neo-Ricardian model a rate of profit which plays a similar role in the market mechanism to the factor market distortions in the neo-classical case, opening the possibility of loss from trade. Such losses, which affect capitalist rather than primary incomes such as wages and rent, can be 'corrected' by the intervention of the state by using tariffs to remove 'wrong' price signals, as shown by Mainwaring (1976). Alternatively, the rate of profit is the independent variable, then international equalisation of the rate of profit can remove the incentive for an 'incorrect' specialisation pattern, as shown by Samuelson (1975). However, the transition between different trading regimes may result in unemployed plant, labour or other resources, problems which are easily exacerbated by the operation of market forces. This is illustrated by Mainwaring (1979), where a market-guided transition from autarky to free trade is explicitly analysed, showing the generalised possibility of gains from trade cannot be guaranteed. Thus, whereas for 'pure' capitalism in the neo-classical case, free trade must lead to a gain in economic welfare, capitalism in the simplest case is fundamentally flawed in the neo-Ricardian model and is unable to guarantee gains from trade.

4 'Unequal Exchange' Route to a Neo-Ricardian Critique of the Theory of Comparative Advantage

Under the general title of the theory of 'unequal exchange' (a term given widespread currency by the

French economist Emmanuel), a critique of the accepted theory of international values has been mounted,[12] which attempts to place economic, social, political and historical forces and their interaction as central determinants of the terms of trade and the distribution of the gains or losses from trade. In time, the 'unequal exchange' theory appeared several years in advance of the neo-Ricardian trade theory discussed in the previous section and, as far as the present author is aware, the work by the 'English' neo-Ricardians has been quite independent of the 'unequal exchange' literature. Emmanuel's theory of 'unequal exchange' was first developed using Marxian reproduction schemes in the theoretical exposition, but as Emmanuel (1972, Appendix V) argues, a Sraffa or neo-Ricardian framework could just as easily have been used. Similarly, the other main 'unequal exchange' theorists, surveyed in Evans (forthcoming), have utilised the neo-Ricardian framework. However, unlike the 'English' neo-Ricardians, the analytical arguments in the 'unequal exchange' literature are often crucially dependent on particular strong assumptions (quite apart from numerous analytical flaws). In my view, Emmanuel's 'unequal exchange' theory remains the most interesting one, which I concentrate on here.

Emmanuel's attack on the theory of comparative advantage challenges first the assumptions made about factor mobility made by Ricardo. (As already noted in section 2, altering the assumptions about factor mobility is of no real consequence to the neo-classical model.) Whilst retaining the assumption of labour immobility internationally, Emmanuel argues forcefully for the treatment of capital as internationally mobile, with the rate of profit tending towards equality in all countries. In this respect, Emmanuel's model is but a special case of the 'English' neo-Ricardian model discussed in the previous section, which formally encompasses the case of both mobile and immobile capital. Secondly, he rejects the lack of explicit treatment of capital in the Ricardian model, and the treatment of capital as having a marginal product equal to its profit, as in the neo-classical case. He treats capital as produced input as in the tableaux of Marx and the 'English' neo-Ricardian system discussed in the previous section. Thirdly, he adopts a specific theory of income distribution, namely, that money and real wages are determined independently by institutional, historical and moral forces. From this model, Emmanuel establishes the direct relationship between the international terms of trade and wages, as measured by the bundle of commodities required to maintain labour.

Simply put, the Emmanuel thesis is about the effects of a persistent inequality of wages between the 'centre' and 'periphery' in the context of a given pattern of international specialisation and tendency towards the equalisation of the rate of profit. With equalised profits internationally, hypothesised differences between 'centre' and 'periphery' worker bargaining power over money *and* real wages lead to an unequal international distribution of wage income. 'Unequal exchange' is defined in relation to what would pertain with *equal* wages. Thus, 'It thus becomes clear that the inequality of wages as such, all other things being equal, is alone the cause of the inequality of exchange' (Emmanuel, 1972, p. 61). 'In relation to what, is this exchange unequal? In relation to the situation where wages would be equalised. It is as simple as that' (Emmanuel, 1975, p. 137). The problem of 'unequal exchange' is often associated with adverse double factoral terms of trade, by both Emmanuel himself and his commentators such as Findlay (1978, p. 19). It is important to note, however, that Emmanuel (1972, p. 61) presents the analytical argument in terms of a comparison of two sets of prices of production, a price–price comparison in which the double factoral terms of trade are in fact irrelevant. That Emmanuel chose his numerical examples so the 'unequal exchange' is associated with adverse double factoral terms of trade is perhaps a confusing but unimportant detail. Crucial to Emmanuel's definition of 'unequal exchange' is the assumption that the international rate of profit is equalised in both the 'unequal' and 'equal' exchange situations. My own earlier confusion in Evans (1976, Appendix) about Emmanuel's definition of 'unequal exchange' (a confusion also made in Van de Klundert, 1971a, and Samuelson, 1973, 1975, 1976), involved a misunderstanding of the role played by the process of equalisation of the rate of profit in the development of 'unequal exchange'. Emmanuel's hypothesis is about developing inequalities of wages internationally in the context of specialised trade and *equalised* international profits, with no reference to the process of the opening of trade and the equalisation of the rates of profit.

The formal definition of 'unequal exchange', elaborated diagramatically in the Appendix and analytically in Evans (1980, forthcoming) is simply an exercise in comparative dynamics which does not take into account what might be called the 'laws of motion' or the dynamic development of 'unequal exchange' through time. Behind the simple analytical model outlined in the Appendix lies a complex set of considerations which lead to the hypothesis that 'unequal exchange' is likely to be reproduced and intensified through times. Thus, in Emmanuel's view, the alleged worsening of 'unequal exchange' over time is caused by an underconsumptionist view of the process of capital accumulation in which rising real wages play a central determining role in the development of productive forces. Rather than a rise in real wages being the effect of technical progress and industrialisation, high wages precede and are a cause of development in many important cases:

> . . . technical progress and industrialisation, where they precede wage increases, do not seem to be the cause of these increases, or even determining cause of

> the political and trade-union actions that bring them about, but merely a favourable condition. Are they, though, at least a necessary condition? Within the framework of each country taken separately, certainly not. There are many examples where technological progress and industrialisation do not *precede* the increase in wages, but follow it . . . the level of wages acts *directly* – that is, by the mere operation of the law of value – upon the economic factors, *by determining the necessity for an intensification of the organic composition of capital and by encouraging investment through the expansion of the market.* (Emmanuel, 1972, pp. 123–4; emphasis in original).

And: '. . . clearly, the process of interaction between economic development and the movement of wages is accompanied by a cumulative effect. Once a country has got ahead, through some historical accident . . . this country starts to make other countries pay for its high wage through unequal exchange . . .' (Emmanuel, 1972, p. 130). High wages cause both higher levels of development and, because of the differential 'centre–periphery' worker bargaining power, push the 'periphery' farther into 'unequal exchange' over time. Thus, the 'centre' workers are in effect a labour aristocracy exploiting the 'peripheral' worker.

Many criticisms have been made of the Emmanuel 'unequal exchange' model in the literature, not all of which are valid. In the latter category, perhaps the Samuelson (1973, 1975, 1976) critique is worth singling out. As I have shown in greater detail in Evans (1980), the Samuelson argument is incorrect first because he deals with the simultaneous processes of the opening of trade and the equalisation of the rate of profit, rather than Emmanuel's problem of unequalisation of wages given equalised profits and an unchanged pattern of specalised trade. Secondly, Samuelson reinterprets Emmanuel using a model in which profits rather than real wages are given, a procedure which might be justified if it made no difference to the point at issue. Since this is not the case, Samuelson's claim that 'unequal exchange' can be removed by international capital movements is entirely beside the point. More pertinent is the argument of Bettelheim (1972) and others that Emmanuel's attempt to justify the choice of wages as the independent variable both by his own analysis and by reference to Marx fails. Not only can it be argued that this approach is a misreading of Marx, but Emmanuel has offered no convincting theory as to how wages are determined over time.

The problem with the choice of real wages as the independent variable can be put another way. The analytical argument in its simplest form is based on a model of the world economy divided into a 'centre' and a 'periphery'. Thus, for internal consistency, Emmanuel must not only explain how the 'centre' and the 'periphery' differ in the process of wage determination, but he must also show that *in principle* it is possible to make a causal connection between worker bargains for money/real wages and the terms of trade. However, both the 'centre' and the 'periphery' are in fact aggregations of many large and small national units. Given the international mobility of capital, an increase in the money/real wage rate in the short run in one country will lower the rate of profit below international levels, leading to a short-run capital outflow and a balance-of-payments crisis. Regardless of the exchange rate mechanism assumed, there will be very strong competitive pressures leading to a lowering of real wages (either through unemployment or devaluation of the exchange rate) to restore the rate of profit to long-run levels, thus undermining the central mechanism required for Emmanuel's theory to work. Quite apart from such an internal critique, there are many other problems with Emmanuel's analysis not dealt with here such as the empirical estimates of the order of magnitude of 'unequal exchange' (discussed in Evans, 1979, pp. 272–3), and the unsubstantiated hypothesis that higher wages not only improve the terms of trade but lead directly to higher levels of accumulation and technical change.

5 Generalisation of Lewis and Prebisch-Singer Terms of Trade Models

The formal neo-Ricardian trade model underlying the Emmanuel 'unequal exchange' model can be regarded as a generalisation of both the Lewis surplus labour model and the Prebisch-Singer terms of trade model. In the former model, real wages are determined by the subsistence factor so that gains from trade in plantation sectors using surplus labour from the subsistence sector are transmitted to the richer high wage country either via the terms of trade or through profits derived from the ownership of plantations. Since real wages are determined by the subsistence sector, there is no immediate competitive pressure via international capital movements to undermine the independent determination of the real wage. In the Prebisch-Singer model, institutional factors in the wage bargaining process lead to a transfer of the benefits of technical progress in low-wage countries to the high-wage countries via a deterioration of the terms of trade of poor countries. (It is noteworthy that neo-classicists, in such standard texts as Södersten, 1971, were unable to deal with institutional factors in the wage-bargaining process. They dismiss this part of the Prebisch-Singer terms of trade argument, using demand and factor augmentation arguments to explain shifts in the terms of trade to poor countries as described in section 2. A notable exception is the neo-classical dismissal of such arguments by Bacha (1978). In terms of the 'unequal exchange' model, technical change in the export sector of the poor country leads for given real wages to a deterioration of the terms of trade of the poor country and a rise in the international rate of profit. If the capitalists of the rich country have strong unions, but no institutional pressure to increase wages in the poor country, then at a constant rate of profit the gains from technical change in the poor country can be used to increase wages in the rich country. However, the Prebisch-Singer results are dependent, as in the Emmanuel case, on the independent determination of real wages in general along the lines argued in section 4 may wish to reject such independent determination of real wages in general along the lines argued in section IV above, this does not rule out the possibility of independent determination of real wages for more fully specified cases. Thus, whilst the case of generalised Emmanuelesque 'unequal exchange' or adverse Prebisch-Singer terms of trade movements may not hold, the neo-Ricardian trade model does open the way theoretically for the explicit inclusion of such empirically identified institutional bargaining effects on the analysis of the distribution of the gains from trade. The great advantage of the neo-Ricardian analysis is that the inclusion of such bargaining effects can be achieved without reference either to 'marginal productivity' as the long-run determinant of factor rewards or to an assumed drive towards full employment of factors, including labour. For a simple exposition of some of the technical points behind this exposition, the reader is referred to the Appendix.

6 Concluding Remarks

There are at least four major problems with the neo-Ricardian critiques of the theory of comparative advantage as developed so far. First, although the issue of income distribution is dealt with in a more satisfactory manner than in the neo-classical model, it remains determined by factors which are not the subject of systematic analysis. This is a problem at the level of specification of abstract models in which alternative distribution closures are merely stated for the simplest cases without further analysis, as can be seen from a reading of the collected essays by the 'English' neo-Ricardians in Steedman (1979). More generally, in Marxian terms, the neo-Ricardian approach tends to concentrate on issues of circulation rather than production. Secondly, the theory remains essentially static with no attempt to move beyond comparative statics or comparative dynamics to a more fully dynamic view. A problem here is the gap between formal theoretical models which cannot deal satisfactorily with such matters, and more general analyses which can potentially reach beyond the precision of formal theoretical model building but which run the danger of being reduced to more or less interesting speculation or empty theorising. Thirdly, there has been little analysis of concrete situations to establish likely tendencies or patterns in the movement of a more dynamic system. The neo-Ricardian theory, still in its infancy, has so far performed mainly a critical function. Fourthly, there has been little or no attempt to relate the economic with political, social and historical factors to build a more unified theory of international trade and value.

Appendix. Diagrammatic Exposition of 'Unequal Exchange' Model

In this Appendix, I deal only with the relationships between real wages, profits and the terms of trade. In all cases, I have not examined here the determinants of the level of activity or implications of substitution in production or consumption between the two commodities. For a fuller analysis of these issues, see Bacha (1978) and Evans (1980). In the relation to the appendix in the earlier version of this article (Evans, 1976), there are some important changes. Briefly, I now argue that the three 'definitions' of 'unequal exchange' referred to in the appendix of Evans (1976) are due not so much to Emmanuel's change in position, but to misunderstandings arising from textual difficulties in the presentation of his argument. The definition of 'unequal exchange' given in Diagram 1 of Evans (1976) is irrelevant to Emmanuel but corresponds to the definition of 'unequal exchange' Amin (1973) and Saigal (1973). The definition shown in Diagram 2 of Evans (1976) corresponds to a misunderstanding of Emmanuel's concept similar to that made in Van de Klundert (1971a). Diagram 2 of Evans (1976) also corresponds to the Samuelson (1973, 1975, 1976) interpretation of Emmanuel. The 'correct' Emmanuel definition of 'unequal exchange' corresponds to Diagram 3. I have elaborated on these issues in Evans (1980).

Identical techniques in both countries

Assume that there are two countries, A and B, and two commodities, 1 and 2, produced with identical techniques of production in each country under constant returns to scale. The organic composition of capital differs between sectors and there are no joint products or externalities. It is assumed that the balance of trade is zero. Then for a given but different (up to a scalar multiple) bundles of commodities which enter the worker's consumption basket, the level of wages being expressed by the scalars w^A and w^B, it is possible to show the relationship between the long-run steady state rates of profit and the terms of trade (p_1/p_2) as in Diagram 1. It is assumed that country A is the high-wage country, so that $w^A > w^B$. Assuming that sector 1 has the higher organic composition of capital, it follows that under autarky (*a*) in each country,

$$(p_1/p_2)^A a < (p_1/p_2)^B a$$

and

$$r^A a < r^B a$$

Now if country A specialises in the production of commodity 1, then the relationship between the terms of trade and the rate of profit for given real wages is shown by $\bar{w}^{A1}$; as the terms of trade improve the rate of profit will rise. The $\bar{w}^{A1}$ curve to the left of $(p_1/p_2)^A a$ is shown with a dashed line to indicate that specialisation is taking place in the 'wrong' direction with profits and growth rates less than under autarky. Similarly, the $\bar{w}^{A2}$ curve shows the relationship between the rate of profit and the terms of trade when country A specialises in producing commodity 2. The $\bar{w}^{B1}$ and $\bar{w}^{B2}$ functions are for country B when specialising in commodities 1 and 2 respectively. Given the above assumptions, when the rate of profit is equalised internationally there are two possible equilibrium terms of trade denoted by $(p_1/p_2)^*$ and $(p_1/p_2)^{**}$ with associated rates of profit r^* and r^{**}. In both cases, the equilibrium terms of trade lie outside the Ricardian limbo region $(p_1/p_2)^A a$ and $(p_1/p_2)^B a$. Further, the equilibrium rate of profit is higher with trade for the high-wage country and lower for the low-wage country in comparison with autarky.

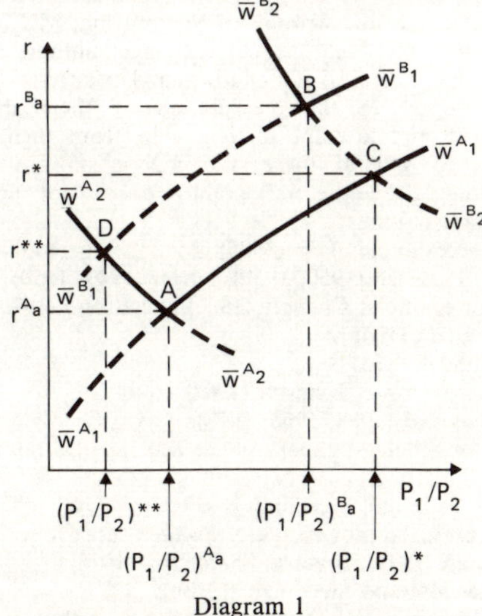

Diagram 1

It can easily be seen that the point C (D) is not a sustainable equilibrium point under free trade, and perfect competition for it will always pay capitalists in country B(A) to produce commodity 1 (2) domestically rather than importing it. By shifting from C (D) to B, the price of the imported commodity 1 (2) falls and the rate of profit will rise. Capitalists in country A, given capital mobility, will always try to export capital to country B, but will be unable to export enough (under the given assumptions) to equalise the rate of profit in the two countries. This result is not Emmanuel's 'imperialism of free trade' but the Amin-Saigal case in which equilibrium at C is sustained by assumed extra-market forces. The Emmanuel case arises when, in spite of international mobility of capital, there remain differences in the techniques of production. Such differences in technique of production could be due to unspecified specific factors not included in the model, as in the traditional Ricardian case.

Different techniques between countries

If there are both different techniques of production and different wage rates, then equilibrium terms of trade inside the limbo region is possible. In this case, both countries will have a higher profit rate after trade. Such a situation is depicted in Diagram 2.

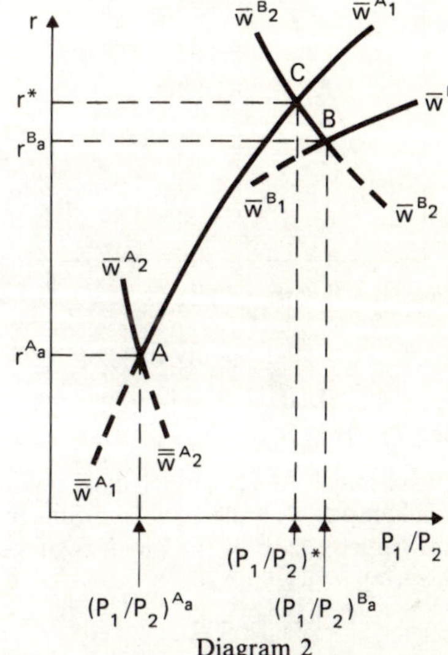

Diagram 2

As before, the pre-trade frontiers are represented by $\bar{w}^{ij}$ for $i = $ A, B and $j = 1, 2$, but in country A technology is now different from country B. Here the post-trade, post-equalisation of the rate of profit equilibrium is given by C at terms of trade $(p_1/p_2)^*$ inside the Ricardian limbo region. Note that in this case, the equilibrium rates of profit and growth are higher at C in *both* countries when compared with the pre-trade equilibrium positions A and B. Since $\bar{w}^A > \bar{w}^B$, equilibrium at C is a situation of 'unequal exchange' for country B in Emmanuel's terms. However, Emmanuel has in mind a slightly simpler case in which both countries A and B have a given pattern of specialisation. Taking $\bar{w}^A = \bar{\bar{w}}^B$, and assuming that a positive rate of profit is still possible, it is possible to show the relationship between 'unequal' and 'equal' exchange in the Emmanuel sense.

Thus, in Diagram 3, the higher wage rate in country B simply shifts the $\bar{w}^{B2}$ frontier downwards to $\bar{\bar{w}}^{B2}$. The point C and the terms of trade $(p_1/p_2)^{UE}$ represents 'unequal exchange' in relation to equilibrium at D and terms of trade $(p_1/p_2)^{EE}$ or 'equal exchange'.

Note that since price substitution effects are not included and the level of activity is abstracted from, there is no consideration of any possible offsetting price or income effects from an improvement in productivity in either country. Such effects, considered in Bacha (1978) and Evans (1980), modify but do not fundamentally alter the implications of the above analysis.

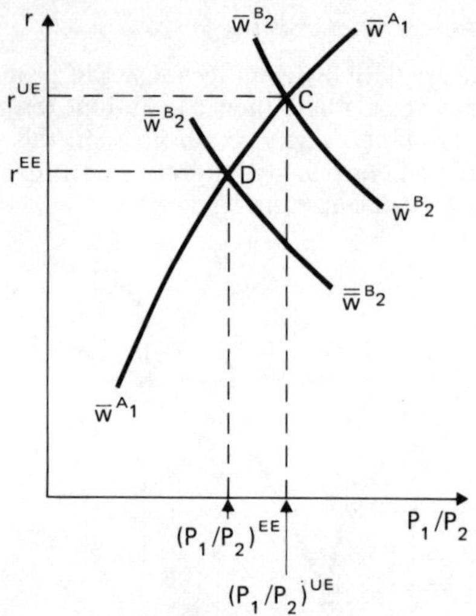

Diagram 3

The generalised Lewis model

The 'unequal exchange' model can be used to show the generalised Lewis model, or the Prebisch-Singer model of inequality of transmission of the benefits of technical change (Diagram 4).

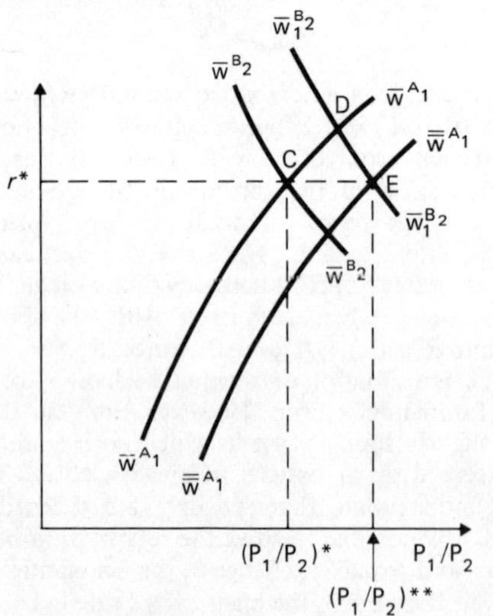

Diagram 4

Taking as the starting point the international equilibrium with wages given autonomously and the rate of profit equalised internationally, note:

1 An improvement in the productivity of labour in economy B will shift the w^{B_2} function upwards say to $\bar{w}_1^{B_2}$ in Diagram 4.
2 An increase in wages in country A will shift the function downwards, say, to $\bar{\bar{w}}^{A_1}$ in Diagram 4.

Hence, when there is an improvement in productivity in country B at unchanged wages, shifting $\bar{w}^{B_2}$ to $\bar{w}_1{}^{B_2}$, the terms of trade worsen for country B and there is a rise in the rate of profit. If there is a subsequent rise in wages in country A shifting the specialisation frontier to $\bar{\bar{w}}^{A_1}$ and restoring profits to the previous levels, there is a further deterioration in the terms of trade for the low-wage country shown by the new equilibrium point E. Thus, if there is a difference in bargaining power of workers between the rich and poor countries, the poor country will be pushed farther and farther into 'unequal exchange'.

Notes: Reading 15

1 The term 'neo-Ricardian' has been used within Marxist debates in a rather loose and often pejorative sense. In this text, I mean by 'neo-Ricardian' the grafting of Sraffa on to Ricardian trade theory. Amongst the authors covered, a distinction should be made between the careful analytical development of a new theoretical basis for international trade theory in the writings of Mainwaring, Metcalfe and Steedman, and the 'unequal exchange' authors such as Emmanuel, Saigal, Amin and Braun. The latter writers are often sloppy in the presentation of their analytical argument and attempt to generalise from their simple models to general theses on imperialism and underdevelopment. See the bibliography for a list of their most important writings.
2 See, for example, List (1885), Manoïlesco (1932), Lewis (1954), Prebisch (1950, 1959), Singer (1949, 1950).
3 See, for example, Chenery (1961) and Bruno (1970).
4 See Graham (1948).
5 See Mundell (1957).
6 See, for example, Johnson (1967).
7 See Bhagwati (1958, 1968, 1973).
8 For an excellent summary of the neo-classical position see Södersten (1971), ch. 12.
9 See Metcalfe and Steedman (1973a).
10 The most important essays in this literature are collected in Steedman (1979). See also Samuelson (1975).
11 See Metcalfe and Steedman (1973b).
12 See Emmanuel (1972). Other main contributors to the development of the Theory of Unequal Exchange are Amin (1973), Saigal (1973) and Braun (1974).

References: Reading 15

Amin, S. (1973), *L'Echange inégal et la loi de la valeur: la fin d'un débat* (Editions Anthropos-Idep); English translation in S. Amin, *Imperialism and Unequal Development* (Harvester, 1977).

Bacha, E. L. (1978), 'An interpretation of unequal exchange from Prebisch-Singer to Emmanuel',

Journal of Development Economics, vol. 5, no. 4, pp. 319–30.

Bettelheim, C. (1972), 'Theoretical comments', Appendix I in A. Emmanuel, *Unequal Exchange: A Study in the Imperialism of Trade* (Monthly Review Press).

Bhagwati, J. N. (1958), 'Immiserizing growth: a geometric note', *Review of Economic Studies*, vol. 25, no. 68, pp. 201–5.

Bhagwati, J. N. (1968), 'Distortions and immiserizing growth: a generalisation', *Review of Economic Studies*, vol. 35, no. 104, pp. 481–5.

Bhagwati, J. N. (1969), *Trade, Tariffs and Growth* (MIT).

Bhagwati, J. N. (1973), 'The theory of immiserizing growth: further applications', in M. B. Connolly and A. K. Swoboda (eds), *International Trade and Money: The Geneva Essays* (University of Toronto Press).

Braun, O. (1974), 'L'Echange inégal, in G. Amoa and O. Braun, *Echanges internationaux et sous-développement*, présentation par S. Amin (Éditions Anthropos-Idep), pp. 141–264; English translation forthcoming.

Bruno, M. (1970), 'Development policy and dynamic comparative advantage', in R. Vernon (ed.), *The Technology Factor in International Trade*, National Bureau of Economic Research, New York).

Chenery, H. B. (1961), 'Comparative advantage and development policy', *American Economic Review*, vol. 1, no. 1, pp. 18–51.

Emmanuel, A. (1972), *Unequal Exchange: A Study in the Imperialism of Trade* (Monthly Review Press); originally published as *L'Echange inégal* (Maspero, 1969).

Emmanuel, A. (1975), 'Unequal exchange revisited', Discussion Paper No. 77, Institute of Development Studies, Brighton.

Evans, H. D. (1972), *A General Equilibrium Analysis of Protection: The Effects of Protection in Australia* (North-Holland).

Evans, H. D. (1976), 'Unequal exchange and economic policies: some implications of the neo-Ricardian critique of the theory of comparative advantage', *Economic and Political Weekly*, vol. 11, nos 5–7, annual number, pp. 143–58.

Evans, H. D. (1979), 'International commodity policy: UNCTAD and NIEO in search of a rationale', *World Development*, vol. 7, no. 3, pp. 259–80.

Evans, H. D. (1980), 'Emmanuel's theory of unequal exchange: critique, counter-critique and theoretical contribution', Discussion Paper No. 149, Institute of Development Studies, Brighton.

Evans, H. D. (ed.) (forthcoming), *The Political Economy of Trade* (Harvester).

Findlay, R. (1978), 'The fundamental determinants of the terms of trade', paper presented to the symposium on The Past and Prospects of the Economic World Order, Institute for International Economic Studies, Stockholm.

Garegnani, P. (1970), 'Heterogeneous capital, the production function and the theory of distribution', *Review of Economic Studies*, vol. 37, no. 3, pp. 407–36; repr. in E. K. Hunt and J. G. Schwartz (eds), *A Critique of Economic Theory* (Penguin, 1972).

Graham, F. D. (1948), *The Theory of International Values* (Princeton University Press).

Halevy, E. (1928), *The Rise of Philosophical Radicalism and Utilitarianism*, tr. M. Morris (Faber); new edn 1934, paper edn 1972.

Harcourt, G. C. (1972), *Some Cambridge Controversies in the Theory of Capital* (Cambridge University Press).

Johnson, H. G. (1967), *Economic Policies Towards Developing Countries* (Allen & Unwin).

Klundert, Th. van de (1971a), 'Labour values and international trade: a reformulation of the theory of A. Emmanuel', Research Memorandum No. 26, Tilburg Institute of Economics (early draft of Klundert, 1971b).

Klundert, Th. van de (1971b), 'Labour values and international trade: a reformulation of the theory of A. Emmanuel', mimeo.; published in French in *Interrogations récentes sur la théorie du commerce internationale*, Cahiers d'Analyse Economique (Editions Cujas, 1974).

Kravis, I. (1956), 'Availability and other influences on the commodity composition of trade', *Journal of Political Economy*, vol. 64.

Lewis, W. A. (1954), 'Economic development with unlimited supplies of labour', *Manchester School*, vol. 22, no. 2, pp. 139–91.

Linder, S. B. (1961), *An Essay on Trade and Transformation* (Almqvist & Wicksell).

List, F. (1885), *The National System of Political Economy* (Longman).

McKenzie, L. W. (1954), 'On equilibrium in Graham's model of world trade and other competitive systems', *Econometrica*, vol. 22, no. 2, pp. 147–61.

Mainwaring, L. (1974), 'A neo-Ricardian analysis of international trade', *Kyklos*, vol. 27, no. 3, pp. 531–53.

Mainwaring, L. (1976), 'The correction of neo- Ricardian trade losses', *Economica Internazionale*, vol. 29, nos. 1–2, pp. 3–10.

Mainwaring, L. (1979), 'On the transition from autarky to trade'. Essay 12 in I. Steedman (ed.), *Fundamental Issues in Trade Theory* (Macmillan).

Manne, A. S. (1974), 'Multisectoral models in development planning: a survey', *Journal of Development Economics*, vol. 1, no. 1, pp. 43–69.

Manoïlesco, M. (1932), 'The theory of protection and international trade', *The Journal of Political Economy*, p. 121.

Metcalfe, J. S., and Steedman, I. (1973a), 'Heterogeneous capital and the Heckscher-Ohlin-Samuelson theory of trade', in M. Parkin (ed.), *Essays in Modern Economics* (Longman); repr. in I. Steedman (ed.), *Fundamental Issues in Trade Theory* (Macmillan, 1979).

Metcalfe, J. S., and Steedman, I. (1973b), 'The non-substitution theorem and international trade theory', *Australian Economic Papers*, vol. 12, pp. 267–9; repr. in I. Steedman (ed.), *Fundamental Issues in Trade Theory* (Macmillan, 1979).

Metcalfe, J. S., and Steedman, I. (1974), 'A note on the gain from trade', *Economic Record*, vol. 50, no. 132, pp. 581–95; repr. in I Steedman (ed.), *Fundamental Issues in Trade Theory* (Macmillan, 1979).

Mundell, R. A. (1957), 'International trade and factor mobility', *American Economic Review*, vol. 57, no. 3, pp. 321–35.

Prebisch, R. (1950), *The Economic Development of Latin America and its Principal Problems* (UN).

Prebisch, R. (1959), 'International payments in an era of coexistence: commercial policy in the underdeveloped countries', *American Economic Review*, vol. 49, no. 2, pp. 251–73.

Roncaglia, A. (1978), *Sraffa and the Theory of Prices* (Wiley).

Saigal, J. C. (1973), 'Réflexions sur la théorie de l'échange inégal', appendix in S. Amin, *L'Echange inégal et la loi de la valeur* (Editions Anthropos-Idep); English translation in S. Amin, *Imperialism and Unequal Development* (Harvester, 1977).

Samuelson, P. A. (1973), 'Deadweight loss in international trade from the profit motive?', in C. F. Bergsten and W. G. Tyler (eds), *Leading Issues in International Economic Policy. Essays in Honour of George N. Halm* (D. C. Heath).

Samuelson, P. A. (1975), 'Trade pattern reversals in time-phased systems and inter-temporal efficiency', *Journal of International Economics*, vol. 5, pp. 309–63.

Samuelson, P. A. (1976), 'Illogic of neo-Marxian doctrine of unequal exchange', in D. A. Belsley *et al.*, (eds), *Inflation, Trade and Taxes. Essays in Honour of Alice Bourneuf* (Ohio State University Press).

Singer, H. W. (1949), 'Economic progress in underdeveloped countries', *Social Research*, vol. 16, no. 1, pp. 1–12.

Singer, H. W. (1950), 'The distribution of gains between investing and borrowing countries', *American Economic Review*, vol. 40, no. 2, pp. 473–85.

Södersten, B. (1971), *International Economics* (Macmillan).

Steedman, I. (1979) (ed.), *Fundamental Issues in Trade Theory* (Macmillan).

Whitin, T. M. (1953), 'Classical theory, Graham's theory and linear programming in international trade', *Quarterly Journal of Economics*, vol. 67, no. 4, pp. 520–44.

Reading 16

The Terms of Trade between Primary-Producing and Industrial Countries

P. T. Ellsworth

Inter-American Economic Affairs, vol. 10, no. 1, 1961.

1

There are few hardier perennials among discussions of international economic relations than the problem of the terms of trade between primary-producing and industrial countries. Of the various views expressed on this topic, the most challenging is probably that of Raul Prebisch. Referring to the period of some sixty-odd years between 1876 and 1938, during which there appears to have been a decline of 36 per cent in the terms of trade of primary for industrial products, Dr Prebisch has attributed this worsening of the position of the primary-producing or peripheral countries to elements of monopoly in the economies of the industrial or center countries.

> Speaking generally, technical progress seems to have been greater in industrial than in the primary production of peripheral countries. . . . Consequently, if prices had been reduced in proportion to increasing productivity, the reduction should have been less in the case of primary products than in that of manufactures. . . . Had this happened . . . the benefits of technical progress would thus have been distributed alike throughout the world. . . .

This did not occur, however:

> from the 1870s until the Second World War, the price relation has turned consistently against primary products – only 63.5 per cent of the finished manufactures which could be bought in the 1860s were bought in the 1930s; in other words, an average of 58.6 per cent more primary products than in the 1870s are needed to buy the same amount of finished manufactures (UN Economic Commission for Latin America, 1950, p. 8).

The explanation of this phenomenon is to be found in the relative cyclical movement of the prices of industrial and of primary products. 'The prices of primary products rise more rapidly than industrial prices in the upswing, but also they fall more in the downswing, so that in the course of the cycles the gap between prices of the two is progressively widened. . . . The reason for this is very simple.' Owing to imperfect competition among industrial producers and to the superior organization of labor in the center countries, prices of industrial products and wages of industrial workers are relatively rigid during the downswing.

> The pressure then moves toward the periphery, with greater force than would be the case if, by reason of the limitations of competition, wages and profits in the center were not rigid. This is the clue of the phenomenon whereby the great industrial centers not only keep for themselves the benefits of the application of innovations to their own economy, but are also in a more favorable position to obtain a part of those deriving from the technical progress of the periphery (UN Economic Commission for Latin America, 1950, p. 13).

2

This view has by no means gone unchallenged. With his usual acumen, Professor Viner has pointed out that long-period comparisons are largely vitiated by the fact that the price indices used for manufactures give no weight 'to the gain in utility from the new commodities which have become available, such as the automobile, the tractor, and penicillin'. Moreover, even 'where the manufactures are nominally the same, they have over the years become incomparably superior in quality', whereas the primary commodities used in their prices indices 'are for the most part . . . not superior in quality and in some cases are perhaps inferior' (1957, p. 143). A modern nylon cord tire serves the same purpose as ten or more of the earliest tires, and does so better, but a ton of copper is still a ton of copper. Hence if the copper producer can today get only twenty tires for a ton of his products as against say forty some fifty years ago, the exchange has moved in his favor, in terms of real satisfaction, rather than against him.

Viner also notes that the more rapid the increase in a country's population (whether it be predominantly agricultural or predominantly industrial) the larger will tend to be the volume of its exports and therefore the worse its terms of trade. We might add that were it not for the relative restraint on population growth in the industrial centers, retention of part of the gains of increased productivity in the form of higher wages would have been most unlikely, and that similar restraint in the primary producing countries would have tended to produce the same results. Thus it may be said that in a sense the peripheral countries chose to take the gains of increased productivity in the form of a larger population rather than in higher *per capita* incomes and better terms of trade.

3

My main concern in this paper, however, is not with considerations which bear upon the total change in the terms of trade over the entire period 1876 to 1938, but with impressions which arose from examining movements within the long-term trend. Examination of the figures used by Prebisch, as well as other similar series, indicate that the net downward movement of the terms of trade of primary as against industrial products took place in three clearly marked stages. The first of these covered the period from 1876–80 to 1901–5, and was followed by a relatively level plateau until 1913. (During the First World War, the terms of trade turned sharply in favor of primary producing countries. This is shown in one of the indices in Table 1, but not in the figures used by Prebisch, which appear to have been column (3) using 1876–80 = 100. He omits the war years from consideration.) A sharp drop occurred between 1913 and 1921, followed by substantial recovery during the mid-twenties, though the pre-war level was never attained. Finally, there is the decline from the late twenties to 1933, again followed by partial but incomplete recovery.

It is my contention that each of these stages of decline in the terms of trade of primary countries requires and is susceptible to a distinct and specific explanation, and that when this is given, relatively little remains to be accounted for by any all-encompassing theory such as that advanced by Prebisch. And what remains for explanation can surely be fully or more than fully countered by Viner's argument with respect to the improved quality and composition of manufactured exports.

Table 1 **Terms of Trade of Primary for Manufactured Goods**

Period	*UK primary imports to manufactured exports (a) (1913 = 100)*	*Primary to manufactured commodities in world trade (b) (1938 = 100)*	*UK imports to exports (c) (1938 = 100)*
	1	*2*	*3*
1876–80	116	147	163
1881–5	119	145	167
1886–90	111	137	157
1891–5	105	133	147
1896–1900	101	135	142
1901–5	100	132	138
1906–10	100	133	140
1911–13	101	137	140
1913	100	137	137
1914	101		
1915	109		
1916	114		
1917	120		
1918	100		
1919	83		
1920	78		
1921	61	94	93
1922	67	103	102
1923	74	114	107
1924	78	121	122
1925	81	123	125
1926	70	121	119
1927	81	125	122
1928	81	121	123
1929	80	118	122
1930	70	105	112
1931	61	93	102
1932	63	89	102
1933	63	89	98
1934		96	101
1935		98	103
1936		102	107
1937		108	107
1938		100	100

(a) Based on W. Schlote (1952), Appendix, Table 26. The two groups of which primary imports are composed, foodstuffs and livestock and raw materials, are given equal weight, in accordance with their relative total values in the period 1910–13.
(b) Source: UN (1949) p. 22.
(c) Source: Same as (b). (Current year weights. Based on W. Schlote, 1952.)

4

With respect to the (apparent) downward movement in the terms of trade between 1876–80 and 1901–5, I suggest that this can be in large part if not wholly accounted for by the sharp decline in railway and shipping rates which occurred during this period. This decline was marked and fairly continuous over the thirty years in question; it was the accompaniment of a rapid expansion of the world's railway network, great technical improvement in shipping and increase in its supply, and the ancillary development of harbors, docks, warehouses and canals. The immense growth of railway mileage is shown in Table 2. Both relatively and absolutely, expansion of the railway network was most rapid in the thirty years between 1870 and 1900, though its growth continued apace until 1930.

Steam shipping replaced the slower and less capacious sailing vessel in this interval, its share of total tonnage rising from 12.5 per cent in 1870 to 64 per cent in 1900, while total tonnage itself approximately doubled. The first refrigerated ship was introduced in 1876, the Suez Canal opened in 1869, and all through this period the major ports of the world were provided with more ample, more specialized and more efficient facilities. By

Table 2 **Railway Mileage, 1870–1930**

	1870	*1900*	*1930*
World	130,361	490,974	795,213
North America	56,106	223,454	319,100
Europe	65,192	176,179	261,545
Asia	5086	37,470	82,487
South America	1770	26,450	58,809
Africa	1110	12,499	42,450
Australasia	1097	14,922	30,822

Source: Ashworth (1952), p. 63.

bringing hitherto remote regions into contact with the industrial centers of western Europe and the United States, the expansion of the railway network greatly extended the area of profitable cultivation of wheat, corn and cotton, and stimulated the raising of livestock. 'By the early nineties every farmer within a zone of 300 kilometers around the city of Buenos Aires had a railway station within ten to 15 kilometers of his farm. In the next decade extensions and feeders to the main lines were built . . . and where the railway reached, land and climate being suitable, cultivation of wheat began' (Hanson, 1938, p. 119).

With the extension of railways went a reduction of freight rates which brought down the delivered cost of grains and other foodstuffs and raw materials at seaboard. The average rate per ton mile on five major US railways fell from £1.44 to £0.78 between 1876 and 1892, or by 46 per cent (Senate Report, 1893, Pt 1, Appendix K, Tables 123 and 130). In the same period, the average carload rate on seven commodities from the west coast to New York declined by 63 per cent (ibid., Tables 123 and 128). The commodities were dried fruit, hides, leather, nuts, beans, wine and hops.

Strongly reinforcing this trend was a parallel reduction in ocean shipping rates. Table 4 shows that UK

Table 3

Year	*Average price per bu. of US wheat in Liverpool*	*Average freight charge per bu., NY to Liverpool*	*Average freight charge per bu., Chicago to NY*
1876	$1.415	$0.1540	$0.143
1891	1.179	0.0625	0.076
Decline:	0.236	0.0915	0.067
		0.067	
Total drop in shipping costs:		0.1585	

Source: Senate Report (1893), p. 1, Table 62, Appendix K, Tables 45 and 129.

inward freights from various ports declined by nearly two-thirds. (If the peak level of 212 in 1877 is taken, the decline by 1901–5 was more than two-thirds.)

Table 4 **UK Inward Freights (1900 = 100)**

1876–80	184
1881–5	143
1886–90	106
1891–5	86
1896–1900	89
1901–5	67
1906–10	68

Source: A. K. Cairncross (1953), p. 176.

The comments of Layton and Crowther vividly express the consequences of this remarkable slashing of transport costs.

> It will perhaps help to put the various elements affecting prices in their right perspective when it is pointed out that, according to an investigation carried out by Powers in the State of Minnesota, the value of farm crops *on the farm* in inland states actually rose per unit in the twenty years preceding 1895, but owing to the fall in the cost of freight to the seaboard, the producers could place their produce on board ship at a lower price than before, while retaining a larger sum as their own share. This, of course, damaged the position of the seaboard farmers relatively to their inland competitors. but though the fall in prices on the seaboard was considerable, it was even more severe in Europe, owing to the steady but rapid fall in the cost of carrying grain across the Atlantic. Thus the railway and shipbuilding mania, which had been so large a cause of the boom of 1870–4, became the leading factor in producing a subsequent decline of commodity prices (1935, p. 90).

The significance of the sharp decline in both railway and ocean freight rates between 1876 and 1905 with respect to the terms of trade of primary producing countries derives from the fact that the price indices used for the exports of these countries are the c.i.f. prices of imports in British markets, whereas the indices used for their imports are the f.o.b. prices of British exports. The apparent relative decline in the prices of primary exports is therefore heavily weighted by the significant reduction in freight rates. It appears certain that a large part of the fall in primary product prices in European markets must be attributed to this cause. What proportion of the change in the index of primary product prices can thus be accounted for could only be determined by a careful, commodity-by-commodity investigation. Limits of time have prevented me from making such a study, but I have obtained a limited amount of evidence in support of the view presented here. (It is my hope that research now under way will throw fuller light on the problem.)

Most of the readily available data relate only to the period between 1884 and 1903, and ocean freight rates alone are given. These are shown in Table 5. For wheat, however, the effects of changes in both railway and ocean shipping rates can be shown for the interval 1876–91. As the following tabulated data indicate, the price in Liverpool of North American wheat fell £0.236, while shipping costs declined £0.1585. Thus 67 per cent of the drop in the price of wheat in this period alone is accounted for by the fall in shipping charges. Lowered costs of transport from the average farm to Chicago *could* account for most of the rest. Since warehousing, loading, and landing costs were also being reduced at this time, the probable real fall in price was negligible.

From Table 5, we can see that a drop in ocean freight rates explains all of the apparent decline in the price of wool, 88 per cent in the case of mutton, 37.5 per cent for corn, but only 12.8 per cent for sugar. From Layton and Crowther (1935, p. 89) we learn, however, that the wide-spread use by European countries of the bounty system on beet sugar 'superimposed on a rapidly increasing world's production, accounts for the fact that sugar fell 58 per cent in England' between 1871–5 and 1894–8. As for jute and rice, the fall in their prices in London was greatly exceeded by the decline in ocean shipping rates. It would therefore appear that the f.o.b. price in Calcutta and Rangoon rose instead of fell between 1884 and 1903.

From the foregoing evidence, it would seem reasonable to conclude that a large proportion, and perhaps all, of the decline in the British prices of primary products in the period between 1876 and 1905 can be attributed to the great decline in inward freight rates, whose collective trend is shown in Table 4. Since the price of British manufactured exports fell in this period by 15 per cent, the terms of trade of primary countries, were f.o.b. prices used for their exports as well as for their imports, may well have moved in their favor.

This conclusion is supported by a recent study of cyclical price movements, which indicates that:

> . . . the price fall which usually took place in a bulky commodity in London in years of economic recession was frequently paralleled by an *increase* in the local price of the same commodity in the frontier area. . . . A few examples will illustrate the price movements in recession years of bulky frontier products which experienced a moderate price fall in the London or Liverpool market and benefited from a considerable decline in freight costs to the centres of consumption. In the recession from 1873 to 1879 wheat prices in the United Kingdom fell 19 per cent, while they increased 9 per cent in Illinois and 29 per cent in Iowa. From 1883 to 1886 the price of Chilean nitrate fell 13 per cent in London and increased 22 per cent in Chilean ports. In the recession from 1890 to 1894 the price of soft-wood lumber fell 8 per cent in London and

Table 5 **Decline in Prices and in Ocean Freight Rates**

	Price			*Freight rates*			*Per cent freight decline is of fall in price*
	1884	*1903*	*Decline*	*1884*	*1903*	*Decline*	
Corn (d. per bu.)	35.34	29.88	5.46	3.51	1.46	2.05	37.5
Sugar (d. per bu.)	310.2	166.8	143.4	42.5	24.0	18.5	12.8
Jute (s. per ton)	282.2	269.6	12.6	37.5	19.38	18.12	143.0
Wool (d. per lb.)	8.5	8.25	0.25	0.625	0.375	0.25	100.0
Rice (s. per ton)	153.33	145.0	8.33	38.92	22.08	16.83	202.0
	1885	*1899*		*1885*	*1889*		
Mutton* (d. per lb.)	4¾	2⅝	2⅛	3½	1⅝	1⅞	88.0

Note: Prices (except mutton) are average unit values; freight rates are inward ocean freight rates from New York (corn), Java (sugar), Calcutta (jute), New Zealand (wool), and Rangoon (rice). Source: Board of Trade (1904).

*Freight charges on mutton include handling and unloading charges in Australia and New Zealand and in London. Source: Hanson (1938, pp. 88–9).

increased 12 per cent in Canada. From 1900 to 1904 wool prices in London fell 8 per cent, while prices in Argentina in terms of gold pesos increased 12 per cent. From 1907 to 1908 the price of oats in London fell 9 per cent, while the price in Australia increased 9 per cent, and in the United States 13 per cent. As a result of such increases in local prices, it has frequently happened that the general export price indices in frontier countries have increased in recessions. In Argentina the export-price index in terms of gold increased in the recessions from 1866 to 1868, from 1889 to 1893, and from 1900 to 1904 and from 1907 to 1908.

The explanation of the above price movements is that the savings in transport costs amounted to more than the decline in the London price (Wright, 1955, pp. 425–6).

5

We turn now to the course of prices and of the terms of trade between 1913 and 1929. Three distinct phases stand out: prices generally rose by some 200 per cent during the war and immediately after, crashed after 1920 to a level about 50 per cent above prewar in 1922, and then moved gradually downward until 1929.

During the 1913–20 period, food and raw materials prices, contrary to their usual behavior in years of expansion, rose less than the prices of manufactured goods. With 1913 = 100, the index for foodstuffs and livestock imports reached 282 in 1920, that for raw materials 292, while British manufactured exports climbed to 370. The terms of trade of primary-producing countries consequently fell to 78. No less conspicuous than this exceptional movement was the marked disparity in behavior of individual prices. Out of thirty-four primary commodities,[1] twelve rose substantially more than the average (218 per cent), while sixteen rose substantially less. This disparity is explainable partly in terms of differences in supply conditions (for some commodities, accumulation of stocks depressed prices in 1920), partly by the distribution of shipping, and partly by the varying incidence of wartime controls.

Our interest, however, is less in the situation during and immediately after the war than in the low point reached by the terms of trade of primary products in 1921–2, and in particular in the failure of the terms of trade to recover fully during the prosperous years of the 1920s. First we must attend briefly to relative price movements in the short-lived postwar depression. The terms of trade went still further against the primary-producing countries. In 1921 they reached a low of 61, recovering moderately in the following year to 67. Considering the situation in 1922, since the rapid fall of all three price indices continued until that year, we find the fall was greatest for raw materials prices, amounting to 54 per cent from their 1920 level, while the decline in foodstuffs and in manufactures was closely similar, amounting to 44 and 42 per cent respectively.

There is no simple explanation for these relative price movements, although two developments appear to have been of outstanding importance. First, British labor obtained a moderate increase in real wages during the war which it was able to retain in the succeeding depression, since the declines (1920–2) in wages and in the cost of living were almost identical. Higher wages were thus built into the cost structure of manufactured goods. Moreover, there can be no doubt that the administrative decisions of manufacturers, who chose to reduce output and employment instead of cutting prices, was also a factor. There is clearly some support for the Prebisch thesis in this period. It is surely worth pointing out, however, that the rise of unemployment in Great Britain – to over two million – meant that the shock of the depression was borne most heavily by this group. In the primary-producing countries, on the other hand, there was relatively little unemployment, the burden of the depression being borne more widely in the form of generally lower prices and money incomes.

Another element of great importance in accounting for the relative decline in primary prices immediately after the First World War was the sharp response of producers to demand during the war, followed by excess capacity and the accumulation of stocks as demand shrank in the postwar period. This expansion and accumulation operated strongly to depress many primary prices – notably those of tin, nickel, copper, coffee, sugar and wheat.

Rubber is a special case. Systematic plantation cultivation of this crop began only in the years just before the war (1905–10). Supplies increased rapidly (from 118,000 tons in 1913 to nearly 400,000 tons in 1919), and costs were substantially reduced. Rubber was unique in that its price actually fell during the 1914–20 inflation; its decline thereafter was also one of the sharpest.

The depression of 1921–2 was of short duration. Why did the terms of trade fail, during the ensuing period of expansion and general prosperity, to recover fully to their 1913 level? By the late 1920s, the terms of trade had reached only 81, still some 19 per cent below the prewar position. The price indices of foodstuffs and raw materials both declined, contrary to their usual movement in cyclical upswings, but the index of prices of manufactures declined even more. The percentage fall in each of these indices between 1922 and 1929 was 12, 9 and 25 per cent respectively.

In spite of moderate improvement in the terms of trade of primary-producing countries, a number of exceptional factors operated to prevent an even greater improvement. These were: a continuation of overproduction in many lines, and in others, expansion of output relative to demand; an aggravation of overproduction by the 'side effects' of a number of restriction schemes; and the impact of specially rapid technological advance in some lines of raw material production.

Among agricultural crops, the prices of sugar, silk, rubber, cotton and wool all fell appreciably more than the average (Layton and Crowther, 1935, p. 185). Although the output of sugar was substantially larger in 1922 than in prewar years, demand had recovered from the collapsed level of 1921, and the European beet sugar industry was contributing less than its earlier proportion to total output. Continued increases in production during the 1920s, especially in Cuba and Europe, led the Cuban government to attempt to restrict sales. The principal effect of this effort was to stimulate production elsewhere, with a steady weakening of the price. Rubber provides a similar case. The collapse in its price during the postwar depression led to the inauguration of the Stevenson restriction scheme in Malaya, the principal producing region. Until 1926 the price soared, but growth of production in non-control areas, especially the Dutch East Indies, finally forced abandonment of restriction. At the end of 1928, the price was only slightly above the low level of 1922.

Cotton prices also moved strongly downward in the 1920s, largely as a result of increasing output in the United States, where the ravages of the boll weevil were successfully countered. Wool production increased by about a third between 1925 and 1929, while wool prices declined in almost the same proportion.

In minerals, the general picture at the end of the war was one of greatly expanded capacity. Recovery from the general price collapse of 1921–2 was fairly general, and was followed by rising demand as industrial output expanded. The response was so vigorous, however, that in many lines prices sagged throughout the later twenties. Thus a new flotation process in zinc production led to the accumulation of stocks which after 1924 depressed the price below the 1921 level. The situation was similar in lead; although demand rose substantially in the early twenties with the increased use of storage batteries in motor cars, new discoveries together with improved technology and increasing recoveries from scrap caused a large rise in production accompanied by a decline in price, which by 1929 was barely above the 1921 average (data on minerals from Elliott *et al.*, 1937). Consumption of tin grew rapidly after the postwar recovery, raising this price by 1926 almost to the peak reached in 1920. Many new companies were floated in the next year or more, raising capacity by more than a third by 1929, and driving the price down by a similar proportion. Even with a continued rise in consumption, it became clear that overproduction was upon the industry. Nickel, whose output had expanded nearly 50 per cent during the war, responded to rising industrial demand in the United States with a further sizeable increase in production in the late twenties. Though the price rose to an average of 35c per lb. in 1929, it was still below the 1921 average of 37c. (It had averaged only 27c in 1924.) Copper, which entered the postwar period with excess capacity and accumulated stocks, also responded to growing demand with an increase in output of almost a third, largely from expansion in Chile and the Congo. It was chiefly these new, low-cost producers who were benefited. Although the price recovered from the 1922 low of £62.1 per long ton (annual average) to £75.4 in 1929, it was then only slightly above the 1913 figure of £68.4.

The experience of petroleum producers was similar to that of producers of the non-ferrous metals. Demand rose steadily, but production more than kept pace.

Two commodities were subjected to severe and growing pressure from synthetic substitutes: silk and nitrates. With the introduction of improved methods of production in Japan, output of raw silk rose by about a third between 1925 and 1929; in this interval rayon production more than doubled, its price was practically halved, and the price of silk fell by 26 per cent. Synthetic production of nitrates in Germany and other European countries introduced a threat to the natural nitrate of Chile, whose share of world inorganic nitrate production fell from nearly 65 per cent before the First World War to just under a quarter in 1928–9.

Finally, brief mention may be made of the resumption, in more moderate degree, of the role of ocean freight rates. These declined from a level of 142 in 1922 to 113 in 1929, or by 20 per cent (*The Economist*, 1938, p. 484). Correction of the prices of primary imports into the UK for this factor would raise them, at least a few points, relative to the prices of manufactured exports.

6

Between 1929 and 1933, the terms of trade of primary-producing countries underwent their third stage of decline, falling from 80 to 63. Although the prices of manufactures slumped some 24 per cent during these years, the drop in prices of foodstuffs and of raw materials was considerably greater – 39 and 42 per cent respectively. As in the first of our three periods, ocean freight rates also fell, in this instance by 25 per cent. Were this taken into account, f.o.b. primary prices would be somewhat higher, though of course by no means enough so to do more than moderate the fall in the terms of trade.

Here we have a major cyclical decline in prices, which Prebisch would explain in terms of resistance to cuts in wages and profits at the center, with contraction of output and of demand there exerting pressure on the periphery and causing prices and wages in that sector to fall more sharply. There can be no doubt that this explanation has considerable validity for this period. Output in the industrial countries fell markedly, and was reflected in unemployment amounting to 20 per cent and upwards of the labor force (this being the principal form in which the burden of the depression is borne in the industrial centers, as contrasted with a greater price

Table 6 **Production of Leading Crops (in Millions of Metric Tons)**

	Wheat	*Corn*	*Rice*	*Barley*	*Oats*	*Sugar*	*Coffee*	*Cotton*
Av. 1909–13	82.2	102.9	77.5	28.7	52.1	14.6	0.77	4.53
1922	86.0	105.2	89.5	26.5	49.3	17.07	1.36	4.14
Av. 1924–8	97.1	107.2	79.7	31.0	52.3	25.4	1.61	5.70
1929	98.3	110.9	80.6	37.7	52.9	27.9	2.52	5.74
1930	105.9	99.6	85.5	36.1	52.1	28.6	1.64	5.63
1931	105.3	111.5	83.4	31.4	48.2	26.8	2.24	5.96
1932	104.3	121.0	82.0	35.7	53.2	24.4	1.83	5.14

Source: 1909–13, 1922: *International Yearbook of Agricultural Statistics 1925–26*; Tables 81 ff.; 1924–32, *The Agricultural Situation in 1932–33*, International Institute of Agriculture, Rome, 1933, pp. 59–93.

fall in peripheral countries, as we have already noted). Real wages in the United Kingdom, which were higher in 1929 than in 1914, rose still further in the next four years.[2]

With demand for raw materials and foodstuffs compressed in the industrial centers via reduced output and employment (though sustained to a degree by the rise in real wages), one would expect a relative price fall for these products even were the response of primary output of the usual economically appropriate kind. That is, even had the decline in industrial demand been met by a reduction of output, however modest, the reduction of primary-products prices would have been greater than that of industrial products, which were subjected to comparatively severe output restrictions.

The relative decline of primary prices, to be expected on the grounds of the Prebisch analysis, was greatly aggravated, however, by the inverse response of the agricultural sector to the fall in demand and prices. Instead of diminishing, the output of many major crops increased. As Table 6 shows, wheat, corn and rice crops were all larger in 1930, 1931 and 1932 than in 1929 (except corn in 1930); the decline in barley was very modest,[3] while oats and cotton production was greater in one of the three depression years. Sugar output at first increased, but by 1932 was down more than 10 per cent. Coffee production alone was notably lower in all three of the depression years.

Producers of non-ferrous metals reacted in the normal fashion to declining demand and price – they reduced output by 40 to 50 per cent in most instances. Yet the prices of these products fell by about the same amount as food prices, owing in their case to previous overproduction and accumulation of stocks (especially noteworthy in the case of copper, zinc and tin).

7

Surveying the entire period 1876 to 1933, during which the terms of trade of primary for industrial products (as reflected in the indices used) declined some 46 per cent, I urge that the evidence shows that this trend is in part spurious, and even where genuine, is not to be explained by any single, simple set of relations. The downward movement was by no means uniform, but consisted of three distinct phases. The first, from 1876 to about 1905, accounting for over one-third of the total decline, was largely spurious, explainable almost entirely if not completely by the huge drop in rail and ocean freight rates. The second phase, 1913 to 1929, includes the postwar collapse of prices and in particular the failure of primary prices to recover to their 1913 level. Here we found overexpansion of output in many lines of primary production during and after the war years reflecting partly exuberant response to rising demand, partly the effects of restrictionist schemes and partly the impact of technological change. The third and final phase, from 1929 to 1933, conforms in part to the explanation given by Dr Prebisch, though the picture was complicated and the worsening of the terms of trade seriously aggravated by the perverse response of suppliers in agriculture, and by previous overexpansion of the production of minerals.

Notes: Reading 16

1 These commodities are those in the list given by Layton and Crowther (1935), p. 137. The index numbers cited are from Schlote (1952), Table 26, and were used to compute column 1 of Table 1, p. 130.

2 With 1914 = 100, real wages in the UK were 118 in 1929. Although money wages fell during the depression, the decline in the cost of living was sufficiently greater so that real wages rose to 130. Results based on data in Layton and Crowther (1935), p. 195.

3 This was also true of wool and raw silk.

References: Reading 16

Ashworth, W. (1952), *A Short History of the International Economy, 1850–1950* (Longman).

Board of Trade (1904), *Memoranda, Statistical Tables and Charts on British and Foreign Trade and Industrial Conditions*, Cmnd 2337 (HMSO).

Cairncross, A. K. (1953), *Home and Foreign Investment, 1870–1913* (Cambridge University Press).

Elliott, W. Y., *et al.* (1937), *International Control in the Non-Ferrous Metals* (Macmillan).

Hanson, S. (1938). *Argentine Meat and the British Market* (Stanford University Press).
Layton, Sir W. T., and Crowther, G. (1935), *An Introduction to the Study of Prices* (Macmillan).
Schlote, W. (1952), *British Overseas Trade from 1700 to the 1930s* (Blackwell).
Senate Report (1893), *Wholesale Prices, Wages and Transportation*, No. 1394, 52nd Congress, 2nd Session.
The Economist (1938), 'Shipping freight index (1898–1913 = 100)', vol. 130, 26 February.
UN (1949), *Relative Prices of Imports and Exports of Underdeveloped Countries*, UN, 11.B3, based on *Industrialization and Foreign Trade* (League of Nations).
UN Economic Commission for Latin America (1950), *The Economic Development of Latin America and Its Principal Problems*, UN E/CN 12/89/Rev. 1 (UN).
Viner, J. (1957), *International Trade and Economic Development* (Clarendon Press).
Wright, C. M. (1955), 'Convertibility and triangular trade as safeguards against economic depression', *Econ. J.*, vol. 65, September.

Reading 17

Export Instability and Economic Growth: A Statistical Verification

C. Glezakos

Economic Development and Cultural Change, vol. 21, 1973, pp. 670–9.

Because less developed countries (LDCs) export mainly primary products, it has been claimed that their economic growth suffers from the deleterious effects of the export instability they experience. The detrimental effects of export instability have been attributed to either the price instability of primary products per se or to the resulting fluctuations of export proceeds.

The argument concerning the effects of export instability on economic growth are usually made on a priori basis with no, or at best, very little empirical evidence. Recent empirical studies,[1] however, have claimed that there is no statistical evidence to support the hypothesis that fluctuations in export proceeds 'inflict any significant damage on the stability and growth of the average underdeveloped country,'[2] or that there is 'any relation between growth in per capita real income and export instability.'[3]

The purpose of this paper is to point out methodological deficiencies in the above empirical studies that significantly weaken their findings and to test in a more systematic way the validity of the a priori arguments regarding the effects of export instability on the economic growth of both LDCs and developed countries (DCs). In addition, an attempt is made to determine the effects of export instability on the growth of exports and to evaluate the relative importance of the export price and export quantity instability effects on economic growth.

1 Recent Empirical Evidence

MacBean based his conclusion that there are no significant effects of export instability on economic growth on the following pieces of evidence: First, on the lack of association between the instability index of exports and that of national income for 35 LDCs using Coppock's data and, second, on the lack of significant regression coefficients in the multiple-regression analysis between the growth rate of the gross domestic product (GDP) and the export instability index, the growth rate of import capacity, the ratio of foreign trade to the national income, etc., for 23 LDCs for the period from 1950 to 1958.

Similarly, Coppock considered as evidence the lack of correlation between his export-instability index and the rate of growth of GNP (1951–7) or the percentage increase in per capita GNP (1951–7) for *all* countries for which he had data.

Both studies, however, seem to suffer from several drawbacks which distort the true relationships the authors seek to estimate.

1. Coppock's instability index, which is merely the antilogarithm of the log-variance of the yearly rates of change of a time series, is greatly influenced by the choice of the first and the last year of the series. Therefore, this measure, especially when it is used for a short-range time series, is an almost random estimate of instability.

2. For the income growth rate, Coppock used the 'percentage increase in GNP per year' adjusted for price changes, while MacBean used the 'compound annual rate of growth of GDP, 1950/1–1957/8' in current prices.[4] Both authors, therefore, invite distorting errors. At first, due to the fact that the LDCs have higher population growth rates than the DCs, the use of the total GNP or GDP growth rates rather than the respective per capita growth rates introduced an upward bias into the rates of the LDCs.[5] Also, since the rate of inflation in the LDCs has generally been greater than in the DCs, the use of income data in current prices for the estimation of the income growth rates results in an additional overestimation of the growth rates of the LDCs.

3. Additionally, Coppock makes two other methodological errors. On the one hand, while he uses export instability indexes for one period (1946–58), his income growth figures cover a rather different period (1951–7). It cannot reasonably be claimed that the existing instability over a given period of time has any significant effect on the incomes of a different period.

Table 1 **Summary of Income Growth, Export Instability, and Export Growth Regressions**

Equation	Sample	Dependent Variable	Constant	Explanatory Variables I_x	X_r	$\bar{R}^2$	F-Ratio/ df
(1-1)	LDCs	Y_r	4.483*	−0.259*	. . .	.226	11.24*
			(6.144)	(3.352)			(1,34)
(1-2)	LDCs	Y_r	0.869**	. . .	0.274	.373	21.82*
			(2.520)		(4.671)		(1,34)
(1-3)	LDCs	Y_r	2.571*	−0.164**	0.225*	.446	15.09*
			(3.229)	(2.341)	(3.805)		(2,33)
(1-4)	LDCs	X_r	8.504*	−0.423**	. . .	.102	4.98**
			(4.746)	(2.230)			(1,34)
(1-5)	DCs	Y_r	3.067**	0.095	. . .	−.050	0.19
			(2.494)	(0.433)			(1,16)
(1-6)	DCs	Y_r	−0.162	. . .	0.454*	.673	36.01*
			(0.246)		(6.001)		(1,16)
(1-7)	DCs	Y_r	−0.298	0.028	0.453*	.652	16.96*
			(0.325)	(0.221)	(5.775)		(2,15)
(1-8)	DCs	X_r	7.430*	0.149	. . .	−.054	0.14
			(3.294)	(0.368)			(1,16)

Sources: Y_r, UN, *Yearbook of National Accounts Statistics* (various issues). OECD, *National Accounts of Less Developed Countries* (1950–66); UN, *Demographic Yearbook* (various issues); I_x, Statistical Appendix; X_r, IMF, *International Financial Statistics* (various issues).

Note: Y_r = annual real per capita GDP growth rate; I_x = instability index of export proceeds; X_r = annual growth rate of exports; $\bar{R}^2$ = coefficient of determination corrected for the degrees of freedom. The figures in parenthesis below the regression coefficients are the *t*-values of the coefficients, and below the *F*-test are the degrees of freedom.

*Significant at 1%.

**Significant at 5%.

On the other hand, the sample of countries he employs in estimating the relationship of export instability and income growth includes a large number of DCs which, according to a priori arguments, are not significantly affected by export instability.

On the basis of the methodological errors pointed out above, we feel that the Coppock and MacBean results should not be taken as evidence against the hypothesis that export instability is detrimental to economic growth in the LDCs.

2 Statistical Testing of the Effects of Export Instability

The instability index

In view of the fact that for every empirical study of export instability the measure of instability is of crucial importance, we paid special attention to the development of a meaningful export-instability index. Our index (I_x) is the arithmetic mean of the absolute values of the yearly changes in a time series corrected for the trend and expressed as a percentage of the average of all observations. That is,

$$I_x = \frac{100}{X} \frac{\sum_{t=2}^{n} |X_t - X_{t-1} - b|}{n = 1}$$

where b is the slope of the linear trend $X_t = a + bt$ fitted by the ordinary least-squares (OLS) method.

Not only does this index possess some desirable properties for a good instability index,[6] but it can also be given a logical economic interpretation. The yearly change in export proceeds can be divided into two components. Part of the change would be expected on the basis of the positive or negative trend in export proceeds experienced in the past. The other part, that is, $|X_t - X_{t-1} - b|$, would be the unexpected and probably the most disturbing part of the change.

The data

Figures of export proceeds in US dollars were used for the estimation of the export-instability indexes, in order to avoid the difficulty of having to correct each country's export proceeds with its terms of trade needed to obtain purchasing power or capacity to import measures. Also, since most of the effects on economic development that have been attributed to export instability stem from the impact of export instability on import capacity, of countries whose import capacity was found not to depend on their exports were excluded from the sample.[7]

The estimated export-instability indexes are presented in the Statistical Appendix. As it can be seen from this table, the export-instability indexes of the LDCs are, in general, higher than are those of the DCs. What a casual examination does not reveal, however, is that the average instability index for the LDCs (10) is approximately twice the size of the average instability index of the DCs (5.3). It can also be seen from the Statistical Appendix that only five of the LDCs have export instability slightly lower than the average export instability of the DCs. These findings contradict MacBean's statement that the difference in export instability betwen LDCs and DCs suggests only 'a fairly weak tendency' and that the differences are not large.[8]

To avoid the methodological error of the previously mentioned empirical studies with regard to the income growth rate, the 'real per capita income growth rate' was estimated by fitting a logarithmic trend to annual per capita GDP data in constant prices for the period 1953–66.[9]

The findings

The results of the regressions of income growth rate on export instability based on the data described above are shown in Table 1. As these findings show, export instability seems to have a significant negative effect on the real per capita income growth rate of the LDCs included in the sample. Specifically, as it can be seen from the determination coefficient of equation (1-1) the export instability is responsible for about one-fourth of the observed variation in the income growth rates of the LDCs under consideration, which is well within reasonable expectations.

More striking, however, is the comparison of the relationship of export instability and income growth between LDCs and DCs. The results presented in Table 1 convincingly confirm the a priori claim that export instability is harmful only to the economic growth of the LDCs.

3 The Growth of Exports

It has been argued that export instability inhibits economic growth in the LDCs, not only through the destabilizing effects on the capacity to import investment goods vital for their economic growth, but also via its detrimental effects on the growth of exports.

To provide evidence in support of this argument it is necessary to show the relationship between export instability and the growth rate of exports as well as that between the growth rate of exports and the income growth rate.

The results presented in Table 1 clearly support the above argument. On the one hand, as shown by the results of equations (1-4) and (1-8), export instability is significantly harmful to the growth of exports only in the LDCs. On the other, as indicated by equations (1-2) and (1-6), the growth rate of exports is an important factor for the economic growth of both developed and less developed countries. It appears, however, that the growth rate of exports is a more important factor in the economic growth of the DCs than it is for that of the LDCs. This result might be more or less expected on a priori considerations. For, even though it is highly probable that rapid growth of the export sector for most countries will result in a noticeable growth of their economies as a whole, the degree with which any expansion in the export sector would be transmitted to the other sectors depends on the nature of the export sector of the country. Since the exports of the LDCs consist mainly of primary products with limited 'backward' and 'forward' linkage effects, a given growth rate of exports would not result in income growth of the same magnitude as in the DCs. However, it should be pointed out that tests for both the equality of regression equations (1-2) and (1-6) as well as for the equality of the regression coefficients (b's) of the same equations do not reveal significant differences at the 10 per cent level.

The implications one can draw from the results of the multiple regressions (shown by eqq. [1-3] and [1-7]) with regard to the variables involved and the importance of their effects are the same as those drawn from the simple regressions between the individual variables.

4 Price Stabilization and Economic Growth

We conclude the present empirical study with an attempt to determine the relative importance of export prices and export volume in the observed instability of export proceeds. Such a determination is relevant to the discussion of the still unsettled issue about the most proper or advantageous stabilization policy.

For this purpose, instability indexes of export prices and export volume, for all countries for which information existed, were obtained separately. Since one of the properties of our instability index is that the index is unaffected when the entire time series (for which the index is estimated) is multiplied by a constant, this index is particularly appropriate to the estimation of instability in a times series of index numbers.

The instability indexes for both volume and unit value of exports are presented in the Statistical Appendix. A detailed examination of the information presented there shows that the instability indexes for both the volume and unit value of exports for the average LDC are more than twice the size of the respective indexes for the average DC. Also, on the average, export volume instability is higher than price instability for both LDCs and DCs.[10]

For 20 out of the 36 LDCs included in the Statistical Appendix the instability index of export proceeds is greater than both the price and quantity instability indexes. This implies that for more than one-half of the LDCs the fluctuations of the prices and the quantities exported during the period under consideration did not tend to offset each other but rather tended to be reinforcing. The same phenomenon is true also for the DCs.

As was mentioned above, export *volume* instability is, on the average, larger than export *price* instability. However, as can be seen from equations (2-1)—(2-4) of Table 2, the most significant relationship for the LDCs is that between export price instability and the growth rate of exports. Although export quantity instability shows a negative effect on the income and the export growth rates, it is not significant. These results support the hypothesis that price instability acts as a more serious deterrent to export and income growth than volume instability. It is not surprising, therefore, to find that farmers more frequently demand government protection against price fluctuations than against crop fluctuations. Since prices are likely to be easier to control, these results suggest that the government of a LDC which wishes to promote domestic stabilization should concentrate on a producers' price rather than on a producers' income stabilization scheme.

Table 2 **Summary Results of Effects of Export Quantity and Price Instability on Income and Export Growth Rates**

Equation	*Sample*	*Dependent Variable*	*Constant*	*Explanatory Variables* I_q	I_p	R^2	*F-Ratio/ df*
(2-1)	LDCs	Y_r	2.714*	−0.052	. . .	−.020	0.06
			(3.409)	(0.598)			(1,32)
(2-2)	LDCs	Y_r	3.270*	. . .	−0.144	.037	1.60
			(4.543)		(1.510)		(1,32)
(2-3)	LDCs	X_r	6.475*	−0.151	. . .	−.009	0.69
			(3.905)	(0.832)			(1,32)
(2-4)	LDCs	X_r	8.430*	. . .	−0.469*	.133	6.08**
			(5.897)		(2.465)		(1,32)
(2-5)	DCs	Y_r	1.847**	0.408**	. . .	.171	4.52**
			(2.091)	(2.125)			(1,16)
(2-6)	DCs	Y_r	3.960*	. . .	−0.118	−.032	0.47
			(5.748)		(0.684)		(1,16)
(2-7)	DCs	X_r	4.306*	0.926*	. . .	.296	8.16*
			(2.889)	(2.857)			(1,16)
(2-8)	DCs	X_r	9.070*	. . .	−0.260	−.019	0.68
			(7.236)		(0.825)		(1,16)

Sources: For Y_r and X_r see Table 1, I_q, I_p, UN, *International Trade Statistics* (various issues) and IMF, *International Financial Statistics* (various issues).

Note: Y_r and X_r denote the same variables as before; I_q = export quantity (volume) instability index; I_p = export price (unit value) instability index.

*Significant at 1%.

**Significant at 5%.

The results for the DCs shown in equations (2-5)–(2-8) seem to be exactly opposite to those for the LDCs. Not only is export price instability less significant than the export quantity instability, but, in addition, the latter is positively related to the growth rates of income and exports.

5 Conclusion

In conclusion, we feel that the empirical evidence presented here (in contrast to that presented earlier by Coppock and MacBean) supports the a priori arguments that export instability is generally larger in the LDCs than in the DCs and that this instability is detrimental to economic growth in the former but not in the latter.

The policy implications which can be derived from the present study may be better understood if one takes into consideration the different mechanisms at the 'micro-' and 'macro-level' through which the effects of export instability are exercised. It may be argued that a country can conceivably act unilaterally to mitigate the micro-level effects of export instability by implementing an appropriate price stabilization scheme. Unfortunately, the very limited success that existing price stabilization schemes have apparently enjoyed—which is mainly due to administrative problems—together with the doubt cast by the previously mentioned empirical studies on the effects of export instability have diminished the attention given to domestic price stabilization policies in the recent years.

Since the empirical evidence presented in this study shows that instability in export proceeds and export prices is indeed harmful to the economic growth of the LDCs, it would seem reasonable and appropriate to suggest that the effects of the fluctuations in the prices of exported commodities should not be allowed to be superimposed on the 'macro-effects' stemming from the instability which the same LDCs experience in their export proceeds. Although it is not possible to define or apply an 'optimum' price stabilization scheme that would be suitable for all circumstances, it would seem appropriate to recommend that much more attention be paid to the evaluation and the choice of alternative schemes that would fit the conditions of particular LDCs.

Statistical Appendix. Instability Indexes (1953–66)

Country	Export Proceeds I_x	Export Quantities I_q	Export Prices I_p
Less developed:			
Argentina	6.50	8.00*	6.13*
Bolivia	14.17	10.14	6.79
Brazil	7.36	9.16	9.14
Burma	8.62	. . .	. . .
Ceylon	6.43	4.48	4.87
Chile	10.75	9.24	9.87
China (Taiwan)	13.64	12.82	8.78
Colombia	9.32	6.18	8.57
Costa Rica	10.09	10.66	8.36
Cyprus	9.96	5.10	7.68
Dominican Republic	14.27	11.43	12.96
Ecuador	6.88	. . .	. . .
Egypt	9.63	. . .	. . .
El Salvador	7.28	. . .	. . .
Ethiopia	8.63	9.35†	6.11†
Ghana	8.65	8.89†	15.52†
Greece	6.87	5.67	5.47
Guatemala	9.12	9.37	11.09†
Honduras	12.57	10.03	5.64†
India	5.03	5.44	5.60
Indonesia	9.24	. . .	. . .
Iraq	7.40	. . .	. . .
Ireland	8.22	7.54	2.09
Israel	7.40	6.13	7.03
Jamaica	6.09	4.95	5.72
Kenya	6.40	7.65	3.55
Libya	41.62	3.77	9.39
Malaysia	12.60‡	. . .	. . .
Mauritius	16.02	10.62	7.36
Mexico	5.15	. . .	. . .
Morocco	4.84	6.28	4.86
Nicaragua	12.81	12.80	9.29
Nigeria	7.81	6.50	5.12
Pakistan	8.74	15.29§	11.82§
Panama	12.13	11.57	5.88
Paraguay	10.36	. . .	. . .
Peru	8.50	6.11	4.94
Philippines	6.74	5.27	4.11
Portugal	6.67	5.14	3.50
Spain	12.23	13.30	4.43
Sudan	15.15	19.10	9.49
Syria	10.92*	. . .	. . .
Tanganyika	11.29	9.28	5.08
Thailand	9.01	7.45	3.19
Trinidad and Tobago	4.36	5.59‖	4.28‖
Tunisia	10.51	11.96	7.37
Turkey	11.77	. . .	. . .
Uruguay	17.23	. . .	. . .
Venezuela	3.97	. . .	. . .
Yugoslavia	6.88	. . .	. . .
Developed:			
Australia	9.38	3.78	7.86
Austria	3.73	3.33	2.17
Belgium	5.70	4.60	3.00
Canada	5.20	4.69	1.19
Denmark	3.31	1.99	4.14
Finland	4.58	3.86	4.01
France	5.26	4.42	2.79
Germany	3.58	2.81	1.57
Iceland	7.19	6.05	9.82
Italy	6.85	7.16	3.11
Japan	7.95	8.85	2.42
Netherlands	4.03	3.29	1.78
New Zealand	6.76	2.80	5.24
Norway	5.29	4.39	3.34
Sweden	3.71	2.71	1.86
Switzerland	3.76	2.97	1.72
United Kingdom	2.51	1.85	1.65
United States	6.94	6.55	1.20

Sources: I_x IMF, *International Financial Statistics* (various issues); I_q and I_p, UN, *International Trade Statistics* (various issues), and for some countries the above IMF publication.
*1953–65. †1953–64. ‡1953–63. §1955–66. ‖1951–60.

Notes: Reading 17

1 J. D. Coppock, *International Economic Instability*, McGraw-Hill, 1962; and A. I. MacBean, *Export Instability and Economic Development*, Harvard University Press, 1966.
2 MacBean, pp. 32 and 127.
3 Coppock, p. 107.
4 This rate also depends greatly on the choice of the two extreme years of the series.
5 Evidence of this error is shown in Coppock's results. His correlation coefficient between the export instability index and the GNP growth rate is −0.003. However, when he used the per capita GNP growth rate, the correlation between the same variables was found to be −0.15, despite the fact that his 'growth in per capita real income' rate is merely the total percentage change of this variable over the period 1951 to 1957 (p. 106).
6 This index, as it can be easily shown, has the following desirable properties: (i) reversibility with regard to time, (ii) symmetry with regard to a common trend, (iii) multiplicity (that is, it takes into account the relative importance of the variation), and (iv) independence of the size of the trend.
7 The primary criterion for the exclusion of countries from subsequent testing was the significance of the regression coefficient of imports on exports of the same year or on exports of the previous year. The countries for which no significant regression coefficient of imports on exports, at 5 per cent, was found are: Argentina, Burma, Guatemala, Libya, Mauritius, Nigeria, Panama, Sudan and Syria. This might be due either to severe restrictions on imports prevailing in these countries or to the existence of other sources of foreign exchange such as tourism, royalties and foreign aid that allow for imports to vary independently of exports. In addition to the above-mentioned nine countries, China (Taiwan) was also excluded from the sample because of the large amounts of foreign aid it received throughout most of the period under consideration, which was well over 30 per cent of its imports. To test the sensitivity of the results of this particular decision to restrict the number of countries included in the sample, comparable tests were made with data including these countries, the results of which indicated slightly inferior relationships, particularly for the LDCs. The evidence, therefore, seems to justify the

approach followed, although it does not appear to have been totally responsible for the results obtained.

8 MacBean, p. 36.

9 The fitted trend line is $Y_t = ab^t$, where Y_t denotes the annual real per capita GDP and t the time in years. Now it is obvious that if $b = 1 + Y_t$, Y_t would be the 'fitted' annual growth rate.

10 These average instability indexes are: for the LDCs, average I_q, 8.67; average I_p, 7.09; for the DCs, average I_q, 4.23; average I_p, 3.28.

Reading 18

The Structure of Dependence

T. Dos Santos

American Economic Review, 1970, pp. 231–6.

This paper attempts to demonstrate that the dependence of Latin American countries on other countries cannot be overcome without a qualitative change in their internal structures and external relations. We shall attempt to show that the relations of dependence to which these countries are subjected conform to a type of international and internal structure which leads them to underdevelopment or more precisely to a dependent structure that deepens and aggravates the fundamental problems of their peoples.

1 What is Dependence?

By dependence we mean a situation in which the economy of certain countries is conditioned by the development and expansion of another economy to which the former is subjected. The relation of interdependence between two or more economies, and between these and world trade, assumes the form of dependence when some countries (the dominant ones) can expand and can be self-sustaining, while other countries (the dependent ones) can do this only as a reflection of that expansion, which can have either a positive or a negative effect on their immediate development.[7]

The concept of dependence permits us to see the internal situation of these countries as part of world economy. In the Marxian tradition, the theory of imperialism has been developed as a study of the process of expansion of the imperialist centers and of their world domination. In the epoch of the revolutionary movement of the Third World, we have to develop the theory of laws of internal development in those countries that are the object of such expansion and are governed by them. This theoretical step transcends the theory of development which seeks to explain the situation of the underdeveloped countries as a product of their slowness or failure to adopt the patterns of efficiency characteristic of developed countries (or to 'modernize' or 'develop' themselves). Although capitalist development theory admits the existence of an 'external' dependence, it is unable to perceive underdevelopment in the way our present theory perceives it, as a consequence and part of the process of the world expansion of capitalism—a part that is necessary to and integrally linked with it.

In analyzing the process of constituting a world economy that integrates the so-called 'national economies' in a world market of commodities, capital, and even of labor power, we see that the relations produced by this market are unequal and combined—unequal because development of parts of the system occurs at the expense of other parts. Trade relations are based on monopolistic control of the market, which leads to the transfer of surplus generated in the dependent countries to the dominant countries; financial relations are, from the viewpoint of the dominant powers, based on loans and the export of capital, which permit them to receive interest and profits; thus increasing their domestic surplus and strengthening their control over the economies of the other countries. For the dependent countries these relations represent an export of profits and interest which carries off part of the surplus generated domestically and leads to a loss of control over their productive resources. In order to permit these disadvantageous relations, the dependent countries must generate large surpluses, not in such a way as to create higher levels of technology but rather superexploited manpower. The result is to limit the development of their internal market and their technical and cultural capacity, as well as the moral and physical health of their people. We call this combined development because it is the combination of these inequalities and the transfer of resources from the most backward and dependent sectors to the most advanced and dominant ones which explains the inequality, deepens it, and transforms it into a necessary and structural element of the world economy.

2 Historic Forms of Dependence

Historic forms of dependence are conditioned by: (1)

the basic forms of this world economy which has its own laws of development; (2) the type of economic relations dominant in the capitalist centers and the ways in which the latter expand outward; and (3) the types of economic relations existing inside the peripheral countries which are incorporated into the situation of dependence within the network of international economic relations generated by capitalist expansion. It is not within the purview of this paper to study these forms in detail but only to distinguish broad characteristics of development.

Drawing on an earlier study, we may distinguish: (1) Colonial dependence, trade export in nature, in which commercial and financial capital in alliance with the colonialist state dominated the economic relations of the Europeans and the colonies, by means of a trade monopoly complemented by a colonial monopoly of land, mines, and manpower (serf or slave) in the colonized countries. (2) Financial-industrial dependence which consolidated itself at the end of the nineteenth century, characterized by the domination of big capital in the hegemonic centers, and its expansion abroad through investment in the production of raw materials and agricultural products for consumption in the hegemonic centers. A productive structure grew up in the dependent countries devoted to the export of these products (which Levin labeled export economies[11]; other analysis in other regions[12, 13]), producing what ECLA has called 'foreign-oriented development' (*desarrollo hacia afuera*).[4] (3) In the postwar period a new type of dependence has been consolidated, based on multinational corporations which began to invest in industries geared to the internal market of underdeveloped countries. This form of dependence is basically technological-industrial dependence.[6]

Each of these forms of dependence corresponds to a situation which conditioned not only the international relations of these countries but also their internal structures: the orientation of production, the forms of capital accumulation, the reproduction of the economy, and, simultaneously, their social and political structure.

3 The Export Economies

In forms (1) and (2) of dependence, production is geared to those products destined for export (gold, silver, and tropical products in the colonial epoch; raw materials and agricultural products in the epoch of industrial-financial dependence); i.e. production is determined by demand from the hegemonic centers. The internal productive structure is characterized by rigid specialization and monoculture in entire regions (the Caribbean, the Brazilian Northeast, etc.). Alongside those export sectors there grew up certain complementary economic activities (cattle-raising and some manufacturing, for example) which were dependent, in general, on the export sector to which they sell their products. There was a third, subsistence economy which provided manpower for the export sector under favorable conditions and toward which excess population shifted during periods unfavorable to international trade.

Under these conditions, the existing internal market was restricted by four factors: (1) Most of the national income was derived from export, which was used to purchase the inputs required by export production (slaves, for example) or luxury goods consumed by the hacienda- and mine-owners, and by the more prosperous employees. (2) The available manpower was subject to very arduous forms of superexploitation, which limited its consumption. (3) Part of the consumption of these workers was provided by the subsistence economy, which served as a complement to their income and as a refuge during periods of depression. (4) A fourth factor was to be found in those countries in which land and mines were in the hands of foreigners (cases of an enclave economy): a great part of the accumulated surplus was destined to be sent abroad in the form of profits, limiting not only internal consumption but also possibilities of reinvestment.[1] In the case of enclave economies the relations of the foreign companies with the hegemonic center were even more exploitative and were complemented by the fact that purchases by the enclave were made directly abroad.

4 The New Dependence

The new form of dependence, (3) above, is in process of developing and is conditioned by the exigencies of the international commodity and capital markets. The possibility of generating new investments depends on the existence of financial resources in foreign currency for the purchase of machinery and processed raw materials not produced domestically. Such purchases are subject to two limitations: the limit of resources generated by the export sector (reflected in the balance of payments, which includes not only trade but also service relations); and the limitations of monopoly on patents which leads monopolistic firms to prefer to transfer their machines in the form of capital rather than as commodities for sale. It is necessary to analyze these relations of dependence if we are to understand the fundamental structural limits they place on the development of these economies.

1. Industrial development is dependent on an export sector for the foreign currency to buy the inputs utilized by the industrial sector. The first consequence of this dependence is the need to preserve the traditional export sector, which limits economically the development of the internal market by the conservation of backward relations of production and signifies, politically, the maintenance of power by traditional decadent oligarchies. In the countries where these sectors are controlled by foreign capital, it signifies the remittance abroad of high profits, and political dependence on

those interests. Only in rare instances does foreign capital not control at least the marketing of these products. In response to these limitations, dependent countries in the 1930's and 1940's developed a policy of exchange restrictions and taxes on the national and foreign export sector; today they tend toward the gradual nationalization of production and toward the imposition of certain timid limitations on foreign control of the marketing of exported products. Furthermore, they seek, still somewhat timidly, to obtain better terms for the sale of their products. In recent decades, they have created mechanisms for international price agreements, and today UNCTAD and ECLA press to obtain more favorable tariff conditions for these products on the part of the hegemonic centers. It is important to point out that the industrial development of these countries is dependent on the situation of the export sector, the continued existence of which they are obliged to accept.

2. Industrial development is, then, strongly conditioned by fluctuations in the balance of payments. This leads toward deficit due to the relations of dependence themselves. The causes of the deficit are three:

(a) Trade relations take place in a highly monopolized international market, which tends to lower the price of raw materials and to raise the prices of industrial products, particularly inputs. In the second place, there is a tendency in modern technology to replace various primary products with synthetic raw materials. Consequently the balance of trade in these countries tends to be less favorable (even though they show a general surplus). The overall Latin American balance of trade from 1946 to 1968 shows a surplus for each of those years. The same thing happens in almost every underdeveloped country. However, the losses due to deterioration of the terms of trade (on the basis of data from ECLA and the International Monetary Fund), excluding Cuba, were $26,383 million for the 1951–66 period, taking 1950 prices as a base. If Cuba and Venezuela are excluded, the total is $15,925 million.

(b) For the reasons already given, foreign capital retains control over the most dynamic sectors of the economy and repatriates a high volume of profit; consequently, capital accounts are highly unfavorable to dependent countries. The data show that the amount of capital leaving the country is much greater than the amount entering; this produces an enslaving deficit in capital accounts. To this must be added the deficit in certain services which are virtually under total foreign control—such as freight transport, royalty payments, technical aid, etc. Consequently, an important deficit is produced in the total balance of payments; thus limiting the possibility of importation of inputs for industrialization.

(c) The result is that 'foreign financing' becomes necessary, in two forms: to cover the exisiting deficit, and to 'finance' development by means of loans for the stimulation of investments and to 'supply' an internal economic surplus which was decapitalized to a large extent by the remittance of part of the surplus generated domestically and sent abroad as profits.

Foreign capital and foreign 'aid' thus fill up the holes that they themselves created. The real value of this aid, however, is doubtful. If overcharges resulting from the restrictive terms of the aid are subtracted from the total amount of the grants, the average net flow, according to calculations of the Inter-American Economic and Social Council, is approximately 54 per cent of the gross flow.[5]

If we take account of certain further facts—that a high proportion of aid is paid in local currencies, that Latin American countries make contributions to international financial institutions, and that credits are often 'tied'—we find a 'real component of foreign aid' of 42.2 per cent on a very favorable hypothesis and of 38.3 per cent on a more realistic one.[5] The gravity of the situation becomes even clearer if we consider that these credits are used in large part to finance North American investments, to subsidize foreign imports which compete with national products, to introduce technology not adapted to the needs of underdeveloped countries, and to invest in low-priority sectors of the national economies. The hard truth is that the underdeveloped countries have to pay for all of the 'aid' they receive. This situation is generating an enormous protest movement by Latin American governments seeking at least partial relief from such negative relations.

3. Finally, industrial development is strongly conditioned by the technological monopoly exercised by imperialist centers. We have seen that the underdeveloped countries depend on the importation of machinery and raw materials for the development of their industries. However, these goods are not freely available in the international market; they are patented and usually belong to the big companies. The big companies do not sell machinery and processed raw materials as simple merchandise: they demand either the payment of royalties, etc., for their utilization or, in most cases, they convert these goods into capital and introduce them in the form of their own investments. This is how machinery which is replaced in the hegemonic centers by more advanced technology is sent to dependent countries as capital for the installation of affiliates. Let us pause and examine these relations, in order to understand their oppressive and exploitative character.

The dependent countries do not have sufficient foreign currency, for the reasons given. Local businessmen have financing difficulties, and they must pay for the utilization of certain patented techniques. These factors oblige the national bourgeois governments to facilitate the entry of foreign capital in order to supply the restricted national market, which is strongly protected by high tariffs in order to promote industrialization. Thus, foreign capital enters with all the advantages: in many cases, it is given exemption from exchange controls for the importation of machinery; financing of sites for installation of industries is provided; government financing agencies facilitate industrialization; loans are available from foreign and domestic banks, which prefer such clients; foreign aid often subsidizes such investments and finances complementary public investments; after installation, high profits obtained in such favorable circumstances can be reinvested freely. Thus it is not surprising that the data of the US Department of Commerce reveal that the percentage of capital brought in from abroad by these companies is but a part of the total amount of invested capital. These data show that in the period from 1946 to 1967 the new entries of capital into Latin America for direct investment amounted to $5,415 million, while the sum of reinvested profits was $4,424 million. On the other hand, the transfers of profits from Latin America to the United States amounted to $14,775 million. If we estimate total profits as approximately equal to transfers plus reinvestments we have the sum of $18,983 million. In spite of enormous transfers of profits to the United States, the book value of the United States's direct investment in Latin America went from $3,045 million in 1946 to $10,213 million in 1967. From these data it is clear that: (1) Of the new investments made by US companies in Latin America for the period 1946–67, 55 per cent corresponds to new entries of capital and 45 per cent to reinvestment of profits; in recent years, the trend is more marked, with reinvestments between 1960 and 1966 representing more than 60 per cent of new investments. (2) Remittances remained at about 10 per cent of book value throughout the period. (3) The ratio of remitted capital to new flow is around 2.7 for the period 1946–67; that is, for each dollar that enters $2.70 leaves. In the 1960's this ratio roughly doubled, and in some years was considerably higher.

The *Survey of Current Business* data on sources and uses of funds for direct North American investment in Latin America in the period 1957–64 show that, of the total sources of direct investment in Latin America, only 11.8 per cent came from the United States. The remainder is in large part, the result of the activities of North American firms in Latin America (46.4 per cent net income, 27.7 per cent under the heading of depreciation), and from 'sources located abroad' (14.1 per cent). It is significant that the funds obtained abroad that are external to the companies are greater than the funds originating in the United States.

5 Effects on the Productive Structure

It is easy to grasp, even if only superficially, the effects that this dependent structure has on the productive system itself in these countries and the role of this structure in determining a specified type of development, characterized by its dependent nature.

The productive system in the underdeveloped countries is essentially determined by these international relations. In the first place, the need to conserve the agrarian or mining export structure generates a combination between more advanced economic centers that extract surplus value from the more backward sectors, and also between internal 'metropolitan' centers and internal interdependent 'colonial' center.[10] The unequal and combined character of capitalist development at the international level is reproduced internally in an acute form. In the second place the industrial and technological structure responds more closely to the interests of the multinational corporations than to internal developmental needs (conceived of not only in terms of the overall interests of the population, but also from the point of view of the interests of a national capitalist development). In the third place, the same technological and economic-financial concentration of the hegemonic economies is transferred without substantial alteration to very different economies and societies, giving rise to a highly unequal productive structure, a high concentration of incomes, underutilization of installed capacity, intensive exploitation of existing markets concentrated in large cities, etc.

The accumulation of capital in such circumstances assumes its own characteristics. In the first place, it is characterized by profound differences among domestic wage-levels, in the context of a local cheap labor market, combined with a capital-intensive technology. The result, from the point of view of relative surplus value, is a high rate of exploitation of labor power. (On measurements of forms of exploitation, see[3].)

This exploitation is further aggravated by the high prices of industrial products enforced by protectionism, exemptions and subsidies given by the national governments, and 'aid' from hegemonic centers. Furthermore, since dependent accumulation is necessarily tied into the international economy, it is profoundly conditioned by the unequal and combined character of international capitalist economic relations, by the technological and financial control of the imperialist centers by the realities of the balance of payments, by the economic policies of the state, etc. The role of the state in the growth of national and foreign capital merits a much fuller analysis than can be made here.

Using the analysis offered here as a point of departure, it is possible to understand the limits that this productive system imposes on the growth of the internal markets of these countries. The survival of traditional relations in the countryside is a serious limitation on the size of the market, since industrialization does not offer hopeful prospects. The productive structure created by dependent industrialization limits the growth of the internal market.

First, it subjects the labor force to highly exploitative relations which limit its purchasing power. Second, in adopting a technology of intensive capital use, it creates very few jobs in comparison with population growth, and limits the generation of new sources of income. These two limitations affect the growth of the consumer goods market. Third, the remittance abroad of profits carries away part of the economic surplus generated within the country. In all these ways limits are put on the possible creation of basic national industries which could provide a market for the capital goods this surplus would make possible if it were not remitted abroad.

From this cursory analysis we see that the alleged backwardness of these economies is not due to a lack of integration with capitalism but that, on the contrary, the most powerful obstacles to their full development come from the way in which they are joined to this international system and its laws of development.

6 Some Conclusions: Dependent Reproduction

In order to understand the system of dependent reproduction and the socioeconomic institutions created by it, we must see it as part of a system of world economic relations based on monopolistic control of large-scale capital, on control of certain economic and financial centers over others, on a monopoly of a complex technology that leads to unequal and combined development at a national and international level. Attempts to analyze backwardness as a failure to assimilate more advanced models of production or to modernize are nothing more than ideology disguised as science. The same is true of the attempts to analyze this international economy in terms of relations among elements in free competition, such as the theory of comparative costs which seeks to justify the inequalities of the world economic system and to conceal the relations of exploitation on which it is based.[4]

In reality we can understand what is happening in the underdeveloped countries only when we see that they develop within the framework of a process of dependent production and reproduction. This system is a dependent one because it reproduces a productive system whose development is limited by those world relations which necessarily lead to the development of only certain economic sectors, to trade under unequal condition,[9] to domestic competition with international capital under unequal conditions, to the imposition of relations of superexploitation of the domestic labor force with a vew to dividing the economic surplus thus generated between internal and external forces of domination. (On economic surplus and its utilization in the dependent countries, see[1].)

In reproducing such a productive system and such international relations, the development of dependent capitalism reproduces the factors that prevent it from reaching a nationally and internationally advantageous situation; and it thus reproduces backwardness, misery, and social marginalization within its borders. The development that it produces benefits very narrow sectors, encounters unyielding domestic obstacles to its continued economic growth (with respect to both internal and foreign markets), and leads to the progressive accumulation of balance-of-payments deficits, which in turn generate more dependence and more superexploitation.

The political measures proposed by the developmentalists of ECLA, UNCTAD, BID, etc., do not appear to permit destruction of these terrible chains imposed by dependent development. We have examined the alternative forms of development presented for Latin America and the dependent countries under such conditions elsewhere.[8] Everything now indicates that what can be expected is a long process of sharp political and military confrontations and of profound social radicalization which will lead these countries to a dilemma: governments of force which open the way to fascism, or popular revolutionary governments, which open the way to socialism. Intermediate solutions have proved to be, in such a contradictory reality, empty and utopian.

References: Reading 18

1 Baran, Paul (1967), *Political Economy of Growth* (Monthly Review Press).

2 Balogh, Thomas (1963), *Unequal Partners* (Blackwell).

3 Casanova, Pablo Gonzalez (1969), *Sociologia de la explotación*, siglo XXI (Mexico).

4 Cepal (1968), *La CEPAL y el Análisis del Desarrollo Latino-americano* (Santiago, Chile).

5 Consejo Interamericano Economico Social (CIES) OAS, Inter-American Economic and Social Council, External Financing for Development in LA (1969), *El Financiamiento Externo para el Desarrollo de América Latina* (Pan-American Union, Washington).

6 Dos Santos, Theotonio (1968), *El nuevo carácter de la dependencia*, CESO (Santiago, Chile).

7 Dos Santos, Theotonio (1968), 'Le crisis de la teoría del desarrollo y las relaciones de dependencia en América Latina', *Boletín del CESO*, no. 3 (Santiago, Chile).

8 Dos Santos, Theotonia (1969), 'La dependencia económica y las alternativas de cambio en América Latina', *Ponencia al IX Congreso Latinoamericano de Sociología* (Mexico, November).

9 Emmanuel, A. (1969), *L'Echange inégal* (Maspero).

10 Frank, André G. (1968), *Development and Underdevelopment in Latin America* (Monthly Review Press).

11 Levin, I. V. (1964) *The Export Economies* (Harvard University Press).

12 Myrdal, Gunnar (1968), *Asian Drama* (Pantheon).

13 Nkrumah, K. (1966), *Neocolonialismo, ultima etapa del imperialismo*, siglo XXI (Mexico).

14 Palloix, Cristian (1969), *Problèmes de la croissance en economie ouverte* (Maspero).

Reading 19

Transnationals, Domestic Enterprises, and Industrial Structure in Host LDCs: A Survey

S. Lall

Oxford Economic Papers, vol. 30, no. 2, 1978, pp. 217–48.

1 Introduction

This paper reviews the literature on the relationships between transnational corporations (TNCs) in the manufacturing sector and domestic enterprises as well as industrial structures in host LDCs. There are two broad sets of relationships involved, both of which are of significance for understanding the effects of TNCs on host economies and to the formulation of policy. The 'direct' relationships that TNCs strike up with local suppliers or purchasers (backward and forward 'linkages' in the Hirschman sense) can constitute powerful mechanisms for stimulating (or retarding) economic, and particularly industrial, growth in LDCs. The 'indirect' effects that the entry and operations of TNCs may have on local industrial structure, conduct, and performance may be equally important: TNCs may change the nature and evolution of concentration; they may affect the profitability and growth of indigenous firms; they may alter financing, marketing, technological, or managerial practices of the sectors that they enter; they may, by predatory conduct, drive domestic firms out of business; and so on.

2 Direct Linkages

Direct linkages may be defined to constitute those relationships between TNCs and domestic enterprises trading with them that have led the latter to respond, positively or otherwise, to technological, pecuniary, marketing, or entrepreneurial stimuli provided by the former.[1] A 'linkage' in this sense is clearly different from a normal transaction in a competitive market; it refers essentially to *externalities* created for domestic industry by the entry of TNC investment. The classic general discussion of the role of linkages in the development of LDCs is by Hirschman (1958), who proposes a deliberate strategy of creating imbalances to harness the forces of entrepreneurship and growth that lie latent in every economy. Particular investments are thus supposed to create such strong external economies in sectors that supply or buy from them that new investments are undertaken in order to exploit them; foreign investment is assigned a vital role, 'to enable and to embolden a country to set out on the path of unbalanced growth . . . [and] to take the first "unbalancing" steps in growth sequences'.[2]

While it is obvious that TNC investments can create strong local linkages in this sense, and indeed the policies of many host LDCs to compel TNCs to maximize their purchase of local inputs have aimed at exploiting these linkages, it is far from clear how the actual experience of TNCs in LDCs is to be evaluated. The normal procedure, of using the proportion of local to total purchases by TNCs as an indicator of backward linkages, is inadequate, since it does not take account of externalities and does not enable us to assess the 'efficiency' of linkage creation. Though it may serve as a crude approximation to the outer limits of the stimulus provided by TNCs to local enterprises, it does not, for instance, show (*a*) if the local enterprises would have been set up in the absence of TNC investments; (*b*) whether they gained or lost by having TNCs as major customers (where this is the case); (*c*) if the host economy could have created the same linkages at lesser cost, say by replacing the TNC by a local firm; (*d*) if the linked local enterprises are desirable from the social point of view (where the linkages are fostered behind heavy protective barriers); and (*e*) whether negative linkages were created by stifling potential local investment. The proper economic evaluation of linkages must be based on a case-by-case cost/benefit examination of actual situation and plausible alternatives, necessarily a difficult and impressionistic procedure; however, the existence and desirability of TNC linkages can only be judged by some such method.

Let us now consider how the existing literature has treated the issue. Our review is confined to *backward* linkages, since there appears to be hardly any empirical work on forward linkages created by TNCs: perhaps not a great omission, since forward linkages cannot be expected to be very strong. We may consider backward linkages for the two main forms of TNC investment—import-substituting and export-orientated—separately, as the issues raised are rather different.

2a Import-substituting TNCs

The vast bulk of foreign manufacturing investment in LDCs has gone into protected import-substituting activities, where governments have been able, especially in the larger and more industrialized areas, to push firms into buying large proportions of their inputs from local sources. TNCs have, consequently, developed extensive and long-standing relationships with local enterprises in countries like India, Mexico, Brazil, Argentina, and so on. Despite the significance of the phenomenon, however, the existing work on TNCs has paid scant attention to examining the economic benefits and costs of the linkages created.

Most of the studies of foreign investment in LDCs have simply noted the extent of local purchasing by TNCs and sometimes remarked on the general difficulties of local procurement (due to technological backwardness, small scale, high cost, poor quality, or unreliability) without attempting to analyse the linkages created in any detail. Thus, a study of six developing countries commissioned by UNCTAD produced data on the import propensities of 159 firms, foreign and domestic, in Kenya, Jamaica, India, Iran, Colombia, and Malaysia, without going into the economics of domestic purchase.[3] Similarly, studies of US investment in LDCs in general,[4] Peru,[5] Iran,[6] South Korea,[7] Malaysia,[8] and some others,[9] have discussed the use of local inputs by TNCs. The general findings, that TNCs buy relatively few inputs within the less industrialized host economies but may be forced or persuaded to increase local content by the more advanced ones, add little to our understanding of the significance or desirability of the externalities created in LDCs.

There are three other studies which may be mentioned separately because they tackle the issue of TNC linkages more directly. Reuber and associates (1973), using information provided by the head offices of TNCs, noted that import-substituting investments created far more local linkages than export-orientated ones, and found, for sixty-four sample firms, that 45 per cent of inputs in 1970 came from local sources. Parent companies were asked whether their operations had given rise to local suppliers or distributors, and their answers indicated that some one-third of the investments had directly given rise to such local activity. Reuber made no attempt to assess the costs and benefits of such linkages, and also qualified the estimates by noting that 'such figures must be viewed with some suspicion both because of the many conceptual and practical difficulties in deriving estimates of this kind and because of the vested interest of respondents in presenting the spin-off effects of their activities in as favourable a light as possible' (p. 156).

Watanabe (1972a and 1974b), in his examination of subcontracting in LDCs, presents a general but useful analysis of this particular (and rather strong) form of linkage. Though he is not concerned exclusively with TNCs, he cites examples of foreign firms (like Singer in South East Asia) which have used subcontracting successfully, and concludes that such activity, 'by stimulating entrepreneurship and encouraging industrial efficiency, can help to promote the industrialization of the less developed countries and thus create the additional employment opportunities they badly need'.[10] He analyses the conditions for success of such linkages (which he terms 'within-border industrial subcontracting'), briefly notes the contribution that TNCs may make by providing assistance with investment, technology and quality control, and recommends policies for increasing linkages; he does not, however, examine in detail any specific instances of subcontracting by foreign firms. In his 1974b paper he examines the problems of subcontracting in India (though without discussing the role of TNCs), and compares its experience to the highly successful one of Japan.

A more pessimistic view of the virtues of local purchasing emerges from Baranson's study of the Cummin's diesel-engine project in India and his analysis of the automotive industry in LDCs generally.[11] He comments at length on the problems raised by the high cost, poor quality, and unreliability of local suppliers in cases where the government has forced the pace of buying local inputs,[12] and discusses the reasons for this state of affairs (protection, technological and skill shortages, lack of experience, small scale, and the like). We must not, however, draw unfavourable general conclusions about the desirability of linkages or the capabilities of local enterprises from this experience: there are several other industries (see below) where domestic linkages have been economically viable, and even for India the recent boom in exports of medium-to-high technology goods (including transport equipment, chemicals, and engineering goods) indicates that some of the problems described by Baranson for the 60s may have been the teething difficulties of launching new and complex industrial processes.

To return to TNCs, however, we find that we are left with very little empirical work on the process and value of creating linkages. The general impression conveyed by the literature is that TNCs establish relatively few linkages in small or industrially backward economies;

that in larger economies they may create extensive linkages, mostly because of government pressure; and that a substantial part of these linkages in import-substituting industries may be excessively costly and uneconomical. This is all in line with *a priori* expectation, but it is sadly inadequate in explaining the specific nature of the linkages that have been created, and in providing the sort of evaluation of their social value that was described earlier.

2b *Export-orientated TNCs*

The recent growth of manufactured exports from LDCs by foreign firms has attracted a great deal of attention, and the creation of linkages, especially by subcontracting, has often been mentioned in this context. In contrast to the inefficiency usually associated with linkages in import-substituting industries, it may be expected that linkages created by firms competing in world markets will be more efficient and beneficial for the host economies (at least in a narrow technical sense, without referring to distributional, social, or political effects). It would be useful to start by distinguishing four types of export-oriented TNCs which have different implications for the creation of domestic linkages.

First, there are TNCs which started by substituting for imports and have grown internationally competitive enterprises with substantial export interests (VW in Brazil or Singer in Asia may be good examples). Such activities usually involve technologies which are stable and not very sophisticated, and they are based in areas with a cheap but relatively skilled labour force and an experienced indigenous sector. The use of the TNCs' marketing networks and established brand names are important in such export activity. These TNCs may have established considerable domestic linkages in the early phases, though, of course, the extent and nature of these linkages may change as they gear themselves for world markets.

Second, there may be foreign firms which produce and export 'traditional' products like footwear, textiles, processed foods, or sports goods. For those industries (like textiles) where technology is easily available and product differentiation is insignificant, the foreign firms involved may be buying groups, retailers, or small manufacturers (sometimes from other LDCs, like Hong Kong firms in Malaysia) rather than TNCs proper. For those (like food processing) where product differentiation, marketing, or product innovation are important, however, large TNCs may predominate in production and export activity.[13] In both cases, there exists a vast potential for linkages with domestic producers, who may manufacture components or whole products for foreign firms.

Third, there are new TNC investments in 'modern' industries in LDCs undertaken specifically for export, transferring fairly complex technologies to LDCs to service established world markets. A constellation of factors (labour and transport costs, the nature of the technology, need for short production runs, managerial requirements, and, of course, political stability)[14] influences the decision to locate such investments, good examples of which are the Philips and General Electric complexes in Singapore, or some 'border industries' in Mexico; the availability of local components is not, however, one of the important factors attracting them. In most cases, such investments are tightly controlled from abroad, the components and processes may be quite advanced, and there may not be much scope for local linkages. It is possible, nevertheless, that local enterprises may be able to provide some products at the right price and quality, and a few linkages may develop in the more advanced of the host economies.[15]

Fourth, there are 'sourcing' investments where only a particular (labour-intensive) process is transferred to LDCs, the more capital-intensive processes being retained in the home countries where the requisite equipment, skills, and R and D facilities exist. The best-known example of this is the electronics industry, especially the semiconductor sector, where the demanding specifications, the rapidly changing technology, and requirements of cost minimisation reduce the scope for domestic linkages to practically nothing.[16]

Of these four types of TNC investment, the first two are likely to create the most linkages, the third rather less, and the fourth least of all. The extent of linkages created in particular LDCs depends upon the stage of development of indigenous industry, the availability of local skills and technology, institutions and government policies, changes in demand and technology in world markets and their political attractiveness to TNCs.[17] The main benefits of such investment are generally supposed to be employment creation, export promotion (though net foreign exchange benefits may be very low for the third and fourth groups that depend heavily on imported components), skill and technology transfer (particularly in the first and second, sometimes the third, groups), and the stimulation of local linkages (see below). The main costs mentioned are the generous fiscal and infrastructural incentives that LDCs have to offer (especially for investments in the fourth category), the socio-political constraints of having to ensure a docile and low-cost labour force, the danger of losing 'footloose' TNCs when costs rise, the risk of getting poor terms from monopsonistic buyers, and the instability of demand for exports. Of these, the danger of 'footloose' behaviour does not seem to have been realized;[18] fiscal concessions certainly have been generous; TNCs have clearly shown a marked preference for stable regimes with little or no labour problems; the incidence of 'squeezing' local firms needs further investigation; and export market instability is not a particular feature of TNC exports. On the whole, the benefits seem to have outweighed the costs with LDCs, and many of them are now seeking to attract TNCs or foreign buying groups.[19]

Besides the general studies of this phenomenon mentioned above, a number of country studies have discussed export-orientated foreign investment (and subcontracting) for Mexico,[20] Hong Kong,[21] Singapore,[22] the Caribbean,[23] and Taiwan.[24] Nearly all of them—with the exceptions of Evers (1977) and Fernandez (1973)—have come to favourable conclusions about the net benefits of such activity to host LDCs, but their discussion of linkages as such has remained desultory and unsatisfactory. There are some impressionistic and anecdotal accounts[25] of the potential for creating beneficial linkages which confirm the general analysis given above, but none of these studies has attempted a systematic evaluation of the extent, costs, and benefits of linkages from the viewpoint of the host economy or the local enterprises. Of those which have touched on linkages, the following may be mentioned:

(*a*) Evers *et al.* (1977), on the textile and clothing industries in Hong Kong, discuss the role of trading companies in developed countries that subcontract to local manufacturers. They find that local linkages for clothing manufacture, in terms of the purchase of local cotton textiles, has weakened rather than strengthened in recent years with the growth of exports, for two reasons: discrimination in developed countries against cotton, and the demand for higher quality products, both leading to a greater dependence on imported textiles (often supplied by the buyers). The authors comment extensively on poor working conditions, use of child labour, excessive working hours (up to 105 hours per week for men), and low wages that support the success of the industry in Hong Kong, and draw unfavourable conclusions for the distribution of benefits resulting from such export-led growth. Conditions are apparently worse in small establishments, since large ones have themselves become multinational and gone to cheaper areas like Malaysia and Indonesia.

(*b*) Lim and Pang (1976), who survey the electronic industry in Singapore, note that European firms buy a fair amount of their inputs (40–50 per cent) locally, while US (under 10 per cent), and Japanese (about 20 per cent) buy much less. This is due to the fact that US firms are specialized in the semi-conductor sector and Japanese firms in high-technology components, beyond the technological capabilities of domestic firms, while European firms manufacture mainly consumer electronics where the scope for local purchase is higher. However, local products tend to be rather costly, and are purchased chiefly in order to qualify for GSP privileges in selling to Europe (a minimum local content is required for these exports). Local firms face the usual problems of quality, technology, high costs, and so on, and are sometimes assisted by the local TNCs from whom they subcontract by free technology transfers. Firms which subcontract to foreign buying groups seem to face greater problems; their wage costs are higher than Hong Kong or Taiwan so that they are constantly threatened with losing their markets; they complain of little assistance from the government; and they are short of finance and new technology.

(*c*) UNCTAD (1975) reviews the electronics industry in LDCs generally, and reaches optimistic conclusions about the effects and prospects for subcontracting. It finds that several finished electronic products can be successfully manufactured by local enterprises in South East Asia, and subcontracting has led to 'a whole network of small manufacturers that were set up as a result of the backward linkages created' (p. 26).[26]

Clearly, much more evidence is needed on the experience of different industries in different LDCs before we can generalize about the impact of TNC linkages in export-based industries. It is obvious that substantial linkages have been created, and that in some sectors, like electricals they have been beneficial to host countries; however, it is possible that in some other industries, like textiles, linkages have been weakening and have had undesirable effects on distribution and welfare. A related question which has been almost totally neglected is whether such exporting activity (perhaps excluding very high-technology products) could have been undertaken more economically by local firms in countries like India, where the bulk of 'modern' manufactured exports are not in fact accounted for by TNCs, and whether this would have created more beneficial linkages. This whole area is of vital importance to policy-making, and cries out for detailed empirical research.

3 Industrial Structure, Conduct, and Performance

What we have termed the 'indirect' effects of TNCs on domestic enterprises can be conveniently reviewed under the standard industrial economics format of structure, conduct, and performance.

3a Structure

Before we come to the effects of TNCs on industrial structure in LDCs, let us note that there are relatively few systematic studies comparing the industrial structures of developing countries[27] or analysing the structures of particular LDCs. A forthcoming (as yet unobtainable) study[28] shows measures of concentration for ten Latin American countries (excluding Brazil) and finds that 'there exists a similar pattern of industrial concentration in Latin American countries. . . . [Industries] with the highest levels of concentration are tobacco, rubber, basic metals, and the manufacture of paper. Latin American countries which have smaller market size have systematically higher levels of concentration than others.' Most country studies, which include those of Pakistan,[29] Chile,[30] India,[31] and Kenya,[32] are forced to rely on poor data, are often not comprehensive, and generally do not (with the exception of Ghosh (1975)) analyse the determinants of changes in structure over time.

It is notoriously difficult to trace the exact causal relationships between industrial structure, the conduct of firms, and their performance,[33] all of which seem to interact in complex ways. Given the nature of data in developing countries, moreover, it may be expected that studies of the impact of TNCs on the structures of host LDCs would face severe informational and methodological problems. The literature on TNCs in developed countries is not clear on the nature of their effect on industrial structures:[34] initially the entry of foreign competition may reduce the existing level of concentration, but in the longer run the oligopolistic nature and large size of TNCs may well increase it. The fact that industrial concentration has tended to increase in developed countries, and that the growth of TNCs has taken place mainly in sectors characterized by growing oligopoly, may suggest the TNCs have actually caused a rise in concentration in the sectors in which they are active. However, it is not clear to what extent TNCs have contributed *independently* to concentration (by, say, unwarranted takeovers or predatory behaviour based on advantages conferred by size or financial power), as distinct from simply embodying or transmitting changes caused by technological, marketing, financial, or organizational developments. Thus, efficient production and trade may, in some industries, require larger firms and increased concentration over time; financial or economic factors may cause takeovers or mergers independently of the nationality of firms; marketing and R and D economies may compel larger size; and so on—these factors must be disentangled from TNC presence before their separate effect is apparent.

Unfortunately, the few studies that exist for LDCs have not tried to grapple with these problems. Most of them, concentrating on Latin America, have tried to show the extent of 'denationalization' (the proportion of foreign ownership) in particular sectors or countries, and to relate TNC presence (but not other variables) to concentration levels. While the results have been useful and suggestive, they have not been able to answer the central question concerning the effect of TNC entry on structure. Let us quickly review the literature by country.

(*a*) *Mexico*. Newfarmer and Mueller (1975) have used data on a sample of 197 US TNCs to analyse the degree of denationalization in 1972. They find that of the 100 largest firms, 61 were foreign (of which 39 were US); of the 300 largest, 150 were foreign (97 US). Foreign subsidiaries were on average much larger than local private firms, but smaller than public-sector enterprises. US firms accounted for 36 per cent, and other foreign firms for 16 per cent, of the assets of the top 300 firms; of total GDP, TNCs accounted for 18 per cent in 1962 and 23 per cent in 1970 (US firms for 15 per cent and 18 per cent respectively). Thus, TNCs represented a large and growing force in Mexican manufacturing. As for structure, Newfarmer and Mueller found that Mexican industries were highly concentrated relative to the US, with over three-fourths of production coming from industries where one or more leading producers was a TNC. They also found 'a high correlation between the presence of MNCs in various markets and their overall concentration' (p. 62).[35]

(*b*) *Brazil*. Newfarmer and Mueller also provide similar data on Brazil, where the US accounts for 36 per cent of foreign capital stock, and where of the 500 largest non-financial corporations in 1972 TNCs number 158 (US firms 59). TNCs are again much larger than domestic private firms, but smaller than state enterprises. They increased their share of assets in five out of seven advanced industrial sectors, the main countervailing force in the other two coming from the government rather than private enterprises. As in Mexico, industry is highly concentrated, with four plants accounting for 50 per cent of output in 176 out of 302 manufacturing industries. TNC presence is associated with concentration:[36] this association would be stronger if data were available by firm rather than by plant, since TNCs are very likely to operate several plants.

(*c*) *Argentina*. Some data on Argentina are given by Sourrouille (1976), who finds that foreign firms contributed some 30 per cent of total manufacturing output in 1970, far more than 20 years previously. Moreover, 'in 1970/73 two-thirds of the foreign industrial produce stemmed from sub-groups where they dominated over 75 per cent of the market . . . and 75 per cent came from sub-groups where they dominated over 50 per cent of the market' (p. 27).[37] The growth of TNCs was 60 per cent higher than average industrial growth.

(*d*) *Central America*. Willmore (1976) calculates the degree of foreign dominance for Guatemala, where he finds that in twenty-two industries in which at least one leading firm is foreign, 'the degree of concentration rises as foreign control of leading firm rises' (p. 506). He concludes that foreign entry raises the level of concentration.

Scattered data of this sort are available for other countries—Chile,[38] Colombia,[39] India,[40] South Korea,[41] Malaysia, and Singapore[42]—but they do not contribute greatly to our understanding of the problem at hand. The general upshot of the work done seems to confirm *a priori* expectations, that TNCs are a significant and growing force in the manufacturing sectors of most LDCs, that they are present in industries with high degrees of concentration, and that they are generally larger than domestic private firms. We are, however, unable to say confidently from the evidence whether or not TNCs *cause* higher levels of concentration. TNCs certainly flourish in sectors that are marked by high levels of oligopoly, but the causes of oligopolization may well lie elsewhere, in scale economies of production, R and D, marketing, finance, or some such factor: to the extent that several modern industries are inherently oligopolistic, the presence of TNCs may not as such cause higher concentration. However, it is quite plausible that in LDCs their entry does *speed up* the natural process of concentration, and that the weakness of local competitors (with the exception of enterprises fostered by the state) enables them to achieve a much *higher degree of market dominance*, in sectors in which they are active, than would be the case in developed economies. Much more detailed empirical work, with more sophisticated tests than have been used till now, will be needed before these matters are clarified.

3b Conduct

In this section we shall consider only two aspects of TNC conduct—takeover as a means of entry, and financing behaviour.

While there is a vast literature on the theory and experience of firms' conduct in expanding or entering new markets, especially on *takeover and merger behaviour*,[43] relatively little work in this area has been done on LDCs. Several host governments in LDCs have, however, expressed concern about takeovers of local firms by TNCs; it has been generally felt that TNCs have, in their immense financial and other resources, an 'unfair advantage' over local competitors, and can, therefore, buy them out at a price which understates their true value. Furthermore, TNCs may, by predatory market conduct, stifle local competition, or so emasculate it that local firms are forced to sell out to them, thus speeding up the process of 'denationalization' and increasing 'dependence' on foreigners.[44] Such fears are not confined to LDCs; they have been voiced in European countries in the 1960s, and the control of acquisitions by large firms (mostly transnational) remains the major concern of anti-monopoly policy.

The US Tariff Commission's (1973) study of US TNCs noted their preference for entering new markets by mergers or takeovers, and gave various reasons for this preference: immediate access to markets and brand names; control over proprietary technology; access to operating plant and personnel; and valuation at less than true worth. In LDCs the second and third reasons may not be important, but the others may be significant enough to explain Vernon's (1974) finding that by the end of the 1960s almost 65 per cent of 2,904 subsidiaries of 396 US and other TNCs in LDCs had been set up by acquisitions rather than by new investments.

The Newfarmer and Mueller (1975) study produces data on Brazil and Mexico which show a lower over all figure for takeover activity in TNCs than those given by Vernon, but which suggest that such activity has risen sharply in recent years, and that TNCs strongly prefer entry by takeover in low-technology sectors (like food processing, textiles, paper, and others) where established local firms offer clear advantages to new entrants. Thus, in Mexico, less than 10 per cent of affiliates were established via acquisitions before 1950, but by 1971–2 this had risen to 75 per cent; for the period 1960–72, 20 per cent of the growth of US TNCs' assets was accounted for by takeovers. Similarly, in Brazil, less than 10 per cent of new entries before 1950 took the form of acquisitions; by the early 1970s takeovers accounted for well over half of new affiliates. Almost 25 per cent of the growth of US assets in Brazil was accounted for by acquisitions during 1960–72.

Similar data are not, as far as I can tell, available for other LDCs, but it seems likely that where takeovers by TNCs are permitted, they have been actively used as a method of entry into sectors where successful local firms offered distinct benefits to new entrants, like established market networks, efficient plant, or a skilled labour force. These factors apply with much less force to high-technology industries, where TNCs would gain little from acquiring local enterprises. If this is indeed true, it would appear that TNC takeovers, generally adding little by way of technology, may not have been very beneficial to host LDCs: they may have yielded high profits to TNCs by the injection of famous brand names supported by sophisticated marketing, but their social gains may have been quite small. Only detailed work on the economic effects of particular takeovers can show how true this is; and such work has not yet been undertaken.

Let us now consider *financing*. A great deal of the literature on TNCs suggests that they use their strong financial position to gear themselves exceptionally highly in LDCs, thus raising the profitability of their equity investment (and depriving local enterprises of domestic savings) and reducing their exposure to exchange risk.[45] While general presumptions of this sort are too numerous to list here, empirical support for them has usually been provided by showing figures on the sources of financing (parent firm, retained profits, local equity, and local/foreign debt) of TNC subsidiaries: in the absence of comparisons with patterns of financing of the TNCs in their home countries, and of local firms in the host country, however, such figures may be quite misleading. A counter to the usual arguments is provided by Lall (1976) in his examination of the comparative financing patterns of a sample of firms (divided into TNC and others, as well as into locally and foreign controlled) in India and Colombia. Lall finds that financing patterns differ markedly between the countries, testifying to the importance of the different institutional and economic environments, but that 'there is little evidence to support statements that MNCs have significantly different borrowing requirements from other firms'. Even if TNCs have privileged access to local finance, the evidence for the two countries suggests that they 'conform to local financing practices rather than using their borrowing power to an abnormal extent'. Lall's argument is supported by Gershenberg's (1976) findings for a sample of TNCs and local firms in Uganda.[46]

An aspect of TNC behaviour which has received a great deal of attention recently is *transfer-pricing*; as this does not directly involve domestic firms, however, readers are referred to the existing literature.[47] Other aspects of conduct—such as the pricing of final products, advertising, innovation, dividend remittance[48] —have not been studied in detail with a view to assessing the impact of TNCs on local industry, or to comparing their respective practices. Some impressionistic evidence exists, but not of sufficient coverage or weight to merit separate discussion.

3c *Performance*

There are several issues which may be considered under 'performance', but we shall concentrate on three which have attracted attention in the context of TNCs, and which fall within the general scope of industrial economics: profitability, productivity, and the choice of technology. Other issues such as employment creation[49] (part of this comes under the choice of technology), exports[50] or management efficiency[51] are deliberately excluded from this survey. We have already remarked on evidence from Brazil and Mexico that, in terms of *size*, TNC subsidiaries seem to be much larger than domestic firms. This difference is found to be confirmed and statistically significant for India but not for Colombia; a general inference is drawn that the larger and more industrially advanced a host economy, the more will TNC affiliates tend to exceed their local competitors in size.[52] This is an interesting observation, but needs greater empirical examination.

It was noted above, and may bear repeating, that practically all the work on profitability, productivity, and technological choice relating to TNCs and local firms has contented itself with comparing these aspects of their performance rather than trying to evaluate the impact of one on the other. Clearly, the latter question is the more important one, but in view of the grave difficulties in empirically investigating it, the present survey can only discuss the former.

i. *Profitability*. While some scattered data are available on the profitability of TNCs in LDCs,[53] there are relatively few studies which try to statistically analyse and explain the relative profitability of TNCs and other firms. The aggregate data indicate that TNCs are fairly profitable in LDCs, and on average perform better than local firms. While this accords with the general theoretical consideration that TNCs possess certain oligopolistic advantages that give them an element of market power (and thus superior profitability) not possessed by other firms,[54] it may be misleading if the average profitability of TNCs reflects, not their superior performance, but the fact that they happen to be concentrated in industries with higher profits (due, say, to higher risk, greater barriers to entry, better capacity-utilization or higher rates of growth), or that they are larger (if size is associated with profitability). If the explanation lies in industrial composition or size, local firms of comparable size and specialization may show equally high profitability—'transnationality' as such may not add to earning capacity.[55]

The main problem in studying the profitability of TNCs is the potential for undeclared profits remitted abroad by transfer pricing, which by its nature is practically impossible to detect and allow for. All studies for LDCs mention this, and we may bear it in mind in interpreting their results.

Willmore (1976) is unable, for a sample of thirty-three foreign and thirty-three matched local firms in Costa Rica, to reject the null hypothesis that the former are no more profitable than the latter. He reports a similar finding by Rosenthal (1973) for Guatemala that 'if anything, average rates of return on domestic industrial plants were higher than those for foreign plants'. Lall (1976) has compared the profitability of TNCs and other firms, and foreign- and locally-controlled firms, for a sample of 109 firms in India and Colombia; he comes to the conclusion, after using analysis of variance, that the declared profits of TNCs and others do not differ significantly from each other. Gerschenberg (1976) arrives at the same result for his sample in Uganda.

All these studies are at variance with *a priori* expectation about TNC performance and with many of the findings for developed countries. Part of the explanation may lie with transfer pricing problems (but this would not be very significant for countries like India where the extent of import-dependence in manufacturing is very small and where a large part of imports is channelled through the State Trading Corporation); part may lie with the relative smallness of the samples, or with accounting and measurement problems; part may lie with host government policies that may have affected the profitability of foreign firms; and part may lie with market structure and entry-barrier variables that affect foreign and local firms equally.[56] If market structure and policies are stronger influences on profitability than origin of ownership or the fact of transnationality, as seems likely from the evidence, some widely held beliefs about the nature of TNCs in LDCs may need to be revised.[57]

ii. *Productivity*. The measurement and comparison of inter-firm productivity is fraught with difficulties. It is not clear how inputs (especially different kinds of labour and capital) and outputs should be measured nor how their relationships should be interpreted. Productivity varies widely with the nature of the industry, the technique of production used, scale economies, managerial efficiency, capacity, utilization, labour-force skills, market power, and so on.[58] Since the purpose of such productivity comparisons (in this case of TNCs with local firms) is presumably to gain an insight into how 'efficiently' firms use 'labour' and 'capital',[59] ideally one should separate out extraneous factors not related to individual firms' efficiency. However, depending on how 'efficiency' is defined (e.g. the ability to maximize value added for a given size of firm, in a given industry, from a given bundle of inputs with a given technology, or to bring new technologies into use, or to improve technology over time, or to realize economies of scale, or simply to 'learn'), different influences may be regarded as relevant or not. There are problems of methodology which need careful handling: to simply compare local and foreign firms, of different sizes, in different industries, facing different market conditions, or using vastly different technologies in the same industry, may be misleading if these factors are not explicitly accounted for. These points should be borne in mind in reviewing existing studies.

Vaitsos (1976) has collected estimates for labour and capital productivity for a large sample (about 3,200) of firms in Peru. He has allowed for different sizes of firms, but his measures of productivity (total output over balance-sheet figures for fixed assets and total employment) leave much to be desired. Since he does not distinguish between different industries, his general findings[60] that foreign firms seem to be more efficient than local ones, particularly in their use of labour, need to be carefully interpreted. Average productivity differences may be caused mainly by the industrial composition of the two groups of firms, a presumption which is supported by figures given in the appendix tables to the report. The absence of statistical tests makes it difficult to say how significant industrial differences are, but it appears from the figures given that in low-technology sectors[61] foreign firms have similar capital productivity but much higher labour productivity, perhaps indicating a more efficient use of similar technology; in high technology sectors[62] foreign firms have much higher capital as well as labour productivity (sometimes with less capital/worker), indicating the use of more advanced technology, scale economies, or better management.

Fajnzylber's (1975) study of Mexico groups firms into light consumer goods, consumer durables, intermediates, and capital goods. Measuring productivity by value-added over employment and capital, he finds that foreign firms have higher labour productivity overall than local firms (2.0 times), with the difference being greatest in light consumer goods (2.5) and least in consumer durables (1.4). Somewhat surprisingly, he finds that the capital productivity of foreign firms is uniformly lower, being 0.8 of that of local firms on average, highest in light consumer goods (0.9), and least in intermediate goods (0.6). Whether this is due to the nature of the technology, the distribution of firms within these broad groups, their size, the existence of excess capacity, or poor management is impossible to say.

On Argentina, Sourrouille (1976) provides information on labour productivity of foreign and local enterprises (measured by output per employee) by industry groups.[63] For 1967, foreign firms' productivity was 2.1 times that of local firms on average, with the difference being highest in transport equipment (5.1), electrical appliances (5.0), machinery (2.6) and petroleum products (2.6), and lowest in chemicals (1.4), textiles and rubber (1.3), and food (0.9). Again, the figures do not enable us to trace the sources of these differences, since data on size, technology, capacity utilization, and so on are not given.

Jo (1976) compares the capital intensity and labour productivity of foreign and local firms in different industries in South Korea. He finds that on average foreign firms have labour productivity 1.8 times that of local firms, lower than local firms in sectors like clay, metal products, food, wood, and electrical machinery, and higher in textiles, chemicals, machinery, and transport equipment. As this pattern is closely related to differences in capital intensity between the two groups (more capital intensity being associated with higher productivity), we may infer that differences in productivity are explained more by the sort of technology used (and perhaps size) than by efficiency in the running of operations.

None of these studies allows us to say whether TNCs *as such* are more efficient in their use of capital and labour than domestic firms. Differences between them certainly seem to exist, but whether this is due to industrial distribution, size, technology, market conditions, x-efficiency, or other factors cannot be determined from the evidence presented.[64] Lall and Streeten (1977) examine labour and capital productivity of different groups of firms in their Colombian and Indian samples, but fail to find statistically significant differences between TNCs and other firms. Industry groupings turn out highly significant, as may be expected, but the sample is too small to test for differences within industry groups.

Balasubramanyam (1973) compares productivities and capital-intensities *within* industries for a sample of 85 Indian firms of which 28 are local without foreign licensing, 42 local with foreign licensing, and 15 foreign. He finds such a diversity of experience across different industries for different measures of productivity that foreign licensing or ownership as such does not seem to exercise an independent influence; in any case, the smallness of the sample of foreign firms does not permit any general inference about their performance.

In his study of Central America, Willmore (1976) finds that capital output ratios of foreign firms is significantly lower than that of local firms, but is unable to explain whether this is because of differences in labour-output or capital-labour ratios.

We are, therefore, led to adopt an agnostic position

about the relative productivities of TNCs and local firms, at least as far as 'efficiency' is concerned. It is likely that TNCs achieve greater output or value-added per worker because they are concentrated in industries which are capital-intensive, they use more modern technology or are able to reap economies of scale.[65] Depending on the nature of the technology, they may or may not achieve higher capital productivity. Not much more can be said about their performance with the evidence that we possess. There is certainly no firm basis for saying that TNCs are more efficient or more productive than local enterprises of similar size, in similar activities and using similar technology: on the other hand, they do seem to be larger, specialized in oligopolistic sectors, and use more advanced technology than firms in LDCs.

iii. *Choice of Technique*. One of the areas of great interest and controversy in the study of TNCs in developing countries has been that of the 'appropriateness' of technology. There are several recent works reviewing the general literature on the choice of technology and employment creation in LDCs,[6] so we shall confine ourselves to the narrower issue of the role of TNCs. There are three separate questions involved:

—whether the technologies used by TNCs are *adaptable* to low-wage labour-abundant conditions in LDCs;
—whether TNCs *do in fact adapt* the technologies they transfer; and
—whether TNCs adapt *better or worse* than local firms.

As far as the *adaptability* of TNC technologies is concerned, the position is far from clear. Much of the general literature on capital-labour substitutability in developing countries has argued that technologies are fairly flexible, using anecdotal evidence from particular industries or production functions derived from aggregated data.[67] However, doubts have been expressed about whether the technology is really flexible once the products (and so income distribution and tastes) are specified,[68] about the production function methodology used to produce high elasticity estimates,[69] and about the economic and commercial viability of labour-intensive technologies, even for simple products where alternatives actually do exist.[70] This is not the venue for a discussion of general factor-substitution problems, but it does appear that efficient technologies may be fairly 'rigid' in a plausible range of economic conditions in LDCs. This 'rigidity' applies especially to TNC technologies (since they tend to predominate in complex, continuous-process, capital-intensive, and modern industries), with the qualifications that (*a*) 'peripheral' processes like handling, transport, storage, administration, etc., may be amenable to substitution, (*b*) the 'core' process itself may, by adaptation of machinery, greater machine speeds and more shifts, subcontracting, use of lower quality inputs, and less rapid changes of technique and models, also be made to use more labour.[71] The total resultant adaptability may not be very great as far as TNCs are concerned, but some flexibility does exist.

The evidence on the *actual* adaptation by TNCs is in line with this reasoning. One of the main sources of the TNCs' special 'advantage' which enables them to grow is precisely the possession of advanced technology, combined in a profitable package with marketing, administrative and financial factors, which can be applied with little adaptation to different areas. It is not to be expected, therefore, that they will undertake *major, expensive alterations* to suit the relatively small markets of LDCs, or to take advantage of differences in labour costs which form a small proportion of total cost. Minor on-the-spot adaptations may be made to suit local conditions, to meet official requirements, or to save foreign exchange, but by their very nature TNCs do not specialize in the simple, labour-intensive products which can be adapted to LDC factor endowments. To recount the evidence on this:

(*a*) Reuber (1973) finds for his sample that about 70 per cent reported no adaptations. The changes in technique that were made were mainly to scale down plant and equipment to lower production volumes; 'there were relatively few instances of adaptation to take advantage of low labour costs or to make up for the absence of skilled labour in the host country' (p. 126). Government regulation, raw material quality, and demand characteristics also induced some changes.

(*b*) Stewart (1974) collects evidence from different sources that very little adaptation was made to basic production technologies in several cases; she also notes, however, that Philips, Ford, General Motors, and some other TNCs were trying to develop appropriate *products* for LDCs. (There is little evidence in more recent years that such attempts have been very successful. All these firms are still operating their modern, capital-intensive plants, producing the latest array of products, in LDCs.)

(*c*) Baranson (1967) lists several minor technological adaptations in the Cummins diesel plant in India, mainly to suit the smaller scale of production. While these tended to use old techniques that were more labour intensive, they were not made explicitly in order to exploit low-wage costs in the host country.

(*d*) Courtney and Leipziger (1975) study nearly 1,500 US affiliates in LDCs, using Cobb-Douglas production functions to estimate two sorts of adaptation: to the technique transferred by the parent (ex ante substitution) and to the running of a given plant (ex post substitution). While the production function approach, especially at the two- and three-digit industrial classification level used by the authors, is open to serious criticism,[72] and the findings are crucially dependent on these estimates, they argue that ex ante technology exported by TNCs differs between developed and less developed areas but not systematically in a capital or labour-intensive direction. In nine out of eleven cases, however, the given process is run more labour-intensively in LDCs to take advantage of lower wage rates.

(*e*) Morley and Smith (1974) in their plant-level investigation of TNCs in Brazil, find little scope for adaptation of technology to low-wage conditions. The main adaptations come, as noted by Reuber and Baranson, from the need to scale down plants.

(*f*) Allen (1973a, b), in his study of US and Japanese firms in South East Asia, fails to find any significant technological adaptation by TNCs to local conditions.

(*g*) A study of can-making in Kenya, Tanzania, and Thailand by Cooper *et al.* (1975) finds that there does exist some scope for efficient factor substitution, and that different TNCs behave differently in response to conditions in LDCs. Some TNCs (vertically integrated and innovative can-makers as well as good packagers for whom can-making is a peripheral activity) prefer to use 'standardized' plant in different areas; however, one TNC shows greater flexibility in searching out and adapting technology. The precise reasons for this difference are not clear from the available evidence.

Several studies have noted the adaptability of peripheral activities[73] and remarked on the willingness of TNCs to use more labour in LDCs.[74]

As for the question of whether TNCs adapt *better or worse* than local firms, the findings are extremely mixed and based on rather shaky data and methodology. The ideal procedure would be to compare matched sets of foreign and local firms, making similar products, with equal access to the relevant technology and facing identical market conditions. While existing studies cannot, for obvious reasons, live up to this ideal, most of them have contented themselves with comparing large and diverse groups of local and foreign firms. Only two studies have, in my knowledge, tried to compare matched pairs: Cohen (1975) and Mason (1973) both fail to find consistent patterns of factory intensity in their samples of local and foreign firms once industry differences are accounted for, and are, therefore, unable to conclude whether or not TNCs are better or worse at adapting technologies.[75]

There are several more general comparisons of the factor intensity of foreign and local firms, some using data aggregated over different sectors, others differentiating between industries. For all of these, we may bear in mind the conceptual and practical problems mentioned previously:

Balasubramanyam (1973) compares factor intensities of Indian firms without foreign technology or capital with those of Indian firms with foreign licensing and those with foreign capital. He finds, within given industries, that the first and third groups are less capital-intensive than the second, but does not provide any clear evidence on the performance of foreign investors as such.

Reidel (1975) finds for Taiwanese export-based industries that there is no consistent pattern of difference between the factor-intensities of foreign and local firms within specific sectors, especially when multivariate analysis is used.

Lall and Streeten (1977) do not find that transnationality makes a statistically significant difference to capital-intensity for their aggregated sample of 109 Indian and Colombian firms, but that the industry grouping does.

Vaitsos (1976) finds that foreign firms are more capital-intensive in Peru for all sizes except the largest ones, where local firms are more capital-intensive. The value of this finding is much reduced by its aggregation over industries.

Fajnzylber (1975) finds in Mexico that foreign firms use 2.5 times more capital per employee on average than local firms. He differentiates between light consumer, durable, intermediate, and capital goods, but the degree of aggregation is still high.

Jo (1976) reports for South Korea that relative capital-intensities vary markedly over industries with no consistent pattern emerging for TNCs, though on average foreign firms are more capital-intensive. Import-substituting firms are far more capital-intensive than export-based ones.

Agarwal (1976) finds for thirty-four Indian industries (at the three-digit level) that TNCs are more capital-intensive than local firms. This is contradicted by Leipziger's (1976) comparison of US and local Indian firms. Using Cobb-Douglas production functions, which has drawbacks noted above, Leipziger finds that US firms import less capital-intensive technology ex ante, but use more fixed capital per man ex post because they have to pay higher wages.

Solomon and Forsyth (1977) find for Ghana that foreign firms are more capital-intensive than local firms within given sectors, but that they are markedly less skill-intensive. The usefulness of this finding is limited by the fact that they cover industries (furniture, bread, footwear, shirts, etc.) where large TNCs hardly exist.

Wells (1973) notes that TNCs may be better at adaptation than local firms in Indonesia, especially when put under competitive pressure.[76]

Pack (1976) finds that in Kenya engineering-trained managers (of whom more are possessed by TNCs) are better at adapting technology than commercially trained ones. Pack's study, unfortunately, focuses on 'traditional' sectors not much frequented by TNCs; in any case, his findings are challenged by Solomon and Forsyth above and by Gershenberg (1976) for Uganda. Gershenberg argues that TNCs use more capital-intensive techniques than local firms.

A number of studies under way are investigating this problem,[77] and may cast more light on a confused situation. The mass of conflicting evidence, the occasional use of imprecise methodology, the inherent problems of definition and measurement, all do not support any strong statement about the relative performance of TNCs and local firms as far as adaptation is concerned.

Notes: Reading 19

1 See Scitovsky (1954) and Hirschman (1958).
2 Hirschman (1958), pp. 205–6.
3 For a summary see Lall and Streeten (1977). This study found that over half the sample firms imported goods worth over 30 per cent of their total value of sales – over 65 per cent of India is excluded – but that this high degree of import dependence did not differ significantly between TNCs and other firms.
4 See Mason (1967), who attempts to quantify the local linkages of US foreign investments using aggregate industry data, measuring backward linkages simply by the 'ratio of local expenditure to total sales' and forward linkages by the 'ratio of local sales to total sales'. See Hufbauer and Adler (1968) for estimates of local and foreign buying propensities of US TNCs.
5 Vaitsos (1976) gives comparative data on the import propensities of local and foreign firms in Peru for 1973, which show that foreign firms had higher imports in eleven out of twelve broad industry groups. He notes, however, that this does not necessarily imply that local firms created more linkages (p. 40); such aggregate data do not permit a detailed examination of the technologies and products involved.
6 Daftary and Borghey (1976) provide rather sketchy data on local purchases by thirteen TNCs, and conclude that few of these have set up significant local linkages, except with the domestic packaging industry (pp. 75–6).
7 See Jo (1976), who reports that foreign firms have higher import propensities than local firms, and that supply, cost, and quality problems limit the growth of local purchasing.
8 Thoburn (1973), in the course of his study of the tin and rubber sectors, touches upon the role of foreign engineering firms in Malaysia. He finds that they helped in the development of local suppliers in processes of low capital intensity and few scale economies; 'but in all cases the firms concerned were already in existence when the link with foreign firms was formed' (p. 113).
9 See chapters 5 and 14 of the annotated bibliography on TNCs by Lall (1975) for other references on LDCs.
10 Watanabe (1972a), p. 425.
11 Baranson (1967, 1969).
12 Lall (1977) notes that foreign automobile assembly plants in Malaysia have not created significant domestic linkages; despite the government's expressed desire to increase local content, the absence of statutory controls on imports has led the TNCs to continue to depend heavily on imports.
13 See de la Torre (1974) and Helleiner (1976).
14 For a detailed analysis of these factors see Sharpston (1975).
15 UNCTAD (1975) notes that this is happening in South Korea, Taiwan, Hong Kong and Singapore. However, König (1975) finds that Mexico, despite its industrial development, is unable to provide 'border industries' with even 1 per cent of their inputs; he places the full blame for this on inefficiencies caused by protection.
16 See UNCTAD (1975), Chang (1971), Finan (1975), US Tariff Commission (1970) and Lim and Pang (1976). Some products of the electronics industry, mainly in consumer electronics, *are* amenable to local manufacture in their entirety, and so fall into the third group.
17 For general discussions of the determinants of export-orientated foreign investments and their costs and benefits see Helleiner (1973, 1976), Adam (1972, 1975), Michalet (1977), de la Torre (1974); for an analysis of the significance of labour skills in trade see Hirsch (1975) and for a recent theoretical analysis of TNCs and trade see Hirsch (1975, 1976); for a description of the role of multinational buying groups see Hone (1974); and for an examination of the tariff provisions in developed countries which lead to 'offshore assembly' see Finger (1975).
18 Rising wage costs in Singapore have led TNCs to upgrade the skill content of their activities rather than leave the country. See Lim and Pang (1976) and Lall (1977).
19 East European countries are also entering the field, and their use of 'industrial co-operation agreements', under which Western firms provide technology, and usually also equipment and intermediate inputs, in return for processed goods, seems to have provided major benefits to their smaller establishments without incurring the problem of direct TNC investment. This arrangement, discussed by Hewett (1975), may serve as a model to the more advanced LDCs.
20 See König (1975), Baerresen (1971), Walker (1969), Fernandez (1973), Sahagun (1976) and Watanabe (1974a).
21 Reidel (1974) and Evers *et al.* (1977), the latter concentrating on textiles.
22 Lim and Pang (1976) on the electronic industry.
23 Van Houten (1973).
24 Reidel (1975).
25 Especially in Helleiner (1976), Watanabe (1972a) and Sharpston (1975).
26 As noted above, however, this has not occurred for 'border industries' in the advanced but highly protected economy of Mexico, even in textiles, despite the efforts of some TNCs to increase local content in order to qualify for GSP privileges. See König (1975), pp. 92–4.
27 For general international comparisons of industrial structures of developed countries see Bain (1966), Pryor (1972), Horowitz (1971), Dyas and Thanheiser (1976) and Panic (1976).
28 Meller (forthcoming), mentioned in the 1976 *Annual Report* of the National Bureau of Economic Research, Washington, DC.
29 White (1974) and Sharwani (1976). White finds that overall concentration in Pakistan is higher than in the US, UK or Germany, and about the same as Japan and Chile.
30 Petras (1969) and Zeitlin (1974).
31 Hazari (1966), Ghosh (1974, 1975), Gupta (1968), Sawhney and Sawhney (1973). Most Indian studies show a marked decrease in overall concentration with the process of industrial growth.
32 House (1973, 1976).
33 Industrial organisation literature is replete with controversies on these problems of theory and methodology; for some recent studies see Needham (1976), Schmalensee (1976) and Phillips (1976).
34 See Caves (various), de Jong (1973), Horst (various), Rowthorn (1971) and Hymer (1976).
35 The growing proportion of foreign ownership and the relationship between TNC presence and concentration in

Mexico are also noted by Fajnzylber and Tarragó (1976) and Sahagún (1976).

36 Also see Evans (1971, 1974), on Brazil. M. C. Tavares of FINEP, Rio de Janeiro, is presently conducting a study of 800 firms (foreign and local) in Brazil, covering their effects on industrial structure and comparing their performance.

37 Also see Chudnovsky (1976) and Katz (1974) for data on Argentina.

38 Zeitling (1974), and a CORFO study mentioned by Vaitsos (1976) in a footnote on p. 24.

39 Chudnovsky (1973).

40 The Reserve Bank of India *Bulletins* publish periodic data on sales of foreign companies, but these have not been utilised to calculate the evolution of foreign ownership in the country. Kidron (1965) gives some early figures.

41 Jo (1976) distinguishes export-oriented from other foreign firms, and finds that foreign dominance is much stronger in import substituting than exporting industries. Surprisingly, the bulk of foreign firms in South Korea are quite small, presumably because of their concentration in textiles, apparel, and electric and electronic components.

42 Lall (1977) finds that 48 per cent of manufacturing output and 51 per cent of fixed assets in West Malaysia were foreign controlled in 1972; and that up to 77 per cent of manufacturing output and 88 per cent of manufactured exports were contributed by foreign-controlled firms in 1975 in Singapore.

43 For general reviews see Singh (1971, 1975), and de Jong (1976); for the relevance of merger theory to TNCs see Baumann (1975).

44 For a colourful expression of such beliefs see Barnett and Müller (1974).

45 See, for instance, Reuber (1973), pp. 88–91. Data on financing patterns of US TNCs are given by Leftwich (1974), while financial strategies open to TNCs are analysed in general terms by Robbins and Stobaugh (1974).

46 In their study of the Singapore electronics industry, Lim and Pang (1976) found that small local firms complained of having much more difficulty than large TNCs in obtaining bank finance. Their data did not, however, permit a testing of whether this was due to difference in size or to the 'foreignness' of TNC subsidiaries.

47 See Lall (1973), Kopits (1976a, b), and Vaitsos (1974a).

48 See Kopits (1976a) for a survey of attempts to explain TNC remittance behaviour in response to different tax rates. Few of these deal with LDCs, and those that do use over-simplified models of TNC behaviour (which ignore the existence of oligopolistic rents and interdependence as well as risk and uncertainty) that greatly reduce their practical interest. No systematic comparisons of the reinvestment behaviour of TNCs and local firms are available, but see Lall and Streeten (1977) for some evidence.

49 For recent surveys see Sabolo and Trajtenberg (1976) and Vaitsos (1974b, 1976).

50 See Helleiner (1976) and Lall and Streeten (1977), ch. 7.

51 See Negandhi and Prasad (1975) for a comparison of the management performance of US TNCs and local firms in selected LDCs.

52 Lall and Streeten (1977), ch. 6.

53 See the references on Mexico, Brazil, Argentina, India and Korea above.

54 See Caves (1971), Dunning (1973), Horst (1975, 1976), Hymer (1976) and Vernon (1971).

55 Empirical work on US TNCs in developed countries (Horst, 1975; Wolf, 1975) does seem to confirm the superior profitability of TNCs over other firms: it also suggests that TNC earnings are less volatile during business cycles than those of firms confined to particular national markets.

56 On the importance of market structure and policy in affecting corporate profitability in different developed countries, see Adams (1976).

57 It may be the case, however, that TNC entry itself changes market structure and so the profitability of different industries.

58 See Bhalla (1975), Lim (1976b), Merrett (1971) and OECD (1966).

59 The problem of technological choice is closely related, but is considered separately below. On the measurement of technical efficiency in LDCs and an interesting analysis of firms in Chile see Meller (1976); unfortunately, this study does not distinguish between foreign and local firms.

60 Vaitsos finds that foreign-controlled firms (20 per cent or more foreign equity) have higher labour productivity for all sizes of firm than locally controlled ones, the differential being highest for intermediate-sized firms and fairly low for the smallest and largest ones. Foreign firms have lower capital productivity for small sizes, slightly higher for the intermediate, and much higher for the largest firms.

61 Food and beverages, textiles, wood and furniture, pulp and paper, leather, construction and glass.

62 Chemicals, rubber, petroleum, metal products and automobiles. Rather oddly, tobacco falls into this group in terms of its productivity.

63 See Sourrouille (1976), appendix tables on pp. 84–5.

64 Meller (1976), in his study of over 11,000 firms in twenty-one Chilean industries, is unable to distinguish between efficient and inefficient establishments on the basis of size, capital–labour ratios, or administration–worker ratios within particular industries. Clearly, the role of managerial efficiency, technology (not measured by simple capital–labour ratios) or other factors is extremely important.

65 Lim (1976a) finds that in Malaysia foreign firms operate their plant longer and more intensively than local counterparts. This is due, according to him, not to their greater x-efficiency or managerial superiority, but to larger size and greater capital intensity.

66 See Bhalla (1975), Gaude (1975), Morawetz (1974), Stewart (1974) and White (1976b).

67 See references to note 66 as well as Pack (1974, 1976), Cooper *et al.* (1975) and Pickett, Forsyth, and McBain (1974).

68 Stewart (1974).

69 O'Herlihy (1972), Morawetz (1976), Gaude (1975) and Pickett and Robson (1977), p. 211.

70 On sugar manufacturing see Forsyth (1977), and on textiles see Pickett and Robson (1977). It is interesting to note that Pickett and Forsyth seem to have considerably modified their views since their 1974 paper, where they showed a much greater belief in the feasibility of extensive factor substitution.

71 See Helleiner (1975) for a good survey of the issues relating technology transfer to LDCs by transnationals. Also see Hellinger (1976) on Latin America and Pack (1976) on Kenya. On a visit to a foreign car-assembly plant in Singapore, I was informed that considerably more labour was employed than in advanced countries by using old equipment, though it was also necessitated by the large number of models that were assembled on one line.

72 The parents and affiliates may be using technologies of different ages, producing different products, having different degrees of capacity utilisation, and so on, all of which would affect the calculation. The Courtney and Leipziger finding that constant returns to scale apply to seventeen out of twenty-two cases is also highly suspect. On methodical issues see O'Herlihy (1972) and Gaude (1975).

73 See references in Helleiner (1975), Pack (1976) and Vaitsos (1974b).

74 This willingness may not be due solely to economic consideration. Social and political factors may, as Pickett and Robson (1977) note for textiles, cause all types of firms in LDCs to indulge in a certain 'prodigality' in their use of capital and labour.

75 Cohen's sample covers Singapore, Taiwan and South Korea; Mason's covers Mexico and Singapore.

76 The role of competition in stimulating appropriate adaptation is supported for Pakistan by White (1976), though he does not study TNCs separately.

77 Helleiner (1975) reports a study by Helen Hughes of 1,400 firms in Israel, Colombia, Malaysia and the Philippines, which finds that TNCs had higher capital-in-place to labour ratios, but used their capital more intensively than local firms. Anne Krueger of the NBER is investigating 1,000 US TNCs' factor substitution in LDCs, as reported in the 1976 *Annual Report* of the NBER.

References: Reading 19

Adam, G. (1972), 'Some implications and concomitants of worldwide sourcing', *Acta Oeconomica*, pp. 309–23.

Adam, G. (1975), 'Multinational corporations and worldwide sourcing', in H. Radice (ed.), *International Firms and Modern Imperialism* (Penguin).

Adams, W. J. (1976), 'International differences in corporate profitability', *Economica*, pp. 367–79.

Agarwal, J. P. (1976), 'Factor proportions in foreign and domestic firms in Indian manufacturing', *Economic Journal*, pp. 589–94.

Allen, T. W. (1973a), *Direct Investment of United States Enterprises in South East Asia* (ECOCEN, Bangkok).

Allen, T. W. (1973b), *Direct Investment of Japanese Enterprises in South East Asia* (ECOCEN, Bangkok).

Baerresen, D. W. (1971), *The Border Industrialization Program of Mexico* (D. C. Heath).

Bain, J. S. (1966), *International Differences in Industrial Structure* (Yale University Press).

Balasubramanyam, U. N. (1973), *International Transfer of Technology to India* (Praeger).

Baranson, J. (1967), *Manufacturing Problems in India: the Cummins Diesel Experience* (Syracuse University Press).

Baranson, J. (1969), *Automative Industries in Developing Countries* (IBRD).

Barnet, R. J., and Müller, R. (1974), *Global Reach: the Power of the Multinational Corporations* (Simon & Schuster).

Baumann, H. G. (1975), 'Merger theory, property rights, and the pattern of US investment in Canada', *Weltwirtschaftliches Archiv*, pp. 676–98.

Bhalia, A. S. (1975) (ed.), *Technology and Employment in Industry* (ILO).

Brown, M., and Perrin, J. (1977), 'Engineering and industrial projects', (OECD Development Centre), CD/R/(77)2, mimeo.

Caves, R. E. (1971), 'International corporations: the industrial economics of foreign investment', *Economica*, pp. 1–27.

Caves, R. E. (1974a), 'Causes of direct investment: foreign firms' shares in Canadian and United Kingdom manufacturing industries', *Review of Economics and Statistics*, pp. 279–93.

Caves, R. E. (1974b), 'International trade, international investment and imperfect markets', Princeton University, Special Papers in International Economics, No. 10.

Chang, Y. S. (1971), *The Transfer of Technology: Economics of Offshore Assembly, the Case of Semiconductor Industry*, Report No. 11 (UNITAR).

Chudnovsky, D. (1973), 'Foreign manufacturing firms' behaviour in Colombia', D.Phil. thesis, St Antony's College, Oxford; published in Spanish as *Empresas Multinacionales y Ganancias Monopolicas*, siglio XXI (Buenos Aires, 1974).

Chudnovsky, D. (1976), *Dependencia Technologica y Estructura Industrial: El Caso Argentino* (FLASCO, Buenos Aires), mimeo.

Cohen, B. (1975), *Multinational Firms and Asian Exports* (Yale University Press).

Cooper, C., Kaplinsky, R., Bell, R., and Satyarakwit, W. (1975), 'Choice of techniques for can-making in Kenya, Tanzania and Thailand', in A. S. Bhalla (1975) above.

Courtney, W. H., and Leipziger, D. M. (1975), 'Multinational corporations in less-developed countries: the choice of technology', *Oxford Bulletin of Economics and Statistics*, pp. 297–304.

Daftary, F., and Borghey, M. (1976), 'Multinational enterprises and employment in Iran', World Employment Programme, Working Paper No. 14, ILO, mimeo.

De Jong, F. J. (1973), 'Multinational enterprises and the market form' in G. Bertin (ed.), *The Growth of the Large Multinational Corporation* (Centre National de la Recherche Scientifique).

De Jong, H. W. (1976), 'Theory and evidence concerning mergers: an international comparison', in A. P. Jaquemin and H. W. De Jong (eds), *Markets, Corporate Behaviour and the State* (Nijhoff).

De la Torre, J. (1974), 'Foreign investment and export dependency', *Economic Development and Cultural Change*, pp. 135–50.

Dunning, J. H. (1973), 'The determinants of international production', *Oxford Economic Papers*, pp. 289–336.

Dyas, G. P., and Thanheiser, H. T. (1976), *The Emerging European Enterprise: Strategy and Structure in French and German Manufacturing Industry* (Macmillan).

Evans, P. B. (1971), 'Denationalization and development: a study of industrialization in Brazil', PhD thesis, Harvard University.

Evans, P. B. (1974), 'Direct investment and industrial concentration', unpublished manuscript.

Evers, B., de Groot, G., and Wagenmans, W. (1977), 'Hong Kong: development and perspective of a clothing colony', translated summary of Progress Report No. 6, Development Research Institute, Tilburg, Netherlands, mimeo.

Fajnzylber, F. (1975), 'Las empresas transnacionales y el sistema industrial de Mexico', *El Trimestre Economico*, October–November.

Fajnzylber, F., and Tarragó, T. M. (1976), *Las Empresas Multinacionales: Expansion a Nivel Mundial y Proyyeccion en la Industria Mexicana* (Fondo de Cultura Economica, Mexico).

Fernandez, R. A. (1973), 'The border industrialization program on the US–Mexico border', *Review of Radical Political Economics*, Spring, pp. 37–52.

Finan, N. (1975), 'The international transfer of semiconductor technology through US based firms', Working Paper No. 118, National Bureau of Economic Research, New York.

Finger, J. M. (1975), 'Tariff provisions for offshore assembly and the exports of developing countries', *Economic Journal*, pp. 365–71.

Forsyth, D. J. C. (1977), 'Appropriate technology in sugar manufacturing', *World Development*, pp. 189–202.

Gaude, J. (1975), 'Capital-labour substitution possibilities: a reviewer of empirical evidence', in A. S. Bhalla (1975) above.

Gershenberg, I. (1976), 'The performance of multinational and other firms in economically less-developed countries: a comparative analysis of Ugandan data', Discussion Paper 234, Institute of Development Studies, Nairobi, mimeo.

Ghosh, A. (1974), 'The role of large industrial houses in Indian industries, 1948–68', *Indian Economic Journal*, April–June.

Ghosh, A. (1975), 'Concentration and growth of Indian industries, 1948–68', *Journal of Industrial Economics*, pp. 203–22.

Gupta, V. E. (1968), 'Cost functions, concentration and barriers to entry in twenty-nine manufacturing industries of India', *Journal of Industrial Economics*, pp. 57–72.

Hazari, R. K. (1966), *The Structure of the Corporate Private Sector: A Study of Concentration, Ownership and Control* (Asia Publishing House).

Helleiner, G. K. (1973), 'Manufactured exports from less-developed countries and multinational firms', *Economic Journal*, pp. 21–47.

Helleiner, G. K. (1975), 'The role of multinational corporations in the less developed countries' trade in technology', *World Development*, pp. 161–89.

Helleiner, G. K. (1976), 'Transnational enterprises, manufactured exports and employment in the less developed countries', *Economic and Political Weekly*, annual number, February, pp. 247–62.

Hellinger, D., and Hellinger, S. (1976), *Unemployment and the Multinationals: A Strategy for Technological Change in Latin America* (Kennikat Press).

Hewett, E. A. (1975), 'The economics of East European technology imports from the West', *American Economic Review*, May, pp. 377–82.

Hirsch, S. (1975), 'The product cycle model of international trade', *Oxford Bulletin of Economics and Statistics*, pp. 305–17.

Hirsch, S. (1976), 'An international trade and investment theory of the firm', *Oxford Economic Papers*, pp. 258–70.

Hirschman, A. O. (1958), *The Strategy of Economic Development* (Yale University Press).

Hone, A. (1974), 'Multinational corporations and multinational buying groups', *World Development*, February, pp. 145–50.

Horowitz, I. (1971), 'An international comparison of the international effects of concentration on industry wages, investment and sales', *Journal of Industrial Economics*, April, pp. 166–78.

Horst, T. (1972), 'Firm and industry determinants of the decision to invest abroad: an empirical study', *Review of Economics and Statistics*, pp. 258–66.

Horst, T. (1974), 'Theory of the firm', in J. H. Dunning (ed.), *Economic Analysis and the Multinational Enterprise* (Allen & Unwin).

Horst, T. (1975), 'American investment abroad and domestic market power', Brookings Institution, mimeo.

Horst, T. (1976), 'American multinationals and the US economy', *American Economic Review Papers and Proceedings*, pp. 149–54.

House, W. J. (1973), 'Market structure and industry performance: the case of Kenya', *Oxford Economic Papers*, November.

House, W. J. (1976), 'Market structure and industry performance: the case of Kenya revisited', *Journal of Economic Studies*, pp. 117–32.

Hufbauer, G. C., and Adler, F. M. (1968), *US Manufacturing Investment and the Balance of Payments* (US Treasury Department).

Hymer, S. (1976), *The International Operations of National Firms: A Study of Direct Foreign Investment* (MIT).

Jo, Sung-Hwen (1976), 'The impact of multinational firms on employment and incomes: the case study of South Korea', World Employment Programme, Working Paper No. 12, ILO, mimeo.

Katz, J. (1974), *Oligopolio, Empresarios Nacionales y Corporaciones Multinacionales*, siglo XXI (Buenos Aires).

Kidron, M. (1965), *Foreign Investments in India* (Oxford University Press).

König, W. (1975), 'Towards an evaluation of international subcontracting activities in developing countries', UN ECLA, mimeo.

Kopits, G. F. (1976a), 'Taxation and multinational firm behaviour: a critical survey', *IMF Staff Papers*, pp. 624–73.

Kopits, G. F. (1976b), 'Intra-firm royalties crossing frontiers and transfer-pricing behaviour', *Economic Journal*, pp. 791–805.

Lake, A. (1976), 'Transnational activity and market entry in the semiconductor industry', Working Paper No. 126, National Bureau of Economic Research, New York.

Lall, S. (1973), 'Transfer-pricing by multinational manufacturing firms', *Oxford Bulletin of Economics and Statistics*, pp. 173–95.

Lall, S. (1975), *Private Foreign Manufacturing Investment and Multinational Corporations: An Annotated Bibliography* (Praeger).

Lall, S. (1976), 'Financial and profit performance of MNCs in developing countries: some evidence from an Indian and Colombian sample', *World Development*, pp. 713–24.

Lall, S. (1977), 'Transfer pricing in assembly industries: a preliminary analysis of the issues in Malaysia and Singapore', Commonwealth Secretariat, London, mimeo.

Lall, S., and Streeten, P. P. (1977), *Foreign Investment, Transnationals and Developing Countries* (Macmillan).

Leftwich, R. B. (1974), 'US multinational companies: profitability, financial leverage and effective income tax rates', *Survey of Current Business*, May, pp. 27–36.

Leipziger, D. M. (1976), 'Production characteristics in foreign enclave and domestic manufacturing: the case of India', *World Development*, pp. 321–5.

Lim, D. (1976a), 'Capital utilization of local and foreign establishments in Malaysian manufacturing', *Review of Economics and Statistics*, pp. 209–17.

Lim, D. (1976b), 'On the measurement of capital utilization in less developed countries',*Oxford Economic Papers*, pp. 149–59.

Lim, L., and Pang, Eng-Fong (1976), 'The electronics industry in Singapore: structure, employment, technology and linkages', Economic Research Centre, University of Singapore, mimeo.

Little, I. M. D., Scitovsky, T., and Scott, M. F. (1970), *Industry and Trade in Some Developing Countries: A Comparative Study* (Oxford University Press).

McLinden, J. E. (1972), 'World outlook for electronics', *Columbia Journal of World Business*, May–June, pp. 65–71.

Mason, R. H. (1967), 'An analysis of benefits from US direct foreign investments in less-developed areas', PhD thesis, Stanford University.

Mason, R. H. (1973), 'Some observations on the choice of technology by multinational firms in developing countries', *Review of Economics and Statistics*, pp. 349–55.

Meller, P. (1976), 'Efficiency frontiers for industrial establishments of different sizes', *Explorations in Economic Research*, pp. 379–407.

Meller, P. (forthcoming), 'International comparisons of industrial concentration in Latin America', National Bureau of Economic Research, New York, 1976 (submitted for publication).

Merrett, S. (1971), 'Snares in the labour productivity measure of efficiency: some examples from Indian nitrogen fertilizer manufacture', *Journal of Industrial Economics*, November, pp. 71–84.

Michalet, C.-A. (1977), 'International subcontracting', in OECD Development Centre's 'Experts' Meeting on International Subcontracting and Reinforcing LDCs' Technological Absorption Capacity', OECD, mimeo.

Morawetz, D. (1974), 'Employment implications of industrialization in developing countries: a survey', *Economic Journal*, pp. 491–542.

Morawetz, D. (1976), 'Elasticities of substitution in industry: what do we learn from econometric estimates?', *World Development*, pp. 11–15.

Morley, S. A., and Smith, G. W. (1974), 'The choice of technology: multinational firms in Brazil', Rice University Program in Development Studies, No. 58, mimeo. (Later published in *Economic Development and Cultural Change*, 1977.)

Morrison, T. K. (1976), 'International subcontracting: improved prospects in manufactured exports for small and very poor LDCs', *World Development*, pp. 327–32.

Moxon, R. W. (1974), 'Offshore production in the less-developed countries: a case study of multinationality in the electronics industry', *The Bulletin*, New York University Graduate School of Business Administration, July.

Müller, R., and Morgenstern, R. D. (1974), 'Multinational corporations and balance of payments impact in LDCs: an econometric analysis of export pricing behaviour', *Kyklos*, pp. 304–21.

Needham, D. (1976), 'Entry barriers and non-price aspects of firms' behaviour', *Journal of Industrial Economics*, pp. 29–43.

Negandhi, A., and Prasad, B. (1975), *The Frightening Angels* (Kent State University Press).

Newfarmer, R. S., and Mueller, W. R. (1975), *Multinational Corporations in Brazil and Mexico: Structural Sources of Economic and Non-Economic Power* (US Senate Subcommittee on Multinational Corporations).

OECD (1966), *Productivity Measurement*, Vol. III (OECD).

O'Herlihy, C. St J. (1972), 'Capital/labour substitution and developing countries: a problem of measurement', *Bulletin of the Oxford University Institute of Economics and Statistics*, pp. 269–80.

Pack, H. (1974), 'Capital–labour substitution – a microeconomic approach', *Oxford Economic Papers*, pp. 388–404.

Pack, H. (1976), 'The substitution of labour for capital in Kenyan manufacturing', *Economic Journal*, pp. 45–58.

Panic, M. (1976), *The UK and West German Manufacturing Industry 1954–72: A Comparison of Structure and Performance* (National Economic Development Office, London).

Petras, J. (1969), *Politics and Social Forces in Chilean Development* (University of California Press).

Phillips, A. (1976), 'A critique of empirical studies of relations between market structure and profitability', *Journal of Industrial Economics*, pp. 241–9.

Pickett, J., Forsyth, D. J. C., and McBain, N. S. (1974), 'The choice of technology, economic efficiency and employment in developing countries', in E. O. Edwards (ed.), *Employment in Developing Countries* (Columbia University Press).

Pickett, J., and Robson, R. (1977), 'Technology and employment in the production of cotton cloth', *World Development*, pp. 203–16.

Pryor, F. (1972), 'An international comparison of concentration ratios', *Review of Economics and Statistics*, pp. 130–40.

R.B.I. (1974), 'Survey of foreign financial and technical collaboration in Indian industry – 1964–70', *Reserve Bank of India Bulletin*, June, pp. 1040–83.

Reidel, J. (1974), *The Industrialization of Hong Kong* (Institut für Weltwirtschaft).

Reidel, J. (1975), 'The nature and determinants of export-oriented direct foreign investment in a developing country: a case study of Taiwan', *Weltwirtschaftliches Archiv*, pp. 505–28.

Reuber, G. L. *et al.* (1973), *Private Foreign Investment in Development* (Clarendon Press).

Robbins, S. M., and Stobaugh, R. B. (1974), *Money in the Multinational Enterprise* (Basic Books).

Rosenthal, G. (1973), 'The role of private foreign investment in the development of the Central American Common Market', Guatemala (manuscript).

Rowthorn, R., in collaboration with Hymer, S. (1971), *International Big Business, 1959–1967* (Cambridge University Press).

Sabolo, Y., and Trajtenberg, R. (1976), 'The impact of transnational enterprises on employment in developing countries: preliminary results', World Employment Programme Working Paper No. 6, ILO, mimeo.

Sahagùn, V. M. B. *et al.* (1976), 'The impact of multinational corporations on employment and incomes: the case of Mexico', World Employment Programme Working Paper No. 13, ILO, mimeo.

Sawhney, P. K., and Sawhney, B. L. (1973), 'Capacity-utilization, concentration and price-cost margins: results on Indian industries', *Journal of Industrial Economics*, pp. 145–53.

Schmalensee, R. (1976), 'Advertising and profitability: further implications of the null hypothesis', *Journal of Industrial Economics*, pp. 45–54.

Scitovsky, T. (1954), 'Two concepts of external economies', *Journal of Political Economy*, pp. 143–52.

Sharpston, M. (1975), 'International subcontracting', *Oxford Economic Papers*, pp. 94–135.

Sharwani, K. (1976), 'Some new evidence on concentration and profitability in Pakistan's large-scale manufacturing industries', *Pakistan Development Review*, pp. 272–89.

Singh, A. (1971), *Takeovers* (Cambridge University Press).

Singh, A. (1975), 'Takeovers, economic natural selection and the theory of the firm: evidence from the postwar UK experience', *Economic Journal*, pp. 497–515.

Solomon, R. F., and Forsyth, D. J. C. (1977), 'Substitution of labour for capital in the foreign sector: some further evidence', *Economic Journal*, pp. 283–9.

Sourrouille, J. V. (1976), 'The impact of transnational enterprises on employment and income: the case of Argentina', World Employment Programme Working Paper No. 7, ILO, mimeo.

Stewart, F. (1974), 'Technology and employment in LDCs', *World Development*, March, pp. 17–46.

Thoburn, J. T. (1973), 'Exports and the Malaysian engineering industry: a case study of backward linkage', *Oxford Bulletin of Economics and Statistics*, pp. 91–117.

UNCTAD (1975), *International Subcontracting Arrangements in Electronics between Developed Market-Economy Countries and Developing Countries* (UN).

United Nations (1973), *Multinational Corporations in World Development* (UN).

US Tariff Commission (1970), *Economic Factors Affecting the Use of Item 807.00 and 806.30 of the Tariff Schedules of the United States* (Government Printing Office, Washington, DC).

US Tariff Commission (1973), *Implications of Multinational Firms for World Trade and Investment and for US Trade and Labour* (Government Printing Office, Washington, DC).

Vaitsos, C. V. (1974a), *Intercountry Income Distribution and Transnational Enterprises* (Clarendon Press).

Vaitsos, C. V. (1974b), 'Employment effects of foreign direct investments in developing countries', in E. O. Edwards (ed.), *Employment in Developing Nations* (Columbia University Press).

Vaitsos, C. V. (1976), 'Employment problems and transnational enterprises in developing countries: distortions and inequality', World Employment Programme Working Paper No. 11, ILO, mimeo.

Van Houten, J. F. (1973), 'Assembly industries in the Caribbean', *Finance and Development*, June.

Vernon, R. (1971), *Sovereignty at Bay* (Basic Books).

Vernon, R. (1974), 'Multinational enterprises in developing countries: an analysis of national goals and national policies', UNIDO, Vienna, mimeo.

Walker, H. O. (1969), 'Border industries with a Mexican accent', *Columbia Journal of World Business*, January–February, pp. 25–32.

Watanabe, S. (1971), 'Subcontracting, industrialization and employment creation', *International Labour Review*, pp. 51–76.

Watanabe, S. (1972a), 'International subcontracting, employment and skill promotion', *International Labour Review*, pp. 425–49.

Watanabe, S. (1972b), 'Exports and employment: the case of the Republic of Korea', *International Labour Review*, pp. 495–526.

Watanabe, S. (1974a), 'Constraints on labour-intensive export industries in Mexico', *International Labour Review*, pp. 23–45.

Watanabe, S. (1974b), 'Reflections on current policies for promoting small enterprises and subcontracting', *International Labour Review*, pp. 405–22.

Wells, L. T. (1973), 'Economic man and engineering man; choice of technology in a low wage country', *Public Policy*, pp. 39–42.

White, L. J. (1974), *Industrial Concentration and Economic Power in Pakistan* (Princeton University Press).

White, L. J. (1976a), 'Appropriate technology, x-inefficiency and the competitive environment: some evidence from Pakistan', *Quarterly Journal of Economics*, pp. 575–89.

White, L. J. (1976b), 'Appropriate factor proportions for manufacturing in less developed countries: a survey of the evidence', Research Program in Development Studies, No. 64, Woodrow Wilson School, Princeton, mimeo.

Willmore, L. (1976), 'Direct foreign investment in Central American manufacturing', *World Development*, pp. 499–518.

Wolf, B. N. (1975), 'Size and profitability among US manufacturing firms: multinational versus primarily domestic firms', *Journal of Economics and Business*, Autumn, pp. 15–22.

Zeitlin, M. (1974), 'Economic concentration, industrial structure, national and foreign capital in Chile, 1966', *International Industrial Organization Review*, pp. 195–205.

Part Four

Industrialisation Strategy

The Readings here cover the import-substitution strategy (Readings 20 and 21), the 'growth pole' strategy (Reading 22), the case for a capital goods industry (Readings 23 and 24) and for the promotion of small industry (Reading 25).

Though Perroux's discussion of growth poles is of the process of economic development in the world economy (and to that extent anticipated the recent increasing interest in transnational enterprises) rather than specifically in the poor countries, he does consider the latter at some length. Perroux has been influential among French-speaking economists and policy-makers for many years, although English-speaking economists are less familiar with his work. Perroux's view of a Schumpeter process of growth involving imbalance and disequilibrium anticipates Hirschman, while his description and use of 'industrie motrice' (propellent industry) and growth poles is close to Rostow's later use of the idea of 'leading industries'. One section also anticipates some of Baumol's (1967) discussion of the relation between oligopolistic business enterprise and growth in underdeveloped countries.

Rosenberg's article is a brief but insightful discussion of the role of a capital goods industry in facilitating technological change, while that by Frances Stewart usefully brings together the earlier Mahalanobis-Feldman argument for a heavy capital goods industry with the more recent arguments based on technological progress.

Reading 20

The Import-Substitution Strategy of Economic Development: A Survey

H. J. Bruton

Pakistan Development Review, vol. 10, no. 2, 1970, pp. 123–46.

Over the past several years, the import-substitution strategy of development has been examined in considerable detail by numerous economists. For the most part, these studies have been concerned with one or another side of this many-sided approach to development policy. It now seems useful to review this literature in an attempt to isolate major themes and arguments and to try to put together a cohesive and comprehensive picture of where we stand now. This paper is not intended as a summary of the individual articles and books on import substitution, but rather is aimed at bringing together the theoretical issues and the empirical results that not only are of interest in themselves, but which also seem to add up to something that might legitimately be called an approach to development. To do this, I asked three general questions: (1) what appears to be the essential mechanics of import substitution as it has been practised in various countries that have been investigated; (2) what problems have emerged, and why, as a consequence of the conventional import-substitution (IS) strategy; (3) what has been found that suggests or leads toward an alternative approach to development that incorporates the good and eliminates the bad of this conventional approach.

The general conclusions that emerge from this survey may be summarized in the following way. Although the countries that have built their development policies around import substitution have experienced great difficulties, there are reasons to believe that a satisfactory approach to development can be built around this approach. The difficulties have arisen as a consequence of the activities selected for domestic development and of the methods employed to provide the incentives to bring about their development. Part of these difficulties arise from a view of the economic development process that now appears misleading, and part arise from assumptions about the developing economies that the empirical evidence shows to be unacceptable. More specifically, it appears that the distortions and misallocations that have been imposed on the economy by the conventional approach to IS have themselves created difficulties that contributed significantly to the widespread failure of the approach to work as satisfactorily as many expected. To repeat the previous sentence in a slightly different way: to implement their IS policy, countries have chosen instruments and techniques that seem, in effect, to prevent that very policy from being successful.

On the other hand, there are important aspects of the IS approach that appear most useful indeed. The concept of a strategy is useful, as is the idea of policies designed to create readily apparent investment opportunities. Similarly, the notion that new activities must be established in the developing countries is equally acceptable and equally important. What appears needed, then, is a way to achieve these advantages of IS without creating the distortions and misallocations that to-date appear so ubiquitous, and that appear responsible for its failures. The work on remodelling the IS strategy is just beginning, and its difficulties are more clearly understood than is where and how to modify it. This review, therefore, spends more time on the difficulties with IS than with more positive recommendations. The latter have, however, begun to receive attention and are implicit in many of the criticisms of the IS strategy as it has been used to-date. It is important to keep in mind from the outset that the general thrust of the literature does *not* show that IS is necessarily futile. What emerges is not a recommendation for abandonment, but rather one for a more careful approach to its implementation.

To a very large extent import substitution was arrived at by default, and is not only the most common (frequently observed) strategy in practice, but it is indeed perhaps the only one. This is true partly because IS encompasses some other possible strategies and partly because it is easily initiated. Indeed, it seems clear that most developing countries tend to slip into an IS approach to development. In this case, then, IS is not a strategy in the sense of a carefully planned approach, but rather a situation into which a country tends to find itself as the development effort is made.

It is this ease of initiation that seems to be the major

(but not exclusive) source of the prevalence of IS's popularity. To curtail imports in order to create investment opportunities or to change the structure is a relatively simple matter. If a country decided on an export-promotion strategy, however, it is not so evident how to begin. Similarly, to build a development strategy around industrialization *without* IS does not lend itself to an obvious set of policies. The same may be said of a strategy built around increasing agricultural productivity.

One may, then, visualize the origins of IS in somewhat the following way: policy-makers become aware (or convinced) that conventional optimizing criteria cannot (do not) lead to policies that produce as rapid a rate of growth as desirable either because the need for an explicit prime mover or because the existing structure of the system is (or is thought to be) alien to growth. The policy-maker then searches for an alternative guide to policy-making—one that will step up the rate of investment and create a larger number and more obvious investment opportunities. Even if it is assumed that a number of strategies are examined, the IS strategy is likely to be selected because it apparently calls merely for keeping out imports, a task most governments can be expected to accomplish. The fact that the country is likely to be experiencing balance-of-payments difficulties adds to the attractiveness of this approach. Also IS will create gaps in the economy where very obvious investment opportunities exist, thereby creating the kind of situation that will generate Hirschman's *primum mobile*. Finally, the IS policy will keep out goods previously imported, thereby encouraging their domestic production, and thereby (again) contributing to structural change. Such a strategy would then seem to meet all, or at least a wide range, of difficulties believed to be blocking development.

That few policy-makers have, in fact, systematically surveyed the range of policy opportunities and concluded that IS is the best hope is not especially important. That they have in fact most often backed into such a policy to meet a balance-of-payments (or some other) crisis is indeed not inconsistent with the preceding arguments. It merely means that the situation that precipitates action is a crisis, not that the crisis is the rationale of the action taken.

Import Substitution

Import substitution has a variety of meanings in the literature, and a frontal attack on a simple definition is no small undertaking (Winston, 1967a). When attention is limited to a single product, there is little difficulty. Here IS refers to a policy that reduces or eliminates entirely the importation of the commodity and, hence, leaves the domestic market exclusively for domestic producers. Measures of IS that are based on changes in the ratio of imports of specific products to their total domestic absorption are if course concerned with this definition. Difficulties emerge when we seek to aggregate. A policy that reduces the proportion of the quantity of a product that is imported may, at the same time, increase that proportion for another product. Whether the policy in this case should be called IS becomes ambiguous. Similarly, changes in the aggregate import-GNP ratio may hide the impact of IS policies on specific sectors. It is a bit misleading, therefore, to rely on changes in the aggregate ratio to identify the effectiveness of IS policies aimed at changing the proportion of total absorption of a good that is imported.

The issue can be put into an understandable framework by identifying the objective of IS policies that are aimed at reducing imports of specific commodities. Few policy-makers actually wish to shut out all imports. Rather, as already noted, the objective is structural change or some kind of investment-incentive-creating idea. Part of the rationale of the structural-change objective is that the existing structure makes the economy undesirably dependent on matters outside its own control. One of the guides to action, then, is how can the structure be changed so that the economy is less at the mercy of its foreign-trade activities? The extent of the achievement of such an objective is not easily measured at all, and certainly not by means of changes over time in the import-GNP ratio.

The picture then seems to be this. Developing countries have not achieved sustained growth because of their structure or their lack of a prime mover. The IS strategy to change this structure and to provide a *primum mobile* is to replace imports by domestic production of *certain* commodities. Thus, IS in the narrow sense is limited to specific activities and is measured by increases in the ratio of domestic production to total domestic absorption. In the broader sense, import substituting within individual sectors is a means to the more far-reaching objectives just stated. These latter objectives mean that the long-run success of IS rests heavily on the specific sectors in which import substitution is carried out, and the methods chosen to bring about their domestic expansion. An analysis of the IS strategy of development, therefore, involves an examination of the rationale of the selection of these activities, and the consequences of the methods and policies used to bring about the import substitution. On this latter issue, interest is primarily directed toward the effect of these policies on the growth of the economy.

1

In this section, we first examine the broad pattern of IS as it has evolved over the last several years or so. Then, we look at a number of features of this pattern that stand out in the broader, overall picture. In the following section, we try to establish a series of positive conclusions that follow from this discussion of the main characteristics of the IS model.

A. The general nature of import substitution

As noted in Section I, the immediate approach of an IS policy is to replace imports of specific activities with domestic production. Without a doubt, the simplest way to do this in a market economy is to impose limitations on imports. This limitation on imports has a variety of impacts. (Power, 1966). It creates gaps in the economy that make for obvious investment opportunities in non-traditional activities of the economy, usually manufacturing. Resources are then directed into new industrial channels (structural change) and the capitalist sector is enlarged. In the latter sector, expected new profits may lead to an increase in the saving rate and to further increases in investment, as capitalists are assumed to be high savers and accumulators. The new capital goods are imported and are paid for with the foreign exchange released by the reduction in the imports of the commodities whose domestic production is being encouraged. In this simple picture, two not so simple questions arise: what markets should be sealed off from foreign competition and what method should be employed to seal them off? Most of the literature under review has something to say directly or indirectly on these two issues. Consider first which products to protect.

In practice the answer is consumer goods in almost all countries. This is certainly the case at the outset of the IS process. There are several reasons for this concentration on consumer goods.

The simplest reason is that the cost disadvantage between domestically produced and imported consumer goods is less than for capital goods or for intermediate goods. Thus, it appears to policy-makers that by preventing the importation of consumer goods, the advantages of IS can be achieved at minimum costs. The cost argument is supplemented by the existence of an obvious demand, *i.e.* the consumer goods are being imported, while the demand for capital goods, intermediate goods, or raw materials depends on the mounting of an investment programme. Finally, consumer goods (especially durables) are universally deemed inessential to development, and an increase in their costs and in their prices assumed to be less harmful than increases in the prices of capital goods. The latter goods are, thus, imported with few impediments and frequently at exchange rates that greatly understate their costs to society. Thus, not only is the domestic production of capital goods discriminated against by the tariffs and exchange-control policies, but also by exchange-rate policies that keep their imported costs below real costs. The rationale of these latter policies favouring the importing of capital goods rests in general on assumptions as to the essentiality or to the strategic role of physical capital in the development process. The relatively low tariff rates on raw materials and intermediate goods mean further that the protection afforded the value added of many consumer-goods producing activities is markedly higher than the rate of protection on the good itself would indicate. Hence, both the extent of protection afforded a given activity and the extent of the cost disadvantage of that activity probably are understated by an examination of nominal tariff schedules.

This first stage of the IS process ends when the expansion of finished consumer-goods capacity hits the limit of the domestic market. At this point, the economy has a number of new activities whose survival depends on some form of protection and whose expansion cannot continue. Further, growth, then, must take place in activities which are now importing or the recently established IS activities must enter the export markets. When this second stage is reached the hurdles the developing country must surmount seem to rise for a number of reasons.

1 Since this second stage is difficult (and the first so easy), the first stage is extended to its maximum extent. Thus, protection is provided on as wide a range of consumer goods as possible. One gets, then, what David Felix (1964) has called 'premature widening' of the productive structure, *i.e.* an expansion into a large number of relative small-scale activities rather than a concentration on a few. Advantages accruing from scale effects are at best limited to a handful of activities, and may well be absent entirely.

2 If IS is to continue, the economy must move more heavily into intermediate- or capital-goods production. This shift not only raises the direct cost of growth (the cost of the domestic production of capital goods or intermediate goods is larger relative to their import costs than is the case with respect to the consumer goods for which domestic supply has already replaced imports), but it also affects the costs of production and the level of existing protection on the new consumer-goods industries. Evidently, if a new producer of consumer goods had been using imported intermediate (or capital) goods in the first stage, and is now forced into using higher cost (and probably lower quality) domestically produced inputs, his production costs will rise. Similarly, at the prevailing tariff rates, protection on the value added of consumer-goods activities will decline. To maintain the same level of protection on the original IS consumer-goods activities, therefore, requires an increase in the rate of protection. This pushes up the cost in these activities, and (barring devaluation) thereby lessens their chance of exporting.

3 At the same time that investment costs are rising, at least two other developments are occurring that tend to reduce the country's saving capacity. As the economy expands its domestic production of consumer goods, their prices may fall relative to those of domestically produced capital goods (Power, 1966) and income probably shifts away from government as customs duties decline (Lewis, 1967). In the second place as the

domestic output of consumer goods rises so too does demand for foreign exchange for the importation of spare parts and raw-material inputs, not all of which can be produced domestically. If these inputs are not forthcoming, underutilization in the consumer-goods sectors appears. The evidence of this underutilization creates obvious pressure for increasing consumption simply because, if the capacity to produce consumer goods exists, it would appear nonsense not to use it. To use it means of course to reduce the saving rate below that which might be achieved (Khan, 1963). To maintain the saving rate in these circumstances will not produce investment because there is no way to use the resources released from producing consumer goods to produce capital goods, *i.e.* capacity built to produce consumer goods cannot be used to produce capital goods (Winston, 1967b) and exporting is not possible because of high costs. Added to these two reasons is the possibility that the misallocation imposed on the economy by the IS policies will reduce total output below the level it would have reached in the absence of such policies, and hence total saving would tend to fall even if the saving-income rate remained constant.

The outcome appears rather clear: at the very point that the economy must save more in order to maintain its rate of growth of capacity, it has major incentives and pressures to reduce that rate. Essentially, the choice of consumer goods—or the investment criteria of least disadvantaged—as the items to import substitute for leads to developments that dampen and may eventually halt the growth that the original protection induced. These growth-dampening effects have to do with investment moving into new areas of higher costs—consequent to the failure of the new activities to enter the export market—at the same time that saving declines.

This is not, however, the end. There is the further question of the complications arising from the nature of the protection afforded the newly created activities. The most common protection package consists of two aspects: (1) an exchange rate that undervalues foreign exchange and adds extra burdens to the effort to enter the export markets. As already noted, the usual rationale of such a policy is that it keeps the price of imported investment goods relatively low and so encourages investment, plus the assumption that foreign demand for most export items is assumed to be inelastic. (2) If foreign exchange is undervalued, then of course equilibrium in the balance-of-payments must be achieved by means of tariffs or the direct licensing of imports or both.

The overvalued local currency may encourage investment, but it has other characteristics much less likely to facilitate growth. It makes for a capital intensity in production higher (due either to choice of technique or to choice of product) than would be the case if foreign exchange were priced right. It thereby dampens the employment effect of the IS activities. It also creates a level of import intensity in production that is incompatible with foreign-exchange-earning power, *i.e.* it penalizes export competing and increases the need for imports. further distortions are imposed by the tariffs and licensing necessary to keep the balance of payments under control. And as tariffs rise and exchange controls become more rigid, for the reasons already noted, the distortions increase. As the latter occurs, supply bottlenecks appear and the economy's capacity to transform its resources into capital (or other) goods and services is increasingly impaired. These developments are hardly conducive to sustained growth.

The picture just described is perhaps a bit extreme when applied to any one country, but the basic pattern seems applicable to a wide range of countries in Latin America and Asia. To summarize briefly: an IS strategy imposes a necessity of selecting activities to protect and conventional selection procedures have left a residue of high cost, nongrowing activities in many countries. Added to the problem of the selection of activities is the method of their protection. Again, conventional procedures have left a residue, this time of distortions which seem to increase as IS is pursued. We usually think of distortions as simply resulting in a lower level of output than would be possible with no distortion. This it surely does, but there is evidence of a much more important consequence, namely a major reduction in the capacity of the economy to maintain its growth of output in the manner noted above. Clearly, then, a successful IS policy must find ways to select the right activities to protect, and must protect them in ways that will not so distort the system that growth is effectively thwarted.

B. *Some specific aspects of import substitution*

In order to consider how these latter objectives might be accomplished, it is helpful to look more closely at some specific results that conventional IS practices foster and which seem to be especially damaging. This will enable us to emphasize as well a few hints as to how such effects might be avoided.

These points may be considered under the following headings:

(1) A structure of production emerges in which it is impossible to use all available capacity without large-scale capital inflows. The argument is clearest if one assumes that prior to the construction (or purchase) of the capital goods, there exist several options as to techniques of production and to choice of product to produce, but after construction both technique and product are fixed. At the time of investment (of the construction of the capital) the consequences of import-substitution policies are reflected in import prices (essentially of capital goods) that are below the costs of producing the exports to buy the imports, in the under-pricing of domestically produced goods, and in the thorough protection from outside competition. In such a situation, investors have numerous incentives to

choose a product and a technique to produce it that are incompatible with relative supplies of inputs. Thus, a structure evolves that can function efficiently only with a rising flow of imports. The growth of exports, however, is discriminated against by the very same factors that produce the alien structure. Unless then a rising flow of unrequired imports is available, we will eventually see underutilization appear. Given an existing alien structure of this sort, correcting the source of the distortions (by devaluation, raising the price of capital, labour subsidies, etc.) will not immediately eliminate the difficulties unless one is willing to assume that technique and product-mix can be adjusted on existing physical capital in a rapid and painless way. Indeed, seeking to correct the distortions in these ways can exacerbate the problem, *e.g.* devaluation may lead to inflation, raising interest rates reduce investment. If the latter events do occur they may drive policy-makers to more direct controls which add to the distortions. An important by-product of the same policies that produce the under-utilizations is that they also result in a rate of increase in labour employment that, independently of the level of utilization, is well below that which might be achieved with different policies.

(2) The above developments lead to the position that specific shortages are brakes on development. Thus, Gordon C. Winston (1967b, 1968) suggests that a capital-goods sector can be too small given the potential saving rate and export capacity. In the former he offers evidence to support the view that in the early years of the Pakistan development effort, the size of the capital-goods sector did seem to be the limiting factor in that country's growth. More generally, the IS strategy leads to the development of an economy whose various sectors are consistent and are feasible only by fluke as the mechanisms for creating and maintaining structural consistency have been destroyed by the IS policies.

External aid may then be claimed on the grounds that if the specific shortage is relieved by aid then the capacity made idle by that shortage will be brought into use, and the economy will in consequence begin to grow very rapidly (Bruton, 1967). This result does hold for a given period, *i.e.* for a situation already distorted. But aid that simply provides the missing input can in fact do more harm than good. It can enable the economy to continue to function despite the existence of the distortions, *i.e.* aid can be used only to permit the economy to continue to live with the policies that produced the specific shortages to begin with. Aid used in this way may hinder the correction of the distortions or even knowledge of their existence (Bruton, 1969). Aid used to permit correction of the sources of distortions will have a much more permanent effect on the growth capacity. In order to use aid in this way, however, the distortions must be barred, their origins understood, and their method of elimination known.

(3) A further complication arising from most approaches to IS has to do with the extent and sources of the distortions imposed on the economy. This issue is seen most clearly in terms of tariffs and indirect taxes. A tariff on the imported product plus any sales tax on the imported product less any sales tax on any domestically produced competitive product provides an initial approximation to the extent of 'nominal protection' (Lewis, 1969). The extent to which a process (in contrast to a product) is protected depends as well on the 'nominal protection' afforded the inputs used by the particular process and the indirect taxes on *these* inputs. Similarly, the not uncommon overvaluation of the domestic currency adds a further element that must be introduced as one tries to untangle the consequence of (*e.g.*) tariffs and indirect taxes. Less evident, but no less important, is the fact that the several markets in an economy vary markedly in the extent of their competitiveness, in their pricing policies, and in the extent that they absorb or pass on taxes. There are two main consequences of all this. In the first place, consideration is almost always limited to the specific target actually aimed at with the given instrument. Rarely does one find evidence of an examination of the many policy instruments that act on the same target, and that act on the efficacy of the specific instrument under consideration.

The second place follows from the first place, namely tracing out the consequences of a single policy—*e.g.* understanding the distorting effects of a tariff—can be extremely difficult, even practically impossible. This issue is particularly relevant in a situation where policies (tariffs) that would, under some circumstances, distort are instituted to correct another policy (overvaluation) that also distorts. In developing countries where the price system does not (or is assumed not to) work effectively, and hence direct controls are widely used, this point has considerable practical relevance.

The studies of the structure of protection by Stephen R. Lewis (1969) and Paul G. Clark (1967) shed considerable light on these issues. They try to estimate empirically the extent and nature of protection by correcting the nominal tariffs for indirect taxes, input taxes, and overvalutions. The computations worked out for Pakistan (Lewis, 1969) and for Brazil (Clark, 1967) and the discussion of Mexico (Reynolds, 1967) show substantial differences between the nominal tariff rates, and these rates modified to take into account overvaluation, indirect taxes, and all the rest. Similarly, the Lewis study shows that one sector may also be protected by virtue of discriminatory government policies against another sector. In the case of Pakistan, the agricultural sector is estimated to have (in the early 1960's) received about 35 per cent less when trading domestically than it could have received if it traded in the international market. This disadvantage of the agricultural sector, the chief supplier of wage goods to the manufacturing sector, contributed to keeping real wages for manufacturing workers favourable, and hence to keeping wage-cost presure in the manufacturing sector modest.

Evidently just looking at the tariff schedule on final

goods does not enable one to predict its consequences in terms of investment allocation. Similarly, correcting distortions due to tariffs requires more information than simply the tariff schedule. It also means that a wide range of policies must be seen in the context of existing policies, and examined in the context of whether these existing policies are institutional constraints or are themselves subject to manipulation. The unravelling of all this in an economy with widespread indirect taxes, direct controls, import and investment licensing, and an overvalued currency is obviously a task of considerable magnitude, and one that does not lend itself to simple formula.

(4) Underlying the IS approach to development is the notion of an economy that is, as noted in Section 1, to be altered. In this sense then investment is aimed at creating a new and different structure that is consistent with the achievement of this objective. Most of the new activities cannot be operated domestically at rates competitive with similar activities in other parts of the world, and hence protection of some sort is required. Implicit in much of the policy-making of IS is the assumption that costs in the new activities will decline and a new structure will emerge whose routine functioning produces a rising GNP. The argument may be put this way: the products produced and the techniques employed in the developing countries are becoming increasingly obsolete. This fact is reflected most clearly, but not exclusively, in deteriorating terms of trade. The country then has a choice with respect to the allocation of its investments: it may put its new resources into traditional activities which are facing increasingly unfavourable terms of trade, or it may put them into new activities that are currently operated at costs well above those that prevail abroad. If it chooses the latter, it must be with the expectation that costs will fall secularly, and at some point the new structure would be composed of activities that can meet world competition (Bruton, 1968b). Evidently, then, a key question has to do with the rate of fall in costs, *i.e.* the rate of growth of productivity, in the IS activities.

The evidence developed in Bruton (1967, 1968a) suggests not only that productivity growth has been generally low relative to that achieved in advanced countries,[1] but also that the very policies designed to implement the IS approach have been significantly responsible for their poor showing in the productivity growth race. To repeat a point made earlier, to implement their IS policy, countries have chosen instruments and techniques that seem, in effect, to prevent that very policy from being successful. Evidence on this latter point is not without ambiguity, but the kind of distortions noted under item (1) above appear at the heart of the explanation. Added to this is the existence of a situation in which it is generally impossible to expoit economies of scale, in which competition is lacking, and in which the imported technology is unsuitable to factor endowment. More generally, one may say that the failure of the conventional IS policy package to take into consideration the strategic role of productivity growth has resulted in it being not only ignored but discriminated against in the same sense that exports and a domestic capital-goods activity are penalized.

The neglect of productivity growth can in part be traced to the widespread acceptance of a growth model in which physical capital formation is at the heart of the growth process. In paying primary, if not exclusive, attention to physical capital formation, the policymaker neglects not only that (productivity growth) which is crucial to the success of an IS strategy, but, as many studies have shown, that which is responsible for well over half of observed GNP growth in all currently rich countries.

(5) Finally, it is useful to mention a few rather more specific consequences of most IS policies. Most developing countries depend quite heavily on import duties as a source of government finance, and as consumer-good imports usually carry a high tariff relative to capital goods, the complete protection of the former can contribute to a government finance problem. (Lewis, 1967). It indeed may do more. Since income taxes are difficult to enforce, an IS strategy may push the government into greater reliance on excise duties, and possible export duties, as a means of acquiring finance. A second point that merits a specific note has to do with the effect of IS on the trade balance. There is little evidence that even hints that the trade balance improves as a consequence of IS policies. This is surely the case in the short run, but seems true as well in the longer run. This is partly explained by the widespread tendency of IS policies to discriminate against exports, but also by the failure of IS to reduce imports or import-GNP ratios, *i.e.* IS policies do not reduce the demand for imports. This point comes through in many papers (see especially Sheahan, 1968).

Following on the heels of this evidence is the point that as the composition of imports changes from heavy concentration on consumer goods to emphasis on capital and intermediate goods, the economy becomes increasingly vulnerable (as to the maintenance of the level and the growth of output) to interruptions in the flow of imports. For example, curtailing the imports of 1000 dollars of shirts will have less impact on an economy than will the curtailing of 1000 dollars of chemical cellulose used in the manufacture of shirt material (Winston, 1967a). A corollary of this point, and indeed all of the points mentioned here, is that the economic structure that the IS approach to development spawns is no more flexible and adaptable than the one that is sought to be replaced. Flexibility, adaptability, responsiveness are attributes thee advantages of which are disputed by no one, and their acquisition is part of the goal sought after. Again, however, the evidence shows that policies aimed at this goal have the opposite impact and tend to solidify the structure rather than to grease the wheels on which it operates. Although little evidence exists that helps our understanding of why some economies appear much more flexible and responsive than other economies, the evidence does suggest that the very alienness of the imposed new structure does play a relevant role (Bruton, 1967).

A simple example may illustrate this point. A machine imported by a low-income, nongrowing country not only creates a required flow of imported spare parts and raw materials, but it can also impose new skill demands, supply and marketing demands, work attitude and organizational demands. This latter group of demands is such that the importing economy cannot respond quickly and easily to meet effectively a situation other than that called for by the exact formula envisaged in the operation of the new machine. The situation is somewhat similar to a firmly established, well-groomed bureaucracy that works splendidly as long as the routine is uninterrupted, but virtually collapses when a file goes astray. In the same sense, an economic structure created by conventional IS policies is so incompatible with the rest of the system that adjustments to changes in demands, in technology, in any part of the routine are accomplished painfully, if at all.

The five preceding categories of characteristics seem to be inherent in the IS approach. Obviously, this package does not apply *en toto* to all the various countries that have been researched. It would be correct, however, to insist that the range of issues just reviewed reveal accurately the nature of the consequences of a widely employed approach to development. It is quite evident how and why these consequences can slow up the growth of GNP, can reduce productivity growth, can increase the need for rising levels of aid, can impede, indeed reduce, the extent to which the economy can exploit its domestic resources, can in fact create a situation that finds continuing development virtually unachievable. Also, evident in the above list are ideas and arguments that lead to reformulations and modifications that suggest alternative approaches to development and alternative sets of policies. These positive results may be considered a bit more explicitly now.

2

Our positive results may be considered under three broad headings: distortions, productivity growth, and what earlier was called alienness.

(1) Distortions of IS policies

The most pervasive impact of IS policies has been that it distorts the economy, and these distortions do not, except in rare instances, correct themselves. Indeed, as shown above, economies become increasingly distorted as the IS process continues. Three assumptions seem to underlie much of the analysis that leads to the policies that in turn produce the distortion. One has to do with the assumptions about the responsiveness of the various sectors of the system to relative price changes, the second to the existence and impact of external and internal economies that accompany the establishment of new activities, and the third to the role of capital formation in development. If one assumes that relative prices have no effect on anything then they can be safely ignored, and distortion loses much of its meaning. Consequently, the policy maker can ignore the impact of misleading price signals on his economy. Similarly, if expected external (or internal) economies are assumed great enough, then *any* activity can be justified, and there appears great, and unsupported, optimism implied by many policies as to the existence of such economies in the newly established activities. And, an assumption seems to prevail that amounts essentially to the assertion that a high rate of physical capital formation can overcome any obstacle. Evidence from several of studies strongly suggests that none of these assumptions can support the weight that it is asked to bear.

The most specific evidence on the role prices can play has to do with foreign trade. Sheahan and Clark (1967), for example, present regressions that leave little doubt that maintaining reasonably correct exchange rates does have a significant effect on export earnings from Colombia's exports other than coffee and oil. In Paul Clark's equations explaining Brazilian imports show price elasticities ranging from -35 to -1.62 for the construction material industry. While elasticities with respect to investment (the stand-in for GNP) were higher than the price elasticities for four of the six groups for which both investment and price elasticities were available, this evidence indicates again that sufficient substitutability between domestic and imported goods exists in Brazil, that to ignore it will induce distortion. The extent to which the Colombian and Brazilian equations represent demand or supply parameters can not be told from either set of equations. Doubtless to some extent both are effective so that the computed coefficients are probably not estimates of a structural parameter. Nevertheless, these results do indicate that a price effect does exist and which in turn indicates substitutability and responsiveness in the economies of significant magnitude.

There is evidence on this issue on a more general level. In a study of Mexico, Clark Reynolds (1967) suggests that postwar policies were somewhat different from those of many other countries. Nominal tariff rates have been much lower than in most other developing countries, and have risen only moderately, if at all, since the 1930's. Also the more established firms have to supply products of reasonable quality and at a reasonable price within a few years of their initiation or their protection is reduced. The findings on Mexico also indicate that considerable substitution exists between domestic skilled labour inputs and imported intermediate goods. Finally, Mexico's IS activities appeared more heavily concentrated in labour-intensive industries than has been the case elsewhere. (Though this latter is not necessarily a desirable condition, it appears to be so in this case.) Evidently, Mexico's relatively strong showing since 1950 is explained by a great number of factors and cannot be attributed exclusively to the points just enumerated. It is, however, appropriate to emphasize that these attributes of Mexican policy did prevent the marked distortions from appearing that would impede the other advantages of Mexico from having their full effect.

A last example has to do with Pakistan. In Chapter VII of Lewis's (1969) discussion of the effect of economic policy on the growth rate and composition of output shows that policies that tended to correct the distortions in the system did produce changes that resulted in a more efficient use of both domestic and aid-provided resources. Both the Export Bonus Scheme and the import-liberalization policies seemed to affect allocations in a manner that facilitated a more rational use of her resources. Other policies examined by Lewis to some extent offset these effects, but the point remains relevant.

On the question of external effects, the evidence is less clear and, what there is, is of a more negative kind than that just mentioned. It is surely clear that structural change itself does not automatically contribute significant external economies. There is virtually no empirical evidence that the often referred to, seldom specifically identified, 'external' effects of new activities—labour training, technological improvement, economies of scale, *etc.*—occur with the establishment of import-replacing activities. Indeed the same distortions that result in activities in the developing economies being less productive than in the advanced countries also have negative effects on the realization of possible externalities. More positively, one may say that these matters must be considered explicitly with respect to individual activities, and general assumptions as to their sources are not acceptable. This is not to suggest that structural change as an end in itself may not be important. If often is, and rightly so. The point here is to emphasize that our studies do not show that such changes do, in themselves, bring about major external economies.

The third implicit assumption underlying much of IS philosophy has to do with the role of capital formation in development. This is a broad question which our studies do not directly consider. The evidence is now overwhelming that merely more investment does not mean a higher growth rate. This does not mean of course that capital formation is not important in producing growth. It does mean that merely generating a high rate of investment is not sufficient to assure growth. More specifically it means that a higher rate of investment will not in itself solve—or prevent from arising—other, growth-defeating issues. A still more important conclusion, noted in several studies, is that concentrating attention on capital formation irrespective of other matters creates growth-defeating developments.

These arguments have two broad categories of implications. In the first place they mean that distortions are very real and must be taken into account in devising and appraising policies. For example, if there were no substitutability between labour and capital (and among products), then the relative cost of labour and capital would not be relevant to the distortion issue. Efforts to affect the distribution of income via wage policies (minimum wage rates, high severance pay, *etc.*) will have no effect on choice of technique or product selected. Where there is such substitutability, however, these policies do introduce distortions. Similarly, if the exchange rate's role as an allocation device is negligible, then to undervalue foreign exchange to encourage investment is acceptable policy. If, as now seems clear, the exchange rate does perform an allocative function, then to keep it below its equilibrium level does impose distortions, the damage of which cannot be overcome by the mere fact of a high rate of capital formation. In general then, we can say that the degree of flexibility and adaptability suggested by recent studies shows that many policies aimed at specific targets do impose distortions on the system that make it difficult or impossible to achieve the specified target.

The second implication is even broader than the first and follows from it. The results suggest that the misallocations produced by conventional IS policies not only reduce total output below the level that it might have otherwise reached, but it also reduces the growth rate, principally through its effect on productivity growth and the flexibility of the economy. This means simply that the distortion issue is a most strategic concept, strategic to the point that to ignore it is to court failure. This we believe to be a vital point, and more will be said on its specific policy implications later.

(2) *IS-created alienness*

We have emphasized that IS seems to create activities that are broadly alien to the economic and social environment of the community. Alien here applies not only to the factor endowment as such, but refers also to the whole range of characteristics and attributes of a society that affect its capacity to produce goods and services and to respond to unpredicted opportunities (and setbacks). Alienness is not independent of, but also not simply a component of, the distortion issue just discussed.

The clearest case of the point appears in Bruton (1967) where evidence is presented that Latin American countries exploited the opportunities offered them during World War II in a more effective way than in later years. During the war there was no inflow of physical or financial capital. The countries were forced to use what they had, to build with what they had, and to rely exclusively on their own saving. They did all this in such a manner that productivity rose at a much higher rate than in the postwar period when foreign capital was relied on to a much greater extent. Also domestic resources were much more fully utilized in the war period than after, despite the fact that the rate of capital accumulation was much less. In being forced to use what they had, the economic structure created was much more consistent, much less alien than in later years when IS policies became so paramount.

In Lewis's (1969) discussion of changing relative prices and the manner in which costs of new activities in Pakistan decreased shows a similar picture. In activities where the inputs fit well with what Pakistan could offer and could do, relative prices—hence presumably costs—declined. Other sectors, less suitable, were also less successful. Natural resources played some role in this, but certainly the whole story is not simply one of natural resources.

Sheahan's (1968) model of the Colombia economy shows how that economy became more rigid, more dependent on imports as the alienness of its economic structure evolved. This may be contrasted somewhat with Mexico, the structure of which evolved in a manner much more consistent with her social and cultural heritage, entrepreneurial ability, organizing capacity, and management skills.

These matters are difficult to separate from the distortion issue already emphasized. The key point seems to be this: that if a country's economy evolves in a manner consistent with its resource endowment, then that endowment can be near fully exploited.

(3) Productivity-growth dampening effects of IS

The argument above indicated that the conventional approach to IS creates conditions that dampens productivity growth, and rapid productivity growth is essential to a successful IS. So an important positive notion emerging from our studies is that countries *must* pursue policies that lead to a high productivity growth or IS *must* fail. The question of course is what are such policies? The first point to emphasize is simply that productivity growth does not just happen. It is not a time trend to be appended. It is rather a phenomenon to be explained, and despite the absence of data and argument it seems clear that it (productivity growth) is and can be affected by economic policies. In many studies where this issue is treated most explicitly, evidence seems to indicate that productivity growth is more likely to reach acceptable rates in economies where distortions and alienness are at a minimum. Certainly it is correct to say that there is nothing incompatible between distortion free economies and the achievement of an acceptable growth of productivity.

Stronger positive statements are more difficult. In general it does seem clear that most developing countries are not paying sufficient attention to the possibilities of adapting and modifying imported physical capital in such a way that it more nearly fits their domestic economies. To do this probably means the allocation of more resources explicitly to this task. It certainly means a conscious recognition of the necessity of this sort of activity by both government and the private sector. General considerations indicate that this can best be done at the firm or plant level. Hence, policies that put pressure on firms or that provide an incentive to them to seek ways to increase the productivity of their resources are an essential ingredient of development policy.

With respect to the effect of education on the productivity of labour, two general points emerge from the literature on education. In the first place, the shortage of the kind of skills learned in the classroom do not appear to be a specific bottleneck. The educational establishment does not turn out individuals who are immediately employed to break a bottleneck. Rather, the productivity effect of education is to equip a person to adapt and to respond to opportunities as they appear. Perhaps most directly they equip a person to profit from on-the-job training. The second point has to do with the quality of education. In economies where productivity is generally low, it is unlikely that it is high in the difficult tasks of educating. This means that many countries that are spending large sums on education may be doing it on rather low productivity activities. The not very startling idea emerges then that the developing countries may not need more education of the kind currently being provided, but rather improved productivity of the educational activities.

Productivity growth probably is not completely explained by allocation, by technological improvements, and by raising the quality of labour. These, however, are surely a significant part of the key to its understanding. The evidence that productivity growth is a strategic element in the picture of a successful IS policy means, therefore, that these matters are equally a significant part of the key to the devising of effective development policy.

What then can we say about strategic variables and mechanisms of growth on the basis of the preceding discussion of our findings? Our analysis suggests that three items, distortion, alienness, and productivity growth, are more demanding of attention, *i.e.* more strategic, than those variables which have occupied attention in the conventional IS model. Since governments cannot do everything, they should then concentrate on these issues. Specific policies would then be appraised as to the extent to which they (*i*) distort or undistort the system, (*ii*) encourage projects consistent with the other characteristics of the economy, and (*iii*) encourage productivity growth. If policies are successful in these areas, then other conditions necessary for continued growth (*e.g.* capital formation) may be expected to be induced or to be achievable without major policy measures. To repeat our well-worn theme, it is attacks on these other, these 'nonstrategic', growth-producing variables that violate our strategic variables and cause the difficulties which we have found to inhere in the IS strategy.

Note: Reading 20

1 Productivity growth here, and elsewhere, refers to labour productivity or 'total' (labour and capital) productivity.

References: Reading 20

Bruton, H. J. (1967), 'Productivity growth in Latin America', *American Economic Review*, December.

Bruton, H. J. (1968a), *Export Growth and Import Substitution*, Research Memorandum No. 22 (Williams College, Williamstown, Mass.).

Bruton, H. J. (1968b), 'Import substitution and productivity growth', *Journal of Development Studies*, April.

Bruton, H. J. (1969), 'The two gap approach to aid and development', *American Economic Review*, June.

Chenery, H. B., and Strout, A. M. (1966), 'Foreign assistance and economic development', *American Economic Review*, September.

Clark, P. G. (1967), *Brazilian Import Liberalization*, Research Memorandum No. 14 (Williams College, Williamstown, Mass.).

Clark, P. G., and Weisskoff, R. (1967), *Import Demands and Import Policies in Brazil*, Research Memorandum No. 8 (Williams College, Williamstown, Mass.).

Felix, D. (1964), 'Monetarists, structuralists, and import substituting industrializing: a critical appraisal', in W. Baer and I. Kerstenetzky (eds), *Inflation and Growth in Latin America* (Homewood, Illinois).

Khan, A. R. (1963), 'Import substitution, export expansion, and consumption liberalization: a preliminary report', *Pakistan Development Review*, vol. III, no. 2, Summer.

Lewis, S. R., Jr (1967), 'Revenue implications of changing industrial structure: an empirical study', *National Tax Journal*, December.

Lewis, S. R., Jr, and Guisinger, S. E. (1968), 'Measuring protection in a developing country: the case of Pakistan', *Journal of Political Economy*, October.

Lewis, S. R., Jr (1969), *Economic Policy and Industrial Growth in Pakistan* (Allen & Unwin).

Power, J. H. (1966), 'Import substitution as an industrialization strategy', *Philippine Economic Journal*, second semester.

Reynolds, C. W. (1967), *Changing Trade Patterns and Trade Policy in Mexico*, Research Memorandum No. 17 (Williams College, Williamstown, Mass.).

Sheahan, J. B. (1968), 'Imports, investment and growth: Colombia experience since 1950', in Gustav F. Papanek (ed.), *Development Policy—Theory and Practice* (Harvard University Press).

Sheahan, J., and Clark, S. (1967), *The Response of Colombia Exports to Variations in Effective Exchange Rates*, Research Memorandum No. 11 (Williams College, Williamstown, Mass.).

Winston, G. C. (1967a), 'A preliminary survey of import substitution', *Pakistan Development Review*, vol. VII, no. 1, Spring.

Winston, G. C. (1967b), 'Consumer goods or capital goods—supply consistency in development planning', *Pakistan Development Review*, Autumn.

Winston, G. C. (1968), *The Composition of Output and Economic Growth*, Research Memorandum No. 24 (Williams College, Williamstown, Mass.).

Industrialisation in Pakistan: A Case of Frustrated take-off?

J. H. Power

Pakistan Development Review, 1963, pp. 191-207.

. . . in reviewing the progress of Pakistan's economic development in the light of the requirements for take-off, the focus will be on industrialization, saving, and the balance of trade. Since a regional breakdown of the data is not yet available, the record relates to the experience of the economy as a whole.

Table 1 shows the growth since 1949/50 of national income in aggregate and per-capita terms, the change in the shares contributed by agriculture and manufacturing, and the trend of imports and exports. Four facts clearly emerge from these data. First, the past thirteen years have witnessed a significant pace of industrialization. While national income rose by 37 per cent, the percentage share contributed by manufacturing doubled, and agriculture's share correspondingly declined.

Second, population grew at about the same pace as national income, so that per-capita income was virtually unchanged over the period. What slight gain occurred was achieved in the very early years. Annual average per-capita income was virtually the same in the three years just prior to the First Plan, during the five years of the First Plan, and in the first three years of the Second Plan.

Third, though the trends of imports and exports are somewhat obscured by the Korean War and erratic fluctuations in the stringency of foreign-exchange licensing, it appears nevertheless that imports have risen substantially while exports have not. On a per-capita basis, exports have actually declined. The aggregate data, of course, hide considerable change in the composition of both exports and imports. Within the latter, there was a great rise in machinery, metals, transport equipment and chemicals; while cotton textile imports declined drastically. On the side of exports, the shift was from raw cotton and jute to their manufactures. Still the rise in manufactured exports was not sufficient to raise total exports significantly, nor was import substitution adequate to raise the share of domestic saving in development expenditure. The result was a rising trend in the dependence on foreign financing.

The fourth fact of importance from Table 1 is, then, the failure of the saving rate to rise. While its behaviour appears erratic, there is no evidence of a rise above the range of five to six per cent. The rate of 7.9 per cent for 1955/56 was undoubtedly due to the temporary effect of devaluation on the trade balance; and the rate of 7.4 per cent for 1961/62 seems to be equally abnormal for reasons I have discussed elsewhere.[1] In any case with the fall in agricultural production and national income in 1962/63, a drop in the saving rate is likely. The unhappy conclusion is that the saving rate is still at a pre-take-off level.

To sum up, we find over the thirteen years a significant pace of industrialization, some import substitution, but stagnant exports, saving, and per-capita income. I turn now to some of the implications of the above findings.

Has industrialization, first of all, contributed to the correction of the first disequilibrium described above—the gap between average labour productivity in agriculture and nonagriculture? Note that our index of industrialization is nonagriculture's share of output, not its share of the labour force. Is the former a good indicator of the latter?

To answer this (and some subsequent questions), consider the identity

$$\frac{Y_n}{Y} \equiv \frac{L_n}{L} \cdot \frac{Y_n/L_n}{Y/L}$$

where Y and L are, respectively, national income and total labour force; and Y_n and L_n are nonagricultural income and nonagricultural labour force. That is, the share of nonagricultural income is the product of the proportion of the labour force in nonagriculture and the ratio of average labour productivity there to average productivity in the whole economy.

Assume initially that labour productivity is constant in both agriculture and nonagriculture, but that it is

Table 1 **Selected Growth Indicators, 1948–1963**

Year	National income (1949/50–1952/53 prices): in crore rupees	National income: index (1949/50 = 100)	Population (millions)	Income per capita: Rs.	Income per capita: index (1949/50 = 100)	Gross saving as per cent of gross national product	Value added in agriculture as per cent of national income	Value added in manufacturing as per cent of national income	Value of imports (1949/50 = 100)	Value of exports (1949/50 = 100)
1949/50	1,753	100	78.9	222	100		61	7	100	100
1950/51	1,839	105	80.4	229	103		60	7	125	214
1951/52	1,852	105	81.8	226	102		59	8	172	168
1952/53	1,906	109	83.3	229	103		59	8	107	126
1953/54	2,025	116	84.8	239	108		59	9	86	108
1954/55	2,034	116	86.3	236	106		58	10	85	102
1955/56	2,022	115	88.2	229	103	7.9	56	11	72	105
1956/57	2,149	123	90.1	239	108	4.5	57	11	127	94
1957/58	2,154	123	92.1	234	105	5.3	56	12	111	83
1958/59	2,155	123	94.1	229	103	6.1	55	12	85	78
1959/60	2,267	130	96.2	236	106	5.6	56	12	133	108
1960/61	2,348	134	98.7	238	107	5.7	56	12	172	105
1961/62	2,420	138	101.3	239	108	7.4	55	13	168	108
1962/63	2,400	137	103.9	231	104		53	14	198	113

Notes: 1 For national income, Central Statistical Office (CSO) estimates are used through 1961/62, except that the terms-of-trade adjustment is not included. The 1962/63 figure was calculated on the basis of estimated changes in value added in agriculture and manufacturing, assuming income from the rest of the economy to have grown in proportion to the growth of population. Weights are 55 per cent for agriculture, 13 per cent for manufacturing, and 32 per cent for the remainder.

2 Value added in agriculture was estimated to have declined five per cent in 1962/63 on the basis of official crop reports.

3 Value added in manufacturing was calculated on the basis of an estimated 10.8 per cent increase in the index of industrial production. The latter was derived by assuming that the average of the indexes for the last two quarters would equal the index for the second quarter (a relationship which has roughly held in recent years, owing to an invariable seasonal decline in the fourth quarter).

4 The population figures are the author's own estimates based on a bench-mark for 1960/61 and the assumption of growth rates of 1.8 per cent for the pre-Plan period, 2.2 per cent for the First Plan and 2.6 per cent for the Second Plan. I have had the benefit of discussion with Dr Karol J. Krotki, Research Adviser to the Institute of Development Economics, about these estimates, but the responsibility for them is entirely my own.

5 The import and export figures are from the CSO, adjusted for the devaluation of 1955, but not corrected for price changes. The figure for 1962/63 is an estimate based on the first seven months.

6 Saving rates are from Planning Commission data in *The Second Five Year Plan* (p. 28) and the *Mid-Plan Review* (p. 49). The calculation differs from that in the *Mid-Plan Review*, however, as explained in the author's 'Two Years of Pakistan's Second Plan', *op cit.*, pp. 129–30.

higher in nonagriculture. Then a rising Y/L is possible only in association with a rising L_n/L. In this case L_n/L must rise faster than Y_n/Y because of the rise in Y/L. If, however, we abandon the assumption of constancy and permit productivity in nonagriculture to rise relatively to overall productivity, the rise in Y_n/Y can equal or even exceed the rise in L_n/L. Thus, in the general case nothing can be inferred about the magnitude of the shift in allocation of labour from the change in the sectoral distribution of income.

In the Pakistan case, however, because of the stagnation of per-capita income we must add the assumption that Y/L is roughly constant (since the labour force as a percentage of the population did not change significantly over the period studied). We can in this case draw a direct inference about productivity in agriculture, as well as the shift in the sectoral allocation of the labour force. For if Y/L is constant, then a rise in Y_n/Y implies a rise in the product of L_n/L and Y_n/L_n. Ruling out a fall in productivity in nonagriculture as extremely unlikely,[2] the remaining possibilities all imply a fall in the average productivity of agricultural labour. For otherwise a rise in either or both of these ratios (L_n/L and Y_nL_n) would raise Y/L. A decline in L_n/L, coupled with a more than proportionate rise in Y_n/L_n (however improbable), would also imply a reduction in productivity in agriculture because of the adverse shift in labour allocation.[3]

Moreover, a rise in L_n/L is much less likely than a rise in Y_n/L_n to be associated with a fall in agricultural labour productivity because the labour shift in this case is favourable. The most reasonable inference in the case of constancy of Y/L is, then, that the rise in Y_n/Y has been due more to a rise in Y_n/L_n than to a rise in L_n/L. This means that the shift in labour allocation has not only failed to match the shift in income proportions, but has failed also to prevent an actual decline in productivity in agriculture. (CSO data indicate a decline of more than 11 per cent over the period 1949/50 to 1961/62.) And only a rise in nonagricultural labour productivity has prevented an economywide decline of output per worker. Thus, we can conclude that in Pakistan the rise in the relative share of nonagricultural value added has depended too much on rising productivity in nonagriculture and too little on shifting labour from lower to higher productivity employment to provide any relief from the first disequilibrium.

It could be argued that a given unit of capital invested to raise productivity in this way creates a greater fund for saving and reinvestment, and thus contributes more in the long run to the correction of all three disequilibria. This remains to be proved, however. And in the absence of a clearcut demonstration of the 'economic' superiority of such a strategy, planners would do well to avoid the political and social (dare I say regional?) problems to which it would give rise. In any case, in Pakistan the saving ratio has not risen noticeably with the rise in nonagriculture's share of income, so it is very difficult to justify the sacrifices such a strategy implies.

Turning to the failure of the saving rate to rise, one might be tempted to explain this as a result of the failure of per-capita income to rise, but in the analysis of growth dynamics we would be more inclined to explain the latter as a result of the former. In any case even without a rise in per-capita income, we might have expected a high marginal saving and reinvestment mechanism to emerge from the rapid increase in the share of income originating in manufacturing. This shift in the distribution of income plays a leading role in many theories of the take-off.[4] Why has it failed thus far in Pakistan?

I would like to venture the hypothesis that the character of the industrialization itself, with its emphasis on import substitution—especially the replacement of imported *consumption* goods—has something to do with it. In so doing I do not mean to downgrade the importance of other explanations any one of a number of which may deserve equal consideration. My reason for focussing on this one is not that I firmly believe it to be more important than any other, but rather that it has been relatively neglected.

I think that it is fair to say that import substitution was not the result of a carefully planned balance-of-payments strategy. Whatever were the reasons for adopting import licensing as the primary control over the foreign-exchange position, I doubt that they included a considered judgement as to the relative merits of various export- and import-competing industries based on comparative advantage, economies of scale, external economies, marginal saving rates, *etc*.

Nevertheless, the licensing system undoubtedly did influence the direction of industrialization. Since it gave greater protection to finished consumption goods than to intermediate goods or capital equipment, it encouraged investment in the former rather than in the latter. Moreover, since the least essential imports were the most stringently licensed, the system gave a special encouragement to investment in nonessential consumption-goods production.

How strong this influence was, whether industrialization would have taken this direction anyway, are questions I will not attempt to answer. What matters for what follows is not so much *why* as the *fact* that industrialization in Pakistan has been very heavily oriented toward production for domestic consumption some part of which could hardly be called essential for economic development.

Why should industrialization, oriented toward the production of consumption goods, be less effective in contributing to selfsustaining economic growth than one which emphasizes capital-goods production or production for export? On the surface, the former would seem to have definite advantages. There is an existing market which can easily be reserved for domestic industry by import restrictions. The products are familiar and the marketing system is already established. And there may be fundamental comparative-advantage reasons for developing consumption-goods industries first.

Moreover, the contribution to saving is potentially just as great for replacement of consumption-goods imports as for replacement of capital-goods imports or promotion of new exports. This can be seen with the aid of another identity,

$$C_d + I_d + X_d \equiv C_m + C_d + S$$

where C_d, I_d, and X_d are value added in domestic production, respectively, for consumption, investment, and exports. S is domestic saving and C_m is the imported component of consumption. The left-hand side is the national product and the right-hand side is the disposal of national income.

An increase in the national product in the form of a rise in either I_d or X_d will mean an equal rise in S if consumption $(C_m + C_d)$ is not permitted to rise. But a rise in domestic production of consumption goods for domestic absorption will also raise saving to the extent that C_m is correspondingly reduced. Thus in a case of pure import substitution (the rise in C_d being matched exactly by a fall in C_m) S will rise by the increase in national product just as in the case postulated above of a rise in I_d or X_d.

The analysis could be extended to the more general case where consumption is permitted to rise with the rise in national product, but the conclusion is the same. The change in saving associated with a rise in output depends on the change in consumption regardless of the kind of goods the output increase embodies. This also emphasizes, however, that if the consumption function is affected by the investment choice, this must be taken into account along with all of the other factors in determining investment strategy.

With this I will turn now to what appear to me to be some of the dangers inherent in a strategy of primary emphasis on replacement of imported consumption goods. First, such a strategy must meet Nurkse's balanced-growth requirement.[5] There can be no specialization for the home market. This means encouraging investment in the production of a little bit of a lot of things, with all of the disadvantages that this implies. It means in some cases an uneconomically small scale of production. In others it means too few firms for the kind of competition that enforces efficiency and progress. It means scattering thinly scarce capital, foreign exchange, and technical and organizational talent. It means, in short, doing many things poorly instead of fewer things well.

As a consequence, the rise in the value added in manufacturing includes a lot of just plain inefficiency in production. Turning the terms of trade against agriculture (by substituting high-priced domestic manufactured goods for cheaper foreign ones) can be justified when a reasonable degree of efficiency turns the high prices into profits for reinvestment. If the high prices are matched by high costs of production, however, the hope of generating selfsustaining growth *via* such a strategy tends to be frustrated and the rationale for a transfer of saving from agriculture to industry is less evident.

The second danger inherent in this kind of import-substitution strategy is the possibility that the early momentum of industrial development will not be maintained because of a failure to develop a self-generating mechanism of industrial growth. This is clearly related to the first danger since a profits-saving-reinvestment sequence is a necessary part of any such mechanism. But even if this condition is met, what about the market inducements to invest after the painless takeover of the existing market from foreign competition has been accomplished?

The pace of investment and industrial growth will be gradually slowed as these market limits are reached[6] unless some combination of three things happens. The first is a rapid growth of productivity across the whole economy (and especially in agriculture) which moves real income per capita ahead fast enough to warrant continuing high investment in industrial growth. The second is the operation of a 'backward linkage'[7] effect inducing investment in the production of the equipment and intermediate goods used in the consumption-goods industries. That is, import substitution must be extended to the prior stages of production. Third is the opening-up of export markets for the surpluses that would develop inevitably if the pace of industrialization is maintained.

Now none of these will happen automatically. There is no natural, spontaneous evolution from the kind of 'hot-house' industrial growth induced by shutting out imports to this kind of permanent, selfsustaining growth. A rapid rise in productivity is itself inhibited by the implications of the balanced growth strategy, as discussed above. The same can be said for the development of export markets, with one additional comment. A few markets will even initially be large enough in a country the size of Pakistan to support a number of firms of economical size. These will be for the consumption goods which have a heavy weight in budgets of low-income families, *e.g.* cotton cloth. While these have great natural advantages for import substitution they have definite disadvantages for export promotion. The usual low income-elasticity of demand for such goods means that demand in the advanced countries is not growing rapidly. And as the less developed countries nearly unanimously select such industries for early import substitution, the export market is further limited.

This leaves the backward linkage effect on investment to replace imported capital equipment and intermediate goods. What is required is that profits from consumption-goods industries be diverted away from reinvestment there to investment in equipment and material supplying industries. This should be a natural development, but there are some influences working against it. First, the capital market is not sufficiently developed to make this kind of reallocation of profits easy. The most likely place for reinvestment of profits is in the industry where they are earned. Nor has the government's taxing and relending activities developed sufficiently to fill this gap. Eventually giant, diversified monopolies of the Japanese *Zaibatsu* type might substitute for a capital market, but this development is still at an early stage in Pakistan.

Second, since final goods are given greater protection in the import-control system than intermediate and capital goods, investment in the production of the latter always seems less profitable anyway. Ultimately, the growing supply of consumption goods would reduce the profitability of investment there, but this might occur only after the aggregate consumption function has been permitted to rise steadily, defeating all attempts to raise the saving rate.

This brings me to the third danger of such an industrialization strategy—the danger of consumption liberalization.[8] We have seen above that replacement by domestic production of imported consumption goods contributes effectively to growth only to the extent that consumption is simultaneously constrained. Unfortunately, however, this strategy carries within it an automatic decontrol of consumption. Let us see how this is so.

We must start with a recognition that some sort of control over consumption was essential right from the beginning of the development effort in Pakistan, even to achieve a five-per-cent saving rate. The principal instruments of control have been the controls on imports—duties and the licensing system. When most manufactured consumption goods had to be imported, this worked not only to curb imports, but to constrain consumption as well. With substitution of domestic production for imports, however, the proportion of consumption-goods demand so constrained has steadily dwindled with the consequence that consumption has been automatically liberalized.

The objection might be raised that import controls did not really curb consumption effectively, but instead simply diverted it away from imported goods. To a considerable extent this is undoubtedly true, but it is the import substitution itself that made this easy. More important, no doubt, was the shift in income distribution that occurred. As import substitution took place, income was transferred from the government (customs duties) and from the profits of favoured importers to income recipients in the new industries. We can guess that because of the relative inefficiency of these industries, a substantial part of the value added there became nonprofit income, a much higher proportion of which is consumed. This guess is at least consistent with the empirical evidence cited above.

Finally, we must note the natural tendency for the emergence of pressures to minimize the constraints on consumption when the business community is overwhelmingly committed to the output of consumption goods. As domestic production rose, the constraints on consumption steadily took more the form of restrictions on the licensing of materials, parts and equipment for the consumption-goods industries, and less the direct limitation of imports of finished goods. And so the phenomenon of excess capacity due to scarcity of imported supplies emerged. While this was clearly the result of a misallocation of investment—too much capacity installed to produce finished consumption goods and too little to produce materials and equipment—and while to justify the full use of the existing capacity would have required such a rise in consumption as to emasculate the saving plan, all of the pressures were on the side of liberalizing the licensing of supplies. For the excess capacity was there, and the cheapest way to get an increase in production (never mind what kind of production!) was to import supplies. What the economy really needed, of course, was a stiff increase in taxes on consumption to offset the steady erosion of control over consumption, but how can one call for higher consumption taxes when there is excess capacity in the consumption-goods industries? This is the kind of trap into which the industrialization strategy followed by Pakistan (albeit inadvertently) naturally leads.

No doubt there are other important reasons why industrialization in Pakistan has failed to raise the saving rate or even to begin to correct the agriculture/industry disequilibrium. I believe, however, that the foregoing explains a good part of it.

Notes: Reading 21

1 J. H. Power, 'Two years of Pakistan's second plan', *Pakistan Development Review*, Spring 1963, pp. 131–2.

2 Since this would have to be accompanied by a rise in L_n/L greater than the rise in Y_n/Y (which doubled in the period studied), it implies a massive transfer of labour out of agriculture into low-productivity employment or unemployment elsewhere. While it is very doubtful that this has happened, it would not affect the main argument of this paper, since it means simply a transfer from agricultural to non-agricultural underemployment.

3 $\frac{Y_a}{Y} \equiv \frac{L_a}{L} \cdot \frac{Y_a/L_a}{Y\ L}$ where the subscript 'a' designates the agricultural sector. Since $\frac{Y_a}{Y}$ has fallen over the period and $\frac{L_a}{L}$ must have risen in this case, $\frac{Y_a}{L_a}$ *a fortiori* must have fallen.

4 See, for example, W. A. Lewis, *The Theory of Economic Growth*, Irwin, 1955, pp. 233–8.

5 R. Nurkse, *Problems of Capital Formation in Underdeveloped Countries*, Oxford University Press, 1960, pp. 11–17.

6 There is some evidence that this has occurred in Pakistan. Between 1950 and 1955 industrial production grew at an annual average rate of 26 per cent. In the first plan period the rate was 11 per cent, while in the first three years of the second plan, it has been between 9 and 10 per cent.

7 A. O. Hirschman, *The Strategy of Economic Development*, Yale University Press, 1958, pp. 100–16.

8 For a fuller discussion of this plus empirical evidence for Pakistan, see A. R. Khan, 'Import substitution, consumption liberalization and export expansion', in the *Pakistan Development Review*, 1963.

Reading 22

Note on the Concept of 'Growth Poles'

F. Perroux

Economie Appliquée, vol. 8, 1955, translated from the French by I. Livingstone.

Cassell (1918) has presented a model of steady growth in which there are no changes in proportions between flows. Population grows: aggregate production grows in the same proportion as the population; the relation between the flow of capital goods and the flow of consumer goods is constant; the propensity to consume and to save, coefficients of production, hours of work remain the same; real capital increases exactly in proportion to production and consumption; real income per head of population stays constant; the index of the general price level and relative prices do not change. . . . In brief 'the economy in one period is the exact replica of the economy in a preceding period; the quantities are simply multiplied by a certain coefficient' (Tinbergen and Polak, 1950, cited by Kraus, 1954, p. 84).

Schumpeter has similarly constructed his enlarged circular flow in which, in contrast with the stationary model, population, production, capital increases from period to period, in exactly the same proportions; in which goods, services, money follow the same paths, and the flows increase without change in structures, or in fluctuations.

As we know, static equilibrium and the stationary model are proper logical tools for clarifying changes and for classifying types of changes. Similarly, growth without change of proportions or of fluctuations (which represents contemporary processes of equilibrium growth) is a tool for understanding and classifying structural changes, fluctuations, progress (eventually regress) which are concomitant with all observable growth.

No observable growth of an economy is expressed by the model which has just been outlined.

One aspect of structural changes consists of the appearance and disappearance of industries, in the varying proportion of various industries, in the flow of total industrial output in the course of successive periods, in the different rates of growth for different industries, during one period and in successive periods.

Another aspect characterizing structural changes in a national economy is the diffusion of the growth of an industry (or group of industries.) The appearance of a new industry, the growth of an existing industry, are diffused through prices, through flows, through expectations. In the course of longer periods, the products of an industry or of a group of industries, profoundly transformed and sometimes hardly recognizable compared with their initial forms, permit new inventions giving birth to new industries.

The fact, rough but solid, is this: growth does not appear everywhere at the same time; it manifests itself in points or 'poles' of growth, with variable intensities; it spreads by different channels and with variable terminal effects for the economy as a whole.

To investigate this process of growth is to make explicit and scientifically manageable a view already presented in several theoretical models,[1] inspired by the observation of underdeveloped countries,[2] apparent in the politics of modern states.[3]

We shall consider: first, the propellent industry and growth; second the industrial complex and growth; third, the development of growth poles and the growth of national economies.

Propellent Industry and Growth

In observable economic growth, attention is attracted to certain industries. In advance of others, they develop in forms which are those of large modern industry: the separation of the factors of production from each other, the concentration of capital under one control, the technical separation of tasks and mechanization.

They have, during given periods, rates of growth of their own output higher than the average rate of growth of industrial output and of national output.

Their rate of growth, accelerated at first during a series of periods, attains a limit, past which they experience a relative decrease (see the series studied by Kuznets, 1930, 1953, 1954). Apart from accidental causes, there are general reasons for this rhythm. The technical progress of the launching of the industry is ordinarily followed, for a time, by less progress. The demand for the product becomes less elastic. Speculation, if it has been set off by the launching, dies out or is reduced, and shifts elsewhere.

The observation of industries which offer these characteristics poses two questions:

1 Is it possible to construct analytically the action exercised by a propellent industry on another industry?

2 How is the action of the propellent industry exerted on the total output of the economy?

1 In the general equilibrium of perfect competition, the maximization of total output at the optimum point results from the profit maximization of each individual firm. The profit of each individual firm is a function of its sales and of its purchases of inputs.

In these conditions, each firm maximizes its own profits by its own decisions, taking into account price, which is the sole indicator by which its decisions are bound to those of the other firms; firms are interdependent only through price.

Quite different is the situation in which the profit of one firm is a function of its own sales, its purchase of inputs, the sales of another firm, the purchase of inputs by another firm (see Scitovsky, 1954). In this second situation, the two firms are no longer connected only by way of price; they are also connected by sales and by the purchase of inputs, that is to say, since these elements depend on methods of production and changes therein, by methods of production employed by the firms and changes in them.

This is one of the recent definitions of *external economies*.

If we consider the industry as one firm, what is said about interrelations between firms can be said about interrelations between industries; if we eliminate the concept of the industry and retain only a collection of firms, the application of external economies is immediate.

Profits, instead of being produced by the decisions of each firm concerning its sales and purchases of inputs, are *induced* by the sales and purchases of inputs of another firm. Insofar as profit is the driving force of capitalist expansion and growth, the propellent action no longer stems from the research and acquisition of profit by individual firms, related to the others by a single price, but by the research and acquisition of profit by individual firms each of which experiences the effects of the level of sales, the level of purchases of inputs, and the methods of production employed by the others. In this way are introduced non-Paretian relationships.

This change produces two consequences important to the understanding of growth: first it shows how (short-term) expansion and (long-term) growth of large collections of firms can take place.[4] Second, it brings out the difference between investment the volume and nature of which are decided on the basis of the proceeds obtained only by the investing firm; and the investment the volume and nature of which are or would be decided taking into account the induced profits and other advantages (Scitovsky, 1954).[5]

2 How is the action of the propellent industry exercised on the *total output* of the economy?

The birth of a new industry is always the fruit of an expectation. An agent or agents consider a new situation; they judge it possible; they assume the risks of its achievement. The project depends on the breadth of their economic horizon,[6] takes the form of a plan or more precisely of alternative plans susceptible to corrections in the course of successive short periods. To the extent that these plans are or become compatible with the plans of other agents,[7] forming a whole, the expectation becomes creative.

If all the factors used were unemployed and if the creation does not impose costs on any other sector, the output of the industry comes as a net increase in the aggregate output of the economy during the preceding period.

If all the factors used are furnished by means of replacement during a process of growth (the depreciated capital being replaced by more productive capital equipment, the retiring means of production giving way to qualitatively superior means of production, with no loss being imposed on sectors outside those in which the replacement operates), aggregate output will again show a net increase.

If a fraction of the factors used are pulled away from previous units, with losses of productivity in certain of their sectors, the net increase in aggregate output is the algebraic sum of the gains and losses in output.

Once a new industry appears in the economy, its effect on total output, from period to period, can, equally well, be followed analytically by distinguishing: first, its own share in total output (the size of its output in total output); second, the supplementary output which, from period to period, it *induces* into its environment. Since a new industry does not generally appear alone, as new industries grow in overlapping fashion, the increase in total output is a function of: the level of additional output in the new industries themselves, taken together, and the levels of additional output induced by the new industries taken together.

Again these *ex post* relationships through sales, through purchases of inputs and through methods of production are insufficient to account for the historical facts observed. The appearance of one or of several industries changes, it is currently said, the 'atmosphere' of the period, creates a 'climate' favourable to growth and progress. These are metaphors, words; they indicate, nevertheless, significant chain-relationships which can be submitted to analysis. *Innovation* introduces different and (or) additional variables in the economic horizon and plans of dynamic entrepreneurs or groups of entrepreneurs: it has a destabilizing effect. Successful innovation by some entrepreneurs acts as an example to others and provokes imitations, themselves creative. In effect, successful innovation, in giving rise to an *increase of inequalities* between entrepreneurs, aware, all of them, of their activities and the results of these activities—intensifies their *relative* desire for gain and their *relative* will for power.

Since every economic dynamic equilibrium is tied to a social dynamic equilibrium, an accumulation of shocks in the first has repercussions on the second. Innovations in the functioning of the economy call forth innovations in the structure of the economy; more precisely, changes in the technical and economic characteristics of the *functions* give rise to changes in the judicial and political characteristics of *institutions*. Since these influences do not work only, or even chiefly, *ex post, there are not in these relationships sequences which are one-way, constant or necessary*. During a period, in the presence of a set of innovations, all entrepreneurs capable of creative expectations are stimulated and pulled along. These may be connected with a given series of operations, during a relatively short period: this is the 'canals fever', the 'railways fever' or the 'gold fever'. Or they may be connected with a large number of new operations (even if the diffusion of their total effect is slow or very slow): these are (to use expressions which are popular, although they are now known to be very imperfect) 'industrial revolutions' or 'agricultural revolutions'.

This analysis, it will have been observed, although it accepts the central idea in which innovation and routine are contrasted, is very different from that offered us by Schumpeter. The latter focused attention unilaterally on the role of the private entrepreneurs, in particular the large-scale private entrepreneurs; but public agencies and their initiatives cannot be forgotten, and neither can minor innovations of adaptation. Schumpeter argues from a stable stationary equilibrium, the observable analogue of which would be furnished by cyclical contraction in a developed capitalist economy or by the stagnation of economics preceding capitalism; but the analysis used here accepts fundamentally that there is *no real situation* which is expressed by stable stationary equilibrium and that the latter is no more than a tool to bring together and classify changes and instabilities. Schumpeter works out his theory for a situation of full (or nearly full) competition; the present analysis integrates the numerous forms of monopolistic competition in the widest sense of this word (monopolies and oligopolies).

It is therefore open to the notion of industrial complexes.

Industrial Complexes and Growth

In saying 'industrial complexes', we have in mind not simply the presence of several industries in communication with each other through Paretian or non-Paretian links; we wish to introduce three elements into the analysis: (1) the key industry; (2) the non-competitive system of the complex; (3) the fact of territorial concentration.

1 This is an industry which has the property, when it expands its sales (and its purchases of productive services), of increasing the sales (and purchase of services) of another or several other industries. Let us call the first, for the moment, the propellent industry, the second (or second ones) the impelled industry.

The propellent industry can increase its sales to utilize its fixed capital more fully, that is, in order to operate at lower and lower points on its cost curves. Once it has reached its optimum output, if it is not a monopoly keeping up its price, it can make further price reductions inducing further increases in the sales of the impelled industries. It is in its interests to do this if it is aware of the consequences which its increase in sales and reduced price will bring about. The increase in the sales of the propellent industries may thus result from anticipation of the effects produced in the impelled industries or, if there is hesitation or slowness on the part of the heads of propellent industries, from State encouragement through, for example, a subsidy.

This property exists in different degrees from one industry to another: let us call a key industry that which induces in a larger group, for example a national economy, an aggregate increase in sales very much larger than the increase in its own sales.

This means that we cannot set up once and for all a list of key industries according to their external and technical characteristics. Raw materials, energy, transportation certainly tend to become key industries, but for them to take this character other conditions must hold at the same time.

The concept of a key industry, essentially relative, is an analytical tool which, in each concrete case, involves the precise definition of the impelled industries of the period considered, of the link between propellent industry and impelled industries. What is decisive is that in all articulated economic structures there exist industries which constitute *special points of operation of the forces or dynamics of growth*. When these forces provoke an increase in the sales of the key industry they will produce powerful expansion and growth in a larger whole.

2 Often the system of the industrial complex is itself 'destabilizing', because it is a combination of oligopolistic firms.

We know numerous types of market structures which, even when their static equilibrium position can be constructed theoretically, appear unconvincingly stable if they are considered dynamically and in conditions closer to reality.

The partial monopolist can impose an agreement on small satellite firms or take shares in them using its accumulated reserves. The duopolist with large capacity and low cost can act in the same way towards the duopoplist with less capacity and high cost. In a tacit agreement the respective positions of the parties are not given once and for all, nor are they in a group constituted around a price *leader*. Oligopolistic warfare, conflicts to eliminate firms, or to subjugate other firms, or agreement, are possible and frequently observed consequences of these situations. The 'destabilizing' action of each of these positions taken in isolation is a propellent for growth when, over a longer period, the dominant firm raises the productivity of the industry and achieves an efficient accumulation of capital superior to that which would have been the case in an industry operating under a more competitive regime.

Again these industrial systems do not show, by themselves, the instability of a complex of industries each of which is in an oligopolistic position and who are each other's suppliers and clients (Perroux, 1955). We might look at the relations between an industry producing a raw material under partial monopoly and an industry manufacturing steel under a partial monopoly, the latter normally absorbing most of the output of the first. We might relate these industries to transport industries benefiting from a monopoly and to a State which, through its purchases as well as by regulation, exerts an influence on the previous industries. We get a rich collection of indeterminacies and dynamic instabilities of prices and quantities. Even if a regulating policy is followed by the large firms, combinations, and public authorities, the modification of these relations will produce changes. Conflict or co-operation among the plans of the large units and their groups co-ordinated and regulated by the State act on prices, sales and purchases of inputs.

It is the result of these forces which provoke the expansion and growth of impelled industry.

3 Territorial concentration adds its specific effects to the process of key industries and to the non-competitive structure of the complex.[8]

In a complex industrial 'pole' which is geographically concentrated and growing, economic activities are intensified because of proximity and human contacts. The urban-industrial conurbation produces types of consumers with more varied and progressive consumption patterns than those of rural agricultural environments. Collective needs emerge (accommodation, transport, public services) and link themselves up. Site rents are added to business profits. Various types of producers, entrepreneurs, skilled workers and industrial labour are formed, influence each other, create their traditions, and eventually share common interests.

To these intensifying effects are added the effects of regional disparities. The complex industrial pole, geographically concentrated, modifies its immediate geographical environment and, if it is powerful, the entire structure of the national economy in which it is situated. Being a centre of accumulation and concentration of human and capital resources itself, it gives birth to other centres of accumulation and concentration of resources. When two of these centres are put into communication with each other by physical and intellectual highways wide changes show themselves in the economic horizons and plans of producers and consumers.

The growth of the market in space, when it comes from the linking up of industrial poles, and more generally poles of activity, geographically concentrated, is quite the opposite of growth equally shared; it operates through concentrations of the means of production in points of growth from which then radiate arrows of exchange. Changes in technique, political vicissitudes, the direction of world traffic flows between major poles favour or otherwise the various poles of concentration. The concentration of men and fixed capital, the rigidity of the structures which accompanied the development of the pole also make their consequences felt when it starts to decline; the pole which was a seat of prosperity and growth becomes a centre of stagnation.

Historians and geographers, even if they do not use the terms 'propellent industries' and 'poles of growth' are familiar with these facts. To adopt the sort of analysis which we propose is then, it seems, to reject some unjustified narrowness which customary theory imposes in treating market and price phenomena.

Once this new approach is adopted, the history of national economies and the theory of their development must be considered again from scratch: we shall limit ourselves to pointing out the most general consequences of the change in viewpoint.

Growth of Poles and Growth of National Economies

The national economy in growth no longer appears simply as a politically organized territory in which a population lives, nor as a supply of factors of production the mobility of which stops at the frontiers.

It appears now as a combination of relatively active groups (propellent industries, geographically concentrated poles of industry and activity) and relatively passive groups (impelled industries, regions dependent on geographically concentrated poles). The former induce into the other phenomena of growth.

The changes thus imposed in appreciating the comparative *economic size or strength* of nations are evident. But two fundamental consequences for the analysis of economic growth must be pointed out:

1 There is today (and there was formerly, under other forms) a conflict between the economic regions of the large economic units (firms, industries, poles) and the politically organized regions of the national states. The first do not coincide with the second; their growth depends on imports, exports, sources of supply, and markets, outside the national territory. Now these great economic units are the instruments of prosperity and weapons of strength of the state. There results a frequent combining of private and public interests in the

management of these great units; a struggle between these great national capitalist units, on a world scale; forms of imperialism both private and political exercised by the economically 'real' and 'active' nations over the economically weak and relatively 'passive' nations (see Byé, 1955). The Marxist dialectic, which stresses the conflict between forces of production and institutional forms, takes up some of the attention which we ought to give to another dialectic active in the modern world, the conflict between growth regions produced by poles of growth and politically organized territories.

2 Insofar as national and nationalistic policies persist in a world in which they are overtaken by technology and the development of economic life, wastes are sustained which, *even in the absence of violent conflicts*, constitute brakes on growth. Each state tries to exploit for the exclusive or principal benefit of its nationals the poles under its control within its own territory or which it has conquered outside. It uses part of its limited means in terms of men, real capital, money capital, to exclude its partners from the advantages which it claims to draw from the exclusive exploitation of poles of growth; from which come quasi-public oligopolistic struggles which endanger prosperity and peace. The elimination or reduction of these practices is not the least of numerous aspects of a policy of growth harmonized on a world scale.

Notes: Reading 22

1 Schumpeter explains by innovation, that is to say by the creation of new industries (in the wide sense), the Juglar cycle as well as the long Kondratieff cycle. J. Maurice Clark stresses the role of *strategic factors* in the short cycle and there is obviously no reason not to trace their influence over periods which encompass several cycles. On the contrary: it is important to distinguish between structural changes (of proportions and of relationships) observable in the short cycle (of two or of four phases) and the structural changes over the course of a century.

2 The approach recommended suits the so-called underdeveloped countries. In a number of these countries, capitalistic industries are planted in economies of which vast parts remain in the state of a natural or peasant economy. The economy as a whole is not yet articulated through networks of prices, flows and expectations. It becomes so through the creation of several poles of growth, linked by the channels and means of transportation, which make up, bit by bit, the infrastructure of the market economy. The geographical and economic isolation of the poles of growth in this case shows up clearly the obstacles to the spread of the cyclical expansions and contractions which afflict the 'imported' capitalistic industries; this isolation also permits us to see the changes of system (types of organisation) and of structure which allow us, little by little, to refer with justification to the movements of a 'national economy'.

3 The approach gives access to growth policies practised by Soviet Russia just as much as to the free world; these policies would be foreign to the general equilibrium analyses or abstract models of combinations of aggregate flows. We have in mind the creation of industrial poles in the Urals, in Russian Asia, as well as the policy of industrial complexes recommended and even already initiated in Africa. One of the processes characteristic of the operation is this: a centre of raw material extraction is linked up to a centre of energy production and, through channels of communication, to transport and manufacturing centres. What in the past has often been obtained through successive foundations, by projects or plans working by trial and error towards co-ordination, is attempted by the formation of a complex pole. (The lover of metaphors would perhaps say: the separate parts of the motor, instead of finding out the rules of their adjustment, are erected together.) In any case a *motor* is certainly what is involved. The complex pole calls up new creations, puts regions into motion, and changes the structure of the environment which it disturbs.

4 The growth of one industry (see Scitovsky, 1954, p. 149) can induce profits:

in an industry B which buys factors produced by industry A;
in an industry C the product of which is complementary with the product of industry A;
in an industry D the product of which is a substitute for the factors used by industry A;
in an industry E the product of which is consumed by individuals whose incomes are increased by the growth of industry A.

5 The optimum level of investment according to the general equilibrium theory of small firms under competition is only realisable if each firm can make perfectly divisible additional investments. . . . We know that today the condition of perfect divisibility is not satisfied.

6 Number of variables, length of anticipation.

7 Producers and consumers.

8 On all these points numerous examples relating to the Ruhr are to be found in Perroux (1955).

References: Reading 22

Byé, M. (1955), 'The large inter-territorial business unit and its plans', *Cahiers ISEA*, serie F, no. 2.

Cassell, G. (1927), *Theoretische Sozialökonomie*, 4th edn (Leipzig; 1st edn 1918).

Kraus, W. (1954), 'Multiplikator, akzelerator, wachstumsraten und konjunkturzyklen', *Weltwirtschaftliches Archiv*, vol. 73, p. 84.

Kuznets, S. (1930), *Secular Movements in Production and Prices* (Riverside Press).

Kuznets, S. (1953), 'Retardation of industrial growth', in his *Economic Change* (Norton), ch. 10.

Kuznets, S. (1954), *Towards a Theory of Economic Growth*, contribution to the second centenary of the university (University of Columbia).

Marczewski, J., *Histoire quantitative de l'économie français*, 13 vols. (ISMEA, Paris).

Perroux, F. (1955), *Matériaux pour une analyse de la croissance économique*, bk. 1, ch. 2, 'The phenomena of growth observed in an industrial pole: the Ruhr', *Cahiers ISEA*, serie D, no. 8.

Perroux, F. (1956), 'Prises de vues sur la croissance de l'économie francaise', *Income and Wealth*, serie V, ed. S. Kuznets (London).

Perroux, F. (1975), *Unités actives et mathématiques nouvelles.*

Revision de la théorie de l'équilibre économique general (Dunod).

Scitovsky, T. (1954), 'Two concepts of external economies', *J. Polit. Econ.*, April, pp. 143 *et seq.*

Tinbergen, J., and Polak, J. J. (1950), *The Dynamics of Business Cycles: A Study in Economic Fluctuations* (University of Chicago Press).

Reading 23

Capital Goods, Technology, and Economic Growth[1]

N. Rosenberg

Oxford Economic Papers, vol. 15, no. 3, 1963, pp. 217 – 27.

One of the things which we all 'know' about American economic history is that the relative scarcity of labour in the United States has led to the development of our well-known, much admired labour-saving technology. But why, in underdeveloped countries, with abundant supplies of labour and scarce capital, has not the scarcity of capital led to the development of capital-saving techniques?

It is at once apparent that there is a confusion with respect to what we all 'know' about American economic history—or, at least, that there is a highly important distinction which is typically glossed over. Scarcity of labour has, in the United States, resulted in the adoption of labour-saving techniques, just as, in underdeveloped countries, the abundance of labour has led to the adoption of labour-intensive, capital-saving techniques. So far there is complete symmetry in our treatment. Differences with respect to factor endowment, and therefore with respect to factor prices, dictate different optimum techniques along an existing production function.

What is frequently asserted with respect to American economic development is an additional and much more important proposition, namely that labour scarcity has in fact led to the development of a new, labour-saving technology, to *shifts* in the production function, and not merely to movements along an existing production function in accordance with factor endowment and prices. But, on reflection, it appears reasonable to ask why this should be the case only when it is labour which is scarce, and not capital. If the relative scarcity of a factor of production has been responsible for innovations which economize on the use of that factor in the United States, why have poor countries not had similar experiences with respect to their scarcest factor of production? For the common observation is not so much that technical change in underdeveloped countries has any particular sort of bias, but rather that it is entirely or virtually non-existent.

Here, then, is the lack of symmetry between factor endowment and technical change which calls for explanation. It is a generally accepted proposition that the scarcity of a particular factor of production—labour—has led to a dynamic technology in the United States. However, in economies where another factor of production has been relatively scarce—capital—the result has been technological stagnation. Why didn't the underdeveloped countries develop their own—capital-saving—technology? If the following explanation, which Hicks offers to account for the labour-saving bias of Western technology, has any validity, why has there not been a parallel capital-saving path of technological innovation in the poor, capital-scarce countries of the underdeveloped world?

> The real reason for the predominance of labour-saving inventions is surely that which was hinted at in our discussion of substitution. A change in the relative prices of the factors of production is itself a spur to invention, and to invention of a particular kind—directed to economising the use of a factor which has become relatively expensive. The general tendency to a more rapid increase of capital than labour which has marked European history during the last few centuries has naturally provided a stimulus to labour-saving invention.[2]

It is suggested here that an important aspect of the nature and impact of technological change is illuminated if we focus attention more explicitly on the role of the capital goods sector and, more particularly, on the relationship between the capital goods and consumer goods sectors as technological change occurs. The capital goods sector obviously plays a crucial role in the process of technological innovation. All innovations—whether they involve the introduction of a new product or provide a cheaper way of producing an existing product—require that the capital goods sector shall produce a new product (machine) according to certain specifications. We may usefully look upon the capital goods sector as one which is, in effect, primarily engaged in custom work. That is, firms in this industry are typically highly specialized in the sense that each firm produces a relatively narrow range of output (at least when the aggregate demand for capital goods is sufficiently large) in response to specifications laid down by a wide range of customers in the consumer goods and other capital goods industries.

The efficient operation of this sector, in turn, is dependent upon the achievement of a sufficiently high level of demand for capital goods. We revert here to Smith's time-honoured dictum (the full implications of which are not yet completely appreciated) that 'the division of labour is limited by the extent of the market'. However, it is extremely important to realize that the strictures imposed by limited market size are much more serious in the case of capital goods than in the case of consumer goods. An economy may be sufficiently large to make possible all the economies of specialization available to the producers of consumer goods without being nearly large enough to generate optimum conditions for the producers of capital goods. There exists, in other words, a discontinuity with respect to minimum size requirements between the capital goods and consumer goods industries.[3]

It should also be pointed out that economists, in attempting to account for improvements in efficiency, have been far too much preoccupied with bigness (economies of scale) at the firm level, and have devoted insufficient attention to changing patterns of specialization within industries (or sectors) which do not involve bigness in the size of the individual firm. The importance of the growth in markets is not necessarily bigness but rather an increased division of labour among firms in the specific sense of a narrowing down of the product range and the ability to concentrate on a limited range of products possessing certain specified properties, performing specific functions, and meeting highly specialized requirements. This is strikingly evident in the machine-tool industry which has never attained to bigness at the individual firm level, has consisted of large numbers of firms, and has been—since the last few decades of the nineteenth century—highly specialized by firm in the sense defined above.[4]

For this reason we wish to distinguish between capital goods industries, whose output constitutes replacement of or additions to the economy's stock of physical capital, and producer goods industries, an imprecise term generally used to designate not only the capital goods industries but also all intermediate goods which are used as inputs by firms. We suggest that capital goods producers (machinery producers), who typically produce a heterogeneous output, usually enjoy economies of specialization, while many producers of intermediate goods, whose output is typically homogeneous (chemicals, iron and steel, metals generally), enjoy economies of scale. Economies of scale, then, is a more comprehensive concept: firms which achieve economies of scale are also specialized, but firms may also achieve economies of specialization of a sort which do not involve significant economies of scale. The economies of specialization referred to derive not from the production of a completely homogeneous product but from the concentration upon a relatively narrow (heterogeneous) product range which in turn requires a relatively homogeneous collection of resources in their production. The point is that the typical machine-producing firm produces small batches of output drawn up to specifications reflecting the unique requirements of the user, but each such batch differs only slightly, and all draw upon a homogeneous collection of resources—each firm possessing plant facilities, designing abilities, and other technological 'know-how' which is geared to the effective solution of a very limited range of production problems. Thus, in the American economy, not only do individual machine-tool firms concentrate on a very limited range of tools (single firms producing only milling machines or boring machines or turret lathes) but frequently also they produce only various modifications of a single basic machine type for firms in a single industry. The truly mass-production industries, such as automobiles, are served by an extraordinary complex of relatively small specialist firms, each constructing very limited numbers and ranges of tooling devices for specific mass-production processes—dies, jigs, fixtures, gauges, moulds, &c.[5] The obvious advantage of this arrangement is that there is an important learning process involved in machine production, and a high degree of specialization is conducive not only to an effective learning process but to an effective *application* of that which is learnt. This highly developed facility in the designing and production of specialized machinery is, perhaps, the most important single characteristic of a well-organized capital goods industry and constitutes an external economy of enormous importance to other sectors of the economy. But for such a pattern of specialization among firms to develop, capital goods producers must be confronted with an extremely large demand for their output.

Thus, even in a domestic market as large as the British a recent study has concluded that the market was insufficiently large to generate an environment conducive to the emergence of technically progressive machinery-producing specialist firms.

> In certain industries the British market has not been big enough to encourage the growth of specialist producers of equipment—who themselves might have created new possibilities of progress. We have found examples of this relating to paper, bread, rubber, plastics, fine chemicals, aircraft, and scientific instruments. There are some cases where one or a few specialist producers exist, but progress in design is slow; in a bigger market there would be more

specialist producers, more competition in design, and a better chance that good designs would be produced.[6]

Now, if we really take seriously what we say about the beneficent forces of competition, the situation confronting underdeveloped economies must be dreary indeed, since they may be unable, in certain cases, because of limited demand, to support even a single modern firm, to say nothing of a competitive industry. The competitive pressures which normally act as a spur to innovation and change and which compel individual firms, on pain of extinction, either to explore new techniques or to adopt superior techniques which have been developed elsewhere, will be virtually non-existent. If, in J. M. Clark's phrase, we conceive of 'competition as a dynamic process', the sources of such dynamism may unfortunately not be available in important sectors of underdeveloped economies. The absence of salubrious competitive pressures thus reinforces the handicap resulting from the inability to achieve an optimum degree of specialization by firm.

Within this context a further point about our own industrial development may be made, pertaining to the especially crucial role of the 'transportation revolution' in making possible the growth of our capital goods sector. It was surely not an historical accident that specialized machine producers emerged on the national scene in the thirty or forty years after 1840—coinciding exactly with the laying down of a national railway network. Until roughly 1840 machinery production was not only relatively unspecialized—each producer typically undertaking a wide range of output— but it was also, because of the very high cost of transporting machinery, a highly localized operation—each producer typically producing for a very limited geographical radius. The growing specialization in machine production after 1840, the emergence of large numbers of producers each of whom typically concentrated on a very narrow range of machines, was closely linked up with the transportation improvements and consequent reduction in freight costs during the period. Highly specialized machinery could not be produced for a severely restricted geographic market for the reason already discussed with respect to underdeveloped countries—insufficiency of market demand. The growth in the size of the market to individual producers of machines, resulting from the reduction in freight costs, was therefore peculiarly important to the process of specialization in the production of capital goods.

We are now in a position to examine the nature of the handicap which confronts underdeveloped economies and also to appreciate more fully the role of the capital goods sector in the process of economic growth. Economists who have been concerned in recent years with the prevailing technology of underdeveloped countries have concentrated their attentions primarily on the question why underdeveloped countries have not developed a modern labour-intensive technology appropriate to their factor endowment. This is, of course, a highly important question.[7] But the manner in which the question is formulated is such that it bypasses an important part of the factor adjustment process for the economy as a whole—specifically the unique role played by the capital goods sector. What is important is not just the development of capital-saving innovations—although this is certainly very important. What is also important is improving the efficiency with which the existing types of capital goods are produced. Underdeveloped countries have been deficient on both accounts, but the latter deficiency has received practically no attention. They have therefore missed a major source of capital-saving for the economy as a whole.

Historically, a major source of capital-saving innovation has been improvements in the efficiency of capital goods production. The important analytical point is that any cost reduction in the capital goods sector—whether it is immediately labour-saving or capital-saving in its factor-proportion bias—is a capital-saving innovation to the economy as a whole. Recognition of the necessarily capital-saving nature of innovations in the capital goods sector goes back at least to vol. iii of Marx's *Capital* (chaps. iv and v), but has appeared in the theoretical literature dealing with technical progress only very recently.[8]

Many of the major innovations in Western technology have emerged in the capital goods sector of the economy. But underdeveloped countries with little or no organized domestic capital goods sector simply have not had the opportunity to make capital-saving innovations because they have not had the capital goods industry necessary for them. Under these circumstances, such countries have typically imported their capital goods from abroad, but this has meant that they have not developed the technological base of skills, knowledge, facilities, and organization upon which further technical progress so largely depends.

A capital-saving stage is an inevitable but later stage of the sequence by which an industrial economy accommodates itself to an innovation. When a new machine is introduced there exists, by definition, no established system of organization to produce the machine. As Marx stated: 'there were mules and steam-engines before there were any labourers whose exclusive occupation it was to make mules and steam-engines; just as men wore clothes before there were such people as tailors.'[9] Currently developed economies, then, have gone through the following historical sequence: with the growth in the demand for machinery the capital-goods industry became gradually more and more highly specialized and subdivided in order to undertake the production of machines, the cost of producing machines was thereby sharply reduced, and as a result capital-saving for the economy as a whole was achieved.

Some remarks by Stigler in a somewhat different

context may be cited on this point:

> If one considers the full life of industries, the dominance of vertical disintegration is surely to be expected. Young industries are often strangers to the established economic system. They require new kinds or qualities of materials and hence make their own; they must overcome technical problems in the use of their products and cannot wait for potential users to overcome them; they must persuade customers to abandon other commodities and find no specialized merchants to undertake this task. These young industries must design their specialized equipment and often manufacture it, and they must undertake to recruit (historically, often to import) skilled labor. When the industry has attained a certain size and prospects, many of these tasks are sufficiently important to be turned over to specialists.[10]

If, then, we consider the process of innovation over time, there is a high probability that labour-saving innovations are likely to be followed by capital-saving innovations, and this may provide an important key to understanding the dynamics of technical change. If we start with a new innovation which is labour-saving and capital-intensive, the new machine itself will, almost inevitably, be produced inefficiently in the early stages. This is not only because it is experimental or because there are 'bugs' in the early stages, although this is often certainly the case, but also because the capital goods (machinery-producing) sector is, itself, not tooled-up or equipped for producing the machine at low per unit cost. The introduction of the new product requires a process of adaptation and adjustment in the capital goods industry which did not initially exist. There is, as it were, a period of technical gestation during which time the resources of the capital goods industry accommodate themselves to the specific requirements of the new product. This entire 'breaking-in' process is a capital-saving process for the economy as a whole, and its final result is an upward shift to a new production function.[11]

It may well be that, historically, this has been the most important path which capital-saving has taken. If so, it carries the implication that it may be very hard for an underdeveloped country to start right off upon a capital-saving path. Perhaps it is necessary first to take the labour-saving path—at least until one has built up a substantial stock of capital and a capital goods industry catering for a market which exceeds some critical minimum size.

Here we may point to a somewhat different reason from the one typically emphasized for the importance of accelerating the rate of domestic capital formation in achieving economic development. A high rate of capital accumulation may be crucial in that it is a precondition for the growth in the absolute size of the capital goods sector. Such an enlargement is essential if this sector is to achieve the minimum size which it requires in order to achieve the high degree of specialization which is so critical to its effective operation. In this sense it may be possible to argue that a high rate of investment is an important determinant of rapid technological change. If this is so, then underdeveloped countries are doubly handicapped: low rates of capital formation perpetuate low capital/labour ratios and therefore low levels of labour productivity: and the failure to achieve a well-developed capital goods sector means a failure to provide the basis of technical skills and knowledge necessary to the development of capital-saving techniques and therefore a reinforcement of their state of technical backwardness. The kinds of skills which are needed to develop a technology more appropriate to their own peculiar factor endowments are, themselves, undeveloped.

In this sense—the absence of the appropriate pool of mechanical skills, knowledge, and facilities—there may be an important asymmetry, reflecting factor endowment. *Not* with respect to the selection among existing alternatives (labour-abundant economies select labour-intensive alternatives, capital-abundant economies select capital-intensive ones) but with respect to the preconditions for technical innovation and progress. Labour-scarce economies are likely to generate labour-saving technical progress, because such economies are likely to develop the pool of mechanical skills necessary for innovation. A critical aspect of the labour-saving path, then, is the 'production' of skills and familiarity with technical processes upon the part of the human agent which are essential preconditions for technical change of any sort. However, labour-abundant economies are not likely to generate a stream of capital-saving innovations because labour-abundant economies, largely because of the stagnation and backwardness of their capital goods industries, are not likely to provide the necessary skills and aptitudes conducive to technical progress in the first place.[12]

A closely related point may be made. Although labour scarcity does not, by itself, lead to innovation, it does lead to the adoption and utilization of technques at the capital-intensive end of the spectrum. And this, in turn, may be expected to have important consequences. Specifically, it leads to the establishment of a sizeable capital goods industry. As a result, such an economy (via economies of specialization, acquisition of knowledge and skills, and familiarity with the technology of capital goods production) may become an efficient capital goods producer and achieve all the conditions, in its capital goods sector, which are indispensable to innovation (and therefore capital-saving) in that sector.

Via this somewhat circuitous route, then, with its intermediate steps concerning the role of the capital goods sector, we arrive at a position in essential agreement with Hicks's conclusion that 'the general tendency to a more rapid increase of capital than labour which has marked European history during the last few centuries has naturally provided a stimulus to labour-saving invention'. But the different *route* by which this agreement has been reached—the special role of the capital goods sector—has important implications to the analysis of economic backwardness. For we have here at least a partial explanation of the perpetuation of low rates of capital formation which, it is generally agreed, is such a central feature of non-developing economies. Although there is general consensus that non-developing economies are characterized by very small annual increments to their capital stock, there is little agreement on the reasons for this deficiency. The reader of the literature is treated to a curious amalgam of economic and sociological explanations, with supposedly 'irrational' preferences playing an important role.[13] Our analysis, however, suggests that, in underdeveloped countries, the investment decision is likely to be heavily weighted by an unfavourable relative price structure which acts as a serious impediment to investment activity. The investment decision, after all, involves computation of a prospective rate of return which is determined by the present price of capital goods and the anticipated future price of consumer goods. But it should be clear that the relative inefficiency of the capital goods industries in underdeveloped countries and therefore the high price of capital goods is responsible for yielding low or even negative rates of return on a wide range of prospective investments. A major handicap of underdeveloped countries, then, is located in their inability to produce investment goods at prices sufficiently low to assure a reasonable rate of return on prospective investment.[14] Reasoning symmetrically, one of the most significant propelling forces in the growth of currently high-income countries has been the technological dynamism of their capital goods industries which has maintained the marginal efficiency of capital at a high level. Empirical evidence lending support to this point has recently been adduced by Kuznets, who found that the ratio of capital goods prices (most particularly producers' durable equipment) to consumer goods prices was substantially higher in less developed countries than in the more advanced countries.[15] Kuznets's data conform with what we should expect to find on the basis of our analysis of the role of the capital goods industries and reinforce our conclusion that underdevelopment can be explained as a basically economic phenomenon.

Notes: Reading 23

1 The author has benefited from helpful comments by his colleagues, Edward Ames and June Flanders, and from a reading of H. J. Habakkuk's recent book, *American and British Technology in the 19th Century*, Cambridge University Press, 1962, which raises some of the problems discussed in this paper, although in a different context. Whereas Habakkuk is concerned with the British and American economics in the nineteenth century, we shall be primarily interested in the problems of underdeveloped countries.

Our special interest in this Reading is in the production of machinery. Throughout, therefore, 'capital goods' should be taken to refer to producers' durable equipment and to exclude the output of the construction goods industry.

2 J. R. Hicks, *The Theory of Wages*, Macmillan, 1932, pp. 124–5. Similar statements may be found in numerous other places, such as N. Kaldor, *Essays on Economic Stability and Growth*, Duckworth, 1960, p. 229, and K. Rothschild, *The Theory of Wages*, Blackwell, 1956, p. 118.

3 This is a point which Hicks has recently emphasised in a discussion of the problems of underdeveloped countries: '. . . a market may be large enough to call forth all possible economies of scale in the production of final consumers' goods, but may not be large enough to do the same in the production of the capital goods which are to make those consumer goods, or in many ancillary industries. All the stages of production must be taken into account. . . . It is especially important . . that many of the most "advanced" capital goods are among the things which are most affected by economics of large-scale production' (J. R. Hicks, *Essays in World Economics*, Clarendon Press, 1959, pp. 184–5). And later, with respect to Ceylon: 'It is only the simplest sorts of capital goods (building materials being the obviously important case) which can expect to command a market within Ceylon sufficient to enable their production to be carried on at an efficient size. One has only to consider that there are plenty of countries that can produce textiles efficiently; but there are very few countries which can keep a textile machinery industry going without considerable reliance on an export market. This is the kind of situation which repeats itself with one sort of specialized capital good after another' (ibid., p. 205)

4 In 1954 the machine-tool industry consisted of 639 companies, the four largest of which accounted for 18 per cent, and the twenty largest companies for 49 per cent, of the value of all industry shipments. Of the industry's 81,000 workers, only 15,500 were employed by firms with over 2,500 employees. (See M. Brown and N. Rosenberg, 'Patents and other factors in the machine tool industry', *The Patent, Trademark and Copyright Journal of Research and Education*, Spring 1960, pp. 45–6.)

5 W. Paton and R. Dixon, *Make-or-Buy Decisions in Tooling for Mass Production*, Bureau of Business Research, School of Business Administration, University of Michigan, Ann Arbor, 1961, pp. 1–4.

6 C. Carter and B. Williams, *Industry and Technical Progress*, Oxford University Press, 1957, p. 155.

7 In fact, late developers have never adopted Western technology wholesale and indiscriminately, and it may be suggested that the proponents of the technological dualism hypothesis have been preoccupied with the emergence of particular industries – such as oil extraction and refining – where the elasticity of substitution between labour and capital is very low. Japanese development is a case in point. In the early years after the Meiji Restoration (1868) the adoption of advanced Western techniques was highly selective. In some industries – e.g. textiles – Western methods were introduced at selected stages and processes, while old-fashioned cottage industry techniques survived elsewhere. Moreover, where Western machinery was introduced it was both operated and serviced more intensively than was the practice in the West. (See G. Ranis, 'Factor proportions in Japanese economic development', *American*

Economic Review, September 1957, pp. 594–607). In the Russian case, Granick has argued that the development of Soviet metal-working industries was characterised, not by adoption of the most advanced, highest labour productivity technology, but by an attempt to minimise the capital–output ratio, and that the substitution of labour for capital was undertaken wherever possible. Granick cites such examples as the persistence, until fairly recently, in the use of general-purpose as opposed to special-purpose equipment, and the failure to substitute mechanised techniques where possible in individual processes such as hand-scouring, manual moulding, and hand assembly tools. Furthermore, throughout a wide range of auxiliary operations – materials-handling, inspection, repair work, clerical and book-keeping work – very little substitution of capital for labour has taken place. (David Granick, 'Economic development and productivity analysis: the case of Soviet metalworking', *Quarterly Journal of Economics*, May, 1957, pp. 205–33).

8 C. Kennedy, 'Technical progress and investment', *Economic Journal*, June 1961, p. 294; J. Robinson, *The Accumulation of Capital*, Irwin, 1956, p. 169; Habakkuk, op. cit., p. 168.

9 Karl Marx, *Capital*, Vol. I, Random House, 1936, p. 417.

10 George Stigler, 'The division of labor is limited by the extent of the market', *The Journal of Political Economy*, June 1951, p. 190.

11 Cf. Habakkuk, op. cit., pp. 167–8.

12 Cf. Habakkuk, op. cit., pp. 163–4.

13 N. Rosenberg, 'Capital formation in underdeveloped countries', *American Economic Review*, September 1960, pp. 706–15.

14 The obvious alternative, of course, is to import capital goods from the low-cost foreign producers of such goods, and this has been a common practice. But, in addition to the fact that this alternative largely deprives the under-developed country of many of the external economies resulting from the possession of a well-developed domestic capital goods industry, it has also posed serious problems due to the following related points: (1) the capital goods of the industrial countries are highly capital-intensive in their use, and therefore not appropriate to the resource endowment of the importing country; (2) the imported capital goods frequently embody a high degree of complementarity to skilled labour rather than to unskilled labour and are therefore difficult to operate successfully; (3) the problems of adequate servicing and replacement of parts are often difficult to handle satisfactorily when dealing with a foreign supplier.

15 Simon Kuznets, 'Quantitative aspects of the economic growth of nations: the share and structure of consumption', *Economic Development and Cultural Change*, July 1960, pt II, pp. 23–4.

Reading 24

Capital Goods in Developing Countries

Frances Stewart

Employment, Income Distribution and Development Strategy: Problems of the Developing Countries: Essays in Honour of H. W. Singer, eds Sir A. Cairncross and M. Puri, Macmillan, 1976.

The role of heavy industry has been a subject of considerable controversy, both in practice – see the Indian and Soviet debates[1] – and in theory. Neo-classical economists distinguish between *projects* rather than *industries*: that is to say, their methodology tends to assume that no particular merit (or demerit) may be attached to a project because it is in a particular industry – rather each project is to be evaluated for the effects to be attributed to it. In contrast, Marxist tradition has been to make a sharp distinction between capital goods industry (category I)[2] and consumer goods (category II), and much analysis hangs on this distinction. Developments of this distinction – in particular those of Feldman and Mahalanobis respectively – provided the justification for the build-up of heavy industry in Russia in the 1920s and 1930s and in India in the 1950s and 1960s.[3] This essay is concerned to explore these differences in approach, and to suggest other considerations, particularly technological development, which may justify special treatment for capital goods industries in developing countries.

It is tempting to spend considerable time on definitions, and impossible to avoid the question altogether. After all, definition and measurement of the capital stock have raised the major stumbling-block to the production function approach in macro-economic analysis. In that debate objections to measurement of the capital stock are chiefly concerned with the problems involved in aggregating a collection of items which are heterogeneous within and particularly *over* time. Questions of *aggregation* need not worry us here – we require rather the possibility of *classification*. Those involved in the debate for the most part accept the possibility of classifying goods into capital and consumer goods. While it may be impossible to achieve an overall watertight definition, it is surely useful to ask whether one should devote current resources to expanding production of steel or food, to production of machines which make machines, or machines which make textiles, and this is what the whole debate is about. Thus it will be assumed in what follows, as it is by the authors under discussion, that the distinction between capital goods (I-goods, or Department I goods) and consumer goods (C-goods, or Department II goods) is unproblematic. Broadly, we shall follow the same kind of classification adopted by national income statisticians, which is also much the same as that used by Marx:

> The total product and therefore the total production of society may be divided into two major departments:
>
> I. *Means of production*, commodities having a form in which they must, or at least may, pass into productive consumption.
>
> II. *Articles of consumption*, commodities having a form in which they pass into the individual consumption of the capitalist and the working class.[4]

The Harrod-Domar identity,

$g = s/v$, where g is the growth rate,
s the savings ratio,
and v the capital output ratio,

provides a good starting point in looking at the role of the capital goods industry.

Given a constant incremental capital output ratio (ICOR), the growth rate is proportionate to the savings ratio. One may look at the determinants of the savings ratio in this identity in four ways: from the point of view of *savings capacity* – in the economy – or the extent to which current consumption may be reduced, releasing resources for investment. Secondly, from the point of view of *investment capacity* – or the availability of the investment goods necessary to enable investment to take place. Thirdly, from the point of view of *absorptive capacity* – or the availability of projects. Shortage of managerial and administrative capacity, lack of skills, absence of required infrastructure and the need to do much investment sequentially rather than simultaneously may limit the number of projects possible at any point of time, in many LDCs. This limit is described here as constituting an absorptive capacity limit on investment. In practice it is likely that, rather than a sudden and complete ceiling, absorptive capacity limitations sharply reduce the returns on investment projects (or raise v for any extra s). We shall return to this point later. Finally, in a capitalist economy in which investment decisions are made privately *willingness to invest* is another determinant of the investment rate. Willingness to invest is related to absorptive capacity, since lack of absorptive capacity has the effect of reducing the returns to investment and, therefore, willingness to invest. But in addition to technical conditions presented by absorptive capacity, business psychology and expectations and government incentives also help to determine willingness to invest.

For *ex post* investment to take place all four types of capacity must be present – that is sufficient resources must be released and investment goods available, there must be projects in which to invest and a willingness to invest in these projects on the part of decision makers, for investment actually to take place. In a socialist economy one might wish to emphasise the first three types of capacity and possibly exclude the fourth category altogether as an independent factor. In a mixed or capitalist economy willingness to invest on the part of decision makers is an important determinant of the level of investment. While *ex post* all four (or three) types of capacity must be present – and equal to the actual level of *ex post* investment – *ex ante* the potential investment capacity – in terms of these four categories – may differ. The level of investment and the subsequent course of the economy depends on the relationship between the *ex ante* capacities and the *ex post* reality.

The maximum possible level of investment is set by the lowest of the four capacities. Assuming a constant and independently determined capital output ratio, then the maximum growth rate is also determined by the lowest of the four capacities. Different approaches to problems of development may often be reduced to different assumptions about which type of capacity provides the constraint on the level of investment. The starting point and distinguishing characteristic of the Feldman/Domar and Mahalanobis models (for brevity referred to as the Feldman model in what follows) is that the investment capacity, or availability of investment goods, determines the level of investment. The model is one of a closed economy, so that it is also assumed that the availability of investment goods is determined by the output capacity of the domestic capital goods industries.

Starting with a given capacity to produce I-goods, the initial savings rate is determined by that capacity. But subsequent capacity to produce I-goods will depend on how far the initial investment is devoted to expansion of the capacity to produce C-goods, and how far to expansions of I-good capacity. Let us assume that λ represents the proportion of initial investment devoted to investment in the I-good sector, and $(1-\lambda)$ the proportion devoted to investment in the C-sector. The higher the proportion of λ, the faster the expansion of the I-good sector, and the greater the production of I-goods possible in later years. With a constant ICOR (the same in both sectors), the higher λ, the higher the ultimate growth of the economy because the higher s. While growth in consumption will initially be lower, the higher λ, eventually growth in C-good capacity will speed up, as the larger size of the I-sector compensates for the smaller proportion of its output going to investment in the C-sector.

Suppose Mt represents the initial capacity output of the I-sector, and Ct the initial capacity output of the C-sector, so $Yt = Mt + Ct$. The initial maximum savings ratio possible is then determined, at Mt/Yt. Subsequently, investment capacity depends on the proportion of investment going to the I-good sector, since

$$M_{t+1} = I_{t+1} = S_{t+1} = M_t + \frac{\lambda}{v} \cdot M_t$$

Growth of the investment sector, in the first period,

$$\frac{M_{t+1}}{M_t} = \left(1 + \frac{\lambda}{v}\right)$$

The level of investment possible in the nth period,

$$I_n = S_n = M_t \cdot e^{(\lambda/v)n}$$

The consumption level depends on the initial C-goods capacity, and subsequent additions to that capacity, or

$$C_{t+1} = C_t + \frac{(1-\lambda)}{v} \cdot M_t$$

in the nth period,

$$Cn = C_t + M_t \left(\frac{1-\lambda}{\lambda}\right) \cdot (e^{(\lambda/v)n} - 1)$$

The rate of growth of investment is thus always determined by λ, assuming v is given and invariable. In the long run the exponential term dominates in determining consumption, so that the rate of growth of consumption and of income is also, in the long run, positively related to the proportion of investment going to the I-sector.

This, very crudely summarised, is the case for building up the capital goods sector as presented by Feldman and others – the justification for the concentration on expanding I-goods at the expense, in the short run, of light industry in both Russia and India. In Russia the policy did appear to lead, in the end, to a higher overall rate of growth, including a higher rate of growth of consumption output. In India perhaps it is fair to conclude that it did not.[5] The applicability of some of the assumptions on which the model is based may in part explain this varying experience.

The Feldman model is subject to two types of

criticism: first for assuming that the operative constraint, and consequently determinant of the investment rate, is domestic investment goods capacity and not one of the other types of capacity discussed earlier. In so far as domestic investment goods capacity does provide the operative constraint then there is a clear case for building up the local capital goods industry. But if one of the other types of capacity provides the operative constraint then building up the local capital goods industries will result in unused resources. It can be argued that this is what has happened in India. In what follows therefore we shall be concerned to discuss the kind of conditions in which it is reasonable to expect local I-goods capacity to provide the constraint. Secondly, the model, along with many others, might be described as a *bottleneck* model. As such it is subject to the criticisms which generally are levelled at *any* bottleneck model. Indeed many of the criticisms of the model are specific applications of these general criticisms.

Bottleneck models, as the name implies, assume that a particular resource is available abundantly at a constant cost up to a certain limit, and then suddenly the supply is completely exhausted and no more is available at any cost. In the Feldman model this is the assumption made about the output of investment goods. It is also assumed that other resources cannot substitute for the resource in question, so that once it is exhausted in quantity, a total limit is imposed on all activity. The assumptions behind such models, therefore, are in complete contradiction to the assumptions of substitutability, diminishing returns and continuity that are at the heart of neo-classical economics. If we make these neo-classical assumptions then no single resource such as I-goods capacity can limit the total level of output. Domestic resources in the C-good industry may move into the I-good sector, foreign resources may substitute for local resources. Similarly, with other postulated bottlnecks – e.g. absorptive capacity – resources from elsewhere may move in to release the bottleneck. In practice therefore there can be no bottleneck sectors; rather there are diminishing returns as output of each sector increases and more costly and less efficient resources have to be drawn in. The pure neo-classicist would reject any bottleneck model for these reasons. Any theory which picks out one sector for special treatment – be it the capital goods sector, or the agricultural sector, energy or industry – is thus denying (often implicitly) that the assumptions of substitutability and continuity are applicable. Given some degree of substitutability then a project approach – using prices that reflect the degree of substitutability – becomes appropriate rather than a sector approach.

Applying this to the Feldman model it would be argued that it is wrong to assume that investment goods are abundantly available up to a point, and thereafter not available at all – even in a closed economy. Rather investment goods would become gradually more expensive (and/or less efficient, depending on which way you look at it) as the quantity of investment increases. This sort of criticism does strike at the heart of the model – indeed it means that the concept of 'investment capacity' loses meaning. It also means that it is wrong to assume v constant, and hence growth uniquely determined by the savings rate. As savings rise v rises continuously and this must be taken into account in determining the optimal savings rate. In a neo-classical model all constraints operate continuously; as with investment goods, similarly with savings capacity. There is no point at which savings are abundantly available at constant cost, nor a point at which savings suddenly 'run out'; rather they are continuously expandable at increasing cost. The same goes for the other types of capacity discussed. Absorptive capacity does not present a potential bottleneck – there are always some possible projects but prospective returns are continuously reduced as investment increases.

Reality is probably more complex than either the pure neo-classicist or the bottlenecker would allow. While there may be some substitutability and elasticity of supply, it is often reasonable to postulate steeply rising costs, and falling elasticity, so that the bottleneck model may provide a good approximation to reality, without being totally accurate. On the other hand some types of capacity fit better into the neo-classical framework than the bottleneck framework. In particular it might be more accurate to view absorptive capacity as causing (a possibly sudden) fall in returns rather than a complete bottleneck. This would mean that the constant v assumption of the model had to be dropped; as the savings rate rose v might rise so that the maximum s would not necessarily lead to maximum growth.

The other type of criticism of the model accepts a bottleneck approach but argues that, for most LDCs, the wrong bottleneck has been selected. The key assumption in the Feldman model is the assumed identity of investment with the capacity output of the I-goods sector. Even assuming that it is the availability of investment goods that provides the operative constraint, only in a closed economy can this be identified with the output of domestic I-goods industry. In an open economy I-goods may also be imported. Thus the *ex-post* identity,

$Id \equiv Sd$, for a closed economy, becomes

$$Id + If \equiv Sd + Sf.$$

While in a closed economy, total investment cannot exceed – though it may fall below – total investment goods capacity, in an open economy I-goods may be imported, and consequently even with zero I-goods capacity, all the savings capacity potential of the economy may be realised by importing I-goods. In terms of the identity above, total savings and investment, $Sd + Sf$, can and is likely to exceed domestic I-goods capacity, the difference being made up by imported I-goods. In fact most LDCs do import a large proportion of their I-goods, so their domestic I-goods capacity is hardly relevant to the amount of investment they may do. Some part of investment consists of non-importable goods such as energy and construction: the model might therefore be applicable to these industries rather than heavy industry as a whole. But since I-goods to build up these industries may be imported, the model would need substantial modification. In an open economy, an upper limit to possible investment is imposed not by domestic I-capacity, but by that capacity *plus* foreign exchange available to buy I-goods from abroad, i.e. $Mt + F$, which sets the upper limit to investment. Assuming zero local I-good capacity, then foreign exchange availability provides the upper constraint on possible investment. If this constraint is reached before the other savings constraints, the savings and investment ratio, and the growth rate, is determined by foreign exchange availability. This, of course, is what occurs in the well known two-gap model of Chenery and others.

The Raj and Sen model shows how a rigid foreign exchange restraint of this kind may justify the build-up of heavy industry. If the limited foreign exchange is used to import consumer goods, the economy will not grow at all. If it is used to import investment goods which produce consumer goods, there will be a steady rate (or level, depending on the nature of the foreign exchange restriction) of investment and a steady rate of growth. If the exchange is used to import I-goods to produce I-goods (i.e. for the build-up of heavy industry) then the capacity to produce I-goods will show a steady rate of growth, and consequently the savings ratio will rise steadily and the economy as a whole will grow at an accelerating rate.

These possibilities are illustrated in the diagram below.

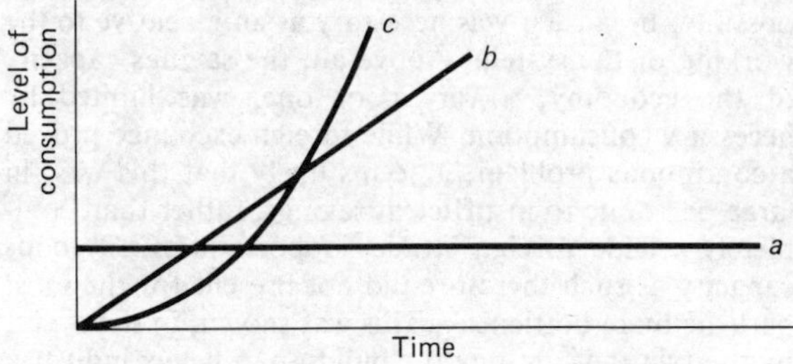

$a =$ all F used for C-goods
$b = F$ used for I-goods to make C-goods
$c = F$ used for I-goods to produce I-goods

The Raj and Sen model is similar to the Feldman model except that the question at issue is the allocation of foreign exchange rather than the allocation of goods produced in the I-sector.

The assumption of a rigid foreign exchange constraint is the key assumption and also most subject to attack. Joshi and others[6] have shown the conditions necessary for an economy to be subject to a foreign exchange gap, distinct from a savings constraint. Joshi argues that there are two conditions necessary for 'a pure foreign exchange constraint': '(*a*) that the underlying rate of transformation in domestic production is zero over the relevant range and (*b*) that the rate of transformation through trade is zero signifying that the elasticity of reciprocal demand is unity or less.'[7] Unless these (somewhat unlikely) conditions are met, then the foreign exchange constraint merges into a savings constraint. Then additions to savings potential will be realisable in some increase in the savings and investment rate. However, while a pure foreign exchange constraint may be unlikely, with very low trade elasticities, the extra investment obtainable from a given reduction in consumption may be very small. In terms of the justification for a build-up of heavy industry, the pure Raj and Sen model requires a pure foreign exchange constraint. In the absence of such a constraint, then there is no special case for building up heavy industry as distinct from other industries. Very low elasticities, but not sufficiently low to create a pure foreign exchange constraint, may *in practice* justify the build-up of heavy industry for the same sort of reasons as those that lie behind the Raj and Sen model. But *in theory* in such a situation project evaluation should produce the required build-up, if appropriate shadow prices are applied, without giving any special weight to heavy industry. In practice, as an alternative to the continued application of shadow rates, the build-up in heavy industry might be encouraged directly (by subsidies or government expenditure) in economies with very low trade elasticities and unrealised savings potential.

All the models which postulate that the investment rate depends on the capacity to make or import investment goods, deny savings an independent role. It is assumed that in one way or another – by a shift to profits in a Keynesian (closed economy) distribution model, by a government tax and/or interest rate policy, investment rules the roost, and savings will not act as an independent constraint. But in LDCs savings may present an independent constraint, even if the Keynesian distribution model operates and/or government can tax as much as it likes. This is because *consumption* is an essential input into the productive process, and cannot be depressed, below certain limits, without affecting the efficiency, and even sometimes the possibility, of further investment. It is a well established fact that real wages in the modern sector tend to be substantially higher (two or more times as much) as subsistence incomes outside. Some believe this is due to trade union pressure and government regulation. But the very widespread prevalence of this differential, more or less irrespective of institutional (i.e. trade union and government) circumstances in the particular country, suggests that the differential has an economic origin. That is to say, the additional real wages, and consumption, are essential for efficient operation in the modern sector. This view is supported by the positive correlation to be found between wages per man and productivity per man. Generally speaking the more modern the technology, the higher labour productivity and the higher wages. Technology is a package designed for particular circumstances: these circumstances include the general well-being, physique, educational level and habits of the workers, all of which are closely related to the level of consumption. Consequently, technology imported from advanced countries requires higher wages than the local subsistence sector.

Whatever the direction and nature of causation – causation may well work both ways, with higher wages leading to more capital intensive and modern technology, which leads to higher wages – extra consumption is a requirement of extra employment in the modern sector. Suppose w' represents the net extra consumption for each additional worker employed, then necessary consumption is

$C = E \cdot w'$, where E is employment in the modern sector.

Hence the maximum savings possible is constrained by this requirement, or

$$S\ \text{max.} = Y - E \cdot w'.$$

Capital goods output capacity (home produced or imported) will only act as a constraint, when,

$$S\ \text{max.} > I\ \text{max.}$$

$$Y - E \cdot w' > Mt + F.$$

The level of necessary consumption is determined by the level of employment and the technology adopted. The literature on choice of techniques is largely concerned to show how choice of technique may influence the level of employment associated with a given amount of investment, and how, by appropriate choice of technique, s/v, or growth, may be maximised. In addition to necessary consumption, most economies also exhibit luxury consumption, that is consumption which can be curtailed without affecting productive efficiency. In practice, governments find it difficult to suppress luxury consumption, and thus in practice maximum savings may be lower than $Y - E \cdot w'$.

In a capitalist economy, what appears to be luxury consumption may in fact be necessary for the efficient training and allocation of labour, and for the provision of adequate investment incentives. One of the most powerful determinants of investment in such economies is expectations about the rate of change of consumption. Thus one reason why consumption cannot be reduced to the minimum level necessary for an efficient work force may be the need to keep up consumption to ensure sufficient investment. In terms of the previous discussion, a high level of consumption is required to prevent the fourth constraint – willingness to invest – becoming operative.

To summarise: growth may be limited by

(*a*) limitations on investment set by absorptive capacity;
(*b*) limitations on investment set by willingness to invest;
(*c*) limitations on savings and therefore investment set by difficulties in restraining luxury consumption;
(*d*) limitations on savings set by necessary consumption;
(*e*) limitations on investment set by the sum of local I-goods capacity and foreign exchange availability.

Special emphasis on build-up of the capital goods sector is only justified where (*e*) sets a lower limit than (*a*) to (*d*) above. Such a situation will only arise where the economy is closed, or where foreign exchange elasticities are very low, leading to a pure or near pure foreign exchange constraint. The USSR in the twenties and thirties probably came close to fulfilling these conditions: the economy was sufficiently advanced so that absorptive capacity did not constrain investment opportunities. Luxury consumption could be ruled out, and since the economy was relatively advanced workers' consumption could be limited without affecting efficiency substantially, while willingness to invest did not arise as an independent factor. The economy was near closed, so that local investment capacity plus limited foreign exchange set the upper limit to investment. Hence the build-up of heavy industry would seem to have been justified to speed up growth, and in the event (qualifying the model to allow for the war and heavy arms expenditure) the speed-up predicted did occur. In contrast, India in the 1950s and 1960s fulfilled few of the conditions. In particular, limited absorptive capacity reduced the returns from investment, though it did not impose a rigid bottleneck; luxury consumption proved unresponsive to government tax policy, partly, possibly, because it was necessary as an incentive to the working of the system. Above all, the savings capacity of the economy, a very poor one, was limited by necessary consumption. While foreign exchange proved a continuous problem, it seems likely that this was, in large part, due to insufficient savings, rather than completely rigid foreign trade opportunities. I-goods capacity as such therefore did not present for the most part the main bottleneck. This was shown, in the event, by the fact that, despite the build-up in heavy industry, the growth rate did not accelerate substantially, there was substantial spare capacity in heavy industry, and a continual savings problem.

The discussion has focused on Russia and India, but may easily be extended. Whether or not LDCs would be justified in building up heavy industry, according to the models discussed, depends on which of the limitations (*a*)—(*e*) operate and whether foreign exchange is a constraint.

Few countries exhibit the relative high-income closed-economy characteristics of the USSR that would justify concentration on heavy industry. It seems likely that most LDCs will come up against absorptive capacity and savings constraints before rigid foreign exchange limitations, and special build-up of heavy industry would not therefore be justified. One might conclude, therefore, that the neo-classical position, discussed earlier, was close to being vindicated: such a position permits a premium on *savings* without giving any special premium to the capital goods industry. However, if a premium on savings is combined with low foreign trade elasticities and a high shadow foreign exchange rate, in effect this will boost returns to projects in the capital goods industries, as compared with other projects.

An Alternative Approach

All the models discussed have assumed away the problem of technology. All assume that the technology adopted is a given of the situation, a parameter and not a variable. The models may or may not[8] assume a choice of techniques, but the range of choice is itself part of the parameters of the system. But technology – that is the nature of methods of production – is itself a product of the economic system. This has an important bearing on the question of the role of the capital goods industry.

Historically, the capital goods industries – particularly machine tools[9] – have been the prime developers of technology. In Britain, the US and France in the nineteenth century machinery producers, rather than machinery users, led the way in innovation.[10] Freeman has shown that in the twentieth century the greatest concentration of research and development and innovation lies among heavy industries.[11] The central role of capital goods industry in the development and diffusion of technical change arises for a number of reasons: first, and most obvious, new products and new processes generally require new machines.[12] Thus without capital goods production many new ideas will remain on the drawing-board. But the capital goods sector does more than simply enable ideas to be realised: it is also a major initiator of change. One reason for this is that a major source of market expansion for machinery producers lies in the replacement of existing machines; development of new machines, and hence rapid obsolescence of old machines, is a powerful instrument for securing rapid replacement. In addition, there is considerable technological feedback within the machine making sector with developments at one stage stimulating and often requiring developments elsewhere. An innovation may induce subsequent innovations in consuming or supplying industries because of the changed scale of requirements following the innovation, or because of changed technical requirements. Strassman has emphasised the scale factor; Rosenberg (1963a and 1963b) technological imbalance. Innovations in the machine sector are most likely to stimulate further innovations because they are both input and output, part of the circular process of production. In contrast, innovations in consumer goods – since they do not form an input into further production – are likely to stimulate fewer further innovations. Strassman has stressed that the greater interrelatedness of capital good production is likely to make an innovation in this sector more productive of innovation in the economy as a whole, than innovations elsewhere. The net result is that innovation is likely to be concentrated in the capital goods sector – as observed; and that economies without a capital goods sector are more than proportionately weakened when it comes to innovatory activity. Their innovations tend to be dead-end innovations, rather than a cumulative process. Put in another way there are greater externalities to innovation in the capital goods sector than innovation elsewhere, and the capital goods sector is likely to benefit more than other parts of industry from externalities associated with innovations elsewhere.

Historically, the capital goods sector has also diffused innovation, spreading new ideas across sectors as well as within them.[13] There is also an important learning and training dimension to capital goods production, particularly in relation to innovation. Countries which have no capital goods sector also tend to lack 'the base of skills, knowledge, facilities and organisation upon which further technical progress so largely depends'.[14]

Historical and analytic approaches both conclude that a capital goods sector is essential for innovatory activity. Lacking such sectors, underdeveloped countries have to import not only their machinery, but also their technical progress. The nature and direction of technical progress are thus determined from the outside.

Capital goods are part of an intrinsic package: that is, associated with each capital good imported is a whole set of requirements that go with it, and are very difficult to separate from it. The package includes

The nature and specification of the product;
scale of production;
requirements at other stages of production – raw materials;
raw material processing, packaging, selling, marketing;
skill and managerial requirements;
nature of work force, education, wage levels as discussed earlier;
marketing arrangements and brand names are often part of the package.

The extent to which items of the package are separable varies, according to the historical development of the technology, and the monopolistic elements connected with it. Sometimes monopolistic elements prevent any break-up of the package; at other times physical requirements arising from machinery design cause association between different elements in the package.

Countries with no local capital goods capacity, then,

are forced to import not only the capital goods but very often the whole package that goes with it. In so far as various aspects of the package are inappropriate they have to accept inappropriate patterns of development. Major differences between the economic circumstances of the advanced countries and LDCs mean that many of the elements of the technology package when designed in and for the rich countries are inappropriate. The inappropriate nature of the technology package imported from the rich countries has been much discussed.[15] Inappropriate characteristics include excessive scale, excessive capital intensity, skill intensity and excessively sophisticated products leading to and requiring unequal income distribution. Much of the dualistic nature of economic development in poor countries can be attributed to the technology package.

There is not, of course, a single technology available from advanced countries, but a variety of technologies, some new, some second-hand, some recently designed, some of earlier origin. Older designs, embodied in new or second-hand machines, generally come closer to presenting an appropriate package.[16] Nonetheless, they are not ideal. First, they may be associated with low productivity, since they do not make use of later technical advances. Secondly, very often they are only available as second-hand machines, in limited supply and with the difficulties of breakdowns and lack of parts associated with old machines. As the second-hand machines need replacing, a newer vintage with less appropriate characteristics is then available second-hand. For this reason, Pack and Todaro have suggested that capital goods capacity in LDCs should be built up, based on old designs from advanced countries.

However, social, historical, geographical and economic circumstances among LDCs today may make 'old' technology from advanced countries as inappropriate (though in different ways) to their needs, as modern advanced-country technology. There is a tendency to assume that LDCs today are more or less identical to advanced countries at previous stages of development. This view has been attacked in a general way by the dependency theorists.[17] From the point of view of technological requirements there are obvious differences between LDCs and advanced countries some at earlier stages of development. These include the land/labour ratio, the rate of growth of the labour force, the availability of different types of materials, and the world technological system in which the LDCs must operate. Thus it is perhaps too readily assumed that old technology from the advanced countries is likely to be appropriate to their needs.

To get technological change responsive to the conditions in the LDCs the change must originate in the LDCs. For this capital goods capacity is essential as much to build up skills associated with technological change, as to realise the ideas others may initiate.

The diagram illustrates the potential role of capital goods industries in LDCs in increasing the range of choice open to them. With no capital goods industry of their own, they have to import their technology from the advanced countries. Technological developments in the advanced countries can be thought of as a historical chain in which successive vintages of machines tend to be associated with higher labour productivity and higher

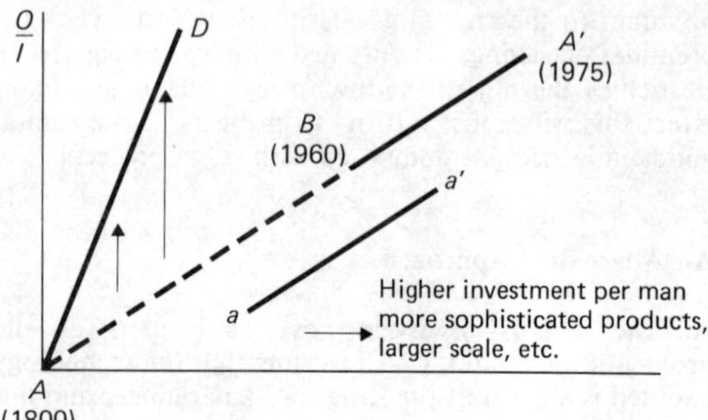

Bracketed figures show dates of design of technology

income characteristics. These characteristics include investment per employee, skill use, and product sophistication. The line *AA′* illustrates technological development from 1800 to 1975. Not all this equipment is on sale today – much is obsolete because the products associated with it are obsolete, because it was of low all-round efficiency, and because it no longer corresponds to the economic circumstances of the developed countries. Only a portion of total developments, say 1960–75, *BA′* on the diagram, are currently being produced and available for purchase by LDCs. In addition LDCs may buy second-hand machines: these cover a greater historical period but tend to be of lower productivity and are represented by *aa′*. Development of their own capital goods industry enables LDCs to extend their choice in two ways: first they may reproduce the older equipment – shown by the dotted line *AB*. Secondly, they may develop new types of equipment with higher productivity and more suitable characteristics than this old equipment. The arrows show the potential productivity improvements; the development of suitable characteristics involves retaining some of the old characteristics (e.g. low I/L) but changing others. Movement is towards *AD* if *AD* is thought of as being in a third dimension and representing more suitable characteristics.

The generation of more appropriate technical change should speed up growth and improve its distribution, by spreading income-generating activities and producing more appropriate low-income products. The current paradox is that labour-intensive techniques, which would suit the LDCs, are often associated with higher ICORs than capital-intensive. In theory, the greater use of labour ought to make the capital equipment used more rather than less efficient. The paradox is to be explained by the near monopolisation of capital goods production and technical change in the advanced countries. Consequently, technical advances have been concentrated on capital-intensive and large-scale technology, making it far more productive than earlier more labour-intensive alternatives, as illustrated in the diagram. Thus instead of benefiting, in terms of productivity of investment, from their reserves of labour, LDCs find them an increasing embarrassment. Appropriate technical change would enable these reserves to be used, *and* should be associated with a lower ICOR.

Twenty years ago Hans Singer succinctly presented the problem: 'The absence of a technology which is both modern and in harmony with existing factor endowments is a major problem of underdeveloped areas.' But, he argued, 'at present the possibilities of developing labour-intensive technologies are limited *because such development itself marks economic advance*' (my italics).[18]

While accepting the relationship between technological development and economic advance, it is argued here that capital goods industries would contribute to both.

The existence of a capital goods industry is, of course, not a sufficient condition for appropriate technical change, though it is a necessary one. The Indian capital goods industry has for the most part imported advanced technology; it has neither adopted (on a significant scale) old designs, nor has it adapted new ones.[19] One explanation of this may be the philosophy behind the development of the industry, which was the Mahalanobis one of a rapid build-up in capacity, rather than any idea of generating appropriate technical change. To secure this rapid build-up required the use of extant foreign technology. The emphasis was on expansion of the industries which contributed most quantitatively to I-goods capacity, e.g. the iron and steel industry, rather than of those industries most likely to generate technical change. For rapid quantitative expansion of I-good capacity, large-scale firms using modern Western technology and employing Western technicians may be necessary.

The type of capital goods industries likely to lead to technical change is very different. Small-scale, locally financed firms, with limited access to foreign sources of technology, catering for firms similarly placed, are most likely to be productive, while a Mahalanobis-type approach suggests concentration on the big input sectors, like iron and steel, and chemicals. Technical change is more likely to come from machine-tool makers. One difficulty facing underdeveloped countries is that a specialised capital goods manufacture is more likely to innovate, but specialisation requires scale, and most countries' markets are too small to provide the required scale. Scale in the market for capital goods might be attained through specialisation – and hence scale – in the production of final goods. Trade between underdeveloped countries in capital as well as consumer goods would also give substantial help.

Conclusion

The first part of this paper showed that the build-up of capital goods industries in LDCs on the basis of a Feldman type analysis is rarely justified, because the assumptions behind the model rarely apply. However, to conclude that there is therefore no justification for giving special encouragement to capital goods industries in LDCs, beyond that suggested by the immediate returns on the projects, is rejected in the second part of the paper, on the grounds of technological development. It is argued that a capital goods sector is an essential condition for local technological development, and that without such development LDCs are forced to accept the technical change of the advanced countries, with deleterious consequences for the rate and pattern of development. Build-up of capital goods industries is therefore justified on technological grounds. However, this leads to a very different type of capital goods industry from the sort of industry which would be justified by the earlier Mahalanobis-type models.

Notes: Reading 24

1 For the Soviet Union see Erlich, Preobrazhensky; and for India see Mahalanobis, Raj, Bhagwati and Chakravarty, and Bhagwati and Desai.

2 Marx includes raw materials production along with capital goods in category I.

3 Popularised in the West by Domar. Hans Singer (1952) put forward a similar model. Raj and Sen further developed the Mahalanobis categorisation to allow for different types of investment goods, for intermediate goods and for limited amount of international trade.

4 Marx, *Capital*, Vol. 1, ch. xx, section II.

5 For some empirical evidence see Wilber on Russia, and Bhagwati and Desai on India.

6 See, for example, Lal.

7 Joshi, p. 115.

8 Contrast Domar, who assumes a single technique for each sector, and Sen, who is primarily concerned with choice of techniques.

9 See, for example, Rosenberg (1963b) and Habakkuk.

10 See, for example, Landes, Rosenberg (1963b, 1969) and Saul.

11 'The industrial pattern of research expenditure is strikingly similar to Britain and America. In both countries one group of industries – mainly capital goods and chemicals – account for over nine-tenths of research expenditure.' Peck found that, in the aluminium industry, while product innovations originated largely with primary producers, process innovations were initiated by equipment makers rather than end-product users or primary producers.

12 See Freeman, Rosenberg (1963a).

13 Many of the most famous developments of the industrial revolution were due to technological imbalances as one technical development speeded up one aspect of the process, creating a new bottleneck, which required further

innovation to break: the famous innovations in textiles provide examples. For other detailed examples, see Rosenberg (1963b).
14 Rosenberg (1963a).
15 See Schumacher, Singer (1954), Stewart (1974).
16 Peck had provided some interesting data on the textile industry supporting this contention.
17 See, for example, T. Dos Santos.
18 See Singer (1954).
19 For evidence of this on the steel industry in India, see Johnson; see also Leff.

References: Reading 24

Berger, B., Berger, P., and Kellner, H. (1973), *The Homeless Mind* (Random House).
Bhagwati, J. N., and Chakravarty, S. (1969), 'Contributions to Indian economic analysis: a survey', *American Economic Review*, vol. LIX, no. 4, pt 2, September.
Bhagwati, J. N., and Desai, P. (1970), *India, Planning for Industrialisation* (Oxford University Press).
Chenery, H. B., and Bruno, M. (1962), 'Development alternatives in an open economy', *Economic Journal*.
Chenery, H. B., and Strout, A. M. (1966), 'Foreign assistance and economic development', *American Economic Review*.
Domar, E. (1957), 'A Soviet model of growth', in *Essays in the Theory of Growth* (Oxford University Press), ch. IX.
Erlich, A. (1960), *The Soviet Industrialisation Debate, 1924–28* (Harvard University Press).
Freeman, C. (1962), 'Research and development: a comparison between British and American industry', *National Institute Economic and Social Review* (May).
Habakkuk, H. J. (1962), *American and British Technology in the Nineteenth Century* (Cambridge University Press).
Johnson, W. A. (1966), *The Steel Industry of India* (Harvard University Press).
Joshi, V. (1970), 'Saving and foreign exchange constraints', in Paul Streeten (ed.), *Essays in Honour of Lord Balogh* (Weidenfeld & Nicholson).
Kidron, M. (1974), *Capitalism and Theory* (Pluto Press).
Lal, D. (1970), 'Foreign exchange constraints in economic development', *Indian Economic Journal*, July/September.
Landes, D. S. (1969), *The Unbound Prometheus* (New York).
Leff, N. H. (1968), *The Brazilian Capital Goods Industry 1924–64* (Harvard University Press).
Little, I. M. D., and Mirrlees, J. A. (1969), *Manual of Industrial Project Analysis* (OECD).
Mahalanobis, P. C. (1953), 'Some observations on the process of growth in national income', *Sankhya*, vol. 12, pt 4.
Marx, K., *Capital* (Lawrence & Wishart edn, 1970).
Pack, H. (1975), 'The choice of technique and employment in the textile industry', in A. Bhalla (ed.), *Technology and Employment in Industry* (ILO).
Pack, H., and Todaro, M. P. (1969), 'Technical transfer, labour absorption and economic development', *Oxford Economic Papers*, November.
Peck, M. (1962), 'Innovations in the post war American aluminium industry', in *The Rate and Direction of Inventive Activity* (National Bureau of Economic Research).
Preobrazhensky, E. (1926), *The New Economics*, tr. 1965 (Oxford University Press).
Raj, K. N. (1961), 'Growth models in Indian planning', *Indian Economic Review*, vol. 5, February.
Raj, K. N., and Sen, A. K. (1961), 'Alternative patterns of growth under conditions of stagnant export earnings', *Oxford Economics Papers*, vol. 13, no. 1, February.
Robinson, J. (1953–4), 'The production function and the theory of capital', *Review of Economic Studies*, vol. 21.
Rosenberg, N. (1963a), 'Capital goods, technology and economic growth', *Oxford Economic Papers*, vol. 15, no. 3, November.
Rosenberg, N. (1963b), 'Technological change in the machine tool industry, 1840–1910', *Journal of Economic History*, vol. XXIII, no. 4.
Rosenberg, N. (1969), 'The direction of technological change: inducement mechanisms and focusing devices', *Economic Development and Cultural Change*, vol. 18, no. 1, October.
Dos Santos, T. (1973), 'The crisis of development theory and the problem of dependence in Latin America', repr. in H. Bernstein (ed.), *Underdevelopment and Development* (Penguin).
Saul, S. B. (1967), 'The market and development of the mechanical engineering industries in Britain, 1860–1914', *Economic History Review*, 2nd series, vol. XX.
Schumacher, E. F. (1973), *Small is Beautiful* (Blond).
Sen, A. K. (1960), *Choice of Techniques* (Blackwell).
Singer, H. (1952), 'The mechanics of economic development', *Indian Economic Review*, vol. 1, no. 2, August.
Singer, H. (1954), 'Problems of industrialisation of under-developed countries', *International Social Scientists' Bulletin*, vol. 6.
Stewart, F. (1972), 'Choice of technique in developing countries', *Journal of Development Studies*, October.
Stewart, F. (1974), 'Technology and employment in LDCs', *World Development*, vol. 2, no. 3, March.
Strassman, W. P. (1959), 'Interrelated industries and the rate of technological change', *Review of Economic Studies*, vol. 27.
UNIDO (1972), *Guidelines for Project Evaluation* (New York).
Wilber, C. K. (1969), *The Soviet Model and Underdeveloped Countries* (University of North Carolina Press).

Reading 25

Small Industry in Underdeveloped Countries

B. F. Hoselitz

Journal of Economic History, vol. 19, 1959.

In historical studies of industrialization prominent attention is usually given to the development of large-scale industry, and whenever small industry is considered at all, it is usually introduced only as the starting point of, or a contrast to, large industrial enterprises. This concern with large industry also predominated in the earliest post-war discussions on the economic development of underdeveloped countries, and from this period stem the famous and often ridiculed schemes of giant steel plants and other large industrial establishments in little-advanced countries. During the last few years, however, the general climate of opinion has changed, and increasing attention has been paid to small-scale and even cottage industries. This has been especially pronounced in the countries of southern and south-eastern Asia, and is strongly supported by various studies and conferences of the Economic Commission on Asia and the Far East and other organizations associated with the United Nations operating in this part of the world.

Much of the literature resulting from this increased interest in cottage and small-scale industries deals with immediately practical questions relating to such problems as how to improve the design of products turned out by small industries; how to induce small industrialists to produce for export; how to provide more adequate credit for small industry; and how to fit the development of small industries more adequately in the large development plans of national governments. Yet all these proposals, narrow as they may be at times, are based ultimately on some more general theoretical propositions concerning the place and economic performance of small industries in the process of industrialization. I shall survey a few of these general propositions in the remainder of this paper, with the hope of arriving at a clearer understanding of the conditions under which small industries originate and survive in the process of industrialization in general and in the densely populated countries of southern and south-eastern Asia in particular.

What is a 'small-scale industry'? It is doubtful whether a definition can be arrived at which will apply with equal validity to the economically most advanced and the economically underdeveloped countries. A firm which in the United States would be regarded as 'small business' may nevertheless, in terms of fixed investment and employment of labor force, be of such size as to be a 'large-scale enterprise' in some countries of Asia. In order to avoid these difficulties which derive primarily from differences in industrial organization of countries at different levels of economic advancement, it is proposed that for the purposes of this paper all firms employing fewer than fifty persons be classified as small-scale industry. Firms employing fifty persons and more will then be considered medium- and large-scale plants. Within small industry, there is a further subgroup of minute or dwarf enterprises which provide employment for not more than five persons altogether, and which have a number of problems normally not shared by enterprises employing six persons and more. I shall designate these minute firms as 'dwarf industries' or 'handicraft shops'.

Using this distinction between dwarf industry, small industry and medium and large industry, I have presented in Table 1 some comparative cross-sectional and historical data on the shares of the total industrial labor force in plants of different size. Let us first examine the upper half of the table, which shows the share of workers in dwarf and small industries in various postwar years in several European countries. In general between 12 and 15 per cent of the labor force was engaged in handicrafts establishments and around 25 to 35 per cent in small industry. All establishments with a labor force below 50 workers employed roughly between 40 and 50 per cent of the total labor force in industry.' In other words, we find that in postwar European countries small industry plays as yet a rather important role, though its importance varies from one industry to another. In general the proportion of the labor force in small industry is significantly higher than the national average in the food processing, leather, construction, metal

Table 1 **Share of Industrial Labor Force (Including Mining and Construction) in Small and Dwarf Enterprises**

Country	Year	Total labor force	Per cent in firms with 1–5 workers	Per cent in firms with 6–49 workers	Per cent in firms with 1–49 workers
	1	2	3	4	5
1 Austria	1930	936,623	30.9	26.8	57.7
2 Austria	1954	1,166,358	13.4 (e)	28.1 (g)	41.5
3 Belgium	1947	1,189,291 (c)	8.1	27.2	35.3
4 France	1906	6,130,977	51.9	18.7	70.6
5 Norway	1953	428,455	14.1 (e)	37.2 (g)	51.3
6 Sweden (a)	1954	616,461 (c)	n.a. (i)	n.a. (i)	28.9
7 Switzerland	1955	1,143,735	12.6	31.1	43.7
8 Germany	1882	5,933,663	55.1	18.6	73.7
9 Germany	1895	8,000,503	39.9	23.8	63.2
10 Germany	1907	10,852,873	29.5	25.0	54.5
11 Germany	1925	12,704,135	22.3	22.8	45.1
12 Germany	1933	9,152,201	33.6	21.6	55.2
13 Germany (Fed. R.)	1950	8,884,458	15.2 (e)	28.4 (g)	43.6
14 Japan (b)	1920	4,565,230	55.6	14.5	70.1
15 Japan (b)	1930	4,432,530	52.9	17.1	70.0
16 Japan (b)	1939	4,950,881 (d)	23.5	29.1	52.6
17 Japan (b)	1955	5,516,928	10.0 (f)	40.6 (h)	50.6

Notes: (a) Industry and mining only.
(b) Industry only.
(c) Employees only, excluding self-employed and employers.
(d) Employers, self-employed and members of owner's family included in smallest size only; in all larger size firms employees only.
(e) Firms with 1–4 persons.
(f) Firms with 1–3 persons.
(g) Firms with 5 to 49 persons.
(h) Firms with 4 to 49 persons.
(i) Data not available.

fabrication and machinery industries, and significantly lower in textiles, mining, basic metal production, paper and chemical industries. In other words, the 'heavy' industries have, on the whole, considerably larger establishments than the 'light' industries.

Of even greater interest than the cross-national comparison of the relative share of small industry in the post-war labor force of European countries is its development over a long period. I have also assembled, mainly in the lower part of Table 1, some historical data: an estimate for France in 1906, two estimates for Austria in 1930 and 1954, and two series of estimates for Germany, stretching over almost seventy years and Japan covering thirty-five years. Let us examine these last two series in more detail. We find that in the earliest years for which data are available handicrafts or cottage industry provided for about half the persons active in industry and that this proportion declined – in Japan apparently more rapidly than in Germany – to somewhat above 10 per cent of the total industrial labor force. (The figure for Japan for 1955 is exactly 10 per cent, but this is doubtless due to the fact that the most recent Japanese statistics make a breaking point for firms employing not more than three, rather than not more than five persons.) In other words, cottage and handicraft industries show a definite and constant decline, and though they do not entirely disappear, they tend to become a rather insignificant sector of industrial production. The same trend as that exhibited in Japan and Germany is also shown by the Austrian series.

While the declining trend in handicraft and cottage industries is clearly marked, the small industries show at first a rise in their relative importance, and later a surprising stability. In Germany and Austria they continue to employ between a fifth and a fourth of the industrial labor force, whereas in Japan they employ in the later period between a third and two-fifths of this labor force. If we combine the two size classes, we find that the labor force in industrial enterprises with less than fifty workers tends to decline from around 70 per cent to between 40 and 50 per cent in recent years. In this connexion the figures for France in 1906 appear to be instructive, for this country in its industrial labor force distribution approaches a situation approximated by Germany almost twenty-five years earlier, and similar to that of Japan in 1930.

How can we explain the trends suggested by these figures? In particular, how can we explain the relatively larger share of small industry in Japan as compared with European countries at a time when its cottage industry has declined to a significance commensurate with that of Europe? Finally, what do the trends exhibited by these figures, and notably the development for Japan, suggest for the place of cottage and small industries in the underdeveloped countries of south and southeast Asia?

It is probably not necessary to comment on the rapid decline of handicraft and cottage industries. These industries have been unable to withstand the competition of larger, normally more mechanized establishments and hence have been able to maintain themselves only in a few branches in which either special skills, usually of an artistic nature, or special customer services (as in repair services or custom-made commodities), are important. It is the decline of handicrafts and cottage industries that accounts primarily for the decline of the share of the industrial labor force in enterprises providing work for less than fifty persons. In part this decline may also be attributed to the general shift in the composition of industrial output in countries experiencing economic development. This shift has been described by Hoffmann (1931, pp. 134–58) who has shown that there is a gradual secular decline in the share of consumers' goods (light) industries and an increase in producers' goods (heavy) industries. And, as already stated, the relative significance of small industry is substantially greater in the light than in the heavy industries.

Of greater interest than the explanation of the reasons for the decline of dwarf industries, is the divergent development of small industry, employing six to forty-nine persons, in Germany and in Japan. In Germany the proportion of the labor force in small industry increased from 18.6 per cent in 1882 to 25 per cent in 1907, and thereafter began to decline, falling to almost 20 per cent in the late 1930s. Our figure for 1950 shows again an increase of the share of small industry to 28.4 per cent. But 1950 was surely not a typical year. German industrial production was still badly disorganized from the war and the postwar inflation, and many large industries were operating at less than full capacity. Unfortunately we do not have comparable data for a later year in Germany. For although there has been an industrial census in 1956 which showed that 12.3 per cent of the industrial labor force was employed in establishments with less than fifty persons (see Statistisches Bundesamt, 1958, p. 182), this figure is not comparable with earlier data, since all establishments designated as handicrafts (*Handwerk*), were omitted from the 1956 census though included in earlier German censuses of manufactures. Considering the overall employment in handicraft shops in postwar western Germany, we may assume that again approximately 20 per cent or perhaps even a little less of the total industrial labor force were engaged in establishments with six to forty-nine workers.

In Japan, however, the share of the industrial labor force in small firms had risen to over 40 per cent in 1955. Students of the Japanese economy agree that small industry is likely to maintain a place of importance for some time to come (see Reubens, 1947, p. 601, and Kyokai, 1957). The strength of the small Japanese industries is also confirmed by the fact that whereas the total number of employees in Japanese industry increased by 29.5 per cent between 1950 and 1955, employment in firms with over 200 operatives increased by only 17.9 per cent, and employment in firms with four to forty-nine persons increased by 33.4 per cent (Economic Planning Board, 1957, p. 207). In other words, Japanese industry shows the rather unusual feature of smaller plants growing faster than large ones in a period of rising economic prosperity. Such a development has taken place in European countries only in periods of depression, as is evidenced by comparison of the German figures for 1925 and 1933.

Both Marxian and non-Marxian economists in Japan have put forward explanations for the vigor of small industry in Japan. The former attribute it to the only half-accomplished bourgeois revolution under the Meiji and the latter to the lack of a stable, large and uniform demand for many commodities turned out by Japanese industry which makes investment in large-scale plant and machinery too risky. Neither explanation appears satisfactory. The former is merely an unthinking application of some Marxian concepts, the latter stresses only one of the conditions favoring the existence of small industry, but does not explain its growing strength and importance. The indispensable feature in Japanese society, which made the continued survival of small industry possible, is a characteristic of Japanese social structure which may well be regarded as a survival from a pre-industrial era. This feature which has become fully adjusted to industrial society is the *oyabun-kibun*, or, as it has also been called, the boss-henchman system. We have two excellent descriptions of how this system works, one dealing with the iron foundry industry and the other with the lumber industry (see Pelzel, 1954, pp. 79–93, and Bennett, 1958, pp. 13–30). The system is based upon the central position occupied by a person who performs all the co-ordinating functions for the many smaller entrepreneurs in a given industry in any one place. He supplies raw materials, he mediates credit, he takes care of the marketing channels and he allocates orders among the various small firms. The Marxian interpreters of Japanese capitalism have, of course, observed this form of industrial organization and, as they labor under the compulsion of describing all phenomena in terms of Marxian categories, they describe it variously as a form of putting-out system or the survival of commercial capitalism which intervenes between genuine large-scale industrial capitalism and the small industrialist (see Fujita, 1957, pp. 127–8). The position of these local bosses in a number of industrial lines has led to a sharp regional concentration of certain small industries and the system of interdependence among small firms has become highly elaborate. This may be illustrated by the bicycle industry in Sakei City, near Osaka, where different small manufacturers each producing a different part of bicycles, such as handlebars, wheelrims, hubs, spokes, etc., interact to supply producers of the finished commodity (see Minoguchi, 1957, pp. 147–8, who also describes a similar situation for the sewing machine industry on p. 148).

Ultimately the integration of small industry into the overall process of industrial production of Japan depends upon sub-contracting. The middlemen who boss the small industrialists are, in turn, dependent upon larger enterprises who often maintain the same boss-henchmen relationship with regard to these middlemen as the latter *vis-à-vis* their 'clients'. Thus the survival of small industry in Japan is the outcome of a highly complex and hierarchical social structure within industrial production, and presents a feature of industrial organization which is probably not approximated in any western country (see Hatton, 1959, p. 349). We must bear in mind this socio-structural peculiarity of Japanese industrial organization, since it appears to be unique not only with reference to western countries, but also with reference to other Asian countries which share one additional aspect with Japan which tends to favor small industry: the high density of population, and especially the large proportion of densely settled agricultural areas.

This relative distribution of productive factors, sometimes designated as the man—and ratio, is represented more accurately by the relative ratio of human to non-human resources available for production. It appears to be the chief 'natural' factor responsible for the ubiquity of small industry in Japan and other Asian countries which show similar population densities. Small industry is usually much more labor-intensive than large industry. In addition, incremental capital coefficients appear to be somewhat lower in small than in large enterprises. In view, therefore, of the relative abundance of labor and the relative scarcity of capital, a smaller size of the average industrial enterprise than that found in the more advanced western countries appears to correspond quite adequately to the relative factor scarcities characteristic of the densely populated countries of Asia. The small industrial enterprises, moreover, have lower average wage costs than large enterprises, a factor which in view of the relatively high labor-intensity of Asian industry is an important factor influencing costs of production (see Hoselitz, 1957, pp. 131–3). Finally costs of production in small enterprises in most Asian countries are lower because various welfare expenses, which are imposed by law on firms employing more than a certain minimum number of persons, do not apply to them. All these factors jointly tend to make small enterprises attractive in an environment in which the supply of labor is large and, within a wide range, almost perfectly elastic.

The establishment of small industries in newly developing countries results in creating a manufacturing sector which, in terms of wages, productivity of labor and capital structure, is divided into two branches. One branch encompasses the large modern factory establishments, and the other embraces small plants often using highly labor-intensive methods and exhibiting a level of productivity which stands in sharp contrast to that of large industry. It is very difficult to adduce precise quantitative data for these differences, because the statistical study of the economic conditions of small industries in many little developed countries is very poor. Hence we must make the most of the very few figures which have become available.

In a recent essay, Simon Kuznets (1957) has developed a procedure for inter-sectoral comparison of productivity per worker. Kuznets was interested in developing a yardstick, rough as it had to be considering the rather inadequate refinement of available data, to compare product per worker in agricultural and non-agricultural branches of production in a large number of countries. I have used the same procedure to construct Table 2. Kuznets' method and possible inaccuracies resulting from the inadequacy of raw data have been described by him in detail, and the findings presented here are subject to approximately the same degree of error as those presented by him for the larger sectors (see Kuznets, 1957, pp. 32 ff).

The entries in Table 2 are based on the assumption that if productivity in all branches of industry is approximately equal, all figures should be equal to or near unity. For assuming that the proportion of total output of small industry is, say, 30 per cent, and the proportion of the labor force in small industry, say 50 per cent, product per worker equals 0.60 of the industry-wide product per worker (that is, 30/50). If in the same country large industry produces 70 per cent of total output and employs 50 per cent of the labor force, per worker product in large industry is 1.4 times the industry-wide product per worker. It also follows that product per worker in small industry is 0.6/1.4 or 0.43 times the product per worker in large industry. In other words, product per worker in small industry is less than half the product per worker in large industry.

Table 2 presents data for two countries, Japan and Norway. The first three columns of the table show relative productivity per worker in small and large industry ('large industry' is defined, for purposes of this table, as consisting of plants with fifty workers and more), and the last three columns of the table present corresponding data from Kuznets showing the relative productivity per man in the agricultural and non-agricultural sectors. A comparison of the first three and last three columns of this table shows that small industry in the two countries is closer in terms of productivity of

Table 2 **Labor Productivity in Industry and Agriculture, Japan and Norway, Post-War Years**

Country		*Year*	*Small industry (1–49 workers) (S)*	*Large industry (50+ workers) (L)*	*S / L*	*Agriculture (A)*	*Non-agricultural production (non-A)*	*A / non-A*
			1	2	3	4	5	6
Japan	(a)	1950	0.62	1.37	0.45	0.50	1.47	0.34
	(b)	1950				0.85	1.06	0.80
Norway	(a)	1950/52	0.77	1.24	0.62	0.58	1.15	0.50
	(b)	1950/52				0.66	1.10	0.60

Notes: (a) Including unpaid family members.
(b) Excluding unpaid family workers.

labor to agriculture than to the non-agricultural sector of the economy. (In both Norway and Japan productivity per worker in service industries is virtually equal to productivity per worker in manufacturing, so that we may use average productivity of labor in manufacturing as representative of productivity in the entire non-agricultural sector.)

The fact that productivity in agriculture is lower than in industry and services is not surprising. But it has also been found that the ratio in productivity between agriculture and non-agricultural production tends to narrow as *per capita* national product increases. In other words, in the wealthier countries, productivity in agriculture and in non-agricultural production is closer to the national average than in poorer countries. Moreover, the tendency of greater disparity in productivity between agriculture and non-agricultural production with falling *per capita* income is enhanced if unpaid family members are included in the labor force. This again is not unexpected, for it is well known that especially in the poorer countries a relatively larger proportion of unpaid family members are active in farming than in industry or services.

The differences in productivity between large and small industry may be subjected to analogous reasoning. Unpaid family labor is more important in small handicraft shops than in large industrial establishments. Moreover, as *per capita* income rises technological procedures in smaller enterprises tend to become more mechanized and the great gap in technology so characteristic between large and small plants in underdeveloped countries becomes less visible. How wide the disparities in labor productivity may be in an underdeveloped country is shown by some rather crude figures which I have computed from various published and unpublished Indian sources. According to these computations productivity per worker in the small cottage industries was 0.18, or less than one-fifth, of that in large-scale factory industry. This discrepancy is considerably greater than that between the agricultural and non-agricultural sectors as whole, since productivity in the former was somewhat more than two-fifths (0.42) of productivity per worker in the latter (Kuznets, 1957, p. 97).

These facts appear to constitute a serious indictment against small industry as one of the avenues of economic development in the poor, densely populated countries of Asia. If small industry is not more productive than agriculture, a shift of the working population from agriculture to small industry may produce the appearance of more employment, but does not constitute a shift from a less productive to a significantly more productive form of work. Yet, there are a number of advantages in small industry which are hidden by the gross, all-embracing figures that were presented on the basis of published statistics in Table 2. The explanation for the low average productivity of small industry in underdeveloped countries is the heavy weight exerted by cottage enterprises and dwarf establishments in these averages. These firms are usually not mechanized, they use simple hand tools comparable to the primitive ploughs and yokes of the peasant, they produce often only intermittently, and a large proportion of their output is of poor quality and indifferent workmanship.

A significant step forward is achieved when the small cottage or handicraft shop becomes mechanized and expands its work force above the size of the dwarf firm of four or five operatives. From this point on expansion of the enterprise towards medium size is possible, though in this situation the availability of entrepreneurial talent and capital for investment in expansion of plant takes on strategic importance. It is not easy to bring to bear valid evidence for the superiority of small mechanized plants over the minute handicraft establishments, since empirical investigations are almost unavailable. I know of only one study, recently completed in Delhi, which presents reliable data on the comparative economic performance of dwarf and somewhat larger establishments in several industries (see Dhar, 1958). On the basis of this study, which bears careful examination by anyone interested in the economics of small-scale production, two facts are particularly noteworthy. If we measure productivity by the net value added per worker, we find that out of eleven industries in which there are comparable figures for small units (employing up to nine workers) and larger units (employing more than ten but not more than nineteen workers), seven industries show greater value added per worker in the larger than in the smaller units. In some cases the differences are considerable, for example, in flour milling value added per worker in the larger establishments is Rs. 3302 per year as against Rs. 857 in the smaller plants. The corresponding figures for leather footwear production are Rs. 3367 as against Rs. 954, and for electrical goods manufacture Rs. 3787 as against Rs. 650. However, in four industries, printing, manufacture of soap, of drugs and foundries, value added per worker is higher in the small than in the bigger firms. This finding appears to point to the fact that in these industries – at least under Indian conditions – economies of scale require a plant size above twenty workers. A further point presented by Dhar which appears to support the proposition of the superiority of larger mechanized as against the smaller handicraft units, is a comparison of net surplus per worker in the two classes of establishments. In the smaller, non-power using plants the average annual surplus per worker is Rs. 492; in the larger, mechanized plants it is Rs. 828 (Dhar, 1958, pp. 77–81). Differences in productivity between dwarf and small industry are also found in Japan and Norway. For whereas in 1950 in Japan small firms (that is, firms employing between four and forty-nine persons) had a labor productivity equal to 0.66 of the total industrial average, the productivity in dwarf firms was only 0.33 of the industrial average. In other words, productivity in dwarf firms was half of that in small firms. The corresponding figures for Norway, for 1953, are: productivity in small firms (employing five to forty-nine persons) 0.89 of industrial average, and in dwarf firms (employing four persons and less) 0.46 of that average. Hence here also productivity in dwarf firms was approximately half that of small firms.

This discussion suggests that the crucial step in the industrialization process in underdeveloped countries is the attainment of a plant size exceeding that characteristic of the dwarf enterprise. We note also, if we consider the data for Germany presented in Table 3, that the process of economic development was accompanied by a diminution of the number of minute handicrafts firms, and an increase of the number of establishments in the small industry class. A similar pattern is discernible in post-war Japan, though, if we consult annual data, there is some uncertainty about the decline of dwarf establishments, which show some irregularity in behavior.

We cannot conclude from these statistics that dwarf firms were transformed into larger firms, though this process has doubtless taken place. Clearly the small cottage and handicraft establishments are exceedingly vulnerable and many of them have disappeared altogether in the course of time. Yet a sizeable number of these small handicraft shops did develop into small- and medium-sized factories, and this process appears to be of special importance in underdeveloped countries. Though it is well known that in the course of European industrial development the participation of craftsmen was significant, and in some industries, indeed, indispensable, we know little about the actual relative weight which may be assigned to the gradual evolution of small handicrafts shops into medium and ultimately large plants. We have some biographical data on early industrialists who started out as artisans or craftsmen. For example, the first manufacturer of machines in Westphalia, Franz Dinnendahl, started as a carpenter and machine mechanic, and the first four machine manufacturers of Berlin also started as artisans. F. A. J. Egells was a locksmith, August Borsig a carpenter, Freund a mechanic and Wöhlert a cabinet-maker. Other manufacturers of machines also started as craftsmen, as, for example, Richard Hartmann of Chemnitz who began as a smith and set up a small shop in 1837 employing three persons. His factory, at his death in 1878, employed some three thousand persons (see Witt, 1929, pp. 13–15).

It is not a mere accident that all these men founded industrial establishments in the machinery industry, for in such industries as textiles, mining, and the production of crude metals, merchants or bankers were much more prominent in the earlier stages. The machine industries, as against textiles, for example, required a high degree of technical skill, and it is this skill element which has made it possible even today for many more smaller enterprises to maintain themselves by the side of much

Table 3 **Number of Enterprises and Change in Number of Enterprises of Different Sizes in Germany and Japan**

	Country	*Years*	*Number of dwarf establishments (a)*	*Number of small establishments (b)*
			1	**2**
1	Germany	1895	1,989,572	139,459
2		1907	1,870,261	187,074
3		1925	1,614,069	205,909
4	Changes (c)	1895–1907	– 119,311 (– 6.4)	47,615 (34.1)
5		1907–25	– 256,192 (– 13.7)	18,835 (10.1)
6	Japan	1947	2,802,043	410,641
7		1954	2,634,046	584,633
8	Changes (c)	1947–54	– 167,997 (– 6.0)	173,633 (42.6)

Notes: (a) Dwarf enterprises for Germany include those employing one to five persons, for Japan, those employing one to four persons.
(b) Small enterprises for Germany include those employing six to forty-nine persons, for Japan, those employing five to twenty-nine persons.
(c) Figures in parentheses are percentages.

larger ones. We find, in general, that the proportion of craftsmen who founded small (and potentially growing) enterprises is larger in those industries in which the skill element plays an important role than in those in which organizational talent or skill in marketing or financial sophistication is of greater significance. For example, a recent study conducted in the region around Izmir in Turkey shows that whereas in the textile industry 62.2 per cent of the plants were founded by merchants and 29.7 per cent by craftsmen, in the production of metal, wood, rubber and leather products, 59.7 per cent of the enterprises were founded by craftsmen and only 37.1 by merchants (Alexander, 1960, p. 5).

Similar conclusions can be drawn from a study in another underdeveloped country, India. James J. Berna undertook a detailed study on the occupational background of the founders of fifty-two enterprises in the light-engineering industry in Madras State. Of these enterprises fifteen were founded by merchants, twelve by engineers, and eleven by artisans and craftsmen. The remaining firms were founded by men of miscellaneous backgrounds. Here again the role of craftsmen is far from negligible (Berna, 1959, pp. 348–53). Finally, we may mention another study in north India, in which also a detailed analysis of small-scale industrialists in the light-engineering industry was undertaken. Here a clear predominance of the craftsmen-entrepreneurs was found. Seven out of the ten firms studied were owned by highly skilled craftsmen themselves and the other three depended upon the close relationship between the owner (who was usually a merchant) and a craftsman actually in charge of operations (McCrory, 1956, pp. 6–9).

But regardless of whether the establishments were owned by a craftsman or a person from some other occupational background, they all faced the same problem: shortage of working capital and virtual absence of reserves. McCrory lists the reasons why these small craftsmen entrepreneurs grow: they have a long-term outlook, and a high capacity to save; they live frugally and plough back all earnings into more fixed equipment and machinery; finally they are more skilled than workers in competing large plants and they probably work harder and longer hours than the average industrial employee in India. But for all these assets, which sound like a reiteration of the Puritan virtues, these enterprises remain at the brink of disaster because there is no adequate organization of integrating their productive efforts into the overall industrial picture of India. Like their Japanese counterparts, these firms do not have access to the regular loan market. They are too new, too small, and insufficiently rationalized in their operations to constitute viable risks which a banker would be willing to consider. They depend, like their Japanese counterparts, on sub-contracts with larger firms or upon marketing their total output through a wholesaler. But unlike conditions in Japan this relationship is not based on a quasi-kinship relation, but rather like the European putting-out system, on the exploitation of the weaker by the stronger partner in this bargain. The Indian middleman is not interested in his small industrialist client, since if this client should fail he hopes to find another in his place. Moreover, the internal integration among small producers, which has been developed in Japan so admirably and which makes possible the coordinated production of a bicycle or a sewing machine by many independent small producers working side by side, is absent in India. The small Indian industrialist is fully exposed to the 'fresh winds of competition', but these winds sometimes take on the strength of a gale, and then the small producer has difficulty in remaining in his place and must use all his ingenuity and force to keep from being blown away.

In spite of this instability, we find in India, as elsewhere, small establishments which prosper from the very start and grow almost continuously. McCrory himself writes of a manufacturer who started in 1948 with savings of Rs. 300 to make fountain pens. At the time this craftsman was interviewed, his labor force had risen to seven, and he had accumulated not only a sizeable amount of machinery, but also a three-months' inventory of finished goods. To be sure that enterprise was not a proven success, but it had considerable chance not only of surviving but of growing vigorously (McCrory, 1956, pp. 53–67). A similar case study is reported from Beirut in the chocolate and candy manufacturing industry. Here again the owner was a former craftsman, a confectioner. After trying to start an independent enterprise with friends who supplied the capital, and which failed because of resulting disagreements, the founder left the company and sold out his interest. He traveled to Europe to study modern methods of confectionery production and with this new knowledge he returned to Beirut. Here is the rest of the story in the words of its author:

> Back in Lebanon he needed funds and found he could secure none from the banking world. An old friend of his in the confectionery trade put his small savings at his disposal and agreed to provide him with an outlet for the products through his own network. The new firm was founded with a capital of only £L.150,000, which was enough to purchase an old chocolate factory. . . . Every attempt was made to save money; instead of buying a cutting machine for £L.5,000, for instance, one was put together with the help of a mechanic from scrap iron tools. . . . The old factory, typical of the majority of small factories in the country, was filthy with the grime of years. It was thoroughly scoured. Wooden floors and ceilings were added to utilize every inch of space. The old machines were cleaned and repaired, and production began. Daily output was 350 kg. . . . Revenue was coming in. New machines were ordered on the instalment plan . . . within six months daily output was 600 kg. Three months later it was one ton and by the end of 1956 it had reached 1.2 tons. . . . (Mills, 1958, pp. 97–9).

Success stories like these have been reported from every underdeveloped country. But the reason why they are told and retold is because they are rather rare. Given the needs for industrialization which are felt in the poor countries of Asia and the Middle East, too many small firms fail and too few prosper. It is not the fact of vulnerability as such which is characteristic of dwarf and small enterprise in underdeveloped countries, but the high incidence of failure, as compared with European countries or Japan. This is also the reason why numerous proposals for some form of cooperation among small industries have been made. It is expected that in this way a higher degree of stability and a better chance for the survival and growth of these establishments can be assured.

Time does not permit an extensive discussion of the various proposals made in south Asia in support of small industry. One fairly ingenious scheme has been outlined by Dey (1955). It consists essentially in an application of the theory of the 'big push' to small industries within a rather narrowly circumscribed local area. Dey finds that the main disadvantage under which small industries labor is the uncertainty and general insufficiency of effective demand. He proposes that a clearing house be set up at which persons within a village or group of villages register their demand for manufactured goods and the objects they can supply. It is then up to the administrators of the clearing center, which functions in the form of a co-operative of the participating artisans, to adjust incoming supplies of produced commodities to the demands registered by the participants in this scheme. As a method of widening somewhat the market for rural artisans this approach may have some advantages, as, indeed, has been shown by Dey. but it is not likely to bring about a genuine transformation of these small rural handicrafts producers into small industrialists. For although the insufficiency of demand is an important factor impeding the growth of industry, the absence of improved techniques, deficiencies of entrepreneurship, and, above all, the lack of capital will hold back industrial development, even if demand is abundant.

In this context the experience of Japanese small industry is instructive. Several teams of experts from the countries of southern and south-eastern Asia have visited Japan and studied her small industry.They have given attention to production techniques, methods of design, management practices, and sundry other problems concentrating upon the single enterprise, but they have for the most part failed to study the social organization of the small manufacturing industries of Japan. It is possible that a form of cooperative organization may be worked out for the small industries of underdeveloped countries which simulates some of the features of the Japanese model. But, unless some form of organization of small industries analogous to that of Japan is developed, the advantages of costs of production and low capital coefficients of small industries may be lost because of the higher costs of co-ordination, marketing and provision of supplies.

In short, the crucial feature of small industry in the underdeveloped countries of Asia and Africa is that it is an integrated sector of the economy as a whole, rather than a bundle of individual enterprises each with its own resources and prospects. Whereas in the course of economic growth of the western countries small establishments could fit themselves into the interstices which were left unexploited by larger enterprises (either by intention or default), the bulk of small enterprises in the poor countries of Asia are much less capable of doing this. In many industrial fields, but especially in light industry, the alternative for Asian countries is to have an elaborate and well integrated network of small producers or an indefinite survival of uneconomic cottage industries. But in the former case, it is likely that small industry will continue to employ a substantially larger proportion of the industrial labor force probably for a longer time than has been the case in western Europe. We have seen that even here small establishments have been tenacious, especially in some industries, but they have ultimately tended to decline just at the time when productivity in small industry tended to catch up with that in medium and large industry. In Asia the fate of small industry is likely to be different. The share of the industrial labor force in small industry will continue for long to be large, and productivity will for a considerable time be substantially below the industrial average. In other words, small industries will occupy a position between peasant agriculture and modern large industry. Yet if countries like India or Indonesia can reach an industrial plateau commensurate with that of post-war Japan, they will have made a giant step forward.

Note: Reading 25

1 As can be seen from Table 1, the only two countries which do not fall in this class in recent years are Belgium and Sweden.

References: Reading 25

Alexander, A. P. (1960), 'Industrial entrepreneurship in Turkey: origins and growth', *Economic Development and Cultural Change*, July.

Bennett, J. W. (1958), 'Economic aspects of a boss-henchman system in the Japanese forestry industry', *Economic Development and Cultural Change*, vol. 7, October.

Berna, J. J. and S. J. (1959), 'Patterns of entrepreneurship in south India', *Economic Development and Cultural Change*, vol. 7, April.

Bernstein, E. (1899), *Die Voraussetzungen, des Sozialismus und die Aufgeben der Sozialdemodratie* (J. H. W. Dietz Verlag).

Dey, S. K. (1955), *Industrial Development: A New Approach* (Thacker Spink).

Dhar, P. N. (1958), *Small-Scale Industries in Delhi* (Asia Publishing House).

Economic Planning Board (1957), 'Statistical analysis of medium and small enterprises in Japan', *Asian Affairs*, vol. 2, June.

Fujita, K. (1957), 'Management structure of small and medium enterprises', *Asian Affairs*, vol. 2, June.

Gerschenkron, A. (1953), 'Social attitudes, entrepreneurship and economic development', *Explorations in Entrepreneurial History*, vol. 6, October.

Hatton, C. S. (1959), *The Position of Small Industry in Japan*, cited in Henry Rosovsky, 'Japanese capital formation 1868–1940', unpublished doctoral dissertation, Harvard University.

Hoffmann, W. (1931), *Stadien und Typen der Industrialisierung* (Verlag Gustav Fischer).

Hoselitz, B. F. (1957), 'Population pressure, industrialization and social mobility', *Population Studies*, vol. 11, November.

Kautsky, K. (1899), *Bernstein und das Sozialdemokratische Programm* (D. H. W. Dietz Verlag).

Koyodai, A. (1957), *The Smaller Industry in Japan* (Tokyo).

Kuznets, S. (1957), 'Quantitative aspects of the economic growth of nations; 2: Industrial distribution of national product and labour force', *Economic Development and Cultural change*, vol. 5, no. 4, suppl.

Landes, D. (1954), ' "Social attitudes, entrepreneurship and economic development": a comment', *Explorations in Entrepreneurial History*, vol. 6, May.

McCrory, J. T. (1956), *Small Industry in a North Indian Town* (Government of India Press).

Mills, A. E. (1958), 'Private enterprise in Lebanon', unpublished dissertation, University of London.

Ministère des Affaires Economiques (1957), Annaire Statistique de la Belgique et du Congo Belge, 1957 (Institut National de Statistique, Brussels).

Minoguchi, T. (1957), 'Productivity and wage problem of Japan's medium and small manufacturing enterprises', *Asian Affairs*, vol. 2, June.

Niyogi, S. P. (1956), 'A study of the west Bengal village exchange scheme', paper read at 39th Annual Conference of the Indian Economic Association.

Pelzel, J. (1954), 'The small industrialists in Japan', *Explorations in Entrepreneurial History*, vol. 7, December.

Reubens, E. L. (1947), 'Small-scale industry in Japan', *Q.J. Econs.*, vol. 61, no. 4.

Sombart, W. (1913), *Die deutsche Volkwirtschaft im XIX. Jahrhundert*, 9th edn (Georg Bondi).

Statistisches Amt (1898), *Statistik für das Deutsche Reich*, CXIII (Puttkammer & Mühlbrecht).

Statistisches Amt (1910), *Statistisches Jahrbuch für das Deutsche Reich, 1910* (Puttkrammer & Mühlbrecht).

Statistisches Amt (1957), *Statistisches Jahrbuch der Schweiz* (Verlag Birkhäuser).

Statistisches Bundesamt (1952), *Die nichtlandwirtschaftlichen Arbeitsstäten in der Bundesrepublik Deutschland nach der Zählung vom 13.IX.1950* (W. Kohlhammer).

Statistisches Bundesamt (1958), *Statistisches Jahrbuch für die Bundesrepublik Deutschland, 1958* (W. Kohlhammer).

Statistisches Reichsamt (1931), *Statistisches Jahrbuch für das Deutsche Reich, 1931* (Reimer Höbbing).

Statistisches Reichsant (1938), *Statistisches Jahrbuch für das Deutsche Reich, 1938* (Verlag Paul Schmidt).

Statistisches Zentralamt (1958), *Statistisches Handbuch für die Republik Oesterreich, 1958* (Staatsdruckerei, Vienna).

Statistiska Centralbryån (1957), *Statistisk Årsbok för Sverige* (Statistiska Centralbryån, Stockholm).

Statistisk Sentralbyrå (1958), *Statistisk Årbok for Norge* (Statistisk Sentralbyrå, Oslo).

Uyeda, T. (1939), *The Small Industries of Japan* (Kelley & Walsh).

Witt, H. (1929), 'Die Triebkräfte des industriellen Unternehmertums vor 100 Jahren und heute', unpublished dissertation, University of Hamburg.

Part Five

Investment Choice and Project Appraisal

Some of the most interesting theoretical discussion in development economics has centred on the theory of the choice of technique and capital intensity and more recently on the theoretical framework for project choice. Sen (Reading 26) summarises and expands upon some of the former discussion, while Joshi (Reading 28) produces a careful and systematic exposition of the more recent Little–Mirrlees approach. Because of the difficulty which students have with some of the complexities of the latter, it was thought worth while to include also the excellent short 'layman's guide' to Little Mirlees provided by Baldwin (Reading 27). Going on to specific components of project appraisal, the Readings by Thirlwall (Reading 29) and Balassa-Schdlowsky (Reading 30) elucidate the complicated concepts of the shadow price of labour and of foreign exchange, respectively.

Reading 26

Some Notes on the Choice of Capital-Intensity in Development Planning

A. K. Sen

Quarterly Journal of Economics, 1957, pp. 561–84.

1

The criteria for choosing between techniques of production for an underdeveloped economy that have so far been explicitly put forward can, I think, be classified into three groups. We shall examine them one by one, at the end of which an alternative suggestion will be put forward as a fourth criterion.

A *The Rate-of-turnover criterion*

Professor J. J. Polak, while discussing the investment criteria of countries reconstructing after the war, suggested that investment for development should be chosen according to the rate of turnover, i.e. the ratio of output to capital.[1] Along with a few other considerations, like the exporting possibility of the goods produced, a high output to capital ratio was made the basis for selection. The same suggestion was put forward also by Professor Norman S. Buchanan. 'If investment funds are limited, the wise policy, in the absence of special considerations, would be to undertake first those investments having a high value of annual product relative to the investment necessary to bring them into existence.'[2]

That this criterion is very imperfect as a general guide to policy is not difficult to realize. For one thing, a high rate of turnover may be associated with a high rate of depreciation and the rate of *net* output may not necessarily be high. But this difficulty can be avoided to some extent by stating the criterion in terms of the *net* rate of turnover, which is how it is actually put in most cases. The main defect of the theory is that it ignores the cost of employing labor in operating the capital. When the cost of employing labor in an economy is zero, a very good case can be made for the criterion of maximum addition to net output from a given amount of capital investment. If, on the other hand, employment of labor involves some cost to society, we have to take that into account.[3]

B *The 'social marginal productivity' criterion*

From what we have said in the last paragraph it is just one step to arrive at the social marginal productivity criterion as put forward by Professor A. E. Kahn.[4] It is suggested that from the addition to output due to the investment, the alternative output sacrificed as a result of drawing factors of production from other fields into this one has to be subtracted. Thus the factors are valued at their social opportunity cost, i.e. at what they could have produced in other fields had they not been drawn into the investment under examination. This criterion would lead to a different result from that of the rate-of-turnover approach, so long as the social opportunity cost of labor is positive. When, however, there is large-scale unemployment, the opportunity cost of labor is nil, and thus labor becomes according to this approach costless. Ignoring factors other than labor, now there is no need for any subtraction and we find Kahn arguing that in this case the Polak–Buchanan criterion is 'particularly desirable'.[5] Thus in an economy of this sort Kahn recommends the technique with the least capital coefficient, i.e. with the maximum rate of turnover.

Professor W. A. Lewis also puts forward a similar view when discussing the question. 'Special care', he argues, 'has to be taken in those countries which have a large surplus of unskilled labour, for in such circumstances money wages will not reflect the real social cost of using labour. In these circumstances capital is not productive if it is used to do what labour could do equally well; given the level of wages such investments may be highly profitable to capitalists, but they are unprofitable to the community as a whole since they add to unemployment but not to output.'[6] 'It is then [when there is surplus labour] arguable that the real cost of using labour in cottage industry is zero, whereas factory production uses scarce capital and supervisory skills.'[7]

In assessing this criterion, I think, we have to start by asking what it is that we are trying to achieve. If we are trying to maximize immediate output, labor should be valued according to its social opportunity cost and the above criterion seems quite appropriate. If, however, we are interested in the future as well, we have to look at the *rate of growth* of income governed by the accumulation of capital. And there is no reason to believe that the maximum rate of output would also give us the maximum rate of excess of production over current consumption, when employment is a variable. Here even if the alternative social product is nil, the cost of labor will be positive, given by the increase in consumption due to extra employment. Thus the social marginal productivity criterion is all right if we are not interested in the future at all. But if we take a long-term point of view, the criterion need no longer be valid.[8]

C The reinvestment criterion

W. Galenson and H. Leibenstein christened their criterion as that of 'marginal per capita reinvestment quotient'.[9] For clarification of what it means, we may quote the authors:

'To secure a clear notion of what is meant by the marginal *per capita* reinvestment quotient we must consider the basic factors involved in its determination. Briefly stated, the seven basic factors are as follows: (1) gross productivity per worker; (2) "wage" goods consumed per worker; (3) replacement and repair of capital; (4) increments in output as a result of noncapital using innovations such as improvements in skill, health, energy, discipline and malleability of the labor force; (5) declines in mortality; (6) declines in fertility; and (7) direction of reinvestment.'[10]

Galenson and Leibenstein provide the criterion with somewhat more manageable dimensions when they discuss the growth of employment. It is clear that what the authors are interested in, briefly stated, is the flow of net investment that is created by a unit of investment today. From the formula on page 357, the rate of reinvestment is found to be equated to

$$r = \frac{p - ew}{c},$$

where p = output (presumably *net* output) per machine;
e = the number of workers per machine;
w = real wage rate;
c = cost per machine.

This actually turns out to be not much different from the capitalist's rate-of-profit criterion. This coincidence is easy to explain. If the whole of the profit is reinvested[11] and the whole of the wages consumed, the rate of profit and the rate of reinvestment must come to the same thing.

Professor K. N. Raj of the Delhi School of Economics puts forward a similar criterion.[12] But since he considers specifically the case of a change from cottage industrial to factory production, he draws our attention to the necessity of subsidizing those who become jobless due to technological change. Thus he regards the cost of maintaining the new unemployed as part of the total costs. This makes his criterion less favorable to more mechanized production than the Galenson–Leibenstein criterion. This criterion is applicable, given its value judgment, to the case where less mechanized production is being *replaced* by more mechanized production. It would, however, be very difficult to apply when we are contemplating *initiation* of production and wondering whether to make it more or less capital-intensive. In those cases, I think, it would be nearly impossible to separate out, from the pool of the jobless people, those who would have been employed had a less mechanized production technique been chosen.

The essence of the reinvestment criterion (whether the unemployed people are paid doles or not) lies in its use of the rate of growth formula associated with the names of Harrod and Domar. The reinvestment formula can be transformed into the growth economics terminology without much difficulty.

$$r = \frac{p - ew}{c} \quad \left(\frac{p}{c}\right)\left(1 - \frac{ew}{p}\right) \quad = \frac{s}{a},$$

where $a = \text{capital coefficient} = \frac{c}{p}$

and $s = \text{savings ratio} = \frac{p - ew}{p}$,

assuming that the whole of wages is consumed and the whole of the rest reinvested. Thus the maximization of r results in the maximization of the rate of growth.

The Galenson–Leibenstein criterion is based on a number of simplifying assumptions, e.g. the techniques have the same gestation lag, the whole of the surplus is reinvested, and so on. These, however, do not constitute any basic limitation of the theory as in actual calculations they could be taken care of. Some questions can, however, be raised about the fundamental validity of the Galenson–Leibenstein criterion.

First, it is assumed in the criterion that the total amount of investment that one can make in the initial period is fixed, irrespective of the technique chosen. Only with this assumption can one say that the technique which gives us the maximum rate of investible surplus per unit of capital investment will give us the maximum rate of growth. That the assumption need not be valid can be realized very easily if we take cases with different propensities to consume of the factors contributing to the respective investments. If, in the case of investment A, the owners of factors of production consume half of what they get, an investment of $100 will mean an addition to the effective demand for consumer goods of $50 in the next round. If in the case of investment B, the factor owners consume whatever they get, the same amount of investment will lead to an additional effective demand for consumer goods of $100 in the next round. Thus given the real resources available in the economy, we may be in a position to have a larger initial capital investment if we chose technique A rather than B. It is therefore possible that even if technique B gives a higher rate of investible surplus *per unit of capital investment*, it may not give us a higher rate of growth.

The practical importance of this criticism depends, of course, upon the actual size of the difference in the propensities to consume. This difference will vary from case to case, but in some cases it may be quite important, as technological change often implies the replacement of a number of unskilled laborers by some skilled workers with lower propensities to consume. Also the producers of different co-operating factors of production may have different spending habits.

Secondly, the same problem may arise in a different garb in connection with international trade. Galenson and Leibenstein do not distinguish between the costs of buying foreign goods and those incurred in the home economy. When one technique has a higher import-content than another, and when extra foreign aid is not specially available when the first is chosen, the balance-of-payments problem introduced by the adoption of the first technique has to be taken into account. I think the best way of measuring the additional cost of higher import-content is to value the import at its export-equivalent. That is, we have to see how much more exports we have to ship abroad to meet the additional imports. Thus if technique A has no import-content and technique B involves imports worth $100 in addition to expenditures made at home, and if to meet the foreign currency requirement of $100 we have to export $150 (at home prices), by subsidization or other methods, we should add $150 and not merely $100 to home costs in the latter case.

This is a consideration of great practical relevance for very many choices of techniques. Thanks to the lack of a sector producing modern capital goods in an underdeveloped economy, the difference between the import-content of factory production and that of cottage industrial production is simply enormous, and choice between the two is very often the basic question in investment allocation in an underdeveloped economy. The Galenson–Leibenstein approach neglects this aspect of the problem altogether.

Thirdly, the Galenson–Leibenstein criterion neglects the fact that present income may be more valuable to society than future income. While the social marginal productivity criterion pins its attention on the present, the rate-of-reinvestment criterion goes to the other extreme. A higher rate of reinvestment may mean a higher rate of growth of income and thus may promise higher income some time in the future, but that in itself is no reason for choosing that technique. If we value present income more than future income, we may prefer to have a lower rate of growth and a higher rate of immediate income. This preference for the present need not arise from 'irrational telescopic psychology', but, for example, may be due to the very rational consideration that our present income being less than our future income, the value of additional income to us is much more at the present moment. This problem of time preference leads to a number of complexities which we shall encounter when we try to put forward an alternative criterion; but that a complete neglect of the problem is illegitimate seems clear. The SMP and the reinvestment criteria represent the two extreme positions on this time question.[13]

D The time series criterion

In the light of our criticism of the reinvestment criterion we can put forward an alternative suggestion. When confronted with the choice between various techniques, we start by finding out our 'best guess' of the time series of real income flows corresponding to each technique. This is done by applying the rate of reinvestment with corrections due to the variability of the volume of investment as we choose one technique rather than another. The variability, as we have shown earlier, may arise from things like different spending habits of the factors of production and the varying import-content of investments employing different techniques. If $\left(\frac{r_1}{r_2}\right)$ is the ratio of reinvestment with technique 1 and technique 2 respectively, and if $\left(\frac{m_1}{m_2}\right)$ is the ratio of the volumes of investment that can be undertaken when we choose the respective techniques, technique 1 will lead to a higher or a lower rate of growth depending on whether $m_1r_1>$ or $<m_2r_2$. This way the two time series of real income flows are obtained. In deriving the two time series one has to remember that there need not be constant returns to scale, as normally assumed, and the relative factor prices may also change with the scale of production, as factors need not be in equally elastic supply.

After getting the two time series of income flows we have to apply the relevant rates of time discount, and even if $m_1r_1>m_2r_2$, we need not necessarily choose technique 1. The time discount is necessary, it appears to me, because of at least two reasons: (a) the diminishing marginal social utility of income with the rising income level, and (b) the uncertainty of the future. If marginal social utility of income falls quickly and becomes negligible as income rises beyond a certain level, it is possible that a higher rate of growth of income may not give us a higher sum of total social satisfaction. Again beyond a point it becomes very difficult to apply all these rational calculations, as it is too difficult to foresee what is going to happen. Thanks to the imperfection of our knowledge, it is not possible to work out all the results of today's actions, for all time to come. We may choose a high degree of capital intensity and sacrifice some amount of present income for expected future benefit; but a technically advanced war, for example, may settle all problems before that future arrives. Thus in addition to the utility function with the assumption of perfect certainty, we need a valuation of uncertainty discount for a rigorous solution of the problem.

In applying our criterion to actual choices of capital intensity such a rigorous solution is not possible as we cannot get the required utility and uncertainty functions. A less satisfactory but more workable method is to fix the period of time we are going to take into account and see whether the loss of immediate output incurred by choosing the more capital-intensive technique is more than compensated by the extra output from it later, before the period of consideration is over. We may actually conceive of a 'period of recovery' (T) defined as the period of time in which the total output (the sum of yearly flows) with the more capital-intensive technique, is just equal to that with the less intensive technique. Figure 1 illustrates the period of recovery. The H and L curves give the two time series of consumption flows with the respective techniques. OT represents the period of recovery, as the surplus-area for the more capital-intensive technique (BCC') is exactly equal to its deficit-area (BAA'). The period we are ready to take into account is U (given by our judgments). When $U<T$, technique L is preferable; when $U>T$, technique H should be chosen; the point of indifference is given by $U=T$. If we assume $U=1$, we get the rate-of-turnover criterion; being interested in the first period only, the technique with the higher rate of immediate output is preferred. If we assume $U=\infty$, we get the rate-of-investment criterion; being equally interested in all time to come, a higher *rate* of growth is all we want.

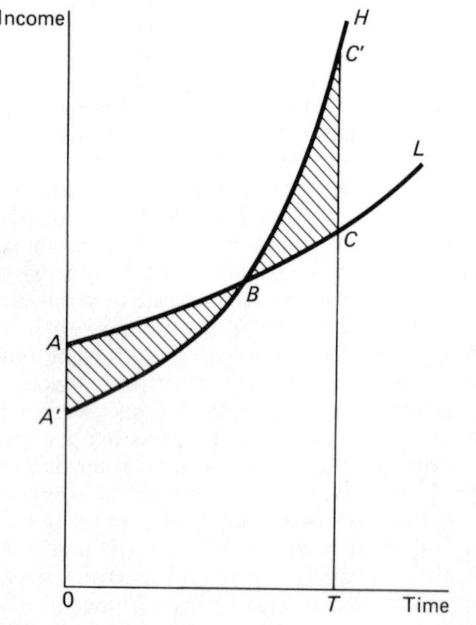

Figure 1

The defect of this approach lies in its arbitrariness. We have to assume that up to the end of the period U, each unit of income is equally valuable and there is no preference over time. But beyond that point no income is of any value at all. This brings in the time factor rather suddenly and with extreme severity. But such arbitrariness is difficult to avoid due to the very nature of the problem, and the approach of the period of recovery may have considerable operational value. In any case by choosing nonextreme values of U it can be made less arbitrary than the approach of the SMP criterion or that of the criterion of reinvestment. It is impossible to arrive at a realistic criterion for tackling this question which will be considered to be fully satisfactory intellectually. The object of the exercise, one has to remember, is not perfection, but minimization of imperfection. The period-of-recovery approach can be properly understood only when this is recognized.

2

We may now apply the criteria to some very simple models and thereby bring out their essential differences.[14] The first model will be chosen in a way that will make the time series criterion coincide with the Galenson–Leibenstein criterion—the assumptions of the model will make the total investment possibility constant in terms of direct outlay and it will be assumed that $U=\infty$. This criterion will be contrasted with the social marginal productivity and the rate-of-reinvestment criteria. As a part of the contrast some observations will also be made on the relationship between the cost of labor and the choice of capital intensity.

(I) The first model

We are looking at a stationary underdeveloped economy which is experiencing no economic growth. The social organization is precapitalistic and production is family-based. There is a big pool of unemployed labor in the economy, though due to the social organization, the unemployment may be 'disguised'. The government is contemplating the initiation of economic development with some public investment. It has decided against using the method of 'forced savings' through inflation and it will invest only to the extent that a technical surplus of production over current consumption is already available. Thus if the subsistence economy provides no surplus at all and if there is no foreign help, the economy is obviously in the grip of complete stagnation. Let us assume that the government has managed to realize some surplus through taxation or other means, and that the problem is in what form to invest it.

The economy consists of two sectors—the 'backward' subsistence sector and the 'advanced' sector under construction. We refer to them as sectors B and A respectively. Labor supply to sector A, we assume, is perfectly elastic in the relevant range due to immigration from sector B.

Sector A can be subdivided into two departments—I and II, the former producing capital goods and the latter corn, which we take as a 'composite commodity' to avoid the index number problem. For analytical convenience all factors other than labor and capital will be ignored. We assume further that all the techniques have the same gestation lag, that a capital good once created lasts forever (i.e. there is no depreciation), that the real wage rate per labor-hour is the same for all the techniques and is constant over time, and that the whole of the wages bill is consumed and that the whole of the surplus over wages is reinvested. In this particular model we also assume that capital goods are produced by labor alone and that the economy is closed. We shall deal with a choice between two techniques—H and L; the former has a higher capital intensity, defined as the number of laborers employed in department I to produce enough capital goods to employ one laborer in department II. We use the following notations for technique L.

- w = real wage rate per period in the production of corn;
- $\bar{w}$ = real wage rate per period in the capital goods sector;
- a = 'capital intensity' as defined above;
- P_c = labor productivity in corn production in department II of sector A;
- L_i = labor employed in department I;
- L_c = labor employed in department II;
- C = total corn produced in sector A;
- W_c = total wages bill in department II of sector A;
- and N = the surplus of corn production over the wages bill ($C - W_c$), in department II.

In the case of technique II we use primed notations. Numerical suffixes refer to the relevant time periods.

As temporary assumptions we have, $w = w'$ and $\bar{w} = \bar{w}'$. We know that $a < a'$. Obviously P_c must be less than P_c'; otherwise there would be little reason to take the more capital-intensive technique seriously.

Let us start with a surplus S of corn extracted from sector B to make the initiation of Sector A possible. We assume that wage earners in department II are paid out of their production.

$$L_i = \frac{S}{\bar{w}} \qquad L_c = \frac{S}{\bar{w}a}; \qquad C = \frac{SP_c}{\bar{w}a}.$$

$$\overline{\bar{w}a}.$$

Similarly $$C' = \frac{SP_c'}{\bar{w}a'}.$$

If we are interested only in the total product for the first period, our choice would depend on whether

$$\frac{P_c'}{a'} >, = \quad \text{or} \quad < \frac{P_c}{a}. \tag{1}$$

This is the rate-of-turnover criterion.[15]

Production in future years will depend not merely on the flow of output from the initial investment, but also on that from additional investments undertaken with the surplus product. So if we are interested in the maximum rate of growth of output, the relevant consideration is the rate of surplus.

$$N_1 = C_1 - W_{c_1} = \frac{S}{\bar{w}} \cdot \frac{P_c - w}{a}.$$

$$N_1' = C_1' - W_{c1}' = \frac{S}{\bar{w}} \cdot \frac{P_c' - w}{a'}.$$

We should choose H or L or be indifferent between them depending on whether $\frac{P_{c'} - w}{a'} >, < \text{or} = \frac{P_c - w}{a}$ respectively. (2)

This is the rate-of-investment criterion.

All this can be represented in diagrammatic form without much difficulty. In Figure 2 there are three axes—the south representing employment in department I, the east employment in department II and the north the corn output of the latter department. OI is the amount of labor that can be employed with the available corn surplus at the prevailing wage rate. Employment in department II depends on the degree of capital intensity chosen, it being defined as the number of laborers that have to be employed in department I to produce enough capital goods for employing one man in department II. Three degrees of capital intensity are used in the figure, represented in the increasing order by the tangent of the angles OL_cI, $OL_{c'}I$ and $OL_{c''}I$ respectively. The employment created as a result of this investment is OL_c, $OL_{c'}$ and $OL_{c''}$ respectively. With increasing capital intensity, the product per unit of labor in department II rises, represented respectively by the tangents of the angles P_cOL_c, $P_{c'}OL_c$ and $P_{c''}OL_c$. Thus the corn output when the first technique is chosen is CL_c, when the second is chosen $C'L_{c'}$ and when the third is preferred $C''L_{c''}$. By taking infinitesimal changes in the degree of capital

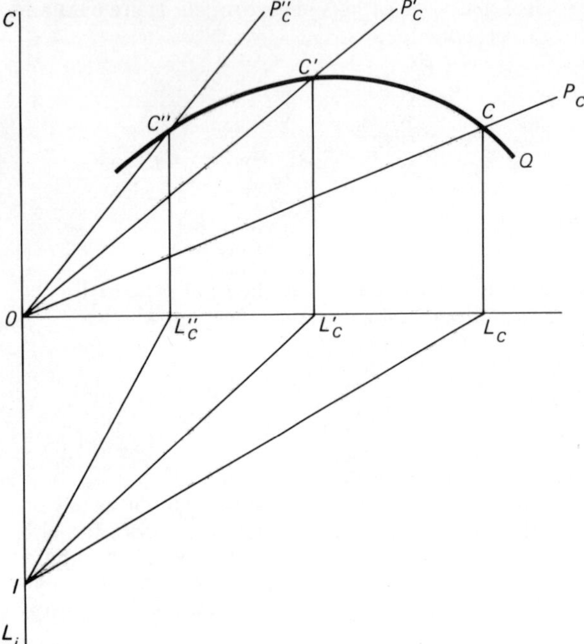

Figure 2

intensity, we derive the curve Q representing the relationship between employment in department II and the output of corn, governed by the technological possibilities. In Figure 3, we have the curve Q and a line Wc representing the total wages bill in department II. As we have assumed a given wage rate, the latter is a straight-line. E represents the point of maximum output. P is the point of maximum surplus of corn production over consumption, as the slope of curve Q at that point is equal to the wage rate. If we adopt the rate-of-turnover criterion, or the SMP criterion when unemployed labor is available without affecting production elsewhere, we should choose point E. If, however, we adopt the rate-of-investment criterion, point P should be chosen.

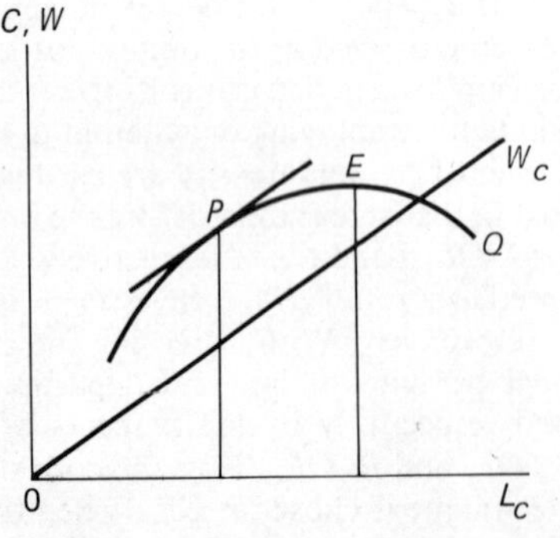

Figure 3

An interesting possibility is represented by point E lying below the wage-line, as in Figure 4. This means that maximization of output would involve negative surplus. Point T gives maximum output consistent with

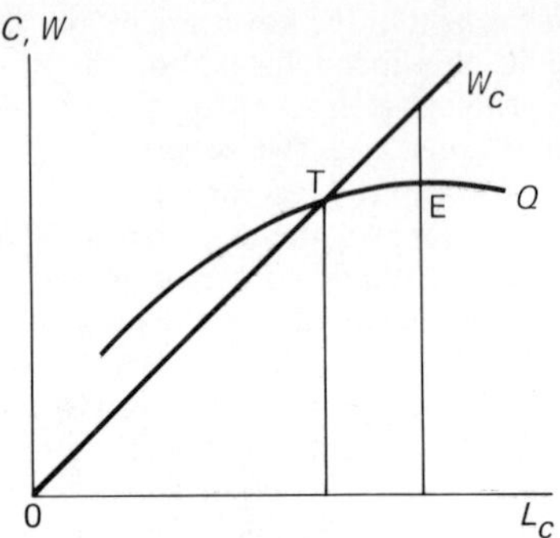

Figure 4

the condition that output covers the wages bill ($P_c = w$). It is thus possible that full application of the SMP criterion or the rate-of-turnover criterion may involve capital contraction rather than accumulation.

In Figure 5, it is illustrated that a rise in the wage rate makes it more profitable to choose a more capital-intensive technique. When the wage-line moves up from W_c *to* $W_{c'}$, the point of maximum surplus becomes A rather than B, as $B_2B_3 < A_2A_3$, although $B_1B_3 > A_1A_3$.[1] This follows also from relation (2), as a technique with a higher rate of surplus per laborer ($P_c - w$) is relatively less affected by a rise in the wage rate.

From this it does not follow, however, that a lower wage economy should necessarily choose a lower degree of capital intensity. In fact, the scope of variation of capital intensity may be very limited, and it may well be that, of the available techniques, the same is best for most wages. In Figure 5, if A and C were the only techniques that existed, a fall in the wage rate from $W_{c'}$ to W_c would have kept the technique unchanged at A, ($C_1C_3 < A_1A_3$). This discontinuity in the production function is a possible explanation of the fact that even low wage economies very often choose techniques that are hardly different from those of the advanced economies.

Lastly, since we equate labor cost to the net increase in consumption due to additional employment, if a part of the former consumption of the laborers previously in sector B can be recovered, the effective wages will be less. If consumption per head in the subsistence sector is k and the proportion of it that can be recovered is q then

$$N_1 = \frac{S}{w} \cdot \frac{P_c - w + kq}{a} \frac{S}{w} = \frac{P_c - w(1-f)}{a}, \text{ putting } f = \frac{kq}{w}.$$

Recovery of consumption of the formerly unemployed is similar to a reduction of wages, and in a borderline case

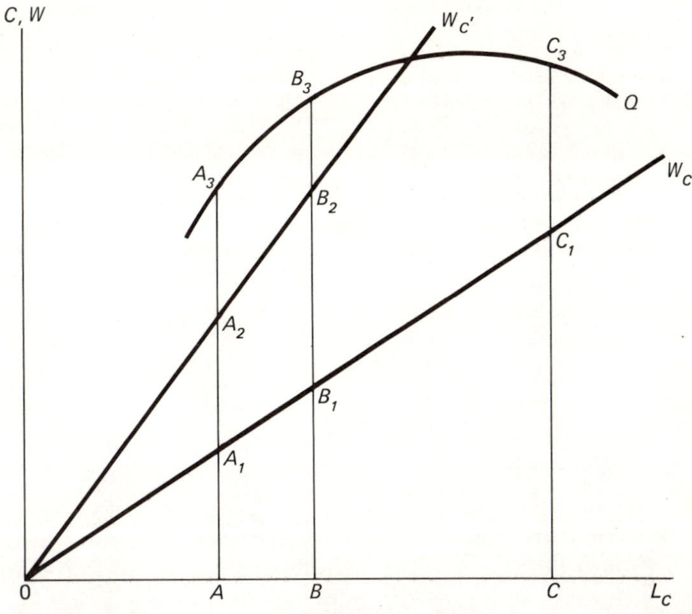

Figure 5

can make us choose a less capital-intensive technique. Left to the free market, however, the scope of recovery is not great, since, in all probability, the remaining rural population will consume nearly the whole of the extra income left by the villagers leaving for the town, as their marginal propensity to consume is very near unity. Taxation linked with the exodus from the rural area, or some system of 'compulsory delivery', may, however, achieve this end. This shows the dependence of technological choice on the fiscal policy in operation in the economy.

We may summarize the observations we have made on the connections between labor-cost and technological choice. (1) Even if there is a lot of unemployment in an economy and the social opportunity cost of using labor is nil, it will be a mistake, if we are interested in the rate of growth of the economy, to treat labor as costless and to substitute capital for labor whenever possible. (2) If the rate of growth is our criterion, lower wages should influence our choice in favor of lower capital intensity, though in many cases, due to the discontinuity of the production function, this point is of only academic interest. (3) The higher the amount of former consumption of the newly employed people that can be recovered through taxation, or compulsory delivery, or other means, the lower should be the capital intensity chosen, given a continuous production function.

Notes: Reading 26

1 'Balance of payments problems in countries reconstructing with the help of foreign loans', *Quarterly Journal of Economics*, vol. LVII, February 1943, p. 208. Reprinted in *Readings in the Theory of International Trade* (American Economic Association, 1949).

2 'International investment and domestic welfare' (New York, 1945), p. 24.

3 See A. E. Kahn, 'Investment criteria in development programs', *Quarterly Journal of Economics*, vol. LXV, February 1951, p. 38.

4 op. cit. See also H. B. Chenery, 'The application of investment criteria', *Quarterly Journal of Economics*, vol. LXVII, February 1953, p. 76.

5 op. cit., p. 51. See also p. 40.

6 'The theory of economic growth' (London and Homewood, Ill., 1955), p. 386.

7 op. cit., p. 140.

8 The criticism of Walter Galenson and Harvey Leibenstein ('Investment criteria, productivity and economic development', *Quarterly Journal of Economics*, vol. LXIX, August 1955, p. 343) also boils down to this point about the valuation of labor though this may not be quite obvious.

9 op. cit., p. 351. For a neat presentation of a basically similar criterion,and also for an interesting study of various other aspects of the problem of choice of capital intensity, see M. H. Dobb, 'Second thoughts on capital intensity', *Review of Economic Studies*, vol. XXIV, 1956.

10 op. cit., p. 352.

11 Galenson and Leibenstein do make this assumption. 'We abstract here from the very difficult problem of ensuring that this Ricardian "surplus" is indeed reinvested . . .', op. cit., p. 352, n. 6.

12 'Small scale industries – problem of technological change', special article, *The Economic Weekly* (India), 7 and 14 April 1956. This point is discussed also by Hans Neisser, 'Investment criteria, productivity, and economic development: comment', *Quarterly Journal of Economics*,

vol. LXX, November 1956, p. 644, and by Galenson and Leibenstein in their 'Reply', ibid.

13 Since this paper was written, two articles on capital intensity have come out in the *Quarterly Journal of Economics*, vol. LXXI, February 1957, namely, by Otto Eckstein, 'Investment criteria for economic development and the theory of intertemporal welfare economies', p. 56, and by Francis M. Bator, 'On capital productivity, input allocation and growth', p. 86. It is particularly necessary to refer to Professor Bator's article, as he denies the importance of the problem of choice over time involved in the question, on which we have put so much emphasis. In fact Bator's model leads him to conclude (p. 99) that there is 'no conflict' between maximising the present output and maximising the growth rate. This conclusion is the result of his assumption that 'the rate of saving is independent of the (as if) market imputed distribution of income' (p. 98). This, of course, amounts to assuming away the problem itself.

14 Unfortunately space does not permit inclusion in this volume of extensions beyond the basic first model. *Ed.*

15 The social marginal productivity criterion coincides with this, as unemployed labour is available in the economy.

A Layman's Guide to Little-Mirrlees

G. B. Baldwin

Finance and Development, Vol. 9, No. 1, 1972, pp. 16–21.

Two well-known Oxford professors, Ian Little and James Mirrlees, have written a manual on industrial cost-benefit analysis which has stirred up a lot of interest and a fair amount of dust.[1] Some important development agencies have already announced adoption of the Little-Mirrlees approach; these include Britain's Overseas Development Administration, West Germany's Kreditanstalt für Wiederaufbau, and the United Nations Industrial Development Organization. The World Bank Group (the Bank, the International Development Association, and the International Finance Corporation, which assists private industry) has studied Little-Mirrlees to see whether any closer move toward it would be a useful refinement of present methods, which are already close to theirs (this is less true of IFC than of the Bank and IDA). Further experiments in applying Little-Mirrlees within the Bank are likely.

One of the major problems in evaluating Little-Mirrlees is understanding it. The *Manual* is not difficult for a reasonably well-trained economist to understand; but some of the subtleties and refinements have got in the way of getting agreement on what is new in Little-Mirrlees and what is not, what is essential and what is not. My own view is that their essential ideas are not new and their new ideas are not essential.

A First Approximation

The *Manual*'s central message can be simply stated. A valid assessment of an industrial project's worth to an economy often requires the use of values that differ from the values used in the normal kind of business or financial appraisals. Economic appraisals frequently must be done with 'shadow' prices, i.e. any assumed prices that differ from those that will actually be realized in the company's own books ('market' prices). The particular shadow prices which Little and Mirrlees believe should be used are 'world prices'; these represent a country's actual trading opportunities. The resulting streams of annual costs and benefits should then be weighted (discounted) to reflect the differing times when they will occur. The discounting operation has the effect of translating future values into their present worth, allowing the streams of future costs and benefits to be summed into single figures. You then subtract the single cost figure from the benefit figure. If there is a surplus the project is said to have a favorable present social value, and is worth doing. Economists will at once recognize that Little and Mirrlees are relying on the familiar discounted cash flow method, using shadow prices, to test for a project's net present worth.

Thus the basic approach of the *Manual* is not new. For those to whom the basic concepts may be hazy or unfamiliar, the *Manual* provides an admirable introductory explanation, free of mathematics or jargon. But the major innovation put forward by Little and Mirrlees —their big idea that has stirred up most of the interest and most of the dust—is their notion that *all* prices used in project calculation should be world prices. They are not satisfied with the procedure followed by many institutions (including, normally, the World Bank Group) whereby partial use is made of international values, e.g. applying them to major inputs and outputs that are or easily could be traded. They argue in favor of valuing all inputs at world prices, even the so-called nontraded inputs that normally cannot possibly be imported (i.e. electricity, construction, local transport and labor). The reason Little and Mirrlees want to go 'all the way' in using world prices for every input and output is to avoid the distortions which they feel creep into the calculations if only partial use is made of world prices. A cost-benefit calculation based partly on world prices and partly on domestic prices has to be put into a single currency through the use of an exchange rate. Little and Mirrlees don't like exchange rates, not even 'shadow' exchange rates based on 'correcting' unrealistic official rates. In their view, no exchange rate, no matter how good, can overcome the distortion in relative values which arises whenever you combine values taken from different sets of prices (such as world prices and domestic prices). The use of one set of prices—world prices—bypasses this problem and, by taking all prices from one common pool, achieves a more valid ordering of the relative values used in constructing costs and benefits.[2]

If by some miracle of wisdom a country had

developed its economic structure under conditions of free trade and free exchange rates, its investment decisions would continuously have been made in the light of world-wide trading opportunities; consequently, the relative values of home prices and world prices would today stand in an undistorted relationship to each other. This is hardly the world as we find it. Protection and other trade restrictions are everywhere, investment decisions have often been made outside the discipline and opportunities of world prices, and many exchange rates now serve to distort rather than to preserve true relationships between domestic and world values. Little and Mirrlees want to prevent this bad history from contaminating investment decisions. They want to avoid using some good prices (world prices of traded items) and some not-so-good prices (the domestic prices of nontraded inputs), which must then be merged by use of a (frequently bad) exchange rate. If all values can be measured in world prices, the problem is solved. In a neat display of inventiveness, Little and Mirrlees have 'solved' this problem. But some of their critics say the cure is worse than the disease. This point is far and away the most controversial part of the *Manual*: just how much trouble is it worth to avoid using a foreign exchange rate, official or shadow?

With this summary introduction we can take a closer look at some of the main features of the Little-Mirrlees approach.

Social Profitability and Private Profitability

Little and Mirrlees begin by pointing out the many similarities between the calculation of an industrial project's private and its economic or social profitability. Both calculations start with the problem of estimating future income (i.e. 'benefits') and costs (capital and operating). The cost and benefit estimates are both made up of two elements: (1) the number of physical units involved plus (2) the price used to value each physical element. 'The essence of a cost-benefit analysis is that it does not accept that actual receipts adequately measure social benefits, and actual expenditures social costs. But it does accept that actual receipts and expenditures can be suitably adjusted so that the difference between them . . . will properly reflect the social gain' (pp. 22–3).

A second but less crucial feature of their system is the emphasis given to savings. Little and Mirrlees feel that resources for investment are so often a critical constraint that they deserve to occupy a central role in evaluating projects. Their handling of this problem, by converting a project's cash flow into a pure savings flow stripped of all consumption elements, is neat, and deserves discussion. But not until we look further at what they have to say about the use of world prices.

Why World Prices?

'If you can get more refrigerators by exporting bicycles to pay for them, than by diverting resources from making bicycles to making refrigerators at home, it is clearly right to make and export the bicycles and import the refrigerators. But whether this is in fact the case, requires a knowledge both of the relative costs of production at home, and of world prices and market conditions' (p. 85). The reason for relating everything to world prices is not because they are 'more rational' than domestic prices but simply because 'they represent the actual terms on which the country can trade' (p. 92). So it is logical to argue that all internationally traded goods —i.e. those which the country actually imports or exports, regardless of whether the project itself will do so—should be valued at their c.i.f. (for imports) or f.o.b. (for exports) prices. But what should we do with nontraded inputs and outputs? (The main nontraded inputs are domestic transportation, construction, electricity, land, and labor; other minor ones can be thought of, e.g. water and waste disposal, telecommunications, advertising, banking services, maintenance and repair services.)

Little and Mirrlees say that since traded goods are valued in world prices, nontraded goods must be similarly valued; 'only thus can we ensure that we are valuing everything in terms of a common yardstick'. Note that a 'common yardstick' may refer either to use of a common currency (e.g. all values expressed in either dollars or rupees), or to the use of a common source of values (e.g. world prices, instead of a mixture of world prices and domestic prices). All methods of project appraisal require the use of a common currency, but only Little-Mirlees require the use of both a common currency and a common source for all values used. The problem of trying to express all values in a single currency where they will stand in a right relationship to each other can be solved either by using 'a special accounting price for foreign exchange' (a shadow exchange rate) or by revaluing domestic resources in terms of world prices; the latter is the method recommended in the *Manual*. Once all values are established in terms of world prices, it does not matter whether they are left in US dollars or converted into domestic rupees (the two illustrative currencies used in the *Manual*). If *a complete set* of costs and benefits are converted from dollars into rupees any exchange rate can be used, since all values will retain a constant relationship to each other. But this is *not* true if some values are taken from world prices and some are taken from domestic prices and the two sets are then put into a single currency by using an exchange rate. This will change the relationships among different values and distort the estimate of the relationship between foreign and domestic resources.

Using Input/Output Analysis to Chase Down Traded Items

Little and Mirrlees advance both pragmatic and theoretical reasons for wanting to anchor all cost-benefit values in world prices. Their pragmatic reason is that world prices represent actual trading opportunities, which heavily influence domestic investment decisions. Every industrial investment decision involves the 'make or buy' decision involved in the refrigerator and bicycle quotation cited earlier. The development process involves a steady expansion of the demand for imports, and the only way to pay for them, in the long run, is to produce for export only those things a country can produce best. To make the most of its opportunities a country must deploy its resources (fundamentally, its land and its labor force) in ways which give it the most for its money, i.e. the most foreign exchange (either earnings or savings) for domestic resources used. And the only way to do this in a complete and theoretically consistent manner is to chase down all the inputs used by a project, direct and indirect, until all the potentially tradable items have been valued in world prices, leaving only land and labor. Land is dismissed as relatively unimportant in most industrial projects. But in valuing labor, Little and Mirrlees argue that even labor's own inputs (i.e. its consumption) should be valued in terms of world prices (they give us some help by suggesting how this refinement might be achieved).

It is not easy to value the nontraded inputs in world prices. The general procedure is to take each such input (power, construction, transport, or labor) and break it down into its own inputs; these in turn will consist of items that are traded and items that are nontraded. The latter are in turn broken down into traded and nontraded items, etc. etc. The only way this chain can be followed back very far is through a detailed input/output table for the economy as a whole. Few less developed countries have in existence a table that is detailed enough to permit the needed calculations for more than a few simple industries. If no such table is available, rough-and-ready approximations to world values can be used. These approximations or 'conversion factors' are based on the ratio of domestic costs of a representative sample, of, say, construction items (wood, cement, steel, fuel, etc.) to the world price of these items. This ratio is based on using the official exchange rate; the reciprocal of the ratio is then used to adjust the domestic cost of nontraded inputs to values closer to what they would be if the complete input/output method had been rigorously followed. This conversion factor is in effect a way of correcting for the overvaluation of an exchange rate; however, it does it on an average basis and not with the precision theoretically achievable if all nontraded inputs could be decomposed into their ultimate traded elements which could then be valued in world prices.

The Price of Labor

There is nothing particularly new or distinctive in the Little-Mirrlees treatment of this much-discussed question. Most of the labor used in industry comes from a labor-surplus rural sector, and its departure involves little or no loss of agricultural production, i.e. its opportunity cost (equal to its marginal productivity) is typically very low. However, industrial labor is usually paid considerably more than the agricultural subsistence wage. Some of this excess over what labor could earn in agriculture is a necessary cost of making it available at industrial locations; but some of the excess is an artificial creation of trade union policies, needlessly high minimum wages, or employer 'softness' in relation to what he could pay if he wanted to pay no more than a competitive wage. So the proper domestic price for valuing labor is a shadow wage that lies somewhere between its actual market rate and an agricultural subsistence wage. A good deal of judgment is involved in settling on a figure (since the cost stream stretches over many years, there is no reason for using a constant shadow price throughout the project life if there is any reasonable basis for varying it).

But Little and Mirrlees do not let the domestic shadow price of labor determine its value in project costs. A domestic shadow price reflects only labor's relative scarcity in the domestic economy; once this has been estimated, this domestic value must then be converted into a world price. In theory this can be done —as explained above—by decomposing labor's consumption into traded items; but in practice either a specific conversion factor or the standard conversion factor would almost always be used.

Adjusting for a Project's 'Commitment to Consumption'

With nations, as with individuals, there is a never-ending tug-of-war between consumption and savings. The ultimate purpose of all economic activity is to raise living standards, which means raising consumption. But it is nonconsumption out of present income (savings) which provides the resources for the investment necessary to assure higher consumption tomorrow. Hence the battle between consumption today and consumption tomorrow. Little-Mirrlees have an unusually clear discussion of this classical problem, although their operational advice seems unnecessarily complicated.

Obviously a dollar's worth of future consumption is never worth a full dollar to us today. Future values always stand at a discount compared to the present, and the more distant the future, the greater the discount. The specific rate at which future consumption is discounted is called the consumption rate of interest (economists often call this the social discount rate, a more ambiguous term). This is not the discount rate

Little and Mirrlees use in discounting cost-benefit streams. Why not? Because projects generate future savings as well as future consumption. Indeed, Little and Mirrlees believe that savings are so difficult to generate, and so important to future consumption, that the main test of a project's economic merit is almost all less developed countries should be its ability to generate savings. There is no reason why future savings should carry the same discount rate as future consumption. So it may look at first as though future consumption will have to be discounted at one rate and future savings at another. To avoid this, Little-Mirrlees revalue future consumption in terms of savings: this gives us a unified benefit stream, a 'cash flow' stripped of its consumption elements so that it represents only savings. These can then be discounted at a single rate; the rate at which savings are discounted is called the 'accounting rate of interest' (ARI). This is the discount rate to use in calculating the present worth of a project's cost and benefit streams.

The social income stream (consumption plus savings) to be generated by a project is stripped of its consumption element by taking the consumption element out of both labor income and returns to capital. On the labor side this adjustment is made automatically by defining labor's cost in terms of its consumption only. Since only this consumption cost is deducted from project income, anything labor saves remains in the net benefit stream. The elimination of consumption from the returns paid to the owners of capital is accomplished by applying to the project's estimated incremental capital income an estimate of the general marginal propensity to consume of those who receive interest and dividends (for some reason no offsetting allowance is made for any extra government consumption which may result from tax revenue generated by a project).

Thus the use of a shadow price for labor increases the benefit stream while the adjustment for consumption out of profits reduces the stream: one wonders how near the truth one would be if neither of these offsetting adjustments were made! But at least Little-Mirrlees give us a complete, easy-to-understand lesson in why a 'commitment to consumption' is 'bad' and how they think it ought to be eliminated from the cost-benefit calculation.

What Discount Rate to Use?

As noted, in the Little-Mirrlees system (as in many others) the investment test used is a project's present social value the difference between the present values of the benefit and cost streams. These present values are, of course, critically dependent on the discount rate used; different rates can change not only the size of the present social value but can make a positive value turn negative. So the specific ARI is important. The Little-Mirrlees rule for choosing the right discount rate is the same as that used by many others, including the World Bank Group: '. . . the accounting rate of interest should be kept as high as possible consistent with there being as much investment as savings permit' (p. 96). ('Savings' here means domestic plus foreign savings, the latter being net capital inflow.) If a too low ARI is chosen there will be excessive investment, a balance of payments deficit, and underuse of resources. Recognizing these limits and choosing a rate that will steer the right course between them is a matter of good judgment. Little and Mirrlees think most developing countries ought to use a rate around 10 per cent in real terms, i.e. after inflation; some countries might use even 15 per cent. Rather than worry about the exact correctness of the ARI, Little and Mirrlees sensibly suggest the trial use of three rates—high, low, and medium—to sort out the 'obviously good' and the 'obviously bad' projects, with marginal ones to be put off until the authorities see how large the investment program will be and whether any clearly better projects come along to displace the marginal candidates.

A Project's Balance of Payments, Employment, and Future Consumption Effects

One of the attractive features claimed for the Little-Mirrlees approach is that it provides a comprehensive project evaluation test. Once it is determined that a project has a positive PSV when world prices are used, one can be confident that it will fulfil all important economic objectives for which projects are often specifically tested. This applies to a project's impact on the balance of payments, on employment, and on society's claims for future consumption. By valuing all project inputs and outputs at world prices (i.e. in terms of their foreign exchange value), 'import-substitution and exporting is encouraged to the maximum desirable extent'. Once the authorities have persuaded project appraisers to use correct values (i.e. world prices) in their cost-benefit studies then 'the right way to control the balance of payments is to concentrate on high-yielding projects, and not to try to do more investment than saving, tax policies, and foreign aid, allow'. By valuing labor's shadow wage also in terms of foreign exchange (which may put a lower value on labor's consumption inputs than domestic prices do) 'producers are encouraged to use labor, instead of imported inputs, to the maximum desirable extent'. Finally, as we have seen, the problem of balancing consumption today against consumption tomorrow is handled by use of a shadow wage rate—e.g. a low shadow wage encourages labor-intensive projects, the main expression of consumption today over consumption tomorrow.

Controversial Points

Toward the end of the Little-Mirrlees volume one comes upon this self-description: 'The methods of project appraisal described in this *Manual*, depending as they do on relatively crude methods of estimating accounting prices, can be thought of as a first step in the harnessing of the whole range of production decisions to social ends. . . . The methods suggested do not depend upon the prior analysis of reliable and sophisticated planning models. They are practicable: and are likely to be accurate enough to exclude all definitely bad projects, and allow all definitely good ones. Small mistakes on marginal projects are less important' (p. 188). Admirable goals for any appraisal method—reliability, simplicity, feasibility. At most points, the *Manual* meets these tests; at a few points it fails them.

Little and Mirrlees do not expect their *Manual* to give individual project analysts everything they need to go out and make valid cost-benefit studies of industrial projects. They acknowledge that they have really written a textbook of appraisal theory, not a how-to-do-it manual for men on the firing line. Furthermore, the textbook is meant for the education and guidance of a small group of high-powered economists who, the authors hope, will be found presiding over development planning at the center of things in every country. They urge every country to prepare a much shorter manual[3] of its own, telling ministries and development banks how to do economic cost-benefit studies and giving them the necessary accounting prices.

The weakest—and certainly the most contentious—of the various steps recommended by Little-Mirrlees is the extent to which they go in using world prices. They want us to use them for *all* cost and benefit values, not just for important items that are actually traded, or could be. To do this involves a lot of trouble for a doubtful advantage. It is a lot of trouble because of the need to use input/output data that usually do not exist with nearly the accuracy needed to yield accurate results—and there seems little advantage in substituting the distortions of bad input/output data, or the approximations of conversion factors, for those arising from overvalued exchange rates. It is not even true that Little and Mirrlees get rid of exchange rates entirely, since some world prices will be in US dollars, some in deutsche mark, some in yen, etc., and these can be merged only by using exchange rates. So part of the exchange rate problem is simply pushed outside the country. In most countries, it appears far simpler and sufficiently accurate to use:

1 world prices for the *actually traded* major capital and current inputs, and for the outputs;
2 domestic factor costs (at either shadow or market prices as judged appropriate) for the *nontraded* inputs; and then to
3 convert these foreign and domestic values into a single currency by resort to an exchange rate (again, using any reasonable rate if the official rate is felt badly out of line).

In a majority of industrial projects distortions in the values of nontraded inputs simply will not be important. Electricity rarely comprises more than 4–5 per cent of manufacturing costs, so a 20 per cent distortion of its value will affect total costs by only 1 per cent. Distortions in internal transport costs for capital and operating costs are unlikely to run more than the same order of magnitude. The construction element in plant capital costs is larger and may run 15–30 per cent; at least half of this will consist of labor costs which, as with operating labor costs, can be adjusted to an 'economic' value through the use of a shadow wage. The distortion arising from using domestic currency to price labor's shadow wage is likely to be less than the margin of error inherent in deciding what shadow wage to use. Thus, when one looks at the relative unimportance of all the nontraded inputs, except labor, in a majority of industrial projects, refinements in these values begin to look relatively unimportant. Cost-benefit analysis simply does not work to the order of precision to which Little and Mirrlees want to take us.

Labor operating costs, which are important in most industrial or agricultural projects, can be handled satisfactorily by sensitivity analysis, i.e. by trying two or three different values to see how much difference it makes to the final result. There is no point in going to a lot of trouble to establish a doubtful accuracy for values that do not change a conclusion reached with more easily established, well-reasoned values. Little and Mirrlees make a good case for using sensitivity analysis when discussing the 'fuzziness' surrounding the ARI; they might well have extended its use to other cost-benefit values. I cannot help concluding that this particular feature of the Little-Mirrlees methodology—the world-pricing-of-nontraded-inputs feature that has caused so much argument—is a tempest in a teapot. I doubt it will catch on, and it will not matter much if it doesn't. There is plenty of wisdom in the basic Little-Mirrlees approach without trying to make everything depend on their controversial method of valuing a project's nontraded inputs.

Notes: Reading 27

1 The Little-Mirrlees manual is Volume II of the Organisation for Economic Co-operation and Development's two-volume *Manual of Industrial Project Analysis in Developing Countries*.

2 The key value of labour is brought into this system of world prices at its proper relative value by first giving it a hypothetical or shadow price in terms of its domestic scarcity and then translating this into its world-price equivalent.

3 Britain's Overseas Development Administration has prepared just such a manual for its own use, based explicitly on the Little-Mirrlees *Manual*.

Reading 28

The Rationale and Relevance of the Little-Mirrlees Criterion

V. Joshi

Oxford Bulletin of Economics and Statistics, 1972, pp. 3–32.

1

There is substantial agreement among economists that less developed countries are characterized by pervasive divergences between market prices and social values. This belief has inspired several attempts to devise criteria for project selection which calculate the benefits and costs of projects on the basis of 'shadow prices' or 'accounting prices' which correct for these divergences. A notable recent attempt in this field is the project selection technique suggested by I. M. D. Little and J. A. Mirrlees in their *Manual of Industrial Project Analysis in Developing Countries (Vol. II)* (10). That this is an original and important contribution to an important subject is already recognized. It has also proved to be a controversial work and is likely to continue to be so for some time. This is partly because its diffuse style leads to misunderstandings and confusions in the minds of both laymen and professional economists to whom it is simultaneously addressed.[1] On the other hand, it is also partly because it makes substantive and fairly radical suggestions about the way projects should be evaluated. In this paper, I shall attempt to elucidate the analytical basis of this method and to discuss critically its underlying assumptions and its practical usefulness. In so doing, I hope to narrow down the area of controversy and to focus it on the relevant issues.

2

Objections to project selection per se

I propose to begin, however, by mentioning briefly some objections to the whole activity of project selection, especially in its application to less developed countries, which appear explicitly in the thinking of some people and implicitly in the views of some others. Some of these objections cannot be conclusively refuted. Indeed, it is my belief that using project selection as an instrument of planning requires ultimately an act of faith—though no more, certainly, than is involved in not using it.

The purpose of this rather general opening discussion is to distinguish, as far as possible, objections to project selection rules *per se* from criticisms of the Little Mirrlees Method.

The first objection comes from people who feel that project selection procedures are unimportant and irrelevant, especially in the context of the less developed countries. The grounds for this belief vary. Revolutionaries feel that replacing the existing social and political set-up is the precondition of development and that everything else is a diversion. Then there are others who think that some general macro-economic strategy is the main requirement and that micro-economic choices do not count for much. There are still others who are impressed by the importance of micro-economic decisions but believe that, in quantitative terms, economic considerations are far less important in the success or failure of projects than technical or managerial considerations. As these arguments stand, it is not quite clear: (a) why micro-economic measures might not be needed to accompany radical change nor (b) why the gains from improved resource allocation should be foregone even if they are not very large. In any case, the recent history of the less developed countries does not lend much support to the view that the gains from economic efficiency are insignificant nor does it throw up any clear recommendations about how to achieve 'significant' gains from non-economic measures or general macro-economic strategies. Of course, any sensible proponent of project selection should admit that it is not, by itself, a guarantee of development.

The second objection comes from purists in economic theory and is really directed against the *approximate* shadow pricing, that is necessarily involved in project selection.[2] At the level of abstract theory, optimal prices and outputs are determined simultaneously, the information problem being handled by the use of iterative decentralization procedures. In practical project selection, there are undoubtedly severe limits on iterative convergence procedures, so that the shadow prices used can at best be 'approximately right'. However, the only shadow prices which have theoretical validity are those associated with the exact solution of the general equilibrium optimum problem. There is, strictly speaking, no theoretical guarantee that decisions based on 'approximately correct' shadow prices will lead the economy 'in the right direction'. Furthermore, given the complexity of objectives and constraints in any actual economy, it may be difficult to derive the relevant shadow prices even as a theoretical exercise: to guess them without solving the entire simultaneous problem may be impossible and foolish. One possible answer to these cosmic doubts is that in certain cases at least shadow prices may not be very sensitive to differences in demand conditions and technological and other constraints. But this is not a very powerful reply: in my opinion, an 'act of faith' has to be made if such cosmic doubts are raised about the whole basis of applied welfare economics. Note also that it would be quite wrong to see these arguments as demonstrating the superiority of centralized planning models for resource allocation decisions. The unreliability of information, the level of aggregation at which such exercises have to be conducted, and the need on the whole to force problems into a linear framework make the shadow prices derived very untrustworthy.

The third objection to project selection, like the second, also concerns the misleading nature of simple shadow pricing rules. The emphasis, however, is not on fine points of economic theory, though it could no doubt be rephrased in those terms. This argument emphasizes the diverse, intangible, unquantifiable effects of every project which can only be allowed for in a qualitative manner and which might render any quantitative criterion irrelevant and useless. However, accurate evidence concerning the impact of projects on various intangible factors is not easy to come by: given this fact, this argument at the very least runs the risk of making too great a demand on the wisdom and judgement of project planners.

The fourth objection to project selection is directed at the institutional framework implied by it. Essentially, this is based on the belief that even the best rules can be perverted by vested interests and therefore that attempts to select projects bureaucratically are a very poor substitute for getting actual prices right. However, there are some goods which by their nature have to be publicly supplied or whose provision must be in the hands of the government due to a lack of development of the market economy. Furthermore, even if the economy is moving towards a more 'rational' price structure, it can only do so slowly, and in the intervening period project selection may have a positive role to play in improving resource allocation.

In the end, one must emphasize that project evaluation is not a subject for a perfectionist. One demands of a project selection criterion that it should be grounded in economic theory, that it should make relevant simplifications about reality, that it should be simple and practical to use, that it should be flexible enough to deal with complex problems. Perhaps one asks for too much and no single criterion can meet all these demands perfectly. Equally important for the ensuing discussion, whether and to what extent any particular project selection method meets the above criteria is itself a matter of judgement.

3

The Little-Mirrlees approach

In principle, the Little-Mirrlees method is capable of dealing with all divergences between private and social values, whatever their source. Nevertheless, a reading of the *Manual* suggests that while the authors mention many such possibilities, they do have a definite view concerning (a) the divergences which are important in the context of less developed countries and (b) the divergences that are usefully taken account of in the choice of individual projects.

Divergences which they consider important on the above criteria and corrections for which they discuss in detail are the following:

(1) The possibility that wage rates in industry overstate the opportunity cost of labour which is drawn from the agricultural sector.

(2) The possibility that aggregate saving and investment in the economy is less than would be socially desirable.

(3) The possibility that the prices of goods are out of line with their social values partly because of the underlying distortions in factor markets and partly because of irrational government interference with the market mechanism. The latter consists of some taxes and subsidies and most controls, especially those on foreign trade.

Distortions (1) and (2) are dealt with by correcting market wage rates and interest rates. The 'shadow wage rate' is an estimate of the social cost of labour which takes into account both the differential productivity of labour in agriculture and industry and the effect of extra employment on total saving. The 'accounting rate of interest' is an estimate of the social opportunity cost of capital. Distortion (3) is dealt with by what is a distinctive Little-Mirrlees contribution. This consists of valuing traded goods at prices which they command on the world market (or more accurately at 'border prices', c.i.f. for imported goods and f.o.b. for exported goods) and valuing non-traded goods by decomposing them into the traded goods and labour embodied in them. Thus, for a project which uses only unskilled labour as a primary factor in production we have:

$$SPV = \sum_{t=0}^{T} \frac{V_t - (SWR)_t L_t}{[1+(ARI)_1][1+(ARI)_2]\ldots\ldots\ldots[1+(ARI)_t]}$$

where SPV = social present value of the project
V = value-added at accounting prices
SWR is the shadow wage rate
ARI is the accounting rate of interest
T is the life of the project
L is unskilled labour used by the project
and t is a time subscript.

There are other sources of distortion with which Little and Mirrlees do not much concern themselves. This is sometimes on the ground that their importance in absolute terms or differentially between projects is slight; sometimes on the ground that it is reasonable to assume that the government can look after them independently of project selection. In particular, we may mention the problem of regional location and the question of external effects. Income distribution between present and future is extensively allowed for; income distribution between contemporaries is also admitted into the project selection criterion to some extent, though it could be argued not adequately. These questions will be discussed later. We begin by considering their treatment of the divergences they do consider important (the estimation of V, SWR and ARI).

The choice of numéraire

A brief discussion is first necessary of the numéraire employed by Little and Mirrlees. The unit of account which they use, while natural enough for their method, is apt to confuse people as it is radically different from units of account ordinarily used. Their unit of account is free foreign exchange in the hands of the government. This involves a double change from usual ways of thinking:

(a) There is the change involved in using *foreign exchange* as the numéraire or, to put it more formally, in setting the shadow price of foreign exchange equal to unity. There are two possible misconceptions which have to be avoided. The first one is that Little and Mirrlees believe foreign exchange to be the only scarcity. This is clearly wrong—using foreign exchange as the unit of account does not mean that it is the only scarce resource. The second misconception, and precisely the opposite one, is that since the shadow price of foreign exchange is absent in their method, they have failed to take into account the scarcity of foreign exchange. This is not the case. The shadow price of foreign exchange is important only as a *relative* price; the relative price between foreign exchange and domestic resources (which should be an indication of their relative scarcities) is not abolished by normalizing all prices with respect to foreign exchange.

(b) There is a further change involved in regarding foreign exchange *at the disposal of the government* as the unit of account. In other words, if aggregate consumption is felt to be too high, increases in income which are devoted to consumption are valued at *less* than their nominal value. This is in contrast to the usual practice among economists of using consumption as the unit of account, in which case increases in national income accruing to the government are valued at *more* than their nominal value. This particular aspect of the change of numéraire is very important in understanding the Little-Mirrlees accounting rate of interest,

4

Estimation of value added at accounting prices (V)

The Little-Mirrlees method consists of valuing *traded* outputs and inputs at border prices. As for *non-traded* inputs they suggest various methods but show a marked preference for one—this consists in valuing such a good at the marginal social cost of producing it broken down into traded goods (valued as mentioned above) and labour (valued at the shadow wage). This is of course an over-simplified account; many qualifications are made to these rules and illustrations given of how to use them in circumstances of varying degrees of complexity.

Now, what is the rationale of valuing commodities in this way? There are, it seems to me, two possible justifications of it; they are both present in the argument of the *Manual*, though they are not always clearly distinguished. One justification is to appeal to an optimum situation and to assume that the economy is moving towards such an optimum. If this is in fact the case then the prices that would prevail in the optimum situation are the appropriate accounting prices. It can then be shown that the accounting prices arrived at by *Manual* methods correspond to these optimum prices. This approach has the advantage of providing a clear standard of reference for the planners; its drawback is that there may be constraints—external or self-imposed—preventing the adoption of optimum policies. The second justification is to allow for such constraints and to show that *nevertheless* the *Manual* rules in their simple form are valid. This requires making certain assumptions about the economy in question and the relevant question then is whether these assumptions are sufficiently close to reality.

The total planning optimizing approach

Consider the first type of justification of the Little-Mirrlees rules. The main points can be made by employing the standard model used in international trade theory. Consider an economy which faces given world prices for all goods. Suppose for the moment that there are no transport costs. Suppose that the planning problem is to maximize social welfare which depends only on the consumption of the various goods at a point of time and on the way in which they are distributed. Suppose further that the only constraints on the maximization are those imposed by technology and trade possibilities—within these constraints the planners are omnipotent.

Now in such an economy the planning rule for production is clearly a very simple one—to equate the social marginal cost of production of each good with its world price. Since the economy cannot affect world prices, the optimal pattern of production is *independent* of the pattern of preferences. Following the above rule will maximize the availability of goods and they can then be distributed in line with social preferences.

Figure 1 shows this for a simple two-good case. If the transformation curve is TT and world prices are given by WW, the optimal production point is P; the optimal 'consumption' point will depend on the welfare function. Note of course that in following the planning rule in practical project selection, the optimal factor prices corresponding to point P would have to be guessed. On the other hand the accounting prices of the traded goods are simply their world prices whatever the domestic production possibilities and whatever the pattern of demand. Thus, at least in this simple case, the Little-Mirrlees procedure of using world prices as accounting prices for traded goods is completely correct. This continues to be true even if we have a large number of goods, some of them intermediate goods and others final goods—the planning rule is clearly the same. The rule also survives consideration of inter-temporal welfare. This is intuitively obvious but has been demonstrated in a simple case by Bent Hansen (6).

The shadow pricing rules for commodities become more complicated, however, if the simple assumptions of this canonical model are dropped:

(a) If the economy is not a price-taker in world trade, then world prices are not given independently of domestic production and consumption. Strictly speaking, in this case, the optimal pattern of production and consumption and the accounting prices of goods and factors must be determined simultaneously. Little and Mirrlees deal with this problem by taking the marginal export revenue or the marginal import cost as a measure of value. This is a useful approximate solution, but if one is taking the 'total planning' line then, strictly speaking, it is the marginal value *at the optimal point* which is relevant; using the marginal value which obtains in a non-optimal situation can lead the economy 'in the wrong direction'.

(b) Even if the economy faces given world prices, admitting the existence of transport costs creates considerable complications, at least in theory. If there are transport costs, we must admit the possibility that some goods should not be traded at all—those whose social marginal value lies between their c.i.f. and f.o.b. prices. However, the category of the goods which should be non-traded and what their accounting prices should be depends on the technological and preference para-

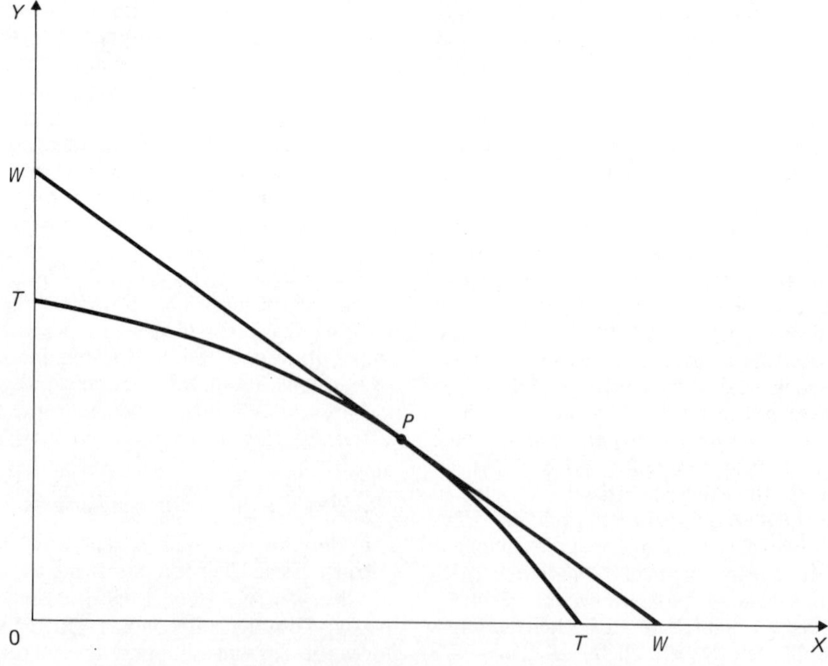

Figure 1

meters. In practice, it is possible to isolate with near-certainty some goods which will turn out to be non-traded in the optimum situation: construction, electricity, internal transport, some services. But with other goods, whether they should be treated as importables, exportables or non-tradables may not be so easy. However, when the difference between c.i.f. and f.o.b. prices is small this problem should not be serious since the border prices give the limits between which the social values of the relevant goods must lie. Determining the accounting prices of the goods which should not optimally be traded is difficult. The accounting prices of all non-traded goods must, in principle, be determined simultaneously since non-traded goods require other non-traded goods to produce them. Further, if the costs of producing non-traded goods vary with the amounts produced, their accounting prices are sensitive to the pattern of demand. These problems are recognized in the *Manual* and fairly exhaustively discussed. It is recognized that, in practice, a simultaneous determination of these accounting prices would be too difficult and various short-cut methods are suggested.

(c) So far we have assumed that the government does not face any constraints in its choice of policy instruments. How does the 'world price rule' stand up when this assumption is dropped? Little and Mirrlees have scattered remarks on this subject but no systematic treatment. A constraint which they build in explicitly is the imperfect control of the government over aggregate consumption; in their scheme, consumption is linked to employment. Such a constraint does not, of itself, provide any argument for abandoning the world price rule for valuing commodities. The reason is simple enough; for any level of employment, the value of output is maximized in an open economy with given world prices by following the world price rule; with consumption determined by employment it follows that the value of investment is also thereby maximized.

Another constraint which Little and Mirrlees consider, though not very explicitly, is the impossibility of levying lump-sum taxes and subsidies. At first sight, this would seem to have serious consequences: it implies that all feasible taxes levied for distributional reasons, must introduce some distortions. Given this deviation from first-best conditions, why should productive efficiency be desirable? In fact, it has been shown by P. A. Diamond and J. A. Mirrlees (4) that in an economy in which the government cannot use lump-sum taxes but is entirely free to choose taxes on *all* final goods, the constrained optimum is characterised by productive efficiency be desirable? In fact, it has been shown by P. A. Diamond and J. A. Mirrlees (4) that in an economy in which the government cannot use lump-sum taxes but is entirely free to choose taxes on *all* final goods, the constrained optimum is characterized by productive efficiency which, in an open economy, involves both in production and in consumption. If it is administratively impossible to separate consumer and producer prices then the intermediate use of such goods may have to be taxed *as part of the optimal structure of taxation* in which case their shadow prices may well diverge from border prices, even if they are traded goods.

It might of course be unrealistic to assume that the government has so much freedom in setting tax rates over the whole economy. One is naturally led to ask what the shadow pricing rules *in the public sector* should be, on the assumption that the government cannot tax private sector activities optimally. This issue is only recently beginning to be explored in the theoretical literature and the following remarks should be regarded as tentative. If the world prices of traded goods are exogenously given, then these are their appropriate shadow prices. The intuitive reason is simply that if world prices are unaffected by domestic activity and the public sector can freely import and export, there must be a social loss if relative marginal social costs in public sector production diverge from the given relative world prices. In this case, distortions in the private sector provide no ground for departing from the Little-Mirrlees rule in the public sector. The prices of non-traded goods are of course not invariant to trade between the public and the private sector. One would thus expect that non-optimalities in the production of these goods in the private sector could be compensated by public sector production decisions; so the shadow pricing rules for non-traded goods would be sensitive to the particular conditions prevailing. Project planners might also be concerned with screening private sector projects which come up for approval. If there are constraints on taxing the private sector, the presumption is that the shadow prices based on the absence of such constraints would no longer be appropriate.

Introducing more constraints leads one to consider the polar case of a project being evaluated in a completely 'locked-in' situation with everything else, including all government policies, assumed given. Do the Little-Mirrlees rules nevertheless provide a correct evaluation of the net social benefit of a project?

The partial planning 'improvement' approach

We turn, therefore, to examining the justification for the Little-Mirrlees approach without making the assumption that the government plans for the whole economy using the appropriate shadow prices (or that it offsets domestic distortions by appropriate taxes and subsidies). In fact, we shall make the opposite assumption—that a project is being evaluated taking everything, including existing (and possibly irrational) government policies, as completely given.

In considering this question, it is useful to separate the class of goods which can be considered to be 'fully traded'. A fully traded good is characterized by the fact that increases in domestic supply of it or increases in domestic demand for it affect only the foreign balance. If the good is an exportable, this requires that foreign demand for it should be perfectly elastic; if it is an importable, it requires that foreign supply of it should be perfectly elastic. Free trade is not necessarily required for goods to be 'fully traded'; a constant tariff or tax will be good enough. Even goods which do not enter into foreign trade could be 'fully traded' in this sense, if they are very highly substitutable for goods which do enter into foreign trade and which are 'fully traded'.

Consider first a project producing a fully traded output. Now, additional supply produced by the project cannot, *ex hypothesi*, change the price. Hence, domestic consumption and other domestic production will be unchanged and the project output will either substitute for imports or increase exports. With free foreign exchange as the numéraire the gross benefit generated by the project is thus equal to the project output times its border price. The same argument applies to inputs as well. It is clear then that if the inputs and outputs of a project all consist of fully traded goods, then the project is worth doing only if the net benefit measured at border prices is positive. This argument is in no way affected by the fact that the value of a *change* in domestic use of a commodity may in the existing situation be different from its border price. On the assumption that all goods are fully traded, the domestic use of no particular commodity is directly affected. The entire effect of the project falls on trade; whether the project finally enables absorption in real terms to increase depends on whether it creates more foreign exchange in the hands of the government to do with it what it likes.

The argument can be illustrated diagrammatically. Consider Figure 2 below.

DD is the domestic demand curve for a certain fully traded importable good. OP is its c.i.f. price, OP′ is the tariff—inclusive internal price. P′P′ is the tariff—inclusive infinitely elastic foreign supply curve. Before the project is undertaken the market is cleared at price OP′, demands OM, imports AM and domestic supply OA. (The domestic supply curve is not drawn to avoid cluttering up the diagram.) Suppose a project is set up producing output AB. Given the perfectly elastic foreign supply, the internal price and demand are unchanged. Imports fall by AB and the value of imports by ABEF. The social benefit of the project output is equal to the cost of the cheapest feasible alternative method by which the economy can obtain the same quantity. In this case the best alternative method is clearly to import; so that the gross benefit of the project output is equal to ABEF and the project should be accepted so long as the social cost of producing the output is less than this amount.[3] In calculating the social cost, all fully traded inputs should, by a similar argument, be valued at their border prices.

Now, the important question is how many inputs and outputs are usefully treated as being fully traded. If a good is not fully traded, then a project which produces or uses more of it will change its internal price and therefore lead to a change in its domestic production or use, in addition to any impact on exports or imports. The marginal value of the extra consumption or the marginal cost of the extra production will, in general, not equal its border price and the conversion of the relevant

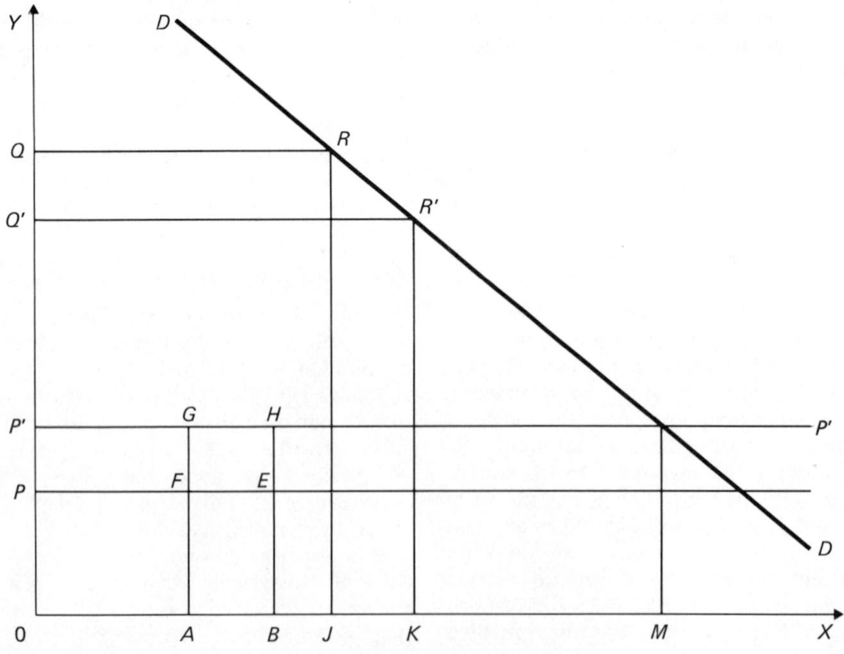

Figure 2

magnitude into its foreign exchange equivalent would pose a difficult problem. The problem is not one of principle. It would be wrong to say that the Little-Mirrlees method gives the right answers only if free trade prevails; it works perfectly well so long as goods are 'fully traded' which is a considerably weaker assumption than free trade. Even when goods are not fully traded, the method is not wrong in principle and there is some discussion in the *Manual* of how to deal with such situations. But in such cases the *convenience* of using the method is seriously affected and the possibility of making errors is that much greater.

I shall now proceed to make several points bearing on this question; the reader should remember that the setting is that of a highly distorted less developed economy.

(i) Clearly, goods whose border prices can change in response to project demand and supply are not fully traded. Domestic production and consumption are in such a case not independent of each other. In this case Little and Mirrlees suggest the use of the relevant marginal values in the world market as the measure of social benefit or cost. There are two difficulties here. *First* there is the difficulty of estimating the elasticities in foreign trade. There is a presumption that less developed countries cannot affect import prices (though they may in some cases have to shift to higher-cost sources of supply as imports are increased) and that they cannot affect export prices in the case of industrial goods. This still leaves exportable agricultural products which are important both in domestic consumption and as inputs into industrial projects. Furthermore, though the shares of the less developed countries in the world market for industrial exports are small, the argument that they face almost perfectly elastic export markets must be treated with caution, given the quality problems and the high selling costs involved. Also, any vigorous export effort may be met by tariff and quota rataliation. *Second*, there is the problem already mentioned of translating the domestic impact of the project into foreign exchange. This is really a question first of estimating the change in consumers' and producers' surpluses (making due allowance for the domestic tax/subsidy structure) and then deflating it by the inverse of the shadow exchange rate. While the *Manual* recognizes these difficulties it does not provide enough guidance about how to deal with them.

(ii) Goods which are produced inland at considerable distance from the port might not be fully traded even if physically similar goods are fully traded nearer the port. The reason for this is that given the poorly integrated markets of less developed countries, the longer the chain of demands involved before the impact on trade, the greater the possibility that a project will change internal prices and that the full impact may not fall on trade. This point becomes more significant still if we bear in mind the very inadequate and highly distorted transport systems that prevail in less developed countries in which private unit transport costs vary with distances and quantities in an economically irrational manner. A further reason for the existence of a number of separate local markets insufficiently linked with each other and to the world market is the lack of information about trading opportunities.

(iii) Goods may not be fully traded as a result of government policy. Consider the case of valuing the output of a project when the product in question is subject to an import quota that is fully taken up. Now, if with the additional output being produced by the project, the quota is unaltered, the price of the product will come down and domestic consumption will increase. If there are no other distortions, this extra consumption should be valued at the increase in consumers' surplus with the old and the new market prices as the limiting values. Certainly, the c.i.f. price understates the benefit. In such a case the project should be approved if the social cost is less than the increased consumers' surplus; valuing the output at its border price could result in the project being wrongly rejected. Of course, this argument depends on the assumption that the quota is unaltered, in other words, that the government behaves irrationally and rejects the readily available cheaper alternative of imports in satisfying demand; the project evaluation unit should obviously point this out. Note also that if the government responds to the extra domestic production by tightening the quota (so as to leave domestic consumption constant) the output is again correctly valued at the c.i.f. price since it once more substitutes for an alternative source of supply rather than increasing domestic availability. Returning back to Figure 2, suppose a fixed and filled import quota which results in market price OQ and consumption OJ (domestic production is not marked, again to avoid complicating the diagram). The project brings the price down to OQ′ and increases consumption to OK. If there are no other distortions, the gross benefit of this extra consumption is JKRR′ and the project should be approved if the social cost is less than that.

(iv) A fourth reason why goods may not be fully traded is the existing underutilization of capacity in home industry. Suppose, for example, that project demand for some input leads to a fuller utilization of capacity in the input-producing industry. This extra demand may neither increase exports nor reduce imports. Indeed, if production in the industry is constrained purely by demand, the social cost of supplying the input is the marginal variable cost of producing it which is below the c.i.f. or f.o.b. price. Two qualifications are in order. *First*, by no means all of the underutilization of capacity to be found in less developed countries is the result of demand factors. If it is due to bad labour relations or inefficient management, increase in demand will not mitigate it. If it is due to a general shortage of inputs, then any fuller utilization of capacity will starve other industries of these inputs; these inputs should then be shadow priced at their marginal value products in alternative use. Second, even if inadequate demand is the cause of under-utilization of capacity, it could be objected that a rational government would not allow such a situation to arise; if it does arise it could and should deal with it independently of the project. This argument is more convincing if the demand shortage is of the overall Keynesian kind which can be corrected by macroeconomic policies. But sometimes the problem is not so much a shortage of overall demand as a regional shortage of demand which is not amenable to easy macroeconomic solutions.

(v) Finally, we come to the case of goods for which the difference between c.i.f. and f.o.b. prices is large and which for that reason do not enter into foreign trade. In the case of such goods, there are of course no border prices to which direct appeal can be made. The Little-Mirrlees argument is that project demand for such goods does affect foreign trade because the increased demand is met by an expansion of domestic production which requires traded goods directly and indirectly. They therefore suggest valuing such goods by their marginal costs of production broken down into traded goods and labour (which is valued at the shadow wage). The difficulty is that the assumption concerning demand for non-traded goods may not in fact be correct. Extra demand may be met by the deprivation of other users rather than by an expansion of supply. Suppose, for example, that the project under consideration demands more electricity. This extra demand might, especially in the short run, be met by starving some other consumer of electricity. Suppose that given the existing distortions, the total production of electricity is below its optimal level, i.e. the marginal social value is greater than the marginal social cost. In this case, the marginal social cost of electricity *understates* the social value sacrificed by employing a unit of it in the project concerned. Of course, the entire impact may be on electricity production in the long run but the later years are the most discounted. The difficulty with taking the marginal social value as the measure of benefit is, of course, how to translate it into its foreign exchange equivalent. The difficulty arises again in valuing non-traded outputs. An assumption which Little and Mirrlees sometimes make and which would rule out the problem is that the government adjusts the production of non-traded goods so as to satisfy the equality of marginal value and marginal cost. Then the cost method of valuing non-traded goods should give correct results. However, this assumption is clearly unrealistic and further gives no concrete guidance about how to plan the production of non-traded goods.

Assessment of Little-Mirrlees accounting prices for commodities

It should be pointed out here that the authors are aware of most of the points raised so far. Inelasticities in foreign trade are discussed in ch. VIII of the *Manual*, though insufficient attention is perhaps given to the problem of estimating the impact on domestic consumption or production in such a case. Quotas are discussed on pages 109, 113 and 128, excess capacity on pages 108 and 113. The possibility of project demand for a non-traded input reducing competing domestic use rather than increasing domestic production is discussed on page 153. In general, the authors admit the possibility that projects affect not only trade but domestic consumption and production, and that in these cases the social value of a commodity cannot be measured by reference to its border price.

But what exactly should one do if these effects are important? Of course, there is no question of principle involved. Foreign exchange can still be used as numéraire. But the method then loses its distinctiveness and its simplicity. There is no alternative to estimating the change in consumers' and producers' surpluses which is difficult enough; but to express these *in terms of foreign exchange* requires an accurate estimate of the shadow price of foreign exchange. Little and Mirrlees's 'standard conversion factor' fulfils the same purpose (in reverse) as the shadow price of foreign exchange. They suggest calculating it by taking the average of the proportions by which domestic prices of traded goods exceed their world prices. But their discussion is somewhat too cavalier for what is a very complex problem. A great deal depends on what weights one uses in the calculation. A great deal also depends on one's standpoint. Is one considering the value of foreign exchange with all taxes and trade restrictions as given or with some of them changing? If the latter, then some allowance would have to be made for the change in price relationships that would naturally occur due to a change in the exchange rate. The Standard Conversion Factor certainly deserves more attention than they give it.

While Little and Mirrlees allow that in clear and important cases the valuation of a good which is not fully traded should take into account all the complications, they nevertheless believe that *as a general rule*, project analysts should lean over backwards to treat commodities as fully traded. Now this is a substantive point and it is worth asking what the justification is for such a general rule. A possible justification is that the border prices *are* the accounting prices of those goods which *should* be fully traded. This, however, raises the whole question of the relationship between the project evaluator and the government machine. Can one assume that the government will follow a rational course of action pointed out by the project evaluation unit? If the project evaluation unit points out that some good *should* be fully traded, will the government accept its advice and modify its trade policy? Not necessarily. The project evaluation unit may have no influence on trade policy which is framed by some other department and consists of extensive quota protection. Certainly, this picture of various government departments pulling in different directions is pretty horrific. This is not the way economic policy should be run, and in actual fact a project evaluation unit once established may be able to persuade other departments to change their policies. Nevertheless, the assumption of a coordinated and rational policy is undoubtedly too extreme. The extensive quota protection and the inefficient tax structures of the less developed countries today surely imply that in many cases projects would have to be evaluated with reference to their effect in the existing situation, rather than in some optimum situation. This considerably widens the range of less than fully traded goods. Further, even if the government refrains from constantly fighting itself, it is possible to imagine quite plausible circumstances in which these complications have to be taken into account. Suppose, for example, that the government is convinced of the need for trade liberalization and is moving towards it. However, it can persuade domestic industry to swallow this only by tying the reductions in tariffs or loosening of quotas to those fields in which projects are proposed which are expected to produce at less than the current domestic cost of production, though still above the c.i.f. price. (This could be because of particular 'infant industries' maturing or particular industries showing increased efficiency.) In such a case, the projects would directly affect domestic consumption and cannot be valued solely by reference to border prices.

The second consideration in assessing the Little-Mirrlees general rule is that goods may be less than fully traded for reasons that have nothing to do with the irrationality of government. In less developed countries it may be true for quite a long time to come that markets are poorly integrated, that information does not flow easily, that internal transport remains very inefficient, resulting in goods which should be fully traded in fact being only partially traded or non-traded. Further, even if governments were rational, they may face severe administrative constraints on instituting the right price structure through taxes and subsidies. This may affect the validity of the border price method in evaluating projects in the private sector. One also should not exaggerate the ease of selling exports on the world market, especially if all less developed countries are trying to do so. *A priori*, the factors which make goods less than fully traded would seem to be extremely important for agricultural projects. Whether they are important for industrial projects will depend on particular circumstances.

There remains the question of convenience. Certainly, working out the impact of projects on domestic production, consumption and trade would be tedious and complicated requiring forecasting of government policy and the empirical estimation of many complicated effects. Using border prices as far as possible is much simpler. This is an important argument —project selection methods would be useless if they cannot be applied—but it is not conclusive. The Little-Mirrlees method works if most inputs and outputs are fully traded with only a few clear and palpable cases requiring special treatment. But what if there are several projects in each of which most outputs and inputs are not fully traded? It might then turn out that using conveniently available border prices would lead to wrong results; while no input or output by itself changes the results of the project analysis, taken together they do. Whether this picture is realistic or not is, in my opinion, the crucial question in judging the applicability of *Manual* methods in their simple form. If projects do in fact have significant domestic effects, apart from any impact on trade, there is no alternative to working out the domestic welfare effects and the trade effects separately and then making them comparable by a 'shadow exchange rate'. This is difficult to do and the Little-Mirrless *Manual* has not made it any easier. In fairness, it must be pointed out that no one has yet come up with practical methods to deal with this problem. For example, the authors of the UNIDO document on project selection (19) emphasize the importance of these problems; but they do not go beyond a statement of general principles which Little and Mirrlees would undoubtedly agree with.

5

The shadow wage rate (SWR) and the accounting rate of interest (ARI)

We now turn to the corrections for market wage rates and interest rates, a question to which Little and Mirrlees devote considerable attention. In shadow-pricing labour, the first step is to estimate its marginal product in alternative use. In surplus-labour less developed economies, the direct or indirect source of extra labour to industry (or to the 'organized' sector) is agriculture. So the marginal product of labour in agriculture has to be estimated. To value this marginal product at accounting prices, one has to take a bundle of products which can represent the marginal physical product and then use the Little-Mirrlees method for pricing traded and non-traded goods to deal with the components of this bundle. This step is not easy; the non-traded goods will present difficulties and may have to be re-priced by using the Standard Conversion Factor. It is an important step, however, as the SWR is a principal way in which the Little-Mirrlees method allows for the 'scarcity of foreign exchange': a lower SWR encourages the use of domestic resources and *vice versa* for a higher SWR.

Suppose now that the minimum industrial wage rate (w) is above the marginal product of labour in agriculture (m) and that this is a genuine distortion. It would seem to follow that SWR = m. Little and Mirrlees argue, however, that in less developed economies, saving and investment are typically lower than socially desirable and that in the presence of this second distortion the

SWR should be set higher than m. While their treatment of this subject bears close resemblance to some others (13), (15), (19), they do attempt to bring the complex intertemporal considerations involved into project selection in a practical way. My discussion of this question will adopt a simple diagrammatic treatment which will attempt to clarify the optimizing framework underlying their analysis. The diagrammatic treatment is a simple development of that adopted by A. K. Sen in 'Choice of Techniques' (15).

Little and Mirrlees take very seriously the idea that saving and investment in a less developed economy could be below the socially optimal level. The possible non-optimality of the prevailing level of savings can be argued on several different grounds. First, it can be argued that even a perfect market would fail to reflect the preferences of contemporaries concerning how much provision they wish to make for future generations. Each man may prefer a state in which he *and* everybody else saves more, to the currently prevailing level of saving; but the market would fail to bring about such a state because it cannot by its very nature offer such collective alternatives.[4] Whether this argument, while logically valid, is psychologically plausible is of course an open question. Second, a more authoritarian line can be taken which relies on correcting for the irrationality of individuals, their 'defective telescopic vision of the future', which leads them to favour present consumption more than is desirable from the point of view of society as a continuing entity. In other words, the planners are trustees for unborn generations; and from the planners' point of view the rate of saving is lower than it should be. Third, in any actual economy the existing tax structure and the risk discounts of private individuals will generally involve a lower than optimum rate of saving.[5]

Whatever the reason for sub-optimal savings, this fact alone is not sufficient ground for taking account of them in the selection of projects. For the best thing to do is clearly to raise the level of aggregate saving and investment to the optimal level by fiscal policy. Allowing the fact of non-optimal savings to influence project selection requires (a) that the saving problem cannot be eliminated independently of the choice of projects and (b) that different projects have different effects on the aggregate balance of consumption and saving so that this is a relevant consideration for choosing between them.

Now, the way in which project selection is affected (by all this) depends on the nature of the saving constraint. In the Little-Mirrlees scheme, this takes the form of a given real wage in the industrial sector. This establishes a link between industrial employment and aggregate consumption. The higher employment is, the lower is total saving. This is why the SWR is crucially affected by the suboptimality of saving. Before I proceed to derive the SWR, an implication of this link between employment and consumption should be noticed. The assumption behind the Little-Mirrlees and other similar schemes is that though saving cannot be increased by extra taxation, it can be increased by restricting industrial employment (i.e. by preventing an increase in the living standards of a particular group, viz. the low productivity workers). It should be noted (a) that the desirability of subsidizing future generations looks very different according to *whose* consumption is being restricted. This point can be allowed for in the calculations of the SWR as will be shown in the next section and (b) even if subsidizing future generations by restricting employment were desirable, it may not be, or may soon cease to be, politically possible.

Consider the following very simple model. The model underlying the *Manual* is more complicated but sufficiently related to the one that follows. Consider the choice of employment in the industrial (or 'organized') sector of an economy producing a single good (or what comes to be the same thing, several fully traded goods with fixed world prices). The output can be consumed or invested (or employed in uses which are as valuable as investment). The marginal product of labour in agriculture remains unchanged as labour is drawn out of agriculture, over the entire relevant range. The terms of trade between industry and agriculture are fixed (say by international trade). Total investment in the economy is equal to the 'surplus' in industry plus some resources taxed away from the agricultural sector. Assume that the maximum tax revenue obtainable by taxing agriculture is invariant to the movement of labour into industry. Production relations in the industrial sector are characterized by constant returns to scale and diminishing returns to labour. Distribution of consumption between contemporaries and the value of leisure are ignored. Less strong assumptions could be made but only at the cost of complicating the exposition.

Consider the problem at a moment of time when the capital stock is given.

In Figure 3 OX is the total product curve relating output (Q), measured in terms of foreign exchange, to employment (L) in the industrial sector. The slope of OW is equal to the institutionally given real wage w; if c is consumption out of wages, $w = c$ by assumption. The slope of OY equals the constant marginal product of labour in agriculture (m). For any level of employment the total industrial wage-bill and hence consumption by industrial workers is given by the corresponding point on OW; with industrial output given by the corresponding point of OX, the contribution of industry to total investment is given by the difference between industrial output and industrial workers' consumption. An extra man moving from agriculture to industry increases *total* consumption by $(c - m)$ and changes *total* investment by $(\frac{\partial Q}{\partial L} - c)$. It is evident that up to employment L′, i.e. so long as $\frac{\partial Q}{\partial L} > c$, both consumption and investment can be increased by additional employment. At L′ where $\frac{\partial Q}{\partial L} = c$, total investment is maximized. At L″

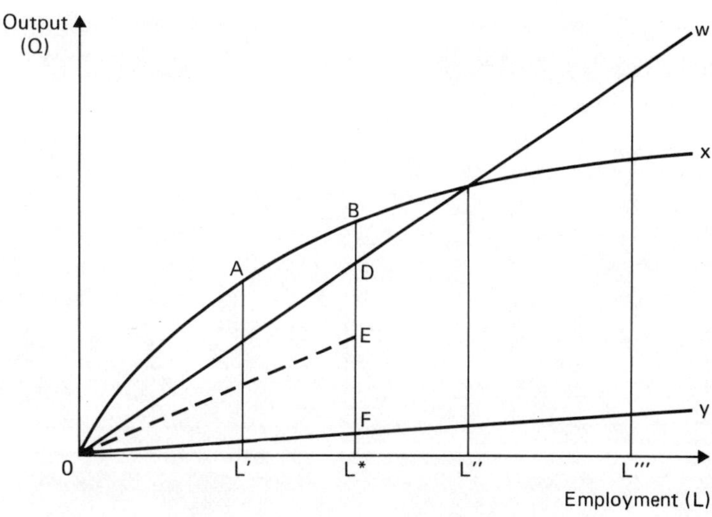

Figure 3

the entire industrial output is exhausted by the industrial wage-bill. Beyond L″, output can still be increased but the increase in consumption of workers must be subsidized by tax revenue raised from the agricultural sector. At L‴, $\frac{\partial Q}{\partial L} = m$, so that output is maximized. Between L′ and L‴ investment decreases at an increasing rate. Beyond L‴, additional employment would be an inefficient way of increasing total consumption since investment would decrease by more than consumption rose. If an increase in consumption is desired beyond L‴ it is more efficiently engineered by reducing taxes in agriculture. In general optimum employment L* must lie somewhere between L′ and L‴, depending on the relative social valuation of consumption and investment.

To see how the model is closed we can first translate the above diagram into a transformation curve between total consumption and total investment in Figure 4.

With industrial employment equal to zero, total consumption (which is equal to consumption in agriculture) is OM and total investment (financed by agricultural taxation) is ON. Remember that ON is invariant to sectoral shifts in the labour force. As industrial employment rises from zero, total investment and consumption can be increased concomitantly till employment L′, corresponding to consumption cL′. Therefore, from the social point of view, any point to the left of A′ would be inefficient. Beyond A′ consumption can be increased but only by sacrificing investment at an increasing rate till at consumption cL‴, output is maximized, i.e. $\frac{dC}{dL} = \frac{dI}{dL}$. Beyond cL‴, increasing industrial employment is inefficient because that means moving along T′ P′; but T′ P′ dominated by the dotted 45° line T′Z which is feasible by simply reducing agricultural taxation.

Given the wage constraint, optimal consumption (cL*) and optimal investment (I*) are determined at the point of tangency B′ between the transformation curve PT′Z and an indifference curve expressing the social valuation of consumption and investment. The choice of B′ fixes the optimal level of employment L* and the optimal output B on the total product curve in Figure 3. The shadow wage of labour, being that quantity to which $\frac{\partial Q}{\partial L}$ should be equated, is also uniquely determined: it is the slope of the tangent at B. If we construct a line OE with a slope equal to the tangent at B then the slope of OE is the SWR. BE is the maximum social profit attainable in the presence of the wage constraint.

We can now show the connection between the SWR and the social valuation of investment in terms of consumption which we denote by s. The value of s is given in Figure 4 by the slope of the tangent at B′ where the marginal rates of transformation between C and I are equated. Given s, we can reason as follows: The net

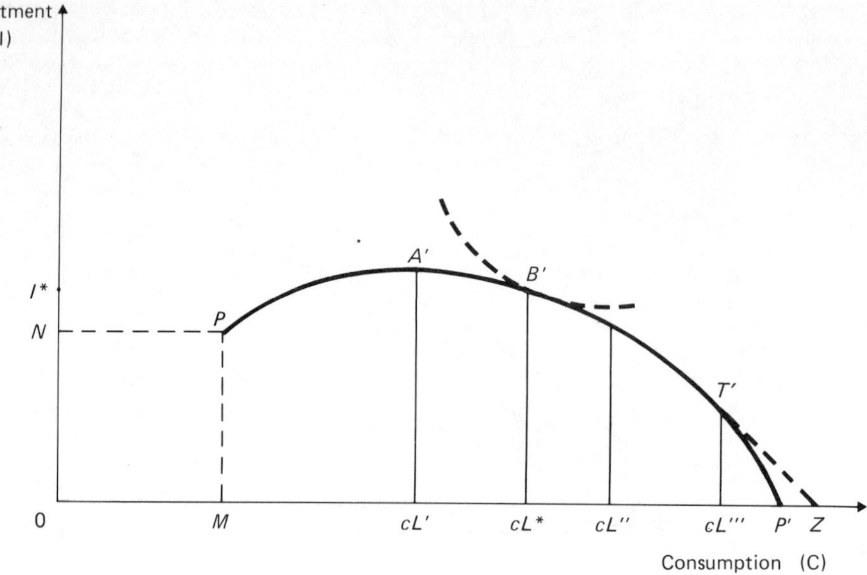

Figure 4

social benefit from employing an extra man consists of a change in investment plus a change in consumption (valued in terms of investment). The change in investment is equal to the change in output $(\frac{\partial Q}{\partial Q} - m)$ *minus* the change in consumption (c – m). The social value of the change in consumption is equal to $\frac{c-m}{s}$. Now, for optimum employment we must increase employment till the net social benefit equals zero, i.e. till

$$(\frac{\partial Q}{\partial L} - m) - (c - m) + \frac{c-m}{s} = o$$

$$\text{i.e. } \frac{\partial Q}{\partial L} = m + (c - m) - \frac{c-m}{s}$$

$$= m + (c - m)(1 - \frac{1}{s}) = \text{SWR}$$

In other words, the SWR or the social cost of labour in employing an extra man is equal to the loss of agricultural output *plus* the increase in consumption *minus* that part of the increase in consumption which is reckoned to be a benefit. In Figure 3 with optimal employment L*, $m = \frac{FL}{OL^*}$, $(c - m) = \frac{FD}{OL^*}$, $s = \frac{FD}{ED}$ = the slope of the tangent at B′ in Figure 4, and $\text{SWR} = \frac{EL^*}{OL^*}$.

It is obvious that so long as the government is being efficient $1 \leq s \leq \infty$. In Figure 4, a tangency at A′ would give $s = \infty$, a tangency at T′ or anywhere to the right along T′ Z would give $s = 1$. Substituting these extreme values of s into the formula for the SWR we see that the limits are SWR = c, when $s = \infty$, and SWR = m when $s = 1$, i.e. the limits for the SWR are given by consumption out of market wages (i.e. by the slope of OW) when extra consumption is valueless, and by the alternative marginal product of labour in agriculture (i.e. by the slope of OY) when extra investment and extra consumption are equally valuable.

As I have already mentioned earlier, with government saving in foreign exchange as the numéraire, m has to be estimated using Little-Mirrlees methods for traded and non-traded goods. The same applies to c: this would involve valuing a representative bundle of commodities consumed by industrial workers at Little-Mirrlees accounting prices and would of course raise the usual problems connected with standard conversion factors.

The SWR has been derived above by making the problem completely static. In fact, it is illegitimate to assume that the social indifference curves between C and I are exogenously given. The value of s today is not independent of the future course of the economy and in particular of the value of s in future periods. Formally, this problem involves maximizing a social utility function over time subject to the wage constraint in addition to the present and future technological possibilities, which are assumed to be known. The solution to this problem, which yields the optimal time-path of the economy, has as the necessary conditions for optimality not merely the static conditions outlined earlier, but also an intertemporal condition linking current s to future values of s. Under plausible assumptions, the feasible and optimal time-path will be such as to make the wage-constraint non-binding over time, i.e. s falls to 1. Heuristically, one can imagine the production function in Figure 3 shifting outwards over time as a result of capital accumulation and eventually desired saving being less than maximum feasible saving, i.e. in terms of Figure 4, as the curve PZ moves out over time, tangency with a social indifference curve occurs in a region analogous to T′ Z.

The intertemporal optimality condition referred to earlier leads naturally to the *Manual*'s treatment of discounting future benefits and costs. Since the *Manual* uses public money as the numéraire, the relevant discount rate is the rate of fall of the utility weight of public money which, if the government acts rationally, should equal the rate of return on public money in terms of itself at every moment. This rate they call the accounting rate of interest (ARI) and clearly the investment budget should be exhausted by projects which show non-negative present value at that rate. Since economists are used to thinking of the consumption rate of interest (CRI), i.e. the rate of fall of the utility weight of consumption, as the social discount rate, it may be useful to show the relationship between the two. If we denote the utility weight of government money by U_I and the utility weight of consumption by U_c, we have $s=\frac{U_I}{U_c}$. Differentiating logarithmically with respect to

time we have: $\frac{\dot{s}}{s}=\frac{\dot{U}_I}{U_I}-\frac{\dot{U}_C}{U_C}$

$$\text{i.e. } \frac{\dot{s}}{s}=\text{ARI}-\text{CRI}$$

In fact, this is one way of stating the intertemporal optimality condition referred to earlier. Note that the rate of discount used depends on the numéraire. If consumption is the numéraire as it is in the UNIDO Guidelines (19), then the social discount rate is the CRI and impacts of the project on saving are multiplied by s in doing the cost-benefit analysis. Little-Mirrlees use public money (or government saving) as the numéraire so the appropriate discount rate is the ARI and impacts of the project on consumption are divided by s. The treatment of workers' consumption on these lines is built into the SWR; but changes in capitalist consumption have to be deflated explicitly. This consideration becomes important in valuing private sector projects as private profits are clearly not as valuable as public money, in so far as they lead to some extra consumption, present and future. In fact, Little and Mirrlees go further and recommend valuing extra capitalist consumption as a pure cost on grounds of income distribution.

Thus, ARI, CRI, s and SWR are all related and values chosen for them must be consistent with each other. In principle, all these are determined simultaneously by solving for the optimal time-path of the economy. But how do we go about calculating them in practice? The Little-Mirrlees procedure is first to guess the time T when the economy (if it can be put on the optimal path) will reach a position where public money is no more valuable than consumption. Then by identifying a 'marginal project' and using the information about its rate of reinvestment (r) and about its labour-capital ratio (n), the value of s in the current period (s_o) is calculated. Essentially, the idea is to estimate the returns from this marginal project up to T and discount them back at the rate CRI to the base period. The crude formula for this is given on page 167 of the *Manual*. Given s_o, the SWR can be calculated. Then the ARI is estimated by trial-and-error, the criterion being that it should not pass more or less projects than the investment budget will permit.

Now, the difficulty with all this is what happens if the initial guesses are wrong. As for the formula for determining s_o and hence SWR on page 167, the results would seem to be sensitive to the r and n chosen. It may be true that if r, n and ARI are chosen correctly, *any* marginal project would give the same s_o and SWR. But if they are chosen incorrectly, the s_o and SWR may depend on which pair of r and n is chosen out of the projects which are thought to be marginal. A further point is that if the ARI is guessed incorrectly, then revising it must involve revising the SWR since it means taking a different r and n. All in all, the r and n procedure seems unnecessarily complicated. Why not guess T, s_o and CRI directly and make some assumption about $\dot{s}/s$ (given that $s_T=1$) and then estimate SWR and ARI using the formulae developed earlier? If the ARI thus estimated passes too many or too few projects then one can go back and change s or $\dot{s}/s$. The question of what practical iteration routines one should follow in estimating the macroeconomic shadow prices is a very complex one. The *Manual* tackles it, but not as successfully as one might wish.

Before closing this section, I should like to make a comment on the Little-Mirrlees shadow wage rate. Its validity is obviously crucially dependent on whether the model underlying it is realistic. Questions which are pretty much ignored by Little and Mirrlees might well be important in particular economies. For example, Little and Mirrlees assume, on the whole, that the supply price of labour to industry is equal to the marginal product (or the average product depending on the set-up) in agriculture. This, however, ignores the fact that because of the various costs involved in moving to an urban life, the need to acquire special skills, etc., the supply price of labour may be higher than the agricultural income sacrificed. If there is a free, unorganized labour market in the urban sector, there may well be an argument for taking the unorganized wage as an estimate of the supply price of labour or organized industry. Another complication is introduced by rural-urban migration which is often very significant in less developed economies. It can plausibly be argued in many instances that migration acts as an equilibrating mechanism linking the earnings in agriculture to the expected value of industrial earnings which in turn equal the industrial earnings times the probability of finding a job. Then it follows that the employment of a marginal man in organized industry would lead to *more* than one man departing from agriculture.[6] In fact, if we believe the equilibrium story completely, the value of the agricultural product sacrificed is equal to the organized industrial wage, i.e. the latter *is* the shadow wage of labour. There are other effects which might be important in particular instances. For example, changes in the terms of trade between industry and agriculture may affect the value of SWR significantly, if they are not fixed by international trade. In summary, we may say that the Little-Mirrlees formula for SWR may have to be substantially modified in particular cases to account for special features of certain labour markets. This is *not* a serious criticism of the Little-Mirrlees method which could be adapted to deal with such cases. Ideally, the authors of the *Manual* might have indicated more strongly the dependence of their shadow wage rate on particular assumptions and the effects of relaxing them. A further important influence on the shadow wage rate is the existing distribution of income which we discuss, in more detail, below.

6

Other distortions

The corrections discussed above occupy the bulk of the *Manual*. Other distortions are mentioned in Part I of the *Manual*, which discusses general principles and they are allowed for to some extent in Part II.

We first take up the question of the distribution of income between contemporaries. It is recognized in the *Manual* that if there is an argument for a positive CRI on the ground of diminishing marginal utility of income, there is on the same token an argument for intra-generational equity (though the effect on incentives must obviously be considered). To some extent the *Manual* assumes this to be looked after by the government through the structure of commodity taxation. But the logic of the *Manual* also suggests a natural extension of the shadow wage rate to achieve distributional objectives if the freedom to tax is limited. However, while this question is considered implicitly in the mathematical appendix, it does not figure very much in the text itself. In principle the 's' factor must be worked out taking into account the standard of living of the particular extra workers employed by the project. Diminishing marginal utility of income implies that the social value of extra consumption generated by employing an extra man is greater and hence 's' is smaller, the poorer this extra man was in his previous occupation. On the other hand, given the agricultural income sacrificed by an extra man employed, 's' is higher the higher is the institutionally fixed wage he receives in industry. Hence the same additional consumption is of higher value if it is spread thinly over a large number of poor people making them each slightly better off than if it is used to make a smaller number of poor people much better off. By a similar argument, one can show that extra consumption by the very rich must have very low social value. Hence, the *Manual* recommends treating consumption out of profits generated by a private project as a pure cost. Private saving is also less valuable than government money because it partly leads to extra consumption in the future by the very rich. This is clarified in ch. X of the *Manual* but it is not sufficiently emphasized in the rest of the text. It should be clear, however, that redistribution objectives *can* be handled satisfactorily within the framework of the *Manual*.

While the distribution of consumption between persons is given some weight, the question of regional equality is hardly discussed. On the whole, the *Manual* view is that 'it is probably politically impractical to give a different quantified weight to the social value of consumption in different regions'. In fact, the question of regional equality is a live issue in several less developed countries and it must be the object of a project selection method to make the resolution of this issue as rational as possible. In so far as the regional question is a question of relative poverty which cannot be looked after by inter-regional transfers, it must clearly affect the choice of projects. The overall pattern of taxation cannot be of much help here because widely different tax rates for the same commodities in different regions of an economy present obvious practical difficulties. But something *can* be done about regional poverty through the SWR. Clearly, given imperfect labour mobility, there should be a lower SWR for a poorer region and perhaps also different weights on the consumption of the richer people. (Obviously, some care will have to be taken in identifying the impact of a project on people in different regions.) But, often the regional question manifests itself in the form of particular regions bidding for a certain volume of industry to be situated within their borders. Even in this case, the *composition* of this fixed allocation of industry could be decided on the basis of the usual accounting prices. Much more difficult is the case where regions want particular industries for their own sake. If this has to be accepted as a political fact, irrational though it may be, the Little-Mirrlees accounting prices for goods would have to be altered.

The next question concerns externalities. On this issue, the *Manual* takes a sceptical line. It doubts their quantitative importance, especially in a differential sense between projects. It doubts on the whole the relevance of 'linkage' arguments on the ground that domestic linkages will generally be a less efficient way of securing goods than foreign trade. The *Manual*'s discussion of externalities must undoubtedly leave many readers dissatisfied. True, the authors admit that if externalities are important, they should be estimated. But the spirit of the discussion is to downgrade their importance and several purely *a priori* and impressionistic arguments are given in this connection. Certainly, no tangible progress has been made in the quantitative estimation of external effects, but to many people this simply indicates the need for more research. The authors can obviously not be blamed for failing to make progress on the question of estimating externalities. But the general tone adopted may have unfortunate effects on simple-minded practitioners.

7

Conclusion

The principal lacuna in the analytical structure of the *Manual* is the lack of a precise statement about the assumptions that are being made about government policy and about the implications of these assumptions. Government rationality is, on the whole, taken for granted; what is not so clear is what is being assumed about its freedom of manoeuvre. The *Manual* scheme has built into it a constraint on the total *volume* of savings that can be raised through taxation combined with considerable freedom with respect to the *pattern* of taxation. Even if we accept this rather odd assumption as reasonable, some issues need clarification. What difference (if any) would be made to the shadow pricing rules for projects in the public sector and in the private sector if there are administrative and other constraints on the government's ability to choose taxes? Of course, this question has to be asked in the context of the government having the maximization of consumption over time as only one of its objectives. In other words, even if the government is rational, do the rational shadow pricing rules in the presence of complex objectives and tax constraints approximate closely to the *Manual* rules in their simple form? And if they differ, in what way would these rules have to be amended? It would be useful if the authors threw some light on this question, at least for the benefit of professional economists.

Taking the *Manual* as it stands, I hope I have shown in this paper that the main question on which the usefulness of the *Manual* is to be judged is the division of goods into fully traded and less than fully traded goods. The larger the number of goods that fall into the former category the greater the applicability of the distinctive *Manual* methods. This is more likely to be the case in relatively open economies than in relatively closed economies, in industrial projects than in agricultural projects. However, even in cases where *Manual* methods are difficult to apply I doubt if they are any more difficult or impractical than other existing or proposed methods of project selection.

Perhaps the truth is that the really difficult problems in project selection still remain difficult. I refer here to the evaluation of projects which have widespread effects both locally and on foreign trade, projects which have significant indivisibilities and externalities. The substantive contribution of Little and Mirrlees—and it is a very substantial one—is twofold: *First*, to bring out the importance for project selection of international trading opportunities and to show how they can be brought into the calculations carefully and thoroughly and, *Second*, to develop a simple, powerful and convenient technique for the appraisal of certain types of projects. Such projects—where the majority of inputs and outputs are approximately fully traded—constitute a fairly special but important case. For dealing with more complex situations, their criterion, if used flexibly and thoughtfully, provides as satisfactory a starting-point as any other method.

Notes: Reading 28

1 A clearer exposition is given in their more recent paper (11).
2 For an extreme statement of this view see A. Rudra (14) and, for a general discussion, A. K. Sen (17).
3 The government loses tariff revenue equal to EFGH when the project is set up. But if it is a public project it can make up for it by selling the output on the domestic market at the internal price OṔ. So, on balance, there is no change in the government's budgetary position. However, if the project is in private hands, we have a loss of government revenue equal to EFGH and an increase in private profits of the same amount. But private profits are less valuable than public money, as we shall see later. So this effect would have to be explicitly allowed for in valuing the project.
4 This argument has been put forward by S. Marglin (12). See also A. K. Sen (15), ch. VIII.
5 See W. Baumol (1).
6 In this connection see M. Todaro (18).

References: Reading 28

1 Baumol, W. (1968), 'The social discount rate', *American Economic Review*.
2 Dasgupta, P. (1972), 'A comparative analysis of the UNIDO guidelines and the OECD manual', *Bulletin*, February.
3 Dasgupta, P. (1971), 'Public sector pricing rules', *Economic and Political Weekly*, annual number, January.
4 Diamond, P. A., and Mirrlees, J. A., 'Optimal taxation and public production', *American Economic Review*, March, June.
5 Dixit, A. K. (1968), 'Optimal development in a labour surplus economy', *Review of Economic Studies*.
6 Hansen, B. (1967), *Long and Short-term Planning in Under-developed Countries* (North-Holland).
7 Hirschman, A., (1967), *Development Projects Observed* (Brookings Institution).
8 Joshi, Heather (1972), 'World prices as shadow prices: a critique', *Bulletin*, February.
9 Joshi, Vijay (1970), 'Foreign trade and investment criteria' in *Induction, Growth and Trade*, W. A. Eltis, M. F.-G. Scott and J. N. Wolfe (eds) (Clarendon Press).
10 Little I. M. D., and Mirrlees, J. A. (1969), *Manual of Industrial Project Analysis in Developing Countries Volume II* (Development Centre, OECD).

11 Little, I. M. D., and Mirrlees, J. A. (1970), 'Shadow pricing as a method of project selection', mimeo.
12 Marglin, S. (1963), 'The social rate of discount and the optimal rate of investment', *Quarterly Journal of Economics.*
13 Marglin, S. (1967), *Public Investment Criteria* (Allen & Unwin).
14 Rudra, A. (1970), 'Use of shadow prices in project evaluation', paper presented at the Second World Econometric Congress, Cambridge.
15 Sen, A. K. (1960), *Choice of Techniques* (Blackwell; 3rd edn 1968).
16 Sen, A. K. (1972), 'Control areas and accounting prices: an approach to economic evaluation', *Economic Journal*, supplement, March.
17 Sen. A. K. (1970), 'Interrelations between project planning and aggregate planning', paper presented at the Conference on Economic Development at Dushambe.
18 Todaro, M. P. (1968), 'A model of labour migration and urban employment in less developed countries', *American Economic Review.*
19 UNIDO (1970), *Guidelines for Project Evaluation*, mimeo.

Reading 29

The Valuation of Labour in Surplus Labour Economies: A Synoptic View

A. P. Thirlwall

Scottish Journal of Political Economy, 1971, pp. 299–314.

There are not many topics in development economics which have provoked so much discussion in recent years as the valuation of labour in surplus labour economies. Moreover, there can be few issues on which opinion has shifted so dramatically in such a short space of time. The dust is now beginning to settle and a consensus reached on a middle view between the former extremes. The purpose of this paper is mainly a pedagogic one of bringing together some of the work in this field—especially that of Sen (1968) and Little and Mirrlees (1969).

The two extreme views on the valuation of labour in less developed countries with surplus labour in agriculture will be familiar. One is the 'traditional' view that if the marginal product of labour in agriculture is zero labour ought to be considered 'costless' to the industrial sector to maximise current total output. This is also the programming solution where the objective function is to maximise current income subject to resource constraints, but where labour is not a scarce resource. The other (opposite) extreme view in the 'modern' one that if the industrial wage is higher than the subsistence wage, and the propensity to consume of wage earners is unity, the transference of labour from agriculture to industry will involve an increase in consumption, and that to maximise growth and output in the future labour ought to be valued at the industrial wage to maximise the current investible surplus.

Both extreme views, basically representing different development objectives, can be illustrated by a simple diagram depicting the industrial sector of the economy (Figure 1).

If the marginal product of labour in agriculture is zero, maximisation of the total product, L_1P, requires that labour be given a shadow wage of zero so that OL_1 workers are employed. If the propensity to consume out of the industrial wage, OW, is unity, however, maximisation of the investible surplus, WRS, requires that labour should be given a shadow wage equal to the industrial wage. To value labour less than OW would encourage the employment of labour beyond OL and involve consumption to excess of production which would reduce the size of the investible surplus and impair future growth.

There are several good reasons, however, for taking an intermediate position between these two extremes. First, it is by no means certain that the marginal product of labour in agriculture is zero. The process of labour transference may well have production effects in the agricultural sector which require explicit consideration in valuing labour. Secondly, there will be consumption (and saving) changes in the agricultural sector as well as the industrial sector which must be taken into account. Thirdly, the objectives of maximising current output and of maximising growth and output in the future represent polar extremes in themselves, and in practice there will be a trade-off between present and future welfare. Fourthly, it cannot be assumed that the size of the investible surplus is determined solely by the valuation of labour when governments have the power to tax and to redistribute income. Lastly, domestic saving may not be the dominant restraint on growth in an open developing economy. A more general formulation of the real cost of labour in surplus labour economies is required which accommodates these considerations.

A. K. Sen (1960) was among the first to react against the traditional view that labour should be regarded as 'costless' in surplus labour economies, even though its marginal product may be zero. Sen goes to the other extreme, however, by adopting the objective of growth maximisation, placing no value on consumption *per se*. Furthermore, while he considers consumption changes in agriculture he ignores the production effects of labour transference from agriculture to industry, and their interaction with consumption, by accepting the traditional assumption of zero marginal product of labour in agriculture.

We can take Sen's framework of analysis as a starting point, however, and then relax the assumptions that the marginal product of labour in agriculture is zero, and that no value is placed on extra consumption at the margin. Further modifications can then be made to allow for government tax policy, and for the fact that foreign exchange may be the dominant restraint on growth rather than a shortage of domestic saving.

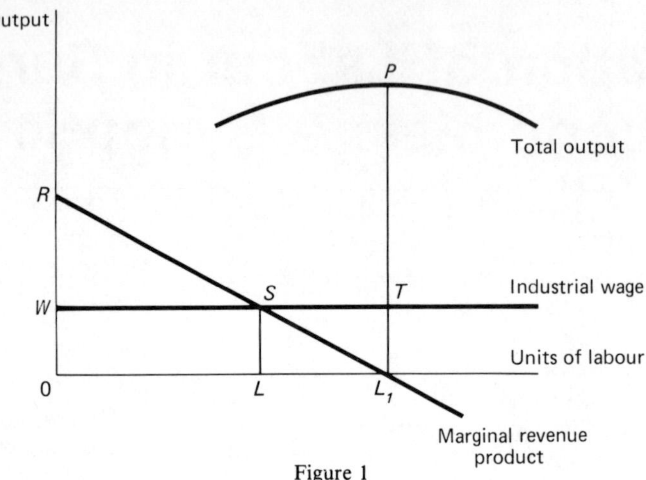

Figure 1

Notation

X = change in consumption.
W = the industrial wage.
c = the propensity to consume of workers in the industrial sector.
d = the consumption of workers when 'unemployed' in agriculture.
$\acute{c}$ = the propensity to consume of the hosts of the former unemployed workers in agriculture.
P_I = the marginal product of workers in industry.
P_A = the marginal product of workers in agriculture.
$\acute{S}$ = the change in the aggregate surplus with respect to labour transference.
W^* = the real cost of labour.
c^* = the propensity to consume of capitalists.

Sen's Model

In Sen's model the objective is to maximise growth and the output of consumption goods at some future point in time. If savings are suboptimal greater importance must be attached to an additional unit of saving than consumption, and the cost of a unit of labour must therefore be put equal to the change in consumption generated by an extra unit of employment in the industrial sector. Taking the industrial and agricultural sectors together, the change in consumption is given by:

$$X = W.c - d(1 - \acute{c}) \qquad ...(1)$$

If we take account of the consumption of capitalists, equation (1) can be extended to:

$$X = W.c - d(1 - \acute{c}) + (P_I - W)c^* \qquad ...(2)$$

If c and $\acute{c}$ are assumed to be close to unity, and $c^* = 0$ (as Sen assumes), the extra consumption will approximate to the wage rate with the implication that labour should be valued close to the industrial wage. The real cost of labour $(W^*) \approx W$. From society's point of view, therefore, the cost of labour is no different from the cost to the private entrepreneur. The maximum investment point represents the free market solution, as Lefeber (1968) has also demonstrated.

The Valuation of Labour when Savings are Suboptimal but Marginal Product in Agriculture Non-Zero

Let us now relax the assumption that the marginal product of labour in the agricultural sector is zero. This assumption is unnecessarily restrictive and is hard to reconcile with the various concepts and definitions of disguised unemployment in surplus labour economies. Zero marginal product is one possible definition of disguised unemployment but is by no means the only one and is certainly a very static definition. We may accept that disguised unemployment implies an elastic supply of labour to the industrial sector at the industrial wage, but the marginal product of labour in agriculture may be zero, positive or negative depending on how agriculture is organised. To illustrate, let us take Sen's diagram, incorporating the distinction between units of labour and units of labour time (Figure 2).

If agriculture is run on fairly capitalistic lines, with a wage-payment system, labour will not be employed beyond the point where the marginal product of a unit of labour time is equal to the agriculture wage (say OW), i.e. beyond OL. Under these conditions the marginal product of labour must be considered positive in the sense that if labour migrated from agriculture total output would fall unless those remaining on the land worked longer to compensate. In this case disguised unemployment must take the form of a low number of hours worked per person. The marginal product of labour can be considered zero only on the assumption that remaining workers compensate for lost production. If agriculture is run on very capitalistic lines disguised unemployment even in this sense will not exist because it is unlikely that an employer will underutilise labour and

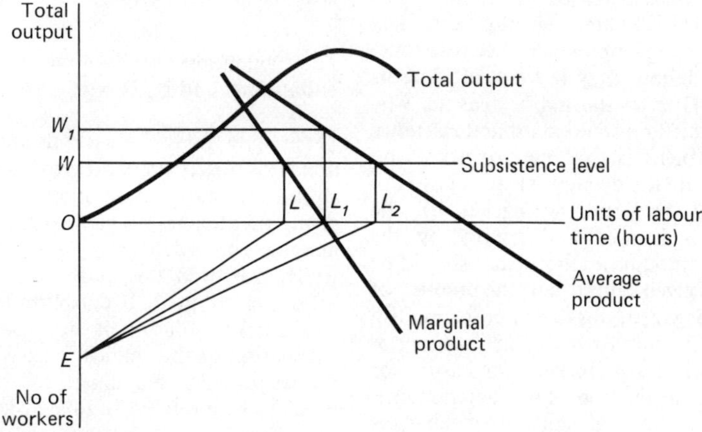

Figure 2

employ labour for what is considered to be less than a working day. In this event, the marginal product of labour is unequivocally positive. Positive marginal product is quite consistent, of course, with models of economic development with unlimited supplies of labour. In Lewis's celebrated model (1954), for example, disguised unemployment includes workers with a positive marginal product since all labour beyond the point where the marginal product is equal to the subsistence wage is unlimited in supply to the industrial sector and hence disguisedly unemployed in the sense that the agricultural sector will not compete for it.

If agriculture is not run on profit-maximising lines but on a family basis, with no wage-payment system, in which the total product is shared, marginal product may be considered zero or negative without any behavioural assumptions concerning the non-migrant work force. Suppose, for instance, that the objective of the family farming unit is to maximise total output or income. In this case OL_1 units of labour time will be worked where the marginal product of labour time is zero. This is possible since the average product, OW_1, exceeds the subsistence level. In fact, OE labour could work OL_2 units of labour time without the average product falling below the subsistence level, in which case the marginal product of labour time would be negative. In theory it is possible to conceive of negative marginal product of labour time if the utility attached to additional hours of work to offset the marginal disutility of leisure exceeds the loss of utility from reducing the average product from OW_1 to OW. Suppose, as in Figure 3 below, the marginal product of a unit of labour time is zero after four hours' work but the marginal disutility of leisure is still negative at this point. The worker may substitute work for leisure, working say six hours, despite the fact that the marginal product of labour time is negative after the fourth hour. This would not be irrational behaviour if the extra utility from working exceeded the loss of utility resulting from a fall in the average product from OW_1 to OW.

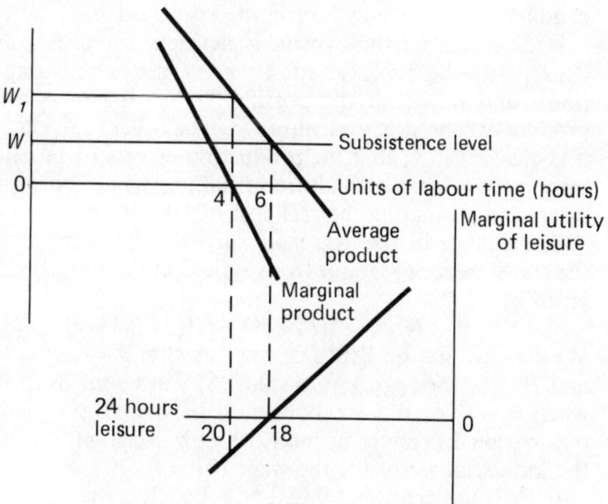

Figure 3

While it is possible to conceive of negative marginal product in the abstract, it is a little more difficult in practice, at least in a static setting; after all, how could workers work two extra hours if there is no product to show for it? Workers could, of course, spin out work but in this case the marginal product of the extra labour time would be zero, not negative, unless it is assumed that the extra time could be spent doing other work which would increase total output. But in the absence of alternative work it would seem that marginal product can only be negative if extra units of labour time impair the efficiency of units of labour time already worked. In a dynamic setting, however, the possibility of negative marginal product needs no elaboration. This is the concept of the dynamic surplus where migration from the land involves or induces a reorganisation of all the factors of production such that output per unit of labour input in agriculture increases as labour transference takes place. The dynamic surplus embraces many 'types' of disguised unemployment because there are many reasons why labour may not be fulfilling its potential to produce. One of the major reasons why estimates and opinions differ on the extent and existence of disguised unemployment is that investigators who have attempted to measure the dynamic surplus have not generally distinguished between the causes of the surplus. If the surplus is measured simply by the difference between the amount of labour that should be necessary to produce a given output and the amount of labour that is actually engaged, this does not distinguish between low productivity due to such factors as poor health; a lack of incentive; a preference for leisure, or the seasonal nature of production. The fact remains, however, that with institutional and other changes accompanying migration from the land, output per unit of input may increase independently of the remaining labour working longer hours, so that if it is labour transference which *induces* these changes the marginal product of labour may be considered negative.

If disguised unemployment is defined, therefore, as $0 \geq P_A \leq d$ (where d is the subsistence wage or consumption), and we admit the possibility that the marginal product of labour in agriculture may be other than zero, it is clear, if $\acute{c}<1$, that the production effects of labour transference from agriculture to industry must be considered in estimating the real cost of labour.

The change in the aggregate surplus with respect to the transference of labour from agriculture to industry is given by:

$$\dot{S} = (P_I - W.c) - c^*(P_I - W) - (P_A - d)(1 - \acute{c}) \qquad (3)$$

We can see that on Sen's assumption that $\acute{c}=1$, $c^*=0$, and $P_A=0$, the aggregate surplus (S) will be maximised when $P_I - W.c = 0$, i.e. labour must be valued to equate the marginal product in industry with consumption in the industrial sector (or the wage if $c=1$).

If P_A is not zero, and $0<\acute{c}$, $c^*<1$, which is the general case to consider, S will be maximised when:

$$(P_I - W.c) - c^*(P_I - W) = (P_A - d)(1 - \acute{c}) \qquad (4)$$

and the real cost of labour is given by:

$$W^* = W.c + c^*(P_I - W) + (P_A - d)(1 - \acute{c}) \qquad (5)$$

The real cost of labour is greater or less than X in equation (2) according to whether $P_A(1-\acute{c}) \gtrless 0$.

Substituting equation (4) into (5) gives $W^* = P_I$, and using equation (5) we get the result that for the surplus to be maximised labour must be employed up to the point where:

$$P_I = W.c + c^*(P_I - W) + (P_A - d)(1 - \acute{c}) \qquad (6)$$

The simple proposition is that if the objective is to maximise growth, and savings are suboptimal, it will be advantageous to encourage labour out of agriculture into industry so long as the increase in the investible surplus in agriculture is greater than the decrease in the investible surplus in industry. If the marginal product of labour is not zero the production effects of labour transference must be considered (in conjunction with $\acute{c}$) in arriving at the shadow price of labour.

The Valuation of Labour when Savings are not Suboptimal and P_A is Non-Zero

Let us now relax the assumption of growth maximisation. It is clearly unrealistic to assume that society places an infinite valuation on additional increments to investment and attaches no value to extra consumption at the margin. This would imply a social discount rate of zero which not even the most austere planned economies have ever adopted. If consumption is valued *per se* the free market solution is not socially optimal and the calculation of the shadow wage rate simply in terms of the wage which maximises the total investible surplus needs to be modified to take account of society's trade-off between investment and consumption, or consumption today and consumption tomorrow. One of the first attempts to do this was by Little (1961), but starting from the 'traditional' view of a zero shadow wage Little takes a two product model, and like Sen assumes that labour's marginal product in the consumption goods industries (agriculture) is zero. His equation for the shadow price of labour (using our notation) is:

$$W^* = Wc \left[1 - \frac{w_x}{w_k} \cdot \frac{P_k}{P_x} \right] \qquad (7)$$

where P_k/P_x is the price ratio of capital goods to consumption goods, w_x and w_k are the weights to be attached to consumption and investment, respectively, and c includes the consumption effects of the withdrawal of labour from the consumption goods sector combined with the propensity to consume in the industrial sector (i.e. the extra consumption is likely to be less than the industrial wage, for even if the migrant labour does not save his family, with one less mouth to feed, will consume less).

Equation (7) says that if the relative prices of capital and consumption goods correctly reflect social utilities (or society's valuation of these goods) then $\frac{w_k}{w_x} = \frac{P_k}{P_x}$, and the bracketed expression in equation (7) is zero giving a shadow wage of zero. If, however (as seems more probable, argues Little) the relative prices of capital and consumption goods undervalue the importance to be attached to investment then $\frac{w_k}{w_x} > \frac{P_k}{P_x}$, and $\frac{w_x}{w_k} \cdot \frac{P_k}{P_x} < 1$, and the shadow wage will be greater than zero. In the extreme cases of $w_x = 0$, or $w_k = \infty$, $W^* = Wc$, i.e. the shadow wage is equal to consumption out of the industrial wage. Depending, therefore, on society's relative valuation of investment in terms of consumption it is possible to arrive at a shadow price of labour between the two extremes of zero and the value of consumption out of the industrial wage.

Recently Little (1969), collaborating with Mirrlees,

has suggested a simple way of valuing investment relative to consumption, which fits in with Sen's time horizon approach to investment planning and the choice of techniques. Suppose within a time period acceptable to society *n* million pounds worth of consumption arises from *q* million pounds worth of investment today, where *n* is the sum of the annual flows of consumption over the time period discounted by the rate of time preference or consumption rate of interest (*r*). The value of investment relative to consumption is simply n/q.[4] The calculation can then be used to estimate the present value of lost saving and investment resulting from the *total* change in consumption exceeding the marginal product of the newly transferred workers in industry. Denoting $n/q = S_o$ and the total level of new consumption as C, the shadow wage is now (including the production effects in agriculture as well):

$$W^* = (S_o - 1)(C - P_I) + P_a \qquad (8)$$

The social optimum requires $W^* = P_I$ so that the optimum shadow wage is:

$$W^* = C - \frac{1}{S_o}(C - P_A) \qquad (9)$$

The higher the valuation given to saving and investment compared to consumption (i.e. the higher S_o), the higher the real cost of labour and the closer the shadow wage will approximate to the industrial wage if all wages are consumed. The equivalence with Little's earlier result (the equivalence of equations (*7*) and (*9*)) is immediately obvious except that (*9*) incorporates the production and consumption effects in the agricultural sector as labour migrates. If no value is attached to consumption at the margin then from (*9*) the real cost of labour is equal to *C*, i.e. the increase in consumption plus the reduction in agricultural output. This is also the result derived in equation (*5*) taking Sen's model. If at the other extreme saving and consumption are valued equally at the margin so that $S_o = 1$, the real cost of labour is simply equal to P_A—the marginal product of labour, which can be zero, positive or negative. In general, the poorer the country, the lower its investment ratio, and the slower consumption is expanding, the greater the weight that will be attached by planners to investment (though not necessarily by the populace) and the higher the shadow wage. Little and Mirrlees do not acknowledge the work of Sen but it is easy to see that their respective models are formally equivalent. The novel feature of Little and Mirrlees' work is that it explicitly takes foreign trade into account by valuing resources at world prices. Thus the *calculation* of *W** may differ. The valuation of labour in an open economy is discussed later.

If the shadow wage lies below the market wage because consumption is a socially desired activity the obvious answer is wage subsidies to increase the employment rate and consumption. In the limit, with no value placed on investment, the entire wage would consist of subsidy (Lefeber, 1968).

Taxation and the Valuation of Labour

It was mentioned at the outset that one of the implicit assumptions underlying the emphasis on obtaining the 'correct' shadow wage is that the investible surplus is a function of the choice of technique and cannot be influenced by fiscal policy. This presupposes that the government can regulate the choice of technique but lacks adequate policy instruments for varying the savings rate to any desired extent. In reality, of course, this is far from the truth. Governments can and do tax and redistribute income for reasons of equity, efficiency and growth, and in practice tax policy can be a substitute for, or used in conjunction with, shadow wages to achieve specific development goals. Wage subsidies themselves would require financing. With policy instruments in the form of subsidies and taxes we can now conceive of the shadow wage not simply as something determined by 'the system' (i.e. by the societal objectives to be maximised) but as an instrumental variable capable of manipulation for the reconciliation of conflicting objectives. In recognition, we shall henceforth refer to the shadow wage as the planning wage. To illustrate the point, the relaxation of the no-tax assumption clearly lessens the conflict between those who put a premium on maximising present employment and consumption and those who emphasise maximisation of the investible surplus for future welfare. The conflict is reduced to the extent that if the planning wage is fixed below the level that would maximise the investible surplus for the sake of increasing employment and consumption (e.g. through wage subsidies), real saving can be prevented from falling (and possibly increased) by a redistribution of income from low savers to high savers. Consider, for example, an extreme situation in which income is redistributed from those with a unitary propensity to consume to those with a zero propensity to consume. In Figure 4 below, a planning wage below OW^*, say OW^*_1, would be compatible with the maintenance of an investible surplus equal to the area W^*WH so long as taxation could be raised from those with unitary propensities to consume (wage earners) sufficient to offset the reduction in saving, HIJ, which would result from the lower wage and the higher level of employment, OL_1.

If at employment level OL_1 tax revenue W^*IT_1T, equal to HIJ, can be collected from those with a propensity to consume of unity and distributed to those with a propensity to consume of zero we can see that the planning wage is capable of manipulation to increase employment without impairing the size of the investible surplus.

The broader question is now raised of how the planning wage might be adjusted by the scope for government to tax to reduce real consumption out of the real wage, and to save and invest on society's behalf, without the uncertainty involved in redistributing income. The government has two main weapons at its

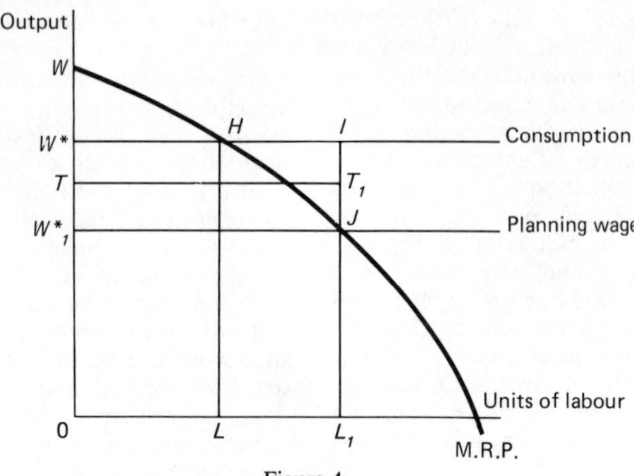

Figure 4

disposal. It can either tax consumption directly by the use of commodity taxation, or indirectly by taxes on income which reduce disposable income. To make the analysis simple for illustrative purposes we shall confine ourselves to taxation in the industrial sector which is where the increased consumption occurs with labour transference.

The scope for taxation to reduce real consumption depends on two interrelated factors: First, on the size of the differential required between the industrial wage and the subsistence wage to ensure an elastic supply of labour to the industrial sector, and secondly on the reaction of workers to a cut in their real disposable income. In recent years there has been a marked tendency for the differential between earnings in the subsistence agricultural sector and the modern industrial sector to widen. Due to the growing income differential many formerly in disguised unemployment in the rural sector have transferred into visible unemployment in the modern urban sector. The increasing income differential may be due to genuine productivity differences between the two sectors or partly the result of labour unions in the industrial sector pushing up money wages in excess of productivity increases. In certain Latin American countries such as Chile, Brazil and Colombia, Meier (1969) suggests that there is considerable evidence that union pressure and minimum wage legislation has raised the wage above the opportunity cost of labour which has also induced the introduction of more capital intensive techniques. Government policies have generally supported urban wage increases, and wages have risen very rapidly in the government sector itself.

Prima facie evidence of the power of monopolistic elements in the industrial labour markets would be an increase in earnings differentials between the modern and subsistence sectors, coupled with a movement in the terms of trade in favour of industrial commodities. Secondary evidence of the power of labour unions would be a rise in the differential between the two sectors, coupled with growing unemployment in the industrial sector itself. There is evidence of both of these tendencies. In many less developed countries in recent years real wages have risen by up to 5 per cent per annum in excess of productivity, and the price of industrial goods has risen faster than the price of agricultural goods within less developed countries (as well as internationally). Furthermore, many countries have witnessed for some time growing unemployment in urban centres. In short, there may be scope for the real wage in the industrial sector to be reduced by taxation without the supply of labour drying up, given some control over monopoly elements in the labour market.

If the existing differential between the industrial wage and subsistence wage is more than sufficient to ensure an elastic supply of labour to manufacturers in the industrial sector and there is no reaction among workers to a cut in their real disposable income it would be advantageous to reduce the planning wage by the product of the amount of the excess differential and the propensity to consume and to tax equivalently. Consider Figure 5 below.

OW^* is the planning wage based on the industrial wage OW as calculated in equation (*5*). WW_1 is the gap by which the actual wage exceeds the necessary wage to ensure elastic supplies of labour to the industrial sector. WW_1 is therefore the possible amount of taxation per worker. If this is the extent of taxation, real consumption would fall by $c(WW_1)$ and the planning wage should be reduced by an equal amount from OW^* to OW^*_1. The amount of labour employed will increase from OL to OL_1 and the excess of consumption over production, STT_1 is fully taxed away. In fact, the total investible surplus rises by an amount $W^*ST_1W^*_1$ which is at the government's disposal. On the assumption that there is no reaction to the cut in real disposable income the real cost of labour is:

$$W^* = (C - cT) - \frac{1}{S_o}\left[C - P_A\right] \qquad (10)$$

where T is total tax revenue.

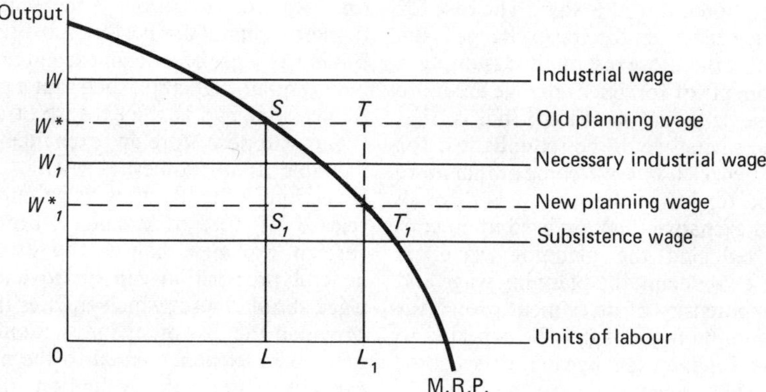

Figure 5

Suppose, however, there is no excess differential between the industrial and subsistence wage. In this event, whether the planning wage can be lowered, without sacrificing growth, by a policy of taxation depends on the reaction of workers to a change in their real disposable income. In the absence of money illusion workers will resist both a reduction in their money wage through direct taxation and also a reduction in their real wage through commodity taxation. If money illusion exists, commodity taxation is a possibility until workers become aware of the cut in their real consumption. Given the valuation of investment relative to consumption the change in the planning wage is equal to:

$$\Delta W^* = (\Delta W - c\Delta T) \qquad (11)$$

where W is the industrial wage.

For a reduction in the planning wage the term $(\Delta W - c\Delta T)$ must be negative which will depend on whether workers react completely to a reduction in their disposable income through an increase in T by bidding for a higher real wage.

The Valuation of Labour in an Open Economy

In an open economy a shadow wage which is calculated in terms of the extra consumption generated by the employment of an additional unit of labour may not be 'optimal' having regard to a country's foreign exchange position. In an open economy dual gap analysis, and the theory of the dominant restraint, becomes relevant, and the scope must be considered for using wages as a policy instrument for equating the two gaps *ex ante*. Again we shall want to refer to the shadow wage as the planning wage. The two gaps referred to are the savings-investment gap and the export-import, or foreign exchange, gap. If domestic saving is calculated to be less than the level necessary to achieve the target rate of growth there is said to exist a savings-investment gap. It is essentially the minimisation of this gap that we have been concerned with so far. In an open economy, however, there may also be a foreign exchange gap if minimum import requirements to achieve the growth target are calculated to be greater than the maximum feasible level of exports. In the absence of foreign borrowing growth will proceed at the highest rate permitted by the most limiting factor. If the largest gap is the foreign exchange gap, growth is said to be trade-limited and domestic saving may go unused despite a 'shortage'.

Whether or not the foreign exchange gap is the dominant restraint, a shortage of foreign exchange obviously has implications for the valuation of resources used in investment projects. If there is excess demand for foreign exchange at the ruling price foreign goods must be worth more to the economy than their domestic price suggests. A shortage of foreign exchange implies that the foreign exchange rate is overvalued and foreign goods are too cheap relative to domestic goods. Foreign resources used in investment projects, if valued in the home currency, will understate their cost to the economy relative to the use of domestic resources. One solution is to adopt a shadow price of foreign exchange.

The alternative adopted by Little and Mirrlees is to make foreign and domestic resources by valuing all inputs and outputs at accounting prices which are derived from world prices. Thus the shadow price of labour in the Little-Mirrlees model fulfils the same function as the shadow price of foreign exchange when domestic currency is the unit of account. In the absence of such adjustments one way to economise on the use of foreign exchange is to encourage the use of 'cheaper' domestic resources in relation to undervalued external resources. A suggestion frequently made is that the planning wage should be reduced. Before recommending this as a policy measure, however, let us follow through its implications. The first repercussion will be to cheapen domestic resources relative to resources from abroad, thereby releasing foreign exchange. On the other hand a lower planning wage will increase the level of employment, which will increase consumption and reduce the level of domestic saving if the planning wage was previously fixed to equate labour's marginal product with consumption out of the wage. The case for lowering the planning wage when foreign exchange is the dominant restraint must therefore rest on the assumption that additional increments of foreign exchange are more useful than the domestic saving sacrificed; that is, that either some domestic saving would be redundant if the foreign exchange bottleneck is not overcome or that more resources are released for investment purposes through the release of foreign exchange than are used up in consumption through reducing the planning wage. A further repercussion of reducing the planning wage and increasing the labour intensity of investment projects is that imports of consumption goods may be expected to rise which will absorb foreign exchange and offset some of the savings of foreign exchange due to the switch in demand from foreign to domestic resources.

In considering a policy of reducing the planning wage to equate, *ex ante*, the savings-investment gap and the foreign exchange gap two considerations must therefore be borne in mind. The first is whether the foreign exchange gap is truly the dominant restraint and the second is the net saving of foreign exchange that can be expected from the policy.

Recently the theory of the dominant restraint has been called into question by many economists (e.g. Kennedy (1968); Bruton (1969)). On the one hand it has been argued that if capital and imports are substitutable for one another there can only be one gap not two, and on the other hand it has been argued that if the capital inflow required to fill the foreign exchange gap is larger than the savings-investment gap this need not imply, as traditional theory argues, that savings will fall below the saving potential of the community or that less productive investment will take place. On the second point, which is the one more pertinent to the present discussion, there are plenty of types of productive investment, e.g. investment in human resources, that do not require imported capital goods. So long as this type of investment can be expanded the existence of a foreign exchange gap should not prevent the translation of potential savings into investment, and the possibility of excess saving disappears. But if this is the case, it is also difficult to argue that foreign exchange is genuinely more valuable than the sacrifice of domestic saving that a reduction in the planning wage would entail. In short, the savings-investment gap, as traditionally calculated from the Harrod growth equation, may be understated due to scope for types of investment with large spillovers to the community.

If it can be demonstrated that domestic saving is just as valuable as foreign exchange, and that there are alternative outlets for domestic saving which do not require capital inputs from abroad which may yield returns equal to the returns from releasing foreign exchange by using cheaper domestic resources in investment projects, the foreign exchange problem must be tackled in ways which do not reduce domestic savings. This is tantamount to arguing that there may only be one gap not two, not in the sense that imports and domestic capital are perfect substitutes for one another, but in the sense of foreign exchange and domestic saving being equally valuable, such that a policy measure which reduces one gap at the expense of another is pointless.

But suppose foreign exchange is genuinely more valuable than domestic saving. The extent of the reduction in the planning wage must depend on the net release of foreign exchange brought about. If the foreign exchange gap is the dominant restraint the general proposition can be advanced that a planning wage should be set which equates the two gaps *ex ante*, provided the loss of saving is compensated by a release of foreign exchange equal to the net release of foreign exchange times the valuation of foreign exchange relative to saving. Ignoring the valuation of investment relative to consumption the change in the planning wage will be equal to:

$$\Delta W^* = (C - F.\frac{w_F)}{w_S} \qquad (12)$$

where C is the total reduction in saving

F is the *net* release of foreign exchange

and w_F/w_S is the ratio of weights attached to foreign exchange and domestic saving.

The term $(C - F.\frac{w_F)}{w_S}$ gives the scope for changing the planning wage to equate the savings-investment and foreign exchange gaps *ex ante*. For a reduction in the planning wage the term must be negative, and it would pay to reduce the planning wage until $(C - F.\frac{w_F)}{w_S} = 0$. The expression will approach zero as C rises and w_F/w_S falls. If no foreign exchange is released because increased consumption good imports match the decrease in foreign resources required for development the expression will be positive and there is no scope for reducing the planning wage since saving would merely fall with no offsetting benefits. In this situation measures such as import controls on consumption goods and devaluation may have to be implemented to remedy the foreign exchange shortage. Devaluation may be particularly efficacious since it tackles the foreign exchange bottleneck and reduces the real wage simultaneously.

Conclusion

The foregoing discussion has suggested that the 'optimum' price of labour must reflect many considerations. The choice between valuing labour at its opportunity cost and the industrial wage is far too stark. Several other factors must be borne in mind such as the valuation of investment relative to present consumption; the scope for taxation and the foreign exchange situation. The models developed, and the policy speculations, now require empirical content and backing. It may transpire, of course, that the planning wage should be close to the industrial wage. On the other hand, given a fairly rapid growth of less developed countries in recent years, coupled with growing unemployment, it may lie sufficiently below to make it worth while for less developed countries to experiment with the subsidisation of labour in the industrial sector, and to encourage greater labour intensity in the productive process for an improvement in the general welfare.

References: Reading 29

Bruton, H. (1969), 'The two gap approach to aid and development: comment', *American Economic Review*, June.

Kennedy, C. (1968), 'Restraints and the allocation of resources', *Oxford Economic Papers*, July.

Lefeber, L. (1968), 'Planning in a surplus labour economy', *American Economic Review*, June.

Lewis, A. (1954), 'Economic development with unlimited supplies of labour', *Manchester School*, May.

Little, I. (1961), 'The real cost of labour and the choice between consumption and investment', *Quarterly Journal of Economics*, February.

Little, I., and Mirrlees, J. (1969), *Manual of Industrial Project Analysis in Developing Countries, Vol. II, Social Cost Benefit Analysis* (OECD).

Meier, G. (1969), 'Development without employment', *Banca Nazionale del Lavoro Quarterly Review*, September.

Sen, A. K. (1968), *Choice of Techniques* (Blackwell; 1st edn 1960).

Thirlwall, A. P. (1970), 'An extension of Sen's model of the valuation of labour in surplus labour economies', *Pakistan Development Review*, Autumn.

Uppal, J. (1969), 'Work habits and disguised unemployment in underdeveloped countries – a theoretical analysis', *Oxford Economic Papers*, November.

Reading 30

Effective Tariffs, Domestic Cost of Foreign Exchange, and the Equilibrium Exchange Rate

B. Balassa and D. M. Schydlowsky

Journal of Political Economy, 1968, pp. 348–60.

1

The use of traditional two-commodity, two-country models had long restricted the theory of tariffs to a consideration of final goods. In recent years, however, attention has been given to the protective effects of Tariffs on commodities at various stages of fabrication, and efforts have been made to evaluate the impact of trade policies on resource allocation.

Two major trends of thought stand out in this development: Michael Bruno (1963; 1967, pp. 88–135) and Anne Krueger (1966) have examined the domestic cost of foreign exchange, while, among others, Bela Balassa (1965), H. G. Johnson (1965), and W. M. Corden (1966) have focussed on the effective rate of protection of individual industries. The purpose of this paper is to indicate the relationship between the two measures and their relevance for the choice among individual industries in a developing country. In this connection, we will also deal with questions of comparative advantage and 'equilibrium' exchange rates.

2

Bruno calculates the cost of foreign exchange saved in the case of import-competing goods and the cost of foreign exchange earned in regard to exports. The analysis of the two cases is basically the same,[1] hence we may speak of 'the cost of foreign exchange' irrespective of whether exchange reserves increase because the country saves or earns an additional unit of foreign exchange. For a given commodity, the cost of a unit of foreign exchange (earned or saved) is taken to equal the direct and indirect domestic resource costs incurred in supplying it domestically, divided by the difference between the foreign price of the product and the foreign exchange cost of direct and indirect imported inputs. The same measure is used, although without reference to Bruno's work, by Krueger.

Let us assume a competitive economy and denote domestic resource costs (value added) at a given stage of fabrication by W, the world market price of the commodity by P, the value of imported inputs per unit of output by N, and elements of the matrix of direct and indirect input requirements by r_{ji}. The cost of a dollar earned or saved for commodity i will be

$$B_i = \frac{\sum_j W_j r_{ji}}{P_i - \sum_j N_j r_{ji}}. \tag{1}$$

For example, if the sum of direct and indirect domestic value added is 240 pesos, the c.i.f. import price ten dollars and, in the event of domestic manufacturing, there is an expenditure of six dollars on direct and indirect imported inputs, the domestic resource cost of a dollar will be 60 pesos. For the sake of comparability with the effective rate of protection, let us reinterpret this measure by expressing foreign values in terms of domestic currency. If the exchange rate is 50 pesos to the dollar, we now get 1.2, indicating that the cost of the dollar in this case exceeds the rate of exchange by 20 per cent.

According to Bruno (1967, p. 106), the cost of foreign exchange criterion 'clearly measures comparative advantage', and the relative desirability of export-promoting or import-substituting projects should be evaluated by ranking them accordingly. Under the assumption of constant costs and infinite foreign demand elasticities, the formula has also been used by Krueger to estimate the cost of protection in Turkey. This cost equals the savings in domestic resources that can be obtained by expanding relatively efficient export industries and contracting relatively inefficient import-substituting activities (Krueger, 1966, p. 475).

In turn, the effective rate of protection is designed to indicate the degree of protection of value added at a given stage of the manufacturing process. It equals the excess of the remuneration of domestic factors of production (domestic value added), obtainable by reason of the imposition of tariffs and other trade barriers, as a percentage of value added in a free trade situation. Tariffs on the product itself raise the effective rate of protection, while duties on inputs have the opposite effect.

If input coefficients are constant in the relevant range and domestic prices equal the world market price plus the tariff, the effective rate of protection on commodity i can be expressed as

$$Z_i = \frac{P_i(1+T_i) - \sum_j M_{ji}(1+T_j) - (P_i - \sum_j M_{ji})}{P_i - \sum_j M_{ji}} = \frac{W_i - V_i}{V_t} \quad (2)$$

where subscripts i and j refer to the product in question and its inputs, Z and T are effective and the nominal rates of tariffs, W and V are value added in the country in question and in a free trade situation, respectively, and M the cost of material inputs per unit of output under free trade.

Developing countries use various protective measures in addition to, or instead of, tariffs. Specific taxes, import surcharges, and prepayment requirements can be considered quasi-tariffs and their tariff equivalent estimated. In turn, in cases where quantitative restrictions rather than tariffs are the relevant means of protection, one should calculate implicit tariffs as the percentage difference between domestic and import prices. These implicit tariffs—the tariff equivalent of quotas—can then be used in the place of nominal tariffs in estimating the effective rate of protection.

Since the effective rate of protection indicates the percentage excess of domestic value added obtainable as a result of protection over value added in a free trade situation, under certain assumptions this measure can be used to rank industries according to their relative advantages. Also, by making assumptions in regard to foreign demand and domestic supply elasticities, the cost of protection can be estimated.

3

It appears, then, that the domestic resource cost of foreign exchange and the effective rate of protection would serve similar objectives. But what is the relationship between these measures, and how can a choice be made between them? To indicate their relationship, let us rewrite equation (2) in regard to commodity j:

$$Z_j = \frac{W_j - V_j}{V_j} = \frac{W_j}{V_j} - 1. \quad (2')$$

With a simple transformation, domestic value added can be expressed in terms of V_j and Z_j,

$$W_j = V_j(1 + Z_j). \quad (3)$$

Substituting (3) into (1) we have

$$B_t = \frac{\sum_j V_j(1+Z_j)r_{ji}}{P_t - \sum_j N_j r_{ji}} = \frac{\sum_j V_j r_{ji}}{P_t - \sum_j N_j r_{ji}} + \frac{\sum_j V_j Z_j r_{ji}}{P_t - \sum_{jN_jr_{ji}} N_j r_{ji}} \quad (4)$$

and

$$P_t = \sum_j V_j r_{ji} + \sum_j N_j r_{ji}, \quad (5)$$

hence

$$B_t = 1 + \sum_j Z_j \frac{V_j r_{ji}}{\sum_j V_j r_{ji}} \quad (6)$$

Accordingly, the cost of a unit of foreign exchange equals unity plus a weighted average of the effective rates of protection, the weights being the contribution of direct and indirect value added to output produced under free trade conditions. It is apparent that the formulas of the cost of foreign exchange and the effective rate of protection will generally give a different ranking of domestic industries.[2] A numerical example may be helpful to indicate the causes of these differences and to appraise the relative merits of the two indicators.

Let us consider two import-competing industries: clothing manufacturing and precision equipment. Assume that, in the country in question, the manufacturing of precision equipment involves the use of steel produced under protection, while the fabrics used by the clothing industry are not protected. It is further assumed that the production of precision equipment is efficient in the sense that domestic value added equals value added under free trade conditions, while this is not the case for clothing manufacturing. Technological coefficients are taken to be constant in the production of both commodities, and costs are expressed in terms of direct inputs as well as in terms of primary inputs (labor and foreign exchange), with a comparison made between domestic and foreign costs. For simplicity's sake, we take value added to equal direct labor cost and disregard non-traded inputs (see Tables 1 and 2). In terms of the domestic resource cost of foreign exchange, the clothing industry ranks ahead of precision equipment manufacturing: the cost of foreign exchange is 1.2 in the first case and 1.4 in the second.[3] By contrast, the rate of effective protection is nil on precision equipment and 50 per cent on clothing (Tables 1 and 2). It follows that the cost of foreign exchange is lower in clothing manufacturing—a relatively inefficient industry—than in the production of precision equipment because the material input of the former (textile fabrics) is produced at world market prices, while the latter is penalized by the protection of the domestic steel industry. Accordingly, while the effective rate of protection indicates the relative performance of processing activities, the cost of foreign exchange saved is affected by inefficiencies in the manufacturing of the product itself as well as in the production of its inputs.

Table 1 **Clothing: Production Costs in Domestic Currency**

	Domestic Production			Foreign Production		
	Labor	*Foreign Exchange*	*Total*	*Labor*	*Foreign Exchange*	*Total*
Fabrics	6	10	16	6	10	16
Direct labor	6	...	6	4	...	4
Total	12	10	22	10	10	20

$$B_c = \frac{\sum_j W_j r_{ji}}{P_t - \sum_t N_j r_{ji}} \quad \frac{12}{20-10} = 1.2$$

$$Z_c = \frac{W_c - V_c}{V_c} = \frac{6-4}{4} = 0.5 \text{ (50 per cent)}; \; Z_f = \frac{6-6}{6} = 0.$$

$$B_c = 1 + \frac{\sum_j Z_f V_j r_{ji}}{\sum_j V_j r_{ji}} = 1 + \frac{0.4 \times 0.5 + 0.6 \times 0}{1} = 1.2.$$

Expressed differently the ranking of domestic industries according to the cost of foreign exchange reflects the implicit assumptions that (1) *all* existing industries will be maintained, and (2) the expansion of the output of any one commodity will require increased output of *all* domestic industries providing direct and indirect inputs into it (that is, the direct and indirect marginal input coefficient of domestic resources and of imports is equal to the corresponding average coefficient). Thus policy changes are assumed not to lead to the substitution of foreign for domestic inputs either in existing output or in future output. Yet one may question the usefulness of this proposition since policy recommendations should properly cover the inefficient input-producing industries also. At the same time, it would be hardly correct if the past establishment of an inefficient steel industry would jeopardize the chances for setting up precision equipment industries if, for example, the high labor content gives a developing country comparative advantage.

But how about the case where relatively inefficient (high cost) input-producing industries are retained following a reform of the system of protection? If our aim is that ultimately all industries should become competitive on the world market, the answer is simple: the desirability of individual industries should be evaluated by the use of the effective protection measure rather than by the cost of foreign exchange, since

Table 2 **Precision Equipment: Production Costs in Domestic Currency**

	Domestic Production			Foreign Production		
	Labor	*Foreign Exchange*	*Total*	*Labor*	*Foreign Exchange*	*Total*
Steel	10	10	20	6	10	16
Direct labor	4	...	4	4	...	4
Total	14	10	24	10	10	20

$$B_p = \frac{14}{20-20} = 1.4.$$

$$Z_p = \frac{4-4}{4} = 0; \; Z_s = \frac{10-6}{6} = 0.67 \text{ (67 per cent)}.$$

$$B_p = 1 + \frac{0.4 \times 0 + 0.6 \times 0.67}{1} = 1.4.$$

temporary inefficiencies (high costs) in input-producing industries should not influence the choice among final products.

Alternatively, we may accept inefficiencies for the sake of non-economic or other objectives and envisage the maintenance of protection in input-producing industries for an indefinite period. This assumption would not affect the conclusions either, provided that the additional inputs necessary for the expansion of the user industries are imported, since, from the point of view of comparative advantage, the marginal rather than the average coefficients are relevant. Were we to assume, instead, that political pressures would entail the expansion of some inefficient input-producing industries *pari passu* with the user industries, the effective rate of protection should be adjusted in the way indicated below.

The above reasoning holds equally well if we assume that the market prices of the factors of production do not equal opportunity costs (shadow prices). The cost of foreign exchange is calculated valuing domestic resources at opportunity costs in this case, while the effective rate of protection measure is replaced by the 'social effective rate' which equals the percentage difference between domestic and free trade value added (that is, the relative costs of the processing activity) measured at opportunity costs.

Neither are the conclusions affected if we introduce non-traded goods (services) that, by definition, have an infinite c.i.f. price. In calculating the effective rate of protection on tradables (actual and potential export and import goods), one may then apply the method suggested by Corden: tradables used directly or indirectly in the production of non-traded goods are considered together with tradables employed directly in the production process, while the sum of direct and indirect domestic factor content (value added) of non-traded goods is in included with the cost of processing (1966, pp. 226–8).

Now, if political pressures were to entail the expansion of the production of some of these inputs, in calculating the effective rate of protection they should be treated in the same way as non-traded goods. But such cases should be judged on their individual merits rather than equating all domestically purchased inputs with non-traded goods as Bruno does, since otherwise one would neglect the possibility that, in expanding user industries, imports rather than inefficiently produced import-competing goods could be used as inputs.

These considerations point to the superiority of the effective protection measure over that of the cost of foreign exchange in evaluating the desirability of individual industries. Accordingly, we have to reject Bruno's claim that his measure ranks industries according to their comparative advantages. But, whichever measure is used for this purpose, several qualifications need to be made. These will be discussed in the following section with reference to the effective rate of protection. The conclusions apply, *ceteris paribus*, to the cost of foreign exchange also.

4

We have seen that protection permits domestic producers to operate with an excess of domestic value added over value added in a free trade situation. Aside from higher labor and capital costs incurred in the process of production, this excess may be due to greater material requirements and higher efficiency wages or rate of return on capital under protection.

In estimating effective tariffs the assumption is made that material input coefficients are invariant to protection. This does not give rise to problems in the case where free trade input coefficients are used in the calculations. If, instead, we use the input coefficients of the country under consideration in estimating the effective rate of protection, a bias will be introduced whenever there is a waste of materials or if the substitution elasticity between any two material inputs or between a material input and a primary factor is greater than zero.

The calculation of the effective rate of protection further assumes competitive factor and product markets. However, labor unions having monopoly power may raise wages in some protected industries. In turn, protection may give rise to excess profits which again increase domestic value added over that obtainable in a free trade situation. To adjust for this, Bruno and Krueger have excluded in their calculations of the cost of foreign exchange any profit that exceeded a 'reasonable' rate of return on fixed capital investment. But the use of a uniform rate of profit in all industries is open to criticism since it does not take account of inter-industry differences in entrepreneurship and risk. Moreover, the choice of the cutoff rate is largely arbitrary. Thus, while Bruno calculates with a standard rate of return of 8 per cent in Israel (1963, p. 109), Krueger has chosen a rate of 20 per cent for Turkey (1966, p. 474).

It follows that, if free trade coefficients are used in the calculations and one adjusts for the effects of the monopoly power of unions and for 'excess' profits in particular industries, the ranking of industries by effective tariffs will provide a ranking according to static comparative advantage. Comparative advantage is defined here in a broader sense to include also the effects of deficiencies in the organization of production and management in individual firms. These are inefficiencies on the 'micro' level in the sense that firms produce given outputs at higher than minimum costs. While the cost minimization assumptions of economic theory are not fulfilled in this case, these sources of inefficiencies should be included among the determinants of comparative advantage since their removal would involve a cost in terms of managerial and other inputs.

In turn, the appraisal of dynamic comparative

advantage would require making adjustments for reductions in costs due to factors such as the exploitation of internal and external economies and learning by doing. Needless to say, it is difficult to carry out such adjustments in practice, in part because information on potential improvements is limited and in part because actual improvements often fall short of potential ones by a margin difficult to estimate.

5

In Bruno's and Krueger's work, as well as in some other writings, references are often made to overvalued exchange rates in developing countries and to the need for estimating 'real' or 'equilibrium' exchange rates. Bruno suggests that in 1958 in Israel the 'real' exchange rate was 2.5 pounds to the dollar as compared to the official rate of 1.8 pounds (1963, p. 91). In turn, in Krueger's view, the estimation of equilibrium exchange rates is an alternative procedure to calculating effective tariffs or the domestic resource cost of foreign exchange (1966, p. 469). It is suggested here that much of this discussion reflects a misconception as to the meaning of equilibrium rates. These misapprehensions, however, originated in earlier writings by Nurkse and Meade whose definitions of equilibrium exchange rates have become widely accepted.

According to Nurkse (1950, pp. 3–34), the 'true' equilibrium rate of exchange is one that maintains a country's external accounts in equilibrium for a period of five to ten years without the need for wholesale unemployment at home, without additional restrictions on trade, and in the absence of temporary capital movements. Meade's definition (1951, p. 15) is similar to Nurkse's except that, instead of 'additional restrictions' on trade, his conditions for an equilibrium rate include the lack of application of trade restrictions for balance of payments purposes.

In regard to Nurkse's definition, the major difficulty lies in the need for separating the restrictions that are in some sense 'basic' and those that are 'additional'. In turn, the definition proposed by Meade is open to criticism on the grounds that trade restrictions serve a variety of purposes and are the result of a historical process. In developing countries, these have been undertaken in response to requests for protection on the part of entrepreneurs and/or in order to improve the balance of payments. The two motives are often difficult to separate, and, at any rate, for the present situation the original motivation is no longer relevant.

Nurkse and Meade pursue a chimera in attempting to define a unique equilibrium exchange rate corresponding to some 'acceptable' measure of tariff protection. For one thing, the extent of protection of domestic industries is affected by the rate of exchange: a given degree of protection can be provided by different combinations of tariffs, subsidies, and exchange rate. For another, the rate of exchange that keeps the balance of payments in equilibrium will depend on the measures of trade policy applied.

If we also take account of the effects of monetary and fiscal policies on the exchange rate, we can define the equilibrium exchange rate with respect to the economic policies actually followed.[4] Unless there is an unplanned loss of reserves and/or temporary capital movements, the equilibrium rate so defined will equal the actual exchange rate. If, however, one alters the system of protection, or monetary and fiscal policies, the equilibrium rate of exchange will also change. One cannot therefore speak of overvaluation without specifying the desired changes in the system of trade barriers or in domestic policies, and an adjustment in the exchange rate as suggested by Bruno is incompatible with the observed price relationships—and balance-of-payments equilibrium.

More generally, for given demand and supply conditions, there are an infinite number of 'equilibrium' exchange rates, each corresponding to a different configuration of trade, monetary, and fiscal policies. Thus, for given domestic economic policies, one may wish to inquire what the equilibrium rate of exchange would be in a free trade situation or in the case of a reduction of tariffs by a certain percentage. The question is, then, how the equilibrium rate corresponding to a new set of policies can be estimated.

Some continue to believe that purchasing power parities, calculated as the ratio of consumer goods prices for a given pair of countries, would approximate the free trade equilibrium rate of exchange between their currencies. One of the authors has elsewhere shown that purchasing power parity calculations are unsatisfactory for the purpose at hand, chiefly because service prices are not equalized through trade. International differences in service prices tend to reflect differences in wages, which in industrial countries roughly correspond to differences in manufacturing productivity (Balassa, 1964). It may be suggested, then, that calculations be made in regard to internationally traded goods only. But in the developing countries such a measure will not give expression to the free trade equilibrium exchange rate either. Rather, for a given exchange rate, it will express the weighted average of nominal (implicit) tariffs and subsidies, adjusted for the cost of transportation.

Neither can we determine equilibrium exchange rates by relying on the relative interpretation of the purchasing power parity doctrine according to which, in comparison to a period where equilibrium rates prevailed, changes in relative prices would indicate the necessary adjustments in exchange rates and hence the degree of over- and undervaluation. For one thing, especially in the present-day developing countries, it is difficult to choose an appropriate base period when 'equilibrium' rates prevailed. For another, one can hardly assume that exchange rates would vary in a parallel fashion with domestic prices. Even if we disregard the problems due to the fact that service prices tend to rise faster than the prices of traded goods (Balassa, 1964, pp. 594–5), differential rates of increase of productivity and other factors will cause a divergence between an index of relative prices and that of the equilibrium rate of exchange.

We have to discard, therefore, the use of purchasing power parities for estimating free trade equilibrium exchange rates. This method is even less appropriate for calculating the exchange rates that would maintain balance-of-payments equilibrium under protection. Thus, if equiproportionate changes in tariffs, subsidies, and exchange rates keep domestic prices unchanged, the equilibrium exchange rate will vary but purchasing power parities will remain the same. In turn, in the absence of such compensating changes, the equilibrium exchange rate corresponding to a new set of trade, monetary, and fiscal policies can be estimated only if appropriate assumptions are made concerning the price elasticities of import demand and export supply at home and abroad. Needless to say, the difficulties of such a calculation are rather formidable.

However, one can indicate the effects of a *given* devaluation, accompanied by changes in tariffs and export subsidies, on effective rates of protection. If, for example, a devaluation is accompanied by compensating changes in tariffs and subsidies that leave domestic prices unchanged, the balance of payments and the ranking of industries by the effective rates of protection will not be affected but effective rates will uniformly decrease by the percentage of the devaluation. Similar conclusions pertain to the case where quantitative restrictions are applied to imports, except that there could be no change in tariffs; rather, devaluation would give rise to a redistribution of 'quota profits' from holders of quotas to the government.

It is easy to see that if some tariff rates (nominal or implicit) and export subsidies are lower than the percentage of devaluation, the above result will not be obtained unless import subsidies and export taxes are introduced. If such measures are not used, both the balance of payments and the ranking of industries by the effective rate of protection will be affected. The re-establishment of balance-of-payments equilibrium through further adjustments in the exchange rate, then, will not restore the original ranking by effective rates.

6

In this paper a comparison has been made between two measures that have come to be used to evaluate the effects of protection on individual industries: the effective rate of protection and the cost of foreign exchange. We have shown that the cost of foreign exchange equals unity plus a weighted average of the effective rates of protection, the weights being the contribution of direct and indirect value added to output produced under free trade conditions. Further, we have provided evidence for the superiority of the effective tariff measure over the cost of foreign exchange for the purpose of indicating the desirability of individual industries.

The paper has also dealt with the relationship of the rate of effective protection on the one hand and comparative advantage on the other. It would appear that if one adjusts for excess profits and disregards the possibility that labor unions have monopoly power in some industries, the ranking of industries by the effective rate of protection will provide an indication of static comparative advantage. However, dynamic comparative advantage will also depend on the possibilities for cost reductions due to factors such as the exploitation of internal and external economies.

Finally, prevailing views on the concept of equilibrium rates have been criticized. It has been suggested that there are an infinite number of 'equilibrium' rates, each corresponding to a different configuration of trade, monetary, and fiscal policies. Thus, if there is no unplanned reserve loss and/or temporary capital movements, the existing exchange rate can be taken as the equilibrium rate for the economic policies followed.

We have also noted that the balance of payments and the ranking of industries by the effective rate of protection will not be affected if a devaluation is accompanied by compensating changes in tariffs and subsidies that leave domestic prices unchanged. Should this not be the case, we face the problem of estimating the new equilibrium rate of exchange and the corresponding rates of effective protection. For reasons explained in the paper, the difficulties of such a calculation are rather formidable.

Notes: Reading 30

1 The only difference is that while c.i.f. prices are used in calculating the cost of foreign exchange saved, exports – but not their imported inputs – are evaluated at f.o.b. prices. This distinction reflects the assumption that freight and insurance are wholly supplied by foreign factors.

2 For Turkey, effective tariffs and the (unadjusted) cost of foreign exchange are: superphosphate fertiliser, 925 and 98.1; plastic, 916 and 292.5; ammonium nitrate fertiliser, 186 and 63.6; truck tyres, 170 and 97.9; electric cables 147 and 49.2; refrigeration units 80 and 24.7; electric motors, 66 and 20.5 (Krueger, 1966, pp. 472–3).

3 Since all variables are expressed in terms of domestic currency, the results are given in index number form with a base of unity. If we multiply B_i by the exchange rate, we get the saving in terms of foreign exchange.

4 We now take economic policies as predetermined and the exchange rate as the dependent variable under the constraint of balance-of-payments equilibrium. One could instead choose the exchange rate and domestic monetary and fiscal policies to be predetermined, and derive the tariff protection needed to keep the balance of payments in equilibrium.

References: Reading 30

Balassa, Bela (1964), 'The purchasing power parity doctrine: a reappraisal', *J.P.E.*, vol. LXII, December, pp. 584–96.

Balassa, Bela (1965), 'Tariff protection in industrial countries: an evaluation', *J.P.E.,* vol. LXXIII, December, pp. 573–94.

Balassa, Bela (1968), 'Integration and resource allocation in Latin America', in Tom Davis (ed.), *The Next Decade of Latin American Development* (Cornell University Press).

Bhagwati, Jagdish (1968), 'The theory and practice of commerical policy', Graham Memorial Lecture, International Finance Secretariat, Special Papers in International Economics, No. 8 (Princeton University Press).

Bruno, Michael (1963), *Interdependence, Resource Use and Structural Change in Trade* (Bank of Israel).

Bruno, Michael (1967), 'The optimal selection of export-promoting and import-substituting projects', *Planning the External Sector: Techniques, Problems and Policies*, Report on the First Inter-regional Seminar on Development Planning (UN).

Corden, W. M. (1966), 'The structure of a tariff system and the effective protective rate', *J.P.E.*, vol. LXXIV, June, pp. 221–37.

Johnson, Harry G. (1965), 'The theory of tariff structure with special reference to world trade and development', *Trade and Development* ('Etudes et travaux de l'Institut Universitaire de hautes Etudes Internationales') (Librairie Droz).

Kindleberger, C. P. (1967), 'Liberal policies vs. controls in the foreign trade of developing countries', AID Discussion Paper No. 14, Office of Program Coordination, US Department of State, Agency for International Development (Washington, DC).

Krueger, Anne O. (1966), 'Some economic costs of exchange control: the Turkish case', *J.P.E.*, vol. LXXIV, October, pp. 466–80.

Leibenstein, Harvey (1966), 'Allocative efficiency vs "x-efficiency" ', *A.E.R.*, vol. LVI, June, pp. 392–415.

Little, I. M. D. (1968), 'Public sector project selection in relation to Indian development' (to be published in a Nehru memorial volume of essays edited by A. V. Bhuleshkat in 1968).

Meade, J. E. (1951), *The Balance of Payments* (Oxford University Press).

Nurkse, Ragnar (1950), 'Conditions of international monetary equilibrium', in H. S. Ellis and L. A. Metzler (eds), *Theory of International Trade* (Blakiston).

Schydlowsky, D. M. (1967), 'From import substitution to export promotion for semi-grown-up industries: a policy proposal', *J. Development Studies*, vol. III. no. 4, July.

Tinbergen, Jan (1963), 'Projections of economic data in development planning', in *Planning for Economic Development in the Caribbean* (Caribbean Organisation, Puerto Rico).

Part Six

Agricultural Development

Agriculture is such a basic sector in the developing countries that it would require a whole book of readings (and there are several such volumes) on this subject to permit reasonably balanced coverage. This mixed bag starts (Reading 31) with Lipton's classic article of the theory of the optimising peasant and follows with a short piece by Livingstone (Reading 32) which attempts to sort out some confusions in the literature on the supply responses of the peasant producer. Given the weight of the literature on peasant production, it is surprising how little has been written on the economics of the plantation sector, and the excellent article by Beckford (Reading 33), bringing into the agricultural sector some of the arguments more often used in the discussion of multinationals and in dependency theory, shows how many different considerations need to be taken into account in appraising the social rather than private costs and benefits of plantations.

From among the many contributions to the discussion of the effects of the 'Green Revolution' in Asia, two pieces have been selected, by Frankel (Reading 34) and Ladejinsky (Reading 35). Also related to the question of equality and inequality in agriculture is the article by Johnston (Reading 36) which discusses the choice between 'bimodal' and 'unimodal' strategies for agricultural extension and other forms of assistance to agricultural producers; one of the most fundamental economic and political choices, made very differently in different countries, facing policy-makers in developing countries, given the importance of the agricultural sector in the economy as a whole.

The brevity of the last piece (Reading 37), on integrated rural development planning, permits it to be immodestly included: the moderate amount of cold water poured on to the concept of integrated rural development planning appears apropos at a time when academics, governments, and especially international agencies, have gone overboard for a concept which, like other terms in the development literature such as 'balanced growth', 'take-off' and 'self-sustained growth', has an intrinsic appeal but is loosely used and seldom closely defined.

Reading 31

The Theory of the Optimising Peasant[1]

M. Lipton

Journal of Development Studies, 1968, pp. 327 – 51.

1

'Peasant conservatism' is out. Economists of underdeveloped countries are beginning to realise that the farmer is no fool. A non-fool, in a static environment, learns to live 'efficiently': to optimise, given his values and constraints, and to teach his children to do the same. Moreover, food-grain output per worker has stagnated, secularly, in many poor countries; that seems to support Professor Schultz's startling conclusion that underdeveloped agricultural communities—not just the individual farmers—are 'efficient but poor' (p. 38).[2] Each farmer, by maximising utility, prevents 'any major inefficiency in the allocation of traditional factors' (p. 39).

Schultz's policy conclusion is that 'no appreciable increase in agricultural production is to be had by reallocating the factors at the disposal of farmers who are bound by the traditional agriculture' (p. 39). This follows from individual utility-maximisation only under perfect competition. In particular, a perfect market in factors and products must exist, and each farmer must be able to predict, with reasonable confidence, the outcome of each array of production, consumption and sale decisions at his disposal.

Schultz's two main sources of evidence are shot through with perfect competition: Dr Hopper implicitly, Professor Tax explicitly. Thus Hopper: 'Are *the people* of Senapur realising the full economic potential of *their* physical resources? *From the point of view of the villagers, the answer must be 'yes' for* in general *each man comes close to doing the best that he can* with his knowledge and cultural background' (pp. 45–6, my italics). This follows for 'the villagers', from individual optimisation, only under perfect competition. And Tax's Guatemalan '*market* . . . tends *to be perfectly competitive*' (p. 43, his italics).

With what sort of perfect competition are we dealing? Not, apparently, with linear-programming (LP) with fixed proportions in each activity and factor substitutions possible only by shifting activities. Schultz's thesis is to be tested, we are told, by the truth or falsity of its 'implications', and a key implication is that 'no productive factor remains unemployed' (p. 40). This implication does not follow in LP. In product-space, we may optimise at a vertex *on an axis*. Hopper's model appears to have only four constraints (land, labour, irrigation-water, bullock-time) and four activities (barley, wheat, peas, grass: p. 46). If it were reinterpreted in LP terms, an axis-vertex optimum would thus be extremely likely. Then at least one factor constraint is not binding, and at least one factor is not fully employed. If that factor is labour, it has zero marginal product—a hypothesis that Schultz spends a chapter in refuting (pp. 53–70).

In any case an LP recasting of Hopper's evidence scarcely supports the 'efficient but poor' hypothesis. Reallocation of factors in Senapur, implies Hopper, could raise food-grain output 10 per cent, without more inputs or loss of other outputs[3]—suggesting substantial 'inefficiency'. Incidentally, it is no disparagement of Hopper's pioneering work to point out that he omits some inputs. If he had measured (and priced) a key input—dung—his conclusions might have been very different.

So Schultz is arguing for something close to neo-classical perfect competition (NCPC): neo-classical because the LP assumption of fixed factor proportions contradicts his own (and the LP evidence does not support his conclusions), perfect competition because otherwise his individual equilibria cannot add up to a social optimum. Agriculture, as a textbook paradigm of NCPC, initially referred to advanced, temperate, monetised and literate agricultures. Can NCPC be applied to underdeveloped, climatically uncertain, subsistence, largely illiterate farming communities? If the peasant in traditional agricultures is a NCPC-optimiser, he must allocate productive factors so as to *equate the marginal value-product of money* in each use.

Some economists with experience of underdeveloped countries have reacted vehemently against the theory of marginal value-product equalisation (hereafter MVPE). They suggest that it is a wicked attempt to retard growth in order to appease free enterprise dogmatism.[4] Right or wrong, MVPE needs a fuller treatment. Some of its supporters—not Professor Schultz, with his pleas for vast extension of State educational provision[5]—may delude themselves that MVPE is a laissez-faire weapon against creeping socialism; but it is the opposite.

MVPE is a doctrine of revolutionary pessimism.

Private enterprise has done its best with the old factors, says this doctrine; but, as we know, the result is secular stagnation. For cultivators have not, of their own volition, introduced new factors on a big scale. The new factors needed—irrigation, education—are huge and indivisible; initial capital costs lie beyond the biggest private cultivator; payoffs are too long-term to be financed by private loan capital; benefits are too diffused, in space and time, to be recoverable by the providers through betterment levies. Thus MVPE implies massive State intervention as a necessary condition for agricultural progress in underdeveloped countries. This writer, while accepting the implication, rejects MVPE.

Opponents of MVPE should thank Professor Schultz for a lucid, non-tautologous and testable statement of his case. That a peasant maximises utility—i.e. does what he wants to do, under the given constraints—is a tedious tautology. Or Schultz might have made his thesis, efficient use of existing factors, tautologous by redefining any improvement in factor allocation as a new technology—or (as when dung becomes compost) as a new factor. Short of tautology, the thesis could have been weakened into unexceptionable dullness. Schultz does not waste time asserting the truism that some incentives affect some farmers; the evidence against the backward-sloping supply curve was needed only by remaining True Believers in subsistence mentality (who, however, will not be swayed by mere evidence). Again, nobody seriously believes that, after centuries of experience, peasant communities can suddenly be taught, by visiting experts, how to double output without increasing any input. But Schultz has not merely advanced a dull tautology, demonstrated that peasants wish to live better, or rejected the wilder claims of the office agronomists. MVPE, the assertion that underdeveloped cultivators are 'efficient but poor', is interesting because it is extreme. The following arguments try to show that it is mistaken.

(a) Owing to rainfall variability, there is no unique marginal physical product (MPP) associated with any factor (for given inputs of all other factors), but only a probability-distribution of MPPs. By acting as if he used the calculus of expected values, an optimising peasant can nevertheless find a long-run profit-maximising algorithm analogous to MVPE. However, in the non-equatorial tropics, rainfall variance is much higher than in most temperate agricultures, so that—for rainfall and hence for MPPs—expected value is a much poorer predictor of actual value. In particular, the smaller is mean rainfall, the greater is the coefficient of variability.

The greater the *impact* of future rainfall upon optimal policy, the smaller is *knowledge* of that rainfall, and the likelier is MVPE to lead to disaster. In two senses, therefore, MVPE has dubious logical status. First, policy is critically dependent on information of which the tropical peasant is deprived in direct proportion to its importance. Second, MVPE for expected values is necessarily a long-run sequential algorithm (as it is not under certainty). Compared with a lower-mean, lower-variance policy, MVPE substantially reduces its practitioner's prospects of surviving to complete the sequence. The more 'underdeveloped' the peasant, the stronger are both objections to the logic of MVPE.

(b) Assuming away this logical problem, and allowing all uncertainty to be reducible to risk, MVPE is possible; but it is not optimal, even for the individual cultivator. He requires risk premium, and the risk is abnormally large owing to the high rainfall variance, and of an abnormally severe outcome, starvation. Utility maximisation can allow for some trade-off between variance and expected profit; MVPE cannot. The constraints or weighting required by such a trade-off, even for a utility-maximiser, ought to be unacceptable to Schultz. His evidence (Hopper, Tax) is relevant only to simple profit maximisation. His policy conclusion—that State measures, from forward pricing (applauded on p. 14) to collectivisation, could scarcely improve allocation of existing factors—also cannot survive a probabilistic, utility-maximising reformulation of MVPE.

(c) Even under certainty, imperfect factor markets (especially for land and, in India, for labour) render it impossible, even secularly, for a utility-maximiser to acquire that set of factors allowing him to approximate as closely to profit maximisation as his utility function allows. The role of taste in determining which crops are grown, different degrees of aversion to labour, different access to free supplies of otherwise scarce factors (e.g. dung), and the unification of production and consumption decisions, combine to render this discrepancy especially serious to MVPE.

(d) Even if factor markets were perfect, inter-farm differences in output from identical inputs, and hence the likelihood that any apparent maximising behaviour results from 'cancelling errors', would still be greatest in underdeveloped agricultures: partly because of differing assets and hence trade-offs between risk and profit, but mainly owing to the fact that some farmers' economic behaviour is trammelled by constraints—heriditary job allocation, land inheritance rules—that prevent the full expression of economic rationality.

(e) The *secular* constancy of environment in underdeveloped countries, needed for learning any optimising algorithm, has been disrupted by population growth and (much less) by development planning. Added to the disruption of *annual* constancy by high rainfall variance, this suggests that an optimising peasant seeks survival algorithms, not maxmising ones. Different peasants learn, and stick to, different algorithms. This hypothesis accords with peasants' descriptions of their own conduct and explains the wide inter-farm differences in the use of similar bundles of resources. MVPE does neither.

(f) In an underdeveloped agriculture, with all its risks and market imperfections, assume that each peasant adopts MVPE and that it maximises the constrained utility function of *each*. The adoption of MVPE by each would still not be optimal for *all*. A planner would reject MVPE in favour of factor allocations allowing for risk, for the effect of income distribution and monopoly on relative prices, for inter-farm differences in reinvestment rates, and for economies of scale to the plot. Even if prices were the only variables directly altered by the planner, these aims would not, in general, be best approximated by setting Langean MVPE price-relatives.

In brief, MVPE is (a) impossible under true uncertainty; (b) even if uncertainty were reducible to risk, not optimal for the peasant; (c) even under certainty, especially divergent from utility maximisation in the imperfect factor markets of underdeveloped agriculture; (d) even with certainty and perfect factor markets, impeded by the framework of custom and law, and demonstrably not adopted; (e) dependent on the untenable assumption of a static environment; (f) socially inefficient even if privately optimal. Evidence for assertions (a)-(f) is provided in sections 2 to 7, mainly from Indian experience.

2

If climatic uncertainty prevails, no resource has a unique marginal physical product (MPP) in any use. Instead there is a probability-distribution of MPPs over states of nature. If price variability is independent of the climate on a particular farmer's land, so that MPPs can stand proxy for MVPs, the policy corresponding to MVPE (long-run profit maximisation) is to equate the marginal-to-expected value-productivity of money in each use. Call this policy MEVPE.

There seems to be no periodicity in yearly rainfall data, however local, in monsoon India.[6] At sowing time, therefore, the best estimate of this season's rainfall, Rs is E(R), the average of seasonal rainfall over the longest period for which data are available. However, the smaller E(R), the greater (i) the impact of Rs on this season's output, (ii) the coefficient of variability of Rs[7] and hence (iii) the unreliability of E(R) as an estimate of Rs. Hence, the greater the impact of R on optimal choice of factor allocations and amounts, the less accurately can R be predicted. MEVPE, therefore, has certain purely logical limitations in the highly variable climates of monsoon Asia.

First, the less E(R), the more likely is an *ex ante* rational policy of MEVPE to be regretted *ex post*. MEVPE asks the farmer to learn from experience, but not to learn the dangers of learning from experience. Since MEVPE maximises profit only in the very long run, this is particularly serious.

Second, the putative long-run maximiser in India and Pakistan is usually a small farmer, with few grain stocks. In extreme cases, long-run MEVPE farmers are dead in the short run, if their risky experiments meet a low $\frac{R_s}{E(R)}$ in the early years. Much more often, this forces sale of land. Small wonder that farmers choose less risky (if ultimately less 'profitable') procedures. MEVPE maximises only in the very long run; yet it shortens the probable 'run' over which the would-be maximiser owns, and hence derives benefit from, his factors of production. This blend is logically odd.

The root of the trouble is that MEVPE, in face of variable climate, yields predictions of rainfall which become less accurate as they become more important (i.e. as E(R) falls). At sowing time, the peasant must employ (or imply employment of) most factor inputs; E(R) is his best estimate of Rs and the reliability of this estimate falls as its importance in picking MEVPE allocations rises.

If all MPPs varied with rainfall in similar proportions, this would matter less in practice (though the logical problem would remain). The climatically critical choice, however, is between (a) crops robust in face of poor rains, but with low average yearly value, and (b) crops with higher average value but worse hit by poor rains. This choice must be made at or before ploughing time—with information that falls in reliability as it rises in importance.

Again, this would matter less if price and output were contravariant for the individual farmer. However, especially in hilly areas, climate can vary drastically between villages. In a typical year, for each crop, some farmers will enjoy favourable Rs and others poor Rs, but 'average' prices will prevail for all. Whatever may apply to country-wide data, the individual farmer cannot rely on price variability to offset rainfall variability.

Uncertainty is confounded and compounded by variations in the price of manufactured goods. Even if the farmer could predict all MVPs, and hence allocate any *given* outlay among productive uses, he would not know how much he could buy with the resultant income. So he could not select the optimal *total* outlay.

All this does not imply that tropical farming is impossible to organise rationally. The alternative to the optimising peasant need not be the pessimising optant. Some practices—covering manure pits, ploughing across the slope—produce more output for almost any Rs, with hardly any increase in inputs. Some allocative decisions —higher seed-rates on poorer soils, appropriate mixed legumes on marshy ground—are similarly always indicated. That, however, is because such decisions and practices reduce the variance of profit, as well as raising the expected value.

3

Suppose that an Indian farmer forms the best possible estimate of monsoon rainfall when he ploughs his land. Suppose, further, that he knows the probability-distribution of rainfall about its likeliest mean value, and can associate with each rainfall-level a probability-distribution of outputs, competitors' outputs, and prices both of his outputs and of the goods he might later want to buy. Even then MEVPE would not be best for him. India is not a welfare state; the collapsing extended family and related caste-panchayat systems have not been replaced by public protection from private disaster. True, improved communications (and universal suffrage) render starvation unlikely. But if an MEVPE farmer is punished with a poor harvest, he must still expect gambler's ruin, i.e. one or more of (a) a crippling burden of debt, (b) the need to sell land at well below normal market prices, (c) attached labour, amounting to bond-slavery for himself and for his family. While Government and cooperative lenders are unable or unwilling to give consumption loans, unenforced legislation to depress interest rates is powerless against market forces.

Thus the risk of harvest failure, associated not merely with MEVPE but with any uninsured risk, assumes immense proportions. Arguments about optimal policies, based on false analogies with the humane, rich and risk-cushioned agricultures of the West, do not impress the subsistence farmer. A bad year or two, in an optimal policy sequence, will not prevent the Western farmer from retaining land and other assets sufficient to follow through the sequence; they will ruin the Indian farmer. His first duty to his family is to prevent such ruin; with growing population, fewer and fewer have enough land left for subsequent optimising experiments. Risk premium is an increasing function of risk *and a decreasing function of assets*.[8] A well-off American farmer can safely prefer a 50-50 chance of $5,000 or of $10,000 to a certainty of $7,000 per year. An Indian farmer, offered a 50-50 chance of Rs X or Rs 1000 as against a certainty of the Rs 700 a year with which he barely feeds his family, cannot set X far below 700. An optimiser maximises utility, not profit. The utility, now, of symmetrically distributed expected harvest is the more reduced by variance about expected value (a) as assets and 'welfare cushions' fall, and as expected value declines—i.e. in poor countries, and (b) as variance increases—i.e. in tropical agricultures. The reduction in family holdings, as India's population grows, will increase the sensible safety-first propensities of the Indian farmer—and probably the annoyance of the agricultural economist who observes them.

4

Divergence of utility-maximising policy from MVPE policy is a familiar problem of economics. When (as in the above section) it is due to risk, not much can be done through factor sales and purchases. Within limits, farmers with relatively low risk aversion can acquire land with high expected value product, but also high variance, from less MVPE-oriented farmers. Each farmer can, in effect, acquire land with greatest comparative advantage for his particular attitude to security vis-à-vis profitability. This, however, merely reduces the divergence between actual and MEVPE policy.

Under certainty, the prospects for equating utility-maximising and profit-maximising allocations might, in the long run, seem hopeful in a community of small family farmers. The standard reconciliation problems concern leisure and tastes. If I inherit land yielding high profit but needing much work, and like an easy life, I can sell the land to a more Puritan spirit, and use the proceeds to buy land producing lower-value output but requiring less managerial effort. If my father's land is suitable only for maize, while I prefer wheat-flour (but wish to go on farming), and you are in the opposite position, we shall exchange land. The transaction will raise psychic income, as well as real output of both crops.

In the Indian village, however, factor markets are seriously imperfect. Farmland hardly ever comes into the market in many cases. The prevailing fragmentation of holdings into numerous tiny plots—which could be consolidated to the advantage of all—demonstrates the inadequacy of the market in reallocating Indian farmland. Ownership is a tenaciously guarded family right, and an insurance policy; because there are substitutes for land in neither function, its price-elasticity of supply is tiny. The labour market (while becoming less imperfect as urban contact and population pressure weaken hereditary job assignments) is still dominated by caste. In some parts of India, a Brahman cannot plough. In almost none would he become a cobbler.

These imperfections in the factor markets have three main effects. They increase the divergence between profit-maximising and utility-maximising factor allocations; they impede (or at least delay) the allocation of productive factors according to the principle of comparative advantage; and they perpetuate a pre-capitalist market structure, in which a few profit-maximising farms exist alongside many risk-avoiding farms, without bankrupting or absorbing them—almost, in many cases, without competing against them.

If there were a perfect land market, differences in taste (i.e. relative utility of different food crops) between farm families would not affect output volume much. Suppose family farmers A and B inherit, respectively, plots X and Y of identical area. Each year X yields 1 bag of millet per man but 7/8 bag of maize; Y yields 1 bag of maize but 7/8 bag of millet. Maize and millet have identical market prices per bag, and producers' marketing costs (including storage) are 1/7 of production costs. Suppose that A and B each have just enough family labour to feed the family on the crop with the comparative disadvantage. Now if A's family strongly prefers maize and B's millet, production of both crops will be suboptimal. Marketing costs are such that A will grow maize and B millet; the socio-hereditary role of land makes it unlikely that they will exchange plots; and a suboptimal factor allocation persists. With many different plots, crops and farmers, the possibility of simple barter declines further. Transport and storage costs (especially for the initial capital needed for the transition from subsistence production) impede even perfect product markets from compensating for imperfect factor markets.

The virtual non-transferability of land titles, then, causes utility differences to impede production (a similar case occurs if in the above example X-land is 'profitable but hard' and Y-land is 'low-profit but easy', but the marginal rate of substitution of leisure for income is higher for A than for B at all relevant levels of labour-input). The social restraints on job transfer mean that many reallocations of labour towards greatest comparative advantage would reduce utility. Like non-transferability of land, this cause of divergence between utility-maximising and profit-maximising also exists in rich countries; extra time spent in Government employment has low marginal utility to many economists who, in such service, would outperform both their colleagues in Government and themselves on campus. Both for land and for labour, however, traditions of factor allocation are backed by strong sanctions in very poor agricultural societies. Hence both factors are especially likely to be allocated in a way that, to attain social harmony (utility maximisation), sacrifices much potential output.

It is vital for advocates of steady reform, whether by planning or by competition, to recognise that imperfect factor markets in very poor countries are not relics of ignorance and conservatism, ready to collapse at the slightest incentive (or executive order). They fulfil a precise function in a tightly knit social structure. The function is to permit the inheritance of security, both of tenure and of employment. The structure is a socio-religious ecology in which tolerance of traditional factor uses alone preserves the harmony between oppressor and oppressed—and hence the acceptance of some residual responsibilities by the oppressor.

The rootedness, the inherence of imperfect factor markets explains many of the disappointments of developmental gradualism, planned or marketeering. It accounts, moreover, for the persistence within a typical Indian (far more than in a US) village of totally different attitudes to farm management. Schultz might well ask, in reply to the arguments of pp. 10–12, 'Why don't MEVPE farmers drive out or buy up the rest?' Over the years, for a farmer strong enough to survive poor harvests, MEVPE must bring an ever-rising share of a village's output. The whole notion of 'taking over' non-traditional occupations and applying MEVPE to them—or even of buying up more land for management (as opposed to rent) may, however, be alien to him. Thus entrepreneurial MEVPE farmers and leisure-oriented risk-averters can exist side by side in a single village.[9] The latter either concentrate on different crops or are eventually 'infected' by the technical advances of the former, and thus survive somehow, but very seldom do they *voluntarily* sell their land, even when sale would be profitable. The likeliest culturally practicable use of capital, raised by such sale, is for moneylending; the ex-landowner would then work on others' land. Agricultural labourers (and small moneylenders) suffer worst in bad seasons; sale of land thus raises risk as well as expected income; hence it is unlikely to be adopted by a risk-averter, especially if he is concerned for his sons.

4

Apart from the imperfections of factor markets, many aspects of the customary and legal framework militate against the adoption, survival or (vis-à-vis other algorithms) 'victory' of MEVPE. Experience in many villages does not suggest that it was adopted. If these facts can be demonstrated, we must ask why the factor allocations in Hopper's study, cited by Schultz, seems to be so close to MEVPE. In 1965 I spent seven months in a typical dry Indian millet village of 800 persons, Kavathe. There, it was hard to identify either MEVPE or any other optimising algorithm. The framework of accounting, enabling the calculated risk-taking necessary for MEVPE, and the institutions of ownership that would support such a framework, are lacking. Where farmers adopt different practices, they are often unrelated to resource differences; when they adopt identical practices, they are often wrong, but based on 'long experience'. An examination of one or two of the major agricultural operations indicates what happens.

Ploughing is a case of failure to push labour and bullock inputs near the optimum, MVPE or any other. In Kavathe, with well-developed bullock-hire and bullock-exchange systems, the reason is not the usual one of fixed labour/bullock ratios and imperfect bullock markets. But each generation of fathers has split its land into ever thinner strips, one for each son, from top to bottom of the slope. Soil quality varies from high to low land according to water inputs, but very little along a contour facing in one direction; and fathers want each son to have some land of each quality. This saddles each generation of sons with longer, thinner sloping strips, increasingly costly and inconvenient to plough properly, i.e. repeatedly and across the slope. Most farmers realise the virtues of such ploughing (soil conservation, water distribution) and claim they adopt it; but so many do not.

This story has two morals. First, cultivators fail to adopt fully understood optimising technologies even when extra input-costs fall far short of expected MVP. Second, institutions restrict optimising possibilities; here, inherited landholding needlessly raises the labour input required to plough a given land area correctly. Specialised ploughing agencies, cooperative or capitalist, would disregard jealously protected strip partitions and are thus seldom practicable. Incidentally, the share of land occupied by the partitions increases with each generation, widening the rift between private and social optima.

If ploughing illustrates how inputs stop well before

(committed) marginal cost falls to (expected) marginal revenue, sowing in Kavathe shows how inherited survival algorithms are preferred to maximising allocation procedures. The standardised sowing practices are traditional, without logical explanation, and not based on remembered experience or experiment. Thus agronomists advocate leaving 12 inches between lines of *bajra* millet (the main monsoon crop), but the seed-drills prepared by the Carpenter all have 9-inch gaps between holes. Confident in the survival value of their sowing practice, the farmers do not press him to change. The mixing rate—three rows *bajra* alone, one row half *bajra* and half pulse-crop—is similarly sacrosanct. So is the 'normal' *bajra* seed rate of 3 kilos per acre.

Some aspects of sowing practice do show inter-farm differences, but these exemplify profit maximisation as little as do the agreed forms of behaviour. The choice of which, among several suitable pulses, shall be mixed with *bajra* millet is partly constrained by soil type, but within these constraints depends on family tastes and cultivating habits (there being hardly any market for these pulses). 'From long experience', about half of my sample of 62 farmers sow 3 kilos of *bajra* seed on good soil, just as on normal soil; one-third raise the rate on good soils; one-sixth (rightly, according to most agronomists) lower it. All three groups may be adopting survival algorithms; but it is impossible that all three are adopting MVPE. The huge variability among deciles in farm efficiency, noted by Hopper himself, supports this evidence.

Manuring practice illustrates the role of custom in prising utility-maximising behaviour away from MEVPE. Most farmers heap up manure; a few bury their manure properly in a pit. The second group is best represented among the *Dhanger* (Shepherd) caste, some two miles distant from the distractions of village social life. In May, while the main body of villagers celebrate each other's marriages, the *Dhangers* give their land a second ploughing and prepare compost pits. The families in this caste, incidentally, have a milk surplus, but regard it as against their *dharma* (customary religious duty) to see it, though they give it away readily. None of this behaviour is MEVPE; nor, given the values that prevail, is it 'irrational'.

Such a structure of custom helps to explain why, in most villages, the 'progressive farmer' is a myth. There is a progressive ploughman, a progressive sower, a progressive composter—but no mechanism to unite the three in a single farmer. On the contrary, the search for a *survival algorithm* leads each family to pick up a bundle of practices, some 'progressive' and others 'conservative', and to show great reluctance to modify part of the bundle. To explain this, we do not need to invoke the peasant's alleged reluctance to interpret events as causal sequences. He may well know that his entire complex pattern of farm practices determines his output level; but how is he to know which element to modify, or which ones must be changed together, to bring improvement? Scarcity sometimes provokes increasingly desperate insurance measures, rather than more accurate allocative procedures. In reply to a question about allocation of manure among crops, I was informed 'There is not nearly enough manure; therefore (*mhanun*) we do not trouble to fix any special division among crops'.

Paradoxically, both the institutions and the reforms of tenancy impede MEVPE. For such few tenancies as exist in Kavathe, the law fixes rent in cash terms, at a value around 20 per cent of average crop. Custom, land shortage and the tenant's preference for safety set actual rents around 50 per cent, crop-share. Thus, even if marginal cost falls below *guaranteed* marginal revenue, landlord and tenant must agree on how that cost is to be borne. The delay, friction and mistrust involved in such agreements in a semi-literate world are costs too.

As the man/land ratio rises, crop-share agreements increasingly commit the tenant to paying all improvement costs. On a half-share basis, marginal revenue must then be double marginal cost (more under uncertainty) before the *tenant* will incur the outlay. Of course a rational MEVPE landlord and tenant would combine to share the cost of investment till its marginal cost rose to the level of expected marginal product!

Selectively enforceable tenancy reform can inhibit MEVPE as effectively as custom. Near Kavathe is the village of Vadagaon, where the numerically dominant Maratha caste is unwilling to work for the Brahman landowner. He cannot easily escape the laws against tenancy at market rents, but he can (and does) exceed the legal ceiling on land holding by *mala fide* transfers to his relatives. Lax laws and strict laws combine to produce half-farmed land.

All this is not a reversion to the Pessimising Optant, the ignorant or stupid peasant conservative. Closely similar farm families with similar resources can *sensibly* adopt different survival algorithms—especially with different tastes, leisure preferences, risk aversions, tenancy arrangements and castes. Many superficially odd village practices make sense as disguised forms of insurance. In Kavathe, most farmer-borrowers prefer to pay interest in grain rather than in cash, though the standard grain rate, in a year of normal harvest, is almost double the cash rate; higher interest buys the borrower an insurance against low crop prices. Share-rent, on the other hand, insures mainly against low crop outputs. The survival of caste rigidity, too, represents *inter alia* a communal sacrifice of income for security.

6

Schultz derives his belief in MEVPE from the long constancy of traditional agricultural environments. 'The economic acumen of people in poor agricultural communities is generally maligned . . . people have been doing the same things for generations. Changes in products and factors have not crowded in on them. . . . The factors of production on which they depend are known through long experience and are in this sense "traditional" ' (pp. 36–7). We have seen that 'long experience' *plus* substantial cultural isolation of (and different preferences among) heads of families in fact produces (a) distinct survival algorithms comprising different practices within a village, not all MEVPE; and (b) agreement on demonstrably non-MEVPE practices to preserve security, ease, etc. We must now ask whether the secular constancy of environment is, in fact, so great as to permit the peasant to learn (and transmit to his sons) what is, for him, best practice.

Schultz writes, 'In modern times, the most pervasive force disturbing the equilibrium of agricultural communities is the advance of knowledge useful in agricultural production. Any poor agricultural community that is adjusting its production to one or more of these circumstances is thus excluded from traditional agriculture to which the *efficient but poor hypothesis* applies' (p. 38). This would still leave many communities where the hypothesis is alleged to apply. However, much more powerful disturbers of community equilibrium in poor tropical agricultures—population growth and planning for development—vastly reduce the number of communities where the secularly constant agricultural environment of (say) 1600–1930 offers adequate lessons to the would-be optimiser in 1950–75.

The attack on malaria and yellow fever means that most agricultural communities are increasing their numbers by 2.5 to 3.5 per cent yearly. In a few environments (slash-and-burn regions of Eastern Zambia, waterholes used by nomadic tribal herdsmen of the Eastern Sudan, the extensible settlement frontier in Colombia), this does not invalidate the assumption of constant environment, since new possibilities of cultivation exist for which the old lessons apply. In most tropical agriculture, however, each new generation of rural decision-takers inherits a man/land ratio about double that of its immediate predecessor—not only because population is growing but because generations are lengthening. In so far as the peasant learns the cheap-land, dear-labour lessons of 'long experience', he is *dis*qualified as a Schultzian.

The political and economic changes since decolonisation, too, have altered the environment. Schultz points out that his hypothesis is not relevant to peasant communities assimilating new knowledge or new factors. Apart from the huge inputs of both, planning provides new opportunities of exerting political pressure, and these require radical revision of the conceptual framework within which the farmer applies *traditional* knowledge to *traditional* factors. If fertiliser is distributed by a cooperative instead of a firm, more or less corruptly; if Indian 'democratic decentralisation' alters the balance among castes, or substantially strengthens or weakens landlords or moneylenders; if improved transport of grain or water renders security against drought less important relative to expected-value maximisation—all these 'ifs' suddenly alter optimising procedures for ever, and in the last twenty years they have come in a rush, whatever one may think of their conception or implementation. Again the man who merely 'learns from experience' is sunk. Just as the year-to-year variability of the climatic environment forces peasants to adopt practices other than MEVPE, so the dramatic shift in man/land ratios and the changed political framework force them to change these practices.

7

Suppose that the objections so far raised are not valid. Assume that climatic information is equally reliable everywhere, instead of varying in usefulness inversely with its importance; that perfect markets, and supporting social institutions and attitudes, bridge the gap between a peasant's utility-function and a policy of MEVPE; and that such a policy is, in fact, carried through. Optimisation by each will not, in general, produce optimisation for all.

First, transfers of land could raise output without variations in input levels, or in MEVPE policy. This is because huge scale economies exist—not, as Professor Schultz rightly argues (pp. 110–24), to the firm (i.e. the farm), but to the plant (i.e. the plot). While land ownership retains its prestige and insurance value, population growth renders the loss of output from tiny, partitioned plots worse in each generation. The potential gains from consolidation correspondingly increase. In theory, voluntary land exchange to consolidate *plots* (with compensation by side-payments) is compatible with MEVPE, provided there are no economies of scale to the *holding*. In practice, however, systematic plot consolidation in a village—as opposed to random mergers as mortgages are foreclosed—requires public encouragement and organisation. Thus, even if each farmer is on his production possibility surface (PPS), the totality of farmers is almost certainly not.

Second, market structures in underdeveloped countries (UDCs) push relative prices far away from any 'optimum', whether defined by Schultz, Lange, Mahalanobis, Friedman or Marx. Of at least five relevant processes, (i) to (iii) are familiar to economists. In UDCs as compared to rich nations,

(i) relatively, and increasingly, inegalitarian income distribution raises wheat and rice prices relative to those of millets, especially as urban incomes grow;
(ii) relatively high inter-product differences in the degree of monopoly raise domestic tea and cotton prices relative to those of food-grains;
(iii) relatively low, slow factor mobility and high time-preference make labour-intensive crops too

expensive compared to land-intensive crops, since relative prices over-reflect the past and under-anticipate the future;

(iv) an aspect of the prevailing urban bias, systematically stronger monopoly in the non-agricultural sector, prevents governments from allowing food-grain prices to rise to market levels, and fear of political instability underlines this decision;

(v) backdoor price effects combine with urban bias when bus drivers strike and riot for lower rice prices, but offset it when farmers (especially cash-crop producers) obtain relief through fertiliser subsidies.

These five effects imply that, even if each farmer produces where his PPS is tangential to the price plane, and even if (which does not follow) the community is on its PPS, it will be at the 'wrong' point on the PPS, however 'wrong' may be defined.

Third, even if all individuals and the community are at a point on the PPS tangential with a socially agreed price plane, this is not even a static social optimum. This point is picked without considering variance, and hence is likely to be subject to a good deal of it. A rational planner in East Pakistan, acting on the above highly unlikely assumption, and seeking to maximise the expected value of output from jute and rice together, would not simply adopt MEVPE with only factor constraints. He would be as unwise as the peasant to disregard maximin survival policies. MEVPE maximisation should be his policy on most land, but some should be set aside for cultivation on a maximin basis. Then 'low-world jute price + poor rice harvest', as a strategy by malevolent Nature, cannot prevent the survival of the planner's population to complete his maximising (MEVPE) policies on the rest of the land area. The selection of the right areas to choose for the maximin policy is an interesting problem.

Fourth, operation at a static optimum, even under certainty, is not sufficient for dynamic optimisation. The weighting of the utility functions of individuals (implicitly by the market, together with initial distribution of income and monopoly power, or explicitly by the planner) implies a social utility function, including a rate of time preference and a rate of diminution of utility. Together with production functions, this implies an optimal rate of investment in each time period. However, the rate of reinvestment will vary among optimising farm units. The reallocation of resources from low-investment to high-investment farmers would usually imply more wheat tomorrow, even if it reduced the total value of wheat today by reallocations from consumption towards seedcorn violating the MEVPE preference of each and every farmer-consumer.

Finally, the concessions of the first paragraph of this section give too much scope to MEVPE as a translator of private into social optima. The institutional constraints upon MEVPE also inhibit its translating powers. In Ruritania, the king decrees that each man shall cut off the right arm of his first-born son. Subject to this irrational constraint, each peasant is an MEVPE-optimiser. Conversion into a static social suboptimum requires the central organisation of training for the left-handed, but such training impedes the urge to remove the decree. The analogy with India's programmes for improving milk-yield from sacred cows, as a second-best to their impossible slaughter but making it impossible for longer, is obvious.

8

How, then, did MEVPE gain any acceptance? Can it have had significance for policy? Can it be replaced by a better theory?

MEVPE gained some acceptance for two main reasons. First, many people accepted the argument that a peasant learns to optimise in a secularly constant environment. Second, quantitative evidence suggested responsiveness to price movements. In particular (and much more surprisingly) it seemed to show that market price-ratios of factors and products stood close to MPP-ratios. Previous discussion has concentrated on the theoretical argument. We have shown that the environment is not secularly constant, that its annual variation makes MEVPE unobtainable, that imperfect markets and institutions render the application of learning difficult, that private optimisation does not imply MEVPE, and that private MEVPE does not imply social optimisation. So how can we account for the quantitative evidence?

The inevitably selective nature of Schultz's data has been justly, if somewhat vigorously, attacked.[10] However, it is now generally agreed that cross-elasticity of supply of acres-sown-to-crops, with respect to last year's relative prices, is positive.[11] It is not obvious that this is rational; two years of continuous rise in the price-ratio of crops requiring similar land, in many observed pairs of Indian price-series, foreshadow a fall in the third year.[12] Schultz rightly puts little weight on such cross-elasticities. The special case of MEVPE needs much stronger evidence.

The sort of evidence provided is, I hope, not caricatured by the following description. Collect a cross-section of physical inputs and outputs of farms or villages. Fit these into a homogeneous production function, imposing constant returns to scale. Differentiate the function with 'best fit' parameters, for each crop, with respect to each physical input. The ratios between derivatives then represent relative input prices under MVPE; the price of a kilogram of Crop X is the value of the output of the factors making the marginal kilogram of X if re-allocated to their next best use; this price is equal to the sum of the marginal value-products of all factors making Crop X, each multiplied by its input per kilogram. (Euler's homogeneous-function theorem implies product exhaustion.) If market prices are 'sufficiently close' to Euler prices, MVPE is not refuted. Analogous tests hold for any homogeneous first-degree production functions, including those implicit in linear programming.

The last sentence contains the implicit weakness of all such testing: its inability correctly to specify the production function. Owing to collinearity (among the majority) of factor inputs, a wide variety of different production functions gives excellent fits. If one picks a function corresponding to an incorrect engineering relationship, the derivatives of such a function cannot be 'marginal products'. Such a function can give an excellent fit to the input data because of their collinearity, but wildly misrepresent the engineering relation. The production functions used by Hopper (and cited by Shultz) omit dung, a factor worth about 4 per cent of total input value in much Indian agriculture[13]—and, of course, capable of making far more than 4 per cent difference to ratios between MPPs of other inputs. Even if all factors of production were included, however, we could never choose among the many production functions with satisfactorily high r^2-values. Hence the ratios between derivatives of an arbitrarily chosen function, while theoretically pleasing if it takes Cobb-Douglas form, have no operational significance.

MEVPE is neither wicked nor absurd. It has plainly convinced many key policy-makers. In 1965, India's former Minister of Agriculture, Mr. Subrahmaniam, outlined his agricultural strategy for the Fourth Five-Year Plan. Peasants on unirrigated land, he argued, had learned to make the best use of their resources in thousands of years of unchanged environment; outlays must be concentrated on the 10 per cent of farmers with the best prospects of raising their output.

The concept of the *survival algorithm*, outlined in this paper, is unlike MEVPE. It would not induce Mr Subrahmaniam to spurn possible low-cost opportunities of raising output by bringing each peasant's ploughing, sowing, manuring, weeding and harvesting practices to the level of the best of his neighbours. It suggests why, in the identical environment of a single village, peasants may develop and inherit various, yet rigid, patterns of farming. It proposes an explanation of 'rational', security-centred peasant conduct remote from the self-confirming tests of collinear production functions, but close to the farmers' accounts of their own conduct.

Finally, the concept of the survival algorithm suggests policies for the use of existing factors, from forward pricing of outputs and crop insurance for innovations to consolidation schemes and demonstration farms. It also suggests the rejection of some policies. In an inadequately watered region, fertilisers raise the variance of net output as well as its expected value. They are thus likely to be wasted or, if adopted, to destroy the peasant's confidence in innovations so irrelevant to his scale of preferences. Their high rate of expected return over cost, therefore, has to be set against their hardening effect on security-centred survival algorithms.

Notes: Reading 31

1 This article is part based on observations in a Maharashtra village, Kavathe, Khandala Peta, in Satara District, Maharashtra, India,. Kavathe is a non-irrigated village (on 90 per cent of land) but has enough moisture to permit double-cropping on slightly over half the plots. Almost all heads of households own land, and cultivate about four acres each, split on average into eight or nine plots. Soil quality is poor because – despite nitrogen deficiency – inadequate, seasonally concentrated rainfall limits fertiliser use.

2 All page references in the text are to T. W. Schultz, *Transforming Traditional Agriculture* (paperback edition), Yale, 1964 (hereafter *TTE*). Schultz's chief sources are Sol Tax, *Penny Capitalism*, Chicago, 1953, and D. Hopper's work in Senapur, summarised in D. Hopper, 'Allocation efficiency in traditional Indian agriculture', *Jnl Farm Econ.*, vol. 47, no. 3, 1966, pp. 611–24.

3 Shown by J. L. Joy in a paper to the Honolulu conference on the Transformation of Traditional Agriculture (not yet published).

4 T. Balogh, *Economic Journal*, December 1964, pp. 996–9.

5 T. W. Schultz, *The Economic Test in Latin America; TTE*, ch. 12.

6 H. H. Mann, *Rainfall and Famine*, Poona, c.1950.

7 S. Naqvi, 'Coefficient of variability of monsoon rainfall in India and Pakistan', *Pakistan Geographical Review*, pt IV, no. 2, 1949; O. H. K. Spate and A. K. Learmonth, *India and Pakistan*, London, 1967, p. 47.

8 M. Kalecki, *Theory of Economic Dynamics*, London, 1954, pp. 94–6.

9 Dr Hopper, in an unpublished paper for the Indian Intensive Agricultural Development Programme, showed that top-decile farmers in Indian villages around Delhi usually outperformed research stations.

10 Balogh, loc. cit.

11 D. Narain, *Impact of Price Movements on Areas under Selected Crops in India,* Asia, 1956, esp. pp. 158–62; E. Dean, *Supply Response of African Farmers*, North-Holland, 1966, esp. pp. 74–9.

12 M. Lipton, 'Should reasonable farmers respond to price changes?', *Journal of Modern Asian Studies*, 1966.

13 Private communication from Professor Schultz, relating to Punjab. See also *Studies in Economics of Farm Management in Bombay: 1954–5 to 1956–7*, Ministry of Food and Agriculture, Delhi, 1962, pp. 86, 88.

Reading 32

Supply Responses of Peasant Producers: The Effect of Own – Account Consumption on the Supply of Marketed Output

I. Livingstone

Journal of Agricultural Economics, vol. XXVIII, no. 2, 1977.

An important question is frequently omitted in the discussion of the supply responses of peasant producers: whether the marketed crop in question is an ordinary cash crop or also a staple food crop with substantial own-account consumption by the smallholder. We first explore graphically the effect of own-account consumption on the supply of a marketable surplus. Subsequently it is shown that this analysis can be extended to cover the case where there is both a food crop and a single cash crop, the food crop being non-marketed. Reference is made to the supply response literature to indicate some of the confusion caused by failure to take proper account of own-account consumption and the income–leisure trade-off.

1

Figure 1(a) shows, on the left-hand side, the farmer's choice between income and leisure. If *AB* is his opportunity-line, he is free to choose any combination of leisure/work and income along this line.[1] If he opts for point C,[2] this means choosing 12 hours of work per day (and the same of leisure) and a cash income of 240 rupees. Figure 1(b) shows how he might choose to allocate this income as between own-account consumption of the staple crop and consumption of other goods. His budget line *DE* starts on the *Y*-axis at $D = 240$ Rs. Point *E* indicates that if he spent all his income on consuming his own product he would consume 24 bags of the staple, implying a price per bag of 10 Rs. This also implies a productivity of two bags per hour worked, since this income is obtained from 12 hours' effort.

According to his tastes he will choose some consumption combination of staple food and other goods, say *F*. In doing so, he will hope to at least 'fill his stomach' with a minimum amount of the staple food before selling the rest of his output to exchange with other goods: and yet there may be a minimum level of expenditure on other items, e.g. tax payments, school fees, some clothing, which he cannot avoid, and for which he is prepared to sacrifice some staple food, even though he is still 'hungry'. At *F* the choice is to consume *OG* of the staple (= 12 bags) and sell *GE* (= 12 bags) in exchange for *DH* (= 120 Rs) of cash income. Consumption of other goods is *OH*.

Suppose now the price of the staple increases by 50 per cent to 15 Rs a bag. The leisure-income opportunity-line would shift from *AB* to *AB′*, and in general any choice of combination along *AB′* could now be made. It will be useful to assume initially that the same number of hours is worked, *C′* being chosen, yielding 360 Rs at the increased price. This will shift the budget line in figure 1(b), which will now run from *D′* to E since, with the same number of hours worked, output (and maximum own-consumption) will still be 24 bags.

The new consumption choice could be anywhere along *D′E*. The interesting point is that any choice between *F′* and *E* to the right of the vertical *JFG*, implies a *fall* in the amount exchanged for other goods, *GE*. For example, at *K* the farmer chooses to consume *OM* (= 16 bags) of staple food and sell only *ME* (= 8 bags) as a result of a combination of income and substitution effects.

However, the implied backward-sloping supply curve for a marketable surplus can be seen to have a quite rational basis. The 'normal' slope will only occur if a consumer choice in the range *F′D′* is made.

We can now relax the assumption that the supply of effort remains unchanged at 12 hours. Suppose *C″* is

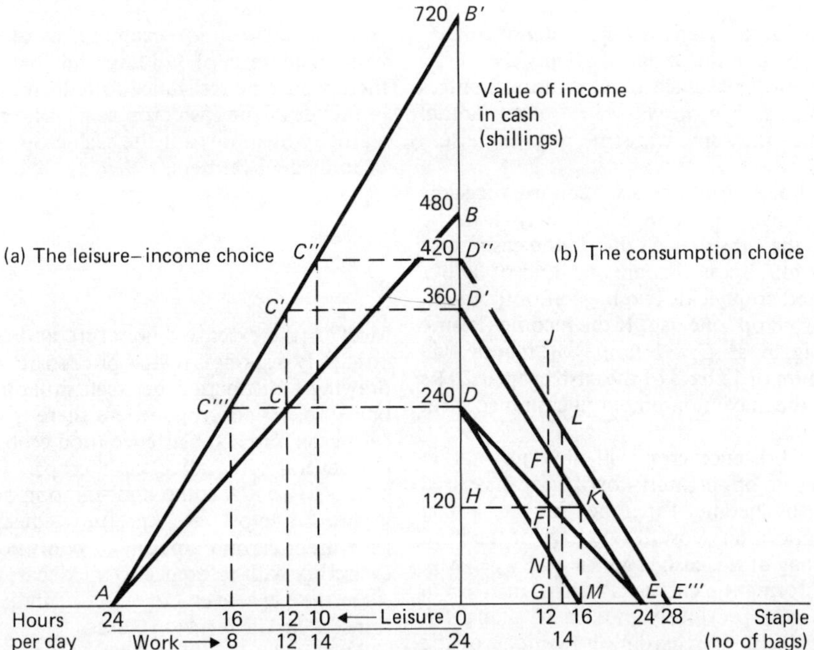

Figure 1 The effect of an increase in the price of a staple on hours worked, own-account consumption, and surplus marketed.

selected, rather than C', with 14 hours worked and income at 420 Rs. With given output per hour,. production will be 28 bags. The budget line in Figure 1(b) will thus shift out to $D'E'$, parallel to $D'E$ since relative prices between the staple and other goods will be as when 12 hours are worked. The amount marketed may not now decrease even if the farmer's consumption choice it to the right of *JFG*. For instance, at *L*, 14 bags are consumed by the farmer, who can still increase his sales to 14, because of the increase EE'' (=4 bags) in his output. On the other hand, if his income–leisure choice were C''', working only 8 hours instead of 12, but obtaining the same 'target' income, 240 Rs, his budget line would be *DM*, again parallel to $D'E$. This time the chances of the marketed surplus decreasing are greater, since the maximum available for own-consumption has decreased, and the farmer may be more willing to cut down on his consumption of other goods for the sake of more leisure, than on consumption of the staple.[3]

Thus, the effect of a change in price on the surplus marketed of a staple crop will depend on the producer's income-elasticity of demand for own-account consumption. More precisely, the change in the surplus marketed will be determined by the size and direction of the income and substitution effects in Figure 1(b) *and* on the income and substitution effects on the demand for leisure in Figure 1(a). There is a simultaneous trade-off between consumption of the staple and of other goods, on the right-hand side, and between income and leisure on the other side. The supply response will be more positive the higher the consumption-elasticity of substitution (the rise in price of the staple makes own-account consumption of the staple more expensive than before, discouraging own consumption and encouraging sales), the lower the income-elasticity of demand for the staple, and the more elastic the supply of effort.

This situation is more likely to hold in the case of a relatively well-to-do farmer with plenty or land and capital, whose income-elasticity of demand for basic foodstuffs will be low. Among small farmers it may apply to those blessed with relatively fertile land, who are able to satisfy their own food requirements with minimum labour input. Such a farmer will have a low income-elasticity of demand for the staple and, since he is not fully stretched in terms of labour input, a high elasticity of supply of effort (unless his leisure-preference is exceptionally high). In contrast, a farmer with low-fertility land, which requires substantial labour effort in relation to output, will have an inelastic supply of marketed surplus for the opposite reasons. In this case or where, in overpopulated areas, he has only a small plot of land, however fertile, which is already intensively used, low or rapidly diminishing returns will reduce the elasticity of supply of effort and output.

2

This analysis can be extended to cover the case where

two crops are produced, if one is a non-marketed subsistence food crop and the other a single cash crop grown entirely for the market since, once more, changes in the price of the cash crop will cause a substantial change in income, thus involving an income–leisure trade-off.

With suitable choice of numbers we can use the same diagram as previously. Labour effort may now be devoted to either the subsistence crop or the cash crop, or some combination. Let us assume one hour of labour devoted to the food crop yields two bags of output and, devoted to the cash crop, one bag. If the income–leisure choice is once again at *C*, 12 hours of labour will produce a maximum of 12 bags of the cash crop at 20 Rs per bag, yielding the maximum potential cash income at *D* of 240 Rs.

Although the subsistence crop will have no market price,[4] it will have an opportunity-cost price, measured in terms of cash income foregone for each bag produced. The opportunity cost of two bags of the food crop will be one bag of the cash crop, or 10 Rs per bag. *DE* is now a transformation curve, as well as, in effect, a budget line. Whereas previously movement along *DE* implied different decisions regarding how much of the food crop to sell for cash (to acquire other goods) and how much to retain, now it means allocating different amounts of labour effort to the two crops, one to be consumed directly and the other for cash to be exchanged with other goods. For instance, at *F*, 12 bags of the food crop would be produced and consumed by the farmer, with six hours allocated to each crop. If there were a 50 per cent rise in the price of the cash crop the opportunity line in Figure 1(a) would shift to *AB′* exactly as before, with the same repercussions. The opportunity-cost price of the food crop would rise relatively to other goods, and the income and substitution effects in Figure 1(b) would be as before. The effect of the rise in its price could in principle be either an increase or a *decrease* in the quantity supplied, still assuming rational behaviour, since any point along *D′E* could be chosen.[5] Any point to the right of *F′* on the line *JFG* implies an increase in the consumption of food crop, made possible by increasing the allocation of labour effort to this crop, and decreasing the production and sale of the cash crop *despite* its rise in price.

The only new element in the analysis is that since *DE* is now a transformation curve, it could in fact be a curve rather than a straight line, reflecting diminishing returns on the farm as output of one crop is increased at the expense of the other, if not all the land is equally suited to both crops or because of different patterns of labour demand. This could be expected to reduce the response to the price rise.

The completely parallel analysis in this case is of some significance in widening its applicability. The situation where farmers are growing one crop mainly for food and one crop for cash, millet and cotton, say, or maize and coffee, is a common one in the developing countries. Thus, for example, in overpopulated areas with small sizes of holding and low income per head, there would be resistance to reducing food crop output in favour of the cash crop as its price rises, reducing the elasticity of supply for the cash crop, at least in the case of individual farmers.

3

Most of the extensive literature and econometric work on supply responses relates price to quantity sold without drawing a distinction between situations where there is one staple food crop, where there is one predominant cash crop and a subsistence food crop, and where there are several alternative cash crops. Thus, neither the effects of own-account consumption or of the income–leisure trade-off are carefully considered. This can generate a certain amount of confusion, which we can exemplify with reference to the debate which took place some time ago over the effect in India/Pakistan of the transfer of US farm surpluses.

Thus, Schultz (1960), commenting on the discussion, interpreted the arguments of other commentators as follows:

> If in the process farm prices decline relatively, this is looked upon as of no economic consequence because of the widely held belief that the price response of cultivators is zero. Lower farm prices by this view will not induce cultivators to reduce production; if anything, it may even cause cultivators to produce more.

Schultz appears here to be making two omissions or misinterpretations. First of all, if we are talking not of one crop among alternatives, but of the total supply of food grains, accounting for a large part of total production, the relevant supply response involved is especially that of total production, the supply of effort. By implication, Schultz is trying to refute allegations in respect of the supply of effort by reference to the only empirical evidence which is available, that on the supply of particular crops. The journal discussion refers clearly to inelastic supply of all food grains taken together in the face of a *general* fall in food-grain prices. It is true that such a general fall *may* be accompanied by significant changes in relative prices, as Falcon (1960) pointed out: but this is something else.

Secondly, Schultz, in referring to the supposition of a backward-sloping supply curve, did not observe that this was supposed to exist here for very special reasons: this was that the commodities concerned were also consumed on-farm, and that the supply in question was specifically of a marketable *surplus*. This point is clearly made by others.

Thus Khakhate (1962) states:

In an economy where the subsistence sector in agriculture looms large, agricultural production does not respond to price changes, while the marketed surplus has a negative response which is totally opposite to what happens in an economy with a preponderance of big landholders. . . .
. . . The situation depicted here cannot, however, be described as one of low or zero price response as Schultz suggests. In fact, the extent of price response is high but negative and it affects marketed surplus and not production. Similarly, this case is also different from the one of a backward-sloping supply curve of agricultural output, where agricultural production is supposed to decline with the rise in prices and vice versa. What happens in our case is that while agricultural production remains unchanged, it is the marketed surplus which assumes the characteristic of a backward-sloping supply curve.

This makes the same distinction as made above between the situation of small farmers with substantial own-account consumption, and larger commercial farmers.

A similar explanation is given by Mathur and Ezekiel (1961):

> An increase in the prices of agricultural products makes it possible for the cultivator to satisfy his monetary requirements by selling a smaller quantity of food grains than before. . . . The residual is (thus) not the amount sold but the amount retained. If prices rise, the sale of a smaller amount of food grains provides the necessary cash and vice versa. Thus prices and marketable surplus tend to move in opposite directions.

This clearly relates the backward-bending supply curve to a marketable surplus, and bases it on a supposition of quite rational behaviour. The argument implied is that cash requirements, while not absolutely fixed, are more fixed than own-consumption requirements, i.e. the demand for food is income-elastic at very low levels of real income compared to demand for other things.

Beringer (1963), in his criticism of Khakhate, makes the valid point that the share of small farmers in terms of total acreage and marketed output is not large. This would cast doubt on the empirical validity of the argument in India/Pakistan, but does not affect the theoretical argument. Khakhate's hypothesis might, for example, apply in many parts of Africa, where large farmers do not predominate. Elsewhere, however, Beringer appears to make the same kind of error as Schultz, when he states:

> My purpose is to suggest that Mr Khakhate has placed too much reliance on the well-known theory of the backward-sloping supply curve in underdeveloped countries as a basis for ruling out potential adverse effects of surplus disposal on agriculture.

As just stated, this was just what Khakhate wished to avoid. The confusion does therefore show signs of persisting.

To summarise, it is essential in discussing supply response to distinguish between:

(1) the supply of particular crops;
(2) the supply of total production, or the supply of effort; and
(3) the supply of a marketed surplus, that is, the supply to the market of a crop for which there is substantial own-account consumption.

We might add:

(4) supply response through expansion of acreage or through increased yields.

Much of the non-econometric evidence offered relating to supply response is of rapid increases in output over time.[6] This is, however, best explained in 'vent-for-surplus' terms, involving expansion of acreage, using surplus labour, rather than by increased yields. Increasing yields involves the supply of 'ingenuity'[7] or quality of effort, and thus the *efficiency* of peasant production, raising a different issue altogether.

Our central point, however, is that when there is a single, major cash crop, a change in price is likely to involve the elasticity of supply of total output, rather than simply substitution elasticity, that substitution between cash production and food consumption will affect the result when the cash crop is also a staple food crop; and that this substitution may also be important when there is a single cash crop, even if it is not a food crop.

Notes: Reading 32

1 With diminishing returns to labour, this would have the usual shape of a transformation curve, concave to the origin. For simplicity of exposition, we assume a straight line. The effect of diminishing returns is discussed later.

2 If we employed indifference curve analysis, C would be the point of tangency between the opportunity-line AB and an indifference curve between income and leisure. However, in both figures 1(a) and 1(b) we shall dispense with indifference curves and assume that the individual's preferences are 'revealed' by his choice of combination along the opportunity-line or budget line.

3 Although a substitution effect should operate against consumption of the staple, in favour of other goods, following a relative rise in price of the staple.

4 This may appear odd, but it is reasonable to assume that the market will be substantially own-account consumption, with farmers unable to sell to each other, and transport costs prohibiting export of the food crop outside the area.

5 This assumes the same point C' on AB' is chosen as before, to yield the same potential cash income OD'.
6 See, for instance, P. T. Bauer (1965).
7 See Smithies (1966).

References: Reading 32

Bauer, P. T. (1965), 'The vicious circle of poverty', *Weltwirtschaftliches Archiv*, vol. 95, no. 2.

Beringer, C. (1963), 'Real effect of foreign surplus disposal in underdeveloped countries: comment', *Q. J. Econ.*, no. 77.

Falcon, W. P. (1960), 'Further comment', *Q. J. Econ.*, no. 77.

Khakhate, D. R. (1962), 'Some notes on the real effects of foreign surplus disposal in underdeveloped economies', *Q. J. Econ.*, no. 76.

Mathur, P., and Ezekiel, H. (1961), 'Marketable surplus of food and price fluctuations in a developing economy', *Kyklos*, no. 14.

Schultz, T. W. (1960), 'Value of US farm surpluses to underdeveloped countries', *J. Fm Econ.*, no. 42, pp. 1010–30.

Smithies, A. (1966), 'Rising expectations and economic development', *Econ. J.*, no. 71.

Reading 33

The Economics of Agricultural Resource Use and Development in Plantation Economies

G. L. Beckford

Social and Economic Studies, Vol. 8, No. 4, 1969, pp. 321–47.

Plantation agriculture has been generally ignored in the rapidly expanding literature on underdeveloped agriculture. To a large extent this reflects a view that plantation agriculture is 'efficient' and 'modern'; that it is particularly suited to certain tropical crops; that the plantation system has served to bring previously isolated areas into the modern world economy; and that large-scale plantation units make possible 'economies of operation by the use of labour-saving machinery'.[1]

More recently, a few development economists have drawn attention to the fact that differences in factor combinations, production technology, etc., among export industries lead to differences in patterns of growth among export economies. And in this connection, the plantation system of resource organization has received some attention.[2]

So far the most important contributions to the study of plantations have come from the sociologists and social anthropologists. The study of Puerto Rico by Steward *et al.* is an outstanding example of this pioneering work and a number of subsequent symposia on The Caribbean have focused on 'plantation society as a sociohistorical determinant of contemporary subcultures'.[3] These studies have provided very useful insights for understanding the internal dynamics of plantation societies. But they emphasize the need for similar work on the economic relations, organization and institutions that characterize the plantation system.

The discussion begins with an examination of the characteristics of plantation agriculture: how it developed, where it exists, and what factors distinguish it from other types of agriculture. Detailed consideration of the internal organization of modern plantation enterprises provides the background for subsequent analysis of the economics of production and resource use. This represents a re-examination of the view that plantation agriculture is 'efficient'. The concern in this paper is not with efficiency of the firm but with efficiency of resource use in the agricultural sectors of countries in which these enterprises operate.

The final part of the exercise is to assess the development potential of plantation agriculture. It is not sufficient merely to state that the plantation system brought backward and isolated areas into the modern world economy. The important question is whether the system makes it possible for these economies to achieve structural transformation and a self-sustaining pattern of growth and development.

1 Characteristics of Plantation Agriculture

The word 'plantation' has fallen into such common use that it denotes different things to different people. Generally speaking, it is considered to refer to a large farming unit. However, as the discussion below indicates, this is an inadequate description.

Plantation production

According to Jones:

> a plantation is an economic unit producing agricultural commodities (field crops or horticultural products, but not livestock) for sale and employing a relatively large number of unskilled labourers whose activities are closely supervised. Plantations usually employ a year-round labour crew of some size, and they usually specialize in the production of only one or two marketable products. *They differ from other kinds of farms in the way in which the factors of production, primarily management and labour, are combined.*[4]

Production on plantations is undertaken not just 'for sale', as indicated above, but specifically for sale in overseas markets (export sale). The special factor combination that distinguishes plantation production from other kinds of farms is the bringing together of as many unskilled farm labourers as possible with each of the few highly skilled supervisor-managers who direct production. As Jones puts it, 'the plantation substitutes supervision – supervisory and administrative skills – for skilled, adaptive labour, combining the supervision with labour whose principal skill is to follow orders'.

Two other aspects of plantation production deserve mention here, although they are considered in more detail below. They are (i) foreign ownership, usually by a corporate enterprise; and (ii) a 'relatively high degree of vertical integration, even of self-sufficiency' – i.e. the plantation enterprise supplies inputs for its agricultural operations and processing and marketing facilities for its agricultural output.

Plantations are mainly involved in the production of certain tropical crops – mainly tree crops and other perennials. Sugar, bananas, tea, rubber and coffee are the main commodities involved. It has frequently been suggested that the 'complementarity between agricultural processing plants and farm-producing units has been one consideration in the establishment of plantations. Many of the major tropical export crops must undergo preliminary processing shortly after harvesting. . . .'

However, the association of plantation production with certain tropical crops cannot be explained in such narrow technical terms. It must be seen in the large context of the way in which these commodities were introduced into the international economy.

The plantation system

Plantation agriculture is the outgrowth of the political colonization of tropical areas by the metropolitan countries of Europe. Temperate areas which had been colonized by Europe – e.g. the United States, Canada, Australia, New Zealand, Argentina, Chile, etc. – involved the movement of people. Those areas developed as 'colonies of settlement' and the pattern of agriculture that emerged was significantly different from that in the tropical colonies where mainly capital and enterprise were involved in the movement from the metropole to produce 'colonies of exploitation'.

As Greaves has pointed out, 'one of the outstanding characteristics of the plantation is that it has brought together enterprise, capital and labour from different parts of the world in an area which offered opportunity for new and increased production'.[5] Enterprise and capital came from the metropole which was usually, though not always, the centre of direct political control. Labour was brought mainly from other tropical areas. With the possible exception of Java, plantations were originally established in sparsely populated areas. And because of the shortage of labour in these areas, the plantation system depended on large-scale (involuntary and voluntary) movement of labour from other tropical areas. Slavery and then indenture provided labour supplies for the establishment and development of plantations in the New World. Chinese, Japanese, and Filipino labourers were brought to develop Hawaii's sugar plantations; the rubber plantations of Malaya and Sumatra drew most of their workers from China, Java and India; and so on. In the New World, even after slavery and indenture, 'new' plantation economies drew labour supplies from 'mature' plantation economies. 'Thus the plantation came to be associated not only with a resident labour force, but more often than not with one of alien origin'.[6]

Perhaps the most important consideration for present purposes is the international dimension of the plantation system. As Greaves puts it:

> Historically and economically the plantation system is fundamentally international in character. Wherever it is found it derives from external stimulus and enterprise; it has always depended on external markets; and it is still largely involved in external finance. Because of this character the plantation has been associated with most political and international developments of modern times; mercantilism and free trade; slavery and independence; capitalism and imperialism. . . .[7]

Further, we are warned that 'although we are apt to speak of a "plantation economy" as though it were in itself a complete and separate economy, *plantations are in practice only a special part of a much wider economic system with a financial and industrial centre usually in a region remote from the plantations*. The extent to which this part of the system is dependent upon the centre is determined by how far the latter controls it; control can take two forms, property ownership, and political connections which affect such matters as prices, tariffs and loan funds'.[8] Thus, for example, nineteenth-century British economists rightly described the West Indies as 'a place "where England finds it convenient to carry on the production of sugar, coffee, and a few other tropical commodities", and the trade between them was similar to the town and country trades at home'.[9]

These characteristics apply as much today as in earlier historical periods. Even where *direct* metropolitan political control is absent, property ownership and indirect political connections still control the pattern of resource allocation and production in countries where plantations are located today. Indeed, even in the absence of property ownership, control from the centre (metropolis) may result from economic connections; for example, financial control through the banking system or the specificity of the raw material export to metropolitan refining capacity. These characteristics of metropolitan control are evident in the case of the politically independent banana republics of Central America which are in fact extensions of the United

States economic system, as well as in the constitutionally independent sugar dominions of the West Indies which still remain extensions of the British and American economic systems.

Plantation economies

Taking note of the fact that plantations form only a part of a wider economic system, the term 'plantation economy' can be used cautiously to describe situations where the *dominant* pattern of agricultural resource organization is the plantation system. It is not necessary that the agricultural sector of countries involved should consist only of plantation units. No such countries in fact exist. Dominant is used in the sense that the bulk of the country's agricultural resources are owned by plantations, and/or plantation production provides the main dynamic for development. The latter condition requires some elaboration. It is used here in the broadest sense to encompass sociological, political and economic dynamics. Thus, for example, there are situations – as in the West Indies – where peasant producers are more numerous than plantation enterprises but where, because the peasantry is a creation of the plantations their behaviour reflects the plantation influence. In the political sphere, political decision-makers are imbued with a psychological dependence on an established plantation sector and agricultural development policy tends to reflect this attitude.

On the basis of this definition, plantation economies are to be found mainly in tropical America and tropical Asia. Although plantations exist in tropical Africa (e.g. oil palm plantations of the Congo), they do not dominate the scene as in the other regions mentioned.

In Asia, countries like Ceylon, Malaya, Indonesia and the Philippines would classify as plantation economies. So would Mauritius and Reunion in the Indian Ocean; and Hawaii and Fiji in the Pacific. The crops involved in these cases are tea, rubber, sugar and to some extent coconuts.

In America, the *locus* of the plantation system is the Caribbean. Indeed, this region is generally regarded as *the* classic plantation area. So much so that social anthropologists have described the region as a culture sphere, labelled 'Plantation-America'. According to Wagley:

> Briefly, this culture sphere extends spatially from about midway up the coast of Brazil into the Guianas, along the Caribbean coast, throughout the Caribbean itself, and into the United States. It is characteristically coastal; not until the nineteenth century did the way of life of the Plantation culture sphere penetrate far into the mainland interior, and then only in Brazil and the United States. This area has an environment which is characteristically tropical (except the Southern United States) and lowland.[10]

Wagley goes on to describe some of the basic common features in this culture sphere. Among these are:

> monocrop cultivation under the plantation system, rigid class lines, multi-racial societies, weak community cohesion, small peasant proprietors involved in subsistence and cash-crop production, and a matrifocal type family form. In addition there are a series of cultural characteristics common to Plantation-America which derive often from similarities in environment, often from the common historical background, and often from the presence of such a large population of African origin.[11]

Common cultural characteristics are said to be reflected in the similarities of peasant crops, production techniques, and marketing arrangements: cuisine, music and folklore with common African influences; and similar traditions or values affecting social life.

Analysis of the development experience in particular plantation regions is outside the scope of the present paper. However, in so far as the discussion requires empirical foundation at various points, the Caribbean is the basic reference area.

2 Plantation Enterprises

The analysis of resource use and production and of the development problem in plantation economies requires prior examination of the characteristics of the major decision-making units – the plantation enterprises. This has largely been ignored in previous contributions; and the result has been a superficial view of the role of plantation agriculture in promoting agricultural development and change in such societies.

Plantation agriculture in the modern world economy is dominated by large-scale multi-national corporate enterprises. The United Fruit Company, the Standard Fruit and Shipping Co. and Unilever are the best known. Several others, less well known, are of particular importance in certain areas. For example, sugar production in the West Indies is dominated by two such companies – Tate and Lyle Ltd, a British sugar-refining firm with wholly owned raw sugar-producing subsidiaries in the region; and Booker Brothers, McConnell and Co. Ltd of London (Bookers).

In addition to the metropolitan basis of ownership, three important characteristics of these enterprises which directly affect resource use in countries where they operate plantations are: (1) a high degree of vertical integration; (2) a lateral spread in their agricultural operations among a number of countries; and (3) each firm accounts for a significant share (often the bulk) of the export output of particular commodities from individual countries.

Bookers is of strategic importance to the economy of Guyana. So far as sugar is concerned, the company has produced well over 80 per cent of the country's output in recent years. In addition the company owns all the bulk storage capacity and sugar shipping facilities and provides ocean transport for most of Guyana's sugar exports. When it is recognized that sugar is Guyana's largest agricultural export and the biggest single employer of labour, it seems reasonable to conclude that Bookers dominates the agricultural economy of that country.

The United Fruit Co. is a giant enterprise, both in respect of banana production in Central America as well as banana imports into the United States. For example, in 1966 U.F.Co. accounted for 55 per cent of total US banana imports. In the same year, the company controlled 100 per cent of export banana acreage in Guatemala, 70 per cent of that in both Costa Rica and Panama and 56 per cent of that in Honduras.[12]

Some significant characteristics

In terms of the scope of their activities, the three firms considered above are, to a large extent, representative of foreign-owned plantation enterprises operating in tropical America. Indeed, together they account for a significant share of plantation output in this region. A factor which is worthy of note is that each firm is large as compared with the agricultural sectors of individual countries in which they operate. For example, the total value of agricultural output in Guyana was estimated to have been in the region of £17 million in 1966, while the 'turnover' (mainly sales) for the entire Bookers organization in that year was of the order of £78 million. Even the sales from Bookers 'tropical agriculture operations' and 'rum and other spirits' alone (£18.7 million) exceeded the total value of agricultural output in Guyana. Another significant feature is that each of the three firms accounts for the major share (in several cases, 100 per cent) of the total output of the particular crop in individual countries where they operate. This means that decisions relating to the adjustment of output for particular commodities in individual countries are made by a central authority located within the structure of a single firm.

A high degree of vertical integration is characteristic of these firms. This vertical integration extends far beyond the stage of the 'factory-farm combines' repeatedly discussed in the established literature on plantation agriculture. In addition to processing of the agricultural raw material, these enterprises are substantially engaged in supplying their own agricultural inputs and, more importantly, in the shipping and marketing of the products at higher stages of production.

Vertical integration has indeed been carried to a stage where the actual plantation operations of the enterprises may no longer represent the bulk of firm investments. What is more, operations at higher stages of production are only partly based on the firm's own supplies from lower stages of the production process. Consequently, the firm is in a position to hedge possible losses on its farming operations against consequent gains further up the scale.

Metropolitan ownership and control is another factor which has much significance. For one thing, it means that the *locus* of decision-making is outside of the countries in which plantation production activities are carried out. This is bound to affect the pattern of production, resource use and development in the countries with which we are here concerned. For example, it is generally recognized that 'foreign investors prefer investments which are directly linked with the foreign exchange-earning ability of the economy' in which they invest.[13] Surpluses for re-investment therefore tend to flow back into established export activities in which these investors have developed an infrastructure of expertise and organization – thus creating rigidities in the overall adjustment process in the agricultural sectors of the countries involved.

The typical geographic spread of plantation operations of individual firms is also significant. The production adjustment process in this event must be considered, not in terms of individual countries but from the point of view of the firm. Decisions relating to expansion or contraction of output in a particular country are made within the context of the firm's overall supply drawn from several countries. The relevant unit for analysis is therefore the plantation enterprise and not the nation state in which only a part of the firm's operations is located.

Yet another feature worthy of note is that the capital investments of these enterprises are highly specific to the production and marketing (including processing) of a particular commodity. In addition to specific capital investment on the agricultural side, complementary investments at other levels tend to be specific to the plantation commodity; for example, bulk terminals, special bulk sugar vessels and refining equipment in the case of sugar; and specially designed banana boats in the case of United Fruit.[14] As we shall see below, this high degree of specificity influences the pattern of resource use and the adjustment process.

3 Agricultural Production and Resource Use in Plantation-type Economies

The concern here is with production and resource use in the agricultural sectors of what we have described as plantation economies; in other words, with the way in which plantation operations influence resource use and overall production in the countries where these enterprises are engaged in agriculture. In this connection, efficiency considerations relate to the agricultural sectors of the plantation economies and not to the firm. The two are not the same. What is good for the firm is not necessarily good for the country where it produces.

Indeed, the general thesis of this paper is that in plantation-type economies efficient resource allocation in individual production units tends to co-exist with inefficient resource allocation for the agricultural sector as a whole.

The efficiency conditions for the agricultural sector can be briefly set out in the conventional way to provide a general background. Resources are allocated most efficiently when the following conditions hold: (1) resources are allocated within each farm in a manner that equates the marginal value productivities of the resource services – i.e. a unit of labour or capital should not be used to grow sugar if it can produce a greater value product in livestock; (2) resources are distributed between farms and farming areas so that marginal value productivities are equal; (3) resources are distributed between farming and other producing areas to equalize value productivities; and (4) resources are allocated over time such that their discounted value products are equal.

Production objectives

The plantation production unit is a corporate enterprise which is chiefly concerned with making profit for its shareholders. Profit maximization is, therefore, one of the primary objectives of plantation enterprises. However, because the plantation itself is part of a wider organizational complex, profit maximization may not be a guiding principle at the level of its agricultural operations. In so far as the firm draws heavily on raw material supplies other than its own at the higher levels of production (and marketing), lower profits on the agricultural side may result in higher overall profits. Furthermore, profit maximization at the farm level is constrained by the firm's specific capital commitments.

In so far as changes in output prices at various levels affect levels of profit, the firm is in a position to hedge losses at one stage against gains at higher stages of production so long as the final disposal (consumer) price does not change proportionately with changes in the prices of primary and intermediate outputs.

One characteristic of the plantation which has been noted by Jones is 'the ability to exploit market imperfections or to manipulate them to its advantage'. This applies not only to the factor market but to the product market as well. The firm is therefore usually in a position to control final disposal prices, perhaps more so than prices of primary and intermediate outputs.

The upshot of the foregoing discussion is that the maximization of total profit for the firm as a whole is not dependent on profit maximization for its agricultural activities. The importance of agriculture in this connection depends partly on the share of agriculture in the firm's total investments. The smaller this share, the less will be the need for using the profit maximization principle on its agricultural operations.

Since the agricultural operations of plantation enterprises are located in the tropical economies with which we are here concerned, this observation has implications for agricultural resource use in these economies. Changes in the structure of output prices (for the whole range of agricultural products which can be grown in these countries) which offer more profitable opportunities than the particular plantation crop do not induce a shift of resources from production of the latter because the profit horizon of the plantation enterprise (which controls these resources) extends beyond these purely agricultural opportunities. Even in the long run, the *adjustment process tends to be limited to output adjustments for the particular crop* rather than to a more flexible deployment of resources over the range of production possibilities in line with differential marginal value productivities.

Capital specificity

It will be recalled from the preceding section that one of the characteristics of plantation enterprises is that the capital stock of these firms is highly specific to the production and processing (including marketing) of particular crops. This produces further inflexibility in the pattern of agricultural resource use. The more integrated is the firm structure the more important is this limitation. For this means that the firm also has investments outside of agriculture which are geared to the particular crop.

The degree of specificity tends to be least at the actual farming level. Equipment used in cultivation, field labour, land, etc., can be used for the production of any number of crops. But the capital required for the processing (in the farm-factory and elsewhere) and shipping is quite specific. For example, sugar mills cannot be adapted to processing vegetables, and banana boats are specially designed to their task. In the vertically integrated structure of the firm it is these specific non-farm investments that help to create rigidities in resource use on the plantation. For capital specificity in related non-farm operations of the firm makes it less profitable to undertake crop switching or diversification at the farm level.[15]

Once ancillary investment commitments have been made, the firm is constrained to a short-run production possibilities curve with a limited scope for the switching of resources to alternative products. This is illustrated below. The first diagram shows the long-run production possibilities for combinations of two crops, sugar and bananas, with a given set of resources. This is denoted by the curve LR. Once the firm commits itself to specific investments relating to one or the other crop the long-run production possibilities (opportunity) curve is no longer relevant. If the investments are specific to sugar production, the operative opportunity curve then becomes $s_c r_c$, while if they are specific to bananas it is $s_b r_b$. The degree of flexibility for product-product

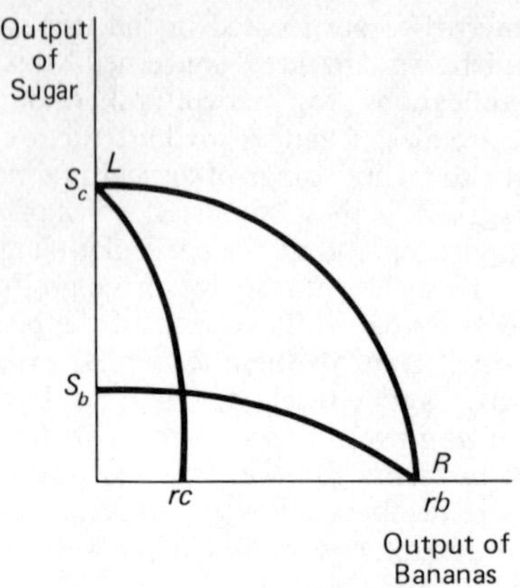

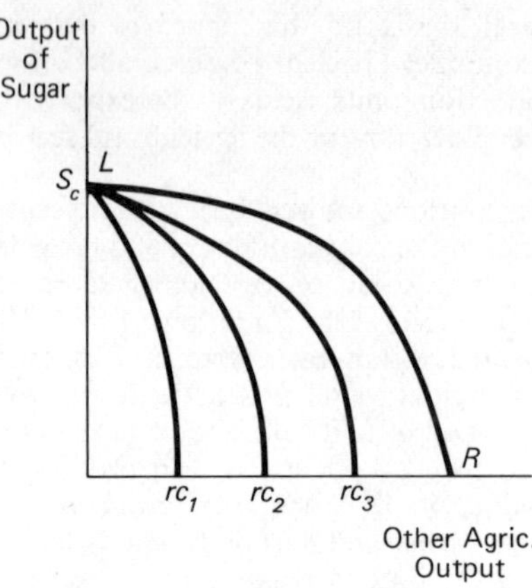

combinations is reduced as a result of the specific commitments.

The second diagram shows different degrees of capital specificity for a set of firms involved in sugar production. The more resources the firm has tied up in activities linked to sugar the greater the degree of inflexibility. Thus in the case of West Indian sugar producers, for example, if rc_1 represents the position of Tate and Lyle subsidiaries, Bookers would operate on a curve to the right of this, say rc_2, since the latter does not have sugar refining investments, while a simple farm-factory combine (sugar estate) without shipping and refining investments would operate further right, on say, rc_3.

The greater the degree of vertical integration the less will be the flexibility of adjusting resource use to changing production opportunities across the range of agricultural commodities which can be produced with available resources.

Land use

The farm-factory operations of plantation enterprises are located in the tropical plantation economies. Here the factory for processing plantation output represents a substantial capital investment. The firm is therefore concerned that adequate supplies of raw material will be available for utilizing factory capacity in a reasonably efficient way. Sufficient land must be acquired to produce the desired flow of raw material. Even where raw material supplies are available for purchase from independent farmers, the firm would be in too vulnerable a position if it relied exclusively on such supplies.

This means that the plantation enterprise will try to secure sufficient land to produce some, or all, of its raw material requirements and to allow for some degree of flexibility of output adjustment over time in response to changing market opportunities.

The land area required by a plantation will be influenced by several factors: the price of land, the size of factory investment, the ratio of factory investment to total farm-factory investment, the availability of raw material supplies from other sources (preferably contract suppliers), and expectations re future market possibilities which influence desired flexibility of output adjustment. The actual land area acquired by plantations will depend on the resources of the firm, the cost of land and the scale economies of processing particular crops. Given a scale of plant, then the minimum area required would be determined by the level of output required to cover fixed costs in processing where non-plantation supplies are available. Where these are not available a larger area will be necessary to make processing profitable.

Normally, plantations would try to secure land well in excess of the technical minimum. Price expectations and the cost of land would mainly determine the maximum area. The lower the cost of land and the brighter the long-term market expectations the greater would be the area secured for plantation production. Because the establishment of plantations has historically been associated with the opening up of new territory, low-cost land was usually available and this led to the alienation of vast areas even beyond expected requirements at the time of establishment.

There is therefore a tendency toward under-utilization of land in plantation agriculture. The extent of under-utilization (i.e. size of acreage reserve) will depend on the cost of securing land and of holding it. So we would expect smaller acreage reserves in countries which are short of land than in land-abundant plantation economies. Under-utilization of land is one means of providing for flexibility of output adjustments over time. Though this may represent an efficient pattern of resource use for the firm, it creates inefficiencies in allocation within the agricultural sector. This is most acute in situations where land is generally in short supply.

Risk and uncertainty considerations

The heavy capitalization and the crop specificity of investments expose plantation enterprises to an inherently high degree of risk and uncertainty – particularly in respect of crop losses from natural or other (e.g. political) causes and of price fluctuations. This induces at least two counter measures which affect resource allocation within the plantation economies.

The first is the exploitation of market imperfections. On the product side this is expressed in enterprise control over disposal prices. United Fruit Company achieved this so effectively in the United States banana market that it had to face a Consent Decree of the Department of Justice to divest itself of part of its capital for the formation of another smaller company. In any event, UFCo. will still be able to maintain its position of price leader in the trade. Tate and Lyle subsidiaries on the other hand achieve this through industry collusion in the West Indies (i.e. Sugar Manufacturers' Associations) and political lobbying in the UK for preferential pricing arrangements. In matters relating to overseas sugar markets it is normal practice in the West Indies for industry leaders to 'speak for the Governments'. The consequences of this counter measure is artificially to distort the structure of output prices for the range of farm products that can be produced in the plantation economies; and thereby to bias resource use in favour of the plantation crop. On the factor side, market imperfections arise from control over supplies of inputs produced within the vertically integrated structure of the firm and from the normally monopsonistic position of the plantation in the labour market. The latter derives from the fact that the land area covered by the plantation enterprise is so vast that it is usually the only source of employment within fairly wide areas.

The second counter measure is the geographic dispersal of the firm's plantation operations. This minimizes the risk of crop losses. In addition to losses from weather and disease, this measure is a hedge against unfavourable changes in the political and economic situation in individual countries and it increases the flexibility of output expansion for the firm itself. But it also leads to perverse supply responses for individual countries. For although the firm may increase overall acreage and output in response to an increase in the relative price of its output it may, in the process, contract acreage and output in a particular individual country. The firm is concerned with efficient resource allocation between its different areas of agricultural operations. And this often results in inefficient resource allocation within a particular plantation economy. Because of the multi-national character of plantation enterprises efficiency conditions tend to be met on the overall operation, i.e. between plantation sectors of nation states but not within the agricultural sectors of individual nation states.

4 Development Problems in Plantation-type Economies

Underdevelopment biases in plantation agriculture

The characteristics of plantation agriculture are such that this type of agriculture tends not to fulfil the basic conditions [generally] set out in the discussion of the role of agriculture in economic development. First, this type of agriculture is not geared to supplying food demand within the plantation economy. Instead, it is geared to metropolitan consumption requirements. As such it fulfils another condition by earning foreign exchange. The question that arises is whether over time the foreign exchange-earning ability will be more than enough to provide for imported food supplies so as to leave a residual of earnings for importation of 'critical capital inputs'.

Plantation export output consists of primary products with relatively low income elasticities of demand. On the other hand, the food import requirements of plantation economies normally consist of high income elasticity products.[16] Therefore for any given increase in consumer incomes in both the metropolis and the plantation economy, the required increase in plantation output will be less than the required increase in food imports. In order to compensate, the export price for plantation output must rise relative to food import prices. In other words, over time the terms of trade must move consistently in favour of plantation export output. But in point of fact the historical pattern has generally been the reverse; so that the export earnings of plantation economies tend toward failing to meet food import requirements unless the rate of income growth in the plantation economy falls consistently behind that in the metropolis.

In addition, it must be noted that the foreign exchange earning capacity of plantation agriculture is limited by the normally high import content of plantation production and consumption. On the production side, this results partly from the fact that metropolitan capital brings with it its own technology, which usually requires inputs not available in the plantation economy; and partly from the vertically integrated structure of plantation enterprises. On the consumption side, because plantation labour has been mobilized for export production there is relatively little production for the home market leading to a characteristic heavy reliance on imports of food and other consumer goods. The actual available foreign exchange is therefore what is left after deducting the value of imported inputs used in plantation production, factor incomes going to the metropole and the consumer expenditure on imports in the second round. On the whole, then, the foreign exchange earning capacity of plantation agriculture seems to be less than is normally assumed.

Another effect of the primary export orientation of plantation agriculture is that the benefits of productivity improvements tend to accrue mostly to metropolitan consumers. This is so primarily in those countries where plantations exist along with farmers producing for their own consumption. In looking at the Jamaican experience, for example, Arthur Lewis observed that although productivity in export agriculture increased by 27 per cent between 1890 and 1930 consumption per head increased only by 13 per cent in the same period because the terms of trade moved adversely from 137 in 1890 to 84 in 1930. Lewis explains this general pattern among tropical exporting countries as follows:

> . . . so long as productivity is constant in subsistence production, practically all the benefit of increases in productivity in the commercial crops accrues to the consumer and not to the producer. . . . Greater productivity is offset by adverse terms of trade.[17]

The same author had outlined the position in greater length in his *Theory of Economic Growth* as follows:

> If nothing is done to raise the productivity of peasants in producing food, they constitute a reservoir of cheap labour available for work in mines or plantations or other export enterprises. . . . So long as the peasant farmers have low productivity, the temperate world can get the services of tropical labour for a very low price. Moreover when productivity rises in the crops produced for export there is no need to share the increase with labour, and practically the whole benefit goes in reducing the price to industrial consumers. Sugar is an excellent case in point. Cane sugar production is an industry in which productivity is extremely high by any biological standard. It is also an industry in which output per acre has about trebled over the past seventy years, a rate of growth unparalleled by any other major agricultural industry in the world – certainly not by the wheat industry. Nevertheless, workers in the cane sugar industry continue to walk barefooted and to live in shacks, while workers in wheat enjoy among the highest living standards in the world. However vastly productive the sugar industry may become, the benefit accrues chiefly to consumers. This is one of the disadvantages to tropical countries (advantages to industrial countries) of the fact that their economic development has concentrated upon the export sector of the economy, and that foreign entrepreneurs and foreign capital have been devoted in the first place primarily to expanding exports. . . .[18]

Lewis has been quoted at length here because he is describing a phenomenon that is characteristic not so much of all export agriculture but of plantation agriculture in particular. For this is perhaps the only type of agriculture that by definition always satisfies the two basic conditions that erode retention of the benefits of productivity improvements: export production and a continuous supply of cheap labour.

It should be pointed out, however, that in recent times productivity improvements have brought more benefit to the plantation economies than in the past. This has resulted mainly from increasing trade union activity which has managed to cream off some of the benefits of improved productivity in the form of higher wages for plantation labour. But against this must be balanced the consideration that improvements in productivity on plantations have invariably involved the oft-neglected cost of increased unemployment.

Plantation agriculture also has a limited capacity for the two other functions mentioned [as] 'conditions of agricultural development'. As concerns transfers of factor supplies there are two important limitations. First, because of foreign ownership capital transfers are to the metropolis and not to the non-agricultural sectors of the plantation economy. And, secondly, because the skill content of plantation labour is low (by the specification of the production function) the adaptability of plantation labour to the requirements of other sectors is extremely slow.

So far as market relationships are concerned, the vertical integration of plantation enterprises stretches across national boundaries. Linkages are established within the structure of the *firm* and not within individual plantation economies. For the latter, then, potential linkage effects are dissipated and this minimizes inter-industry transactions with their potential development-spread effects.

Some other factors which further restrict development possibilities in plantation economies and which deserve elaboration are the inherent rigidities in resource adjustment, the element of foreign ownership, the unequal pattern of income distribution and the characteristic rigid social structure.

In our examination of the economics of resource use, it was observed that the high degree of specificity of plantation enterprise investment and the distorted structure of agricultural output prices create a built-in rigidity in the pattern of resource use in plantation agriculture. Because of this heavy commitment to the production of a particular export crop, and because foreign investors have little or no interest in production for the domestic market, opportunities for agricultural development deriving from changing patterns of consumer food expenditure tend not to be taken up. The normal development pattern, implicit in a model based on more perfectly competitive conditions, does not emerge.

Foreign ownership of plantations limits development in two additional ways not previously considered. First there is the leakage of income in the form of dividends which reduces the investment capacity of the economy. Secondly, when re-investment out of the surplus occurs, there is no assurance that the economy in which the surplus was produced will benefit. This follows from the spatial distribution of the firm's operations among a number of countries. Surpluses produced in one country can be re-invested in any other country where the firm owns plantations or at home-base in the metropolis.

The low wages of plantation labourers stand in dramatic contrast to the earnings of the skilled supervisory and management staffs which operate the plantations. This sets the stage for a generally unequal pattern of income distribution among all households in plantation economies. The adverse development consequences of this are twofold. Aggregate effective demand is low; this limits the size of the market and rules out the establishment of consumer goods industries with significant scale economies. In addition, the low incomes of the bulk of the population restrict household savings and the scope for domestic investment, while the high-income classes engage in conspicuous consumption of luxury imports and invest heavily in non-productive assets.

Finally, the rigid class lines and weak community cohesion of plantation societies serve to restrict social mobility and to impede the development of large-scale units of collective action. Restricted social mobility adversely affects individual incentive for economic advancement and affects labour adaptability as well.

Contributions of plantation agriculture to development

Two factors which are repeatedly mentioned in the literature on plantation agriculture deserve consideration here so as to round off the discussion. The first is that plantation agriculture has served in the past to open up previously inaccessible areas. In so doing, it has developed an infrastructure of roads, ports, water supplies, electricity, etc., in underdeveloped countries much more rapidly than would otherwise occur. This is undoubtedly an important contribution to these economies. But the benefits of this must be weighed against the dynamic underdevelopment biases considered above. What is more, it should be noted that, like everything else, the infrastructure is geared to the specific needs of the plantations and does not necessarily benefit other producers to any significant degree. Thus, for example, we normally find villages and farming areas just outside the boundaries of plantations without water and electricity, though the plantation itself is well supplied with these.

The second consideration is that unlike other types of agriculture in underdeveloped countries, plantation agriculture is 'scientific'. Plantations invest in research which produces a high rate of technological change. Furthermore, the implementation of research findings is quick and easy because of the centralized authority structure of plantations. This can be contrasted with the slow rate of adoption of new techniques by peasant farmers and the overwhelming problem of extension in peasant farming areas. This point is also well taken but requires qualification. Again, the research input of plantations are specific to particular crops and may not apply across the range of technical production possibilities. For example, United Fruit undertakes an elaborate programme of research on bananas, and West Indian sugar plantations maintain their own research stations for studying the problems of sugar. Neither of these invests very much in research on other crops and/or livestock which may offer better economic prospects *to the countries* involved than the particular plantation crop. This raises the problem of the allocative efficiency of research resources. But, in addition, it underscores the existing dynamic bias against high-income production opportunities in the domestic market; for in the absence of technical knowledge such opportunities cannot be readily seized.

Summary and Implications

This paper represents a first attempt to examine the economics of resource use and development in economies based on plantation agriculture. The analysis suggests that the particular character of plantation enterprises of a certain type (multi-national corporate enterprises) and the dependent nature of the economies dominated by these enterprises create certain inefficiencies in resource allocation *within these economies* and, in addition, limit the potential for development.

Allocative inefficiencies arise from the structural characteristics of the plantation enterprises considered here – in particular vertical and horizontal integration across national frontiers, and the high degree of capital specificity that characterizes the production process. The inefficiencies within the agricultural sectors of plantation economies co-exist with efficient resource use for the firm itself, reminding us of the maxim that what is good for the firm is not necessarily good for the country.

Similarly biases toward underdevelopment in plantation economies derive from certain structural factors – foreign ownership and export orientation, the inherent rigidities in resource adjustment, the low skill content of plantation labour, unequal distribution of incomes, and rigid social structure – that inhere in this type of agriculture.

Notes: Reading 33

1 See, for example, V. D. Wickizer, 'The plantation system in the development of tropical economies', *Journal of Farm Economics*, February 1958.

2 See, for example, R. E. Baldwin, 'Patterns of development in newly settled regions', *Manchester School*, May 1956; and 'Export technology and development from subsistence level', *Economic Journal*, March 1963.

3 See J. H. Steward *et al., The People of Puerto Rico*, Urbana, Illinois, 1956; Symposium, *Plantation Systems of the New World*, Pan American Union, Washington, DC,

1959; Vera Rubin (ed.), *Caribbean Studies: A Symposium*, ISER, University of the West Indies, 1957.

4 W. O. Jones, 'Plantations', in David L. Sills, *International Encyclopedia of the Social Sciences*, Vol. 12, 1968, p. 154. My emphasis.

5 Ida Greaves, 'Plantations in world economy', in *Plantation Systems of the New World*, op. cit., p. 13.

6 Greaves, op. cit., p. 15.

7 ibid., p. 14.

8 ibid., p. 15. My emphasis.

9 ibid., p. 16. The reference in this quotation from Greaves is to John Stuart Mill.

10 Charles Wagley, 'Plantation America: a culture sphere', in Vera Rubin (ed.), op. cit.

11 ibid., p. 9.

12 H. B. Arthur, J. P. Houck and G. L. Beckford, *Tropical Agribusiness Structures and Adjustments: Bananas*, Harvard Business School, Division of Research, Boston, 1968, pp. 33–53.

13 R. E. Baldwin, 'Patterns of development in newly settled regions', *Manchester School*, May 1956.

14 In 1966 the forty-one vessels owned by the company accounted for as much as 28 per cent of total investment (see the company's *Annual Report 1966*, pp. 19–20).

15 Certain factors at the farm level tend as well to be highly specific; for example, laboratories and managerial functions. It has been suggested, for example, that these rigidities may derive as much from the circumscribed entrepreneurial horizons of firm managers as from the existence of capital specificity in a physical or engineering sense. Firm managers who have established themselves as 'sugar men' or 'banana men' are unlikely to contemplate crop changes which would erode their established authority. Although this is a factor which is of relevance, it does not really set plantation operators apart from other types of agricultural producers. This same kind of 'psychological attachment' to crops can be found among peasant farmers. It seems therefore that the degree of capital specificity is the more important consideration.

16 Basic starchy staples (the low-income elasticity products in the consumer food basket) are usually supplied from within plantation economies.

17 W. Arthur Lewis, Foreword to Gisela Eisner, *Jamaica, 1830–1930: A Study in Economic Growth*, Manchester University Press, 1961, pp. xviii–xix.

18 W. A. Lewis, *The Theory of Economic Growth*, London, 1955, p. 281.

Reading 34

India's New Strategy of Agricultural Development: Political Costs of Agrarian Modernization

F. R. Frankel

Journal of Asian Studies, 1969, pp. 693-710.

By the spring of 1966, it was abundantly clear in New Delhi that the Third Five Year Plan was a failure. Over the five-year period (1961–6), the rate of increase in national income was less than half the projected level. Per capita income showed no increase at all. At the same time, prices for all commodities rose by over one-half. The price index for foodgrains climbed by more than 56 per cent. By 1966, food shortages were so severe that some thirty million persons in major cities and towns were placed under statutory rationing. By the middle of the Third Plan, the Planning Commission was convinced that persistence of static production levels in agriculture, along with rising prices for food articles and raw materials, would jeopardize the prospects of further industrialization. As a result, in 1964 the planners announced a 'fresh consideration of the assumptions, methods and techniques as well as the machinery of planning and plan implementation in the field of agriculture.'[1]

The new strategy, advanced by the Food and Agriculture Ministry, stood in striking contrast to the basic assumptions of past policies. Whereas the older approach had relied mainly on more intensive utilization of traditional inputs, e.g. reclamation of cultivable wasteland and the more efficient application of underemployed labor, the Ministry now urged the utmost importance of applying 'scientific techniques and knowledge of agricultural production at all stages.'[2] [C.] Subramaniam [the Minister of Food and Agriculture] argued, in particular, that there was 'no use trying (to increase yields) with our traditional (seed) varieties which we have here. Even with the best of practices, with all the resources put in, the potentiality for yield of these traditional varieties is limited.'[3] Instead, the Ministry proposed to introduce improved varieties of paddy and wheat developed in Taiwan and Mexico respectively, with reported yield capacities of 5,000 to 6,000 pounds per acre, some six times the average all-India yield, and almost double the maximum potential output of conventional Indian varieties. They also proposed to extend the use of higher yielding hybrid varieties of maize, bajra, and jowar developed at Indian research stations in the late nineteen-fifties.

Moreover, in order to realize the new technical potentialities in agriculture, the Ministry argued for concessions in the salience of ideological goals which were focused on increasing equality in the rural sector. They pointed out that the policy of all-India coverage under the Community Development Program was causing scarce inputs to be diluted below the critical level needed to achieve significant increases in output. The continuation of this pattern would be all the more damaging in the case of the new seed varieties, where the prospects of achieving optimal levels depended on the availability of assured water supply, and the application of a 'package' of modern inputs, including high doses of chemical fertilizer and pesticides. This, Subramaniam told the Lok Sabha, was the major 'concrete lesson' of past failures. 'If we concentrate our efforts in a given area where we have assured water supply and we have the necessary extension services also concentrated in that area,' he argued, 'then it should be possible for us to achieve much better results than by merely dispersing our effort in a thin way throughout the country.'[4]

Equally important to the success of the new approach, the cultivator had to be provided with economic incentives to adopt the new practices. Once again, the Food Minister insisted, this required not only new initiatives in providing cheap agricultural credit for the majority of poor farmers, but also a reversal of past priorities in the formulation of price policy, from a preoccupation with providing low-cost foodgrains for the urban poor, to a firm commitment to 'remunerative and incentive prices to make the production process reasonably safe for the farmers.'[5] In practice, this meant official guarantee of profitable minimum support prices for foodgrains, as well as higher incentive prices for government purchases of surplus produce.

Through the three-pronged approach of the new agricultural strategy, i.e. the application of scientific knowledge and techniques of agricultural production, concentration of improved inputs in irrigated areas, and price incentives to producers, the Ministry predicted that food production would increase from the base level of 90 million tons in 1965 to 125 million tons in 1971, and thus India would finally achieve self-sufficiency. In percentage terms, the projected increase approached 38 per cent over a five-year period, or over 7 per cent per annum. By contrast, between 1949–50 and 1964–65, the annual increase in foodgrains production averaged approximately 3 per cent.

Ambitious though it is, the new strategy seems quite plausible if one grants the soundness of its three major assumptions: (1) the new varieties can more than double per acre productivity for the major foodgrain crops; (2) concentration of high-yielding seeds and complementary modern inputs in irrigated areas can realize maximum potential gains in output; and (3) incentives prove effective and cultivators do adopt the scientific practices urged on them by government. Unfortunately closer analysis of these propositions reveals serious problems in each one of them.

First, let us consider the high-yield potentiality of the new seeds. The fact is—and Food Ministry officials freely admit it—that the empirical foundations of this assumption were quite weak. The Ministry's strategy was formulated to meet an emergent food crisis at a time when data on the performance of the new seeds under Indian conditions were still insufficient to establish their value. The imported rice and wheat varieties were released only after the most perfunctory testing. The record of the new wheats was actually discouraging. A series of trials conducted on government research stations in 1964–65 showed no substantial difference in yield levels of imported Mexican varieties and the best Indian strains.[6] Meanwhile, new paddy varieties were introduced in Andhra Pradesh and they did confirm the Ministry's expectations.[7] The trial, however, was confined to a pilot area of only 10,000 acres.

Actual experience with the imported varieties on farmers' fields since 1965–66 reveals a very mixed picture. The technical problems associated with the use of the new wheat varieties can apparently be overcome. There is evidence that the earlier disappointing performance of the imported wheats is remedied by a change in cultivation techniques. Traditional Indian plows penetrate the soil too deeply to permit the short-stemmed Mexican varieties to germinate properly. Farm mechanization—at least to the extent of using tractors for the preparation of seedbeds—is necessary to realize the full yield potential of Mexican wheats.

The prospects of the imported paddy seeds, however, are clouded by more serious difficulties. For one thing, the Taiwan seeds mature much more quickly than conventional plants and are ready for harvest in about ninety days. Unhappily, this period coincides with the northeast monsoon in large parts of the rice-growing south. Cultivators not only find it difficult to gather the harvest in heavy rain, but they also are denied the traditional convenience of drying their crops in the sun. Like the Mexican wheats, the new rice varieties require some degree of farm mechanization, particularly mechanical drying equipment to prevent sprouting during storage. In addition, the most popular Taiwan seeds have shown higher vulnerability than conventional varieties to bacterial blight, a plant disease which flourishes in the high humidity of the monsoon season.[8] No remedy for blight has yet been found. A major effort in adaptive research will therefore be necessary before the imported-paddy varieties can be extensively introduced.

Even the hybrid maize, bajra, and jowar seeds, which were developed at Indian research stations and released after three or four years of testing, will require a large and continuing commitment to research in order to develop new disease resistant varieties since the ones currently in use lose their immunity. For example, hybrid jowar has proved highly susceptible to shoot fly which cannot be effectively controlled by pesticides: new varieties are the best solution. Similarly, constant experimentation is needed to protect hybrid bajra from attack by ergot and hybrid maize from mildew and insects.[9]

Much more complex, however, are the policy dilemmas raised by weaknesses in the second and third major assumptions on which the new strategy rests.

Altogether, only some 23 per cent of the total cultivated area currently enjoys assured water from irrigation.[10] No definitive data are available to indicate just what share of the irrigated land is held by small and medium agriculturists. It must be substantial. According to the National Sample Survey Landholding Enquiry, 1961–62, some 40 per cent of all cultivated land is operated in units of 10 acres or less.[11] Agro-economic surveys carried out in the early nineteen-sixties in districts with maximum irrigation facilities show that in eleven of fifteen areas studied, landholdings of 10 acres or less account for 41 per cent to 69 per cent of the total cultivated area.[12] Quite apart from the structural barrier to mechanization these small units of production present, they also face very serious financial obstacles to the introduction of the package of new inputs. Most of them are subsistence holdings; a few perhaps have modest savings. Some may have access to a little credit from the cooperatives. All of this together, though, could hardly finance the Rs. 400 per acre which the Food Ministry estimates is the cost of the 'package' of practices recommended for the most efficient cultivation of new paddy and wheat varieties.

Actually, the initial capital investment is often much

higher. Irrigation projects in most parts of the country have been designed with traditional techniques in mind and to ensure minimal crop yields even in times of drought by spreading available water as widely and thinly as possible. They generally cannot supply the higher water levels per acre necessary for the efficient introduction of modern agricultural practices, especially chemical fertilizer. The new varieties, therefore, often require supplementary water from a private tubewell at the phenomenal expense to an average cultivator of some Rs. 7,500 to Rs. 18,750 ($1,000–$2,500). But even this does not exhaust the full dimensions of the problem. According to official estimates, about 23 per cent of all farmers are tenants.[13] Moreover, official figures are necessarily underestimates since they cannot take into accurate account the large number of share-cropping arrangements which are settled orally. For instance, Wolf Ladejinsky, who made a special study of selected irrigated districts for the Planning Commission in 1963, found that 50 per cent or more of all cultivators were operating wholly or partially leased lands amounting to more than half the cultivated area in two of the most productive rice districts in India—Tanjore Madras and West Godavary, Andhra Pradesh.[14] Most tenant-cultivators pay the entire costs of production, but share the output with the owner on a fifty-fifty basis; in cases where the landowner provides a pump set on irrigated land, the rent is commonly two-thirds of the gross produce.

In consequence, insofar as the majority of small farmers adopt the new practices, they can be expected to do so slowly, cautiously, and partially. They may be able to afford the relatively modest expense required for the new seeds, but probably only a fraction of the additional costs for complementary inputs of fertilizers, pesticides, agricultural machinery, and supplemental irrigation facilities. However, maximum potential gains in productivity can only be realized by adopting the whole package of new inputs, new seeds together with substantially increased amounts of water, pesticides, and especially, fertilizers. In fact, the major advantage of the new seeds—and the reason they are profitable to the farmer even at much higher costs of production—is their capacity to continue to respond positively to additional doses of fertilizer much beyond levels which conventional varieties can tolerate. For example, the imported paddy and wheat seeds show a constant yield increase of 15 to 20 pounds per acre to additional applications of nitrogen up to levels of 50 to 60 pounds per acre, and reach a peak yield (although at diminishing rates of response for each additional unit above this level) at doses of 100 to 120 pounds. In contrast, the fertilizer response ratio of conventional Indian varieties is roughly 1:10, while decreasing rates of return set in at dosages of 18 to 20 pounds per acre, and yield decline occurs at applications above 50 to 60 pounds per acre. If the smaller cultivators with limited funds are not able to afford the price of the entire 'package,' therefore, any strategy which attempts to reach all farmers and saturate selected irrigated areas with improved practices is likely to involve substantial waste in scarce resources. Actually, there is evidence that the Food Ministry recognized this problem. In the summer of 1966, guidelines prepared for the States on the implementation of the high-yielding varieties program included an explicit recommendation for initially concentrating the new inputs among surplus producers having private funds to finance most of the additional costs of the new techniques.[15]

The third major assumption of the new strategy—that economic incentives could be devised to enable the average cultivator to invest in scientific practices on a satisfactory scale—is meant, of course to overcome this difficulty. Specifically, the Food Ministry proposed two major incentives: a crop based system of agricultural credit; and more profitable official prices for foodgrains. Regarding the first, the Food Ministry proposed to provide each participant in the high-yielding varieties program with sufficient credit from the cooperatives to meet their full production requirements. This was to be accomplished by replacing traditional criteria for credit-worthiness based on ownership of property and other assets, with a formula for assessment of each cultivator's repaying capacity according to the value of his gross produce. Again, in theory, the rationale of a crop based loan system is sound. Credit tied to a production plan can generate its own repayment capacity in the sense of leading to additional produce of at least the same value. All that is needed to ensure the recovery of crop loans, therefore, is effective linkage between credit and marketing. In fact, under the new system, each borrower is obligated to sell to the cooperative marketing society to which the credit agency is affiliated, the quantity of produce necessary to meet the principal and interest of his loan; he also agrees to allow the marketing society to deduct the credit agency's dues directly from the proceeds of the sale.

Difficulties arise in practice because the link between credit and marketing is presently too weak to ensure that the credit agency will actually have any control over the sale proceeds of members' crops. The cooperative marketing societies do not have any purchasing agents operating in the village at all. Cultivators wishing to use their services must arrange their own transport to the market town. Worse still, the majority of marketing societies lack funds to make outright purchases of foodgrains from cultivators or even to offer substantial advances against anticipated sale proceeds. They generally act only as commission agents, arranging for sale of members' produce by open bid in the market town. This may be some help to large landholders, but not to medium and small cultivators. The latter, with only limited supplies to sell, usually dispose of their produce immediately after harvest within their own village or neighboring hamlet to private traders who make payment on the spot. As a result, even when provisions are written into loan bonds requiring members to sell their produce through an affiliated marketing society, the credit agency cannot enforce such provisions. Experience with the crop loan system as a pilot project in six maximum irrigation districts since 1961 indicates that under these conditions, 'crop-loans' come to mean little more than a paper exercise to establish the *maximum* amount of credit for which any cultivator is eligible. The village level extension worker prepares a loan application for each farmer based on an approved plan for the introduction of better seeds, fertilizers, and pesticides. In theory, each cultivator is then entitled to borrow up to the full amount of his estimated production costs for improved inputs. In practice, because of the weak link between cooperative credit and marketing, the credit society still calculates the actual limit of each cultivator's loan on the basis of his net assets. Thus, in the six districts mentioned above, in 1963–64, cultivators with holdings of 2.5 acres or less received agricultural loans from the cooperatives averaging approximately Rs. 17. This inched up to Rs. 28 for cultivators with holdings of 2.5 to 5 acres; and only reached an average of about Rs. 67 in the case of medium landowners with five- to ten-acre holdings.[16]

The other major economic incentive proposed by the Ministry and designed to increase investment in improved practices—more remunerative prices for foodgrains—is also likely to have only minimal impact on the economic activity of the smaller cultivator and the subsistence producer. The Food Ministry's proposal concentrates on two mechanisms: (1) assuring 'remunerative' floor prices for all wholesale transactions in agricultural commodities; and (2) raising official procurement prices of major foodgrain crops to 'incentive' levels. The first of these is not likely to be very helpful to the small producer. In the past, the absence of reliable farm cost data has caused minimum prices to be calculated as a simple average of those in the immediate post-harvest period over the previous three years, at the time when they are likely to be lowest. Moreover, the Agricultural Prices Commission has recently directed that 'only the cost of the relatively efficient and innovating farmers' should be taken into account in setting support prices in future years.[17] Even if floor prices were raised, however, there is virtually no way to ensure that private traders and their agents would actually pay the official price to cultivators in the absence of government and/or cooperative procurement machinery in the village. Nor is the second device likely to be much more useful to the smaller producer, as in general he does not dispose of his crop to government purchasing agents. On the contrary, larger farmers are the major beneficiaries of higher price maxima for government purchases of foodgrains. Indeed, the recommendation to pay 'incentive' prices for major food crops represents a departure from established government policy which favored low procurement rates not only to stabilize the general price level and supply foodgrains at reasonable prices to the urban poor, but also to exact an indirect tax on the profits of the larger cultivators.

Taking all these factors into consideration, it seems inescapable that effective implementation of the new agricultural strategy requires greater concessions in the ideological objective of equality than the government is willing to admit. In practice, only a minority of all agriculturist families in selected districts have the surplus to invest in the whole package of inputs. It follows that to achieve maximum gains in output, the actual base of effective operation of the new agricultural programs would have to be even more narrow than that implied by the physical target of concentration of inputs in the irrigated area. Unless the government faces up to this structural limitation—and adjusts the criteria for the selection of areas under the high-yielding varieties program accordingly—increases in productivity from the introduction of the new seeds are likely to remain substantially below the maximum potential levels projected.

The political costs to be paid for the new agricultural strategy are slowly coming into sharper focus. It is clear that agriculture will have to be accorded a much higher priority in the allocation of public expenditure and foreign exchange resources. This means a fundamental adjustment in the industry-oriented grand strategy of economic development with the prospect of retarding the growth of import-substituting heavy and basic industries, and prolonging the period of dependence on (uncertain) foreign aid.

It also seems clear that long-standing ideological objectives of development will have to be subordinated to economic criteria. There is no doubt that the architects of India's five-year plans appreciated that the 'production of an agricultural surplus (was) the key to industrialization'. But scarce capital and foreign exchange resources, already severely strained by large industrial programs, permitted only marginal investments in yield increasing inputs, such as chemical fertilizers. At the same time, the overriding ideological goal of a 'socialistic pattern of society' ruled out concentration of these inputs in the more favored areas of the country where they could be expected to bring the greatest increases in agricultural development. Instead, the planners devised a strategy of agricultural development to actively involve some sixty million peasant cultivators in the difficult task of raising yields through the painstaking application of more labor-intensive techniques. The crux of the approach—the major inducement to greater effort on the part of the small farmer—was the promise of social reform held out by large-scale initiatives for institutional change. The highest priority was assigned to rapid implementation of land reforms, including security of tenure, lower rents, and even some redistribution of land. State-partnered village cooperatives were newly created to fortify the smaller farmers with facilities for cheap credit and economies of bulk purchase and sale of agricultural commodities. The capstone of the rural development effort was the Community Development Program. But by the early nineteen-sixties most legislation on tenancy and ceilings had still not been effectively implemented; the village based network of cooperative societies remained much too weak to provide adequate credit and low cost agricultural services for the mass of poor farmers; and adequate numbers of competent rural extension workers were lacking to train millions of marginal producers in the adoption of more efficient techniques. In fact, the new agricultural strategy signalled a tacit admission by the leadership that they had failed in their fifteen-year effort to make the small producer an effective vector of economic progress through far-reaching institutional reform. Within the agricultural sector, therefore, the political costs of the new strategy are important concessions in socialist goals to the capitalist imperatives of resource concentration and price incentives; and perhaps, even a fundamental break with the egalitarian objectives that have motivated Indian planning since Independence.

The record of 1966–67, moreover, underscored just how limited the Government of India's capacity is to provide even the minimum inputs required by the new strategy. Nitrogen shortages were so severe that the actual size of the high-yielding varieties program was reduced by over one-third, and even in the areas sown with the new seeds, there was a 'more or less universal failure to use the recommended dose of fertilizer'. It became dramatically clear that any effective implementation of the new strategy necessarily involved major reliance upon Indian and foreign private enterprise, including new opportunities for private entrepreneurs in fields of production and marketing previously closed to them or made unattractive by government controls over pricing and distribution. Thus, the new agricultural strategy involved the weakening of socialist objectives not only in agriculture but in the industrial sector as well.

Yet, even if the government made all these concessions, there was, in fact, no assurance that they could meet the total price of the new approach. Nearly two decades of official espousal of a socialist pattern of society has had its impact. Indian and foreign businessmen are suspicious of government motives and have limited faith in government commitments. Many fear a sudden policy reversal once they have made their investment, which would deprive them of their projected profits. Hence, it is quite conceivable that even if government conceded all their demands, they in the end would prefer to remain outside the major agricultural industries.

Potentially far more dangerous is the discontent among small cultivators and landless laborers which such a policy of concentration would almost inevitably trigger. While larger landowners, particularly those in irrigated or high rainfall areas, may be able to increase their net earnings by as much as six times, many smaller producers, especially those on marginal lands, will not be able to take advantage of the new techniques at all. Lester R. Brown reports that in some areas, tenant-cultivators have already been reduced to farm laborers by landlords who have discovered the profitability of the new techniques and resumed their land for personal cultivation. Finally, while the new varieties do require additional amounts of labor, given more complicated cultivation practices and opportunities for double cropping with quick maturing plants, any increase in the income of agricultural laborers is certain to be dwarfed by the gains to larger landowners.

Although the extent of future economic gains under the new agricultural strategy is still problematical, some of the social costs are already apparent. For one thing, there has been an extreme concentration of scarce inputs in irrigated areas, with a corresponding neglect of the rest of the country. Since 1966–67, almost 60 per cent to 70 per cent of the total available supply of nitrogen has gone to priority programs in about 20 per cent of the cultivated areas. Meanwhile, most States have reduced their outlay on the Community Development Program to levels sufficient only for staff maintenance; some State Ministers have even argued in favor of abolishing the Program entirely. At the same time, inequalities have also increased within the irrigated areas, where, the Food Minister, Jagjivam Ram, observed, 'smaller farmers stuck to ancient techniques . . . while the bigger farmers had been quick to take advantage of the intensive agricultural programs involving high-yielding varieties of hybrid seeds'. There is virtually no prospect that the government will be able to siphon off a significant proportion of the income gains to larger cultivators in order to finance bigger public investment programs. On the contrary, at the meeting of the National Development Council in December 1967, the Chief Ministers of the States flatly rejected the Center's proposal to raise irrigation rates or levy a progessive income tax on farmers.

In summary, then, the new agricultural strategy poses fundamental political choices for the Indian government. Certainly, it involves much more than a limited adjustment of past economic policies in the rural sector. At the least, efforts to ensure the essential conditions of success for the new agricultural approach seem bound to commit India more closely to an entrepreneurial or capitalist strategy of development in all sectors of the economy, with the attendant political risks of intensifying economic inequalities and social conflict. They also appear certain to involve her in closer economic dependence on American and other foreign private investors and to increase the constraints on an independent foreign policy. It even seems likely that the new agricultural strategy will weaken the very foundations of central planning by concentrating an ever greater proportion of the agricultural surplus in the hands of larger landowners—the very group all State governments, in

India, regardless of party identification, have found politically impossible to tax.

Notes: Reading 34

1 India, Planning Commission, *Memorandum on the Fourth Five-Year Plan*, New Delhi, 1964, p. 26.
2 India, Department of Agriculture, Ministry of Food and Agriculture, *Agricultural Production in the Fourth Five-Year Plan: Strategy and Programme*, New Delhi, 1965, p. 3.
3 *Lok Sabha Debates*, 7 December 1965, p. 6078.
4 ibid., p. 6075.
5 C. Subramaniam, *New Agricultural Strategy in a Socialist Society*, mimeo, p. 5.
6 Indian Council of Agricultural Research, *Annual Report, 1964–65*, New Delhi, 1965, p. 3.
7 ibid., p. 2. The ICAR reported crop yields as high as 7,500 pounds per acre with the Taiwan varieties.
8 The first reports that the Taiwan seeds were highly susceptible to bacterial blight reached the Food Ministry from officials in Andhra Pradesh only in the summer of 1966, again after the ministry decided to use these varieties as the mainstay of the high-yielding varieties programme for paddy. Moreover, the Taiwanese strains present an even greater problem than the Mexican wheats in consumer preference. They yield thick, round and brownish grain instead of the fine, white rice of the best local varieties. They are also glutinous and stick together when cooked; Indian consumers prefer soft grain which remains separate.
9 B. V. Nimbar, 'A word of warning on hybrids', *Economic and Political Weekly*, vol. II, no. 47, 2 December 1967.
10 This was the figure given to the Lok Sabha on 10 July 1967 by the Minister of Irrigation and Power, Dr K. L. Rae, *The Statesman*, 11 July 1967.
11 Indian Statistical Institute, *The National Sample Survey*, Number 140: *Tables with Notes on Some Aspects of Landholdings in Rural Areas (States and All-India Estimates), Seventeenth Round, September 1961–July 1962, Draft*, Calcutta, 1966, p. 60.
12 India, Expert Committee on Assessment and Evaluation, Department of Agriculture, Ministry of Food and Agriculture, Community Development and Co-operation, *Intensive Agricultural District Programme*, Second Report, 1960–5, New Delhi, 1966.
13 This estimate is from a 1968 report published by the Registrar-General and Census Commission. It is quoted in *The Statesman*, 1 June 1968.
14 Wolf Ladejinsky, *A Study on Tenurial Conditions in Package Districts*, India, Planning Commision, New Delhi, 1964, pp. 13, 21.
15 Interview with the Economic and Statistical Adviser to the Government of India, New Delhi, 2 August 1966.
16 *Intensive Agricultural District Programme*, Second Report, 1960–5.
17 India, Department of Agriculture, Ministry of Food and Agriculture, *Report of the Agricultural Prices Commission on Price Policy for Kharif Cereals for 1965–66 Season*, New Delhi, 1965, p. 2.

Ironies of India's Green Revolution

W. Ladejinsky

Foreign Affairs, July 1970, pp. 758-68.

1

For nearly five years the 'green revolution' has been under way in a number of agriculturally underdeveloped countries of Asia. Its advent into tradition-bound rural societies was heralded as the rebuttal to the dire predictions of hunger stalking large parts of the world. But more than that, those carried away with euphoria at the impending changes saw in them a remedy for the poverty of the vast majority of the cultivators. They were correct in assuming that the new technology stands for vastly increased productivity and income to match. However, the propitious circumstances in which the new technology thrives are not easily obtainable and hence there are inevitably constraints on its scope and progress. Apart from this, where it has succeeded, the revolution has given rise to a host of political and social problems. In short, the green revolution can be, as Dr Wharton correctly pointed out in *Foreign Affairs* in April 1969, both a cornucopia and a Pandora's box.

This is seen very decisively in India's experience. There, extravagant anticipations have been replaced by a more sober and meaningful appreciation of its accomplishments and of the possibilities for expanding the scope of the technology beyond its current narrow limits. It has become obvious that many more farmers must be drawn in to share the benefits of the revolution. The polarization of income between the rich and the poor farmers, and the erosion of the position of the tenantry which has been accentuated by the increases in productivity, should not be part of the model of the new agricultural strategy. While self-sufficiency in foodstuffs is indeed a welcome—and likely—prospect for India, concern is rising that for all its technological feasibility it may fall short in helping solve some of the grave problems of a good many village poor.

Despite the serious social and technological limitations of the new agricultural strategy, one thing is clear: the wheat revolution is a reality, way beyond any expectation. Second, where the ingredients for the new technology are available—new high-yielding varieties, concentrated doses of fertilizers, assured sources of perennial irrigation—no farmer denies their effectiveness. Third, agriculture in the late 1960s has benefited from a guaranteed minimum price for wheat and a general improvement of terms vis-à-vis other sectors. Fourth, the desire for better farming methods and a better standard of living is growing not only among the relatively small numbers using the new technology, but also among countless farmers still outside looking in. This mental attitude, though too seldom supported by the necessary resources, cannot be overemphasized. At long last, in India too the power of ideas to bring about change is being demonstrated. To those concerned with purely physical entities of economic growth, a psychological change of this sort is not subject to numerology and is probably of no moment as a developmental factor. But it cannot be denied that a new, if unquantifiable, factor of growth has been introduced. Finally, the progress in agriculture is a result of major official and private efforts at several strategic points, which have slowly created a milieu radically different from that of the 1950s and early 1960s. These are considerable achievements, regardless of the growth rate.

2

This said, and viewing the new developments as a technological phenomenon, what stands out at this point is the unevenness of their application and the need for patient attention over a considerable period of time in order to achieve basic agricultural changes. Nothing makes this clearer than comparing the progress made with the two pivotal foodgrain crops of India, wheat and rice.

Whereas wheat has been a success story par excellence, rice can claim no such distinction. Between 1964–65 and 1968–69 all the basic indicators of agricultural growth in rice have remained almost unchanged; in contrast, the respective increases in wheat acreage, production and productivity were 19, 52 and 28 per cent. But the character of the technological changes is best seen in the hotbed of the green revolution, in the state of Punjab, India's traditional wheat basket. There, an innovation-minded group of farmers has in a few years succeeded in translating larger crops and income into a new way of life. More precisely, they planted 80 per cent of the land with 'miracle' wheat varieties; increased the number of tubewells for irrigation from 7,000 to 120,000; virtually tripled the consumption of fertilizers within four years—moving, during the last decade, from a mere two to three kilograms per acre to as high as 40 to 60 kilograms in 1968–69—and almost doubled the yield. For this the Punjab farmers deserve much credit, but they were fortunate in a remarkable set of partners: the Ford Foundation, which pioneered and demonstrated the utility of the new 'package of practices' idea; the Rockefeller Foundation, with its invaluable work in developing the Mexican 'dwarf' wheat varieties upon which the wheat revolution is based; the Punjab Agricultural University, which has rapidly become the center of dissemination for new varieties; and finally, the great effort of the central and state agencies which in a variety of ways helped to provide the inputs upon which the upswing in productivity rests.

At the moment, the same cannot be said for rice, despite significant pockets of progress in Kerala, Tamil Nadu, parts of Andhra Pradesh and West Bengal. Since wheat accounts for 15 per cent of the total acreage in foodgrains as against 31 per cent in rice, the latter is most important in determining the overall rate of agricultural growth. If rice productivity had shown anything comparable to that of wheat, India would have been self-sufficient in foodgrains now. The principal reason for the disparity in performance is that tested and proved new varieties are still in the making, and that, generally speaking, rice varieties demand a great number of favorable environmental conditions: they are susceptible to pest and disease, the knowledge of which still is inadequate. The quality of the new strains leaves something to be desired and it markets at a considerable discount. Unlike Punjab, with its successful irrigation program, the lack of irrigation and absence of drainage facilities in some of the major rice-growing parts of the country are serious constraints. In such conditions, with few notable exceptions, the much talked about 'miracle' strains from the Philippines and Taiwan have so far met with limited responses. Additionally, the problems of the 'new' rice, especially in the eastern belt of the country, extend beyond the technological lag: a much larger proportion of the cultivated rice area is in small holdings whose proprietors lack credit and are often tenants on the land, and these impose limitations of their own. For this very reason, if the improved rice technology could become a reality it would achieve something beyond higher productivity.

Nor is the green revolution only a wheat revolution, as its critics taunt; this first stage is a spectacular development in itself but more importantly it will serve as a useful organizational testing ground for general changes in agricultural technology. Only a blind enthusiast could have conceived that the passage from traditional to modern agricultural practices would be effected as if by magic—even in the United States hybrid corn came into its own after much trial and error, and more than a decade after the initiation of the process.

That the changeover is a long-drawn-out affair, or that coarse grains and nonfood crops have hardly been touched by the transformation, or that the total rate of output is still only half of that anticipated is partly in the nature of things and partly a matter for concern. A monsoon failure to which India is so prone might slow down the progress of the new strategy still further, but it would not be fatal. And the most encouraging part about the recent technological developments is not so much the physical output as the use of inputs, or the willingness of the farmers to invest and take risks. Inputs have been sharply and steadily rising, as in the use of chemical fertilizers, improved seed, minor irrigation facilities, plant protection devices, tractors, etc., and the remarkable degree of monetization of the farm economy and the big array of industrial consumption goods increasingly in demand by the farmers. Another sign of the profitability of modern agriculture is the appearance on the scene of a new breed of farmers made up of a motley crowd of retired military and civil servants, doctors, lawyers and businessmen. Not a few of them have 'unemployed' rupees acquired through undeclared earnings, and most of them look upon farming as a tax-haven, which it is, a source of high supplementary income free of any tax burdens.

3

Without minimizing the significance of the accomplishments, however, one must say that the revolution is highly 'selective', even if its spread effect is not inconsiderable in certain areas. Such revolutions must often go slowly under the most propitious circumstances, which are not present in India. It is enough to recall that three-fourths of India's cultivated acreage is not irrigated, and 'dry' farming predominates. If for no other reason, vast parts of the country have not been touched by the transformation at all and equally vast parts can boast only of 'small islands within'. Even in Punjab, with all its advantages, not every small farmer —not to speak of remaining tenants—practises the new technology and much less so in other developing parts of the country. The green revolution affects the few rather than the many not only because of environmental conditions but because the majority of the farmers lack resources, or are 'institutionally' precluded from taking advantage of the new agricultural trends.

In typical Indian conditions of great inequality of land ownership, resources and marketed surpluses, income inequality is the normal state of affairs. It is estimated that in 1969 out of a total rural population of 434 million, 103 million owned no land at all and another 185 million operated less than five acres per family. Taken together they represented 67 per cent of the total rural population, and of these an estimated 154 to 210 million lived in abject poverty, or at a level of 200 rupees ($21) per capita per year.

If the widening gap between the benefits to large and small holdings is to be reduced and the scope of the new technology enlarged, the less privileged cultivators must be enabled to secure the highly productive new inputs. Since it takes 10,000 to 12,000 rupees to re-equip a seven- to ten-acre holding, it is not normally within the reach of the farmer unless he can secure cooperative credit. More often than not he can get only insufficient credit and, on occasion, none at all, for the distribution of credit and inputs in an Indian village reflects a power structure very much biased in favor of the affluent. But whatever the causes, the argument is not against modernization for making the rich farmers richer still, but against the limited scope and that the growing disparity leaves the poor peasants relatively poorer. Many would-be innovators can be likened to tenants who receive land under a reform but nothing else to go with it. They are excluded from the purview of the green revolution altogether, or participate in a limited way at best. For reasons only partly attributable to the new technology, many farmers in areas of great potential are now pointing enviously to better production, higher income and better living 'over there' in their neighbors' fields. India can ill afford any growth in social discontent.

The situation of the multitude of tenants is even more difficult than that of the small farmers. In areas where the agricultural transformation is a potent force—Punjab and the Purnea district of Bihar—the accomplishments are marred by its adverse effects on the already troublesome tenurial conditions. Where the new farm practices are in vogue, land values have risen three, four or fivefold, and unrestricted land control has never been more prized. As a consequence, not only have rents risen from the traditional (though illegal under the reforms) 50/50 to as high as 70 per cent of the crop, but security of tenure and other rights in land a tenant might claim have also been perceptibly weakened. Now that green-revolution land is practically invaluable, the owners would like to get rid of tenants altogether and resume the land for self-cultivation, making use of the plentiful supply of hired labor which has no claims on the land whatsoever. There are too many tenants or sharecroppers to deal with them summarily without courting a good deal of trouble, but the old squeeze whereby tenants are reduced to sharecroppers and eventually to landless workers is being accelerated as more of the bigger owners become involved with the new technology. The basic provisions of tenancy reforms are less attainable than before the advent of the green revolution.

And the landless farm laborers, though their lot is temporarily improved, are eventually due for a setback. The new type of agriculture is labor-intensive, employing more labor due to double-cropping and other labor-demanding practices it is introducing. Not surprisingly, therefore, it has been hailed as a solution of the large problem of unemployment among rural landless. It appears, however, that even in the most advanced state like Punjab this is not as promising as anticipated because the technology is both labor-absorbing and labor-displacing. In recent years, wages have risen sharply, and so to a degree has the number of days of employment; on balance, and despite a steady rise in the cost of living, farm labor in Punjab is somewhat better off. Not so in Purnea, where higher productivity and higher prices have caused a shift in wage payments from kind to cash. This is a distinct disadvantage to the farm laborer, whose wages in kind have insured him a minimum food supply. And looking ahead, additional employment and better wages are not forever, for new farm practices are bringing in a host of labor-saving devices such as tractors and threshers and much in between.

Events are beginning to catch up with Nehru's lament against farm mechanization as a threat to peasant welfare. Agricultural labor has received none of the organizational and legislative benefits which have helped industrial labor. Even at this early stage of modernization of the bigger farms of Punjab the drive is for more equipment and fewer hands. The estimated 35 to 40 million landless laborers are bound to grow in numbers and their rate of employment in any other field of activity is not promising; thus the outlook is for an overcrowded, low-wage farm market regardless of the scope of the green revolution.

4

The new technology is not the primary cause of the accentuated imbalances in the countryside. They are the result of all the social, religious, economic and political forms which govern the village, and which admittedly are mirrored in the shape which the new technology has assumed. It is not the fault of the green revolution that the credit service does not serve those for whom it was originally intended, that the extension service is falling behind expectations, that the village 'panchayats', or councils, are essentially political rather than developmental bodies, that security of tenure is not given to the many, that rentals are exorbitant, that ceilings on land ownership are notional, that even rising wage scales are hardly sufficient to satisfy the basic essentials of the farm laborer, or that generally speaking in those conditions economic necessity and social justice of and for the village poor do not ride in tandem.

To a considerable extent these are man-made issues of long standing. Modernization of agriculture should include a combination of technical factors geared to higher production *and* improvements in the institutional framework to benefit the rural underprivileged. The current emphasis is on productivity, to the exclusion of social imperatives: the first will bring India to self-sufficiency; the second is beginning to yield great vexations.

Under the leadership of leftist parties, the village poor are not averse to forcible occupation of land, harvesting standing crops and violent attempts to secure better wages. According to the Ministry of Foreign Affairs, in the first nine months of the past year 346 incidents of forcible occupation of land (totalling 100,000 to 300,000 acres) with many murdered and injured have taken place in West Bengal alone. That this could be only a foretaste of an enormous 'law-and-order' problem is well understood, and the government of India is deeply disturbed by it. In late November 1969 an emergency conference was held on how to place the agrarian reforms back on the rails. The Prime Minister addressed the Chief Ministers of all the states with an unmistakable sense of urgency, saying: 'The warning of the times is that unless the green revolution is accompanied by a revolution based on social justice the green revolution may not remain green.'

Reading 36

Criteria for the Design of Agricultural Development Strategies

B. F. Johnston

Food Research Institute Studies in Agricultural Economics, Trade and Development, vol. II, no. 1, 1972, pp. 27 – 58.

Discussion of the policy issues of agricultural development has been dominated by a polarization of opinion on whether the principal objective of policy should be equity or efficiency. This has been particularly evident in India, where the direction in which policy has moved depended largely on which of those two divergent views was ascendent at the time. Underlying this professional schizophrenia has been the assumption that equity and efficiency are separate and necessarily contradictory goals.

The Need for Criteria

This paper seeks to define criteria for assessing alternative strategies for agriculture. W. D. Hopper's contribution to the Rockefeller Foundation's Symposium on 'Strategy for the Conquest of Hunger' provides a particularly emphatic statement of the view that agricultural strategies should be based on single-minded pursuit of the goal of increased output. Thus he argues that for countries that cannot afford 'the luxury of mixed goals and of uncertain, unproductive policies . . . the production of food must be accepted as *the* priority objective. . . .' [1, p. 105.] The thesis of this paper is that agricultural strategies can and should be directed at 'mixed goals', or, as I prefer to express it, multiple objectives.

The Multiple Objectives of Agricultural Strategies and the Concept of Total Efficiency

The historical experience in a number of countries, and the recent technical breakthroughs of the Green Revolution, justify major emphasis on increases in factor productivity. It is, however, the experience of Japan and Taiwan that is especially useful in demonstrating that an *appropriate* sequence of innovations based on modern scientific knowledge and experimental methods makes possible an expansion path for the agricultural sector that is characterized by large increases in factor productivity *throughout* the agricultural sector. Such a strategy enables a widening fraction of the working population in agriculture to be associated with increasingly productive technologies, based mainly on expanded use of purchased inputs that are divisible and neutral to scale. It is because the new inputs of seed and fertilizer, that are the essence of the Green Revolution, are complementary to the large amounts of labor and land already committed to agriculture that these increases in factor productivity can have such a large impact on total farm output. At the same time, by involving an increasingly large fraction of the rural population in the process of technical change, such a strategy means that the fruits of economic progress are widely shared.

The thrust of this argument is that it is possible and desirable to devise and implement agricultural strategies which are efficient in terms of a number of objectives, including but not confined to the objective of achieving desired increases in farm output at low cost. The following objectives, which are examined later in some detail, seem to be especially relevant to the design of strategies for agriculture that are efficient in this broad sense:

(1) Contributing to the overall rate of economic growth and the process of structural transformation,
(2) Achieving a satisfactory rate of increase in farm output at minimum cost by encouraging sequences of innovations which exploit the possibilities for technical change most appropriate to a country's factor endowments,
(3) Achieving a broadly based improvement in the welfare of the rural population, and
(4) Facilitating the process of social modernization (including the lowering of birthrates, the extension and improvement of rural education, and the strengthening of entrepreneurial capacities) by encouraging widespread attitudinal and behavioral changes among farm households.

I believe that it is useful to assess the 'total efficiency' of alternative agricultural strategies in terms of their relative success in achieving those four objectives.

The concept of total efficiency is, quite obviously, difficult to define operationally. That is inherent in the nature of the problem. But the problem must be confronted because only when a country's agricultural strategy is efficient in this broad sense is the trade-off between the goal of increased output and other objectives likely to be minimized. Indeed, it is my contention that with an agricultural strategy that is designed with those multiple objectives in view, the trade-off is likely to be small or nonexistent.

A country's overall strategy for agriculture is a composite of substrategies relating to research, education, water resources development, promotion of farmers' organizations, marketing and price policy, credit and the distribution of inputs, agricultural taxation, land tenure, policies affecting the nature and pace of mechanization, and other elements. The total efficiency of the strategy depends on the complementarities among those various activities and the quality of implementation as well as decisions with respect to the allocation of funds and personnel and policies for individual substrategies.

The choice between unimodal and bimodal agricultural strategies

The most fundamental issue of agricultural strategy faced by the late developing countries is to choose between a bimodal strategy whereby resources are concentrated within a subsector of large, capital-intensive units or a unimodal strategy which seeks to encourage a more progressive and wider diffusion of technical innovations adapted to the factor proportions of the sector as a whole. The essential distinction between the two approaches is that the unimodal strategy emphasizes sequences of innovations that are highly divisible and largely scale-neutral. These are innovations that can be used efficiently by small-scale farmers and adopted progressively. A unimodal approach does not mean that all farmers or all agricultural regions would adopt innovations and expand output at uniform rates. Rather it means that the type of innovations emphasized are appropriate to a progressive pattern of adoption in the twofold sense that there will be progressive diffusion of innovations within particular areas and extension of the benefits of technical change to new areas as changes in environmental conditions, notably irrigation facilities, or improved market opportunities or changes in the nature of the innovations available, enable farmers in new areas to participate in the process of modernization. Although a bimodal strategy entails a much more rapid adoption of a wider range of modern technologies, this is necessarily confined to a small fraction of farm units because of the structure of economies in which commerical demand is small in relation to a farm labor force that still represents some 60 to 80 per cent of the working population.

The late developing countries face a wide choice of farm equipment embodying large investments in research and development activity in the economically advanced countries. The performance characteristics of these machines are impressive, and representatives of the major manufacturing firms in the economically advanced countries are experienced and skillful in demonstrating their equipment. And they now have added incentive to promote sales in the developing countries to more fully utilize their plant capacity which is large relative to domestic demand (mainly a replacement demand since the period of rapid expansion of tractors and tractor-drawn equipment in the developed countries has ended). The availability of credit under bilateral and international aid programs temporarily eliminates the foreign exchange constraint to acquiring such equipment; and when such loans are readily available it may even appear to be an attractive means of increasing the availability of resources—in the short run. Within developing countries there is often considerable enthusiasm for the latest in modern technologies. But little attention is given to research and development activity and support services to promote the manufacture and wide use of simple, inexpensive equipment of good design, low import content, and suited to the factor proportions prevailing in countries where labor is relatively abundant and capital scarce.

A recent monograph by W. F. Owen [2] presents an explicit presentation of the case for a 'bimodal' agricultural strategy. He argues that 'sound development policy, as well as more relevant research in the social sciences, likely needs to be based on an explicit recognition of two quite distinct rural sectors: a "modernized" or "commercial farming sector" and a "transitional" or "surplus population-supporting sector".' The commercial farmers, defined rather arbitrarily as those 'capable of generating from the production and sale of farm commodities a continuing standard of living comparable to that earned by skilled workers in the modernized urban-industrial sector', would 'include only a small proportion of the entire farming population'. He goes on to assert that 'it may be posited as a basic condition of economic growth in all countries that most of the available land resources should be incorporated in this commercial subsector' [2, pp. 3–4].

Owen dismisses the idea that the small-scale farm units of the 'transitional sector' might pursue a course of progressive modernization based on gradually increasing commercial sales and use of purchased inputs as a 'myth'. 'If the majority of the population concerned is transitional to anything,' he declares, 'it can only be to potential non-farming employment opportunities, irrespective of how difficult this potential may be to realize' [2, p. 7].

The historical experience of Japan and Taiwan

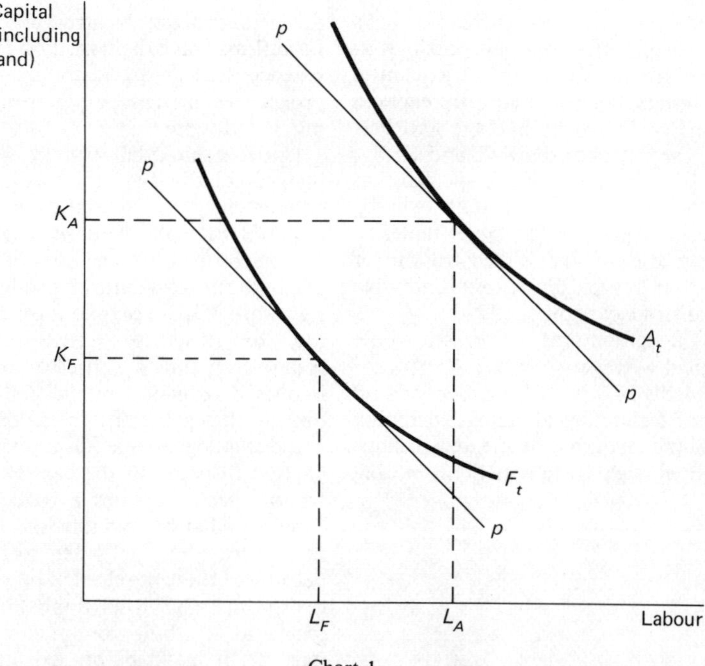

Chart 1

demonstrates, however, that a bimodal pattern is not an inevitable outcome. It is a pattern that is being determined to a considerable extent by economic policies that distort price signals and by failure to take the positive measures that would encourage a unimodal strategy of progressive modernization of agriculture.

Considered in the context of the multiple objectives of an agricultural strategy, a unimodal approach appears to have significant advantages with respect to 'total efficiency' as well as in its effects on income distribution and equity. But before examining those multiple objectives, and the interrelationships among them, in terms of their relevance to the choice of strategy for agriculture, it will be useful to clarify the differences between the two strategies by means of a unit isoquant diagram. M. J. Farrell used this device to define the concepts of technical, price, and economic efficiency, but it also serves as a useful expositional device for clarifying how the 'total efficiency' of the agricultural sector's expansion path is influenced by the new production possibilities that become available [3].

Points on the diagrams represent the combinations of inputs used by different firms per unit of output. By joining the points that represent the minimum input combinations an envelope curve is drawn so that no observation lies between the envelope and the origin. The frontier thus defined represents the least quantities of inputs required per unit of output; firms whose input combinations lie on that frontier isoquant are said to be technically efficient. All other firms are described by points lying within the envelope. A curve fitted to such points can be defined as the 'average isoquant' [3, Chap. 4]. For expositional purposes we imagine that all firms other than frontier firms lie on this average isoquant and employ an 'average technology'.

In Chart 1 the frontier and average isoquants are labeled F_t and A_t respectively. On both isoquants price efficient firms employ the combination of inputs indicated by the tangency of the relative price line PP with the isoquant.

A bimodal strategy in agriculture involves capital-intensive technical change within a modernized subsector. A unimodal strategy involves progressive technical change which only gradually increases the degree of capital-intensity and which involves the entire agricultural sector. These differences are represented in Charts 2 and 3.

As in Chart 1, A_t and F_t represent the average and frontier isoquants prior to the technical change. In Chart 2, F_{t+t*} represents the new frontier isoquant after a capital-using bimodal strategy has been introduced. In Chart 3, F^*_{t+t*} represents the frontier isoquant associated with widespread introduction of improved seed-fertilizer combinations and the investments in research, training, and infrastructure emphasized by a unimodal strategy. Inasmuch as these are innovations that can be used efficiently by small, labor-intensive farm units using only limited quantities of purchased inputs, there will also be an inward shift of the average isoquant. To simplify the diagram, it is assumed arbitrarily that the new average isoquant, A_{t+t*}, now corresponds to the position of the old frontier isoquant.

Under identical relative factor prices (represented by the price line PP) the bimodal strategy involves a much higher capital to labor ratio in those firms that have access to the land and capital that makes it possible for them to operate on the frontier isoquant. Consequently, the bimodal strategy results in substantial differences in the factor proportions employed by average and best firms as indicated by the slopes of the K/L and K′/L′ rays in Charts 2 and 3. In fact, it is to be expected that the K/L ratio for the remaining farm units will be considerably less than would be possible under a unimodal strategy because of the concentration of purchased inputs in an atypically capital-intensive subsector if a bimodal strategy is pursued.

The rate at which the agricultural sector as a whole moves from the original average isoquant, A_t, toward the new frontier isoquant, F_{t+t^*} or $F^*_{t+t^*}$, depends on the rate of diffusion of technological change including the use of purchased inputs required by the new technology. The strategy chosen by governments in promoting agricultural development can have a significant influence on the pace and especially on the nature of this diffusion process. As structural change takes place and farm firms make the transition from predominantly subsistence production to commercial farming, there is a progressive increase in their ability and need to use purchased inputs.

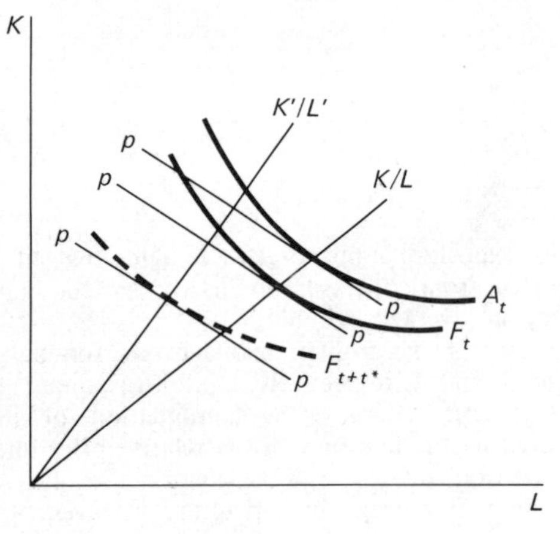

Chart 2

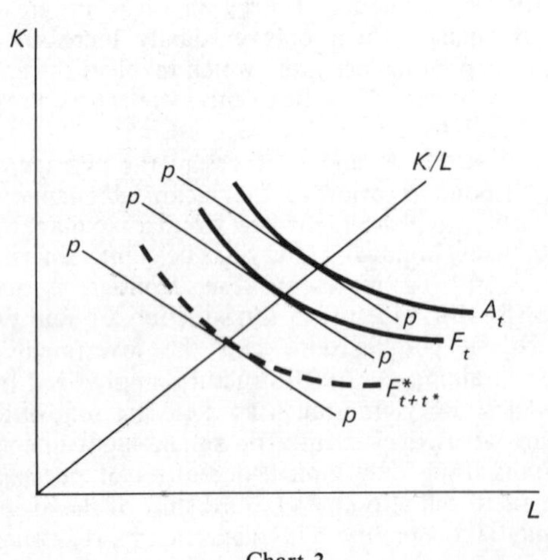

Chart 3

Under a bimodal strategy frontier firms with their high capital to labor ratio would account for the bulk of commercial production and would have the cash income required to make extensive use of purchased inputs. Inasmuch as the schedule of aggregate commercial demand for agricultural products is inelastic and its rightward shift over time is essentially a function of the rate of structural transformation, to concentrate resources within a subsector of agriculture inevitably implies a reduction in the ability of farm households outside that subsector to adopt new purchased inputs and technologies. In addition, the high foreign exchange content of many of the capital inputs employed in the frontier sector implies a reduction in the amount of foreign exchange available for imported inputs for other farm firms (or for other sectors). It is, of course, because of these purchasing power and foreign exchange constraints that it is impossible for the agricultural sector as a whole to pursue a crash modernization strategy. It might be argued that a proper farm credit program could eliminate the purchasing power constraint, but the availability of credit (assuming that repayment takes place) merely alters the shape of the time horizon over which the constraint operates. And capital and government revenue are such scarce resources in a developing country that government subsidy programs are not feasible means of escaping from this constraint. In brief, bimodal and unimodal strategies are to a considerable extent mutually exclusive.

Under the bimodal approach the divergence between the factor intensities and the technical efficiency of 'best' and average firms is likely to become progessively greater as agricultural transformation takes place. Moreover, both the initial and subsequent divergences between the technologies used in the two sectors are likely to be accentuated because the factor prices, including the price of imported capital equipment, faced by the modern sector in contemporary developing countries typically diverge from social opportunity cost. This divergence is obvious when subsidized credit is made available on a rationed basis to large farmers and when equipment can be imported with a zero or low tariff at an official exchange rate that is overvalued. In addition, the large-scale farmers depend on hired labor rather than unpaid family labor. The wages paid hired labor may be determined by minimum wage legislation, and even without a statutory minimum the price of hired labor is characteristically higher than the opportunity cost of labor to small farm units. Market wage rates tend to reflect the marginal productivity of labor in peak seasons, and even in those seasons jobs are likely to be rationed to some extent. This underpricing of capital

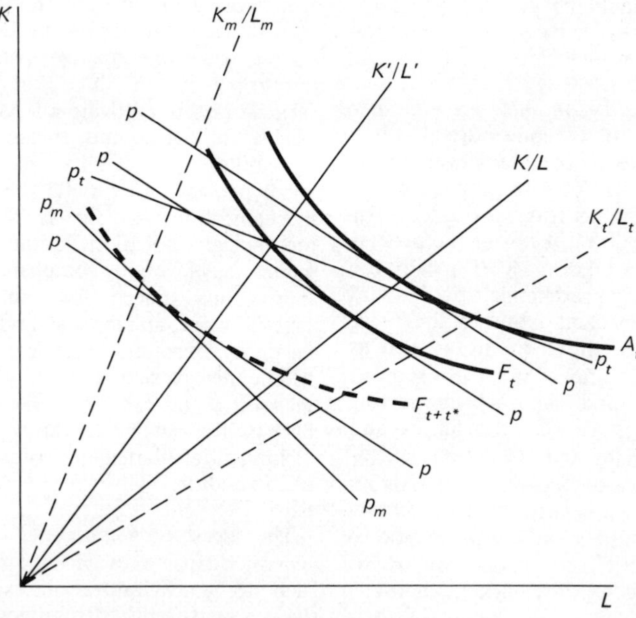

Chart 4

(and foreign exchange) and overpricing of labor means that the relevant price line facing the 'modern' subsector will be the steeper line P_mP_m shown in Chart 4. Various factors, including policies which repress instead of foster the healthy growth of financial intermediaries, would tend to raise the price of capital to the traditional sector above the social opportunity cost of capital, resulting in an opposite bias in relative factor prices as represented by the price line P_tP_t. The price distortions would thus accentuate the divergence in capital-labor ratios caused by biased technical change; this greater difference would be represented by the K_m/l_m and K_t/L_t rays for the modern and traditional sectors respectively.

Under the unimodal strategy with its emphasis on highly divisible and scale-neutral innovations, the best firms in the agrarian sector display essentially the same factor intensities as average firms. Interfarm differences in performance will be large, especially during transitional periods as farmers are learning how to use new inputs efficiently, but this will reflect mainly differences in output per unit of input rather than major differences in factor proportions. Inasmuch as the expansion path for the agricultural sector associated with a unimodal strategy implies a level of capital intensity and foreign exchange requirements that are compatible with a late developing country's economic structure, more firms within the agricultural sector are able to expand their use of fertilizer and the other divisible inputs that dominate purchases under this strategy. Thus, the diffusion of innovations and associated inputs will be more broadly based, and the divergence in factor intensities between frontier firms and average firms will be moderate.

Although the foregoing has emphasized the contrast in the pattern of technical change, it is apparent that the two strategies will have significantly different impacts on many dimensions of economic and social change. Most obvious are the differences in the nature of demand for farm inputs, but the structure of rural demand for consumer goods will also be very different under a unimodal as compared to a bimodal strategy.

A major difference in income distribution is to be expected because of the likelihood that under a bimodal strategy the difficult problem of absorbing a rapidly growing labor force into productive employment would be exacerbated whereas under a unimodal strategy there is a good prospect that the rate of increase in demand for labor would be more rapid than the growth of the labor force. Underemployment and unemployment would thus be reduced as a result of wider participation of the rural population in improved income-earning opportunities. This improvement in income opportunities available to members of the rural work force would result in part from increased earnings as hired labor since rising demand for labor would tend to raise wage rates and the number of days of work available during the year for landless laborers and for very small farmers whose incomes derive to a considerable extent from work on farms that are above average size.

Most important, however, would be the increased incomes earned by farm households cultivating their own or rented land.

The multiple objectives of an agricultural strategy

In the paragraphs that follow I comment briefly on some of the reasons why the design of an efficient strategy for agriculture should be guided by explicit consideration of four major objectives of an agricultural strategy and the interrelationships among them.

Contributions to overall economic growth and structural transformation. It is conventional when considering agriculture's role in economic development to catalog a number of specific 'contributions'. Several of these contributions imply a net transfer of factors of production out of the agricultural sector as the process of structural transformation takes place. Typically the farm sector provides foreign exchange, public and private investment resources, and labor to the more rapidly expanding sectors of the economy as well as increased supplies of food and raw materials to support a growing urban population and manufacturing sector.

The nature of the linkages between agriculture and the local manufacturing sector and the seriousness of foreign exchange and investment constraints on development will be influenced significantly by the structure of rural demand for both inputs and consumer goods. Because of their differential effects on the sequence of innovations and on rural income distribution, a bimodal and a unimodal strategy will differ greatly in their aggregate capital and foreign exchange requirements.

The more capital-intensive bimodal strategy emphasizes rapid adoption of mechanical innovations such as tractors along with chemical fertilizers and other inputs essential for increasing crop yields. Even if that type of machinery is manufactured locally, the foreign exchange requirements for capital equipment and for components are high, and the production processes require a high level of technical sophistication, large plants, and capital-intensive technologies.

The unimodal strategy with its emphasis on mechanical innovations of lower technical sophistication and foreign exchange content, such as improved bullock implements and low-lift pumps, appears to offer greater promise for the development of local manufacturing which is less demanding in its technical requirements and which is characterized by lower capital–labor ratios and lower foreign exchange content. On the basis of experience in Japan and Taiwan as well as an analysis of the nature of the supply response to the two patterns of demand, it seems clear that a unimodal strategy will have a much more favorable impact on the growth of output and especially on the growth of employment in local manufacturing and supporting service industries. The reasons cannot be pursued here except to note the wider diffusion of opportunities to develop entrepreneurial and technical skills through 'learning by doing' that leads to increasing competence in manufacturing. Progress in metal-working and in the domestic manufacture of capital goods are especially significant because they are necessary to the creation of an industrial sector adapted to the factor proportions of a late developing economy. (see 5, Chap. IV; 19.)

Increasing farm productivity and output. The importance of distinguishing between inputs and innovations that are mainly instrumental in increasing output per acre and those that make it possible for each farm worker to cultivate a larger area has already been noted. Biological and chemical innovations increase agricultural productivity mainly through increasing yields per acre. In general the effect on yield of farm mechanization *per se* is slight, although certain mechanical innovations, notably tube-wells and low-lift pumps, may be highly complementary to yield-increasing innovations. Indeed, for some high-yielding varieties, especially rice, an ample and reliable supply of water is a necessary precondition for realizing the genetic potential of the new varieties. This distinction between yield-increasing and labor-saving innovations is significant because the relative emphasis given to these two types of innovations largely determines whether development of agriculture will follow a unimodal or bimodal pattern.

The thrust of a unimodal strategy is to encourage general diffusion of yield-increasing innovations and such mechanical innovations as are complementary with the new seed-fertilizer technology. The bimodal strategy emphasizes simultaneous adoption of innovations that increase substantially the amount of land which individual cultivators can efficiently work in addition to the yield-increasing innovations emphasized in the unimodal approach.

For reasons discussed above, it is not possible for developing countries to pursue the unimodal and bimodal options simultaneously. In placing emphasis on reinforcing success within a subsector of large and capital-intensive farms, a bimodal strategy may have an advantage in maximizing the rate of increase in the short run because it bypasses the problems and costs associated with involving a large fraction of the farm population in the modernization process. In a longer view, however, a unimodal strategy appears to be more efficient, especially in minimizing requirements for the scarce resources of foreign exchange and loanable funds. Because of the scope that exists for obtaining widespread and substantial increases in the productivity of the relatively abundant resources of labor and land, and of other farm-supplied resources such as draft animals that are internal to the agricultural sector and often to the farm unit, the potential impact on aggregate farm production is very large.

Achieving broadly based improvement in the welfare of the rural population. Rural works programs are probably the most frequently discussed measure aimed directly at improving the welfare of the poorest segments of the farm population.

Other programs also merit attention because they offer the promise of substantial benefits relative to their cost, and some of them can also make a substantial contribution to the expansion of output by improving the health and productivity of the rural population. Public health programs such as malaria control are notable examples. Nutritional programs also deserve attention. The effects on well-being of increased farm productivity and incomes can be enhanced considerably if diet changes are informed by practical programs of nutrition education.

Although it is foolhardy to attempt to treat the complex and controversial subject of land tenure in a few paragraphs, the positive and negative effects on rural welfare of land reform programs cannot be ignored.

It is sometimes argued that because of the connection between size of holding and choice of technique, redistributive land reform is a necessary condition for a unimodal strategy. Indeed it is even claimed that the success of unimodal strategies in Japan and Taiwan is attributable to their postwar land reforms, notwithstanding the fact that in both countries the basic pattern of progressive modernization of small-scale, labor-intensive, but technically progressive farm units was established long before World War II.

I am persuaded that an effectively implemented land reform program that brings about a more equal distribution of landed wealth will not only contribute to the goal of equity but will also tend to facilitate low-cost expansion of farm output based primarily on yield-increasing innovations.

The critical factor determining the choice of technique and factor proportions in agriculture is the size distribution of operational (management) units rather than ownership units. Past experience, for example in prewar Japan and Taiwan, demonstrates that a highly skewed pattern of land ownership is not incompatible with a unimodal size distribution of operational units.

Owner cultivation avoids the difficulties that arise when landlords, responding to higher yields, raise the percentage share of output that they demand as rent. But if redistributive land reform is not a realistic possibility, widespread renting of land seems clearly preferable to the further concentration of land in large operational units and the bimodal pattern which is thereby accentuated.

Facilitating the processes of social modernization by encouraging widespread attitudinal and behavioral changes. It seems likely that the broad impact of a unimodal strategy would have favorable effects in three areas important to this process of social change. First, the wide diffusion of familiarity with the calculation of costs and returns and of opportunities to acquire managerial experience would appear to provide a favorable environment for the training and recruitment of entrepreneurs. The same would apply, of course, to the wider diffusion of learning experiences in manufacturing which is associated with a unimodal strategy.

Secondly, a broadly based approach to agricultural development seems likely to generate strong support for rural education as well as the institutions more directly related to promoting increased agricultural productivity. It is sometimes argued that large-scale, highly commercialized farm enterprises are easier to tax than millions of small units. Because of the power structure maintained or created by a bimodal strategy, however, the greater administrative convenience may in practice mean very little. The fact that public education, and especially rural education, in most of South America seems to lag behind progress in other developing countries where average incomes are considerably lower seems to provide some support for this generalization.

Thirdly, and most important, the reduction in birthrates in the countryside, resulting from spontaneous changes in attitudes and behavior as well as behavioral changes induced by government population programs, are likely to be more widespread and have a greater effect on the national birthrate under a unimodal than a bimodal strategy.

The controversial issues today concern the determination of research priorities. These will be quite different depending on whether a country's agricultural strategy is aimed at a bimodal or unimodal pattern of development. If it is the latter, adaptive research on yield-increasing innovations capable of widespread adoption clearly deserves major emphasis. Protective research to minimize losses from disease, pests, or environmental hazards also becomes increasingly important as farmers enlarge their use of purchased inputs and operate at higher yield levels. Research and pilot projects to determine the most feasible and economic techniques of improving the availability and management of water supplies also merit special attention because of the critical importance of investments in agricultural infrastructure required to create environmental conditions that will enable a larger percentage of farm households to take advantage of the new seed-fertilizer combinations. Another research need, and one that has received relatively little attention, is to promote the development of well-designed but inexpensive items of farm equipment that can be widely used on small-scale farm units to ease labor bottlenecks and permit more timely and more precise performance of various operations. The development of a bullock-drawn disc harrow and a seed-fertilizer drill in India are examples of partial success in that type of operation.

Decision-making with respect to the complex and controversial issues of agricultural strategy is complicated by the influence of interest groups and political considerations. The welfare of various social groups is affected quite differently by alternative policies. Increasing land taxes and imposing excise taxes on those farm inputs that are mainly labor displacing in their impact appear to be important policy instruments for implementing a unimodal strategy. Large landowners, who would bear a substantial part of the burden of paying such taxes, can be expected to oppose these measures out of self-interest and a conviction that as the most advanced element in the agricultural sector they should be free of disincentives and benefit from positive measures such as the availability of credit at subsidized rates in order to make a maximum contribution to the growth of farm output.

References: Reading 36

1 Hopper, W. D. (1968), 'Investment in agriculture: the essentials for payoff', in *Strategy for the Conquest of Hunger: Proceedings of a Symposium Convened by the Rockefeller Foundation* (New York).

2 Owen, W. F. (1971), *Two Rural Sectors: Their Characteristics and Roles in the Development Process*, International Development Research Center, Occasional Paper 1 (Indiana University).

3 Farrell, M. J. (1957), 'The measurement of productive efficiency', *J. Royal Stat. Soc.* (London), Series A (General), 120 pt. 3.

4 Timmer, C. P. (1970), 'On measuring technical efficiency', *Food Research Institute Studies*, vol. IX, no. 2.

5 Johnston, B. F., and Kilby, P. (1971), 'Agricultural strategies, rural-urban interactions, and the expansion of income opportunities', draft monograph prepared for the OECD Development Centre (OECD).

Reading 37

On the Concept of 'Integrated Rural Development Planning' in Less Developed Countries

I. Livingstone

Journal of Agricultural Economics, January 1979.

The emphasis in development economics, for many years on industrial development of the LDCs, is now clearly on the agricultural sector, and on rural development generally. Within this there is widespread enthusiasm among academics and operating development agencies alike for what are known as 'integrated rural development plans'. These are based on a concept, however, which is seldom closely defined and which deserves rather more critical attention than it has received so far, despite one 'sceptical' view expressed not long ago by Vernon Ruttan.[1] One reason for caution is that the term 'integrated' bears some similarity to other terms which have emerged in the literature of development economics in having an intrinsic appeal. 'Balanced growth', 'take-off' and 'self-sustained growth' are of the same *genre*. Just as balance must by definition be desirable (until Hirschman expressed a preference for *un*balanced growth), so integrated rural development planning appears preferable to 'non-integrated' planning. In fact there are different ways in which the term 'integrated' rural development planning has been used and might usefully be used, and it will be useful to explore these alternative senses.

Rural development plans are frequently described as being integrated when 'comprehensive' would be a much more accurate and consistent description. Such plans for particular areas are comprehensive in the sense of providing complete coverage of the area's economy, in a number of ways. They cover the whole area, spatially. They cover all productive activities in the area, crop and livestock possibilities, for example, but also non-agricultural rural activities. And they include provision for infrastructure, both productive infrastructure such as roads and social infrastructure such as schools and hospitals. The plans are in effect *multi-sectoral* within the boundaries of the areas concerned. 'Integrated' here may therefore really mean multi-sectoral or comprehensive.

Since integrated rural development planning (IRDP) is simply one form of *area planning*, it is worth first considering the latter in more detail. A useful division here is between (1) primary-level planning, which refers to macro-economic planning or economy-wide plans; (2) secondary-level planning below that level, which may be separated into (a) area planning and (b) sectoral planning, according to whether the economy is divided spatially or by sector; and (3) tertiary-level planning which refers to project planning and implementation. Area planning includes both regional and district planning (depending on the size of the area), in which the boundaries are given by administrative units, [2] and, for example, river basin development, in which the area is defined geographically.

The primary feature of area planning is naturally its *area focus* or spatial element. A second feature is the deliberate establishment of *planning machinery at the local level*. Compared to the vertical or hierarchical system of national planning, this is characterised by a horizontal organisation involving a degree of co-operation between ministries at the local level, is a much more continuous process compared to the discontinuous process of macroeconomic plan preparation, and has a greater emphasis on implementation, being one stage nearer to the tertiary level of project planning. The third feature, going beyond simple project identification, is that area plans generally attempt more or less comprehensive *resource assessment*, that is, to present a comprehensive, integrated view of the area's development possibilities, given its agricultural and natural resource base. This feature of comprehensive resource assessment does mean that the 'plan' may not be phased in the strict manner of a national four- or five-year plan, in which only those projects which are proposed for implementation during the limited plan period are included. In an area development plan the time-scale for exploitation of the resource identified may be considered to be an independent matter, and left open. The plan may therefore be comprehensive in covering the entire resource base and not simply projects for immediate implementation. Finally, the multisectoral nature of the plan, and the ingredient of comprehensive resource assessment, generally implies a fourth feature, that plan formulation has to be a multidisciplinary exercise, involving not only general and agricultural economists, but engineers, agronomists, soil scientists, and others, while plan implementation similarly involves a multi-agency effort.

Plans may be comprehensive or multi-sectoral in the ways described above, however, without being 'integrated'. The point in having an 'integrated' plan exists, first of all, if there is some advantage in *combining* several activities or components: where there is incomplete divisibility in the sense that particular activities cannot be carried out efficiently independently of each other. An area plan which is comprehensive in the senses described already could still be quite divisible, with separate segments quite capable of independent implementation.

The closest form of interdependence is where two projects depend directly on one another, as when, say, the exploitation of iron ore requires the exploitation of an adjacent source of coal. There is also interdependence (by definition) between the production base as a whole and supporting productive infrastructure, but this is generally much weaker. It is stronger where the opening up of a new region 'requires' the building of a major trunk road into the area or where expansion of agricultural production 'requires' the provision of additional feeder roads to facilitate the marketing of the produce. But there may be considerable choice regarding the degree of improvement in communications required, in the quality of the trunk road, for instance, or mileage of feeder roads. Thirdly, integrated plans usually include provision for additional social services such as health and education, if only to maintain the level of social service expenditure per head if population is expected to expand along with the expansion of production: and indeed the goal of increasing the level of economic welfare in an area would require increasing expenditure on social services *more* than in proportion to population. But this interdependence between production plans and supporting *social* infrastructure may be even less strong, since the extra social spending is a desirable concomitant rather than required condition for increased output: this is indicated by the fact that spending on social services in the national plan for the country as a whole will necessarily be below the level which would be desired, due to the low level of income and taxable capacity, and is clearly the subject of choice.

If we use 'integrated' to mean 'interdependent', it means that *national* macroeconomic plans are 'integrated' to an important extent, in that components of the plan are highly interdependent. Thus public sector plans will depend on adequate government revenue being raised from taxation, this in turn depending on the expansion of the public sector; consumption and investment plans will depend on the availability of foreign exchange, and therefore on the accuracy of foreign exchange projections, and so on. This is most obvious in a multi-sector plan based upon input–output analysis, but applies also to one based on a simple aggregate growth model incorporating the main aggregates, C, I, G, X and M. An area rural development plan may actually be *less* integrated, in fact, if the area is small and fairly homogeneous, such as an area specialising in the production of a single cash crop for export, say coffee. Here the main activity of coffee-growing would depend much more on external factors, particularly the coffee price, than on other activities in the area.

The term 'integrated' may usefully be used in a number of other senses, as well as that involving interdependent activities and sectors. It may be used to indicate, related to the area focus of the plan, that the plan incorporates a diagnosis or *analysis* of the area's development problems and prospects. This need not involve a major integrated rural development planning exercise or the production of a mammoth 'master plan', which may even serve to obscure the essentials of the development requirements of the area.

Related to this, an area plan is more likely than a national plan to cover all the *people* and categories of person in the area. This springs in part from a comprehensive approach, which implies taking account of all groups in the area, as well as all sectors and activities. It is also 'integrated', however, in that it may take account of the interdependence between the activities and development of one group on those of others. Thus Ruttan specifically mentions[3] that 'the concern today with integrated rural development in the developing world represents, in part, a reaction against the distortions produced by the production-oriented ("Green Revolution") rural development efforts of the 1960s'. Thus a seed-fertiliser programme or tractor loan service could help progressive farmers while reducing the incomes of smaller farmers or increasing the number of landless. Again, large 'integrated' rural development plans in practice may or may not deal with such interdependencies, and frequently do not.

As mentioned already, sub-national area planning with a more or less comprehensive resource assessment component will be interdisciplinary to the extent that it involves the co-operation of different kinds of experts (soil scientists, agronomists, water engineers, agricultural economists, etc.). The contributed efforts of all of these could then be said to form an 'integrated' plan for the area. In part this greater degree of integration of different aspects is associated with the focus on (natural) resource assessment, but in part also it arises because of the more detailed and specific nature of local area planning involving, for instance, the determination of precise locations for agricultural and other schemes and projects. How far this is *planning*, in the most important sense, rather than implementation, is another matter. It must be realised, also, that obtaining a comprehensive inventory of resources, however desirable, is not costless, and may be attainable for some areas of the country only at the expense of studies elsewhere.

Finally, participation and self-help have often been seen as an important or even key element in integrated rural development planning. Ruttan refers to the community development emphasis in the earlier rural development efforts of the 1950s. Participation and self-reliance were planned to be important features of Kenya's Special Rural Development Programme,[4] in which local project identification and implementation via a decentralised, localised planning machinery was emphasised. Participation by the population at large in actual planning efforts was very limited, however, as it has been generally in rural development planning.

Rather different issues from that considered here regarding the precise meaning which can be attached to the concept of integrated rural development planning are raised in the critical article by Ruttan mentioned earlier. Ruttan starts by commenting on the apparent lack of successful *programmes* of rural development as compared to successful projects. This he puts down to two things. First, 'there is an absence of any well-defined rural or community development technologies around which professional capacity or resources can be organised or institutionalised' (p. 16). Referring perhaps to the same sort of enthusiasm for IRDP as we referred to initially, he states (p. 14) even more directly that 'integrated rural development can be described, perhaps not too inaccurately, as an ideology in search of a methodology or a technology'. Secondly, he argues that rather than planning techniques, successful rural development has depended on specific stimuli, particularly an urban impact, technical innovations 'capable of generating substantial new income flows', or institutional mobilisation and development. Belshaw, in reply,[5] does not comment on the existence or otherwise of successful case studies of integrated rural development, but does deny strongly the absence of available techniques of rural development planning. He claims (p. 14) that 'a set of relatively powerful planning techniques have been assembled from diverse fields of application to provide rural development planning with an effective set of "teeth",' drawing attention to six different areas 'each with an accompanying set of techniques'.

Unfortunately the techniques supposedly available under each of the six heads are not sufficiently specified for a convincing case to be sustained. As regards the first head, regional planning techniques, what is available such as input–output analysis, is more relevant to developed, industrialised countries than to less developed. The second, delimiting rural development planning areas, is necessary, but cannot be described as a technique. The 'design of village production systems' and 'physical planning procedures' are closer to detailed implementation procedures than to diagnostic forward planning. 'Sequential planning for rural development' appears to refer to rolling annual plans at the regional level, not in themselves constituting a technique; and 'information systems for rural plan management', while carrying some potential for the improvement of rural development administration, have not yet been fully developed or widely applied. In general, therefore, we cannot say that there is as yet any coherent 'set' of planning techniques which could constitute a method of 'integrated' rural development planning and thus justify from the side of methodology and approach the concept discussed here.

This is not, of course, to say that regional and area planning in less developed countries is not of extreme importance. These generally mean a desirable increase in the volume of planning activity; better coverage of areas, including backward areas frequently neglected in national macroeconomic plans; attention to all groups within the areas concerned; more comprehensive resource assessment; much needed decentralisation in many cases; improvements in planning machinery at the local level and increases in the supply of manpower for local planning and plan implementation.

All this, however, does not mean that what passes under the head of 'integrated rural development planning' can be usefully so described, or that a 'science' of integrated rural development planning has been evolved which can invariably justify substantial and time-consuming 'master plans'. These could, while providing employment for more expatriate experts, actually obscure a synoptic view of the development possibilities of a region or district.

Notes: Reading 37

1 Vernon W. Ruttan, 'Integrated rural development programs: a skeptical perspective', *International Development Review*, vol. 17, no. 4, 1975.

2 'Region' here is used to refer to an administrative unit within a country. Region and regional planning are, of course, used sometimes to refer to a wide area embracing several countries.

3 Ruttan, loc. cit., p. 9. Since first writing this article I have come to feel that this point is especially important and that interdependencies between groups should be interpreted much more broadly, in political economy terms. Measures to improve standards among the mass of the rural population, for example, or particular target groups within it, should not be developed in abstraction or as purely technical/economic matters.

4 See especially 'An overall evaluation of the special rural development programme', Occasional Paper No. 8, Institute of Development Studies, Nairobi, November 1972.

5 D. G. R. Belshaw, 'Rural development planning: concepts and techniques', *Journal of Agricultural Economics*, vol. 25, no. 3, 1977.

Part Seven

Money and Finance

The systematic survey of the literature on the causes of inflation in developing countries by Kirkpatrick and Nixson (Reading 38) is followed by an article by Chandavarkar (Reading 39) arguing in a neglected area of policy for a much more radical interest rate policy in developing countries.

Reading 38

The Origins of Inflation in Less Developed Countries: a Selective Review

C. H. Kirkpatrick and F.I. Nixson

Inflation in Open Economies, by M. Parkin and G. Zis (Manchester University Press, 1976), pp. 126–74.

1 Introduction

This paper is a selective review of the theoretical and empirical evidence on certain aspects of the post-war inflation experience of less developed countries (LDCs). It is mainly concerned with the factors that are alleged to generate inflationary impulses and the mechanism by which an inflationary spiral comes into being. It does not attempt to provide a comprehensive survey of the many facets of the relationship between inflation and economic development (for a general survey of this relationship, see Thorp (1971)), and it does not directly concern itself with the increases in the world price of traded commodities. Clearly, such price increases are very important (witness the impact of rising oil prices on the LDCs) but they enter the analysis only in so far as the type of development policies pursued by LDCs makes them more vulnerable to this kind of imported inflationary pressure.

2 Comparative Rates of Inflation

Table 6.1 shows the average rates of inflation in different groups of countries during the period 1965–73. The figures reveal that throughout this period the average rate of inflation in the LDCs has been substantially greater than the average rate in the groups of industrial and other developed countries. The data also indicate considerable variation in the average inflation rate in different geographical groups of the LDCs, with the highest rate being experienced in Latin and Central America.

3 The Relevance of 'Orthodox' Analysis to LDCs

The 'orthodox' analysis of inflation is presented in terms of a reversed L-shaped aggregate supply curve and a downward sloping aggregate demand curve. The original Phillips curve hypothesis stated that wage change was caused by excess demand and that the latter could be measured (or proxied) by the inverse of the unemployment rate. This has since been modified to take into account the fact that both sides of the labour market attempt to influence real rather than money wages. It is suggested that the rate of change will equal the expected rate of price change plus an adjustment related to the excess demand for labour (as measured by the level of unemployment) (Parkin (1974)). Expectations are formed by an 'error-learning' process. The reformulated Phillips hypothesis predicts that if a (closed) economy is operated with permanent excess demand (i.e. unemployment is permanently below its equilibrium or 'natural' level) inflation will persistently accelerate. The origins of excess demand are to be found in government monetary and fiscal policies. The 'orthodox' theory of inflation in an open economy attempts to integrate the expectations-augmented Phillips curve analysis with the monetary approach to balance of payments theory. We discuss this in greater detail in section 5 below.

Over the past decade, economists working on the problems of LDCs have become increasingly wary of uncritically applying concepts and theories which have originated in the economic and institutional setting of western, industrialised economies. Seers (1963) early on pointed out the 'limitations of the special case', emphasising the integrated nature of the industrialised economy and the fragmented nature of the LDC, and Streeten (1972) has warned against '. . . the simple transfer of fairly sophisticated concepts from one setting to another without close scrutiny of the institutional differences' (p. 127).

One of the principal ways in which errors enter into analysis has been termed 'misplaced aggregation', that is, it is assumed, incorrectly, that dissimilar items can be analysed in terms of a single category (Streeten (1972)). 'Orthodox' theory places emphasis on the concept of the 'natural' rate of unemployment but we must question the relevance of the more basic concepts of 'employ-

Table 6.1 **Price increases in developed and less developed countries 1965–73(%)**[a]

	Annual average 1965–70	*Change from preceding year*				
		1969	*1970*	*1971*	*1972*	*1973*
Industrial countries	4.2	4.7	5.9	5.4	4.8	7.2
More developed primary producing countries	4.9	4.4	6.2	9.0	9.4	13.2
All less developed countries	13.0	9.1	10.5	10.0	13.0	24.0
Africa	4.0	6.0	4.5	6.0	5.0	7.0
Asia	18.0[b]	6.1	9.3	5.0	7.0	19.0
Middle East	3.0	3.4	4.0	5.0	6.0	10.0
Western hemisphere	15.0	15.8	17.0	15.0	21.0	36.0[b]

Source: IMF *Annual Reports*, 1973, 1974.

Notes:

[a]For the developed countries, the figures are the average of percentage changes in the GNP deflator of each country, weighted by the US dollar value of their GNPs at current prices in the preceding year. For the LDCs the figures are the average of the percentage changes in the consumer prices indices of each country, weighted by the US dollar value of their GNP in 1972.

[b]Excluding one high-inflation country, the Asian figure in the first column would be 7 per cent; with a similar exclusion the western hemisphere figure in the last column would be 21 per cent.

ment' and 'unemployment' within the LDC context. These concepts, as commonly used, imply a homogenous, mobile, adequately trained, wage-earning labour force willing and able to work and responding to incentives. But as Streeten has argued: 'In a society of isolated communities, some of them apathetic or with religious prejudices against certain kinds of work, illiterate and unused to co-operation, the notion "Labour Force" does not make sense' (Streeten (1972), p. 55).

In all LDCs employment in the 'modern' sector represents a small but privileged proportion of the total labour force, strengthened as it usually is by strong trade unions and government legislation (minimum wage legislation, etc.). The great mass of labour is engaged in small-scale, self-employed, low-productivity activities in the 'traditional' sectors of the economy (both rural and urban) and may be idle or underutilised for lengthy periods of time. This has been termed disguised unemployment or underemployment, but differs from the phenomenon, originally noted by Joan Robinson, of workers being forced to accept less remunerative occupations during periods of economic depression, which is of a temporary nature and is eliminated by an increase in the level of effective demand. Disguised unemployment or underemployment in LDCs refers to the mass of the labour force that is permanently engaged in low-productivity activities, and a change in the level of aggregate demand for wage labour has little or no impact on the level of traditional sector underemployment. Concepts such as 'full employment' and the 'natural' rate of unemployment are not meaningful given the disintegrated and fragmented nature of LDC economies.

A second and perhaps more fundamental limitation of 'orthodox' inflation analysis is the use of the concepts of aggregate demand and supply (another example of misplaced aggregation) and the postulation of a ceiling to aggregate demand in real terms that is set by aggregate supply (Myrdal (1968), appendix 2, section 23). The LDC economy is characterised by factor immobility, market imperfection and rigidities and disequilibrium between demand and supply in different sectors of the economy. Substantial underutilisation of resources in some sectors (for example manufacturing; see Little, Scitovsky and Scott (1970), pp. 93–8) coexists with shortages in other sectors of the economy, and market imperfections (and technological constraints) prevent the movement of resources in response to market signals. In these conditions, it is questionable whether the 'orthodox' interpretation of inflation in terms of aggregate demand and supply can be applied. Myrdal rejects the notion of a single ceiling and argues for the 'structural' or 'structuralist' interpretation of inflation which stresses '. . . the fragmentation, the disequilibria, and the lack of balance between supplies and demands in different sectors of the economy and between different groups in the community' (pp. 1926–7).

In other words, there is no overall limitation on aggregate supply; limitations are diverse and specific and inflation can be more usefully analysed in the terms of the structural composition of the economy, taking into account the imperfection of markets and the division of the economy into separate or poorly integrated sectors of economic activity. Inflation is then seen as the result of particular sector bottlenecks in the economy (we discuss what is meant by 'bottlenecks' in Section 4 below) with different types of bottleneck accompanied by '. . . different types of price rigidities, different supply elasticities, different response mechanisms, different degrees of substitutability on the part of the purchaser, and different distributional effects' (Myrdal (1968), p. 1928).

In Section 4 we summarise the 'structuralist' analysis as it has been developed in Latin America. This is not meant to imply that this analysis is relevant only to that area; indeed, Myrdal is referring specifically to South Asia in his discussion of structurally induced (or 'development') inflation. Likewise the lack of references to African economies indicates that until recently, and for a variety of reasons, inflation was not an immediate problem. We would argue that a 'structural' analysis is relevant to that area, although obviously the relative importance of various sectoral constraints will differ between both countries and continents. Inflation in Latin America has posed the greatest problems and has been most intensively studied. It is for these reasons, and because the analyses discussed make it clear that gross imperfections and fragmentation of markets in LDCs make it inappropriate to analyse inflation in terms of aggregate demand and supply relationships, that we devote the following section (with the exception of the empirical, cross-country studies referred to) exclusively to Latin America.

4 'Structuralist' and 'Monetarist' Explanations of Inflation

1 The theoretical issues

The debate over the causes and consequences of inflation in Latin America has largely been between two groups loosely labelled 'structuralists' and 'monetarists'. The two groups do not represent coherent schools of thought; rather they each consist of a certain type of approach to the specific problem of inflation and, more broadly, economic development in general. Roberto de Oliveira Campos (1967) whilst claiming responsibility for having introduced the expressions, at the same time feels the controversy is a spurious one. He argues that structuralists, if in power, would have to adopt monetarist policies as a short-run measure and that monetarists would, in the long run, accept the primacy of structural change. The monetarist is 'a structuralist in a hurry' and the structuralist is 'a monetarist without policy-making responsibility' (pp. 108–9).

Not everyone would agree with this rather facile dismissal of any fundamental difference (apart from one of time period) between 'structuralists' and 'monetarists'. Felix (1961) notes that there is disagreement not only as to the causes of inflation and the efficacy of stabilisation programmes but, as we have already noted above, there is general disagreement on appropriate development policies. Furthermore, he argues that 'structuralists' are usually 'of the left' while 'monetarists' are 'of the right' of the political spectrum. Seers (1964) summarises the argument as follows:

> It is . . . not just a technical issue in economic theory. At the heart of the controversy . . . are two different ways of looking at economic development, in fact two completely different attitudes toward the nature of social change, two different sets of value judgements about the purposes of economic activity and the ends of economic policy, and two incompatible views on what is politically possible (p. 89).

We will first outline the main features of the 'structuralist' and 'monetarist' analyses before returning to the nature of the controversy.

The 'structuralist' argument (often identified with the UN Economic Commission for Latin America (ECLA)) is that inflation is inevitable in an economy that is attempting rapid growth in the presence of structural bottlenecks or constraints, defined as 'certain fundamental facets of the economic, institutional and socio-political structure of the country which in one way or another inhibit expansion' (Thorp (1971), p. 185). Inflation accompanies the transition of the LDC from an 'outward-oriented' export-based economy to an 'inward-oriented' domestic-market-based economy (ISI being the key feature of this process as we shall see below). Such a transition requires massive changes in the socio-economic structure of the LDC which the price mechanism, operating within very imperfect market structures and with limited resource mobility, is unable to achieve: 'Given the imperfections of the system, the result of attempting major structural change had to be shortages and disequilibria on many fronts' (Thorp (1971), p. 186).

The 'structuralist' analysis is concerned largely with the identification and examination of the alleged structural constraints (what Osvaldo Sunkel (1960) in his seminal work refers to as the basic or structural inflationary pressures). These are generally taken to be: (*a*) the inelastic supply of foodstuffs; (*b*) the foreign exchange bottleneck, and (*c*) the financial constraint.

Before discussing these three constraints in greater detail, we must first be clear as to what is meant by the term 'bottlenecks' and its relation to inflation. Edel (1969) points out that there is no reason in theory why an increase in the price of one commodity should raise the general price level and provoke an inflationary spiral. In an open economy, an increase in imports can keep prices constant, and in a closed economy, neoclassical theory would predict that a rise in the relative price of one type of goods (for example food) would lead to a shift in demand to other goods and a reallocation of the factors of production, leading to the restoration of an equilibrium position. But if the prices of manufactured goods are inflexible downwards, a rise in food prices (with other prices constant) raises the average price level. In turn, if industrial wages are tied to consumer prices, they will rise, leading to an upward movement in industrial prices. The change in relative prices may be insufficient to lead to a shift in demand, and thus an inflationary spiral develops. W. A. Lewis in his 'Closing Remarks' in Baer and Kerstenetzky (1964) distinguishes between the factors that start a price rise and the spiral processes that keep prices rising (the above factors plus budget deficits, devaluations and rising import prices) and argues that the inflationary spiral may continue for reasons unconnected with the original cause. In other words, the price increase stemming from the bottleneck is not a once-and-for-all change in relative prices but instead may trigger off an inflationary spiral. However, as we shall see below, an effective propagation or transmission mechanism is necessary for the inflationary spiral to manifest itself.

The structuralists argue that urbanisation and rising incomes have led to a rapidly rising demand for foodstuffs which cannot be met by the agricultural sector. The supply response of the agricultural sector is poor because of the structural constraints within that sector—the domination either by large non-capitalistic latifundia which are not profit maximisers, or by minifundia operated almost at a subsistence level and barely integrated into the market economy (Baer (1967), p. 8)—and this inelastic supply constitutes a structural inflationary factor. Sunkel (1960) notes with respect to Chile (the country in which the structuralist analysis originated) that:

> . . . the stagnation of global agricultural production cannot be attributed to market, demand and, or price conditions, but must be due to factors inherent in the institutional and economic structure of the main part of the agricultural sector itself (p. 115).

The 'monetarist' argues that the alleged structural inelasticity of food supplies is not in fact structural at all but rather results from the all too frequent administrative control of food prices, imposed by the government in order to protect the urban consumer and avoid growing pressures for wage increases. This interference with the operation of market forces has a disincentive effect on food producers, but this is a distortion induced by administrative controls and is not inherent in the structure of land ownership (Campos (1961), p. 112).

Edel (1969), whose study we shall discuss in greater detail below, tested the agricultural supply bottleneck hypothesis for eight Latin American countries. He did not find a perfect relationship between food supply and inflation but he concluded that the direction of the relationship was the one indicated by the 'structuralist' analysis (inadequate food production meant more inflation, relative rises in food prices, more food imports, and slower growth in other sectors of the economy).

The second major bottleneck identified by the 'structuralists' is the foreign exchange bottleneck, dealt with in greater detail in Section 5 below. The alleged bottleneck arises because the rate of growth of total foreign exchange receipts (earnings from exports and capital inflows) is not sufficient to meet rapidly rising import demands generated by accelerated development efforts, rapid population growth and attempts to industrialise which take place within the environment of imperfect factor mobility, technological limitations and structural imbalances noted above. The structurally induced balance of payments deficit is not cured by devaluation, the latter only adding to the inflationary spiral, and the import constraint is an important stimulus to ISI, the nature and consequences of which we discuss in Section 7. Import shortages and rising import prices trigger off cumulative price rises in a fashion similar to the process described above with respect to the agricultural sector bottleneck. Baer (1967) notes that

> control of imports . . . will create shortages of many formerly imported goods. The relative domestic price of these goods will rise and thus contribute to the inflationary forces . . . balance of payments difficulties will sooner or later force countries to devalue their currencies; this will also have the effect of an immediate upward push on the price level, especially if imports consist of many consumer goods, including basic foodstuffs, which the agriculturally inelastic country might be forced to import (p. 9).

It is further argued that instability of export proceeds is inflationary in that when it leads to a reduction in government revenues the government is forced to resort to deficit financing to maintain relatively inflexible levels of expenditure.

The 'monetarist' counter-argument is that part at least of the slow growth of exports is policy rather than structurally induced. Exchange rates are typically overvalued, and development efforts emphasise 'inward-looking' ISI rather than 'outward-looking' policies aimed at maximising traditional exports and developing new lines. It is further argued that the import quantum has been maintained, on the average, for Latin America, despite the alleged external bottleneck, and that therefore there has been no inflationary decrease in the availability of imported goods.

The third bottleneck, identified by some 'structuralist' writers but not others, is the lack of internal financial resources. Rapid urbanisation and the industrialisation effort have increased the range of necessary government activities, mainly in the sphere of physical and social infrastructure facilities, but government revenue has not expanded at a sufficiently rapid rate. Baer (1967) describes the tax-collecting bureaucracies of Latin America as 'antiquated, inefficient and sometimes corrupt' (p. 10). The necessary reform of these bureaucracies is a long-run problem whereas in the shorter run massive infrastructure investment is an essential condition of more rapid economic growth. The dilemma is usually solved by recourse to deficit financing, with inflationary consequences. The problem is compounded by the low rate of private capital formation and its preference for safe, non-productive investments (land and property, foreign bank accounts, etc.) which, it is alleged, forces the government to play a larger role in capital formation than would otherwise be the case and does not provide a sufficient volume of investment to absorb into productive employment the rapidly growing population.[1] In addition to these problems, other writers (for example Myrdal (1968), pp. 1928–9) argue that bottlenecks in other sectors—electricity, fuel, imported raw materials, transport, repair facilities and credit facilities—are also of importance in giving rise to inflationary pressures.

In addition to these basic inflationary pressures, Sunkel (1960) draws attention to so-called exogenous inflation pressures. These would include upward movements in the prices of imported goods and services and major increases in public expenditure arising out of natural disasters or political measures. In addition, we have cumulative inflationary pressures which are induced by inflation itself. In Chile, Sunkel argues that these pressures are an increasing function of the extent and the rate of inflation and they consist of the orientation of investment (already referred to above), expectations, the negative impact of inflation on productivity (including the distortions introduced into the price system by price controls) and the lack of export incentives.

If the structural constraints outlined above are to give rise to price increases, which in turn lead to a rapid and continuous increase in the general price level, it is obvious that there must exist an effective transmission or propagation mechanism which permits the manifestation of the various inflationary pressures. Few 'structuralist' writers (or at least the interpreters of the 'structuralist' position) pay much attention to this mechanism, yet it is clear that if various groups or classes in society did not attempt to maintain their relative positions in the face of price increases, the chances of an inflationary spiral being generated would be much reduced. In Chile, for example, Sunkel (1960) argues that the propagation mechanism has resulted from the inability of the political system to resolve two major struggles of economic interests, that of the distribution of income between different social classes and that of the distribution of the productive resources of the community between the public and the private sectors of the economy. The propagation mechanism is thus seen as:

> . . . the ability of the different economic sectors and social groups continually to readjust their real income or expenditure: the wage-earning group through readjustment of salaries, wages and other benefits; private enterprise through price increases, and the public sector through an increase in nominal fiscal expenditure (p. 111).

One of the main components of Sunkel's propagation mechanism is the budget deficit (the third major bottleneck referred to above) which leads to an increase in the supply of money. Public expenditure is not easily reduced, and we have already noted the insufficient expansion of tax revenue. The public sector deficit thus represents '. . . the existence of a number of structural problems which preclude the realisation of a balanced-budget policy' and the propagation mechanism of the public sector inflationary pressures consists of '. . . the financing of the deficit by loans from the banking system, issuing bonds to the social security institutions, revaluation of monetary reserves and other measures related to the money supply. . . .' (Sunkel (1960), p. 122). For the private sector, 'price increases supported by passive reaction of the monetary and credit system constitutes the propagation mechanism of the inflationary pressures to which the business sector is subjected' (p. 123).

Thus to the 'structuralist' an increase in the supply of money is seen as a permissive factor which allows the inflationary spiral to manifest itself and become cumulative—it is a symptom of the structural rigidities which give rise to the inflationary pressures, rather than the cause of the inflation itself. In other words the increase in the supply of money is a necessary condition for the rise in the overall level of prices, but it is not regarded as a sufficient condition. We return to this point below.[2]

Arising out of Sunkel's analysis of the propagation mechanism is what Thorp (1971) refers to as the 'income shares approach' to inflation. Inflation is seen as the means of reconciling the conflicting objectives of different social groups, with the attempts of weak governments to satisfy all interests inevitably leading to inflation. This is not acceptable as an explanation of the initiation of inflation and is only really an explanation of how various groups attempt to defend their relative economic positions.

It is often assumed that 'structuralist' writers favour inflation as a means of accelerating economic growth, but this is not generally the case. They are concerned with the problem of how to make stability compatible with economic development but they argue that price stability can only be achieved through economic growth, which is a longer-run process. Inflation cannot be curbed in the short run without cost, and although they do not in general question the efficacy of monetary stabilisation policies, they do question the social and economic costs of stability achieved at the expense of full capacity utilisation and economic growth. In other words, inflation is preferred to stagnation.

The Latin American 'monetarist' analysis of inflation is relatively straightforward. Inflation originates in and is maintained by expansionist monetary and fiscal policies, comprising government deficit spending (coupled with the operation of inefficient state enterprises and uneconomic pricing policies), expansionist credit policies and the expansionary exchange operations of central banks. The rate of inflation needs to be drastically reduced (and the concomitant distortions in the economy eliminated) via the curbing of excess demand through monetary and fiscal policies, the control of wage increases and the elimination of subsidised exchange rates, with the help, wherever possible, of international financial assistance.

It is important to note that the 'monetarists' do not deny the existence of 'structural' rigidities and bottlenecks in LDCs, but they argue that such bottlenecks are not in fact 'structural' or 'autonomous' in nature. They result from the price and exchange rate distortions which are generated by the inflation itself and government attempts to reduce the rate of price increases (price controls on foodstuffs, overvalued exchange rates, high tariff barriers and direct import controls, etc.). The causal relationship is reversed, and in 'monetarist' eyes the bottlenecks in the economy retarding growth will be eliminated when inflation is brought under control. Furthermore, with a suitably reformed tax structure and with less inflation and perhaps less government intervention, the private sector would be able to play a larger role in the development process, thus reducing the need for government deficit financing. Campos (1967) maintains that the majority of 'monetarists' appear to recognise the 'social priority of development', but insists that stable and sustained growth can best be achieved in an environment of monetary stability.

Campos (1967) argues that 'monetarists' should perhaps be called 'fiscalists' in that the monetarist approach not only includes the use of traditional monetary weapons (the effectiveness of which may be very limited because of the underdeveloped nature of financial markets characteristic of LDCs) but also places emphasis on the use of fiscal policies. He maintains that the effectiveness of monetary weapons is greater in the case of demand inflation than of cost inflation, and this is also the case if the objective is to curb investment rather than consumption. Finally, monetary policies have an asymmetrical effect in that it is easier to promote the expansion of certain selected sectors than it is to enforce the restriction of certain undesirable sectors. Campos concludes that:

> . . . monetary weapons, though indispensable ingredients in anti-inflationary programs, have to be used in prudent combination with fiscal policies (p. 113).

The 'monetarist' analysis leads us directly to the controversy over the need for, and efficacy of, stabilisation policies. The 'monetarist' solution—the removal of budget deficits, the restraint of credit and the elimination of distortions in the market mechanism (especially the establishment of an 'equilibrium' rate of exchange) —forms the basis of IMF-sponsored stabilisation programmes. 'Structuralists' do not deny that monetary variables are partial determinants of inflation (in so far as inflation could not continue for long without monetary expansion)[3] but they are basically concerned with the underlying forces which put such pressure on the monetary authorities as to make the expansion of the money supply almost inevitable. Even if total demand were reduced, the underlying structural inflationary pressures would still persist and short-term stabilisation would in fact be detrimental to growth because it would prevent the realisation of the longer-run structural changes essential to the eventual elimination of inflation (Grunwald (1961), pp. 96–7; Thorp (1971), p. 198).

Numerous stabilisation programmes have been imposed upon various Latin American economies. Thorp (1971, pp. 204–7) characterises them as 'costly failures' aggravating the basic inflationary pressures and severely depressing output. In Argentina, for example, in 1959 (the first year of a severe stabilisation programme) output fell while prices rose 102 per cent. The improvement in the following two years originated from an inflow of foreign exchange, but when that came to an end in 1961 the underlying structural conditions remained unaltered and the 1959 experience was repeated in 1962–3 (Eshag and Thorp (1965)). Felix (1964, pp. 392–6) argues that IMF stabilisation programmes worked against the necessary reallocation of resources and that '. . . they were based on a misappraisal of where some of the leading difficulties lay, as well as on an erroneous normative perspective'.

The 'monetarists' ' counter argument would be that the stabilisation programmes had not been rigorously adhered to. In Chile, the stabilisation programme introduced in 1956 (the result of the Klein-Saks Mission of 1954) achieved an initial but short-lasting success in reducing the rate of inflation. Grunwald (1961) argues that it was precisely the 'structuralist' aspects of the programme (for example, tax reforms) that were politically unacceptable, and the stagnation of economic activity and the rise in unemployment exerted pressure to ease credit and wage restraints. Sunkel (1960) notes that the monetary manifestations of inflation became less marked but

> . . . the structural, exogenous and cumulative inflationary pressures remained latent, since the other stabilisation measures—devaluation and exchange reform, improvement of agricultural prices and the rise in utility rates—did not actually counteract these pressures but rather allowed them free influence on the price system (pp. 124–5).

As Thorp points out, the two key factors in the success of a stabilisation programme are the impact on the external sector and the ability of labour to maintain its share of national income. An inflow of foreign capital can alleviate the deflationary impact of domestic credit restrictions, and the lack of an organised labour movement (or government repression of that movement) permits a regressive shift in income distribution which further aggravates the disequilibrium between the structure of the production and the composition of demand (Sunkel (1960), p. 126).

Prebisch (1961) maintains that the contraction of economic activity is the result of a particular type of anti-inflationary policy, rather than the inevitable result of checking the inflationary process. Campos (1967) is critical of certain aspects of IMF stabilisation programmes,[4] arguing that they need to be more flexible, and Thorp (1971) notes that towards the end of the 1960s the IMF was prepared to co-operate in more orthodox stabilisation programmes and was beginning to acknowledge the importance of maintaining public investment expenditures.

The 'monetarists' quite rightly point out that the 'structuralists' do not have a coherent, short-run anti-inflation programme to replace IMF-sponsored measures. 'Structuralists' stress the need for economic and social reforms to give greater balance and flexibility to the productive structure and greater social unity. Such measures include lessening the vulnerability of the economy to foreign trade instability, increasing the elasticity of supply of the output of various productive sectors (via government investment in transportation, marketing facilities, irrigation, provision of credit and technical advice) and raising the living standards of the great mass of the population. But they are vague as to what would happen during the transition period when these reforms were working themselves out. Grunwald (1961) argues that it is not surprising that the 'structuralists' do not have such a programme, as they have never been in a policy-making position.

Perhaps of greater importance is the distinction that Felix (1961) makes between those 'structuralists' who would work within the social framework in an attempt to reform it and for whom reconciliation with the 'monetarists' is theoretically possible and those who would see revolutionary change as an essential condition of development.

As we pointed out at the beginning of this section, the debate over inflation is only one aspect of the debate over the objectives and policies of development in general. 'Structuralists' such as Prebisch (1961) argue that:

> the general mistake persists of considering inflation as a purely monetary phenomenon as such. Inflation cannot be explained as something divorced from the economic and social maladjustments and stresses to which the economic development of our countries gives rise. Nor can serious thought be given to autonomous anti-inflationary policy, as if only monetary considerations were involved; it must be an integral part of development policy (p. 346).

Campos (1961), on the other hand, argues that the 'structuralists' have failed to distinguish between autonomous and policy-induced bottlenecks, and restates the 'monetarist' (or 'fiscalist') position:

> . . . the role of old-fashioned monetary and fiscal policy is vitally important. Money factors are not residual but at the very core of the process. The inflated countries are those that choose incompatible targets (p. 73).

There are certainly three criticisms that can legitimately be made of the 'structuralist' analysis (or at least the more popular versions of that analysis). Firstly, their emphasis on two or three bottlenecks and their presentation of a somewhat rigid and mechanical analysis of the operation of the bottlenecks leads to overgeneralisation (often easy to refute with specific examples) and the downgrading in importance of the actual (as opposed to the hypothetical) policy choices that a government is faced with. Within a given socio-political environment, a government is 'forced' to pursue certain policies (inflation is, for example, an 'easier' political alternative than land reform, or a reduction in the consumption of upper-income groups), and although the result may be a policy-induced constraint, it is no less the outcome of a particular economic, political and institutional structure. We do not agree with Olivera's distinction between 'structural inflation' and 'structural proneness' to inflation. We would argue for a broadly defined 'structural' (as opposed to 'structuralist') analysis of inflation and would agree with Sunkel when he states:

> . . . inflation does not occur *in vacuo* but as part of a country's historical, social, political and institutional evolution . . . *the underlying causes of inflation in underdeveloped countries are to be found in basic economic development problems and in the structural characteristics of the system of production in these countries* (Sunkel (1960), p. 108; emphasis in original).

The second criticism is that too little attention in 'structuralist' analysis, with the notable exception of Sunkel, has been given to the nature and the role of the propagation mechanism and the expansion of the money supply that accompanies the inflationary process. We have seen that a propagation mechanism is necessary to transmit basic inflationary pressures and that an increase in the supply of money is necessary (other things being equal) for the manifestation of inflationary price rises. The 'structuralist' assertion that the increase in the money supply is merely a permissive factor may tend to obscure the wider socio-economic framework within which this policy option is chosen. Anticipating the discussion of Section 4 (2) below, both schools of thought can accept the proposition that changes in the money supply occur in response to political factors, but the basic question remains as to whether these changes permit or are the actual cause of the inflationary process (a question to which some of the empirical studies discussed below address themselves).[5]

The third criticism concerns the distribution of income. Logically, this should be the focus of attention of every 'structuralist' analysis. Most LDCs are characterised by a high degree of inequality (Chenery *et al.* (1974)) which is an important determinant of the pattern of domestic demand and the structure of imports, the composition of industrial output and, through the technology adopted, the creation of employment opportunities. Furthermore, the distribution of economic and hence political power determines the range of policy options any particular government is likely to pursue, and the process of inflation itself significantly alters the economic and political power structure of the inflating economy. The fact that many 'structuralist' analyses abstract from distributional questions weakens both their analytical validity and their general applicability.

2 *Empirical tests of the 'structuralist' and 'monetarist' hypotheses*

An important test of one aspect of the 'structuralist' analysis has been carried out by Edel (1969) in his empirical study of the alleged food supply bottlenecks in eight Latin American countries. He tests two propositions: (i) that food has lagged behind the required rate of growth, and (ii) that this agricultural lag is associated with inflation, balance of payments difficulties, and stagnation.

The adequacy of food supply is defined as that rate of autonomous growth of production (resulting from the adoption of new techniques, increases in labour force and area of production, etc.) sufficient to satisfy demand without any change in relative prices. Edel found that Mexico, Brazil, and Venezuela outpaced or at least approximately equalled food requirements. Taking into account price changes, he found that the five countries with inadequate growth rates (Chile, Columbia, Peru, Uruguay, and Argentina) all had increasing relative food prices and thus the inadequate growth could not have been a function of price deterioration. He concluded:

> The trend or autonomous rate of growth of food output would thus seem to be a more important determinant of the adequacy of a country's agriculture than the existence of a positive response to prices. . . . Although it may be incorrect in these countries to speak of 'inelastic supply' as the central aspect of the problem, it seems justifiable to speak of 'inadequacy' of production trends in Chile, Columbia, Peru, Uruguay and Argentina and to add inelasticity as a factor, perhaps, in the last three (pp. 41–2).

He did not find a perfect relationship between food supply and inflation but the evidence justified the conclusion that

> . . . the direction of the relationship is the one indicated by the structuralist theory that less adequate food production means more inflation, as well as relative rises in the food prices, more food imports, and slower growth in other sectors of the economy (pp. 135–6).

Chile, Peru, Argentina and Uruguay in particular showed more clearly evidence of these pressures.

Several factors modified the basic structuralist thesis:

1 Increased foreign exchange earnings allowed imports when production was inadequate (Venezuela and Peru in the early 1960s);
2 The existence of an exportable surplus or a high level of consumption cushioned a country against having to increase imports (Argentina, Uruguay);
3 A change in the distribution of income changed the demand for food (Argentina in 1959), and
4 The possibilities of belt-tightening and the elimination of luxury imports permitted imports to be cut despite the inadequate expansion of food production when foreign exchange was lacking (Columbia).

These factors do not invalidate the 'structuralist' model. Once the *ceteris paribus* conditions are taken into account, the 'production lag' model holds for some Latin American countries. Edel further concludes that the degree of price control on foodstuffs does not appear to be related systematically to agricultural performance for all the countries studied, whereas there is considerable evidence that land tenure and low productivity are related to one another.

Edel considered that Brazil came closest to conformity with the monetarist model, and this conclusion has been strongly supported by Kahil (1973). The four alleged structural constraints that Kahil analyses are the agricultural sector bottleneck, the inadequate mobility of capital, the external sector bottleneck and the effect on demand and costs of rapid urbanisation. His major conclusions are: a rural/urban price spiral was not generated by an inelastic supply of agricultural produce; urbanisation itself has not been responsible for inflationary pressures (specifically, it did not lead to an increase in the purchasing power of migrants); the rigidity of capital supply did not have much influence on the price level; the terms of trade throughout the period studied (1946–63) were more favourable to Brazil than at any time since the mid-1930s, and that the chief cause of increasing balance of payments disequilibria was the stagnation of the export quantum, resulting from inflation and faulty economic policies; and finally, there was no evidence that bottlenecks in transport or energy contributed to rising price levels or that the lack of labour (especially skilled) pushed up industrial prices.

Kahil argues that:

> . . . the structural weaknesses of the economy cannot

> have played a significant role in the evolution of the price level from 1946 to 1964, and . . . their aggravation towards the end of the period was more an effect than a cause of the acceleration of inflation (p. 327).

Price rises were caused by large and growing public deficits, a too rapid expansion of bank credit in the early years, and later unnecessarily large and increasingly frequent increases in legal minimum wages. At the early stages of inflation, these three factors are independent of one another but as inflation accelerates, they interact in such a way that it is impossible to say which is cause, which is effect. As price rises become increasingly rapid, '. . . the Central Bank is *compelled* to supply the public sector with a growing volume of funds, while the commercial banks are *forced* to expand loans to the private sector at an accelerated pace, and wages and salaries *have* to be raised again and again to restore the rapidly declining standard of living of workers and employees' (p. 329; emphasis in original). Thus the basic causes of inflation appear to become mere parts of the structuralist propagation mechanism—'mere passive elements in an uncontrollable process which seems to have a life of its own, and dominates the whole economy' (p. 330).

Having reached a strong monetarist conclusion, Kahil then performs a surprising (and undoubtedly unintentional) *volte-face* and argues that the factors ultimately responsible for inflation were political rather than economic. The two main policy aims of the 1950s were rapid industrialisation and the winning of the allegiance of the urban masses while at the same time serving the interests of other politically important groups. This, he argues, explains the incoherent and inflationary nature of many government policies: '. . . the multifarious and frequently incompatible policy decisions taken by authorities were largely motivated by their strong determination to achieve their two major objectives simultaneously' (p. 331). In other words, inflation was the outcome of the attempt by the State to fulfill its development objectives and grant privileges (albeit temporary and illusory) to mutually antagonistic groups or classes. This conclusion is remarkably similar to the one reached above (and stated in the context of western developed economies by Devine (1974)) and is consistent with the structural analysis of inflation in LDCs advanced in this paper. In Brazil, Kahil argues that it was the big industrialists, bankers, merchants, and contractors who were most favoured by inflation and who were most likely to resist stabilisation measures. But inflation began to accelerate at the end of 1958, social and political conflicts intensified, and a combination of economic and political factors eventually precipitated the military coup of 1964.

The study by Harberger (1963) of inflation in Chile has been the most influential empirical analysis of inflation in the monetarist tradition in Latin America, and subsequent econometric studies by Diaz-Alejandro (1965), Diz (1970), and Vogel (1974) are extensions of the basic Harberger model.

Harberger's study of Chilean inflation covers the period from 1939 to 1958, during which time inflation was almost continuous, and the wholesale price index and the cost of living index increased more than eightfold. The approach is basically a monetarist one, and Harberger tests the hypothesis of a stable demand function for real balances by regressing the annual rate of price change in the cost of living index upon the percentage change in money supply during the present and preceding year and the percentage change in real income during the present year. Expected changes in the cost of holding idle balances are allowed for by introducing past changes in the rate of inflation as an additional independent variable. Harberger also attempts to clarify the role of wage changes in the Chilean inflation, and wage changes are used as an additional independent variable in the regression equation. The role of wages in the inflationary process has been a subject of controversy in Chile (as elsewhere) with, at the one extreme, 'monetarists' arguing that wages simply respond in a passive fashion to inflationary forces which are monetary in origin, while at the other extreme there is the view that wages are the principal factor in explaining the rate of inflation, and that once their effect has been taken into account monetary variables will not add to the explanation of the inflationary process.

During the whole of the period investigated by Harberger, there was a form of minimum wage for public sector employees which was revised upward annually, and was set largely as the result of political negotiations among parties in the congress. Once a certain percentage increase in this minimum wage had been determined, wage contracts in the industrial sector of the economy were adjusted at least to match this percentage increase, and private wages tended subsequently to drift upward in response to the pressures of the labour market and collective bargaining. Harberger argues that in such circumstances wage movements could have played an active part in the inflationary process.

The empirical results obtained by Harberger would appear to support the monetarist interpretation, with each of the monetary variables statistically significant and the inclusion of the wages variable failing to increase the overall explanatory power of the monetary variables. However, Harberger is careful not to adopt the strict monetarist position that would be suggested by a superficial inspection of the results. He argues that:

> these results suggest that one of the major roles of the wage variable was indeed as a 'transmitter' of inflation from one period to the next, responding to the monetary expansion of the past period and including monetary expansion in the subsequent period. The wage variable does not significantly alter the predictions . . . and in this sense one does not 'need' it. . . . The wage variable does not add significantly to the

variation in the rate of inflation explained by monetary factors: in this sense too . . . one does not 'need' it. But none of this denies that if wage changes had tended in the period to be unaccompanied by monetary expansion, prices would have none the less responded. Nor does it deny that prior wages rises were an important factor in inducing monetary expansion during the period. It only says that during this period monetary expansions were typically great enough to 'finance' prior wage changes, and that on top of this, monetary expansions had independent variations, which also influenced the price level in much the same way as if they had been accompanied by wage changes (pp. 246–7).

As previously mentioned, the studies by Diaz-Alejandro, Diz, and Vogel are extensions of the basic Harberger model, and therefore require less detailed discussion. In his study of Argentina, Diaz-Alejandro regresses various indices of inflation (wholesale price index, components of that index, cost of living index) on four independent variables—money supply, real gross domestic product plus merchandise imports, hourly money wage rates in industry, and the exchange rate. All variables are expressed as annual rates of change, with observations covering the period 1945–62. The coefficients are generally statistically significant and have the expected signs. Diaz-Alejandro finds that changes in wage rates are highly correlated with subsequent changes in the money supply, while changes in the money supply do not appear to have a significant influence on subsequent changes in wage rates. He argues that the high rates of inflation combined with the fall in real national product that occurred in several periods reflect the existence of cost-push inflation so that the monetary authority is faced with increasing unemployment if it does not permit the money supply to grow in response to increases in wage rates. The author's main conclusion is therefore that the money supply played only a permissive role in Argentina's inflation and was not the underlying cause.

The study by Diz. also examines the experience of Argentina, covering the period 1935–62. Two dependent variables are used (wholesale price and cost of living indices), and the independent variables used are: money supply (with two definitions, one including and the other excluding savings and time deposits), real income, an index of nominal wages, the official exchange rate, and a measure of price expectations. In the regression results, the money supply, real income, and expectations coefficients are statistically significant and exhibit the expected sign. The wage coefficients are not significant and the exchange rate coefficients, although significant, suggest a highly inelastic response of prices to changes in the exchange rate. Diz interprets his findings that changes in the money supply have a substantial impact on the rate of inflation as evidence in support of the 'monetarist' analysis of inflation. His conclusions are that:

> from 1935 to 1962 the changes in the rate of change in money significantly affected the behaviour of the rate of inflation, through a process of adjustment which involved considerable time. The results indicate that the adjustment of prices to an acceleration of money seemed to require no less than two years and that it involved initial overshooting and later deceleration of prices. Changes in the expected rate of change in prices and real income also affected significantly the rate of inflation. The role of devaluations and wage increases in the Argentine inflationary process was also analysed, but the results show that their influence on the rate of inflation failed to achieve the levels and significance usually attributed to them (p. 123).

Vogel has extended the Harberger model to sixteen Latin American countries for the period 1950–69. The dependent variable is the consumer price index, and the independent variables are money supply (currency plus demand deposits), real income (nominal GNP deflated by the consumer price index), and past changes in the rate of inflation (as a proxy for the expected cost of holding real balances). All variables are annual and are expressed as percentage changes. 'Structural' variables, such as wage changes and exchange rate changes are not included in the analysis. The paper reports the results obtained from using pooled data covering time-series and cross-section observations, and for each country separately. The results obtained from the pooled data exhibited a high level of overall explanatory power, and the coefficients of the independent variables exhibited the correct sign and were statistically significant (with the exception of the lagged change in inflation rate variable). The results of the individual country regressions were less favourable, and they revealed considerable differences between countries. The value of the correlation coefficient ranged from 0.87 to 0.00, and some of the coefficients of money supply and real income variables were either statistically insignificant or exhibited an incorrect sign.

On the basis of these results Vogel concludes that:

> the most important result of the present study . . . is that a purely monetarist model, with no structuralist variables, reveals little heterogeneity among Latin American countries, in spite of their extreme diversity. The substantial differences in rates of inflation among these countries cannot under the present model be attributed to structural differences, but must rather be attributed primarily to differences in the behaviour of the money supply (p. 113).

Ignoring the question of whether his regression results are sufficiently robust to warrant this conclusion, Vogel misinterprets the structuralist position when he implies that structuralists argue that inflation can be explained by 'structural differences', in isolation from or independently of changes in the monetary environment. Vogel's findings are not inconsistent with the 'structural' interpretation of Latin American inflationary experience (although this is not meant to imply that there would be agreement as to the exact nature of the relationship between changes in the money supply and changes in prices), and adherents to the structural hypothesis would be in full agreement with his conclusion that:

> the importance of the money supply suggests that further research is needed on its determination, particularly since the studies of Harberger, Diaz-Alejandro and Diz indicate that the money supply may not be exogenous in every Latin American country (p. 113).

The study by Argy (1970) is an attempt 'to appraise the contribution of structural elements in inflation in developing countries' (p. 73), and it differs from those so far discussed in that it is based entirely on cross-sectional data. The author computed a variety of indices to represent four structural constraints—the foreign exchange bottleneck, the export instability bottleneck, the agricultural bottleneck and the demand shift constraint—for twenty-two LDCs using data averaged over the period 1958–65. Two alternative indicators were used to represent the foreign exchange constraint: the average annual percentage change in net barter terms of trade, and the average import ratio for the period 1954–8. The agricultural bottleneck was tested using two alternative measures of excess demand for agricultural production. For each country, the rate of growth of demand for agricultural output was calculated by assuming that the elasticity of demand with respect to population growth was unity, while the income elasticity of demand was assumed to be 0.6. The first measure of excess demand was taken as the difference between this assumed growth rate of demand and the actual rate of growth of agricultural production in each of the countries in the sample. The second measure was the average annual rate of change in food prices minus the average rate of change in the cost of living for each country. The export instability hypothesis (that, other things being equal, fluctuations in export receipts will tend to create an upward movement in the price level) was tested using two measures of export variability. The first index used was the variance of the annual percentage changes in dollar export receipts. To allow for the possibility of a lag in adjustment, a second index was calculated using the variances for the years 1958–64. The demand-shift hypothesis (that shifts in the sectoral composition of demand will cause an upward movement in the price level) was tested using an index based on the changes in the weights of eight different sectors in each country's economy that occurred between 1958–9 and 1964–5. Two further variables were used in the regression analysis: the government deficit rate and the rate of change in the money supply. The variables were tested in a variety of combinations—structural only, monetary only, structural and monetary—using ordinary least squares linear regression analysis. On the basis of the results obtained, Argy concludes that 'the results for structuralist variables are, not surprisingly, poor' (p. 38) and that 'the monetary variables perform very well. In every case the addition of a monetary variable to structuralist variables improved substantially the results' (p. 83).

However, Argy's findings are subject to a number of serious limitations. First, as Argy himself acknowledges, it is extremely difficult to devise appropriate indicators of structural constraints, and the indices used are in most cases of limited value. For example, changes in the sectoral weights may represent changes in the rates of growth of different sectors, rather than shifts in demand; changes in the barter terms of trade may bear little relationship to changes in import capacity; changes in the import ratio are an inadequate measure of the severity of the foreign exchange constraint; the assumptions of unity elasticity of demand for food with respect to the population and 0.6 with respect to income are arbitrary; the relationship between variability in export receipts and inflation will vary significantly between countries depending upon the economic and institutional features of the economy. Second, there is a strong possibility of significant multicollinearity between the independent variables used in the regression analysis. For example, variations in export receipts can be expected to affect the import ratio, changes in sectoral composition will influence agricultural production: furthermore, the change in agricultural prices used in calculating the agricultural bottleneck index will be an important component of the dependent variable. A third, and more fundamental, criticism of Argy's analysis is that his findings, and conclusion that 'monetary variables predominate in accounting for rates of inflation in developing countries' (p. 84), contributes little to our understanding of the basic causes of inflation in LDCs. As we have already seen, little weight can be given to the statistical tests of the 'structuralist' variables, largely because of the difficulty of deriving testable hypotheses from 'structuralist' theory. The fact that monetary variables are found to have a high correlation with the rate of inflation is a result that will cause little surprise to either 'monetarists' or 'structuralists': evidence of correlation fails to provide us with an understanding of the underlying causal relationships that exist between structural constraints, monetary expansion and inflation.

The various studies that have been described in this section of the paper illustrate the immense difficulties that arise in attempting to assess empirically the relative importance of the 'structural' and 'monetary' factors in inflation in LDCs. The studies of Harberger, Diaz-Alejandro, Diz and Vogel illustrate both how different results can arise from an examination of the same time period, and how very different conclusions about the monetarist-structuralist controversy can be reached from essentially similar findings. In the case of Kahil, an initial monetarist interpretation can in fact be shown to be consistent with the structural analysis of inflation. The fundamental problem of distinguishing cause from effect, as distinct from discovering evidence of correlation, has limited the usefulness of existing quantitative investigations (with the exception of Edel's study). Nevertheless, at the very least it can be said that a careful examination of the empirical studies that have so far been undertaken neither discredits nor disproves the structural analysis of the causes of inflation in LDCs.

5 The Foreign Exchange Constraint

An important element in the structuralist interpretation of inflation is the notion of a foreign exchange bottleneck. Many LDCs are faced with persistent balance of payments difficulties which are the result of the rapidly rising import demands implicit in a programme of planned economic development, imperfect factor mobility, and insufficiently rapid growth in foreign exchange receipts. Both demand and supply constraints frequently prevent the LDCs from achieving significant increases in export receipts, the international reserves of most LDCs are at a critically low level, and inflows of external capital do not, with certain notable exceptions, account for a significant proportion of total foreign exchange receipts.[6] Inadequate foreign exchange receipts constitute an effective structural constraint upon the growth and development of the economy, since

> . . . rapid growth requires a large increase in the supplies of machinery and equipment, raw materials and other manufactured goods that are typically imported in a poor country. The more rapid the rate of growth, the larger the reallocation of labour and capital away from traditional patterns that will be needed to prevent bottlenecks developing. If this reallocation is not sufficiently rapid, shortages of imported goods will provide a limit to further growth quite apart from the investment limitations. The import limit reflects the inability of the economy to provide the composition of output—from domestic sources plus imports—that is required by its level of income, rate of investment and pattern of consumer demand. In cases of acute shortages of imported goods the economy will be unable to transform potential savings into investment because of insufficient supplies of investment goods.[7]

The foreign exchange bottleneck argument implies therefore that the typical LDC will experience persistent pressure on its balance of payments, with a permanent tendency for the foreign balance to move into deficit.[8]

The notion of the foreign exchange constraint is contrary to the predictions of the monetary approach to balance of payments theory, which represents a revival of the price-specie-flow theory originally advanced by David Hume. This analysis showed that the amount of money in an economy would be adjusted to the demand for it through changes in the balance of payments, induced by the effects on relative money price levels of excess demands for and supplies of money. The fundamental element in the monetary theory of the balance of payments is therefore the existence of a stable demand for money function, which is determined by the level of real income and the opportunity cost of holding money. If each of these determinants remains constant the monetary approach can be regarded as a theory of the rate of inflation, whereby the price level will adjust to ensure that whatever the stock of nominal money, the level of money in real terms will be equal to the amount demanded. Thus the nominal money supply determines the price level. In an open economy, the supply of money is given by the sum of domestic credit and international reserves: a change in the balance of payments therefore will affect the nominal money supply. In a world of fixed exchange rates where each economy is operating at the full employment level of output, the rate of inflation in the world price level is determined by the rate of expansion of the international money supply (which is equal to the sum of the increase in each country's domestic money supply), and in equilibrium each economy takes this world inflation rate as its own rate of inflation. However, in the short run, inflation rates will differ between countries. These differences can be allowed for by making a distinction between internationally traded and non-traded goods, with the discrepancies in national inflation rates being explained in terms of lags in the transmission of inflationary movements in the traded goods sector to the non-traded sector. The adjustment mechanism can be envisaged by considering an individual economy that is initially in equilibrium with an inflation rate equal to the world rate of inflation, which generates an expansion of domestic credit. The immediate result will be to increase the supply of money and create excess money balances. Demand will then rise as individuals attempt to reduce their increased money balances. Part of this demand will be for traded goods, and since the economy is assumed to be operating at or near to full capacity output level, the increased demand cannot be met from domestic sources of supply and will lead to an increase in imports. Part of the excess money balances will be used in attempting to purchase non-traded goods, resulting in a rise in their domestic prices. This in turn will lead to rises in wages, and a fall in the supply of traded goods to the external market. The balance of payments deficit is thereby accentuated since both exports fall and imports rise with the transfer of resources into the production of non-traded goods.

The effect of the rise in wages and in the price of non-traded goods is to produce a rate of inflation in excess of the equilibrium world inflation rate. Subsequent events are dependent upon whether the authorities reverse or continue with the policy of domestic credit expansion. If the expansion of domestic money supply is reversed, the deterioration in the balance of payments will, through the loss of reserves, lead to a fall in the supply of money. The level of money balances will then be reduced below the desired level, and in an effort to restore the money balances, exports will be increased and imports reduced. There will therefore be an improvement in the balance of payments and a slowing down of the inflation rate back towards the equilibrium, or world, inflation rate. If the authorities do not reduce the expansion of domestic credit, the loss of reserves will force a change in the exchange rate. The effect of devaluation will be to raise the domestic prices of imported goods, thus putting further pressure on domestic prices and wages.

The implications of the monetarist theory for the conduct of the monetary authorities are clear. If the authorities wish to maintain a fixed exchange rate, then the maintenance of the equilibrium in the balance of payments and a steady rate of inflation (equal to the world inflation rate) will require the adoption of a 'passive' monetary policy which allows the supply of money to be determined by the demand for it. Where the authorities expand the supply of domestic credit, and at the same time attempt to maintain an unchanged exchange rate, the result will be an acceleration in the rate of inflation and a deterioration in the balance of payments. The existence of a balance of payments disequilibrium is the result of pursuing a policy of expanding the supply of money that is incompatible with the maintenance of the existing rate of exchange, rather than the result of fundamental or structural imbalances within the domestic economy. The balance of payments pressure can therefore be eliminated (and the rate of inflation reduced) either by a reduction in domestic credit creation or by an abandonment of a fixed exchange rate policy.

It must be acknowledged that certain exponents of the foreign exchange constraint argument have presented the argument exclusively in real terms, and have ignored the monetary environment within which the constraint arises. However, as we argued in Section 4, structuralists do not deny that monetary variables are a necessary condition for the continuation of inflation, but they would argue that the underlying forces, which may be economic, political and social, that have resulted in the monetary authorities' decision to expand the money supply will not be removed or eliminated by the adoption of orthodox monetary policies. In terms of the foreign exchange constraint, structuralists would argue that there is a fundamental difference between the determinants of the level of imports in an advanced economy and in a LDC where the level of imports is frequently closely related to the availability of foreign exchange. In the developed economy, where there is considerable scope for substitution between domestically produced and imported commodities, the level of imports will be responsive to changes in relative prices. In contrast, the typical LDC is heavily dependent upon imported goods for which domestic substitutes are not available.

It is also true that the foreign exchange constraint argument has often been presented in an unrealistically rigid manner, implying that the constraint is fixed and cannot be relaxed by deliberate policy measures. As Bruton (1969) has pointed out, a literal interpretation of the foreign exchange bottleneck analysis implies that the importation of non-essential consumer goods is zero, that the imported component of investment is technologically fixed and that exports cannot be increased. None of these assumptions is entirely correct. There is obviously some degree of choice available in the proportion of import capacity that is devoted to the importation of investment goods. Technology is seldom so rigid as to result in the rate of transformation in domestic production being zero. Nor can it seriously be argued that the individual LDC cannot, by adopting appropriate policies, influence the level of its export receipts. Nevertheless, the foreign exchange constraint argument draws attention to the fact that many LDCs have inherited an economic structure that is unable to meet the demands that are imposed by the need for economic development. A lack of domestic substitutes coupled with a reliance upon imported technology has resulted in a heavy dependence upon imported investment goods and raw materials. Leff and Netto (1966) make the point with respect to Brazil:

> In Brazilian conditions, the marginal propensity to import, *m*, means something very different than it does in economies with more ample foreign exchange supply. In other economies, imports are determined by the level of income, relative prices of domestic and imported products, and the exchange rate, subject to the constraint that imports be less than or equal the supply of foreign exchange. In such conditions, the marginal propensity to import can be considered a function of national income. In Brazil, however, the constraint imposed by the availability of foreign exchange intervenes long before the desired level of imports is reached . . . within a considerable range, imports would be much higher were it not for the foreign exchange availability constraint. Consequently, the import coefficient, M/y, is simply the ratio of foreign exchange receipts to national income (pp. 227–8).

Leff (1967) has argued that in discussing the economic consequences of limitations of import supplies, a distinction should be made between a 'demand-diverting' effect and a 'supply-constraining' effect. That is, one effect of import limitations is to divert demand from imported suppliers to domestic suppliers. At the same time, however, a lack of raw materials and other inputs imported from abroad may inhibit the ability of domestic producers to respond to the increased demand for their products, so that a shortfall in foreign exchange receipts will have a serious depressive impact on the level of domestic economic activity. Thus, while it is logically correct to argue that, given a fixed exchange rate, there is a rate of domestic credit expansion that will ensure equilibrium in the balance of payments, this view ignores the underlying distortions, imperfections and structural rigidities that exist within the less developed economy, and which ensure that the actual level of imports will frequently be less than that required to achieve the economic development of the economy. Chenery (1969) has made this point in the following way:

> It has become customary to . . . regard . . . limited success in increasing exports or curtailing imports as . . . evidence of bad policy. . . . [However] the limits to government action are set by its diagnosis of the problem, the likely response of the economy, and the political acceptability of the results. . . . A diagnosis of past causes of balance of payments disequilibrium . . . is important primarily for the guidance that it provides as to future possibilities for improved performance. Whether or not disequilibrium in the payments balance could bave been avoided by having a higher peso-dollar exchange rate for the past ten years does not determine whether the current problem in country *X* is structural. The effects of an over-valued rate or other misguided policies are incorporated in the existing distorted structure of production and trade. The fact that it requires a reallocation of investment and other changes extending beyond the short run to expand the trade limit makes the problem structural, whatever its origin (pp. 446–7).

The view that denies that LDCs face a fundamental or structural balance of payments disequilibrium in many instances amounts to arguing that 'the problem would not exist if countries had followed ideal policies in the past. Whether or not this is true, it is not particularly relevant to a description of actual policy alternatives' (Chenery (1969), p. 447). The persistence of the foreign exchange constraint, as evidenced by the persistent balance of payments pressures experienced by many LDCs, has encouraged the adoption of policies aimed at its removal. The widespread pessimism that exists in LDCs concerning the prospects of obtaining a significant increase in foreign exchange from the export of primary products has resulted in a concentration upon policies that attempt to relieve the foreign exchange bottleneck by reducing the economy's dependence on imported commodities. This response to the foreign exchange constraint has taken two main forms. In the short run, policies have been directed at releasing foreign exchange for 'essential' imports by reducing the volume of consumer goods imports. This has been attempted by the use of import controls, quotas, duties, and exchange rate changes (as discussed in Sections 6.1 and 6.2). In the longer run, policies have been directed at the substitution of domestic production for imported commodities through the process of import-substituting industrialisation (as discussed in Section 7.2). The adoption of these policies has had two related, but unanticipated, results. First, they have not in general reduced the foreign exchange constraint: rather, as we shall argue in subsequent sections of the paper, they have frequently increased the economy's dependence on imported commodities. The second result of adopting these policies has been to accentuate the inflationary pressures that result from the structural bottlenecks in the economy. Therefore we turn now to an examination of each of these types of policy-response to the foreign exchange constraint, placing particular emphasis on their implications for the rate of inflation.

6 Import Restraint and Inflation

1 Import controls and inflation

A characteristic feature of economic policy in many LDCs is the widespread use of import controls. This structure was initiated in most countries in response to the economy's balance of payments difficulties, and policy was therefore initially aimed at restricting inessential consumer goods imports rather than encouraging the establishment of domestically produced substitute commodities, with the result that protective effects were incidental rather than planned. Nevertheless, the result has been to give the highest protection to these commodities that are considered to be non-essential for the growth of the economy. The introduction of import controls will result in an initial increase in the domestic price level, either as a direct result of the imported tariffs or indirectly through the black market prices created by the administrative controls. However, the inflationary impact of import controls will vary with the type of control that is employed. If import tariffs which do not limit the volume of imports are used, and if the level of the tariffs is constant, then the imposition of the tariff will simply mean that the commodity will be supplied at a higher constant domestic price: the price will rise with the introduction of the control but there will be no further inflationary impact. However, as we have already argued, in most LDCs the potential demand for imports exceeds the available supply. As a result, import controls and quotas that limit the volume or total value of imports are used, the result being to create domestic shortages which lead to the inflation of the domestic prices of imported goods. Where domestic substitutes are available, their prices will tend to increase in line with those of imported commodities. The increase in prices will lead to demands for increased money wages, and, by means of the propagation mechanism and increases in money supply, inflation will become established.[9] Since most LDCs rely heavily upon discretionary import controls that limit the total volume or value of imports, the impact of the widespread adoption of quantitative import controls in LDCs has, in general, been to add to domestic inflationary pressures.

2 *Devaluation and inflation*

Orthodox analysis would suggest that a persistent balance of payments disequilibrium is evidence that the exchange rate should be devalued to the level at which there is equilibrium between the demand and supply of foreign exchange without import controls: devaluation is seen as a policy substitute for restricting imports by controls. This view, based on the standard analysis of currency devaluation, fails to take into account many of the features that are typical of LDCs, and that limit the impact of devaluation on their foreign exchange situation.

One explanation of the reluctance of policy-makers in LDCs to use devaluation as a tool of economic management is the fact that the foreign exchange rate may be used to pursue many objectives other than the clearing of the foreign exchange market.[10] The objectives may include the encouragement of import-substituting industrialisation, improving the barter terms of trade, avoidance of an increase in the domestic costs of imports or external debts denominated in foreign currency, altering the distribution of income among broad sectors or classes in the economy. Faced with inadequate means of achieving the multiple objectives of economic policy, it need not be considered irrational to use the exchange rate as an indirect instrument with which to pursue these aims. Most LDCs therefore have some combination of an open and a suppressed payments deficit, and, as a result, when the decision to devalue is ultimately taken or forced upon the policy-makers, the nature and impact of the exchange rate alteration is considerably more complex than a simple adjustment of the exchange rate.

The reluctance to devalue is frequently due to pessimism with regard to the potential contribution of devaluation to an easing of the foreign exchange constraint in LDCs. For a number of reasons, the price elasticity of demand for both imports and exports is likely to be low. The first point to be noted is that the elasticity of demand for imports is likely to be low where imports consist largely of raw materials, capital and intermediate goods, the volume of which will be unresponsive to relative price changes. Second, to the extent that devaluation is accompanied by the removal or relaxation of import controls and quotas, the domestic final price of imported commodities may be reduced and consumption increased. Third, in so far as the incomes of exporters are increased, their consumption of imports or import-intensive domestic commodities will increase. On *a priori* grounds, therefore, it seems unlikely that devaluation will have the effect of significantly reducing the value of imports.[11] The burden of adjustment therefore rests largely upon the response of the export sector.

The response of the export sector to the currency devaluation can be expected to be more variable, but nevertheless there are a number of *a priori* reasons for supposing that, in general, the devaluation is unlikely to result in a substantial increase in export receipts. The export receipts schedule is a function of both domestic supply conditions and foreign demand conditions. The price elasticity of demand for many primary products and raw materials is low: in part this may be due to the low proportion of raw material cost in final output, or it may be due to the imposition of quotas or taxes upon these commodities by the importing country. There are also grounds for believing that the supply within the LDCs may be unresponsive to changes in relative prices. We have already referred to the importance of the agricultural sector bottleneck in many LDCs which may prevent any significant increase in the production of agricultural exports. Where the export commodity is a major item of wage goods within the domestic economy there is a greater possibility for an immediate increase by reducing domestic consumption, but this is likely to result in increased inflationary pressures originating in wage and price movements in the urban sector. A re-direction of manufactures from the domestic to the external market may not be easily accomplished. First, the previous pattern of highly protected ISI is likely to have led to the establishment of a relatively high-cost inefficient sector whose products are uncompetitive in world markets. Second, even where manufactures can be competitively exported at the new rate of exchange, the opening up of new export markets requires the establishment of new marketing networks and the identification of consumer tastes and preferences. Furthermore, the export of manufactures from LDCs is subject to substantial trade barriers in the developed countries' markets.

There are therefore good reasons for being pessimistic about the import and export elasticities in LDCs, and for believing that devaluation may fail to make a significant contribution to the removal of an existing trade deficit. On *a priori* grounds it seems unlikely that devaluation alone will reduce the foreign exchange constraint that exists in many LDCs. Since devaluation cannot be expected to alter the value of either exports or imports substantially, it cannot free the LDCs from the necessity of import controls. Devaluation is therefore not an alternative to import controls.

The effect of devaluation in LDCs upon the rate of inflation is more difficult to establish from *a priori* reasoning. The immediate effect of the devaluation will be to increase the c.i.f. price of imported goods, expressed in domestic currency. But if the devaluation is accompanied by a relaxation of import controls, the scarcity rents that previously accrued to those who obtained import licences will be reduced, and depending on the degree of devaluation as compared with the measure of import liberalisation, domestic prices of imports may fall somewhat. On balance, however, it seems more likely that the domestic prices of imports will rise after devaluation. Since most imports consist of intermediate and capital goods, the higher import costs will increase the final cost of manufactured goods. The devaluation may also be used as a 'cover' for increasing the price of non-traded goods and services: for example, a devaluation has frequently been accompanied by a programme of increased consumer charges for public utility services. In those economies where labour is organised, the increased prices will lead to demands for increased money incomes. If these pressures are met by increases in domestic credit, there will be increased inflationary pressure and further deterioration in the balance of payments.

To summarise, it has been argued in this section that the foreign exchange constraint that exists in many LDCs compels the adoption of import controls and devaluation, aimed at the restraint of non-essential imports. The implementation of these policies can be expected to have two major effects, both of which are negative. First, they are unlikely to lead to any substantial reduction in the foreign exchange constraint. Second, they may be expected to contribute to an increase in the rate of inflation.

7 'Openness', Import-Substituting Industrialisation and Inflation

The prominance given to discussion of the foreign exchange constraint concept in the development literature is a recognition of the 'open', dependent nature of the majority of LDCs. The failure of import-restraining policies significantly to reduce the foreign exchange constraint has encouraged the adoption of policies aimed at reducing the 'openness' and dependence of the economy by substituting domestic production for imported commodities through the establishment of import-substituting industrialisation. We begin this section with a brief but critical discussion of the measure of 'openness' that is commonly used in the literature. We then proceed to outline the pattern of import-substituting industrialisation that is occurring in the majority of LDCs, its impact on the 'openness' of the economy, and its relationship to inflation.

1 'Openness' and inflation

Iyoha (1973) has used cross-country regression analysis to test the monetarist hypothesis that where an economy is closely integrated with other economies by international exchange relationships, domestic excess demand can be met, at least in the short run, by an increased import surplus, thus reducing the pressure on the domestic price level. This 'spillover' hypothesis is tested by examining the relationship between the 'openness' of the economy, as measured by the ratio of imports to national income, and the rate of inflation. The observed negative correlation between these two variables is interpreted as evidence in support of the hypothesis that, in an open economy, domestic inflationary pressure spills over into the balance of payments, thus necessitating less price inflation.

In attempting to transfer this 'spillover' hypothesis to the LDCs, Iyoha has seriously misinterpreted the relationship that exists between inflation and the balance of payments in most LDCs. A fundamental criticism of Iyoha's analysis relates to the casual relationship that he envisages between 'openness' and inflation in the LDCs. We are in agreement with Iyoha when he states that '. . . most developing economies are open, and . . . rapid inflation can be a serious obstacle in the process of economic development' (pp. 31–2). But we feel that he has seriously misinterpreted the nature of this 'dependence' and has, as a consequence, utilised an inappropriate definition of 'openness' in his analysis of inflation. We will discuss each of these criticisms separately.

As we have already seen, many LDCs are faced with balance of payments pressures which constitute an effective structural constraint upon the growth of the domestic economy, and the possibility of absorbing potential inflationary pressures through an increasing import surplus is therefore severely limited. As a result, and contrary to Iyoha's argument, the import surplus is not the dependent factor that responds to changes in the pressure of internal demand, but rather it constitutes a structural constraint upon the growth of the economy and contributes to the rate of inflation. The typical LDC does not have a choice between the rate of inflation and the magnitude of the balance of payments deficit: the rate of inflation is, in part, determined by the foreign exchange constraint. The degree to which an individual LDC is constrained by the foreign exchange bottleneck can be established only by detailed examination of the particular characteristics of its economy. It is highly unlikely that a single measure, such as the import ratio, will provide a reliable indication of the magnitude of this constraint and, at the very least, it is necessary to examine the composition of imports to establish the extent to which 'less essential' imports can be reduced.

The import–income ratio is used by Iyoha as a measurement of the degree of 'openness' of a LDC's economy. But the use of this ratio is subject to a number of criticisms and it is very difficult to give an unambiguous interpretation of movements in this coefficient (Robock, 1970). A reduction in the coefficient does not necessarily imply a reduction in the absolute value or quantity of imports, and both imports and the import coefficient are closely related to the availability of foreign exchange.

A LDC will probably (though not necessarily)

experience a falling import coefficient if it is pursuing a policy of ISI, but of far greater significance than a low or falling coefficent is the change in the composition of imports that arises during the ISI process. We discuss this phenomenon in greater detail below and will also comment on the impact of ISI policies on domestically generated inflationary pressures. For the present, it is sufficient to state that if, as we believe to be the case, inflation in most LDCs originates in (although is not exclusively caused by) long-run sectoral bottlenecks and imbalances in the economy, the reduction of inflation will necessitate the adoption of policies aimed at altering the fundamental structure of the economy. An implicit assumption of the 'spillover' hypothesis is that the impact of domestic excess demand is reduced by the importation of consumer goods. However, a development strategy aimed at eliminating inflation must lead to the removal of the inflation-generating structural constraints. Priority must therefore be given to altering the structure of imports in favour of those goods that are essential for the transformation of the LDC.

Iyoha admits to the weakness of his own case when at the end of his paper he states that '. . . the import–income ratio is not a good measure of the true openness of the economy' (p. 37). He argues that changes in imports can result from policy decisions and that '. . . the import value is the thing that can be changed at will, the only degree of freedom'. We will argue below that this is unlikely to be the case, especially for those countries deeply involved in ISI policies and which are unable to face the domestic consequences of a cut in imports. Our analysis of the relationship between ISI and inflation will provide a more plausible explanation of Iyoha's empirical results. But of greater importance than this is the fact that Iyoha, even though admitting to the poor quality of his 'openness' variable, does not hesitate to conclude that, if true, his results have far-reaching implications for development policy:

> Specifically it will have implications for the optimal trade policy ('inward-looking' vs 'outward-looking' policies) and the optimal capital accumulation strategy. If rapid inflation in fact discourages domestic capital accumulation, and if increased capital accumulation is needed for development, it will turn out that an outward-looking trade policy resulting in more openness is optimal (p. 36).

We will strongly dispute this conclusion below. As a more general criticism, the results derived from cross-sectional data cannot be used in this manner to infer the optimal relationship between the import ratio and inflation in a particular economy over time. Cross-sectional data do not necessarily indicate the trend that will be followed by any economy over time, and one of the most frequent criticisms of this approach is that very different patterns of change are observed when time series data are used (Aaron (1967)).

2 *Import-substituting industrialisation and inflation*

The vast majority of LDCs are pursuing policies of ISI. Typically this begins with the manufacture of consumer goods for which a domestic market is already well established, although such production usually takes place behind high protective tariff barriers. As a result of this development, the import of finished consumer goods is reduced but the commodity composition of imports changes towards raw materials, semi-finished inputs and capital goods.[12] One of the main results of this change in import structure is to increase the proportion of domestic value added which is supported by, and dependent on, imports, and this factor introduces an inflexibility into the import structure and generates a trade dependency markedly different from the one that existed prior to the implementation of ISI (Winston (1967)). In this new situation, a decline in export proceeds not counterbalanced by a net inflow of foreign capital leads to forced import curtailments and industrial recession. Looked at from a different angle, 'non-essential' consumer goods imports are converted into 'essential' raw material and intermediate and capital goods imports, needed to maintain domestic production and employment. The import structure may not become completely inflexible and a certain amount of room for substitution between different categories of imports may still exist, but in general the LDC becomes more dependent on foreign trade and more vulnerable to foreign influence and actions. W. Baer (1972) comments that it is ironic that '. . . the net result of ISI has been to place Latin American countries in a new and more dangerous dependency relationship with the more advanced industrial countries than ever before'. Another observer concludes that:

> . . . the economic structure that the ISI approach to development spawns is no more flexible and adaptable than the one that is sought to be replaced . . . [it] . . . is so incompatible with the rest of the system that adjustments to changes in demands, in technology, in any part of the routine are accomplished painfully if at all (Bruton (1970)).

Two further considerations merit brief mention. Foreign private capital has been extremely important in establishing import-substituting industries in the majority of LDCs, and the need to finance the repatriation of interest, profits, management fees, etc., constitutes a growing, and relatively inflexible, burden on the balance of payments. A second feature of the ISI process is that it tends to get stuck at the stage of consumer goods substitution. Instead of achieving a smooth transition from consumer goods to intermediate goods and finally to capital goods production, we observe what D. Felix (1964) has referred to as the 'premature widening' of the productive structure. The fragmented market, the greater risks and uncertainty associated with capital goods production and the reliance on an imported, capital-intensive technology combine to build into the system a bias against the development of intermediate and capital goods industries (which reduces the possibilities for the development of an indigenous technology which in turn might reduce the dependence on imports), and the usual result of the ISI strategy is the establishment of an industrial sector characterised by high cost and inefficient operation, large scale excess capacity and whose continued existence depends upon high levels of protection (Little, Scitovsky and Scott, 1970).

The available evidence points overwhelmingly to the fact that the LDC, pursuing a policy of ISI, increases its dependence on the external sector. The import coefficient may be constant or falling, but of greater significance is the change in the composition of imports and the rigidity introduced into the import structure. The economy's increased dependence on imported inputs increases the likelihood of inflation being imported through rising international prices of essential capital and intermediate goods (Sunkel's exogenous inflationary pressures).[13] Furthermore, fluctuations in export receipts may tend to result in an upward movement of the price level.[14]

Even if we ignore the increased vulnerability of the ISI economy to externally generated inflationary pressures, the ISI process itself can be expected to add to domestic inflationary pressures in the following ways: it does not, inflation, as we have seen, centres on the slow growth of agricultural output and the slow growth in the capacity to import. Shortages and rising prices provide opportunities for ISI, but at the same time ISI adds to inflationary pressures in the following ways. it does not, in general, relieve the balance of payments constraint (that is, it does not increase the capacity to import, at least in the short run); the changed structure of imports, noted above, leaves little scope for reduction or reorganisation; ISI turns the domestic terms of trade against agriculture and thus reduces the rate of growth of agricultural output below what it would otherwise have been (and the lack of investment in agriculture further exacerbates this problem); the concentration on ISI has an adverse effect on exports, aggravated by the neglect of agriculture and the overvalued exchange rate, and the creation of a high-cost, inefficient and monopolistic manufacturing sector adds to inflationary pressures. ISI, as practised in LDCs over the past few years, can thus aggravate the major rigidities in the economy that are the basis of the structuralist view of inflation.[16]

We also reject as a gross oversimplification the distinction between 'outward-looking' and 'inward-looking' development policies.[17] Import substitution, as currently practised, even if it reduces the import coefficient, does not reduce the external dependence of the LDC or promote self-sufficient development. The foreign exchange constraint is not alleviated and the economy becomes heavily dependent upon foreign capital, skills and technology. In other words, ISI has produced results contrary to those expected by its early advocates. Even if it is accepted that the expressions 'inward-looking' and 'outward-looking' are meaningful, the impression still remains that they are in some sense mutually exclusive. This is not the case. ISI by itself has not proved to be a viable development strategy. Such a strategy must aim at structural changes permitting self-sustaining growth, and should include, *inter alia*, measures aimed at the domestic production of goods previously imported, the exploitation of existing and the development of new export opportunities, the transformation of agriculture and the establishment of a fully integrated industrial sector. The far-reaching significance and complexity of such measures are not adequately encompassed by the expressions 'inward-looking' and 'outward-looking'.

To summarise, ISI aggravates the inflationary tendencies that already exist in the LDC and, by changing the structure of imports, increases the vulnerability of the economy to 'imported' inflation. As a result of ISI, the concepts of openness and dependence require reformulation.

8 Conclusions

Our objectives in this paper are threefold. Firstly, we have critically examined the relevance and usefulness of western concepts and 'orthodox' theory to the analysis of the inflationary process in LDCs. We have argued that these concepts and theories are not directly applicable, and their transfer into a different economic and institutional setting is likely to lead to faulty analysis and incorrect policy prescriptions.

Following on from this, our second objective has been to present a concise summary of the state of the debate between the two main schools of thought concerning the origin and nature of inflation in LDCs. The theoretical and empirical contributions have originated largely, although not exclusively, in Latin America, but we argue that a structural approach to the problem of inflation is applicable (indeed essential) to all LDCs.

We distinguish between 'structural' and 'structuralist' analyses in order to focus attention on the broader socio-economic institutional framework which LDC governments both influence and are a part of, and within which development objectives are pursued and policies are formulated, rather than concentrating on specific alleged structural constraints, usually not applicable to all LDCs. Within this framework, the nature of the transmission or propagation mechanism (including necessary increases in the money supply) is of crucial importance. If specific groups or classes within society are unable to regain their previous position relative to other groups after an inflationary increase in prices has led to a deterioration in their real living standards, relative price changes will not lead to an inflationary spiral. They will, of course, lead to a redistribution of income, and the relationship between inflation and income distribution is vital to any understanding of inflation in LDCs. Jackson, Turner and Wilkinson (1972, pp. 31–2) note the relationship in Argentina, and Baer (1973) presents data illustrating the movement towards even greater inequality that has taken place in Brazil in the period 1960–70 (for example, the top 5 per cent of the population have increased their share from 27.4 per cent to 36.3 per cent and the share of the bottom 40 per cent has fallen from 11.2 per cent to 9.0 per cent). Evidently, inflation can be 'cured' or at least brought under some degree of control given a sufficiently strong (and repressive) government.

Two additional conclusions are perhaps implicit in the analysis. Firstly, the problem of inflation cannot be separated from the problems of underdevelopment and development. An asocial and ahistorical analysis obscures the real issues involved and incorrectly reduces a complex economic and socio-political problem to a 'straightforward' technical one. Secondly, broad generalisations and aggregate cross-country studies are of limited value. Sunkel (1960) has stressed the specific nature of each country's inflationary process and we can do no more than strongly endorse that position.

Notes: Reading 38

1 Felix (1961) argues that '. . . Latin American countries entered their industrialisation era burdened with a domestic capitalist class of limited investment horizons and weak propensities to accumulate, and a low and regressive tax structure which hampered public capital formation' (p. 85).

2 Olivera (1964) does not accept the recourse to deficit financing as a structural bottleneck. He argues that it is not useful to describe as 'structural' an inflation which results from the difference between *ex ante* savings and *ex ante* investment. He terms this 'structural proneness to inflation' rather than 'structural inflation'. Thorp (1971) has some sympathy with this viewpoint, but feels that those who argue thus separate themselves from 'structuralists' proper (pp. 189–190).

3 '. . . the structuralist should not deny that monetary variables in some sense determine inflation. Structuralists may write at times as if inflation is a totally non-monetary phenomenon – but implicit in their analysis must be the assumption that the monetary system is having to respond to pressure, in order that a given rate of growth and level of employment be achieved' (Thorp, 1971, p. 193).

4 Campos's main criticisms are: (i) the IMF's approach was too aggregative and failed to distinguish between consumption and investment expenditures and to identify bottleneck sectors where investment would have to be maintained or accelerated, (ii) underestimation of the effects of trade fluctuations, (iii) inflexible attempts to achieve internal and external balance simultaneously, (iv) underestimation of political problems associated with stabilisation programmes (pp. 117–20).

5 Devine (1974) makes the similar point within the developed economy context: 'The expansion of the money supply is essentially a symptom rather than a cause, of inflation. It is either the *result* of the state seeking to make expenditures that socio-political pressures make necessary and that these same pressures prevent from being financed by taxation or by borrowing from the private sector; or it is the *result* of the state being obliged to accommodate pressures elsewhere in the economy for fear of the socio-political consequences that would follow if it did not.'

Furthermore, it is of interest to note that in a recent discussion (IEA, 1974), Milton Friedman stated that 'I always speak of the change in the money supply as a proximate cause, and say that the deeper causes must be found in what are the explanations for the rise of the money supply' (p. 101). E. J. Mishan, in his review of the IEA volume (*The Times Literary Supplement*, 18 April 1975), perceives the cause of inflation as residing in the 'apparent irreconcilability of current aspirations with current institutions' and suggests that the difference between the monetarist and other schools of thought is largely one of semantics. It should be clear from what we have already said that we do not accept the latter conclusion, at least with respect to LDCs. The clearest difference between the monetarist and structuralist schools of thought and one where the issue is obviously not one of semantics is to be seen in the controversy over the necessity and desirability of policies aimed at economic stabilisation.

6 In 1971 the total net resources flow (i.e. Official Development Assistance, other official flows, private export credits, private investment and grants and loans from multinational agencies) to LDCs amounted to a per capita receipt of $9.2 (OECD, 1973, Table 23).

7 Chenery and Strout (1966), p. 682.

8 It is important that a distinction be made between the notion of a foreign exchange constraint and the balance-of-payments deficit. The former concept relates to an *ex ante* situation, whereas the balance-of-payments deficit is an *ex post*, or realised, situation which is dependent upon the amount of external finance available. The existence of a small or zero balance-of-payments deficit is therefore not necessarily evidence of the absence of a foreign exchange constraint.

9 This sequence of events is very similar to that envisaged by the monetarist school. The essential difference concerns the 'cause' of the inflation. The structural approach envisages the foreign exchange constraint giving rise to domestic shortages and relative price increases, which are followed by increases in domestic credit and inflation. The monetary analysis argues that the balance-of-payments disequilibrium arises as a result of the expansion of the money supply, which in turn leads to inflation.

10 The complexity of the devaluation decision in LDCs is emphasised in Cooper (1973).

11 A recent IMF study of the effect of devaluation in non-industrial countries showed that in the majority of the countries studied, '. . . in the post-devaluation period . . . the rate of growth of imports actually exceeded the pre-devaluation growth rate' (IMF, 1974, p. 54).

12 For an analysis of the falling share of consumer goods imports, see Bhagwati and Wibulswasdi (1972). Helleiner (1972) gives data indicating the compositional changes that have taken place in the imports of Brazil, Nigeria, Mexico, Argentina and Tanzania.

13 Sunkel (1960).

14 The evidence linking export instability with inflation is

inconclusive. See MacBean (1966), Argy (1970), Maynard (1962).

15 See Felix (1961) and Grunwald (1961), especially p. 113.

16 Furtado (1970) also places emphasis on the interrelationship between the ISI process and the generation of inflation. ISI requires rapid structural changes if it is to succeed as a development strategy, but such changes have not been forthcoming, and in addition to the conventional structural constraints Furtado draws attention to the inadequacy of infrastructure, the short-term inadequacy of labour (lack of skilled labour and industrial entrepreneurs), the inadequacy of fiscal systems and increased financial commitments aggravated by government policies aimed at increasing investment.

17 Robock (1970) refers to the choice between ISI and export promotion as a 'false dichotomy'. The 'inward-looking'–'outward-looking' distinction has also been questioned by a number of prominent economists. See Streeten (1973).

References: Reading 38

Aaron, H. (1967), 'Structuralism versus monetarism: a note on evidence', *Journal of Development Studies*, January.

Adams, N. A. (1967), 'Import structure and economic growth: a comparison of cross-section and time-series data', *Economic Development and Cultural Change*, vol. 15, January.

Adekunle, J. O. (1968), 'Rates of inflation in industrial, other developed and less developed countries, 1949–65', *IMF Staff Papers*.

Agosin, M. R. (1973), 'On the Third World's narrowing trade gap: a comment', *Oxford Economic Papers*, March.

Ahmad, Z. (1970), 'Inflationary process and its control in less developed countries', in E. A. G. Robinson and M. Kidron, *Economic Development in South Asia* (Macmillan).

Argy, V. (1970), 'Structural inflation in developing countries', *Oxford Economic Papers*, March.

Arraes, M. (1972), *Brazil: The People and the Power* (Penguin).

Baer, W. (1967), 'The inflation controversy in Latin America: a survey', *Latin American Research Review*, Spring.

Baer, W. (1972), 'Import substitution and industrialization in Latin America: experiences and interpretations', *Latin American Research Review*, Spring.

Baer, W. (1973), 'The Brazilian book 1968–72: an explanation and interpretation', *World Development*, vol. 1, no. 8, August.

Baer, W., and Kerstenetzky, I. (1964), *Inflation and Growth in Latin America* (Irwin).

Balogh, T. (1961), 'Economic policy and the price system', *UN Economic Bulletin for Latin America*, March; repr. in T. Balogh, *The Economics of Poverty*, 2nd edn (Weidenfeld & Nicolson, 1974).

Bhagwati, J. N., and Desai, P. (1970), *India, Planning for Industrialisation – Industrialisation and Trade Policies since 1951* (Oxford University Press).

Bhagwati, J. N., and Wibulswasdi, C. (1972), 'A statistical analysis of shifts in the import structure in LDCs', *Bulletin of the Oxford University Institute of Economics and Statistics*, May.

Bhatt, V. V. (1970), 'On inflation and its control', in E. A. G. Robinson and M. Kidron (eds), *Economic Development in South Asia* (Macmillan).

Bruton, H. J. (1970), 'The import–substitution strategy of economic development: a survey', *Pakistan Development Review*.

Bruton, H. J. (1969), 'The two-gap approach to aid and development: a comment', *American Economic Review*, June.

Campos, R. de O. (1961), 'Two views on inflation in Latin America', in A. O. Hirschman (ed.), *Latin American Issues: Essays and Comments* (The Twentieth Century Fund).

Campos, R. de O. (1967), *Reflections on Latin American Development* (University of Texas Press).

Chenery, H. (1969), 'The two-gap approach to aid and development: a reply to Bruton', *American Economic Review*, June.

Chenery, H., and Strout, A. (1966), 'Foreign assistance and economic development', *American Economic Review*, September.

Chenery, H. B. *et al.* (1974), *Redistribution with Growth* (Oxford University Press).

Cochrane, S. H. (1972), 'Structural inflation and the two-gap model of economic development', *Oxford Economic Papers*, November.

Cooper, R. N. (1971), 'Devaluation and aggregate demand in aid-receiving countries', ch. 16 in J. N. Bhagwati *et al.* (eds), *Trade, Balance of Payments and Growth, Papers in International Economics in Honour of C. P. Kindleberger* (North-Holland).

Cooper, R. N. (1972), 'The European Community's system of generalised tariff preferences: a critique', *Journal of Development Studies*, July.

Cooper, R. N. (1973), 'An analysis of currency devaluation in developing countries', ch. 9 in M. B. Connolly and A. K. Swoboda (eds), *International Trade and Money* (Allen & Unwin).

Devine, P. (1974), 'Inflation and Marxist theory', *Marxism Today*, March.

Diaz-Alejandro, C. F. (1965), *Exchange-rate Devaluation in a Semi-Industrial Country: The Experience of Argentina 1955–61* (Cambridge University Press).

Diz, A. C. (1970), 'Money and prices in Argentina 1935–62', in D. Meiselman (ed.), *Varieties of Monetary Experience* (Chicago, Ill.).

Donnithorne, A. (1974), 'China's anti-inflationary policy', *The Three Banks Review*, no. 103, September.

Economic Commission for Latin America (ECLA) (1962), *Economic Bulletin for Latin America*, October.

Edel, M. (1969), *Food Supply and Inflation in Latin America* (Praeger).

Erb, G. F., and Schiavo-Campo, S. (1969), 'Export instability of development and the economic size of less developed countries', *Bulletin of the Oxford University Institute of Economics and Statistics*, vol. 31, no. 4, November.

Eshag, E., and Thorp, R. (1965), 'The economic and social consequences of orthodox economic policies in Argentina in the postwar years', *Bulletin of the Oxford University Institute of Economics and Statistics*, February.

Felix, D. (1961), 'An alternative view of the "monetarist"–"structuralist" controversy', in A. O. Hirschman (ed.), *Latin American Issues: Essays and Comments* (The Twentieth Century Fund).

Felix, D. (1964), 'Monetarists, structuralists and import-substituting industrialisation', in W. Baer and I. Kerstenetzky (eds), *Inflation and Growth in Latin America* (Irwin).

Felix, D. (1968), 'The dilemma of import substitution –

Argentina', in G. F. Papanek (ed.), *Development Policy – Theory and Practice* (Harvard University Press).

Furtado, C. (1967), 'Industrialisation and inflation', *International Economic Papers*, no. 12.

Grunwald, J. (1961), 'The "structuralist" school on price stabilisation and economic development: the Chilean case', in A. O. Hirschman (ed.), *Latin American Issues: Essays and Comments* (The Twentieth Century Fund).

Harberger, A. C. (1963), 'The dynamics of inflation in Chile', in C. Christ *et al., Measurement in Economics: Studies in Mathematical Economics and Econometrics in Memory of Yehudi Grunfeld* (Stanford University Press).

Harvey, C. (1971), 'The control of inflation in a very open economy: Zambia 1964–9', *Eastern African Economic Review*, vol. 3, no. 1, June.

Helleiner, G. K. (1972), *International Trade and Economic Development* (Penguin).

Institute of Economic Affairs (1974), *Inflation: Causes, Consequences, Cures* (IEA).

International Monetary Fund (1972), *Financial Statistics*, vol. XXV.

International Monetary Fund (1973), *Annual Report* (Washington, DC).

International Monetary Fund (1974), *Financial Survey*, 18 February.

Iyoha, M. A. (1973), 'Inflation and "openness" in less developed economies: a cross-country analysis', *Economic Development and Cultural Change*, October.

Jackson, D., Turner, H. A., and Wilkinson, F. (1972), *Do Trade Unions Cause Inflation?* (Cambridge University Press).

Johnson, H. G. (1967), *Economic Policies Towards Less Developed Countries* (Allen & Unwin).

Kahil, R. (1973), *Inflation and Economic Development in Brazil, 1946–63* (Clarendon Press).

Kravis, I. B. (1970), 'Trade as handmaiden of growth: similarities between the nineteenth and twentieth centuries', *Economic Journal*, December.

Laidler, D., and Nobay, A. R. (1974), 'Some current issues concerning the international aspects of inflation', mimeo.

Leff, N. H., (1967), 'Import constraints and development: causes of the recent decline of Brazilian economic growth', *Review of Economics and Statistics*, vol. XLIX.

Leff, N. H., and Netto, A. D. (1966), 'Import substitution, foreign investment and international disequilibrium in Brazil', *Journal of Development Studies*, April.

Little, I., Scitovsky, T., and Scott, M. (1970), *Industry and Trade in Some Developing Countries* (Oxford University Press).

MacBean, A. I. (1966), *Export Instability and Economic Development* (Harvard University Press).

Maizels, A. (1968), 'Review of A. I. MacBean (1966)', *American Economic Review*, June.

Maynard, G. (1962), *Economic Development and the Price Level* (Macmillan).

Modigliani, F., and Tarantelli, E. (1973), 'A generalisation of the Phillips curve for a developing country', *Review of Economic Studies*, vol. L(2), no. 122, April.

Murray, T. (1973), 'How helpful is the generalised system of preferences to developing countries?', *Economic Journal*, June.

Myint, H. (1969), 'International trade and the developing countries', in P. A. Samuelson (ed.), *International Economic Relations* (Macmillan).

Myrdal, G. (1968), *Asian Drama: An Inquiry into the Poverty of Nations* (Penguin).

OECD (1973), *Development Co-operation, 1973 Review* (OECD).

Olivera, J. H. G. (1964), 'On structural inflation and Latin American structuralism', *Oxford Economic Papers*, November.

Parkin, J. M. (1974), 'Inflation, the balance of payments, domestic credit expansion and exchange rate adjustments', in R. Z. Aliber (ed.), *National Monetary Policies and the International Financial System* (Chicago University Press).

Parkin, J. M. (1974a), 'Inflationary policy in the UK: an evaluation of the alternatives', *National Westminster Bank Review*, May, pp. 32–47.

Parkin, J. M. (1975), 'The causes of inflation: recent contributions and current controversies', in R. Nobay and M. Parkin (eds), *Current Economic Problems* (Cambridge University Press).

Prebisch, R. (1961), 'Economic development or monetary stability: the false dilemma', *Economic Bulletin for Latin America*, vol. 6, no. 1; repr. in I. Livingstone (ed.), *Economic Policy for Development* (Penguin, 1971).

Reuber, G. L. (with M. Crookell, M. Emerson and G. Gallais-Hamonno) (1973), *Private Foreign Investment in Development* (Oxford University Press).

Robinson, J. (1936), 'Disguised unemployment', *Economic Journal*, June.

Robock, S. H. (1970), 'Industrialisation through import substitution or export promotion: a false dichotomy', in J. W. Markham and G. F. Papanek (eds), *Industrial Organisation and Economic Development* (Boston, Mass.).

Seers, D. (1962), 'A theory of inflation and growth in underdeveloped economies based on the experience of Latin America', *Oxford Economic Papers*, June.

Seers, D. (1963), 'The limitations of the special case', *Bulletin of the Oxford University Institute of Economics and Statistics*, vol. 25, no. 2; repr. in K. Martin and J. Knapp (eds), *The Teaching of Development Economics* (Cass, 1967).

Seers, D. (1964), 'Inflation and growth: the heart of the controversy', in W. Baer and I. Kerstenetzky (eds), *Inflation and Growth in Latin America* (Irwin).

Sjaastad, L. A. (1976), 'Why stable inflations fail', in J. M. Parkin and G. Zis (eds), *Inflation in the World Economy* (Manchester University Press).

Stein, L. (1971), 'On the Third World's narrowing trade gap', *Oxford Economic Papers*, March.

Stein, L. (1973), 'On the Third World's narrowing trade gap', *Oxford Economic Papers*, March.

Stewart, F. (1973), 'Trade and technology', in Streeten (1973).

Streeten, P. (1972), *The Frontiers of Development Studies* (Macmillan).

Streeten, P. (ed.) (1973), *Trade Strategies for Development* (Macmillan).

Streeten, P., and Stewart, F. (1969), 'Conflicts between output and employment objectives in developing countries', *Oxford Economic Papers*, July.

Sunkel, O. (1960), 'Inflation in Chile: an orthodox approach', *International Economic Papers*, no. 10.

Thorp, Rosemary (1971), 'Inflation and the financing of economic development', in K. Griffin (ed.), *Financing Development in Latin America* (Macmillan).

Triffin, R., and Grubel, H. (1962), 'The adjustment mechanism to differential rates of monetary expansion among the countries of the European Economic Community', *Review of Economics and Statistics*, November.

Turner, H. A., and Jackson, D. A. S. (1970), 'On the determination of the general wage level, a world analysis: or "unlimited labour for ever" ', *Economic Journal*, December.

Vogel, R. C. (1974), 'The dynamics of inflation in Latin America 1950–1969', *American Economic Review*, vol. LXIV, March.

Wall, D. (1968), 'Import capacity, imports and economic growth', *Economica*, May.

Whitman, M. V. N. (1969), 'Economic openness and international financial flows', *Journal of Money, Credit and Banking*, November.

Winston, G. C. (1967), 'Notes on the concept of import–substitution', *Pakistan Development Review*, Spring.

Reading 39

Some Aspects of Interest Rate Policies in Less Developed Economies: The Experience of Selected Asian Countries

A. G. Chandavarkar

IMF Staff Papers, no. 18, 1971, pp. 48–110.

One of the basic problems facing most less developed countries is the scarcity of domestic capital in relation to the size of investment required to achieve high and self-sustaining rates of growth of national and per capita real income. Although the accumulation of capital is not the prime determinant of economic growth, its role as a necessary, even if not a sufficient, condition in the economic development of the less developed countries is widely recognized. But, paradoxically, positive interest rate policies have been conspicuously lacking in the developing economies, apart from a few notable exceptions, such as Taiwan,[1] Korea, and, more recently, Indonesia. Even in the literature the emphasis has been more on the structure, behavior, and determinants of interest rates than on the policies pursued.[2] Discussions of interest rate policy in the less developed countries have been concerned largely with the role of interest rates as 'loan' rates, that is to say, as a means of regulating the cost and availability of credit.[3] But interest rate policy has other relevant aspects than the purely monetary. For instance, interest rates can be viewed as instruments for more effective mobilization of savings (as deposit rates) through the offer of realistic rates on monetary savings, such as time and savings deposits, claims on financial institutions, and government securities. Similarly, interest rates can be viewed as a social rate of discount to determine the optimum allocation of savings between consumption and investment and as a rationing device for efficient allocation among alternative forms of investment. Therefore, a purposive interest rate policy has different aspects, each of which is relevant for particular phases of monetary policy or development planning. Consequently, interest rate policies have to reconcile the conflicting requirements of rates that are appropriate to the desired level and composition of investment and also attractive enough to stimulate savings. This calls for policies aimed at an optimum level of interest rates as well as a proper spread between different rates in keeping with the changing requirement of economic growth and stability.

The role of interest rates in helping to mobilize voluntary domestic savings merits much closer attention, not only because of its bearing on the economic growth of the less developed countries but also because of the general skepticism regarding the efficacy of interest rates in mobilizing savings;[4] this skepticism in turn derives from the lack of a determinate causal link between rates of interest and aggregate real savings in the national accounts sense, or even between interest rates and financial savings. Moreover, even for personal savings, the econometric evidence, while by no means conclusive, does suggest that such variables as the level, distribution, and rate of growth of disposable income, wealth, price levels, industrialization, and urbanization are far more influential than rates of interest in explaining observed variations in the savings/income ratio. In fact, efforts to introduce fiscal and monetary variables, such as taxes and interest rates, into savings functions have not been notably successful. Thus, the inductive evidence appears to justify much of the received doctrine on the relative unimportance of interest as an incentive for saving. All this reflects the complexity of the determinants, motives, and incentives underlying the savings behavior of individuals and households, which is, moreover, subject to life cycles. For instance, saving may be for a specific purpose (the Harrodian 'hump saving'), for old age, for inheritance, or for unknown future contingencies. But while the concept of saving as a residual is true of aggregate saving in the typical Keynesian model of an economy at less than full employment, it does not necessarily hold good for particular components of saving, still less for saving by particular persons or groups in specific forms, such as interest-bearing assets. It would be unrealistic to deny the existence of an *ex ante* savings gap that acts as a constraint on the rate of growth. The question then is this: What role can an interest rate policy play in mobilizing saving in financial assets in developing economies and in influencing the general climate for aggregate real savings?

Interest Rate Levels and Policies in Asia

Instruments and rationale of interest rate policies

An interest rate policy may be defined briefly as any official action designed to influence the level and structure of money rates of interest through statutory means, money market intervention, or moral suasion to attain given ends of credit policy and to help in the mobilization of saving through financial media. Because of the undeveloped character of the money and security markets in most of these countries, and the limited reliance on central bank credit, both open market operations and bank rate changes have limited usefulness. Consequently, in practice, official regulation mostly takes the form of interbank agreements, either voluntary or statutory. This takes into account the statutory powers of central banks to regulate directly the rates on deposits and loans.

But 'it is largely as a result of introducing social considerations that the policymakers face a real dilemma, when it comes to the choice of an appropriate level and structure of interest rates'. In fact, the case for a pragmatic approach to interest rate policy based on modification of the market price mechanism by extra-market criteria is even stronger in the less developed countries, owing to the greater imperfections of the money and capital markets and the stronger element of officially determined priorities in the allocation of capital funds.

Are interest rates low in less developed countries?

Unorganized sector. One of the characteristic features of the less developed countries is the prevalence of high interest rates, ranging typically from 24 per cent per annum to 50 per cent and above in the unorganized sector, where credit is supplied by moneylenders and noninstitutional bankers. But these superficially high nominal rates of interest, which can range up to 300 per cent per annum, overstate the real price of loanable funds in the unorganized sector. As has been noted, 'nominal interest is kept in these conditions, at fantastic levels. But this is mainly a device to keep the peasants permanently in debt. The actual payments exacted cannot exceed the margin between subsistence and rent.'[5] Of course, the fact remains that debtors do owe the high nominal interest charges even if they cannot afford to pay them out of current income. The figures of rural rates based on detailed field investigations, such as those of the All-India Rural Credit Survey, show the normal upper limit of rates to be about 50 per cent. Tun Wai's estimates placed the world-wide weighted average of interest rates in the unorganized sector of the less developed countries within a range of 24–36 per cent.[6] Assuming that effective rates in the unorganized sector are within a range of about 24–50 per cent, those would still be regarded as high in absolute terms as well as relatively to those in the organized sector (typically about 10–12 per cent) of the less developed economies and in the developed economies as a whole. On the other hand, the comparable rates for consumption loans in the developed economies are also recognized to be nearly as high as the lower level of rates for noninstitutional credit in the less developed countries.[7]

Although there are no adequate data, it is reasonable to assume that it is the unorganized sector, with its high interest rates, that finances the bulk of total credit requirements in most of the Asian countries, whereas the organized sector, with its comparatively low rates, finances about one-fourth of the aggregate credit. Indian experience in this matter, which may be assumed to be not untypical of Asia as a whole, is revealing. The Indian Central Banking Enquiry Commission in the 1930s estimated the share of unorganized banking at about 90 per cent. The All-India Rural Credit Surveys in the 1950s and 1960s showed that this ratio had not changed significantly despite the impressive growth of institutional banking facilities; organized banking still accounts for only about 15 per cent of total credit in rural areas.[8]

These facts pose a paradox: what is the role of interest rate policy in countries where nominal rates of interest for the most part are high enough to reward the effort of saving and where the problem therefore is really to reduce the cost of credit. In fact, the existence of usury laws in many developing countries points to the need to reduce the high average rates of interest on loans by eliminating the high-risk premiums and monopolistic profits in the moneylending business. But the paradox presented by these facts is more apparent than real. For one thing, the high rates of interest in rural areas are exclusively lenders' rates that are applicable only to loan transactions and not to deposit transactions. Moneylenders do not usually accept deposits, and in the event of acceptance the rates are far below those for loans. This highlights one of the distinguishing features of noninstitutional banking in developing countries, namely, the virtual absence of any link between deposit rates and loan rates. The latter are therefore in the nature of autonomous rates. The customers of noninstitutional lenders are almost exclusively borrowers (agriculturists and artisans) whose incomes are too low and fluctuating to enable them to save and hold their savings in financial forms for any length of time. The high rates of interest charged by lenders consequently have little influence on the propensity of the rural sector to save. Therefore, from this point of view an appropriate interest rate policy for the unorganized sector should aim at reducing rates to more economic levels through multiplication and diversification of competitive sources of credit and a broad-based program of improved production and marketing in order to enhance the creditworthiness of the rural borrower.[9]

The organized sector (a critique of the Myrdal thesis of low rates). In the less developed countries the level of interest rates in the organized sector (comprising joint-stock banks, other financial institutions, security markets, etc.) tends to be substantially below that in the unorganized sector. They are almost the same as, or lower than, similar rates in the developed countries, where savings are much higher; and even where the rates are slightly higher than in the developed countries, it could be argued that the gap does not fully reflect the relative scarcity of capital that is normally characteristic of such economies. To that extent, the rates are adjudged to be low and therefore unrealistic and inappropriate. Often such judgments tend to partake of obiter dicta not substantiated by any detailed analysis or empirical investigation. A conspicuous exception is Myrdal's analysis[23] of the inappropriateness of low interest rates in the organized sector, which, being among the most substantial of its kind, merits critical appraisal as representative of this point of view even though it was made in the context of the insulated credit and capital markets of India, Pakistan, and Ceylon. Its main propositions may be summarized as follows:

Despite the great scarcity of capital in the less developed countries in comparison with the developed countries, it is paradoxical that rates of interest, despite recent increases, are conspicuously low and in fact not as high as in many developed countries. This paradoxical policy has been sustained by a combination of selective and discretionary controls on credit and investment and by concessional finance, and is thought to be justified on the grounds of inappropriateness of high interest rates in developing countries and the insensitivity of investment to interest rate changes in a highly protected economy.[10]

On balance, according to Myrdal, a substantially higher level of interest rates in conjunction with a dismantling of discretionary controls would be more in harmony with the prevailing scarcity of capital in the South Asian countries and would induce economy in the use of capital. It would stimulate greater inflow of foreign capital and mobilize more domestic saving in productive forms instead of being dissipated in speculation, hoarding (particularly of gold), conspicuous consumption and investment, and purchase of land (at inflated prices) and foreign securities. It would also bring about a decline in oligopolistic profits and in capital and land values; the latter would enhance the feasibility and reduce the cost of large-scale changes in land ownership and tenancy. Since the major portion of government debt is intragovernment debt, higher interest rates would only bring about a change in accounting relationship within the public sector. Insofar as bonds are held by private persons, higher rates would tend to bolster the rentier class but higher incomes from this source would be easy to trace and to tax, even if income from loans in other forms would, as now, be more difficult to trace.

We may now examine critically the validity of the Myrdal thesis in the context of Asian economies and its policy implications.

A comparison of the relative range of interest rates (Table 1) in the developed and less developed countries suggests that Asian countries are in two clearly defined groups, namely, Group I (Burma, Ceylon, India, Malaysia, Nepal, the Philippines, Singapore, and Thailand), which has more or less conventional rates of interest that are about the same as or lower than those in the developed countries, and Group II (Taiwan, Indonesia, and Korea), with interest rates that are far above those in the developed countries or other less developed countries. In fact, the nominal rates in the organized sector in these three countries approximate those in the unorganized sector of the countries that have low interest rates.

In terms of comparative nominal interest rates, Myrdal's generalization would therefore appear to be valid only for some countries in Group I. Even within this group it would be misleading to generalize about countries in which financial saving shows varying degrees of response to more or less similar levels of interest rates. For instance, even with comparatively low and stable nominal rates of interest the growth of financial saving in Malaysia and Singapore, as shown in a subsequent section, has been impressive partly because the real interest rate has been positive, owing to prolonged price stability and the resultant confidence of the investor in financial assets. It would therefore be interesting to compare the real interest rates between the developed countries and the less developed countries that have low interest rates. To illustrate this, the prevailing nominal rate on postal savings in India, the United Kingdom, and Japan and the savings deposit rate in France and Malaysia is deflated by the annual percentage change in consumer prices in the respective countries, using data from the Fund publication, *International Financial Statistics* (December 1963 = 100 for all the countries except Malaysia, in which 1959 = 100). The resultant figures (Table 2) show that the real rate on savings deposits was negative in the developed countries in all the years and in India during 1965–67, whereas in Malaysia it was positive in all years except 1967. Although it is difficult to draw any clear-cut inferences from these data, they do suggest that the gap between the real rates in the developed and less developed countries is perhaps not perceptibly greater than that in the nominal rates.

There is also an interesting parallelism between the similarity of interest rates in the organized sector of the less developed countries and the developed countries, on the one hand, and the relative average capital/output

Table 1 **Developed and Less Developed Countries: Comparative Rates of Interest, 1958–1969**

(Range in per cent per annum)[1]

Country	*Call Money*	*Treasury Bills*	*Savings Deposits*	*Time Deposits*	*Long-Term Government Bond Yields*	*Central Bank Rate*	*Commercial Bank Advances*
Developed countries							
France	3.51–10.41	—	4[2]	4.50[2, 3]	4.94–6.80	3.50–8	—
Japan	—	—	3.60[2, 4]	5.50[2, 3]	—	5.48–8.40	7.40[2, 5]
United Kingdom	—	3.37–7.89	2.50[2, 6]	5[2, 7]	4.82–9.46	4–8	8½[2, 8]
United States	—	1.84–5.35	4[2]	5[2, 3]	3.43–6.51	2.50–6	—
Less developed countries							
Group I							
Burma[2]	—	—	0.50[9]	1¼[3]	4.5[10]	—	4–6
Ceylon	—	—	3½[2]	—	2.70–5.36	2.50–5.50	5½–10
India	1.85–6.28	—	3½–4[11]	—	4.05–5.58	4–6	—
Malaysia	3–5⅜[2]	4[2]	3½[2]	6[2]	6.25[2]	—	7½–8
Nepal	—	—	4½[2]	6–7[2]	—	—	7½–9
Singapore[2]	—	4	3½–4	6[3]	—	—	7½–8
Thailand	6–12[2]	5[2]	3½[2]	—	7[2]	5–8	9–14
Group II							
Taiwan[12]	—	—	5.40–54[9]	9.72–24[3]	—	10.80–14.40[13]	13.32–118.80
Indonesia[14]	—	—	1.5–36[9]	2.5–72[3]	—	—	84–150[15] 48–120[2, 16]
Korea[17]	—	—	16.8–30[9]	15–26.4[3]	—	10.22–23	18–28[5]

Sources: International Monetary Fund, *International Financial Statistics*; national sources.
[1]Approximate range between low and high figures.
[2]1969.
[3]One year.
[4]Postal.
[5]Overdrafts.
[6]Post Office and Trustee.
[7]Seven days' notice.
[8]Prime rate.
[9]Three months.
[10]Certificates.
[11]October 1969.
[12]1949–69.
[13]Rediscounts.
[14]Since October 1968.
[15]1968.
[16]Private banks.
[17]1961–69.

Table 2 **Selected Countries: Estimated Real Rate of Interest on Savings Deposits, 1965–69**

(In per cent per annum)

Country	*1965*	*1966*	*1967*	*1968*	*1969*
India	−1.20	−10.00	−4.60	4.80	−0.30
Japan	−1.40	−1.80	−3.20	−0.40	−3.30
Malaysia	2.00	2.80	−1.20	3.30	4.50
United Kingdom	−1.40	−0.30	−0.20	−1.00	−2.30

Sources: Estimated from Table 1, national sources, and price indices given in International Monetary Fund, *International Financial Statistics*.

ratios* and the average rate of return on capital in manufacturing,† on the other hand. This suggests that as the organized sectors in the less developed economies are developed enclaves they have more in common with the developed economies than with the unorganized sector in their own countries. Borrowing by the organized sector in the less developed countries is likewise from the same sector and hence it is feasible at the lower rates prevailing in that sector. Neither the governments nor the financial institutions borrow directly from the unorganized sector where interest rates are higher. Thus, the dualism of the financial sector and the coexistence of noncompeting capital markets conceal the fact that the borrowing is from the low interest rate sector, which does not necessarily reflect the overall scarcity of capital in the economy.

The feasibility of government borrowing at low interest rates in the less developed countries reflects, first, the existence of a captive or guaranteed minimum market for government loans arising from the statutory requirements stipulating minimum ratios of investments by financial institutions and social security funds in government securities. Such requirements coupled with the paucity of equally safe alternative investment outlets make the market for government securities less competitive in the less developed countries. Consequently, it is arguable that institutional and other investors would hold a substantial portion of their portfolios in government securities even in the absence of statutory regulations. For instance, Indian experience shows that, even before the imposition of statutory investment ratios, banks and insurers held government securities at

*See Raymond W. Goldsmith, *Financial Structure and Development* (Yale University Press, 1969), Table 6-3, p. 294.

†See Bagicha Singh Minhas, *An International Comparison of Factor Costs and Factor Use* (Amsterdam, 1963), Table XVI, p. 88.

or even above the same level that came to be required by statute. It is also not uncommon for financial intermediaries to hold 'excess' (i.e. above the statutory minimum) portfolios of gilt-edged stock. Second, the low rates on government loans are possible because of the strong semimonopsonistic position of governments as borrowers in the less developed countries, which stems from the sheer size of their borrowing operations, and the imperfections of the capital market. Last, the fact that government obligations in all economies, developed or less developed, are virtually risk free makes their yield correspondingly low and uniform by eliminating the risk premium altogether.

Thus, the capacity of the less developed countries to maintain artificially low interest rates below the real cost of capital controverts the belief that the 'floor interest rate' is higher than in developed countries. This in turn is buttressed by the conventional wisdom that favors comparatively low and stable average interest rates in some of the less developed countries, reflecting the cumulative effect of various factors—intellectual, historical, and institutional. Although it is difficult to indicate their relative importance or historical sequence, it is possible to identify some of the more important influences.

A major obstacle to the adoption of bolder interest rate policies is the notion that a historical level of interest rates—say, in the range of 3–5 per cent—is in some sense a 'normal' level. The notion of a normal rate, however, stems from historical experience in the United Kingdom and elsewhere as well as being a survival from the era of war finance when it was both necessary and desirable to finance the war effort on the basis of a given and stable basic rate, such as 3 per cent. This experience appears to have strongly colored the thinking in some Asian countries, where one of the implicit assumptions of policy seems to be the desirability of financing long-term development programs on the basis of low and stable rates. But the notion that a low stable rate is normal becomes increasingly inappropriate in a developing economy, where relative prices, including the interest rate, must necessarily reflect relative scarcities of factors and goods.

The historical experience of interest rates in the organized sector in the less developed countries has been one of variations within a comparatively narrow range of about 3–6 per cent, which has probably conditioned the authorities to low interest rates. It may be that within this range interest rates have had comparatively negligible effects. But really large changes in the rate of interest—say, 10–20 per cent—might well have a significant effect on decisions about savings and investments. Also, the fact that prevailing levels of interest in the unorganized sector are unconscionably high (20–50 per cent) creates a bias in favor of low and stable interest rates. There is an element of paradox in this attitude insofar as the acceptance of low rates in the organized sector goes together with tolerance of abnormally high rates in the unorganized sector. Logically the case is, if anything, for higher rates in the organized sector and much lower ones than those prevailing in the unorganized rural sector.

To sum up, while one may accept the general validity of the Myrdal thesis in the context of low interest rate countries in Asia, it must be subject to appropriate qualifications.

First, the choice is not between low and high rates but between rigid and flexible policies, somewhat along the lines of the Radcliffe Committee's 'three-gears' approach, with rate changes corresponding to low, medium, and high levels. The rate changes can then take the form of fractional variations (fine tuning) or else of larger steps of 1 per cent or more. But in times of high or rapid inflation the three-gears approach may be rendered inoperative, and the situation may warrant dramatic 'quantum' jumps in nominal rates to offset the declines in real interest rates.

Second, even with very high rates it would not be possible to dispense wholly with discretionary credit controls because of the imperfections of the credit market, which give rise to qualitative credit rationing as well as the need to take account of social priorities. But higher interest rates would certainly help to reduce the reliance on discretionary controls and would thereby eliminate the major portion of the massive 'disequilibrium' systems found necessary to maintain the existing low rates.

Third, the effects of higher interest rates on the choice of techniques and the degree of capital intensity may be blunted insofar as purely technological considerations determine the minimum size of plant and equipment in industry and construction. A more salutary effect, however, may be a more rational allocation of capital between the public and private sectors, provided that the public sector borrows its requirements in a competitive market.

Fourth, higher interest rates by themselves may not be sufficiently strong inducements either to drastically alter existing asset preferences, e.g. for land and gold, in less developed countries without a radical change in savings psychology or else to attract foreign loan capital. Moreover, the foreign exchange gap can be more appropriately bridged by an inflow of aid and equity capital than by loan capital.

Finally, higher interest rates would help to extend the organized sector of finance and to promote financial intermediation and the integration of the money and capital market. The maintenance of nominal interest rates in the organized sector below their true economic level results in a steady attrition of organized finance. Since only the rates in the organized sector are controlled, the rise in real rates of interest will be confined to the unorganized sectors, resulting in a steady diversion of savings to that sector in search of higher rates of return. This may result in an increase of either consumption or direct investment in the unorganized sector, since lenders in this sector are more prone to make consumption loans. Thus, attrition of organized finance is accompanied by a rise in consumption, a fall in investment and savings, misallocation of savings to investment, and inefficient use of real resources.

Another consequence of this process is the possible adverse impact on the monetization of the economy, at least in conditions of rising prices. Inflation functions as a kind of tax on cash balances and leads to a steady decline in the holdings of money and also in financial assets. On the other hand, the pace of monetization could not be said to depend on the level of interest rates.

The Scope for Interest Rate Policies

The savings patterns in Asia

The potentialities of an active interest rate policy depend on the extent to which the voluntary financial savings of the household sector are responsive to variations in the level and structure of interest rates. The available data on the savings pattern of some selected Asian countries emphasize, first, the sizable share of the household sector in gross savings (Table 4); second, the relatively small proportion of financial assets—between 35 and 45 per cent—except for Japan, 82 per cent, and Ceylon, nearly 66 per cent; and, finally, the overwhelming predominance—more than 70 per cent—of the voluntary component in household savings and the correspondingly negligible role of compulsory and contractual savings. Together these factors suggest a favorable environment for the use of interest rates to stimulate voluntary financial saving by households. In particular the still negligible role of contractual and compulsory savings, unlike the situation in the developed countries, indicates a much wider potential scope for interest-sensitive savings by households.

Table 4 **Selected Asian Countries: Sectoral Distribution of Gross Savings, 1954–59**

(In per cent)

Country	*Government*	*Corporations*	*Households*
Ceylon			
1955	50.8	6.7	42.5
1956	50.9	14.3	34.8
1957	50.7	18.0	31.4
1958	10.2	18.3	71.5
1959	7.8	18.3	73.9
1955–59	38.4	13.8	47.8
Taiwan			
1958	41.6	4.4	54.0[1]
1959	33.6	7.6	58.8[1]
1958–59	37.1	6.2	56.7[1]
India[2]			
1954–55	5.6	7.2	87.2
1955–56	3.3	7.9	88.8
1956–57	9.4	7.2	84.8
1957–58	13.2	2.1	84.7
1955–58	8.0	5.7	86.3
Korea			
1958	−83.3	48.0	135.3
1959	−36.0	22.0	114.0
1958–59	−51.6	30.6	121.0

Source: United Nations, Economic Commission for Asia and the Far East, *Economic Bulletin for Asia and the Far East*, December 1962, p. 4.

[1]Derived as a residual by deducting identifiable savings in other sectors.

[2]Net savings.

This leads to the more difficult question of interest elasticity of personal savings in Asia, on which the available evidence is inconclusive and sometimes conflicting. According to a recent comparative evaluation by J. G. Williamson of some of the major determinants of personal savings in Asia[24] combining both temporal analysis of individual Asian nations and intertemporal cross-section analysis of a large group of Asian countries, 'higher interest rates are associated, if anything, with lower real saving in Asia. The explanation would appear to lie in the fact that the savings and investment decisions are highly interdependent in the Asian household sector . . . interest rates appear to influence the short-run savings decision far more powerfully than the long-run savings decision.' One of the findings of the study was that for Asia the net impact of real interest rate movements on personal saving was either negative or insignificant.

However, another regression analysis, by K. L. Gupta,[11] using the same variables as Williamson's but a different and more reliable set of primary data on savings for India (estimates by the Reserve Bank of India instead of the National Council of Applied Economic Research) arrived at results just the opposite of Williamson's. Gupta's results (Table 10) show that while the real rate of interest is not significant at the aggregate level it is more influential in determining personal savings at the per capita level. Apart from the use of more reliable primary data, Gupta's analysis, unlike Williamson's, which relies on a single rate of interest as the index of return on financial assets, considers the following real rates of interest as alternatives.

(a) r_r = short-term treasury bills
(b) r_{lg} = long-term government bonds
(c) r_{lp} = private securities
(d) r_t = commercial bank time deposits
(e) r_s = nonbank savings deposits

The results of Gupta's analysis (Table 10) for India show that in all the equations the coefficient has a positive sign, suggesting that higher real interest rates lead to higher real savings.

Table 5 **India: Interest Rates and Personal Savings**[1]

Aggregate

$$S = -982.7 + 0.15019\,Y_d + 25.965\,r_s \quad R = 0.849$$
$$(0.0310) \quad (118.280)$$

$$S = -1008.6 + 0.12875\,Y_d - 0.32175\,Y_d + 112.06\,r_s \quad R = 0.871$$

Per capita

$$S = -94.386 + 0.37249\,Y_d + 3.7892\,r_{lg} \quad R = 0.698$$
$$(0.1327) \quad (2.0322)$$

$$S = -94.979 + 0.3859\,Y_d + 4.9280\,r_s \quad R = 0.677$$
$$(0.1375) \quad (2.9825)$$

$$S = -46.182 + 0.1660\,Y_d - 0.4774\,Y_d + 5.009\,r_{lg} \quad R = 0.723$$
$$(0.2757) \quad (0.1818) \quad (2.501)$$

$$S = -96.442 + 0.39178\,Y_d - 0.38311\,Y_d + 4.912\,r_s \quad R = 0.678$$
$$(0.2613) \quad (0.1788) \quad (3.1846)$$

Source: K. L. Gupta, 'Personal Saving in Developing Nations: Further Evidence,' *The Economic Record*, Vol. 46 (1970), p. 248.

[1]Standard errors are shown in parentheses.

Although the econometric evidence on the interest sensitivity of personal savings in Asia is thus inconclusive and conflicting, it points to the potentially greater role for interest rates in a country like India.

Experience of High Interest Rate Strategies in Asia

Taiwan. Taiwan's experience since 1949 is of exceptional significance in highlighting the potentialities of a conscious and purposive interest rate policy in an economy subject to the strains of civil war and postwar inflation as well as developmental expenditures. Taiwan is rightly regarded as a pioneer and leading exponent of a high but flexible interest rate strategy.

The monetary history of Taiwan since 1949 affords a classic example of conditions in which interest rates become one of the major anti-inflationary instruments. The extent of the inflation that had to be combated and its repercussions on the level of interest rates are brought out in Table 6.

Table 6 **Taiwan: Prices and Interest Rates, 1940–46**

(In per cent per annum)

Year	*Rate of Increase of Wholesale Prices*	*Black Market Rate of Interest*
1940	158	22
1941	177	32
1942	180	33
1943	202	136
1944	224	197
1945	253	270
1946	151	185

Source: United Nations, Department of Economic Affairs, *Inflationary and Deflationary Tendencies, 1946–1948* (Sales No.: 1949.II.A.1), p. 48.

But inflationary pressures and rising prices showed no signs of abatement even after the consolidation of the regime in Taiwan after 1945 and, if anything, were aggravated by the growing volume of military expenditure and the influx of refugees from the mainland. In this situation, apart from the political difficulties of higher taxation and compulsory borrowing, there was not much hope of evoking any public response to government bonds or of increased accruals to savings bank accounts despite an annual average rate of increase of 85 per cent in wholesale prices.[12] Under these conditions, the Taiwan authorities were inevitably led to rely on economic incentives rather than the purely patriotic impulses of the populace. In the monetary sphere this pointed to the use of sufficiently attractive interest rates to induce the public to save more.

But considering the prevailing rate of price rise and the fact that interest rates were already high, evidenced among other things by the payment of interest even on current account deposits (3.24 per cent per annum in 1949), it was evident that the authorities would really need to pitch the rate on new savings instruments at extraordinarily high levels. The Taiwan authorities boldly broke through the psychological barrier, which so often inhibits the raising of nominal interest rates above conventional levels, by introducing in March 1950 a special system of preferential deposits of one-month, two-month, and three-month maturities carrying a rate of 7 per cent a month (i.e. 125 per cent per annum compounded monthly). The choice of very short maturities was significant, inasmuch as with the high liquidity preference prevailing under conditions of hyperinflation, it was unrealistic to expect the public to buy bonds of long-term or even medium-term maturities. Thus, initially, the policy comprised a combination of very high interest rates on very short-term maturities. But there was no irrevocable commitment to a policy of rising rates, since this would have undermined the market by inducing investors to hold back in anticipation of further rises. Encouraged both by the response to the new deposits as well as by the decline in the wholesale price index between May and July 1950, the authorities reduced the rate of interest on one-month deposits in July 1950 by one half, to 3½ per cent a month. This reduction led to a slight fall in time deposits, but even so this reaction of depositors proved to the authorities that they had been able to arrive at the 'critical area' in which monetary savings had become responsive to interest rate changes. Nevertheless, the authorities reduced the rate to 3.0 per cent a month on one-month deposits. The cut coupled with the resumption of a sharp rise in prices may have led to the fall in the preferential interest rate deposits to a very modest level of NT$21 million in January 1951.

The authorities were concerned, however, to ensure that the rise in the deposit rates was not communicated to loan rates, since this would have affected the working capital requirements of trade and industry. Accordingly, the strategy was adapted to ensure a ceiling on loan rates as well as a 'floor' for deposit rates. But the progressive raising of rates on deposits without a corresponding increase in loan rates created an 'inverted' interest rate structure with a negative differential between the preferential deposit and loan rates, since the former were raised to higher levels than the latter. To meet this situation a 'redeposit facility' was created whereby banks were given the option of placing excess deposits (i.e. those for which they had no immediate outlet by way of investment or loans) in the Bank of Taiwan at rates equal to or above those paid by the commercial banks. This, in effect, protected the commercial banks against losses on the preferential deposits. This facility has proved quite popular with the banks, especially since 1951, as evidenced by the rise of redeposits from NT$6 million in March 1951 to NT$329 million in August 1952. The spectacular rise in redeposits reflected the weak demand for credit relative to the growth of bank deposits in response to the high interest rates. The loss suffered by the Bank of Taiwan in paying higher interest on redeposits than its earnings from loans and investments was substantially offset by the earnings from US counterpart funds deposited with it. But, more importantly, the net cost of 'redeposits' to the Bank of Taiwan in financial terms was more than offset by its efficacy in combating inflation, an apt example of external economies of the high interest rate policy.

The years 1958–59, in retrospect, marked the completion of the phase of stabilization that created an environment wherein interest rates could be viewed as a normal instrument of policy. Since that time the authorities have steadily endeavored to reduce nominal rates on deposits and loans in keeping with the improvement in the overall economic situation, the increase in quasi-money, and the relative stability of the cost of living (Tables 7 and 8).

On the whole, the experience of an active interest rate policy in Taiwan has pertinent lessons for other developing countries, even those that may not have encountered rapid inflation or hyperinflation. First, it shows that there is a critical zone even in a hyperinflation within which an appropriate level and structure of nominal interest rates will not only counter the flight from money into goods but also stimulate financial savings. The rationale of the interest rate policy with its primary accent on deposit rates rather than on loan rates derived from the paramount need in a hyperinflation to increase savings by diverting funds from consumption rather than by merely restraining investment. Second, it also emphasizes that an anti-inflationary policy cannot rely merely on the differential between deposit and loan rates unless it also ensures a positive real rate of return to depositors. Consequently, the nominal interest rates were pitched high enough—in fact far above levels that are regarded as conventionally normal—to yield a reasonably attractive real return to the saver. For the greater part of the period 1952–58 the real rates of interest on deposits were positive but well within the conventional range of rates, despite the high nominal rates. Likewise, over the years the gap between the nominal and real rates of interest has been progressively narrowed, attesting to the feasibility of a policy of fixing nominal rates in increasingly closer approximation to the real rates. Third, it highlights the scope of central bank support of an 'inverted' interest rate structure consequent upon a high interest rate strategy.

Another feature is the flexibility of interest rate policies in Taiwan as evidenced by the subsequent lowering of lending and deposit rates that was associated with a corresponding rise in the ratio of liquid assets, including quasi-money, to GNP. Thus, the ratio increased from 9.6 per cent in 1953 to 37.4 per cent in 1969, whereas the rate of interest on one-year savings deposits declined from 24 per cent to nearly 10 per cent. This suggests that the disincentive effects of falling interest rates were more than offset by the stimulus to the general propensity to save by the rising levels of income and the progressive strengthening of confidence in the currency. Thus, the overall strategy had two broad phases. In the first phase nominal rates were pitched sufficiently high, or at rising levels, to stimulate financial savings. The levels at which financial savings became responsive to interest rate increases may be described as the first stage of 'criticality'. This is the point at which the inflationary psychosis may be said to have been effectively countered. But it was obviously not necessary to maintain rates at this level because, once deposits became responsive, the momentum imparted by the initial rise in rates could be depended upon to sustain future increases in deposits, provided that other factors were favorable. The second stage was reached when the impact of falling, or low, rates was more than offset by rising incomes and confidence, so that despite the lowering of rates there was a progressive rise in financial savings.

Table 7 **Taiwan: Interest Rates on Deposits; Quasi-Money; and Private Savings, 1949–69**

(Rates in per cent per annum;[1] amounts in billions of new Taiwan dollars)

	Demand Deposits[2]			Quasi-Money		Real Rates on One-Year Deposits			
	Nominal rates			Nominal rates					
Year	Checking	Passbook	Amount	Three-month deposits[3]	One-year deposits[4]	(A)	(B)	Amount of Quasi-Money[5]	Private Savings as Percentage of Gross National Product at Current Prices
1949	3.24	16.20	0.09	54.00	—	—	—	—	—
1950	1.62	8.10	0.20	39.60	—	—	—	—	—
1951	1.62	8.10	0.34	54.00	—	—	—	—	—
1952	1.62	8.10	0.52	25.80	—	—	—	0.52	—
1953	1.62	5.40	0.70	15.60	24.00	8.88	2.00	0.69	3.9
1954	1.62	5.40	0.93	13.20	19.20	21.63	20.20	0.88	3.5
1955	1.62	5.40	1.15	13.20	19.20	−9.19	5.20	1.03	3.5
1956	0.90	3.60	1.57	12.00	21.60	15.97	8.60	1.07	4.0
1957	—	2.88	1.78	10.20	19.80	18.15	18.80	1.45	3.7
1958	—	2.88	2.57	10.20	19.80	13.93	17.80	2.57	4.3
1959	—	2.88	2.88	9.00	17.04	5.35	5.84	3.46	3.8
1960	—	2.88	3.30	9.00	17.04	5.33	−2.06	4.72	5.0
1961	—	1.44	4.12	7.20	14.40	14.34	10.30	7.75	7.2
1962	—	1.44	4.30	6.48	13.32	6.83	10.52	9.56	7.4
1963	—	1.44	5.76	6.00	12.00	6.50	11.30	12.47	9.5
1964	—	1.44	7.89	6.00	10.80	13.30	10.20	15.81	10.5
1965	—	1.44	9.02	6.00	10.80	12.44	10.10	18.43	10.3
1966	—	1.44	10.27	6.00	10.08	7.84	8.48	23.90	12.7
1967	—	1.44	12.99	5.40	9.72	6.95	7.02	29.57	13.2
1968	—	1.44	15.12	6.48	9.72	8.19	3.42	33.62	11.5
1969	—	1.44	17.14	6.48	9.72	8.13	4.02	41.03	. . .

Sources: Central Bank of China, *Taiwan Financial Statistics Monthly*; Directorate-General of Budgets, Accounts, and Statistics, *National Income of the Republic of China.*

[1]Rates for savings deposits, discounts, call loans, and time loans are monthly rates at the end of December converted to annual rates. Real rates are adjusted for changes in wholesale prices (A) and consumer prices (B); the rates for 1968 are adjusted for price changes between December 1967 and October 1968.

[2]Rates for 1949–56 are applicable only to banks other than the Bank of Taiwan. The rate on Bank of Taiwan demand (checking) deposits was 0.90 from June 1950 to June 1957, when interest was abolished for the Bank of Taiwan. Interest was abolished for all other banks in the following month. The rate on Bank of Taiwan demand (passbook) deposits was 3.6 per cent per annum from June 1950 to July 1957; from that date until 1961 the rate was 2.88 per cent per annum, the same as paid by other banks.

[3]Rate was applicable only to banks other than the Bank of Taiwan until January 1959, when the latter started to accept three-month deposits at the same rate, 9.0 per cent per annum.

[4]From 1953 to 1958 this rate, applicable to all banks, refers to one-year preferential deposits, which from April 1953 could be pledged as collateral on mortgage loans: after that date the privilege was withdrawn. From 1959, the rate refers to one-year savings deposits, which were introduced in January of that year. Since then no new preferential deposits have been accepted. From July 1, 1963, the same rate has been applied to two-year and three-year deposits.

[5]From International Monetary Fund, *International Financial Statistics.*

Although there are no adequate data covering the whole period, there is reason to believe that the share of unorganized finance in Taiwan has gradually declined as a result of the policy of realistic rates in the organized sector. A sample survey of the flow of funds[25] of private enterprise in 1968 showed that the share of the unorganized sector (excluding nonfinancial institutions) in the money and capital market had declined from nearly 45 per cent in 1964 to about 38 per cent in 1967. The impact of the high interest rate strategy on the unorganized sector is also indicated by the progressive decline in the average free market rate for unsecured loans over the period 1949–69 from about 208 per cent to 28 per cent.

It is more difficult to evaluate the efficacy of high interest rates in stimulating total private savings in Taiwan, even though the ratio of private savings to GNP has improved over the period as a whole from about 3 per cent in 1953 to a range of 10–13 per cent in recent years. There is, however, no consistent trend in the aggregate private savings in relation to GNP. This, of

Table 8 **Taiwan: Loan Rates of Interest, 1949–69**

(In per cent per annum)[1]

Year	Central Bank Rate: Rediscounts	Central Bank Rate: Call loans[2]	Time Loans: Bank of Taiwan[3]	Time Loans: Other banks[4]	Average Free Market Rate of Unsecured Loans
1949	...	46.80	46.80	118.80	208.8
1950	...	41.40	21.60	46.80	144.0
1951	...	41.40	21.60	57.60	126.0
1952	...	36.00	21.60	39.60	79.2
1953	...	21.60	14.40	28.80	51.6
1954	...	21.60	11.88	23.76	49.2
1955	...	21.60	11.88	22.32	54.0
1956	...	18.00	10.80–22.32	21.60	46.8
1957	...	18.00	10.80–22.32	19.80	43.2
1958	...	18.00	10.80–20.32	19.80	39.6
1959	...	18.00	10.80–20.88	18.00	46.8
1960	...	18.00	10.80–20.88	18.00	46.8
1961	14.40	16.20	10.80–18.72	16.20	32.4
1962	12.96	15.84	7.50–18.72	15.84	32.4
1963	11.52	14.04	7.50–16.56	14.04	28.8
1964	11.52	14.04	7.50–15.48	14.04	25.2
1965	11.52	14.04	7.50–15.48	14.04	28.8
1966	11.52	14.04	7.50–14.76	14.04	25.2
1967	10.80	13.32	7.50–14.04	13.32	25.2
1968	11.88	14.04	7.50–14.04	13.32	18.8
1969	10.80	13.32	7.50–14.04	13.32	28.8

Source: Central Bank of China, *Taiwan Financial Statistics Monthly*.

[1]Rates for rediscounts, call loans, and time loans are monthly rates at the end of December converted to annual rate. Free market rate is monthly average rate (based on quotation in Taipei City for the fifth, fifteenth, and twenty-fifth of each month) for unsecured loans converted to annual rate.

[2]Bank of Taiwan rate through 1960; Central Bank rate thereafter. The Bank of Taiwan extended credit through call loans prior to the reactivation of the Central Bank. The call loan rate of the Central Bank also applies to its secured advances to other banks.

[3]Beginning on December 8, 1956, differential rates have been charged by the Bank of Taiwan; these figures give the minimum and maximum rates.

[4]Rate for secured time loans through 1955 and thereafter for secured loans of less than one year.

course, follows from the absence of a determinate causal link between interest rate changes in financial media and the aggregate real savings of the private sector.

Korea. The successful experience of Taiwan is the use of interest rates as an anti-inflationary weapon also stimulated the interest of the Korean authorities in the possible adoption of similar measures as part of a wider stabilization program for the Korean economy, which had experienced persistent inflation following the political division of the country in 1945 and the economic dislocation in the wake of the Korean conflict. The Korean authorities sent expert teams to Taiwan to study[13] the techniques used by the Taiwan authorities and their results and to suggest possible measures in the light of their investigations. Thus, long before the implementation of the interest rate reforms in September 1965 there was official recognition in Korea of the desirability of a bold and purposive interest rate policy.[14] The phase of hyperinflation lasted until about 1951–53. But even thereafter attempts to check inflation met with only limited results: despite substantial foreign aid, the growing requirements of defense and economic reconstruction aggravated the inflationary pressures. During 1953–63 the annual rate of increase in money supply and wholesale prices averaged 38 per cent and 21 per cent, respectively. It was not until late in 1963 with the election of a new government that the authorities were able to initiate a resolute anti-inflationary program, which in its initial stages was concerned primarily with restraining monetary expansion and with extending the role of the price mechanism as a means of achieving a more efficient allocation of resources. For many years the Korean authorities had maintained statutory ceilings on interest rates that were substantially below free market interest rates and doubtless did not reflect the real economic cost of capital. One major effect of the unrealistic levels of interest rates was that 'time and savings deposits of banks did not increase at all in real terms between December 1962 and September 1965 (before the interest rate reform) despite strong savings campaigns carried out by both government and financial institutions'.[15] Consequently, there was a drain of funds from the organized to the unorganized sector, which, according to one estimate, financed about one-third of total outstanding loans in Korea.[16]

Apart from their unrealistic levels, the structure of interest rates in the organized sector suffered from an excessively complex and artificial differentiation of deposits by categories, maturities, and rates. There were about 11 classes of deposits with rates ranging from 0 to 1.8 per cent on 'money' accounts and from 3.6 per cent to 16.8 per cent on savings accounts. It has been said that 'so fine a distinction between accounts implies a knowledge by banking officials about the public's elasticities of demand for deposits of different maturity, with slight differences also in some other characteristics, that must be fictitious'.[17] Thus, the situation clearly pointed to the need for raising interest rates to more realistic levels while simplifying their complex structure.

The Korean authorities announced a far-reaching scheme of interest rate reforms in September 1965.[18] Its objectives were to raise deposit and loan rates to realistic levels to reflect the true economic cost of capital; to increase voluntary private monetary savings by providing adequately attractive 'real' rates of return; to promote optimum allocation of savings in productive channels; to facilitate the shift in credit policy from specific and direct controls to global instruments; to attract funds from the unorganized sector (curb market) into the banking system, thereby extending and strengthening the area of effectiveness of the monetary authorities; to encourage the use of equity capital instead of borrowed capital by industrial and commercial firms; and to reduce the degree of 'gearing' in the capital structure.

The Bank of Korea announced an increase in the rates on its loans and discounts, with effect from November 16, 1965, raising its basic rate from 10½ per cent to 21 per cent. Alongside these measures, the Monetary Board dismantled the extensive system of direct quantitative credit controls by abolishing, on September 30, the loan ceilings for individual banks and on specified uses of funds. Likewise, it abolished the 'penalty' interest on central bank loans to banks that had exceeded their loan ceilings.

The actual ceiling rate on bank deposits was set at 2½ per cent a month, which was a little higher than the average yield on the government bonds (1.9–2 per cent a month) in the preceding few years but about one-half of the rate prevailing in the unorganized sector (4–5 per cent a month), following Taiwan's successful experience in this matter.[19] As to loan rates, the authorities also adopted a pragmatic approach, in the absence of information on the interest elasticity of credit demand, in their search for a maximum rate that would not inhibit private investment. In the light of studies of the cost structure of various industries, it was estimated that the average cost of interest to industries would not increase if loan rates were set about 26 per cent per annum, on the basis that if borrowing from the unorganized sector was reduced because of the increased availability of bank credit at such a rate the incidence of increase in the average interest rate would remain largely unaffected and perhaps even be reduced in the long run. These studies also suggested the average rate of return on industrial capital to be about 20 per cent in real terms.[20] Assuming that there would be an annual price rise of 7–10 per cent, an average loan rate of 26 per cent was regarded as reasonable, with a higher rate of 36½ per cent for overdue loans to discourage the use of extended overdrawn positions to profit from the differential between the deposit and loan rates.

The sharp, dramatic increases in deposit and loan rates (see Table 9), in addition to the announced objectives, were intended to demonstrate clearly the determination of the authorities to curb inflation. Thus, the standard loan rate of banking institutions was almost doubled, increasing from 14 per cent per annum to 26 per cent. In terms of annual interest the rise in the maximum interest on the one-year deposit was more than doubled, from 15 per cent to 34½ per cent. It is significant that the rates on long-term deposits were set on a monthly basis in accordance with the practice in the unorganized markets. This gave the depositors the option of either withdrawing the interest earned at the end of each month or accumulating it to have it compounded monthly. This feature was intended to give a sharper edge to the organized banking sector's competition with the unorganized sector. Since the rates prescribed were intended as legal maxima, this meant that within the ceiling rate(s) each bank was free to fix its deposit rates by term structure and its loan rates by purpose, security, etc. In fact, however, all banks adopted uniform deposit and loan rates by an agreement of the Korean Bankers Association, mainly to avoid uneconomic interbank competition. Most banks increased the agreed actual rates to the maximum that was permitted under the law of September 30, 1965.

The lower rate on loans from government funds was considered justifiable for attracting private investment in selected essential sectors. Another consideration was that the rate on long-term loans (of ten years and above) should be geared to long-term expectations on interest, since unilateral changes in long-term loan contracts between banks and customers were considered neither feasible nor desirable. This second consideration indicated that the high interest rate strategy was regarded essentially as a transitory program to cope with low monetary saving under inflationary conditions and that, with the attainment of a relatively stable price level, interest rates would decline to relatively normal levels.

The standard loan rate also did not apply to government-approved borrowing, whether private or official, from foreign sources. This, in a climate of domestic credit restriction, coupled with the relative

Table 9 **Korea: Selected Interest Rates of Banking Institutions, September 30, 1965–June 2, 1969**

(In per cent per annum)

	Date of Change								
	Prior to Sept. 30, 1965	*Sept. 30, 1965*	*Nov. 16, 1965*	*Dec. 1, 1965*	*Feb. 1, 1966*	*June 29, 1967*	*Mar. 1, 1968*	*Oct. 1, 1968*	*June 2, 1969*
	Lending rates								
Bank of Korea									
Export and UN supply loans	3.5	—	3.5	3.5	-	-	3.5	3.5	—
Rice lien loans	4.0	—	4.0	4.0	—	—	4.0	4.0	—
Commercial bills	11.5	—	21.0	28.0	—	—	21.0	23.0	22.0
Other bills	13.5	—	23.0	28.0	—	—	28.0	28.0	26.0
Purchase of aid goods	9.5	—	23.0	26.0	—	—	26.0	25.2	24.0
Commercial banks									
Export bills	6.5	6.5	—	—	6.5	6.0	—	6.0	6.0
Import bills	—	—	—	—	6.0[1]	6.0[1]	—	6.0[1]	6.0[1]
Commercial bills	14.0	24.0	—	—	24.0	24.0	—	26.0	24.6
Other bills	16.0	26.0	—	—	26.0	26.0	—	25.2	24.0
Overdrafts	18.0	26.0	—	—	28.0	28.0	—	28.0	26.0
Overdue loans	20.0	36.5	—	—	36.5	36.5	—	36.5	36.5
National Agricultural Cooperatives Federation									
Rice lien loans	11.0	11.0	—	—	—	—	—	—	—
General fund loans	16.0	26.0	—	—	26.0	26.0	—	25.2	24.0
Agricultural and forestry loans	16.0	23.0	—	—	—	26.0	26.0	25.2	24.0
Cooperative business loans	9.1	12.2	—	—	—	—	—	—	—
	Deposit rates								
Time deposits									
3 months	9.0	18.0	—	—	—	—	15.6[2]	14.4	12.0
6 months	12.0	24.0	—	—	—	—	20.4[2]	19.2	16.8
12 months	15.0	26.4	—	—	—	—	26.4[2]	25.2	22.8
More than 18 months	15.0	30.0	—	—	—	—	27.6[2]	—[3]	—
Savings									
National Savings Association	16.8	30.0	—	—	—	—	28.0[2]	25.2	22.8
Installment	10.0	30.0	—	—	—	—	28.0[2]	25.0	23.0
Short-term									
Notice	3.65	5.00	—	—	—	—	5.00[2]	5.00	5.00
Savings[4]	3.60	7.2	—	—	—	—	—	—	—

Source: Bank of Korea, *Monthly Statistical Review.*

[1]Commercial bank loans for imports of raw materials for earning foreign exchange carry an annual interest rate of 6 per cent, while the rate on loans for importing raw materials and industrial facilities for other purposes is 24 per cent.

[2]April 1, 1968.

[3]The revision on October 1, 1968, abolished time deposits of more than 18 months.

[4]This deposit was abolished in November 1967. The revision on April 1, 1968, created a 'new living' deposit, carrying annual interest of 12 per cent. The June 1969 revision lowered the interest rate to 9.6 per cent.

stability of the exchange rate since 1966 and the greatly reduced exchange risks, naturally led to a large expansion in foreign borrowing.

When allowance was made for these preferential rates and the exemption of foreign loans from the purview of the enhanced loan rates, the weighted average lending rate of commercial banks was estimated to be about 18–20 per cent. Likewise, the average money cost of borrowing for businesses was reduced to levels far below the standard loan rate of banks, and the real cost too was further reduced with the continued increase in prices. Thus, approximately one-third of total commercial bank credit was extended at preferential rates (mostly to the export sector).

In order to counter the rise in commercial bank credit after September 30, the basic rediscount rate of the Bank of Korea was raised on December 1, 1965, from 21 per cent to 28 per cent, which probably represents the highest central bank rate ever.

The effectiveness of the high interest rate structure in October 1965 in stimulating saving is shown by the spectacular rise in monetary saving in 1966 (123 per cent) and 1967 (84 per cent). It is significant that even the lowering of interest rates on deposits in April and October 1968 did not affect the growth of monetary savings, which increased by 94 per cent in 1968. The increase in time deposits was at a higher rate than in other types of saving because of the more favorable rate, and also because some categories of savings deposit, such as installment savings, could not be accelerated in the short run. The rise in quasi-money is indeed impressive, even though a part of the increase reflects the accrued interest that was withdrawable on demand. On the other hand, some of the rise in time deposits might represent merely a diversion of deposits previously held with nonbank moneylenders (the unorganized sector).

The bulk of the increase in time and savings deposits during 1964–68 was accounted for by the household sector (see Table 10). The presumption of interest sensitivity of household savings is also borne out by the results in a multiple regression analysis, which showed a strong correlation between the real deposit rate of interest and the savings of the household sector[21] as well as between gross private saving and gross domestic saving. On the other hand, the behavior of aggregate private savings (i.e. private savings as a percentage of GNP at current prices) was somewhat erratic (see the last column of Table 11 over the period 1962–68. On the whole, it may be conceded that the policy of realistic interest rates has improved the efficacy of the price mechanism in the organized money market in Korea. There are, however, no data to indicate its precise impact on the share of the unorganized sector in total finance. On the other hand, the high interest rates on domestically borrowed funds have also encouraged excessive borrowing from abroad. Since such borrowing requires the approval of government departments and specialized financial institutions, it has in effect created a system of administrative credit rationing. Equally, to some extent, the high rates have doubtless also stimulated an inflow of remittances from abroad. This only highlights some of the problems of an active interest rate policy in a comparatively open economy.

Table 10 **Korea: Changes in Holdings of Time and Savings Deposits, 1964–68[1]**

(In billions of won)

Year	*Total Increase*	*Increase in Holdings of Private Individuals*
1964	3.3	+2.8
1965	26.7	+17.5
1966	56.8	+44.0
1967	76.1	+63.1
1968	152.2	+110.5

Source: Bank of Korea, *Monthly Statistical Review*—based on Flow of Funds Account.

[1]Includes insurance and trust deposits.

While the interest rate policy in Korea has been notably successful in achieving its objectives, some of the concomitant factors that contributed to the result cannot be overlooked in an overall asessment. First, the achievement of overall balance in the government budget virtually eliminated the need for domestic borrowing, except for temporary accommodation from the Bank of Korea. Consequently, the need to keep down the cost of government borrowing ceased to be an inhibiting factor in raising interest rates. Second, the comparatively small ratio of financial assets to total national wealth meant that capital losses, as a result of interest rate increases, were not a material consideration. Third, because, as in Taiwan, government and semigovernment institutions account for a substantial part of commercial banking, the implementation of the reforms was that much easier. Other contributory factors included the active savings campaign of the Government, the lack of alternative financial assets to bank deposits offering comparably attractive rates, and the exemption of deposit interest from income tax. Thus, interest rate policy, although important, was only one element in the overall stabilization program, which comprised appropriate budgetary, credit, and exchange policies.

The interest rate reform of September 1965 is, in retrospect, best viewed not as a once-for-all, high interest rate strategy but as an avowedly transitional phase, since the authorities have steadily endeavored to normalize the interest rate level and structure by progressively reducing and simplifying the general level of rates with the restoration of financial stability. The attainment of price stability has, however, ensured the maintenance of positive real rates of interest.

A conventional interest rate policy (Malaysia and Singapore)

In contrast to the high interest rate strategies in Taiwan and Korea, the experience of high and rising levels of monetary savings in Malaysia and Singapore, despite low and stable nominal interest rates, is equally instructive—not least because of some other distinguishing features of these economies.

The fact that both Malaysia and Singapore have been able increasingly to adopt an autonomous interest rate policy on their treasury bills, in contrast to the earlier tendency to follow the UK treasury bill rate, shows that the openness of an economy need not be a constraint on an autonomous policy geared to local needs. The development of increasingly active local treasury bill markets has created a convenient outlet for short-term banking funds that were formerly invested in UK treasury bills.

The structure and level of deposit and loan rates of interest in Malaysia and Singapore (Table 5) as well as

Table 11 **Korea: Nominal and Real Rates of Interest on Deposits; Quasi-Money; and Private Savings, 1961–June 2, 1969**

(Rates in per cent per annum; amounts in billions of won)

	Time Deposits				*Savings Deposits of National Savings Association*			
	3 Months		*12 Months*					
Year	*Nominal rate*	*Real rate*[1]	*Nominal rate*	*Real rate*[1]	*Nominal rate*	*Real rate*[1]	*Amounts of Quasi-Money*	*Private Savings as Percentage of Gross National Product at Current Prices*
1961	9.0	0.8	15.0	6.8	16.8	8.6	8.92	—
1962	9.0	2.3	15.0	8.3	16.8	10.1	16.57	2.88
1963	9.0	−10.7	15.0	−4.7	16.8	−2.9	17.52	7.17
1964	9.0	−22.9	15.0	−12.9	16.8	−11.1	20.18	6.51
1965	18.0	−5.6	15.0	1.4	16.8	2.9	39.22	5.80
1966	18.0	1.2	26.4	9.6	30.0	13.2	86.74	8.94
1967	18.0	6.8	26.4	5.2	30.0	18.8	128.99	7.03
1968[2]	—	—	26.4	—	28.0	—	—	—
1968[3]	14.4	4.4	25.2	15.3	25.2	—	257.62[4]	6.85
1969[5]	—	—	22.8	—	22.8	—	—	—

Sources: Bank of Korea, *Monthly Statistical Review*; International Monetary Fund, *International Financial Statistics*.
[1]The real rate is adjusted for changes in consumer prices for all cities (1965 = 100).
[2]April 1.
[3]October 1.
[4]End of 1968.
[5]June 2.

the nominal rates on government securities (up to 6½ per cent), are of a comparatively low and stable character in contrast to those of Taiwan and Korea. They therefore represent a more conventional pattern of interest rates commonly found in economies that have not experienced violent economic fluctuations. Thus, apart from the fine and fairly frequent variations in the treasury bill rate, other rates have been remarkably stable over long periods. The explanation for this may be sought in the fact that the volume of monetary savings in both countries has risen impressively despite the low and stable interest rates. This reflects in large part the confidence of the average investor in the stability of the value of monetary assets that has resulted from his experience with prolonged stability of consumer prices, which in turn is due to a variety of factors, such as the openness of the economies and the appropriateness of financial and wage policies. The depositor therefore has been able to earn a real rate of interest at least equal to the money rate and in some years even higher than that, owing to the fall in prices. Significantly, deposits have maintained their rise even in years when the real rate was negative.

More or less similar considerations apply to the pattern of interest rates on government securities because of the positive real rates of interest on them. Because about 80 per cent of the total marketable public debt is held by tax-exempt 'captive' funds (required by law to be invested in government securities), such as the Employees' Provident Fund and other trust funds and the Post Office Savings Bank, the Government is assured of progressively rising support from investors even at stable interest rates. In view of this, paying higher interest on funds that would flow into gilt-edged stock would add needlessly to the cost of debt service. Although the debt service burden is not a decisive argument against higher (realistic) interest rates on government loans, at least two possible considerations might argue against excessive rigidity of existing yields on government securities. The first is the 'equity' argument that the Government should not unduly exploit its monopsonistic position as a borrower. Moreover, pension and social security funds in many countries are increasingly diversifying their portfolios by investing in high-yield, first-class equities to offset the low nominal yields, as well as depreciation in real terms, of gilt-edged stock. Consequently, the availability of a large and growing captive market in Malaysia and Singapore in itself need not preclude examination of the adequacy and equity of the real rate of return to the investor in government securities, even though this has been positive in the past decade. These considerations are, of course, equally applicable to other developing economies.

Another argument for an increase in interest rates on government securities could be its possible efficacy in

Table 12 **Malaysia: Interest Rates on Fixed and Savings Deposits and Private Savings, 1959–69**

(Rates in per cent per annum; amounts in millions of Malaysian dollars)

	Fixed Deposits			*Savings Deposits*			*Private Savings[4] as Percentage of Gross National Product at Current Market Prices*
year	*Nominal rates[1]*	*Real rates[2]*	*Amount[3]*	*Nominal rates*	*Real rates[2]*	*Amount[3]*	
1959	3.50–3.75	—	290	2.50	—	118	—
1960	4.00	4.20	400	2.50	2.70	142	—
1961	4.00	4.20	475	2.50	2.70	154	—
1962	4.00	3.90	485	2.50	2.40	182	17.1
1963	4.00	0.90	543	2.50	−0.60	218	16.3
1964	2.50–5.00	3.00–5.50	600	2.50	3.00	257	17.4
1965	2.50–5.00	1.50–4.00	727	3.00	2.00	291	19.7
1966	2.50–5.00	2.30–4.80	842	3.00	2.80	340	18.6
1967	3.00–6.00	−1.20– +1.80	1,012	3.00	−1.20	434	17.9
1968	3.00–6.00	2.80–5.80	1,260	3.50	3.30	484	18.4
1969	3.00–6.00	4.30–7.30	1,488	3.50	4.80	550	—

Sources: Bank Negara Malaysia, *Annual Reports* and *Quarterly Economic Bulletin*.

[1]The nominal rates in 1959 were 3.50 per cent for the 3–6 month deposits and 3.75 per cent for the 9–12 month deposits; the rates for 3–12 month deposits were 4.00 per cent for the period 1960–63 and 5.00 per cent for the period 1964–66; in 1967 and 1968 the fixed deposit rates were made to vary with the length of deposit, from 5.50 per cent for the 3-month deposits and 5.75 per cent for the 6-month deposits to 6.00 per cent for the 9–12 month deposits. Since 1964 the deposit rates for one month have been fixed at 2.50 per cent for the period 1964–66 and at 3.00 per cent for the period 1967–68.

[2]As adjusted by the retail price index (1959 = 100). Minus sign indicates negative real rates.

[3]At the end of period.

[4]Mid-term review of the First Malaysian Plan, 1966–70 (figures for 1968 are preliminary).

attracting noninstitutional (i.e. personal) savings. This is an unexceptionable objective, but its feasibility is problematic. In Malaysia and Singapore, as elsewhere, the trend is toward a progressively greater 'institutionalization' in the ownership of public debt, and it is arguable whether personal savings (for which there is a wide range of competing assets, such as debentures, equities, consumer durables, real estate, or more simply plowing back into family business) would be induced into gilt-edged stock to any great extent merely through an increase in interest rates. A complementary approach might be to tap noninstitutional savings through means other than a rise in the interest rates, say, through variety in their terms, forms, and maturities, improved institutional facilities, sales promotion, etc.

On the whole, the experience of Malaysia and Singapore shows that price stability is in itself a major factor in sustaining an ideal climate for encouraging financial savings, and to that extent the role of interest rates in an overall savings strategy has been correspondingly less important than in other countries.

Some Implications of an Active Interest Rate Policy

The foregoing analysis suggests that, first, the choice is not so much between particular levels or structures of interest rates as between rigid and flexible policies; second, in the absence of any universally valid a priori criteria, interest rate policies have to be determined in terms of a judicious empiricism as part of an overall savings and development strategy, with perhaps a little more accent on the role of interest rates as a savings incentive than heretofore.

Paradoxically, some institutional features of the less developed countries create an even more favorable environment for positive interest rate policies than in the developed countries. Thus, the comparatively low ratio of financial assets to total assets minimizes problems of capital loss to holders of such assets, and even where a considerable volume of transferable, income-yielding financial assets (other than bank deposits) exists, most of these assets are held until maturity. Consequently, interest rates can be raised more often without excessive regard for protecting the balance sheet position of financial institutions. The comparatively small range of financial assets also minimizes the risk of 'switching' from one asset to another without any net inflow of savings. Likewise, the comparatively low ratio of public debt to national income and of the burden of debt service to government revenues implies that the justification for low interest rates to reduce the cost of government borrowing loses much of its force. On the other hand, the greater 'skewness' of income distribution in the less developed countries would also suggest that higher rates on government securities might favor the higher-income groups. But the redistributive effects of interest rate changes can be mitigated by effective taxation of interest income as well as by subsidizing (i.e.

higher) interest payments on nonmarketable debt (e.g. small savings).

Appropriateness of rates on government borrowing

Concurrently, rates on government borrowing will need to be kept constantly under review, so that the level and structure of interest rates ensure the optimum allocation of resources between the public and private sectors. The very enjoyment of monopsonistic borrowing powers makes it all the more incumbent on governments in the less developed countries to borrow at more competitive rates in keeping with the real cost of capital in the economy, rather than to continue to borrow at artificially low rates in the organized sector. Neither the capacity of governments to borrow at low rates nor the existence of a captive market for private savings can be regarded as a decisive argument against more realistic interest rates. To continue to offer unattractive interest rates to one class of savers, when effective rates in the rest of the economy are much higher, amounts to subsidizing one category of borrowers (public sector) merely because the lenders (private savers) have no alternative. But this argument is based not merely on grounds of equity to the saver but even more importantly on criteria of economic efficacy in allocating scarce investible funds, which are clearly vitiated by permitting excessive diversion of funds to the public sector through the captive market. To the extent that these conditions prevail, the economic rationale of low and stable rates on government borrowing in some of the less developed countries is not well founded, since it disregards the opportunity cost of public borrowing and investment. This issue is of vital importance for developing countries, as the organized sector (public and private), although small in relation to the total economy, accounts for the major share of new investment under development plans.

Admittedly, in both Taiwan and Korea interest rate reforms were only one of the elements in the stabilization program, since there were other and perhaps more significant contributory factors, such as exchange reforms, appropriate monetary and fiscal policies, and foreign aid. Nevertheless, their contribution to the success of the program was certainly substantial, even allowing for the limitations of the evidence and the fact that the use of extremely high money rates of interest in both countries occurred under very special circumstances of high and rising inflation, which both justified the use of and brought success to the interest rate policies implemented. The experience of Taiwan and Korea has, however, many pertinent lessons for other less developed countries, not least because these countries also rank high in the 'growth league' as well as in terms of export performance. Above all, it suggests that there is a critical range within which monetary savings may respond, positively to increases in interest rates. It underscores both the desirability and feasibility of maintaining realistic interest rates on monetary savings, which also helps to improve the climate for aggregate real savings and thereby to promote stability as well as development. Equally, the fact that policies in both countries have been sufficiently flexible to lower interest rates with a progressive increase in monetary savings also implies that the emphasis in developing countries should be on realistic and flexible interest rates rather than on stable average rates, whether high or low, and that there are risks in a 'ratchet-like' interest rate structure.

Perhaps the greatest barriers to realistic rates of interest are the tendency to concentrate on the money rate rather than the real rate of return and the pyschological resistance to raising nominal rates to very high levels. But, equally, countries like Malaysia and Singapore, which have enjoyed a relatively high degree of price stability, have been able thereby to ensure an adequate positive rate of return to savers. Such a rate of return can therefore be achieved either through manipulation of nominal interest rates or through stable prices. The contrasting experience of Taiwan and Korea, on the one hand, and of Malaysia and Singapore, on the other hand, is a salutary reminder of the dangers of dogmatic generalizations on interest rate policies that will need to be tailored to specific situations in conjunction with appropriate price and income policies. One cannot therefore conceive of any purely monistic objective of regulating interest rates. An appropriate overall interest rate policy for a less developed country will have to be based on a delicate balancing of rates realistic enough to stimulate saving but not so high as to inhibit investment in desired channels, a task that will tax the resources of economic management in the less developed countries, considering that 'interest is the most paradoxical of all economic quantities.'[22]

Notes: Reading 39

1 Referred to throughout the original article as China.

2 See U Tun Wai, 'Interest rates in the organized money markets of underdeveloped countries', *Staff Papers*, vol. V, 1956, pp. 249–78, and 'Interest rates outside the organized money markets of underdeveloped countries', *Staff Papers*, vol. VI, 1957, pp. 80–142; Anthony Bottomley, 'Monopoly profit as a determinant of interest rates in underdeveloped rural areas', *Oxford Economic Papers*, new series, vol. 16, 1964, pp. 431–7, and 'The premium for risk as a determinant of interest rates in underdeveloped rural areas', *The Quarterly Journal of Economics*, vol. LXXVII, 1963, pp. 637–47; A. G. Chandavarkar, 'The premium for risk as a determinant of interest rates in underdeveloped rural areas: comment', *The Quarterly Journal of Economics*, vol. LXXIX, 1965, pp. 322–5. A notable exception is the discussion of 'Rates of interest in the organized sector' in Gunnar Myrdal, *Asian Drama*, vol. III, appendix 8, New York, 1968, pp. 2087–96, which questions the rationale of existing interest rate policies in South-East Asian countries.

3 See, for example, S. N. Sen, *Central Banking in Underdeveloped Money Markets*, Calcutta, 4th edn, 1967, pp. 30–51.

4 'It has been admitted from Marshall's time at least that the influence of the interest rate on saving is doubtful even as to its algebraic sign', G. L. S. Shackle, 'Recent theories concerning the nature and role of interest', in *Surveys of Economic Theory: Money, Interest, and Welfare*, vol. I, London, 1965, p. 151. 'An increase in the rate of interest, according to historical experience, does not seem to have an influence on rate of saving', Thomas Balogh, *The Economics of Poverty*, London, 1966, p. 26.

5 Joan Robinson, *The Accumulation of Capital*, London, 1965, p. 290 (fn.).

6 Tun Wai, 'Interest rates outside the organized money markets of underdeveloped countries' (cited in note 2), p. 102.

7 For instance, in the United States consumer loans cost about 24 per cent (consumer finance companies), 16.6 per cent (sales finance companies), 10 per cent (commercial banks), and 9 per cent (federal credit unions). Paul F. Smith, *Consumer Credit Costs, 1949–59*, Princeton University Press, 1964, p. 78,

8 The relative shares of different credit agencies in financing the credit requirements of rural households in India in 1961–2 were as follows:

	per cent
Organised sector	
Government	2.3
Co-operatives	13.8
Commercial banks	0.7
Unorganised sector	
Moneylenders	46.6
Traders and commission agents	10.1
Relatives	8.8
Landlords	0.7
Others	17.0

Source: Reserve Bank of India Bulletin, vol. XIX, 1965, p. 1309.

9 This strategy would be in keeping with the author's hypothesis that the element of monopoly profits in the determination of rural interest rates could well exceed the sum of other components, namely, risk and liquidity premiums and administrative charges. In fact, purely institutional elements, as distinct from such behavioural factors as liquidity preference, appear to be more influential in the determination of interest rates in the less developed countries, an aspect that is insufficiently recognised in the literature. (For details, see Chandavarkar, 'The premium for risk as a determinant of interest rates in underdeveloped rural areas: comment' (cited in note 2), p. 325.) A notable exception is Joan Robinson's observation, 'The most important influences upon interest rates – which account for, say, the difference between 30 per cent in an Indian village and 3 per cent in London – are social, legal and institutional', 'The rate of interest', *Collected Economic Papers*, Vol. II, Oxford, 1960, p. 246.

10 Myrdal cites two statements by a spokesman for the Reserve Bank of India, op. cit., p. 2091:

> Since there are other measures to directly control and regulate investments, is there any point in trying to use the Bank rate for that purpose? ('Monetary policy', *The Economic Weekly*, Bombay, 4 January 1964, p. 7.)
>
> In a largely protective economy like ours, where profit expectations rule high, dear money loses importance as a deterrent to investors. ('How positive is our credit policy?' *The Economic Weekly*, 21 December 1963, p. 2085.)

11 K. L. Gupta, 'Personal saving in developing nations: further evidence', *The Economic Record*, vol. 46, 1970, pp. 243–9. The list of variables (all deflated by P = cost of living index) is as follows: S = personal saving; Y_p = personal income; Y_d = disposable income; Y_w = wage and salary income; Y_e = non-labour income; T = direct taxes on households, *minus* net transfers to households.

12 Reed J. Irvine and Robert F. Emery, 'Interest rates as an anti-inflationary instrument in Taiwan', *The National Banking Review*, vol. 4, 1966, p. 30.

13 Bank of Korea, Research Department, 'High interest rate policy in Taiwan', mimeo., 1965, cited by Kwang Suk Kim, 'An appraisal of the high interest rate strategy of Korea', unpublished, Center for Development Economics, Williams College, Mass., May 1968, p. 9.

The report *The Financial Structure of Korea*, by John G. Gurley, Hugh T. Patrick and E. S. Shaw (United States Operations Mission to Korea, July 1965), which was commissioned by the US Agency for International Development, also made recommendations on an appropriate interest rate policy as part of a comprehensive review of financial and monetary techniques and policies in Korea.

14 See, for instance, *Summary of the First Five-Year Economic Plan, 1962–1966*, Republic of Korea, Economic Planning Board, 1962, pp. 12 and 37.

15 See Kim, 'An appraisal of the high interest rate strategy of Korea' (cited in note 13), p. 4.

16 Kwang Suk Kim, 'Unofficial money market in Korea,' unpublished, United States Operations Mission to Korea, 1964, p. 81. The size of the unorganised sector was estimated at W 40–45 billion in 1964, or almost double the outstandings of commercial bank loans (Gurley, Patrick and Shaw, op. cit., p. 81).

17 Gurley, Patrick and Shaw, op. cit., p. 53.

18 Bank of Korea, *Monthly Statistical Review*, October 1965, p. 62.

19 'High interest rate policy in Taiwan' (cited in note 13).

20 Estimates of the average rate of return in Korean manufacturing industry have ranged (in real terms) from 13.5 per cent (Korean Economic Development Institute, *Analysis of Capital Cost: Selected Industrial Establishments*, Seoul, 1967, p. 79) to 20 per cent, marginal product of capital (Edward S. Shaw, *Financial Patterns and Policies in Korea*, United States Operations Mission to Korea, April 1967, pp. 29–30).

21 See Kim, 'An appraisal of the high interest rate strategy of Korea' (cited in note 13), pp. 16–25. The regression equation was as follows (p. 18):

$$Sm = -124.36 + \underset{(0.03)}{0.21\,Y} + \underset{(0.37)}{1.10}\,(R - \Delta P_2)$$

$$R_2 = 0.9363, \quad S_y = 12.08$$

Where Sm = money saving (constant billion won)
R = nominal maximum deposit rate
ΔP_2 = annual percentage change in the two-year saving average of national wholesale price index.

22 Shackle, op. cit., p. 150.

23 Myrdal, *op. cit.*, p. 2087.

24 Jeffrey G. Williamson, 'Personal Saving in Developing Nations: An Intertemporal Cross-Section from Asia,' *The Economic Record*. Vol. 44 (1968), pp. 194–210.

25 This was conducted by the Economic Research Department of the Central Bank of China.

Index

20 30 40 50 60 70

40 75 120 175 240 315

Do EEC GSP.

Lomé I : II
3